KÁROLY RÉDEI

ZYRIAN FOLKLORE TEXTS

1828—1978
PUBLISHED IN THE YEAR OF THE 150th JUBILEE

BIBLIOTHECA URALICA

3

Redigit

P. HAJDÚ

AKADÉMIAI KIADÓ · BUDAPEST 1978

ZYRIAN FOLKLORE TEXTS

by

KÁROLY RÉDEI

AKADÉMIAI KIADÓ · BUDAPEST 1978

English translation
by IMRE GOMBOS
English translation revised
by GEORGE F. CUSHING

ISBN 963 05 1506 7

PRINTED IN HUNGARY

CONTENTS

Preface 9
Bibliographical Abbreviations 11
Abbreviations for Zyrian Dialects 12

I. *The Vym Dialect* 13
(a) Tales and narratives 14
1. A married couple and a son 14
2. The merchant who was a widower 18
3. The little peasant 26
4. [The Tsarevich and the girl who was driven out] 32
5. The rich brother and the poor brother 36
6. [The soldier and the priest] 40
7. About my life 44
8. About my life 52
9. How I got married 54
10. About the wedding 56
11. [How clothes are made] 58
(b) 12. Riddles 60
(c) 13—14. Proverbs, idioms 66
(d) 15—22. Songs 68
(e) 23—26. Laments 78
(f) 27—28. Children's songs, tales in verse 84
(g) 29. Rhymes 84

II. *The Lower-Vyčegda Dialect* 94
(a) Tales and narratives 96
30. [The priest's cows] 96
31. Tsarevich Ivan 96
32. pipiriśťi falcon 110
33. About Poma 118
34. Uncle Norįmę 126
35. Father Ręman 132
36. [The mother curses her daughter] 134
37. About the three dragons 136
38. [The three sisters] 136
39. Popular customs 138

(b) 40. Riddles ... 144
(c) 41—42. Proverbs, idioms ... 148
(d) 43—58. Songs ... 148
(e) 59—65. Laments ... 168
(f) 66—80. Children's songs, tales in verse ... 174
(g) 81. Rhymes ... 192

III. *The Middle-Vyčegda (Syktyvkar Region) Dialect* ... 200
Narratives ... 200
82. About my childhood ... 200
83. About the wedding ... 202

IV. *The Upper-Vyčegda Dialect* ... 206
(a) Tales and narratives ... 208
84. [Lazy Ivan] ... 208
85. The mouse travels down and up the river ... 216
86. How I was frightened ... 220
87. How I first shot wild-duck ... 222
88. How we caught a pike ... 222
89. About hunting ... 224
90. A summer day ... 230
(b) 91. Riddles ... 232
(c) A proverb ... 234
(d) 93. Charms, curses ... 234
(e) 94—126. Songs ... 236
(f) 127—141. Children's songs, tales in verse ... 308
(g) 142. Rhymes ... 326

V. *The Višera Dialect* ... 330
(a) Tales and narratives ... 332
143. [Petruš and the fugitives] ... 332
144. [Stupid Balakirov] ... 332
145. About the priest ... 336
146. [Ivan and Tsar Grim] ... 340
147. [The miraculous lamp] ... 344
148. [Hunters' stories] ... 352
149. [Our village] ... 354
150. [Picking berries] ... 356
151. Bogorodsk ... 356
152. Something that happened ... 358
153. Something that happened ... 358
154. [About games] ... 360
(b) 155—171. Songs ... 360
(c) 172—178. Laments ... 382
(d) 179. Rhymes ... 394

VI. *The Ižma (Lower Ob) Dialect* ... 397
Tales and narratives ... 398

180. About a lying old man 398
181. Ermine-coat 400
182. [About fishing] 404
183. [About reindeer-breeding] 406

VII. *The Northern Permyak Dialect* 409

(a) Tales and narratives 412
184. About Aľonuška 412
185. About Rich Marko 414
186. [The witch and the two girls] 416
187. [The ghost and the two girls] 420
188. [How Ivan rescued the Tsar's daughters from the dragons] 424
189. [The clever perch] 430
190. [The poor man and the forest ghost] 430
191. About getting married 432
192. About childbirth 436
193. About burial and commemoration of the dead 436
194. About swinging 438
195. About frightening things 440
196. About food and drink 442
197. [About food and drink] 446
198. About the building of the house and household work 448
199. About tilling the land 450
200. Fishing 452
201. Birch-bark 452
202. About the weaving of canvas 452
203. About the Chuds 454
204. About unchaste spirits 454
205. [Meeting a bear] 456
206. [The tempest] 458
207. The elk 458
208. The sable 460
209. The River Ińva 460
210. [About the seasons] 460
211. [About the school-years of V. I. Lenin] 462
212. [At dawn] 462
213. [Moscow] 464
214. [About the Michurin garden] 464
215. [Our peasant women] 466
216. [Our village] 466
217. My grandmother 468
(b) 218. A song 468

VIII. *The Southern Permyak Dialect* 471

Tales and narratives 474
219. The fox and the thrush 474
220. The fox and the crab 476
221. The goat and the fox 478

222. The cat and the fox 478
223. The tom-cat, the lamb and the goat 480
224. The fox and the crane 482
225. Suddenly-enriched Kuzma 482
226. Kroška Xawroška 488
227. Stupid Jemeŀa 490
228. The devils and the soldier 496
229. Mush from a hatchet 498
230. How the landowner hatched horses 500
231. The priest and the soldier 500
232. The wordy woman 502
233. The son made of clay 504
234. The frog tsarevna 506
235. Śiwka-burka 514
236. Go I-know-not-where, bring I-know-not-what! 520
237. Tsarevich Ivan and the wolf 532
238. Our kolkhoz 536
239. [Hare-hunting] 538
240. [Gathering mushrooms] 538
241. [About fishing] 538
242. [About boating] 540
243. [Playing on the river bank] 540
244. [A ride in a snow-storm] 540
245. [My family] 542
246. [About cooking] 542
247. [Picking berries] 542
248. [How I lost my way in the forest] 544
249. [Our village] 546
250. About weddings 546
251. [Our village] 554

Notes to the Texts 558
Appendices 597
Type-Numbers of Tales according to the Aarne-Thompson System 597
Musical Examples 600
Photographs 647

PREFACE

Apart from a few narratives, the texts published in this volume were collected during my tour of three and a half months in the Komi ASSR in 1964. The bulk of the material originates from the following dialect areas: Vym, Vyčegda Lower, Vyčegda Upper, Višera, Permyak Northern and Permyak Southern. A few pages of text have been added from the dialect areas of Middle Vyčegda (the neighbourhood of Syktyvkar) and Ižma (Mi̮ži); these were noted in Moscow and Syktyvkar. My aim was to carry out research in areas which had so far produced little, if any, material for scholarly examination. The texts from Vym, Lower and Upper Vyčegda and Višera are direct field-notations, except for some Višera (Bogorodsk) specimens which I collected in Syktyvkar. For the Permyak material I am indebted to students at college in Syktyvkar; and I noted one of the Southern-Permyak narratives while staying in Moscow. — I should also mention that I had noted some of the Upper-Vyčegda texts in Moscow during my first study tour in the Soviet Union, in 1957. A few pages of this collection were first published in a linguistic periodical (NyK 61: 95—99). The same periodical published some specimens from the Vym and the Lower-Vyčegda dialects (NyK 73: 3—23).

About seventy per cent of the collected material is also available on tape.

While collecting in the villages along the Vym river (in May 1964) I enjoyed the company of the literary historian and folklorist A. K. Mikušev. To facilitate our work, the Komi Branch of the Academy of Sciences of the Soviet Union kindly placed at our disposal one of its small boats called "Nauka" (Science). During my field-work in the Upper-Vyčegda region (June 1964) I received similar assistance from the linguist E. S. Gulyaev, and in Nivšera (July 1964) from the linguist G. G. Baraksanov. In transcribing the texts from tape, the folklorist J. G. Ročev was of greatest assistance to me. It is largely due to their friendly collaboration and generous kindness that the study tour to the North remains an unforgettable memory to me. I express my gratitude to all of them.

The texts as published are divided into dialects and within these by types: tales, narratives, songs, laments, etc. Each dialect-group is introduced by a brief description of the main characteristics of the dialect in question. Notes on linguistic and other relevant topics complement the texts.

I have used the method of phonematic notation, although in certain cases I have also indicated the allophones to ensure that the phonetic characteristics featured in the given dialect should not be blurred.

Names of Russian origin used in Zyrian have been transcribed according to the rules of transliteration adopted in Slavonic linguistic studies.

The Chapter on Type-Numbers of Tales according to the Aarne-Thompson System has been contributed by Ágnes Kovács while the elaboration of the Musical Examples, by Mária Domokos. I am also grateful to Péter Hajdú for his having kindly read the Hungarian manuscript of my book.

I wish to express my indebtedness to the Hungarian Academy of Sciences for having made possible my study tour to the land of Zyrians, as well as to the Komi Branch of the Academy of Sciences of the USSR for all the assistance it offered me during my stay there. Finally, I owe a debt of thanks and gratitude to my informants. Without their zealous devotion I should never have been able to complete this enterprise.

BIBLIOGRAPHICAL ABBREVIATIONS

Даль = Даль, Владимир, Толковый словарь живого великорусского языка. 1—4. С.-Петербург—Москва 1880—1882.

FOKOS, ZürjNépk-Mut. = FOKOS, DÁVID, Zürjén népköltészeti mutatványok [Specimens of Zyrian folk poetry]. NyK. 41, 42; Separatum, Budapest 1913.

FOKOS-FUCHS = FOKOS-FUCHS, D. R., Syrjänisches Wörterbuch, I—II. Budapest 1959.

KRSl. = Коми-русский словарь. Москва 1961.

KT = Karjalainen, K. F., Ostjakisches Wörterbuch. Bearb. u. hg. von Y. H. Toivonen, I—II. Helsinki 1948 (Lexica Societatis Fenno-Ugricae, X).

LYTKIN, DialChrest. = Лыткин, В. И., Диалектологическая хрестоматия по пермским языкам. Часть 1. Москва 1955.

LYTKIN, IstVok. = Лыткин, В. И., Исторический вокализм пермских языков. Москва 1964.

MSFOu. = Suomalais-Ugrilaisen Seuran Toimituksia. Mémoires de la Société Finno-Ougrienne. I–. Helsinki 1890–.

NyK = Nyelvtudományi Közlemények I–. Pest, (then:) Budapest 1862–.

RÉDEI, SLW = RÉDEI, KÁROLY, Die syrjänischen Lehnwörter im Wogulischen. Budapest—Bloomington–The Hague 1970.

Sborn. = Историко-филологический сборник. Сыктывкар 1960, 1966.

SrSlK = Сравнительный словарь коми-зырянских диалектов. Сыктывкар 1961.

VFUJa. = Вопросы финно-угорского языкознания. 1962–.

VJa. = Вопросы языкознания. 1–. Москва 1952–.

WIED. = WIEDEMANN, F. J., Syrjänisch–deutsches Wörterbuch nebst einem wotjakisch–deutschen und einem deutschen Register. St. Petersburg 1880.

WUo. = WICHMANN, YRJÖ–T. E. UOTILA, Syrjänischer Wortschatz nebst Hauptzügen der Formenlehre. Aufgezeichnet von YRJÖ WICHMANN, bearb. u. hg. von T. E. UOTILA. Helsinki 1942 (Lexica Societatis Fenno-Ugricae VII).

ABBREVIATIONS FOR ZYRIAN DIALECTS

I = Ižma
I_L = Ižma Lower
Le = Letka
Lu = Luza
Mez = Mezeń
P = Permyak
PE = Permyak Eastern (on the basis of Genetz; = Ya)
Peč = Pečora
PN = Permyak Northern
Pr = Prup
PS = Permyak Southern
S = Sysola
SC = Sysola Central
SR = Syktyvkar Region (on the basis of SrSlK; = VC)
SU = Sysola Upper
Ud = Udora
V = Vyčegda
VC = Vyčegda Central = SR
VL = Vyčegda Lower
Vm = Vym
VU = Vyčegda Upper
Ya = Yazva (on the basis of Lytkin; = PE)

I. THE VYM DIALECT

My texts from the Vym dialect area originate from the following three villages: Шёшки (Zyr. *śe̮śka)*, Луг (Zyr. *gu-će̮rt*) and Турья (Zyr. *turja*). Шёшки is situated on the left bank of the Vym (Zyr. *jem-va*); Луг and Турья are somewhat further North, on the right bank of the river. My informants were as follows: Шёшки: Evdokija Ivanovna L a p i n a, Lidija Ivanovna P a r c h a č ë v a, Evgenija Grigorjevna P r o š e v a, Aleksandra Semënovna P u d o v a, Anna Ivanovna P u d o v a; Луг: Marija Dmitrievna K o k a n i n a (b. 1926, Луг), Anastasija Petrovna K o z l o v a (b. 1891, Турья), Irina Semënovna M a l'g i n a (b. 1892, Луг), Marija Semënovna M a l'g i n a (b. 1910, Луг); Турья: Natalija Ivanovna K u č m e n ë v a (b. 1892, Кони), Ol'ga Andreevna N e k r a s o v a (b. 1903, Турья).

The main characteristics of the dialect are as follows:

1. As regards the phoneme *l*, *l* ~ ø, in other words, it is of the Ižma type. For example, *ve̮le̮n* 'with a horse' ~*vē̮* 'horse' *pukala* 'I sit' ~*pukōni̮* 'to sit'. Following a palatal vowel, *l* becomes *j*, e.g. *zej* 'very' (in Šoški *zē*:) ~ S *zel*, *pij* 'cloud' ~Ud *piv (< *pil)*. Similarly, *l* becomes *j* if preceded by *a*: *majtni̮* ~ S *maltni̮* 'schmieren, beschmieren'. Followed by two consonants, or by a single one in the final position, *l* is dropped, but the preceding vowels *(u, o, i̮, e̮)* are not lengthened. For example, *sutsa* 'standing', *sut:* 'stand up!' ~ S *sult-* 'aufstehen, stehen bleiben'. Finally, *l* remains unchanged in certain verbal suffixes *(-oll-* ~ S *-all-*, *-i̮l-*, *-li̮ll-)*: *pi̮rolli̮ni̮* 'hineingehen', *aǯǯi̮lni̮* 'sehen', *vetli̮lli̮ni̮* 'herumgehen, gehen' (cf. SrSlK 458).

2. *e̮* and *i̮* remain unchanged in all positions.

3. Assimilation is also a typical feature of the dialect. For example, *bat'tas* 'fathers' ~ V *bat'jas*, *le̮śe̮ćći̮ni̮* ~ V *le̮śe̮d'ći̮ni̮* 'sich vorbereiten'.

4. *js* is sometimes found instead of palatalized *ś*, and *jd* instead of *ʒ́*. For example, *vojsa* ~ V *vośsa* 'offen', *ke̮jdni̮* ~ V *ke̮ʒ́avni̮* 'kalt werden, gefrieren'.

5. The *t* of the *śt* sequence is usually omitted in the final position, e.g., *boś* ~ V *bośt* 'nimm', *ge̮ś* ~ V *ge̮śt* 'Gast'.

6. The forms of the past tense of the negative verb are *ig*, *in*, *iz* etc. (~V *eg*, *en*, *ez* etc.).

7. The dative suffix *-li̮* occurs sometimes with an accusative function, e.g., *pili̮ bi̮ttisni̮* 'they brought up the boy', *mene̮li̮* 'me', *sije̮li̮* 'him' etc.

(a) Tales and narratives

1. *gozja i e̯ťik pi*

1. *olis-vi̯lis gozja | znaćit, si̯le̯n ve̯li e̯ťik pi, i v a n | i v a n, znaćit, sija | zej ki̯jśi̯ś-vijśi̯ś | zej morti̯s | sečе̯m streľeć-kojd | mune̯ | mi̯j ve̯re̯ munas | utka vajas ti̯r | baťli̯-mami̯ | vaje̯ e̯te̯re̯ | bi̯d lun vaje̯ sije̯ nešole̯n | seśśa olis | e̯ťik lun | vetlis | daj si̯li̯ś meľńića prud dorti ve̯li vetle̯dle̯ | i nī̯ sećće̯ pete̯ma | si̯li̯ś veśse̯ mi̯rďďis | mi̯j-ke̯ | utka-pe̯tkate̯ | baťi̯s dine̯ munis da mamis aľi šuve̯ni̯: | "mi̯j-ne̯, i v a n, ńi-ne̯m iz śur?" | "a iz pe̯ śur talun" | me̯d lun munis | vaje̯ ve̯li. e̯pjať sija boštis i e̯pjať abu | "mene̯ pe vajan, on? | jeśľi-ke̯ mene̯ vajan | śeta | on vaj, og śet | i vot sija | dumaććis, dumaććis da ni-ńe̯m iz šu | i mami̯sli̯ viśtalis | šuas: | "mame̯, vot, tačе̯m-tor! | me — šuas — ki̯k lun ńin vaji | da ki̯knan pēse̯ e̯tbe̯ritis e̯ťik nī̯ka | sija pe̯ — šue̯ | — 'mene̯ pe̯ vajan, on?' | a me pe̯ vot og ke̯sji̯śli̯ i oz śet | pre̯mi̯s" | no taja šuis | mami̯s: | "te pe̯ vot meľńića prudśi̯d petas | da vi̯ǯe̯d pe̯! | jeśľi-ke̯ pe̯ ni̯li̯s śin-ki̯ma | znaćit, sije̯ boštni̯se̯ | ke̯sji̯ś vajni̯te̯ | a abu ke̯ pe̯ śin-ki̯mi̯s | in ke̯sji̯ś vajni̯te̯!" | i vot sija | kojme̯d lun munas | kojme̯d lun munas | i bara | ni̯li̯d mi̯j-ke̯ karas | boštas si̯li̯ś | meše̯kte̯ | i šuas: "i v a n, mene̯ vajan, on?" | nī̯li̯ viǯe̯dlas | i šuas: "vaja pe̯" | "no vajan i korošo | i nī̯-baba sija veśse̯ śetis | kujimnan lunśate̯ da i nuis | "vot jeśľi-ke̯ — šue̯ — te vajan mene̯li̯ | te — šue̯ — asi̯ | lok — šue̯ — ta pe̯rajase̯ | tаćće̯ | i me — šue̯ | — seki vetlam bať-mam orde̯ pridanne̯jla pe̯" | nu vot sija | munis | i bať-mamli̯ i viśtali̯s | mi̯j "asi̯ me ni̯li̯s dine̯ muna" | sija munis | ni̯li̯s i petis bara | ni̯li̯dke̯d meľńića-mi̯j-ke̯ad i pi̯risni̯ | znaćit | vae̯ pi̯risni̯ | va ūti munini̯, munini̯ | voisni̯ sija bať-mam orde̯ | i zej una | mi̯j-ke̯ vajisni̯ nali̯ | ge̯śťińǯi śetisni̯ | ge̯śťitisni̯ | mi̯j-ke̯ olisni̯ | i zej una vē̯-ti̯r nī̯li̯ pridanne̯j vajisni̯ | nī̯ zej śuś | bur sija | vajisni̯ | i gortas ve̯li ľokińǯik kerka | ni̯li̯s sije̯ kerka karis i bi̯d-tor | viľ kerka ve̯ćisni̯.*

2. *nu vot voisni̯ | a etija | mi̯jke̯isli̯ loi zavid | no sari̯sli̯ | — važe̯n kuǯ šuasni̯ | — sarjas ved vi̯dajtisni̯ | zavid loi, mi̯j sija e̯ťik voje̯n kerka ve̯ćisni̯ | i korisni̯ i v a n t e̯ sećće̯ | korisni̯ sećće | i šue̯ni̯ | mi̯j-ke̯ pe̯ | dumščikjas i šue̯ni̯: | "vot i v a n pe̯ ke̯sji̯śe̯ karni̯ e̯ťik voje̯ pe̯ | — taje̯ i v a n i̯ s veśke̯ ńi-ne̯m iz šuli̯ — | a i v a n vot pe̯ ke̯sji̯śe̯ karni̯ pe̯ vićko" | no i v a n ćujmis: |*

1. A married couple and a son

1. There lived a married couple. They had a son, Ivan. Ivan is a great hunter, the sort of man who is a good shot. He goes out into the woods, and brings a bag full wild-duck to his parents. He never ceases to bring, to bring a bag every day. Thus he lived. One day he went out and passed by the mill-dam, when a girl came that way. She took everything away from him, er, his wild-duck, his wild-fowl. He went home to his parents; they say: "What's the matter, Ivan, didn't you find anything?" "Well, no, I found nothing today."Next day he went out again. He brought back his bag. But again she took it away. "You will marry me, won't you? If you will marry me, I will give it you back, if not, I'll not give it you back." Well now, he thought and thought and did not say a word. He told his mother about it: "Did you ever hear such a thing, mother! I" — says he —" brought wild-duck yesterday and the day before yesterday, but a girl took them away both times. She asks me: 'You will marry me, won't you?' I don't promise her anything, and she won't give me back the bag." His mother spoke thus: "When she comes out from the mill-dam, take a good look at her! If she has eyebrows, promise you'll marry her; if she has no eyebrows, don't promise her anything!" Well, the third day he goes out again, and the girl takes away his bag again, the bag full of wild-duck, saying: "Ivan, you will marry me, won't you?" He takes a good look at her and says: "I'll marry you." "Well, if you'll marry me, everything's all right." The woman gave him back everything — she had taken three days' bags from him —. "If you'll marry me" — says she — "come here tomorrow at this time, and I" — says she — "then we'll go to my parents for the dowry." Well, he went home and told his parents, "Tomorrow I'm going to the girl." So he went there, and the girl came out. Then both he and the girl walked together into the millpond. They walked and walked under the water, and they arrived at the parents' house. And they brought many presents and gave them to them. They feasted with them living there for a while. And they gave many cart loads of dowry to the girl. The girl is clever and good. The house they lived in was old. The girl made a new house and everything; they built a new house.

2. Well, they arrived at home. The, er, the Tsar — as they used to call him — grew envious of them. The Tsars (counsellors) let it out that they had built a house in a single night. They summoned Ivan, and the counsellors say, "Well now, Ivan promises that in a single night" (this Ivan had not said anything) "Ivan promises that he will build a church." Well, Ivan wondered: "What ever is this?", and he goes home. "If not, they will cut off his head, if it is not done." At this he grew sorrowful and went to his wife; and she

'mij taja?' | munis gortas | "a oz kę pę, jur kerōnį | jeśľi oz lo." | seśśa śogę vojis sija | munis gętir dinę | da i śuę: "mij, i v a n te śog?" | "a mij nę — suas — | ęťik voję čęktisnį vićko karnį | no — śuas — me og vermį karnį. kiʒ nę — śuas — me kara?" | "in pę majiććį! | vęćam pę" | i ić-moń | ęťik vojnas vęćis siję | vićko zej mića loi | "i mun — śuas — vićko dinin toľko čęlkatnį | mij-kę pę meletęn ęťiklaę točęd da mędlaę tučęd da med — śuas — | mij-kę loę | (karę)" | nu vot | sija vęćis | i sar bara ćeććis. aʒʒis: | vęćęma | "vot pę ęd kučęm ńin!" | bara dumčikjas dumajtisnį, dumajtisnį | "a i v a nis pę ęd sija ńin kęsję pę karnį | med pę teeʒ daj gortęʒis vęli pos | sečęm kęrt pos | i med pę veśis sad vęli | a pos | doras | pę med vęli oźero | i oźero doras pę med utkajas i pętkajas i stavis plavajtę". | sija | i v a nęs bara korisnį | "i v a n — śuas — te vot ośjiśęmid tačęm-tor" | "me — śuas — | ńi-nęm ig śulį" | "da — śuas — te ośjiśęmid | jeśľi — śuas — on kar ęťik vojęn | ten — śuas — śmert | i jurtę — śuas — kerōnį" | babalį bara viśtalis | "nu — śuas baba — | mij nę, i v a n, in pō | kuʒ-kę — śuas — | loę daśkęn" | nu | bara vodis | i v a n | asį-voʒ babaįs ćeććęde: | "nolį — śuę — ćeććį, kęźajin! | mun — śuas — da kitęn-kę tį dorjasad mij-kę ęťięn śvućkį da mędęn śvaćkį da mij-kę vęćō — śuas —!" | i v a n munis, mij-kę setęni vek | mij-kę karę | loktis sar | bara śuas: | "nu vot, smotri· pę, mij sija karę" | etija dumčikjaslį bara nalį zavid | i bara śuęnį: | taję — śuas — | ębjaza·ťeľnę kolę kuʒ-kę podvedťitnį, i v a nęs | mij taja | tačęm-torjas vęćalę | seśśa | sija i śuis: | "vot pe — dumčikjasid naja viśtalęnį saridlį — | taja pę i v a nid, vot ńin mij kęsję karnį: | mij pę źverįs vijim | vęras | kučęm źver | oś | kęjin | bidśama pelęssę | veśsę pę kęsję vajędnį | taććę | znaćit, dvoras tenid" | no | i v a nęs korisnį "i v a n — śuas —, te kęsjiśin?" | "ig pę | me pę ńi-nęm og tęd" | "a kiś — śuas — on tęd? | te żę kęsjiśęmid, vot baχvaľiććęmid, ośjiśęmid pę da" | mij bara | mij seśśa — śuas — karnį? | bara seśśa | munis | bara munis gortas | śogęn | śogalis, śogalis da i śuę | babaįs: | "mij nę — śuas — i v a n, tačęm śog taun pukalan?" | "a kiʒ nę — śuas — on pukō | tačęm-tor — śuas — men čęktisnį vęćnį da" | "no — śuas — vod, «утром вечерние мудреннее» — śuę — | vod da i uź | spoko·jnę! | a toľko — śuę — kōmas ćeććinį asį-voʒnad voʒ" | no | siję koris stav źvertę | "ńeńki — manki pę — śuas — | ćukęrtej | stav źversę, mij vęras vįjim | no | źverjas kuććisnį ćukartnį seni | kodi įmzę, kodi mij, kodi mij | stavįs pōźis da med asinas čękte, śuas: | "kiʒi gaźid, bęr vętlalę!" | strak loi silį | petni oz liśtį | dvoras |

said to him: "What's the matter, Ivan, why are you so sad?" "Why?" — says he. "They have ordered me to build a church in a single night." "Well" — says he — "I can't do that. How am I to do that?" — says he. "Don't worry, we shall do it." The young wife built it in a single night. The church was very beautiful. "Go" — says she — " and make a noise by the church! Knock at it with the hammer on the one side, then on the other, to make a noise." Well now, this is what he did. The Tsar got up and caught sight of it: it had been finished. "Look, what a sight!" The counsellors thought and thought again. "Well, Ivan now wants to build an iron bridge so that a bridge may connect your house and his, and also a garden, a pond by the bridge, with wild-duck and wild-fowl in the pond, all swimming." They had Ivan summoned again. "Ivan" — says he — "you boasted of such a thing." "I" — says he — "did not say anything." "But" — says he — "you did boast. If you do not have it finished in a single night, it will mean your death, and your head" — says he — "will be chopped off." Again he told his wife the story. "Well now" — says the woman — "why, Ivan, don't be afraid; somehow" — says she — "perhaps it will be done." So Ivan went to bed; the woman wakes him in the morning: "Hurry up, husband, get up! Go" — says she — "beat away at something with one of your hands, strike away at something with the other somewhere on the shore of the pond, as if you were making something!" — says she. He went there, and busied himself with something. The Tsar comes along and says, "Well now, just see what he is doing!" Again the counsellors grow envious, and say once more, "Certainly we must get this Ivan into trouble somehow for doing things like this." "Just see," — say the counsellors — "what this Ivan is about to do this time: whatever kinds of wild beasts are living in this wood, — all kinds of wild beasts, bears, wolves, and all the rest, — all of these he wants to bring to your court." So they had Ivan summoned. "Ivan" — says he — "have you been making another promise?" "No, I know nothing at all." "What do you mean, you know nothing at all? After all, you have made a promise, you have been bragging, you have been boasting!" So what is then to do? Once again he went home sadly. Full of grief, full of grief he was; and his wife speaks thus: "Why do you sit there, Ivan" — says she — "so sadly today?" "Well, how would you be sitting" — says he — "when you are ordered to do such things!" "Well then, go to bed" — says she — "a man's wiser in the morning than he was last night. Go to bed and sleep in peace!" Well, she summoned all the beasts there. "*Ńeńki, manki*" — says she — "gather together all the wild beasts that live in the wood. They began to gather the beasts together, some roaring, some doing what they usually did. Everybody was terrified. Next morning the Tsar gives

to ke̮jin | to oš sete̮ni | to mi̮j-ke̮ | ke̮ć, to | ruć to | bi̮dśama pe̮le̮s | i be̮r će̮ktis seśśa ve̮tlōni̮ sije̮li̮ | pōźis sije̮ | pōźis | nu vot seśśa | ni-ne̮m iz vermi̮ni̮ i v a ne̮s karni̮ | ńi-ne̮m iz vermi̮ni̮ karni̮.

3. *jeśśe̮ dumajtisni̮ | mi̮j — šuas — tead babai̮d pe̮ | vot le̮śale̮ | seče̮m, seče̮m mortli̮ | i v a n kutis ske̮rōni̮ | i v a n kutis seče̮ma ske̮rōni̮ | "i mi̮j — šuas — taja | menam — šuas — baba bur | oz ske̮rō" | "kuʒ́ — šuas — tenad oz ske̮rō babai̮d? | vot — šuas — vetlam | vot buď oz ske̮rō | vot sije̮ kuʒ́-ke̮ pod-veďitisni̮ | i śorovno seśśa i v a ni̮d | be̮rťi ńin | veritni̮ kutis | seśśa | ʒ́ugśisni̮ | be̮rti ńin | babai̮ske̮d | janse̮ććisni̮ | i | ľoka kutisni ōni̮ | i siʒ́ʒ́i seśśa jansa-lisni̮ | i e̮ni ole̮-vi̮le̮. pom.*

2. *de̮več kupeć*

1. *kupeć olis, si̮le̮n babai̮s kule̮ma. i si̮le̮n ve̮li kujim nī̮. kujim nī̮ ve̮lini̮ i zej jona nī̮jasse̮ sija ve̮li raďejte̮-ľubite̮. a me̮d ʒ́e̮ľase̮ jeśśe̮ jona ľubite̮. i vot sija, znaćit, vetle̮dle̮ bi̮d vo puťešestvujtni̮. puťešestvujtni̮ vetle̮dle̮ i sija i̮ʒ́i̮d nī̮se̮ koris: "mi̮j — šuas — te meni̮m će̮ktan vajni̮?" vot ni̮li̮s sija šuis: "men pe̮ kole̮ ze̮le̮tnej veńeć, sije̮ pe̮ men de̮sta·ńit." a me̮d nī̮se̮ koris: "ten ne̮ — šuas — mi̮j kole̮?" "men pe̮ žemćugnej plaťťe̮ kole̮." "no ten pe̮ verma dostańitni̮." i me̮d iće̮t nī̮se̮ koris: "ľubimej dońka pe̮, ten pe̮ mi̮j kole̮?" "a men pe̮ kole̮ aľenkoj ćvetoćek." no vot, znaćit, baťi̮d šogśis, sije̮ šuas: "me peľe̮n pe̮ ig kī̮li, śinme̮n pe̮ ig aʒ́ʒ́il. ki̮ś pe̮ sije̮ men ćukte̮dni̮? znaćit, nu korošo. sija no vozmo·žno pe̮ i dosta·ńita. znaćit, meam pe̮ bogatsvo ti̮rmas i vozmo·žno pe̮ dosta·ńita". bať muni. "toľko — šue̮ — ti bura ole̮, me vote̮ʒ́ vere̮s saje̮ in mune̮. bura ole̮ i kuʒ́ śle̮dujte̮, gosudarstvo kute̮ menśi̮m ole̮m, me̮d oz ńe-kićće̮ protaskućći̮, me̮d oz, znaćit, ńe-kod oz nu ńe-ki̮ćće̮. śoj i vopšem ti in ľubićće poka me vote̮ʒ́ ńe-kod-ke̮d! korošo!"*

2. *taja kupeć muni, muni — daške̮ mijan viśtōni̮ ke̮ńešne̮ regi̮d, a si̮li di̮r — daške̮ ńin munis i miśić, daške̮ i ki̮ke̮s. sija te̮rgujtis bura, vuzaśis aslas ka-pitanjaske̮d da mi̮j da kodi si̮le̮n ve̮li, ťeloχrańiťeľjasi̮s no sija bura vuzaśis i kuććis ńin korśni̮, znaćit, pe̮darokjas. kole̮ be̮r ńin vozvraťi·ćći̮ni̮ gorte̮. pe̮darok korśni̮ munis. nī̮li̮ śuri veńeć, śujis sije̮li̮ sunduke̮. me̮d nī̮li̮ śuri žemćugnej plaťťe̮. kojme̮dli̮ korśis, korśis i ńe-ki̮ś iz śur [iś‿śur]. me̮d ʒ́e̮ľa nī̮li̮, znaćit, ge̮śťińći iz śur i vois šoge̮ sija. mi̮j kutan karni̮? i kole̮ uže ńin be̮r vozvraťi·ćći̮ni̮.*

orders: "Somehow or other you must chase them back!" He was so scared that he did not dare to go out. In the courtyard he sees here a wolf, there a bear, elsewhere, er, a hare, or a fox. All kinds of beasts. And he ordered him to drive them back. Certainly he was scared, he was very scared. Well, they could not do anything to harm Ivan. They could not do anything at all.

3. In the end, the counsellors thought up a new plan: "Look, so and so, and so and so have taken a fancy to your wife." Ivan began to grow angry. Ivan began to rage exceedingly. "What? My wife is good, she does not hate me." "Well, well" — says he — "you think your wife does not hate you. Let's go and see then if she hates you or not!" Well, they deceived him in some way or other. And then Ivan began to believe them. Then relations between them got worse; then he divorced his wife. They began to become estranged and so finally they were divorced. And he is still alive. That's the end of the story.

2. The merchant who was a widower

1. There lived a merchant. His wife had died. He had there daughters. He had there daughters, and he was very fond of his daughters. But the youngest one he loved best of all. He goes on his travels every year. He goes on his travels and he asked his eldest daughther: "What do you order me to bring you?" The girl said: "I want a wedding-garland of gold, that will be enough for me." He called his second daughter: "What do you want?" — says he —. "I want a pearly dress." "Well, I can get one for you." He called his youngest daughter: "My beloved daughter, what do you want?" "Well, I want to have the purple flower." The father grew sad, saying: "My ears have not heard of it, my eyes have not seen it. Where am I to get it? All right, then. Perhaps I can get it. I have wealth enough, perhaps I can get it." The father went off. "Just you be good" — says he — "and not marry before I come back home! Live well" — says he — "the state is looking after my wealth so that it may not be wasted, so that no one can carry it away anywhere. Eat well and in general do not make love to anyone until I return! That's all right then!"

2. This merchant went on and on — of course, it takes us a short time perhaps to tell the tale although it took him a long time — he went on his way perhaps for a month or two. He made good bargains, trading with his captains; and he had men to guard him. Well, he had made good bargains and then he began to look . . . er . . . for the presents. It was time to return

no vot sije̯ vozvraťi·ććis be̯r. sija kuććis lokni̯ gortas, a si̯li̯ ši̯biććisni̯ kuče̯m-ke̯, seče̯m mi̯j-ke̯jas, piratjas. ši̯biććisni̯ si̯li̯ i mort ńe-ki̯ćće̯ oz vermi̯ spasaćći̯ni̯. sija pi̯šjis da pi̯šjis da munis da munis da. a etija mi̯j-ke̯śi̯s sija ve̯ri̯n ńin ćeććis da sija koľi mi̯j-ke̯śis, karabśis. i vot sija, znaćit, ve̯ras pi̯šjis da pi̯šjis da pi̯šjis da seśśa sija vek munis i be̯re̯ berge̯ćći̯las. ńe-ki̯ćće̯ munni̯ i vek vože̯ mune̯ i mune̯ i mune̯. i vi̯že̯de̯ i sija jona i mi̯žis i vi̯že̯de̯: seni bi̯ťťe̯-ke̯ś bi e̯zje̯, ti̯dale. "no — šuas — mi̯j taja? śorovno — šue̯ — muna." si̯le̯n plaťťe̯-ke̯mkot kiśśis. i si̯le̯n uže ńin śoje̯mi̯ś veś či̯gje̯ vois i bi̯d-tor. no mi̯j ve̯ćan? munis. toko vois sija i̯ži̯d mramorne̯j kerka. znaćit, sija sećće̯ pi̯ris. ńe-kod ńe-ki̯te̯n abu. ńi kerkai̯n mort abu ńe-kod. kerka veśi̯s ubranne̯j, ćiste̯j da šue̯: "me veśke̯, vot ki̯ne̯m śumale̯, śoji̯štni̯." vi̯že̯de̯: stol loi, seni i śoje̯d-jue̯d loi. pe̯žalusta, śoj-ju! śojis-juis da. "eśke̯ — šue̯ — tani-ke̯ — šue̯ posťeľa men loe̯." nu i kre̯vať loi, kre̯vajte̯ vodis. poka raďio ve̯li vorse̯ i̯ži̯da. mije̯n sija vodis, kutis ńe̯žjammi̯ni̯ i ńe̯žjammi̯ni̯ i ńe̯žjammi̯ni̯ i unmōśis sija. vot sija i uźis. sija uźis i "mi̯j — šue̯ — tate̯ni? tan — šue̯ — ńe-kod — šue̯ — abu, ńe-ki̯te̯n abu, a mi̯jla — šue̯ — tače̯m taja veśi̯s — šue̯ — ube̯rite̯m." no śojis i stol be̯r voši, abu. "ćas — me — šue̯ — petala ge̯ge̯rtni̯ kerka ge̯ge̯rse̯, sadse̯." sija i kerka ge̯ge̯r (sad) munis, ge̯ge̯rtis i pomśis ai̯ži̯s, znaćit, ale̯j ćvetok. "vot taje̯ — šue̯ — aľeńke̯j ćveto·kse̯ me — šue̯ — ni̯le̯jli̯ i bośta. vot men — šue̯ — ve̯ľiśťi i šuri." sija ćegis i sećće̯ sije̯li̯ źver ši̯biććis i prame̯ si̯ vi̯le̯ "vot — šuas — te me̯nši̯m śe̯le̯me̯s boštin i mi̯j — šue̯ — te ke̯sjan ta vi̯le̯ plaťitni̯? te — šue̯ — on-ke̯ — šue̯ — plaťićći̯, me — šue̯ — tene̯ bure̯n og leže̯, ten — šue̯ — śmert." "no a mi̯j ne̯ — šue̯ — menam ďeńga vi̯jim, me — šue̯ — teni̯d, mi̯jtta kole̯, śeta. menam i ezi̯ś, menam i ze̯le̯te̯. no mi̯j ńin kole̯, ten sije̯ i śeta." "men — šuas — tenad ńi-ne̯m oz kō, a toľko men — šuas — kujim nī pi̯čke̯śśi̯d e̯ťike̯s i̯sti̯ pe̯ taćće̯!" no dumaććis, dumaććis, dumaććis i šuis: "ladne̯ pe̯, i̯sta. a vot e̯ni — šuas — men kuž-ke̯ kole̯ gorte̯ voni̯." "ten pe̯ śeta kujim lun strok, znaćit, kujim lun strok, kujim lun, med pe̯ kujim ćas, kujim minut, kujim śekund. jeśľi-ke̯ oz vo seććež ni̯li̯d taćće̯ mijan dore̯ i seki — šue̯ — ten śmert. i śorono — šue̯ — te ole̯m tenad pomaśas." no vot, znaćit, sija ke̯sjiśis. "no vot men pe̯

back home. He went out to look for presents. For the eldest daughter he found a wedding-garland, which he put in a chest. For the next daughter he found a pearly dress. He searched for the present for the third one; he searched everywhere but could not find it. For the younger daughter, er, he could find no present and he grew sad. What was he to do? And now he must return. So he started back. He started to return home but he was attacked by some, — what shall I call them? — robbers. They assaulted him, and none could escape. He ran and ran away, and went on and on. He woke up in a wood, a long long away from his ship or whatever it was. He ran, ran and ran in the wood, always going ahead and turning back. There is nowhere to go, so he always goes ahead, on and on and on. He looks, he has grown very tired, and looks: it seems, as if there were a fire burning there. "Well" — says he — "what's this? No matter" — says he — "I'll go there." His clothes and his shoes were in tatters. And he was starving for lack of food and everything. It seems he arrived at a big house of marble. He stepped inside. There is nobody to be seen anywhere. There is no man to be seen in the house. The whole of the house is tidy and clean. And he says: "I should like to eat something, for I am hungry." He sees a table appear, with food and drink on it. "I wish" — says he — "I had place to sleep here." Well, a bed also appeared, and he went to bed in it. There was even a wireless there, playing loudly. As soon as he lay down he began to feel calm, so calm, so calm, and he fell asleep. He slept. He slept and said: "What's going on here? There's nobody here at all, how is it then that everything has been made so tidy?" He had a meal, but the table disappeared again; it is no longer there. "Wait a minute" — says he — "I'll go out round the house and the garden." He went round the house and the garden and at the end of it he caught sight of the purple flower. "Well" — says he — "I shall take this purple flower away to my daughter. At last I have come upon it." He plucked it off, and there a wild beast dashed at him, straight at him. "You've taken away my heart" — says the wild beast. "What will you pay for it? If you do not pay," — says he — "I shall not let you go on your way alive; you shall die." "Well, now what?" — says he — "I've got money and will give you as much as you want. I have silver and I have gold. So tell me how much you want and I will give it to you." "I don't want anything you have," — says he — "I only want one of your three daughters" — says the beast — " just send one of them here." Well, he thought and thought and thought, and then spoke: "All right, I shall send her. But now" — says he — "I must get home somehow." "I'll give you a time limit of three days, three hours, three minutes and three seconds. If your daughter does not arrive here before then" — says he — "you shall die. In any case, your life will

kole̮ i gorte̮ munni.” “vot mun pe̮ da ki̮te̮n pe̮ uźin, kre̮vajtad, mun pe̮ da pe̮duška ulas pe̮ vi̮jim perśťeń, sije̮.” si̮li̮ vodte̮ʒ̮is šuis: “taje̮ ne̮ kepi̮śse̮ śuj, gortad voan i taje̮-že̮ pe̮ kepi̮śnad med loktas ni̮li̮d me dine̮ be̮r: znaćit, kujim lun, kujim ćas, kujim minut, kujim śekund.” no vot seśśa sija be̮r gortas muni.

3. *no vot i vois bať gorte̮, pe̮darokjas śetalis nī̮jasli̮. i e̮ťi lun ole̮ bati̮s, šoga ole̮. i vot už kojme̮d lunas kole̮ ńin i̮sti̮ni̮ nī̮te̮, e̮ťi̮ke̮s. koris i̮ʒ̮id nī̮se̮. “vot — šuas — dorogoj doćka, me — šuas — siʒ̮i i siʒ̮i ke̮sji̮śi aľeńkoj ćveto·k vi̮le̮ e̮ťik ni̮le̮s śetni̮. on-e̮ — šue̮ — baťse̮ vi̮rućit? a baťi̮sli̮, jeśľi-ke̮ te — šuas — on mun, to baťi̮sli̮ loe̮ śmert.” sija i šuis: “kodli̮ pe̮ sije̮ vajin, sija pe̮ i munas.” i vot koris me̮d nī̮te̮. “nu — šuas — on-e̮ — šuas — te mene̮li̮ mi̮nti̮ pe, mi̮j baťse̮, seśśa baťi̮sli̮ śmert loe̮ vot seki, jeśľi-ke̮ te on mun.” ni̮li̮s bara sije̮ šuis, naotre·z — šuas — “te kodli̮ bośtin, sija pe̮ med tene̮ i vi̮rućitas.” i kojme̮d nī̮te̮ koris. sija ve̮li si̮li̮ žaľ med ʒ́e̮ľa ni̮li̮s, potomu što sije̮ jona ve̮li ľubite̮ i oz ve̮li sija ke̮sji̮ me̮de̮dni̮. no vot i nī̮se̮ koris i be̮rʒʒ́is baťi̮s, šuas: “vot milaja doćka, mene̮ — šuas — mi̮j taja aľeńke̮j ćveto·kte̮ pe̮ me oroti i vot — šuas — sečem-seče̮m źver — šuas — me vi̮le̮ ši̮biććis i — šuas — koris e̮ťi nī̮. no i̮ʒ̮id ćojjasid pe̮ e̮tkažiććisni̮. a mi̮j pe̮ te šuan? jeśľi-ke̮ pe̮ te on mun, to meni̮m — šuas — śmert.” i med ʒ́e̮ľa ni̮li̮d i šue̮: “vot dorogoj baťuško — šue̮ —, me — šue̮ — raz kori tenśi̮d, me pondi — šuas — te śmert on asli̮d pe̮lućit, a muna — šue̮ — me. me — šue̮ — źveri̮ś og pō i me — šuas — ńe-kodi̮ś og pō. me — šuas — veśse̮ ubeďita i me — šue̮ — stavse̮ ulaďita.” i baťi̮d i be̮rʒʒ́is. baťi̮d be̮rʒʒ́is da i šuis: “no — šuas — seśśa — šue̮ — śinme̮n — šuas — tene̮ og aʒʒ́i̮l, ńi peľe̮n og kī̮. vot — šuas — me̮de̮da tene̮, loin, znaćit, śmert vi̮le̮. vot seśśa — šuas — tene̮ ńi og aʒʒ́i̮l, ńi og kī̮.” i vot nī̮li̮ kepi̮ś śujis. nī̮ kepi̮ś bośtis, kie̮ śujis daj abu ńin. abu, voši da vśo.*

4. *nu vot nī̮, znaćit, vois si̮ kerkae̮, prame̮ sećće̮ʒ, kerkae̮ vois, pi̮ris. znaćit, sije̮ bi̮ťťe̮ potnale̮ni̮, bajke̮de̮ni̮. nī̮ šuas: “śojni̮!” śojni̮ vajalasni̮. śojasni̮, juasni̮, seśśa be̮r ubiri·tasni̮. vodas pośťelae̮. poka sija vode̮, sije̮ ńin bajke̮de̮ni̮ taʒ̮i, mi̮j-ke̮ raďioe̮n ńe̮žje̮nʒ̮ik, lajke̮de̮ni̮, med sije unmōśas, ki̮ćće̮ʒ sije̮ uźas. i vot das-ki̮k ži̮r. znaćit, munas sija i žirte̮ sija ki̮čotas lunnas i šuas da šue̮: “zej — šue̮ — bur ōni̮ i le̮śi̮d, no toľko — šue̮ — śorńitni̮ ńe-kodke̮d i — šuas — znaćit, meni̮m — šuas — śe̮ki̮d ōni̮. toľko — šuas — śorńitni̮ ńe-kodke̮d.” nu,*

come to an end." "All right", he agreed, "now, I must start for home." "Well, just go to the couch you have slept in, and you will find a jewelled ring under the pillow." Before going to bed, he said to him: "Put on these gloves; when you arrive home, let your daughter come to me with these gloves. So: three days, three hours, three minutes and three seconds." Then he left for home.

3. The father arrived home and gave the presents to his daughters. The father stays (at home) for one day, and a sad man he is. For on the third day he must send away one of his daughters. He called his eldest daughter: "Now" — says he — "dear daughter, this way or that, I have pledged one of my daughters for the purple flower. Are you willing to save your father? If you refuse to go" — says he — "your father must die." She answers: "Let her for whom you have brought it go." He called his second daughter. "Now" — says he — "will you not save me, your father, for if you refuse to go, your father must die?" But the girl replied bluntly: "Let the one you have brought it to save you!" He called his third daughter too. He was very sorry for his youngest daughter because he loved her dearly and did not want to send her there. Anyway, he called his daughter; and the father began to weep, saying: "Well, my dearest daughter, because I have plucked this purple flower" — says he — "some kind of wild beast attacked me and demanded one of my daughters. Your sisters have refused to go. Now what do you say? If you do not go, that will be death for me." The youngest daughter speaks thus: "Dear father, since it is I that asked you for it, on my account" — says she — "you shall not die, so I shall go. As for me" — says she — "I am not afraid of any wild beast. As for me" — says she — "I am not afraid of any wild beast. As for me" — says she — "I am not afraid of anyone. I shall conquer everything, I shall put everything right." Her father began to weep. Her father began to weep, saying: "From this time forth, I shall not see you with my own eyes, not hear you with my own ears. I am sending you away, and handing you over to death! From this time forth, I shall neither see you nor hear of you." He passed the gloves to his daughter. His daughter took the gloves, put them on and all of a sudden she is nowhere to be seen. She is not there, she has disappeared.

4. Well, the daughter arrived at the house, right there, and she entered the house. It was as if she were rocked, and lulled to sleep. The girl speaks thus: "Give me something to eat!" They bring food to her. They eat and drink, then they clear everything away. She goes to lie down in the bed. As soon as she lies down, she is softly lulled to sleep with the wireless, and while she sleeps she is rocked. And, you see, there are twelve rooms there. In the day-time she walks round the rooms and says: "This is a very pleasant place and a

pi̮ris sija med-be̮rja komnatae̮: taje ramorne̮j śťenaad giže̮ma ze̮le̮te̮j bukvae̮n: “te — šuas — menam loan mi̮j-ke̮e̮n, nu, rukovoďi·ti̮śe̮n, znaćit, te taja mi̮j-ke̮nas, ole̮mnas. i te — šuas — veśse̮ ńin ovlaďe·jtin i me — šuas — teni̮d me nin podćińećća — morske̮j ćudoviśše̮ šuas — me teni̮d podćińećća. e̮ni — šuas — te ńin i̮ź̮i̮d, te be̮rśań pe̮ vetle̮dle̮ni̮ das-ki̮ke̮n — šue̮ —, te toľko on aź̮ź̮i̮, a das-ki̮ke̮n pe̮ vetle̮dle̮ni̮ i stavi̮s — šuas — tene̮li̮, mi̮j-ke̮ kare̮ni̮, krańite̮ni̮. te — šuas — ńe-ki̮ćće̮ on voš, ńe-ki̮ćće̮ on lo i tene̮ —šuas — lun i voj krańite̮ni̮.” “nu, med — šuas — pe̮ža·lusta — šuas — pe̮ vot petke̮ćći̮ pe̮ te meni̮m!” a sija i šue̮: “me — šue̮ — petke̮ććini̮ og li̮śti̮. ježľi-ke̮ — šuas — mene̮ te aź̮źan, te — šuas — sećće̮ i kulan, pōźan da. mene̮ — šuas — te vi̮ź̮e̮dni̮ on vermi̮, potomu što te — šuas — pi̮r kulan, pi̮ri̮śte̮m-pir.” no sija bara vette̮dlas sade̮d, vette̮dlas, guľajtas. “i vot — šue̮ — jeśľi pe̮ — šui̮ — toľko men śorńiti̮ś pe̮ kole̮.” i sija kor-ke̮ dumajtis — olis olis da — vot veśke̮ — šuas — piśme̮ gižni̮, ke̮ť baťli̮ — šuas — ki̮k kī gižni̮, mi̮j sije̮ bať šue̮ ve̮li: ’te mi̮j kulan pi̮r’, a me — šuas — ola le̮śi̮da i baťli̮ kole̮ piśme̮ gižni̮. śejćas pojavi·ććis si̮li̮ końvert, buma·ška, rućka: ’pe̮ža·lusta, giž!’ gižis piśme̮, voši. a baťi̮s me̮d asi̮ ćeććis, a mi̮j-ke̮i̮n piśme̮, e̮śiń vi̮li̮n. nu vot baťi̮s li̮ďďis mi̮j »dorogoj bať’, te in pećaľićći̮, in šogśi̮, me ola seče̮m bura morske̮j źver dini̮n. me — šuas — aćim ńin e̮ni i̮ź̮i̮d, mene — šuas — sija li̮ďďe̮ kńaginae̮n ńin, mi̮j — šuas — ’te rukovoďi·ti̮ś pe̮ veśse̮. nu vot sadnas ńin — šuas — te veśnas rukovoďi·tan.’« i sija baťli̮ zej ľubo loi, mi̮j, znaćit, nī ži̮v, zdorov, ole̮ bura. i vot bara sija kutis mi̮j-ke̮ karni̮, olis, olis da mi̮j-ke̮ šuas: “me ľoke̮s ve̮taśa.” bara munis sija, ki̮te̮ni pojavľećće̮ mi̮j-ke̮, bukvajasi̮s, mi̮j — šuas: “vot me — šuas — veśke̮ okota gorte̮ vetli̮ni̮, ebjaza·ťeľne̮ bať dore̮ — šuas —, ke̮ť kujim lun kežle̮. meni̮m kole̮ e̮bjaza·ťeľne̮ baťe̮s i ćojjase̮s vi̮ź̮e̮dli̮ni̮, kuče̮ma ole̮ni̮.” nu si̮li̮ razreši·tisni̮. vot šuas: “toľko kujim lun, kujim ćas, kujim minut, kujim śekund. jeśľi-ke̮ — šuas — te on vo, znaćit, me kula, taja sadi̮s veśi̮s kulas, propaďitas i te čeč propaďitan, jeśľi-ke̮ si̮ ćas kežle̮ on vo.” taja nī bośtis, vot si̮li̮ viśtalis, perśťeńte̮ bara bośtis, sija śujis kije̮ i bara gortas vois. munis i sija ki̮mi̮n lun olis, sije̮ pośľedne̮j lunas i kole̮ ńin si̮li̮ munni̮. kole̮ munni̮, a etija mi̮j-ke̮i̮d, ćojjasi̮d si̮li̮ś veštisni̮ ćaste̮, znaćit, mi̮j-ke̮ karisni̮, podveďitisni̮ sije̮, med sija, mi̮j le̮śi̮da viśtale̮ ole̮m; zavidne̮ loi

nice place to live in, except that there is no one to speak to" — says she — "and so it is hard for me to live here. For there is nobody to speak to." Well, she entered the last room: on its marble walls is written in golden letters: "You will be my guide in this life. You" — it reads — "have already taken possession of all that is here, and I already obey you" — says the sea-monster — "I obey you. Now you are great, you have twelve followers all the time" — says he — "but you cannot see them, twelve of them are following you all the time, . . . er . . . to guard you. You shall not disappear anywhere, you shall not take a step" — says he — "without being guarded night and day." "Well now, show yourself to me!" But he replies: "I do not dare to show myself. If you catch sight of me" — says he — "you will die of fright. You may not see me, for you shall die the very moment you see me." Well, she walks around the garden again, she walks and walks. "What I need" — says she — "is someone to talk to." She went on living there, and one day she thought of writing a letter, even if it were only two words to her father, for her father had said: "You will die immediately." "But as for me" — says she — "I'm doing well, and I ought to write a letter to my father." At once envelope, paper and pen appeared: "Here you are, write!" She wrote the letter which disappeared at once. Next day her father woke and found the letter on the window. Now, the father read it: "Dear father, do not grieve, do not sorrow, for I am having such a good life with the sea monster. I am now a great personage; he regards me as a princess, saying, 'you are the head of everything'. So he says: 'In the garden you are the head of everything'." The father was very glad to learn that his daughter was alive, healthy and contented with her life. She went on living there, and then again she began . . . er . . . to say, "I have had a bad dream." She went again to the place where the letters appeared, saying: "Whatever happens, I must go home and see my father, if only for three days. Whatever happens, I must see how my father and my sisters are living." Well, she was allowed to go. But he says: "Only for three days, three hours, three minutes and three seconds. If" — says he — "you do not return in time, I shall die, this whole garden will die and perish, and you will perish as well if you fail to return by that time." The girl took the jewelled ring — he told her to take it — and put it on her finger, and started for home. She arrived home and stayed there for three days; on the last day she had to leave. She had to leave, but her sisters changed the clock . . . er . . . to get her into trouble, because she had told them about her pleasant life; they grew envious of her, and they put her clock an hour wrong. And the girl says: 'I've got to go, go, go, but what is the matter with this clock?" Then she left before her time-limit was completely over. She arrived there

i si̮li̮ś ćaste̮ ńuže̮disni̮ e̮ťi ćas voǯe̮. i vot taja ni̮li̮d ńin šue̮: “kole̮ munni̮, munni̮, munni̮, a mi̮j taja ćasi̮d?” seśśa sija iz že̮ na eśke̮ spoľne̮ja ti̮r si̮le̮n stroki̮s i munis. a munis, uže sadi̮d sūte̮ma i stavi̮s ši̮ńale̮ma, će̮lale̮ma, ńi-ne̮m ńe-ki̮te̮ni abu. nu taja munis, sadte̮ ki̮čotis, mi̮j taja ki̮te̮n mi̮j-ke̮i̮d. seśśa munis sija da taja kodi źveri̮d uśe̮ma. sija sećće̮ uśe̮ma i uže oz zdi̮χa·jt. i vot sija zi̮re̮dis da sije̮ munis da ši̮gi̮rtis da okalis. šuas: “morske̮j źver, morske̮j tulovi·šše, me — šuas — tene̮ ľubita, me — šuas — tene̮ raďejta. i in — šuas — kū, vaj — šuas — lōźi̮!” i seśśa sija ve̮rźis i ni̮li̮s sećće̮ saďte̮m uśi. i vot seśśa sija seti̮ś si̮ dini̮ś vešjis, med oz aʒ́ʒ́i̮, potomu što sije̮ bara pe̮ pōźas, i vot znaćit, seśśa sija mi̮j-ke̮ karis, lōźis be̮rťi ńin. be̮r sija i veś bara sadjas kuććisni̮ vorsni̮, bara kuććis gaže̮ććini̮ stavi̮s, stavi̮s loi mi̮j-ke̮. taja, znaćit, seśśa kuććis ni̮li̮s bi̮d lun korni̮, vek taja munas i koras. šuas: “lok pe̮žalusta, — mi̮j šuas — lok — šuas — meke̮d vette̮dlam orćće̮n.” i kuććisni̮ naja orćće̮n vette̮dli̮ni̮ i seśśa iz kućći̮ pōni̮. be̮rťi i kutisni̮ orćće̮n vette̮dli̮ni̮.

5. i vot vois, znaćit, strok. vois strok, taja veśi̮s seśśa moloďeć loi sija, mića moloďeć. “mene̮ pe̮ komi̮n vo baťe̮ karis, mi̮j me mića re̮ďićći i baťe̮ pe̮ vot komi̮n vo taćće mi̮j-ke̮ karis i das-ki̮k ni̮li̮d, kode̮s ve̮li viśtala, stavi̮s krasavi·ćajas ve̮lini̮ i ale̮j ćveti̮s bi̮dmis sećće̮, ćveťitni̮ kuććis.” i vot munini̮ i tajajas — kuććisni̮ ki̮k ćoji̮s zavidujtni̮ — i ge̮trašisni̮. i pirujtisni̮-balujtisni̮. mi sete̮n če̮č ve̮lim.

3. ʒ́e̮ľińʒ́ik kreśťańin

1. olis-vi̮lis ʒ́e̮ľińʒ́ik kreśťańin-gozja. olisni̮ da vi̮li̮sni̮, nale̮n i e̮ťi nī̮ re̮ďiććis. puktisni̮ ľ i ď i j a imja. vot sije̮ bi̮ttisni̮, bi̮ttisni̮. sije̮ mam viśmis, mam kuli. sija i koľini̮ (aja-pija) aja-ni̮la. i lois seśśa si̮li̮ ge̮traśni̮. e̮tnas oz vermi̮ ōni̮, ni̮li̮s na i ʒ́e̮ľa. ge̮traśiś sija i vajis seče̮m baba. baba olis, olis da nī̮te̮ ńenaviďitni̮ kutis. sija ńenaviďite̮ i aslas tože̮ ki̮k nī̮ loi, kujim nī̮ kuććisni̮ bi̮tti̮ni̮. sija mi̮j-ke̮ vek i ńenaviďite̮ sije̮ nī̮se̮. ki̮ćće̮-ke̮ većer vi̮le̮ kore̮ni̮ najase̮s, priglašajte̮ni̮. većer vi̮le̮ kore̮ni̮ i ľ i ď i j a veśke̮ zej mića krasavića, sija ić-iń-pom. sije̮li̮, mi̮j-ke̮, koľe̮ni̮ gorte̮, as śemjanas mune̮ni̮. sije̮ gorte̮ koľisni̮. “vot te pe̮ boś etije̮ kujim ćetverik pe̮jim da te pe̮ sije̮ voj-bi̮d požnav!” aśni̮s većer vi̮le̮ mune̮ni̮.

and in the garden she found that life had stopped, everything was silent, motionless, there was no sign of life anywhere. Well, she walked round the garden to see what had happened. As she was walking she saw . . well, whom did she see . . . this monster fallen down on the ground. He had fallen down there on the ground and was no longer breathing. She leaned over him, embracing and kissing him. She says: "Sea monster, I love you," — says she — "I adore you. Do not die, come to life !" Then he stirred, and the girl fell into a swoon. Then he moved away from her, so that the girl might not see him, lest she might be frightened again. And, see, once again . . . er . . . she came to. And everything in the garden began to recover in joy and gladness, everything was restored . . . er . . . to life. Then every day the girl called him, always walking about and calling: "Come, I beg you" — says she — "let us take a walk together." And they began to walk together, and she had no more fear of him. Then they began to walk around together.

5. Well, the time came when the spell was ended. The spell was ended, and he turned into a handsome young man. "Thirty years ago my father laid a spell on me because I was handsome at birth, and thirty years ago my father spirited twelve girls to come here as well; I have told you about them. All of them were beautiful, and purple flowers grew there, blooming." They went home and though the two sisters grew envious they got married. There was feasting and rejoicing, and we too were there.

3. The little peasant

1. There lived a little peasant couple. They lived their life and a daughter was born to them. They called her Lidia. Well now, they raised her and brought her up. The mother became ill, the mother died. The father and the girl were left by themselves. Then he had to get married. He cannot live alone, his daughter is still so young. He married and brought home a wife. The woman lived and as she lived she began to hate the girl. She hates her, she too gave birth to two daughters, now they began to bring up three girls. She always hates that girl. They are invited to a party one evening; they receive an invitation. They are invited to an evening party, and Lidia, although a wonderful beauty, is a stepdaughter. They leave her at home, taking their own family to the party. She was left at home. "And you must take these three *četvert's* full of ashes and sieve them the whole night long !" They themselves go off to the party. The stepdaughter was left at

i sije̮ vot ić-iń-pomse̮, sije̮ koľisni̮, si̮li̮ re̮be̮ta, sije̮ pe̮ med e̮ni vote̮ʒ ve̮li ešte̮-de̮ma, požnale̮ma. no naja većer vi̮le̮ munisni̮.

2. *sija nī̮ be̮rdi̮šte̮, końe̮r. be̮rdis i be̮rdis, zavoďitas sija re̮bitni̮. zavoďitas re̮bitni̮ i vois seče̮m, kuče̮m-ke̮ ťe̮tka. "atte̮ pe̮ ľ i ď i j a pe̮, mi̮j ne̮ pe̮ końe̮re̮j pe̮ te tan mućiććan pe̮? vaj pe̮, većerńika vi̮las vetli̮!" "a ki̮ćće̮ ne̮ pe̮ me vetla? men pe̮ e̮d etije̮ kole̮ re̮bitni̮ da na vote̮ʒ pe̮ med ešte̮ma da uberi·te̮ma da med pe̮ i ge̮to·v ve̮li." i sija końe̮r be̮rʒʒis da. "a in be̮rd, vaj, mun, mun, vetli̮, paśtaś! me ten plaťťe̮, ke̮m-kot śeta." sija śetas plaťťese̮, ke̮m-kotse̮, seče̮m mića krasavića loe̮. "me pe̮ ten ge̮to·v kara vote̮ʒi̮d. te pe̮ mun da se̮mi̮n pe̮ gaže̮ćći̮!" no sija i munis tože̮, viʒe̮dni̮ munis. sija kuče̮m-ke̮ kupeć-ľi, sar-ľi, kuče̮m-ke̮ zej bur orde̮ munisni̮. seśśa sija esće̮ śurja doras sūtis. sen same̮j i je̮kte̮ni̮, no tanćujte̮ni̮. i sija aʒʒis, seče̮m nale̮n moloďeć. i sija aʒʒis da sije̮ bośtis. da zej jona je̮ktis, zej jona ľubitis da jeśśe̮ ke̮ť ńin oz i leʒ. "atte̮, me — śue̮ — i̮llae̮ te̮ke̮te̮ petala." petis da końe̮r e̮djeʒi̮k med uďitas sija uďiraj daj pi̮šjis gortas. i kor-ke̮ voisni̮ ić-ińńas, kor-ke̮ voisni̮ sija ajjas-ćojjas. "atte̮ — śue̮ —, kuče̮m mića nī̮ — śue̮ — volis (da naja naverne̮ oz i te̮dni̮ že̮), atte̮ pe̮ jona pe̮ i je̮ktis a mi pe̮ eśke̮ kuče̮m mićaa paśtaśe̮maeś da mijan vi̮le̮ pe̮ sar-pi̮i̮d iz pe̮ i viʒe̮dli̮." sija seśśa zej ćē̮ ole̮, mi̮j seśśa sija oz e̮d sija viśtaś.*

3. *no kor-ke̮ be̮rti olisni̮-vi̮lisni̮, kor-ke̮ i bara sija loi većer. bara kore̮ni̮. sije̮ veśke̮ nī̮se̮ sije̮ vek te̮dmale̮ni̮, bara većer vi̮le̮ sije̮ veśke̮ kore̮ni̮. bara as śemjae̮n munisni̮, bara sije̮ koľisni̮. si̮li̮ jeśśe̮ una koľisni̮, pe̮jim vek požnōni̮ če̮kte̮ni̮, mi̮j-ke̮, śu da med ve̮li ge̮to·v. si̮li̮ kvajt ćetverik koľisni̮, sije̮ med ve̮li ge̮to·v. seśśa i bara ťetkai̮d vois sija bara zej jona voćis da voćis da "vaj pe̮, in majićći̮, meam pe̮ ge̮to·v loe̮. te pe̮ mun, tanćujt pe̮, je̮znad pe̮ gaže̮ćći̮! to pe̮ końe̮re̮, mi̮j pe̮ tan mućiććan?" i nu i bara sija me̮de̮ććis. e̮ni i śe̮le̮mi̮s ńin si̮le̮n te̮de̮, mi̮j 'ńin meam kuče̮m-ke̮ ťe̮tka loi.' sija bara me̮de̮ććis, sije̮ voćis seče̮m mićaa sija. bara sećće̮ muni, tanćujtis, bara bośtis sija moloďećis. sije̮ eśke̮ sije̮ i kvaťitis, bara pi̮re̮ na i kvaťitis sija ńin sije̮ i viććiśe̮. no seśśa bara tanćujtisni̮, tanćuj-tisni̮, śorńitisni̮, mi̮j karisni̮. sije̮ oz leʒ ńe-kuʒi. sija eśke̮ ke̮sje̮ gortas munni̮, oz leʒ ńe-kuʒi. "mi̮jla pe̮ te munan, in vaj mun! kuʒi munan, vaj pe̮ tanćujtam da te pe̮ koľćći̮ me dine̮ ōni̮." sija "no, no, ladne̮, ladne̮" — śue. sija peti i̮llae̮*

home; she has work to do, and by the time they arrive home it must all be finished all sieved. So they went to the party.

2. The girl bursts into tears, poor soul. She wept and wept, then she begins to work. She begins to work, and an old lady came there. 'What a pity ! Lidia, my poor little dear, why are you toiling away here ? Come along, go to the dance !" "Come now, where should I go ? You see, I have to do this work so that by the time they arrive home everything is finished, tidy and made ready !" And the poor girl began to cry. "Don't cry, come on now, and go along to get dressed ! I will give you a dress and a pair of shoes." She gives her a dress and a pair of shoes, and she made a really beautiful girl. "I will finish this before you return. Just you go and have a good time !" So then she went away, she went to have a look at the place. It was a merchant or a Tsar, some better sort of people whom they had gone to a visit. Then she stood by door-post. There happened to be a dance there. She saw they had a son, a well-grown lad. He also caught sight of her and took her off to dance with him. He danced with all his might, and fell deeply in love with her, not letting her go for a moment. "Oh" — says she — "I am going out for a little while." She went out and off she ran, dashing home, to arrive there in time. Soon her stepmother and the rest of the family arrived, soon her father and her sisters came home. "Oh" — they say — "what a beautiful girl appeared there, and how she danced ! Although we were very beautifully dressed, the Tsarevich did not even look in our direction." Then she kept silent, than she did not say a word.

3. They lived their lives, and then another party took place. Once again they are invited. They are for ever making enquiries about the girl to see whether they might perhaps invite her again. Once again they went with their own family, and again they left her at home. They ordered her to do even more work, commanding her to sieve ashes all the time . . . and, . . . er . . . grain, and to finish it all in time. Then the old lady came again, and once again she made her look beautiful and dressed her up. "Do not grieve, I will finish all this. You just go, dance, and have a good time with those people ! Poor soul, why are you toiling here ?" So she started off there again. Now she feels in her heart, "I have got some king of an aunt". She set out on her way, so beautifully had she dressed her. She arrived, she danced, and the young man again took her off to dance. He seized her, he went in and seized her, he had been longing to see her. Then they danced and danced, and talked together. He will not let her go at all. Although she wants to go home, he will not let her go. "Why should you go ? Don't go ! How should you go ? Come along and let us dance, stay and live with me !" "Well, well, all right, all right" — she answers. She went out and again went home

i bara tube·ń gortas końer vois, med ńin uďitas edje voteznis. 'mene pe ed vijasni.' no vot sizik i loi. seśśa bara sija kor-ke voisni ić-ińńas, ćojjas, aj, voisni na dine.

4. *bara, mij-ke, olisni, olisni i bara nin [*sic!*] koreni. vežōlun gaške i olisni, edjezik ńin terepiććе sija med sija edjezik ńin sija nilis kole, śure, med kuz-ke. bara sili rebetase koľis ić-ińid una: "oj pe vaj pe med pe veli getov, weśis karema ćist!" etija sar-piid ńi-nem iz vermi karni da piris sija nilid tanćujtniad. da sija kerka-vozse śiren majtis, med silen, mij-ke, kučem-ke znak koľe. ńe-kiś oz vermi korśni. śiren majtis. sija seśśa kološa — no važen ved kološa sapožkijas nōleni — kološa sapožkien munis. seśśa sija bara jektisni zej jona, bara jektisni. sija ńin sar-piid kiśis oz ćetli. sije i kuććis zirajtni, oz ńin seśśa ńekiććе vizedli beke. seśśa sija tanćujtisni, tanćujtisni, jektisni, bara silen peraid, nilen vois. bara kole gorte munni. "atte, i v a n s a r e v i ć, me — śue — petala — śue — illae." "a me pe čeč peta." "no vaj pe, me dir og, regid pe og pe pisji, og pe." petis nilis, munis. a vizedlis, a kološ-pelid i koľema. "kološ-pelid silen koľema. seśśa sije i kolośen i kuććisni korśni. sar-pi sija kuććis keretaa velen kološ-pelen vetledlini. kuz-ke sili nīli znakomitni kole, kiz-ke korśni. kiś sije tedeni? ńe-kiś oz tedni. kole korśni. korśeni sijeli. bidlae piraleni. si kerkae voisni. voisni sija nilis kerkae i vot mij-ke. "no vot vajli ne nījasse! vajli, kološse pe śetla." no vot sili oz śet aslis, a ić-ińis bośte. "me pe aćim, vajli, kemedala, kodli pe taja ladmas." sija izid nīse kemedis aśśis, aśśis nīse kemedis, a izid nīse koľis. kokas veli oz ter, a kok-ćuńńasse ćińtis da mededis siked. munis, munis, a gorzeni guľujas, petemaś da. "i v a n s a r e v i ć pe kokis vir, kokis vir, i v a n s a r e v i ć, kokis vir." kvaťiććas, a dođďis stavis vir verne. kuľis kem-kotse, a sije ber mededis. 'vaj pe taja ńe-ladne keźajka pe śetema nīte.' "kodlen pe taja mij-keid?" med nīli svić śetis da bara kemedis, bara aśśis mededis, a etije ić-ić-ń-pomse oz meded. seśśa sija bara munis, munis. azzisni guľujasis, bara naja kutisni gorzini: "a i v a n s a r e v i ć, kokis vir, kokis vir!" bara i v a n s a r e v i ć: "mij taja bezobra·źije!" bara kosis. "mijla te, keźajka, tazi mij karin? vaj pe me aćim kemeda nīte." seśśa i boštis sija, mij-ke, ľ i ď i j a p r e k r a s n a · j ate, sije boštis sije aćis. "lok!" ke-*

directly, poor soul, so that she might get home before they arrived. "They will kill me." Well, so it happened. Later her stepmother and her family arrived, her sisters and father came home.

4. They lived their lives, and once again they received an invitation. Perhaps it was a week they lived; he is a great hurry now; he needs the girl as soon as possible; she must be found somehow. Her stepmother again left her much work to do. "Oh dear, everything has got to be finished and tidy!" This Tsarevich did not know what to do. The girl went in to dance. And he smeared the front of the house with pitch, he wanted to make some kind of mark. He cannot find her anywhere. (This is why) He smeared the front of the house with pitch. On this occasion she was wearing overboots — well, in the old times people wore boots with overboots — so she went there in boots and overboots. Again they had a good lively dance. This time the Tsarevich will not let her out of his hands. She began to look this way and that, till in the end she did not look either way. Then they danced and danced and danced till it was again time for the girl to leave. "O, Tsarevich, Ivan" — says she "I am going out." "I'm coming out as well." "Well, I'll not be long . . . soon . . . I'll not escape, no." The girl went out, and left. She looked back, well, one of her overboots had been left behind there. Then they began to search for her with the overboot. With one of the overboots the Tsarevich himself began to search for her, in a horsed carriage. Somehow he must make the girl's acquaintance, somehow he must find her. Where is she known? She is not known anywhere. They search for her. They enter each house. They reached that house. They reached the house where the girl was living. "Come along, bring out the girls! Let's try them on! Here is the overboot." Well, he did not pass it to the stepmother, but she took it away. "I myself will see which one it fits." She pulled in on the foot of her elder daughter, she herself drew it on her daughter's foot, and then she left her. The overboot was too small for her foot, so she cut off her toes and sent her off with him. He went on and on and the pigeons called out: "Tsarevich Ivan, her feet are bleeding, her feet are bleeding." He makes a snatch at it, and indeed, the whole sledge is covered with blood. He took off the shoes and sent her back. "Damn it! This wife has not given me the right girl." "Whose is this thing?" Quickly she gave it to her other daughter and pulled it on her foot. Again she sent her own daughter, and did not send her stepdaughter. Then again he went on and on. The pigeons caught sight of him and again they began to call out: "Tsarevich Ivan, her feet are bleeding, her feet are bleeding!" Tsarevich Ivan says: "What a disgrace!" And he turned back again. "Goodwife, why did you do this? Now I myself will put it on the foot of your daughter." Then he himself took hold of the beautiful

me̮dis da munis. (seśśa iz śet mi̮j-ke̮.) te̮disni̮, kaźalisni̮, mi̮j podveďite̮. no vot sija ke̮me̮dis, paśte̮dis seśśa, a etija ki̮ś-ke̮ i ťe̮tkai̮s sećće̮ vois mi̮j-ke̮as da sije̮ paśte̮dis da ke̮me̮dis da seče̮m prekra·snaja krasavi·ća loi. da seče̮m veśi̮s sija briľľante̮vej plaťťe̮ paśte̮dis da seče̮m krasavi·ća. munis gozja seśśa. no vot seśśa sobira·jtis i mamse̮, ić-inńse̮ iz i boś. pir vi̮le̮ iz boś ńi-ne̮m seśśa. "vot te pe̮ on kō, te pe̮ in lok!" baťli̮ bośtis, nue̮dis mi̮j-ke̮li̮ bara. seśśa veśse̮ ćuke̮rtisni̮. sen naja pirujtisni̮-svaďbujtisni̮. ve̮ľiśťi nali̮ ľube̮ da doli̮d da bur loi ole̮m. no vot seśśa olisni̮-vi̮lisni̮, nalen i kor-ke̮ ćeľaď loi. zej bura kutisni̮ ōni̮. baťi̮s si̮le̮n kuli. aći̮s sare̮, me̮di̮s sarića loi. e̮ni ole̮-vi̮le̮ i pom.

4.

1. *važe̮n olisni̮-vi̮lisni̮ gozja. nale̮n mamni̮s kuli i nī̮ koľi, eťi nī̮ koľi. aji̮s ve̮li si̮le̮n meľńiki̮n, sija ge̮traśis. seśśa kor-ke̮ di̮rji naja petni̮ kuććisni̮ geśťitni̮ ić-ińi̮ske̮d. a sija ni̮li̮s kori̮ś loi da si̮li̮, meľńiki̮n aji̮s ve̮li da si̮li̮ pi̮ź śetis. pi̮ź śetis daj sija kiśkaśis. voisni̮ geśťitan-inśi̮s da i kuććis ić-ińi̮s sije̮li̮ pińōni̮. seśśa sije̮li̮, nī̮se̮ i ve̮tlisni̮. ić-ińi̮s si̮li̮ś sojse̮ keralis.*

2. *nī̮ i dumaćće̮: 'a ki̮ćće̮ pe̮ me voštiśa? ki̮će̮ bara veśke̮ me muna?' si̮le̮n ńi-ne̮m abu. munis da munis da munis da sije̮ ki̮ćće̮-ke̮ vois. seśśa si̮li̮ kujim tuj-vož vois. kujim tuj-vož vois i oz te̮d, ki̮ćće̮ pi̮rni̮.'a inli pe̮ me pe̮ etaćće̮ pe̮ še̮r tujas pi̮rala pe̮.' seśśa še̮r tuje̮d sija munis da munis da munis da, seśśa vois sećće̮ sad. sad vois, seni veśi̮s e̮śale̮ jablońa. jablońa e̮śale̮ seni veśi̮s i soj-te̮m pi̮rni̮ oz vermi̮. kuǯ-ke̮ sija sojte̮gi̮s sećće̮ jablońaad? ki̮nemi̮s si̮le̮n śumale̮. sija sojte̮g muni. seśśa pi̮ris sećće sadas sija da jablońate̮ i kite̮m da, oz vermi̮ da, vomnas kuććis sija jablońase̮ mi̮j-ke̮ karni̮, śojni̮, kurććōni̮. sari̮sle̮n ve̮li sija jablońa-sadi̮s. sadi̮s ve̮li sari̮sle̮n da sija sari̮s et-pir i̮sti̮lis sija e̮ťi ste̮re̮že̮s: "menśi̮m pe̮ jabloke̮s pe̮ kod-ke̮ kurććale̮, veśi̮s pe̮ ǯi̮nja jabloke̮, veśi̮s pe̮ jabloke̮ ǯi̮nja menam." seśśa sija: "me pe̮ ńe-kode̮s pe̮ ig aǯǯi̮l, karauľiti da ig aǯǯi̮l." seśśa sija i̮stis i me̮de̮s, sari̮s, me̮d karaul. me̮d karaul bara iz aǯǯi̮l. kurććale̮ma, jablok kurććale̮ma, a ńe-kode̮s iz aǯǯi̮l sija. a kojme̮d pe̮ i̮stis sija asśi̮s pise̮: "mun pe̮ pije̮ pe̮, vetli̮ pe̮ da kodi pe̮, noli̮ pe̮! karaulščikjasi̮s pe̮ ńe-kode̮s pe̮ iz viśtōni̮, a jabloknime̮s pe̮ veśse̮ pe̮ śojisni̮. noli̮ pe̮, vetli̮ pe̮ da on-e̮-ke̮ kode̮s-ke̮*

Lidia: "Come along!" He put the shoe on her foot and went away. Then they realized and perceived that the stepmother was false. Well, then he put the shoe on her foot, and dressed her up. From somewhere that old lady also arrived by some means or other; she dressed her, and she turned into a real beauty. She dressed her in a dress adorned with jewels, and a beautiful girl she was. Then the pair left. He summoned his mother, but did not take the stepmother with him. She did not take anything to the wedding. "You are not wanted, you must not come!" He took the father with him. Then they assembled everybody. They arranged a wedding there. And now they started a happy, gay and good life. Then they lived on and on, and later children were also born to them. They lived very well. The father died, he himself became a Tsar and the other a Tsarina. They are still alive. That's the end of the story.

4. [The Tsarevich and the girl who was driven out]

1. Once upon a time there lived a married couple. The mother died. The mother died and left a daughter. The father was a miller; he got married. Then some time later they went visiting, he and the stepmother. The girl became a beggar and — the father was a miller — so he gave her flour. He gave her flour, and she scattered it about. They arrived home from the party, and the stepmother began to chide her. Then they drove her out, the girl. Her stepmother cut off her arm.

2. The girl thinks hard: "Where shall I do away with myself? Where shall I go?" She has nothing at all. She went on and on and on, and arrived somewhere. Then she arrived at three crossroads. She arrived at three crossroads, and did not know where to go. "Let's just see. I'll go this way, along the middle road." Then she made her way along the middle road, she went on and on, and then she arrived at a garden. She arrived at a garden quite full of apple-trees. It is quite full of apple-trees, but she cannot enter without an arm. If only she could somehow climb the apple-trees without an arm! She is hungry. She entered without an arm. She entered the garden there without her arm, and she cannot pick an apple . . . she began to eat apples and bite at them with her mouth. It was the Tsar's garden. The garden belonged to the Tsar, and the Tsar once sent a guard there: "There is somebody who keeps biting at each of my apples, eating half of them." Then he answered: "I have not seen anybody, I have been on guard, but I have not seen anybody." Then the Tsar sent someone else, another guard. The other guard did not see anybody either. And there were the apples bitten and bitten away, yet he did not see anybody. The third time he sent his own

pe̮ aǯ́ǯ́i̮?" pii̮s sija aǯ́ǯ́is soj-pe̮la nī̮te̮ seti̮ś. pii̮d aǯ́ǯ́is sije̮li̮ da i sije̮li̮ gortas nue̮dis sija. gortas mue̮dis da seśśa mami̮s-ajani̮sli̮ i šuis (sija ńin krasavi·ća ve̮li, sečem mića ve̮li sija): "a me pe̮ aje̮ pe̮ da mame̮, keť pe̮ meni̮m mi̮j šue̮, taje̮li̮ pe asli̮m pe̮ reve·śńića vi̮le̮ bośta, ge̮ti̮r vi̮le̮." no aj-mam si̮ke̮d pre̮ťiv iz munni̮. "no pije̮ pe, mi̮j pe̮ seśśa mi pe̮ og pre̮ťiv ime·jte̮, bośtan-ke̮, boś!" seśśa sije̮li̮ i bośtis sija. seśśa i e̮tlaaśisni̮ naja. e̮tlaaśisni̮. pii̮s si̮le̮n tom ve̮li da si̮li̮ś i armijae̮ nuisni̮ pite̮. sije̮ armijae̮ bośtisni̮. armijae̮ bośtisni̮ i si̮le̮n ke̮ńe·šne̮ koľi ńin, sija čučkua koľi babai̮s.

3. seśśa sije̮ kor-ke̮ armija kosti i babai̮d i vajis kaga. kaga vajis da seśśa sar gozjai̮s i saldate̮s i̮stisni̮ pii̮s dine̮: mi̮j si̮li̮ ńimse̮ bośni̮? i̮stisni̮ siji̮li̮, saldate̮s. a sija saldati̮s munis da munis da munis da sija ri̮te̮-bure̮ vois i pi̮ris kerkae̮ uźme̮ćći̮ni̮. sija same̮j ić-ińi̮s orde̮ sle̮jme̮ma da seśśa sija seni uźis. a piśme̮se̮ ić-ińi̮s sija źepśi̮s vojnas ki̮ski̮lis da si̮li̮ i gižis sija giže̮maas, mi̮j pe̮ ńimse̮ bośtas: "a tenad pe̮ re̮ďićće̮ma pe̮ pon-pi da mi̮j pe̮ si̮li̮ ńimse̮ bośni̮, si̮le̮n pon pe̮ re̮ďićće̮ma." sija munis, śetis armećidli̮. me̮d asi̮ ćeććis, asja-bure̮ vois. asi̮-vo̮ǯe̮ munis, munis da munis — men viśtōni̮ regi̮d, ke̮ne̮šne̮ si̮li̮ i di̮r, sija e̮d abu me̮d kerkai̮ś — sija kuźa mune̮. seśśa i vois kor-ke̮ sija armeći̮d dine̮. armeći̮d dine̮ vois da si̮li̮ śetis piśme̮te̮. da piśme̮as si̮li̮ gižis sija — bara piśme̮te̮ gižis —, me̮d pe̮ keť pe̮ mi̮j re̮ďite̮ma, sija me̮di̮m pe̮ ńimse̮ puktasni̮, pon keť mort. seśśa sija i kor-ke̮ i di̮rji i bara armeć śujis źeptas mi̮j-ke̮li̮ i bara muni, gortlań ńin lokte̮. gortlań lokni̮ kuććis. munis da bara sija ić-ińi̮d orde̮ vois. ić-ińi̮d orde̮ bara uźni̮ad vois. ić-iń si̮li̮ś bara źepśi̮s ki̮skis piśme̮, vojnas unmōśis da. seśśa i sija gižis: "me̮d pe̮ ubirajććas pe̮ me vote̮ǯ pe̮, me̮d duki̮s pe̮ iz ve̮!" ić-ińi̮d si̮li̮ gižis piśme̮ vi̮lad. piśme̮ be̮r źeptas śujis, saldatli̮ źeptas śujis. munis da munis da munis da kor-ke̮ i sar dine̮ vois. sar dine̮ vois, sar gozjali̮ śetis piśme̮. sar gozja li̮ďďisni̮ i kaga śetisni̮ si̮li̮ i sije̮li̮ ve̮tlisni̮. ve̮tlisni̮ sije̮ gortśi̮d.

4. seśśa sija munisni̮, da munisni̮ da munisni̮ da seśśa sija kor-ke̮ i va-dore̮ loktisni̮. more dore̮ loini̮, more vois nali̮, mama-pijali̮. seśśa more dore̮ vodisni̮ vojnas uźni̮. seśśa moreidle̮n vaćkis valji̮s da sija i asi̮ vo̮ǯnas ćeććis da ki̮knan

son: "Go, my son, go, and whoever it may be, bring him here! The guards told of nobody, yet all our apples have been eaten. Bring him here, go and see if you can see someone!" The young man caught sight of the girl with one arm and took her home. He took her home and said to his parents (she was so very beautiful, so fair): "Father and mother, whatever you say to me, I am going to marry her, and she will be my partner for life." Well, his parents did not object to it. "Well, my son, we have no objection to it, and if you want to marry her then marry her!" So then he did marry her. They live as a married couple. They lived as a married couple. The Tsar's son was young, and his son was taken off to the army. He was enrolled in the army. He was enrolled in the army, and of course, his wife was left behind pregnant.

3. Then one day, while he was away with the army, the woman gave birth to a child. She gave birth to a child, and then the Tsar and the Tsarina sent a soldier to their son, saying, "What name shall the boy be given?" They sent him, the soldier. The soldier went on and on and on, and it grew dark. And he entered a house to sleep. He happened to go into the stepmother's house and there he went to bed. During the night the stepmother pulled the letter out of his pocket and wrote down for him that a name was to be given to the child: "Well, your wife has given birth to a puppy, and what name shall we give it, she has given birth to a dog." She went to him, and stuck the letter in the warrior's pocket. He got up next day, when it was morning, and left early in the morning; he went on and on — of course, it takes no time for me to tell, but it took him a long time since he was not from next door — so took him a long time. Then some time later he found warrior. He gave him the letter. In the letter he wrote — he too had written a letter — that a name should be given to the thing she had given birth to, be it dog or human. Then the warrior put the letter in his pocket and set out again. He was now on his way home. He began the journey home. He went on his way, and again he stepped into the stepmother's house. This time again he arrived at the stepmother's house to sleep. The stepmother again took the letter out of his pocket as he was sleeping at night. "Get it out of the place; by the time I get home let not even a whiff of it remain!" This is what the stepmother wrote in the letter. She put the letter back in his pocket; she stuck it into the soldier's pocket. He went on and on and on, and at last he arrived at the Tsar's. He arrived at the Tsar's, and handed the letter to the Tsar and Tsarina. The Tsar and Tsarina read the letter, gave her her child and drove her out. They drove her from home.

4. Then they went on and on and on, and they arrived at a shore. They came to the shore of the sea; the mother and her son arrived at the sea-shore. At night they lay down to sleep on the sea-shore. Then the waves of the sea

ki̮i̮s si̮le̮n, kija ńin. seśśa kagate̮ bośtis sija da seśśa bara mama-pija me̮disni̮. munisni̮ da munisni̮ da munisni̮ da seśśa ʒ́e̮ľa kerkae̮ naja voisni̮. ʒ́e̮ľa kerkaas seni vodisni̮ da unmōśisni̮.

5. *a sećće sija tale̮n sari̮dle̮n, seśśa pii̮d gortas vois. sari̮dle̮n pii̮s gortas vois da mamjasi̮dli̮ viśtalis sije̮ da sija i babase̮ korśni̮ me̮de̮ććis. seśśa sija munis da munis da munis da seśśa sija ʒ́e̮ľa kerkae̮ sle̮jmi, pete̮. (sija ke̮ńe·śne̮ sar-pii̮s saldatke̮d tože̮ munis, iz e̮tnas, saldatke̮d munisni̮ ki̮ke̮n.) seśśa ʒ́e̮ľa kerkai̮s sija ľikmis da seśśa i śuis sija saldatli̮: "te pe̮ ō pe̮ — śue̮ — a me pe̮ unmōśa pe̮." seśśa sija sar-pii̮d vodis da unmōśis. no sije̮ vojse̮ naja uźisni̮ kuʒ́-ke. seśśa asi̮ voʒ́e̮ bure̮ voisni̮, seni olisni̮-vi̮lisni̮. sija kija-koka veśis si̮le̮n, pi̮risni̮ pe̮ kerkae̮ mama-pija, kor ruale̮-vaale̮ veśis. veśi̮s ruale̮-vaale. sije̮ naje̮ ve̮li ge̮śťite̮dis, a sar-pii̮dli̮ sija kažiććis babai̮s kojd ge̮śťite̮ććiśi̮s, mama-pijai̮s. "inli̮ pe̮ me pe̮ ton pe̮ aći̮m pe̮ karauľita taje̮li̮ pe̮ vojnas." seśśa vodisni̮ naja da sar-pii̮s sija aći̮s karauľitni̮ kuććis. da seśśa petis sija babai̮s da si̮li̮ tože̮ muži̮ki̮s kojd kažiććis da sije̮li̮, ćeććis da śi̮gi̮rtis da śi̮gi̮rććisni̮ da okaśisni. da seśśa ćeććisni̮ asi̮-voʒ́nas da munisni̮. kagase̮ boštisni (saldat) da munisni̮ gortani̮s da sete̮n piruško da baruško karisni̮.*

5. *ozi̮r da ge̮ľ vok*

1. *olisni̮-vi̮lisni̮ ozi̮r vok da ge̮ľ vok. ozi̮r vok zē bura ole̮, a ge̮ľ vok zē ge̮ľa ole̮. ćeľaď zē una si̮le̮n, śojni̮se̮ ńańi̮s abu. si̮li̮ meľńića vi̮le̮ kōmis munni̮ i ve̮li̮s iz śur, abu. sija ozi̮r vok orde̮ peti. "vajli̮ meni̮m vē̮te̮, kole̮ meľńićae̮ vetli̮ni̮." "bośtli̮, vetli̮ meľńića vi̮le̮!" — sija śue̮. vē̮ bośtis, ićet ťeľegaa. munis meľńića vi̮le̮. ize̮ććig kostii̮s ve̮li̮s ćańalas. ćańi̮s ťeľega ulas pi̮ras. da i śue̮, pete̮ da ge̮ľ vok: "meam pe̮ ťeľegai̮s ćańale̮ma." gorte̮ vois da śue: "baba, mijan ta-lun ťeľegai̮s ćańale̮ma, mijan ćań vi̮jim. seśśa vē̮ loe̮, taje̮ mi bi̮ttam."*

2. *vićće̮, ozi̮r vokle̮n vē̮ ti̮ra, vićće̮ vek ćańale̮m. vē̮ iz ćańō. a ge̮ľ vok orde̮ loktis da i śue̮: "ten — śue̮ — kiś ćańi̮s?" "me — śue̮ — meľńića vi̮las kor vetli, ťeľegai̮s vajis seče̮m mića." "sija — śue̮ — iz vaj ťeľegai̮d, a sija meam ve̮li̮s*

began to beat upon her, and when she got up early in the morning she had two arms, she now had both arms. Then she took her child, and the mother and her son started off again. They went on and on and on, and at last they arrived at a small cottage. In that small cottage they lay down and went to sleep.

5. Then this Tsar's son arrived home. The Tsar's son arrived home and told his parents about everything. And he set out to seek his wife. He went on and on and on, and at last he came across the small cottage, and went in. (The Tsarevich went with the soldier; he was not alone; he and the soldier went together.) Then they reached the small cottage, and he said to the soldier: "You stay awake while I go off to sleep!" — says he. Then the Tsarevich lay down and fell asleep. Well, they slept that night somehow. Then dawn came, and they stayed there. The mother and her son entered the house — and her hands and feet were now whole — and when the food was steaming, and everything was steaming she feasted them. But to the Tsarevich it seemed as if the woman who gave the feast, the mother, resembled his wife. "Just wait, this night I shall stay on watch!" Then they lay down, and the Tsarevich began his watch. And then the woman came out, and to her too it seemed that he was her husband. She sprang towards him and embraced him; they embraced each other and kissed each other. Then early in the morning they got up and started on their way. They took the child and went home and then they made a great feast.

5. The rich brother and the poor brother

1. There lived a rich and a poor brother. The rich brother lives very well, and the poor brother lives a wretched life. He has many children and no bread to eat. He had to go to the mill and he could not find a horse. There is no horse. He went to his rich brother. "Give me your horse, I have to go to the mill." "Take it, and go to the mill!" — says he. He took the horse, the one used with the small cart. He went off to the mill. While he is grinding, the horse drops a foal. The foal goes under the cart. The poor brother comes out and says: "My cart has dropped a foal." He arrives home, and says "Wife, our cart has had a foal today, we have a colt. Then we shall have a horse; we shall rear this one."

2. He is waiting — the rich brother's mare is in foal — he is waiting all the time for the mare to foal. The horse does not foal. He came to the poor brother, and says: "Where" — says he — "did you get the foal?" "When" — says he — " I went to the mill, my cart gave birth to such a nice foal." "It is not your cart that gave birth to the foal" — says he — "but my mare

ćańale̮ma. ješše̮ i̮le̮dan!" ozi̮r voki̮s sude̮ śetas. seśśa i suďďa šue̮: "ti — šue̮ — kodni̮d te̮danni̮d, mi̮j źemľa vi̮las kodi medśa musa da kodi medśa si̮la da kodi bi̮stre̮j, si̮li̮ — šue̮ — i ćań loas." leććisni̮ gortani̮s. i naja, ozi̮r vok gozja dumać-će̮ni̮, kodi pe medśa musa. a baba i šue̮: "a mei̮ś musa — šue̮ — ńe-kod abu." seśśa šuas: "s o b e̮ ľ pon vi̮jim, s o b e̮ ľ ponśi̮s bi̮stre̮j pe̮ tože̮ ńe-kod abu." seśśa bara dumaććis, dumaććis da: "a i̮ǯi̮d porśśis si̮laǯi̮k tože̮ ńe-kod abu." siǯi naja śorńitisni̮, nale̮n śuri kī̮jas. a ge̮ľ vokle̮n ve̮li je̮j vok. je̮j moze̮n pukale̮ sija i ki̮vzi̮śe̮. gortas loktis da i bať-mamli̮ šue̮: "naja vot — šue̮ sije — dogovo-riććisni̮." "a ti — šue̮ — i viśtale̮! ti — šue̮ — viśtale̮, mi̮j źemľa vi̮las musase̮ kor jualasni̮, će̮ski̮dse̮, sija — šue̮ — unmi̮d meććen će̮ski̮d, a kodi medśań si̮la, sija pe̮ źemľa, a kodi pe̮ medśań bi̮stre̮j, sija pe̮ śinmi̮d. ti pe̮ mune̮ da siǯ i viśtale̮!" naja munasni̮, ke̮ńešne̮ siǯ i viśtalasni̮, ge̮ľ vokli̮ i vē̮ loe̮. mi̮j-ke̮ sija te̮keńǯi ole̮.

3. *seśśa ozi̮r vokle̮n i ńim-lun ta-lun. ge̮ľ voke̮s sije̮ oz kor. a sen pirujte̮ni̮ ozi̮r je̮z, geśťite̮ni̮. seśśa vot i šue̮ ge̮ľ vok: "vaj — šue̮ — vetlam mi taun na orde̮, oz-e̮ pe̮ mijan ńań-tor śet-ľi, verd-ľi?" munini̮. ge̮ľ vok voisni̮, ke̮časas pukale̮ni̮. komnataas śi̮le̮ni̮, mojde̮ni̮, jue̮ni̮, śoje̮ni̮. na vi̮le̮ oz i viǯe̮dli̮ni̮. pukalisni̮, pukalisni̮, pi̮zan sajas vajlisni̮ i̮reš kružka nali̮. seśśa, mužik i šue̮: "vaj pe̮, munam! mi̮j pe̮ tan karam? mijanni̮me̮s oz pukśe̮dni̮ a, gorte̮ — šue̮ — munam." mede̮ććisni̮ gorte̮ munni̮. mune̮ni̮, a mužik i šue̮: "vaj — šue̮ — śi̮lam! je̮zśis — šue̮ — janǯim, nale̮n pe̮ bal, a mi pe̮ će̮le̮n munam. naje̮ — šue̮ — abu juktale̮-mae̮ś, med — šue̮ — ćajtasni̮, mi̮j pe̮ mi kode̮ś." a baba i šue̮: "kuče̮m — šue̮ —, śi̮lam da mi̮j da? me — šue̮ — og!" "a me — šue̮ — śi̮la" — mužik šue̮. mužik gore̮das śī̮ni̮. śi̮le̮, a kod-ke̮ be̮rśańi̮s ńebiďińǯia tože̮ śi̮le̮. babali̮ i šue̮: "te taj — šue̮ — čeč śi̮lan. in pe̮ ke̮sji̮, a čeč śi̮lan"' "me — šuas — og śī̮." "a kod ne̮ — šue̮ — medi̮s śi̮le̮? kod-ke̮ — šue̮ — med ńebi̮d ge̮le̮se̮n śi̮le̮. viǯe̮dasni̮: daške̮ ćuń-ǯi̮n soda mort lokte̮ be̮rśańi̮s, etače̮m soda. seśśa i šue̮ni̮: "te ne̮ pe̮ kodi, taja?" "a me pe̮ tijan nuždai̮s, be̮rśańi̮d pe̮ vette̮dla, nuždani̮d tijan". seśśa meše̮ke̮ keźajin sije̮ śujas. "ten pe̮ śe̮ki̮d munni̮te̮. vaj pe̮, me tene̮ meše̮ke̮ śuja da nue̮da gorte̮." gorte̮ nue̮das. voasni̮, babali̮ šue̮: "vaj te, vod, a me poka og na vod." baba vodas, mužik mi̮j-ke̮ voj-bi̮d tučke̮-točke̮. kare̮ gort nuždali̮. gort*

that gave birth to it. Do you think you can deceive me?" The rich brother takes him to court. The judge says: "Whichever of you can tell me what is loveliest, what is richest in fat and what is swiftest in the world, his" — says he — "shall be the foal." They went home. And they, the rich brother and his wife, ponder on what might be loveliest. Now, the wife says: "Well now, nobody" — says she — "is lovelier than I." Then she continues: "We have a dog called *sobel'*, and there is nobody swifter than our dog *sobel'*." Then again she pondered and pondered: "Likewise there is nobody richer in fat than our big swine." Thus they talked, and they did not fail to find words. Now the poor brother had a stupid brother. He just sits there stupidly and listens. He came home and says to the parents: "Why, they have a greed." "Well, you must not say the same! You must say, when they ask what is loveliest, and what is sweetest on earth, that dreams are the sweetest; and as for the richest in fat, well, it is earth; and as for the swiftest, well, it is eyes. Go and speak in this fashion!" They go and, of course, they speak in this fashion. The horse is given to the poor brother. There is hardly any sign of life in it.

3. Now today is the name-day of the rich brother. He does not invite his poor brother. Well, the rich people are marry-making and feasting there. The poor brother speaks up: "Come" — says he — "let us go to their house today and see if they are willing to give us a piece of bread, if they are willing to offer us something to eat. They went there. The poor brother and his family went there, and they sat at the corner by the door. Inside, in the room, they are singing, telling stories, drinking and eating. They do not even cast a glance at them. They just sat and sat there, and a jug of *kvas* was brought to them at table. Then the husband says: "Let us go! What are we to do here? They do not even ask us to take a seat. Let us go home!" — he says —. They started for home. They go on their way, and the man says: "Let us sing! It is a shame before all these people" — says he — "there is a ball at their place, and we are walking in silence. As for them" — says he — "they did not give us to drink; just let them think we are drunk!" The wife answers: "How should we sing? Just think of it! As for me" — says she — "I will not." "Well, I will" — says the man. And he starts to sing a song. He sings and why, behind him somebody else sings in a low voice. He says to the woman: "Why!" — says he — "you are singing as well. You didn't want to sing, yet you are singing!" "Me?" — says she — "I'm not singing." "Then who else is singing? Somebody else" — says he — "is singing in a low voice." They look round; a man no more than half a finger tall perhaps, as big as that, is coming after them. "And who are you?" "I am your misery, I always follow in your tracks; I am your misery."

karas, seśśa gorte̮ śujas i manasti̮re̮ nuas. gu kodjas, sije̮li̮ gue̮ śujas i ti̮rtni̮ kuććas. ti̮rtni̮ kuććas, zastupe̮ si̮li̮ vit śure̮, ze̮le̮te̮j kuso·k-tor. sije̮li̮ sije̮ bośtas. gortas voas, babali̮ oz viśtō. a me̮d asī̮nas i śue̮: “me — śue̮ — ton bazar vi̮le̮ vetla, mi̮j-ke̮ — oz-e̮ śur ńe̮bni̮?” śojni̮se̮ ńi-ne̮m a, bazar vi̮le̮ vetlas sija. munas, ze̮le̮te̮j kusok-tor nuas. seśśa sija si̮ vi̮le̮ ńe̮bas ki̮k vē̮, ki̮k vē̮-ti̮ri̮s ńań ńe̮bas. sija ki̮k ve̮la lokte̮ daj ki̮k vē̮-ti̮r ńań vajas. baba i śue̮: “ki̮ś ne̮ — śue̮ — ten ta mi̮tta ńańi̮s?” babali̮ viśtalas: “vot siǯi i siǯi.” sija e̮ťi lun vetlas da siǯ e̮ťie̮s bośtas da, me̮d lun vetlas da sija te̮var daške̮ vajas, paś-ke̮m da.

4. *seśśa ozi̮r vok — sija ōme̮ććisni̮, kuććis ge̮ľ vok — a ozi̮r vok i śue̮: “te — śuas — zē ge̮ľ ve̮lin, a mi̮j-ke̮ — śue̮ — drug kuććin ōme̮ćći̮ni̮.” seśśa sija ge̮ľ voki̮d i viśtalas: “vot pe̮ me siǯi i siǯi. mi pe̮ ti ordi̮ś kor munim, nuždase̮ pe̮ ǯebi manasti̮re̮.” seśśa si̮le̮n śe̮le̮m kuććis puni̮. oz vermi̮ ōni̮. “vaj — śue̮ — pukśi̮ da i ćaj ste̮kan ju!” “me — śue̮ — og ešti̮, kole̮ — śue̮ — munni̮ gorte̮, mi̮j-ke̮ uǯali̮šta.” sija gorte̮ vois, zastup bośtis, e̮dje̮ǯika manasti̮re̮, nuždali̮ be̮r ćukte̮dni̮, med ge̮ľ vok orde̮ munas nužda be̮r. nuždali̮ ćukte̮dis, kodjis, seśśa vośtis. “no vaj — śuas —, mun te ge̮ľ vok orde̮ be̮r!” me — śuas — ge̮ľ vok ordad e̮ni og mun. sija — śue̮ — mene̮li̮ tūjalis gorte̮ da gue̮ śujis, a te — śue̮ — še-de̮din. me — śue̮ — te śi̮lie̮ kuććiśa da te śi̮li̮n i ola.” ozi̮r vok śi̮lie̮ kuććiśis. sija ge̮l vokśi̮s kuže loi. a ge̮ľ vok ozi̮rmis da zē bura ōme̮ććis, a ozi̮r vok kori̮śni̮ petis.*

6.

1. *starik gozja olisni̮-vi̮lisni̮. nale̮n pi re̮ďiććis. pili̮ bi̮ttisni̮. naja, starik gozja, e̮ťiki̮s e̮ťi vo kuli, me̮di̮s me̮d vo kuli. tom mortli̮ bi̮ť loi ge̮traśni̮. ge̮traśis armijae̮ munte̮ǯ. starikli̮ś pise̮ armijae̮ bośtisni̮. ge̮ti̮r koľi e̮tnas. tom ge̮ti̮r zē mića. praźńik lois, re̮švo. pop vetle̮. pop loktis śilig-ti̮r moľitva. vośtis e̮ǯe̮sse̮. “vot — śuas — molodka, bura bur — śuas — da vot — śuas — te siǯ kagase̮ ke̮sjan vajni̮, a mužiki̮s — śuas — abu kok pukte̮ma. me ten kok pukta. “no,*

Then the man puts him in his bag. "It's difficult for you to walk. Come, I'll put you in the bag and take you home." He takes him home. They arrive. He says to his wife: "You go to bed; I'm not going to bed yet." The wife goes to bed, the man is busy all night knocking something together. He makes a coffin for the misery. He makes ready a coffin, then puts him in the coffin and takes him to the monastery. He digs a grave, puts him in the gave and begins to bury it. He begins to bury it; he comes across five pieces of gold with his spade. He picks them up. He goes home, not saying anything to his wife. In the morning he says: "Today I'm going to the fair to see if there is something to be bought." They have nothing to eat, yet he goes to the fair. He goes off, taking a gold piece with him. Then he buys two horses, and as such corn as two horses can carry. He arrives home with two horses and brings two horses' load of corn as well. His wife says: "Where did you get all this corn?" He tells his wife: "Well, it happened in this way." He goes one day and brings home one thing; he goes the next day and brings home goods and clothes.

4. Then the rich and the poor brother began to live. The rich one says: "Well" — says he — "you were very poor and all of a sudden you have begun to become rich." Then the poor brother tells him: "Well, it happened in this way. When we had left you last time I buried the misery in the monastery." Then he grew hot with envy. He could not live in peace any longer. "Come" — says he — "sit down and have a glass of tea!" "I have no time to" — says he —, "I must go home to do a bit of work." He went home, took a spade, and hurried to the monastery to free the misery so that it might return to the poor brother. He freed the misery, dug it up, and then opened the coffin. "Now" — says be — "go back to the poor brother!" "As for me" — says he — "I will not go back to the poor brother again. He nailed me into the coffin and put me into the grave, while you" — says he — "you have released me. I shall cling to your neck and live on your neck." He clung to the neck of the rich brother. His lot turned out worse than that of the poor brother. The poor brother grew rich, the rich brother went begging.

6. [The soldier and the priest]

1. There lived an old man and his wife. A son was born to them. They brought up the son. The old man and his wife died, the one in one year, the other in the next. The young man necessarily had to marry. He married before going to join the army. The lad was taken into the army. His wife stayed alone. The young wife is very beautiful. There came a festival — it was Christmas.

no, a mi̯j ne̯? . . ." ić-moń šogśi̯ni̯ kuććis. "me — šuas — be̯rnas, ri̯tnas — šuas — vola." "no ladne̯ — šuas. no ić-moń šogśi̯ni̯ kuććis. pop ge̯ti̯rli̯ šue̯: "me — šue̯ — ďak orde̯ vetla, asi̯ — šuas — me̯d ďerevńae̯ kole̯ munni̯ da." pop ďak orde̯ pi̯ďďi de̯va orde̯ loktis. "no, no, vaj — šuas — lokta — šuas — kokte̯ kara." no davaj, kokte̯ karis ke̯ńešne̯.

2. *no ladne̯, kor-ke̯ saldat lokte̯. i końešne̯ zonmi̯d prejďitis, i̯ži̯d ńin, kikoke̯n vetle̯. a saldat vois da pike̯d radućće, znaćit: "oj, menam pi, menam si̯no·k, viďiš ti̯ kak, kuče̯m, no, viže̯d te, kuče̯m! oj, menam ge̯ti̯r, te viže̯d, kiććež pili̯ bi̯ttemi̯d!" "da, 'bi̯tte̯mi̯d' te šuan. vot a eške̯ kuče̯me̯s me bi̯tti, kok-pē̯te̯g kare̯mi̯d!" "no kod — šuas — kok-pē̯te̯ karis, m a r u ś a?" "baťuško" — šuas. "e̯! baťuško karis kok-pē̯te̯!" "a mi̯j ne̯? te kok-pē̯te̯gi̯d kare̯mi̯d da." "no, no, no, no, korošo, korošo."*

3. *no vot, znaćit, kor-ke̯ tuli̯s vois. pop ge̯re̯ karta sajas, ńe-i̯li̯n. pop dine̯ saldat muni. "no — šuas —, baťuško, me te̯-ri̯t — šuas — ge̯ri, menam agsōni̯ kole̯, a te — šuas — ge̯rani̯d oz na ešti̯, a men agasse̯ — šuas — on śetli̯?" "śetla — šuas — śetla. mun, ge̯ti̯rliś — šuas — juaś!" ge̯ti̯r dore̯ leććas. naja mama-ni̯la ve̯lini̯. poplen nī̯, sija tom nī̯, seče̯m mića pople̯n. mama-ni̯la gorti̯n ve̯lini̯, pue̯ni̯-pe̯že̯ni̯ muži̯kli̯. a saldat vois da. "vot — šuas — popaďďa — šuas —, men sija če̯ktis, muži̯kidliś juaśni̯ kali da." loktis, migńitis. "uźni̯ on lež?" "ńi me og verićći̯. me vot . . ." "a lok — šuas — petavlam sod vi̯las, jualam — šuas —, ki̯ke̯n pe̯talam." no petisni̯ ki̯ke̯n. "baťuško!" "mi̯j?" "če̯ktin te śetli̯ni̯ meni̯m?" "śetli̯, śetli̯, in žaľit, ńi-ne̯miś in žaľit, śetli̯!" "pe̯ža·lusta." "no vot — šue̯, saldat šue̯ — no vot" — šue̯. no pi̯risni̯. "pervoj molodkase̯ kole̯, nī̯se̯." nī̯li̯ ge̯ris, ge̯ris, berťi i popaďďali̯ ge̯ris. pop vois śojni̯. "ke̯ni — šuas —, puin-pe̯žin? mi̯j puin-pe̯žin?" "pua-pe̯ža taj, besse̯vesne̯j?! mi̯jla ne — šuas — mene̯ ńin, med mene̯ a nī̯te̯ ne̯, mi̯jla če̯ktin nī̯te̯ saldati̯sli̯?" "mi̯j — šuas*

The priest walked around. The priest arrived there singing prayers. He opened the door. "Look, young wife, it is very good" — says he — "that you want to bear a child, but your husband" — says he — "has failed to make legs for him. I am going to make legs for him." "Well, well, whatever do you mean . . . ?" The young wife began to grow sad. "I will come" — says he — "this evening." "Well, all right" — says she. So the young wife began to grow very sad. The priest says to his wife: "I am going to the precentor's" — says he — "in the morning we must go to another village." Instead of the precentor, the priset went to visit the grass-widow. "Well, well, here I am, I'm going to make legs." — says he. So away he went — of course, he made the legs.

2. Well now, everything is all right; then suddenly the soldier comes home. Of course, the child has come into the world, he is big already, and crawls around on all fours. Well, the soldier arrived home and was happy with his son. "Oh son, my little son, see what he is like! Oh wife, look what a size you have reared the child to be!" "Yes, 'You have reared him', you say. But what kind of a child should I rear? You made him with only one leg!" "Well, Marusya, who made the other leg?" "The Father." — she answers. "Damn it! so the Father made the other leg?" "Well, why not! When you made him with one leg." "Well, well, all right, all right."

3. Now spring came at last. The priest is ploughing not far behind the stable. The soldier goes over to the priest. "Father" — says he — "I did the ploughing yesterday, now I have to harrow, and you" — says he — "will not be finished with the ploughing today, will you lend me your harrow?" "I will lend it to you" — he answers — "of course. I will. Go and ask my wife to give it to you!" He goes to his wife. The mother and her daughter were both at home. The priest's daughter is very young and beautiful. The mother and her daughter were at home, baking and cooking food for the husband. The soldier arrived. "Well, mistress" — says he — "I have been to make enquiries of your husband and he ordered me to do it." He moved closer and winked at her. "Will you let me sleep with you?" "I don't believe you. I . . ." "Well, come on then" — says he — "let's go out on to the steps and ask him, let's both go!" — says he. Both of them went out. "Father!" "What's the matter?" "Did you order me to give it?" "Give it, give it, never mind a bit, spare no pains, just give it!" "As you please." "Well, well" — says the soldier. They went into the house. First he had to deal with the young lady, the daughter. He fucked the girl, then he fucked the priest's wife too. The priest came home to have a meal. "Where is it?" — he asks. "Have you baked and cooked?" "Do you want me to bake and cook as well, you lewd man! Why did you force me and

— če̮kti?" "no te že̮ če̮kte̮mi̮d mijanni̮me̮ siǯi, vopšem uźni̮-ōni̮." "ńeužeľi! — šuas — a menam sija voǯe̮s — šuas.

7. *as ole̮m ji̮li̮s*

1. *bať-man kuli da me oli pe̮ri̮ś mam dori̮n. da seśśa źať ve̮li menam, ćoj ve̮li menam. ćojle̮n ćeľaďďas ve̮lini̮, me med ǯe̮ľa ve̮li mamle̮n. a me koľi okmi̮s are̮n baťśi̮d da me jona vetle̮dli je̮z strošńićae̮, kazaćina. me ve̮li das-e̮ťi are̮sa, etače̮m da me ker dore̮ kai, je̮zli̮ strošńićae̮ da vetle̮dli. lunnas ve̮li paśtalam ľok sukman da źipun. koki̮d ve̮li etače̮m, ki̮šuna vaľe̮k abu, etače̮m gi̮n sape̮g sije̮n ki̮šuna vaľe̮knad. sije̮ mijan kokni̮m ki̮nmas da ki̮nmas. da aći̮d sukman gać karan da sija sitani̮d kuš; etati be̮knad vi̮jim, a sija i vir ľadvejśi̮d i̮skōte̮, ker dorad munan da. tē̮-bi̮d kole̮ ker dorad ōni̮, je̮z trošńićae̮n, das e̮ťi are̮s ve̮li. tē̮-bi̮d olan ǯik, aći̮d i ki̮nmalan. a šaľi̮d abu! etače̮m šaľ śetasni̮ trošńićai̮si̮dli̮. etaje̮n seśśa tē̮nas ki̮nman, on?! seśśa mam meni̮m i̮ste̮ma sukman, kare̮ma da (etaja nojse̮, kode̮s viśtali), śeti sukmante̮, da je̮z trošńićaad siǯ i vetle̮dlan da olan. seče̮m men mi̮ntisni̮ ďeśiť kopejoke̮n lun, lun re̮bitan ďeśiť kopejok. omeľǯiki̮sli̮ na mi̮j-ke̮, ďeveť kopejok, kodli̮ oďinnaćiť da śete̮ni̮. lunnas re̮bitan da sije̮ lun-ti̮r ker ki̮skalan. i̮ǯi̮d ge̮rae̮d leććan da leććan da ve̮li̮d voje̮de. a mi̮j ne̮ das-e̮ťi are̮s mort, sija kuče̮m mort?! žeńšina. ve̮lad kuććiśan esiǯi da vē̮ sija voje̮de̮. kvaťiććan, a kerji̮d uśe̮ma. kvaťiććan, doďďi̮d žugale̮ma, esija doď-niri̮d, esče̮m doď-ni̮ri̮d, sija doď-ni̮ri̮d ľapki̮d. seśśa i bara ńi-ne̮me̮n . . . kani̮d og li̮śti̮, je̮z kor, ke̮ť ke̮źajin: "oj-oj, m i k a j l e̮, doďďe̮ žugali." "med, n a t a ľ e̮, žugali-ke̮. vaj, śet mi̮j-ke̮, čupam da gezje̮n ke̮rtalam da leććam, gorte̮ leććam da karam". vot kuǯ seśśa olim. seśśa ajte̮g bi̮dmi siǯi, źať dori̮n bi̮dmim, jona śe̮kta. seśśa i das-śiźim are̮ǯ oli, mi̮j-ke̮, mam-źať dori̮n.*

2. *seśśa vere̮s saje̮ peti, ǯik e̮ťi kerka-kolas. a me̮d kerkaas muni, sećće vere̮s saje̮ peti. "don e̮gi̮r vi̮lin-ke̮ verman sulōni̮, n a t a ľ e̮, munan da i sen pe̮*

your daughter to do that? Why did you force your daughter on the soldier?" "What did I force you to do?" — he asks. "Well, look here, you forced us to sleep with him." "Really?" — says he — "Well, it was to discharge my debt".

7. About my life

1. My father and mother had died and I was living with my grandmother. I had a brother-in-law and a sister. My sister had children; I was my mother's youngest daughter. I was left fatherless when I was nine years old, and I had to work hard as a day-labourer, as a farm-worker. When I was eleven, as big as this, I went to the timber works as a day-labourer. We wore old clothes and caftans of frieze in the day-time. As for our feet, there were no *ki̯šuna vaľek* available, *ki̯šuna vaľek* are long felt boots like this (thigh-boots with fulled cloth upper parts and feet legs sewn together). Our feet are cold, always cold. And you have to make your own frieze caftan and trousers, and your bottom is bare: your trousers come up here, on the side, and your thighs bleed when you walk to the timber works. Throughout the winter I had to work as a day-labourer at the timber works; I was eleven years old. Throughout the whole winter you live like this, you freeze, you have no scarf. This is the kind of scarf day-labourers get. You'll catch cold with such a scarf in the winter, won't you? Then mother sent me some frieze cloth; she made and sent frieze clothes to me, the sort I have mentioned. This is how you live and work as a day-labourer. They paid me ten kopeks a day, you earn ten kopeks a day. The weaker ones get nine kopeks, some even receive eleven kopeks. You work in the day-time, pulling tree-trunks the whole day. You come down and down from the high hills, and the horse gallops. What is an eleven-year-old; what sort of a person? And a woman at that! You cling tight to your horse, and the horse gallops. You clutch at your horse, the timber falls off, you clutch at it, the sleigh breaks, the front of the sleigh breaks; the front of the sleigh is low. Then there is no way of going on . . . I daren't go up to call the people, perhaps the master: "Oh dear, oh dear, Mikajlę my sleigh has broken." "Never mind, Nataľ, if it has broken. Give us something, and we'll repair it, and we'll tie it up; we'll go home and put it right." You see how we were living. I was brought up without a father, I grew up at my brother-in-law's house, in very hard conditions. Then I lived with my mother's son-in-law until I was seventeen.

2. Then I married a man living exactly a house away. I married into the next house but one; that's where I went to live. "If you are able to stand on live coal, Nataľ, you can go and live there." I went there and lived there

verman ōni̮." me si̮će̮će̮ munli da oli me seni (saši̮k ve̮li das-e̮ťi are̮s) das-ki̮k vo, das-kujim vo oli me seni. seśśa ve̮jnad loi da mužikte̮ menśi̮m ve̮jna vi̮le̮ nuisni̮ da me seće̮će̮ koľi, końe̮ruško. seśśa ve̮jna vi̮las mi stradujtim ve̮li i̮li̮n jui̮n, vers śo saji̮n. gaške̮ i̮li̮nǯi̮k jui̮n mi stradujtam mi̮j-ke̮ gozja da ǯe̮ľińǯik ďever. i̮čkam da kurtam jona. a voʒ́ǯa ri̮tad me vakśi da śerali da vakśi da, sija be̮rde̮mi̮d voʒ́se̮n. vakśi da śerali da men šue̮ mužik: "mi̮j-ne̮, n a t a ľ e̮, te śeralan, mi̮j-ne̮ ďive̮?" "vot taj, meśa, ś e m a n, śerame̮ pete̮ da seśśa kuććisni̮, meśa, og vermi̮, śerame̮ pete̮." seśśa me̮d ri̮tad — sija kerka dore̮ katigad — me̮d ri̮t vois, seśśa i lokta be̮rdig-ti̮r. una mi kurtam, a pi̮ža ki̮te̮: "ś e m a n, ge̮te̮vićći̮ pe̮!" "ki̮će̮će̮?" "ve̮jna pe̮ loi." da e̮dje̮ǯi̮k pe̮ etija jage̮di̮s veśtas munini̮, vi̮le̮ kaisni̮ da. sija pe̮ m i ť v a ń ve̮la da mi̮j-ke̮ "e̮dje̮ǯi̮k pe̮ ge̮te̮vićći̮, voasni̮ pe̮ e̮statki pi̮žajas." pi̮žajas ńin ki̮tisni̮ da taja e̮statki pi̮ža ńin koľi. a meam mužiki̮d i šue̮: "me pe̮, n a t a ľ e̮, in pe̮ tače̮ma be̮rd, me pe̮ og mun ve̮jna vi̮lad, me ńe-stre̮jeve̮j da me be̮r kosa. me pe̮ t u r j a e̮ ǯ leććila i be̮r voa." s a ši̮d i etačem kvajt miśećća kaga ve̮li. sija bab da ďed vi̮ǯe̮ni̮. seśśa me i be̮rda zej jona. "mi̮jla be̮rdan?" seśśa kor-ke̮ i luni̮d koľi, kuǯ koľi. men viśtōni̮ re̮gi̮d, a seśśa zavoďitim katni̮. e̮statki pi̮ža oz na lokni̮. katim da etani ti̮dale̮ seni vonjasni̮m, ćomjasni̮m, olam ke̮ni, viǯ vi̮śi̮s, katidǯikin. seśśa pi̮ža i lokte̮. zej mića li̮a, i̮ǯi̮d li̮a. naja i šue̮ni̮ k a ľ v a ń i ľ ľ a j a s: "no, ś e m a n, s e ś ś a pe̮ śibe̮ćći, seśśa pe̮ i teni̮d šabaš! koľ pe̮, n a t a ľ, te be̮rdig-ti̮r!" seśśa śibeććim da seśśa i be̮rde̮ni̮, meśa, babajasi̮d ne̮ kuǯ koľini̮. babajasi̮d pe̮ mijan be̮rdig-ti̮r i koľini̮ veśi̮s baď dore̮ pe̮, be̮rde̮ni̮. "oj-oj, meśa, mi̮j-ne̮ taja me, meśa, taće̮će̮ vaas pi̮ra." ś e m a n šue̮: "mi̮j pomla te vaas pi̮ran? tead na pe̮ e̮d i ďiťa vi̮jim, sije̮ pe̮ kole̮ viǯni̮, a in pe̮ n a t a ľ be̮rd, me pe̮ taćće be̮r voa. tan na pe̮ ti stradujtanni̮d, a me pe̮ t u r j ae̮ǯ vetla da me pe̮ ve̮le̮n taće̮će̮ kaa stradujtni̮ad ti dore̮ be̮r." seśśa pi̮že̮ śibećći̮lim da mi̮j-ke̮ zapas boštis da de̮re̮m-gaććas, mi̮j ve̮li si̮li̮ kole̮ da pi̮že̮ se̮lisni̮. da mi ı koľim ǯe̮ľa ďeverke̮d, etače̮m-kojd. me li̮a kuźai̮d vete̮ćći da vete̮ćći da vete̮ćći da be̮rdi da be̮rdi. uśla da mute̮ ćapišta da be̮rda da be̮rda da be̮rda. ki̮će̮će̮ǯ mužiki̮d munis, etačem ćiki̮ľ-ni̮rd da ćikiľtis da seśśa oz, ćiki̮ľe̮di̮s i oz ti̮dō mužiki̮d. seśśa i me kor-ke̮ i voi, seśśa be̮r pi̮ž dore̮ voi da be̮rdi da be̮rdi da. seni be̮rdi, gorzi. seśśa katni̮ petim, a meni̮m i šue̮ni̮, sen kerka doras kodi ole̮ni̮: "mi̮jla, n a t a ľ e̮, taǯi be̮rdan? mi̮j-ke̮ taj e̮tnad,

(Sašyk was eleven years old), I lived there for twelve or thirteen years. Then war came, my husband was taken away from me to the war, and I, poor soul, was left by myself. Then during the war we made hay far away by the river, a hundred versts away. We were making hay perhaps even farther away by the river, my husband, I and my younger brother-in-law. We were mowing and raking hard. The night before I was laughing, laughing and weeping alternately. I was laughing and laughing, my husband asks me: "What are you laughing at, Natal', what the deuce is that?" "Śeman" — I say — "a fit of laughter has come over me, and I can't keep it back, it has come over me so hard." Then next day, in the evening, as we were coming home down the river, next evening I came in tears. We were doing a lot of raking, and a man in a boat comes down the river: "Śeman, get ready to go!" "Where?" "War's broken out." And they went away in a hurry, right through this pine-wood, upstream. Mit' Vań came with a horse: "Make haste, get ready, here come the other men in boats." The men in the boats had already gone down the river, only this boat stayed behind. My husband says: "As for me, Natal', don't cry so bitterly, I'm not going to the war, I'm in the reserve and I'll come back. I'm going down to Turya and I'll come back." Sasha was such a six months old child. Grandmother and grandfather will take care of her. Then I wept bitterly. "Why are you crying?" Then the day passed somehow; it passed away. It does not take long for me to tell the tale. Then we began to go up the river. The remaining boat had not yet arrived. We rowed upstream, and the tents and huts where we were living began to appear beyond the meadow, along the upper course of the river. Then also the boatman arrives. The bank of the river is very beautiful; there is sand, much sand there. They, Kal' Vań Il'l'a and the rest say: "Well, Śeman, join us, for now you may call it a day! Stay here, Natal', and weep!" Then we joined them, the wives were crying. Well, how should they have been left behind?! All the women stayed behind at the willow tree. "Alas, alas" — I say — "What am I to do? I shall drown myself in the water here." Śeman says: "Why should you drown in the river? After all, you have a child, you must bring it up, so do not weep, Natal', for I shall come back here. You will be mowing the hay here, I shall go to Turya, and I shall come back on horseback, to make hay with you." Then we walked to the boat, he took spare clothes, underwear, the things he needed, and got in. I and the little brother-in-law stayed behind, he was as big as that. I ran and ran and ran after him along the sandy bank and I cried and cried. I stumbled and I clawed at the earth, and cried and cried and cried. There was a bend in the river where my husband was going, and then my husband was not to be seen at the bend. Then, some time after,

n a t a ľ ȩ loktan? kȩn-nȩ ś e m a n͔id?" "meśa, ś e m a n͔id i vȩjna v͔ilȩ nuisn͔i da abu ńin ś e m a n." seśśa vot meam ku͔ǯi i koľi!

3. *seśśa mi kor-kȩ seni i stradujtim, seśśa i kı̄tim gortȩ, ǯȩľa ďeťinkakȩd, d͔ir stradujtim da. seśśa kı̄tim da sečȩm na ińka-ajkaȩ. seśśa sijȩ na ȩd kolȩ mijan turuntȩ il͔iśtȩ ȩd purjȩn vajn͔i. seśśa purjȩn vajn͔i da bara ǯȩľa ďeťinkakȩd mijann͔imȩj k͔ilȩćć͔in͔i petisn͔i. me eśkȩ ńin tȩda, b͔idȩnȩs kuža karn͔i. ajka mijan pȩr͔iś vȩli, kȩsjȩ 'me pȩ čȩč vetla k͔ilȩćć͔in͔ias med narad͔is v͔ilȩ', mikȩd iz i mun. mi ǯȩľa ďeťinkanad menȩ i mȩdȩdis ajka͔id. bȩrdig-t͔ir muni da, muni bȩrdig-t͔ir, a veś ńin bȩrdȩn͔i mamjas mijan orćća da bȩrdȩn͔i, me bȩrda da. m͔ij-nȩ takȩd me da kom͔in doď turun vaja, abu ȩd eča! sija šuȩn͔i r ȩ m a n m i š ȩ (da sija seśśa munim da, mi bȩrdam jona da): "in pȩ n a t a ľ bȩrd! ćȩ̄l͔i! me pȩ tijan otsala." "mijan-kȩ, meśa, otsalan i bur." mijan seśśa eča ōmȩćći bȩr. a katn͔iad ȩd il͔in, porogjas͔id g͔ir͔iś, ńe-ku͔ǯi on lo katn͔iad: s͔i g͔irśa. ȩnija moz ȩd on motorȩ sȩ̄, sek ȩd zib-pom moľľȩdan, sȩlan. da a vȩl͔id kučȩm zboj! śľega͔id ȩd eta kuźa, das-kȩkja·m͔is aršin kuźa. vot pȩńimajtan das-kȩkja·m͔is aršinsȩ? eta g͔irša śľega͔is. sijȩ dined͔is on l͔iśt͔i kȩrtōn͔i vuž-doďďad. dined͔is-kȩ kȩrtalan, sija etaǯ vaľiććas da. etaǯ vaľiććas da on i volȩ, a sijȩ kolȩ vek jı̄-doď śľegatȩ pȩrȩdn͔i kolȩ, etaǯi ńı̄. esija med din͔is, esti loktȩ, k͔iz͔is, a vȩsńisȩ, k͔iskan sijȩl͔i. seśśa k͔iskalim, k͔iskalim sijȩ, kujim pur-t͔ir mi. seśśa mi seś pur karim da sijȩ seśśa gruźitim i͔ǯ͔id m͔ij-kȩ . . . kodi mat͔inǯ͔ik, a k͔irti il͔inǯ͔ik turun͔is versś͔isǯ͔ik k͔iskalim, sijȩ vȩlȩn jursȩ k͔iskalim. a etija purj͔is, a etija stogj͔is, etija beregis. seććȩ karasn͔i eta paśta pes-pom k͔ik pu͔iś! k͔ik pu͔iś pes-tor karasn͔i da sijȩl͔i kes vı̄ti͔is seććȩ k͔ik nar-vı̄ vaćkasn͔i, ľibȩ kujimȩs, med sijȩ esiǯ oz katlaś. seśśa nȩśila, etaććȩ śujan, turuntȩ sȩ̄tan. seśśa mužik͔id esti bośtas, a me etaja berdti͔is bośta da menim šuas sija tȩvarišid, m i k a j l ȩ i d: "ok, n a t a ľ, te verman, on, n a t a ľ, pȩ in uś!" "no, meśa, uśa-kȩ ȩd, bȩr ćećća. muna, og i uś. vek muna." vȩli menim šuȩ: "menam pȩ n a t a ľ v͔ile naďej v͔ijim, s͔il͔i kȩť vȩla jur, kȩť prȩstȩj jur, n a t a ľ pȩ śorovno k͔iskas bȩrȩ." seśśa mi sijȩ gruźitim da mi seśśa sijȩ purjȩn kı̄tim, kujim kuźanas. kujim kuźanas sijȩn purjȩn kı̄tam da va͔is kos! k͔ilȩ, va͔is kos, sija gaškȩ eta ǯuǯta, śľega͔id eta g͔irśa: seśśa mi sijȩl͔i*

I came back to the boat, and I cried and cried and cried there, and wailed. Then we started upstream, and people living there in the house say to me, "Why are you weeping so bitterly, Nataľ? Why have you come back alone, Nataľ? Where is Śeman?" "Śeman has been taken to the war" — I say — "Śeman is no longer." Then see how I was left behind!

3. Then once we were mowing hay there, and I was going down the river with my little child, we were going home, we had been mowing long. We went down the river afterwards, I have a father-in-law, and a mother-in-law like that. You know, we have to raft our hay a long way. I and my child went again to raft. I know how to do it, already I know how to do everything. My father-in-law was old: "I'll go with you to raft, if only to guide you." But he did not come. My father-in-law sent me with my little child. I went weeping and weeping, but we mothers all weep together, side by side, so I weep as well. Well now, I bring thirty loads of hay, and that's no little thing. Ręman Mišę and the rest (we were passing by them and crying at the time) say: "Do not weep, Nataľ! Calm yourself! I'll help you." "If you will help us, all's well." Then we breathed somewhat more freely. But it is a long way up the river, there are big rapids, there's no way of going upstream, so big are they. You don't go by motorboat as you do nowadays, in those times you just sat in a boat and wore the end of the pole smooth. And the horse, how wild it is! The hay-pole is as long as this, eighteen arshin long. Do you know how long eighteen arshin is? That's the length of the hay-pole. You never dare fasten the thick end of it to the hay-load. If you fasten the thick end to it, it will fall apart like this. It will fall apart, and you will not get there, it is always the thin end that must be fastened slantwise, like this. This is the thick end of it, it is placed like this, and you pull on the thin end. Then we pulled and pulled and pulled three loaded rafts. Then we loaded a big one . . . er . . . whoever was nearest loaded it, but the hay is further away where the bank is steep, we pulled it from a kilometre away, we had a horse pull the stack of hay. Here is the raft, here is the haystack, and here is the bank. We made a wooden sledge this wide out of two logs. You make a sledge of two logs, and you put two cross-laths over them, or three, so that it does not wobble. Then you put the rack on here, and load the hay on it. Then one grasps it here, while I hold it at this end, and Mikajlę, the man helping me, says: "On Nataľ, can you hold it? See that you don't slip!" "Well" — say I — "if I slip I shall get up again. I shall go on, I shan't slip, I shall go on and on." He said to me: "I trust Nataľ, it is the same to her whether it be a horse-drawn load or a simple stack, Nataľ will pull it." Then we finished loading, and went downstream with three rafts, one after the other. We were going downstream with three

kostę — vot etani biįs tįdalę — etaććęʒ bięʒis mi i munam sį mįtta i vermam munnį. vot kuʒi kįlęććim, ęni i viśam. seććę ęt'i pur, etaja, įʒįd stogsę jitam da męd da kojmęd da seććę stog das jitan pom-vī̦ tęvarįšjaslįś, med sija ęt'iįs kosęd̦is munę, a kodįs va vįlas voęma, med sija kįskę. seśśa mi siʒi vot i kįlęććim vek. a mij-kęįd, ćikįl'is, etačęma porogjasįs, kośśasįs, kučęm sija? sečęm: zibtę, zibtę esiʒ, purtę vek kutan esiʒ da vek čukędan da. on i vejjō, bara ńin nuę pęlęsinti. esiʒi vek kī̦tam, vek. vot kuʒi vek rębitim da olim da. vot seśśa ęni taję kuʒi, gosudarsvę mijannimę verdę siję. — seśśa vajam, siʒi kįlędam kiʒ-kę bęrdig-tįr. seśśa siję vajam da seśśa gortę voam. oj-oj, petam j e m - v a vįlad da seśśa ʒęl'a ju kojdįś na vajam da. j e m - v a vįlad petam da tęlįd petę! sutki kįk ęt'ilaįn viʒas. zej įʒįd koz pęrędasnį da zej įʒįd kozsę siję kęrtalasnį purjas da sija med mij-kę karas, pursę kįskę va tujędis, med oz beregas pįrtnįas vęl'asę śet. sija kozjįs ęd vęję da sija aćįs kįlalę. seśśa kī̦tam, kī̦tam da (k o ń i vomįnįn sija zej veśkįd, vot v e s l' a n aad kaigęn aʒʒilin?), seśśa seććę voan da seććę i įlalan vojnad. on tęd, kodorę munan. kī̦tan-ę, katan? pur-vī̦śįd-kę ćeććasnį pįžajasįd, eśkę gortanįs munęnį, kī̦tįd kī̦tęnį, a naja katįd katęnį, naja. ćuksaśnį kuććan: "kįććę munan?" "gortę." "ti ęd ńe-ladnę munannįd, ti ęd męd̦orę munannįd!" vot seśśa siję vajan da kor-kę leptalan bara įʒįd sabrię. da gortę voan da seśśa i verdan.

4. *seśśa ęt'i d'ad' mikęd vęli čeč kī̦tę — sįlęn nī̦, kįk nī̦ pur vįlas — da šuę: "no, mi taććę į b ę s dinad śibęććam." į b ę s dinad śibęććęnį naja. naja seśśa unmōślasnį kor-kę. unmōslasni da: "oj-oj-oj-ej pę, mij nę pę ńin taja? mi pę taj nę voęmaś . . . k u a - v i ʒ katįdinęś, o ń e ž j e kī̦tįdad. mi pę taj k u a - v i ʒ katįdę voęmaś! edję ćeććę, v a r u k ę, da mij-kę, m a r e, ćeććę edję da katamę jęzis ćeććōtęʒ setįś pę pur vī̦śis, domalę pę purtę da!" seśśa pur vįlįś ćeććasnį da eśkę į b ę s dinįnęś na eśkę vęlęmaęś, k į ʒ - d i n kī̦tįdad, k o ń i katįdad, vomįnad seśśa purtę kor-kę vajim, sija bara na ćē̦tam da.*

5. *kerkatę mijan karęma, mužikįs karlis: matićaįs da pereveďinaa ʒoʒįd. seśśa i menę jukisni. menę i oz vermįnį dęmśįd vętlįnį da i menam i nįlįd vįjim. "menęlį kvart'ira pę śetan męd̦or bęksę." "ińka-ajkaįd menę oz lęʒnį. da me*

rafts, and the river was dried up! Just look! The water has dried up! The hay-pole is perhaps that deep. Then we went on along the dry land — look, you can see the fire — we must reach that fire if we can manage to reach it! That's how we had been rafting, and we are still sick. There we link one raft-load, a great stack, with the second and the third one, you can link ten stacks together, so that the one in the water can draw those of the others on dry land. This is how we always rafted. And the bends, the rapids, the waterfalls, what are they like too! This is how you do it: you hold the pole, the pole like this, always pushing the raft this way. You do not go straight ahead, again it goes to one side. This is how we make our way down the river, and you see how we toiled and lived all the time. Well, then, how is it nowadays? It is the state that looks after us. — This is how we carry the load, this is how we come down the river, weeping. We transport it, and come home. Alas, alas, we go out to the Vym, and then bring it from a small river to the Vym. We reach the Vym, and the wind is blowing. It takes two days to work in one place. They fell a very tall spruce, and tie the big spruce to the raft for it to pull the raft along the mainstream, and not let it bump against the bank. You see, the spruce just sinks into the water and so floats downstream. Then we go down and down the stream (on the *kośi* stretch it is quite straight; you must have seen it when you were going to *vesľana*). Then you arrive there, and lose your way at night. You do not know which way you are going, up or down the river. When the boatmen leave the raft and land, they go home, to be sure. They think they are going down the river, but they are going up the river. You begin to shout: "Where are you going?" "Home." "You're going the wrong way, you live in another direction!" Well, at last you bring home the hay and some time you store it in the big barn. You arrive and then feed the animals.

4. Then an old man was travelling with us down the river, his two daughters were also on the raft. He says: "Well, here is *i̮be̮s*, and we'll land here." They landed at *i̮be̮s*. Then they fall asleep. They fall asleep, and: "Alas, alas, alas, whatever is this? Well, we have been coming . . . coming, we are above *kua-viǯ*, downstream from *ońežje*. Why, we have arrived somewhere above *kua-viǯ*. Get up quickly, Varuk and Mare, get up at once and let's go upstream, against the current, before the people on the raft wake up, untie the raft there!" They spring up on the raft, and they were really perhaps at *i̮be̮s*, below *ki̮ǯ-din*, on the stretch above *kośi*. Then some time we brought home the raft and again we unloaded up the hay.

5. Our house was built by my husband: the main beam, the joists and the floor-planks. Then I got my share. I cannot be expelled from the house, I have a daughter. "Give me the other side!" My mother-in-law and

seśśa mam orde̯ kvarťirae̯ peti. men me̯s śetisni̯ i. a meam me̯sse̯ viǯa e̯ťilai̯n, a turuni̯s me̯dlai̯n, aći̯m ola kojme̯dlai̯n. kuǯ oli me, vek oli! seśśa kor-ke̯ i tē̯nad me e̯ťili̯ś vē̯ korla da me̯dli̯ś vē̯ korla da mame̯ mene̯ otsali i. da me seśśa i kerse̯ leǯi, jirtte̯, etaćće̯ pe̯te̯le̯kte̯. da seśśa me kor-ke̯ i re̯be̯tńikjas bośtali. re̯be̯tńikjasi̯dli̯ me kodli̯ sija vi̯jim voǯese̯n čupśan, nake̯d voǯese̯n doľie̯n piľiććan mužikjasi̯ske̯d. (vot be̯rda! abu taje̯ le̯ž, veśi̯s ina.) seśśa kodli̯ i zuaśan, kodli̯ i vuran. bi̯d-nog kole̯ morti̯sli̯ ōni̯. seśśa meni̯m kerkate̯ leptisni̯, juralisni̯, seśśa i jirtte̯ puktisni̯, i ǯoǯte̯ puktisni̯ i veś. sije̯ karisni voǯlas-dorse̯ meni̯m. seśśa i e̯be̯sse̯ vośtan i i̯lla! paćse̯ karis źaťi̯d. źaťe̯ maśťer ve̯li da paćse̯ karis. źaťe̯ pi̯dďi kare̯ vetli, s i̯ k t i̯ v - k a r e̯, ńańla gruze̯n, gruzla. seśśa me sije̯ jurśi̯m bur patkase̯ źaťe̯li̯ śeti, mužiki̯dli̯ś šeńeľte̯ śeti, mužiki̯dli̯ś ćasite̯ śeti kerkapi̯čke̯s kare̯mi̯d vi̯le̯. me śťente̯ le̯sali, aćim veśse̯ kerali, a s a ši̯ske̯d i stružitim. me i̯ǯi̯d, s a ši̯d ǯeľa, oz vermi̯. a stružjas e̯d te̯dan? etaćće̯ gez ke̯rtale̯ni̯ da sija s a šte̯ verstak vi̯le̯ sūte̯da da s a ši̯d i ďergajte stružte̯, a me esti i kuta esiǯi. stružte̯ me i kuta, a sije̯ s a ši̯d ďergajte̯, stružite̯. vot, kuǯ me stre̯jićći, oli. seśśa i menam kuče̯m-ke̯ ńe-śćasne̯j-li, mi̯j-ľi, ni̯le̯ ńin loi das-e̯ťi are̯s. seśśa me aći̯m muna, turun ki̯le̯dni̯-katni̯ ke̯sja ńin, a meni̯m kuče̯m-ke̯ korać voi da vot ki̯ćće̯ǯ voi. da kerkate̯ vuzali seś da i tan kuče̯m śe̯kta oli. tani e̯ťi lun je̯zi̯n olan, me̯d lun je̯zi̯n lunjan. vot kuče̯m juan-ine̯ voli da vek loi ōni̯, da oli da e̯ni ni̯le̯ ńevesta. e̯ni i pe̯ri̯śmi, e̯ni i śinte̯mśi. seśśa i ľokman. ōni̯ bur, ōni̯ le̯śi̯d da śinmi̯d da i zdorovjei̯d iz lo.

8. as ole̯m ji̯li̯ś

1. mijan zej bur oli̯śjas ve̯lini̯. etija i ve̯li kerkai̯s, etaćće̯ i muni tože̯. zej bur oli̯śjas ve̯lini̯, vit ćoja-voka ve̯lini̯. ajni̯m kuli i koľim vit ćoja-voka. me okmi̯s are̯s ve̯li, okmi̯si̯s na lokte̯. a ćojjas sija, e̯ťi i̯ǯi̯dǯi̯k ćoj, a seśśa ǯeľa veśi̯s. seśśa mi olim zej jona, zej śe̯ki̯da, mam das-ńoľ koľi, das-ńoľ are̯snad koľim da mijan same̯j ve̯jnai̯d. ve̯jnai̯d. ńe-kodli̯ stradujtni̯ abu, ńańi̯d abu. vok armijae̯ munis,

father-in-law will not let me in there. Then I moved to my mother's house. They gave me a cow. But I keep my cow in one place, the hay in another, and I live at a third place. How I have had to live all the time! Then in winter I ask one person for a horse, and another for a horse, my mother also helped me. Then I rafted logs, and had a ceiling, a ceiling with beams made here. Then once I hired workers as well. You and the workers have to be quits; you do carpentry for this one, go sawing with other men, in return. (Look, I am weeping! I'm telling no lies, all this is true.) Then down there you card wool for this one, and sew for that one. One must live in some way or other. Then they erected my house, roofed it, put up the ceiling and laid the floor and everything. They made me a front. You just open the door, and there is the yard! The oven was built by my brother-in-law. My brother-in-law was a master-craftsman and he built ovens. Instead of my brother-in-law I went to town, to Syktyvkar, to fetch corn, to arrange transport, to bring home loads of goods. Then I gave my good headscarf to my brother-in-law, I gave him my husband's overcoat, I also gave him my husband's watch for having built the inside of the house. I trimmed the walls smooth, I myself trimmed everything smooth, and Sasha helped me with the planing. I am big, Sasha is little, she does not know how to do it. Do you know what a plane is? You fasten twine here, and I stand Sasha at the planing bench, and Sasha pulls the plane while I hold it like this. I hold it and she, Sasha, pulls it and planes. Just imagine how I built, how I lived! Then my unfortunate daughter or what shall I call her, was eleven years old. Then I myself went to the river, to transport hay up and down the river, but some sort of measles attacked me, and see where I am now! I have sold my house, and I have led such a hard life here. Here you live one day among people, and you spend the next day among them too. Look, how full of drunkards this place is! But one must live on, and I have been living, and my daughter is engaged already. I have grown old now, and already I have grown blind. Then you become ill. To live is good, to live is fine, but you have no eyes and no health.

8. About my life

1. Very kind people lived in our place. This was the house, and this is where I came when I was married. They were very kind people; I had five brothers and sisters. My father died, and the five of us were left behind. I was nine years old then, just entering my ninth year. As for my sisters: one of them was older than me, then all the others were younger. Then we were living a hard life, and mother left us too; I was fourteen when we were left by

mi ǯeľa vokked koľim. ćojnim veres saje munema, ńe-kod abu, ǯik kiken. vot mijan i ilin stradaid zej že. stradujtni kaim mi, sek na i gožemnad ńańid iz vē da i ig verme, mi na arnas kaim, kor-ke taj p r o k o p e j *dirji vois ńańis voǯ.*

2. *seśśa i kik peľe kaim, ćoje i tože mužikis armijain, tože sija etnas. sija kais vokeked, ǯeľa vokeked, a menim śelsovetiś śetisni pomošńića, sečem ńe śe jej, ńe śe prestuž kojd. mi ileǯik kaim siked. mij ne me ńi-nem og kuž karni. das-ńoľ aresnas mij kužan karni? sabri kole karni, kole i kosate keslini. ńinem on kuž karni. seśśa mi i bidenes veleććim. eťiliś jualam, viśtalasni, naraďitasni, medliś viśtalan, bara naraďitasni. seśśa veśse kōmis aslid karni. seśśa mi kor-ke stradujtim da i voim gorte. kuǯ karim, karim, sket vijim mij-ke tir na, kik mes na vijim daj vē na vijim. seśśa i ćoj, sija kir ulin ole, a mi tan olam vokked. seśśa i sija turun kole vajōni tēnad, velen kole vajōni mijan, velen, ńeľamin kilometra sajiś (vers veli važen). sije vajalan verdan sketli. me berdlam, gruz na ed kole kiskōni. bidenes kole karni, veśse, a eni ed ńi-nem sije oz vermini karni das-ńoľ-aresjasid. naverne mijan demas demni oz kužni, a vot mijan loi ōni. seśśa oli da i kor-ke i vok vois armijaiś i getraśis sija.*

3. *kuǯ olan, olan sija. seśśa vek siǯ olim, olim. seśśa i mužikked olim, mužik zej bur eśken veli, pośis ōni da seśśa i bara vejnaid loi. bara seśśa sije nuisni da i seśśa vok. kuǯi olan, olan. kik vok koľi.*

9. *veres saje munem jiliś*

me muni das-śiźim aren, mene vajisni. mene god ńin viććisni muked žeńikjasid da ig mun, a me sećće saldat sajas muni ćerez demse. žeńik bur, žeńik mića, te kojd že ǯeľińǯi, abu iǯid tušaa. i ne mića veli. abu ľok, bur, mij-ke das-śiźim aresa nili vaje. seśśa muni da menim koraśisni ǯoń śo aršin, derase śo aršin koraśisni menim da śo aršin pridanneje mi. ińkali nui, ajkali nui, ďeverjasli, seśśa i mužikli derema-gaća, žeńik derema-gaća. seśśa i vejpśim,

ourselves, and there happened to be war in our country. There is nobody to cut the hay and we have no bread. My brother went into the army, I stayed with my little brother. My sister married, we had nobody, there were just the two of us. Well, the hayfield is far, far away. We went to mow the hay. That summer we still had no bread, so we could not go, and we went in the autumn, somewhere around Prokopij's day, rather early, the corn was ripe.

2. Then we went in two directions. My sister's husband was at the war too, so she also lives alone. She went away with my younger brother, my little brother, and the village council gave me somebody to help, who was not quite stupid nor quite sane. We went farther away with her. What then? I cannot do a thing. What can one do at fourteen? You have to build a barn and sharpen the scythe. You cannot do anything. Then we had to learn how to do everything. You ask one man, people will tell you, instruct you, you ask another one, and again you are told how to do it. Theny you had to do everything by yourself. Then somehow we finished hay-making at last and came home. We did as best we could, we have animals, some of them with young, two cows and even a horse. My sister lives at the foot of the hill and I and my little brother live here. Then we have to fetch hay in the winter, we have to fetch it with the horse, with the horse a distance of forty kilometres (people used to say *verst*). You bring home the hay and feed the animal. We weep, for we have to pull the load. We have to do everything, all sorts of things, but young people of fourteen today cannot do a thing. These young people here probably cannot put a patch on, but we had to live. This is how I went on living. Once my elder brother also came home from the war and married.

3. You live as best you can. Then we went on living like this all the time. I was living with my husband. My husband was a good man, you could live with him; then war broke out again. He was also taken away, then my brother. You live as best you can. Two brothers were left behind.

9. How I got married

I married at seventeen, then I was taken away from home. Other fiancées had been waiting for me a year, but I did not marry any of them, I married him, the soldier, one house further along. The bridegroom was good, the bridegroom was handsome, as short as you are, he was not tall in stature. And, well, he was handsome. He was not bad, he was good, and he married a girl of seventeen. I married him, they asked my hand, and I had to give

seni be̮rdi jona. mij-ne̮ das-śiźim are̮sa?! ve̮jpśanse̮ pirujtni̮as kole̮. me pola ve̮li že̮ńikśi̮d. a ve̮jpśe̮ni̮, sije̮ ve̮jp-ine̮ ćukarććam mi, nī̮ ordas. perve̮j ve̮jpśe̮ni̮ sije̮li̮, seśśa veś sija voas že̮ńikle̮n re̮d. že̮ńikle̮n re̮d voasni̮ da seśśa [naja] si̮li̮ i koźin me seti veśi̮sli̮, daške̮ i ki̮ź ki̮mi̮n koźin, veśi̮sli̮ ći̮šjan. sija ve̮li seče̮m ći̮šjan, ǯe̮ľaǯi̮k-ke̮ i ǯe̮ľaǯi̮k ći̮šjan. ći̮šjanse̮ sije̮ bośtasni̮ da ńi-ne̮m ten oz śetni̮. seni pi̮zan vi̮li̮n eta mi̮tta vajale̮maeś veśse̮, seśśa »kuź ńem da bur šud« da mi̮j da šualasni̮ »kuź ńem, bur šud da bura ōni̮« da. seśśa mi sije̮ koźnaśim, seśśa be̮re̮-voǯe̮ ńevesta pukśi̮lan že̮ńik dore̮ orćća da že̮ńiki̮d sija me eśke̮ esiǯ kise̮ kara, sija mene̮ eśće̮ ľićkalasni̮ da že̮ńiki̮sle̮n vežańi̮s, med i̮ǯi̮d tuj pe̮ on boś. sećće̮ǯ ľićkalasni̮ tene̮. te esiǯ końe̮r i pukalan, naja eśće̮ puktasni̮ sojjasse̮, a te siǯi i pukō! seśśa i be̮rdni̮ munim, seśśa be̮rdim aśśi̮d nī̮ ole̮mse̮.

10. *svaďba ji̮li̮ś*

1. *me muna koraśni̮ ńevesta orde̮. "ńevesta, te ke̮sjan, on munni̮?" "baťli̮ś juala." "no juō vaj! mijan kōmas laďiććini̮, tene̮ me lokti koraśni̮." "baťli̮ś kōmas pre̮šeńńe korni̮, kuče̮ma sija śetni̮ kuććas se̮glašeńńe̮." "no vaj, juō, gaške̮ di̮r ōni̮." "me ke̮sja munni̮ kuče̮m ine̮, se̮glaśiććan? meam sija že̮ńik." "no, bať ke̮sji̮śis?" "ke̮sji̮śis." "no ke̮sji̮śis-ke̮, me pe̮ og ǯug tijane̮s. vajas." "a kor ne̮ svaďbase̮ ke̮sjan teke̮d karni̮?" "a ton-ke̮ laďiććam, dvaćeť pjatoje ton laďiććam, med surjas eštalas, ki̮k vežon mi̮śťi karam svaďba." . . . "kōmas mijan de̮re̮ma-gać, mijan kōmas ći̮šjan, komi̮n ći̮šjan, e̮d menam re̮d i̮ǯi̮d." "vaj ladne̮! śorńitim da seśśa on ńin janse̮ćći̮, bi̮ť loe̮. on, loe̮ ńin bi̮ť laďiććini̮." "jurli̮, baťli̮ loe̮ lepti̮lni̮, med lepte̮." "seśśa mijan seki, svaďba vi̮las loas, tene̮ na mi ve̮jpśi̮lam. volam ve̮jpśini̮ unae̮n. no vot seki komi̮n ve̮jpśan ći̮šjante̮ i koźnalan. a ke̮li̮ś di̮rji esije̮ i koźinte̮ mijan koźnalan bať-mamli̮. sije̮ ńin e̮bjazaťeľne̮ kolan-tor." "loe̮ ge̮te̮vitni̮. kodse̮-ke̮ ge̮te̮vite̮ma, kodse̮-ke̮ na abu." "svaďba vi̮las mi karam ki̮k ri̮t pirse̮. ki̮k ri̮t karam pirse̮ da karam bura da*

them a full hundred *arshin* of linen, a hundred *arshin* as dowry. I gave part of it to my mother-in-law, part of it to my father-in-law, to the brothers-in-law, and then to my husband I gave shirt, pants, a bridegroom's shirt and pants. Then we had a gay time, but I cried bitterly there. Well, of course I did, I was seventeen! The betrothal had to be celebrated. I was afraid of the bridegroom. Well, they had a celebration, we gathered together at the place where the celebration was held, at the girl's home. She is fêted first, then all the bridegroom's relatives arrive. The bridegroom's relatives arrive, then I gave presents to him and to all of them, perhaps twenty presents or so, a kerchief to each of them. It was a sort of kerchief, a kind of small kerchief. They accept the kerchief and do not give you anything. There on the table they had brought such a mass of everything, then they wished me "long life and good luck" or something like that: "long life, good luck and a good life". We gave presents, then the bride sits by the bridegroom, back to back; I place my hands like this, they press me against him, the bridegroom's godmother, so that you may not undertake a long journey. They press you so tightly. You, poor soul, sit like this, they place their arms here, and you sit like this! Then we went to lament, we lamented our maiden life.

10. About the wedding

1. I go to propose to the girl at the fiancée's house. "Fiancée, you want to marry, don't you?" "I'll ask my father." "Well, go and ask him! We must make preparations, I have come to ask you to marry." "I must ask for father's permission and find whether he is willing to give his consent." "Well, hurry up and ask him, perhaps it will take a long time." "I want to go to such and such a place. Do you agree? He is my fiancé." "Well, has your father given his consent?" "Yes, he has." "Well, if he has given his consent I shall not trouble you any longer. He will marry you." "And when do you want to arrange the wedding?" "When we are quite ready; we have agreed upon the twenty-fifth as the date when the beer has to be brewed, and a fortnight later we'll hold the wedding." . . . "We need shirts, pants, and we need kerchiefs, thirty kerchiefs since I have plenty of relatives." "All right! We have talked things over, and you cannot separate from this day on, the wedding will be held in any case. We shall certainly have to make preparations." "The head, the father must organize it, let him organize it." "Then another thing is essential for the wedding: we must get you engaged. Many of us will come to the engagement. Well, then you must give us thirty engagement kerchiefs as presents. At the wedding you

bura pirujtam. mi ćukartam una je̮ze̮s da med ve̮li mijan gaža, bur, med ve̮li je̮z kvaľite̮ni̮." "ke̮ńešne̮, tijan i̮ǯi̮d re̮d, mijan i̮ǯi̮d re̮d. una i ćukarmasni̮." "una, vot seśśa mijan svaďba loas trićatoje, šuan?" "ďeśatoje, ďeśatoje!" "ďeśatoje, no, no. vot svaďba mijan kole̮ karni̮ bure̮s. seśśa ōni̮ kōmas mijan sija, bura." "seśśa loe̮ ńin ōni̮, ge̮te̮vićći̮ni̮ jona ńin kole̮." "jona ge̮te̮vićći̮ni̮ da . . ." "i̮ǯi̮d mi̮j-ke̮ ńin taja, zabota. no vot seśśa i stavi̮s bur, siǯike̮n i siǯi.i karam bura . . ." "med mijan jur aslani̮m ve̮li abu jande̮ma, mi svadbai̮ś!" "oz, mijan bať sija mi̮j-ke̮ da sije̮ oz sija jane̮d." re̮dstvo mijan i̮ǯi̮d, bur, mijan kole̮ bura karni̮, lepti̮śni̮." "mejam bať-mam tože̮ bur, nali̮ bur koźin kole̮." "bure̮s śetam." "aśśi̮d jurte̮ in jane̮d!" "og, og, in pondi̮, bespokojićći̮ni̮ oz kō."

2. *no vot siǯi i kole̮: bura karni̮ da bura pirujtni̮ da bura koraśni̮ da bur ńevesta da ńimalan že̮ńik da ńimalan ńevesta da med ńin ve̮li bur, je̮zli̮ med abu śeram, bur med ve̮li. no vot! seśśa svaďba loe̮, pirujtam. no i śo seśśa svaďba ji̮li̮ś ńin.*

11.

pi̮š da šabdi karam da sije̮li̮ mi ti̮alam. da seśśa sije̮ pi̮š-šabdise̮ ti̮alam da seśśa sije̮li̮ mi karam arnas maľićae̮n. maľićanas karam da seśśa sije̮ trepajtam jona da seśśa sije̮ zualam. da sije̮ arťeľe̮n ćukarććam, voǯe̮se̮n zuaśam, seśśa nualam da sije̮li̮ mi seśśa pećkam. da seśśa sije̮ mi̮śkam še̮rtse̮ veśse̮ da seśśa mi de̮ra panam da seśśa de̮ra ki̮am sije̮li̮, kuǯi kužam, bi̮dśama śernas kare̮ni̮. no me ve̮li kuža i śer vi̮li̮ś karni̮. kuče̮m, etače̮m śeri̮ś. seče̮mse̮ me ve̮li kuža karni̮. no i katertte̮ bi̮d-nog kare̮ni̮, ke̮m-paśte̮ sije̮ karam. seśśa seś karam mi źipun, mi̮j-ke̮ de̮ra panana vurun pećkam, da i̮ž vi̮li̮ś i ši̮ram, kode̮s vurun pećkam. da seś karam sukman da źipun da seś i gaćte̮ karam: etati, sitani̮s abu, eta kuź be̮ki̮s. seśśa sije̮ nōlam. a paśi̮s, kuče̮m i̮ž-ku paś sija? ježi̮d paś sija. ke̮ǯi̮d voas da esiǯ pi̮ralas, ki̮nmas daj. sije̮ ve̮li nōlam. seśśa mi̮j-ke̮ de-

give these presents to the parents. This is absolutely necessary." "We have to make arrangements for the wedding. Some things have been arranged already, other things have not." "At the wedding we shall give a feast on two evenings. On two evenings we shall give a feast and have a good time. We shall invite a lot of people, so that everything may be merry and proper among us, and people will praise us." "Of course, you have many relatives and we also have many relatives. There will be a lot of people there." "Well then, our wedding will be on the thirtieth, you say?" "On the tenth, on the tenth." "On the tenth, well, all right then. You see, we must make proper arrangements for the wedding. Then we must have a good time." "Then we shall have to prepare it very carefully . . . !" "And this is a great worry for us. Well, then, everything is all right, we shall manage it properly in some way or another." "So that we don't bring shame on our head because of the wedding." "No, our father is not the man to shame us." "We have a lot of relatives; all right, we must arrange everything well, we must pride ourselves on it!" "My parents are fine people too; they must have good presents." "And we'll give them good presents." "You must not bring shame on your own head!" "No, no, do not start off again, you need not worry!"

2. Well, this is the way to do it: you must do it properly, and you must have a good time, you must ask for the girl's hand properly, for a good bride. A respectable bridegroom and a respectable bride — everything must be done properly so that people may not hold anything up to ridicule, that everything should be all right. Well, you see! Then there will be a wedding, we shall have a good time. Well, this is all to be said about the wedding.

11. [How clothes are made]

We ret the hemp and flax; we do the soaking. We ret the hemp and the flax, then in the autumn we make *malitsas*. We make *malitsas:* we beat them thoroughly, then comb them. Then we meet at a bee and do the combing for each other, then we take it away and spin it. Then the yarn is washed, all of it, and we weave canvas. We weave it into canvas as we can, people do it with all sorts of patterns. Well, I myself knew how to do it following a pattern. What is it like? It follows a pattern like this. This was the sort I could make. Yes, and they make all kinds of tablecloths; we make clothes. We make frieze caftans from it, we weave the wool that can be woven into linen, it is shorn from the lambs from which comes the wool we weave. It is this from which frieze clothes, frieze caftans and pants are made: it has no bottom here, this is the long side. Then we wear them. And the wide

rate̮ karam sije̮li̮, una de̮ra. etija še̮rtase̮ kare̮ni̮, ki̮ka še̮rtase̮ kare̮ni̮, ve̮sńi de̮rase̮ kare̮ni̮, śera de̮rase̮ kare̮ni̮. bi̮de̮ne̮s kare̮ni̮. seśśa sije̮li̮ še̮ralam da vuram da vot sije̮li̮ nōlam. sije̮ i ve̮li nōlam.

(b) Ne̮d-kī̮jas (ne̮dan kī̮jas)

12.

1. *ki̮k ńiź pi̮šje̮, bi̮d te̮vari̮s vi̮li̮sas. — śor.*
2. *vai̮n ćuže, bii̮n bi̮dme̮, mamse̮ aǯǯas da be̮r kule̮. — sō.*
3. *i̮ǯi̮d, i̮ǯi̮d dub, dubjas das-ki̮k ū, (das-ki̮k ūji̮n) bi̮d ūji̮n ńoľ ke̮šeľ, a ke̮šeľas śiźim koľk: kvajti̮s je̮ǯi̮d, a śiźime̮di̮s ge̮rd. — vo, te̮li̮ś, vežon, lun.*
4. *pe̮ri̮ś, pe̮ri̮ś starik, paśi̮s śo rotasa. — pī̮śan-gor.*
5. *veś kuźa ge̮nte̮m, ki̮k veś kuźa ge̮na, śe̮le̮mi̮dli̮ burman-tor, jaji̮sli̮ kolantor. — kore̮ś.*
6. *mića, mića moloďeć da še̮re̮di̮s ge̮re̮da. — i̮ǯas-juk.*
7. *mića, mića moloďeć da bi̮d be̮ž-ū aǯǯi̮le̮. — tage̮s.*
8. *das-ki̮k ćoj da e̮ťi zońťik uli̮ne̮ś. — ruǯe̮g-ćumaľi.*
9. *luni̮n skamja, voji̮n kalać. — pon.*
10. *sunduk pi̮čki̮n zarńia le̮ška. — paći̮n e̮gi̮r.*
11. *mića, mića moloďeć da me̮d-me̮dore̮di̮s ńeče̮ni̮. — e̮be̮ś.*
12. *veśse̮ ki̮čōtasni̮ da be̮r e̮tlaśasni̮. — či̮n.*
13. *ńol vok e̮ťi dozje̮ kuǯale̮ni̮. — me̮s-li̮śte̮m.*
14. *ćań ćire̮ste̮, vē̮ ge̮re̮de̮, j a r o s l a ve̮ǯ ki̮le̮. — virdi̮šte̮, gi̮mi̮šte̮.*
15. *tan keralan, m o s k v à (m o s k v a e̮) ćagi̮s ćeććе̮. — piśme̮.*
16. *luni̮n ve̮li̮ś ǯuǯi̮d, a voji̮n me̮s-siti̮ś pe̮ ľapki̮d. — megi̮r.*
17. *bi̮d kerkàn ańaeś e̮ďďala. — paćće̮r.*
18. *śo koka, śten dore̮ sūte̮tte̮g da oz sūt. — ge̮ľik.*

coat, what kind of sheepskin coat is it? It is a white sheepskin coat. It grows cold and it comes in like this, you catch cold! That's what we wore. We make linen, a good deal of linen. They make it from such yarn, they make two-ply linen, they make thin linen and they make mottled linen. All kinds are made. Then we cut them out and sew them, and you see, we wear them. This is what we wear.

(b) Riddles

12.

1. Two pine-martens run along, they have all their belongings on them. — A cross-beam.

2. It is born in water, grows in fire, and when it sees its mother, it dies. — Salt.

3. There is a big, big oak-tree, with twelve branches on this oak-tree, there are four bags on each branch, and seven eggs in each bag: six of them are white, the seventh is red. — The year, the months, the weeks, and the days.

4. There is an old, old daddy; with a hundred patches on his sheepskin coat. — The stove in the bath-house.

5. For one span it is hairless, two spans hairy: it is satisfying to your heart and necessary for your body. — A bath brush.

6. A handsome, handsome lad with a knot in the middle. — A straw-stack.

7. A handsome, handsome lad that can look under every tail. — A threshold.

8. Twelve sisters under one umbrella. — A stook of rye.

9. A bench in the day-time, a cake in the night-time. — A dog.

10. A gilded spoon in a chest. — Coal in the fireplace.

11. A handsome, handsome lad that is pulled to and fro. — A door.

12. They go round everything and then reunite. — Smoke.

13. Four brothers pissing into one vessel. — Milking the cow.

14. The colt shrieks, the horse neighs, it is heard as a far as Yaroslav. — Lightning and thunder.

15. You cut it here, and its shavings leap to Moscow. — A letter.

16. It is taller than a horse in the day-time and shorter than the rump of a cow in the night-time. — A curved yoke.

17. A dirty covering in each house. — The top of the stove.

18. It has a hundred feet, yet if you do not put it against the wall it will not stand up. — A brushwood besom.

19. *bi̯d peľesi̯n šomja bekar. — te̯li̯ś.*

20. *kerka ge̯ge̯r site̯ś gez. — ńič.*

21. *ćikľa-mukľa, ki̯ćće̯ munan? ši̯re̯m gogi̯n, mi̯j ten ďela? — ju da vi̯ǯ.*

22. *bi śe̯le̯ma, va ki̯ne̯ma, i̯rge̯n sarapana. — same̯var.*

23. *sitte̯m, śūte̯m śo šor vuǯe̯, kite̯m, kokte̯m pue̯ kae̯. — pišćaľ da puľa.*

24. *mune̯, mune̯, tuji̯s abu, kerale̯, kerale̯, viri̯s abu. — pi̯že̯n mune̯m va vī̯ti.*

25. *kok-vož kolas ve̯le̯ga, a sitan-dor ćeś. — jē̯-li̯śte̯m da koľk-vaje̯m.*

26. *ńoľ ćoj da e̯ťi gue̯ kuǯale̯ni̯. — me̯s-li̯śte̯m.*

27. *ńoľ ćoj da e̯ťi patka vi̯li̯n ti̯škaśe̯ni̯. — pi̯zan.*

28. *bi̯d kerkàn oš-lapa. — pać-ći̯škan li̯s.*

29. *ge̯na vomse̯ vośte̯, viľi̯d jurse̯ śuje̯, more̯se̯n ľićkaśe̯ni̯, koke̯n tažjaśe̯ni̯. — de̯ra-ki̯je̯m.*

30. *ši̯-ti̯r i̯ž da e̯ťi be̯ž. — ńań-pe̯žale̯m.*

31. *ši̯-ti̯r i̯ž da bi̯de̯n ke̯rt koka. — pać-e̯gi̯r.*

32. *mu-gu, mu-gu mu uli̯n, śe̯rti̯n, śe̯rti̯n, śe̯d sete̯r, vomi̯ni̯n ki̯d-ań. — mu uli̯n oš ole̯, śe̯d sete̯rse̯ śoje̯, śe̯rtas ole̯; sabri.*

33. *ge̯na vomse̯ vośte̯, viľi̯d jurse̯ śuje̯. — paśtaśe̯m.*

34. *ki paśta śe̯d, śe̯d še̯ras ruź, ruź še̯ras kī̯ vi̯jim, moľi̯d poma volī̯le̯. — toman da kľuć.*

35. *piruľľi-paruľľi saraj-moľitva. — petuk.*

36. *mu-gu, mu-gu mu uli̯n, śe̯rti̯n, śe̯rti̯n śe̯d sete̯r, kure̯g-će̯ski̯d baď dori̯n, śe̯le̯m vi̯ǯan ǯaǯ dori̯n. — re̯dka, oš, vote̯s, sō.*

37. *ki̯k doras ľe̯m-pu, še̯ras kuk-ku. — ćap.*

38. *śe̯d ve̯r še̯ri̯n mića moloďeć sulale̯. — ge̯rd šľapa.*

39. *bi̯d kerkai̯n śe̯d tasma. — paz.*

40. *bi̯d kerkai̯n śinme̯n aǯǯi̯te̯m. — šoni̯d.*

41. *aći̯s sī̯ kuźa, lapai̯s veś kuźa. — lojli̯śan vor.*

42. *komi̯n vok e̯ťi jur uli̯n. — pe̯te̯le̯k.*

43. *bi̯d kerkai̯n bordte̯m kača. — rukomejka.*

44. *ćiki̯ľi-muki̯ľi, ki̯ćće̯ munan? ćē̯, veže̯m ure̯s, aśte̯ le̯sale̯ni̯ i gognale̯ni̯. — kosa.*

19. A glass of coal in every corner. — The moon.

20. A mucky string around the house. — Moss.

21. Crooked and twisting, where are you going? Shear-knife, what is it to do with you? — A river and a meadow.

22. Fiery-hearted, wet-bellied, with a copper sarafan. — A samovar.

23. It has neither bottom nor bowels, yet can cross a hundred brooks; it has neither hands nor feet, yet in can climb trees. — A gun and a bullet.

24. It goes on and on, though there is no track, it cuts and cuts, but there is no blood. — Travelling by boat on the river.

25. Nutriment between her legs, and the width of her bottom is her honour. — Milking and egg yield.

26. Four sisters pissing in one bucket. — Milking the cow.

27. Four sisters quarrelling over a silken kerchief. — A table.

28. A bear's paw in every house. — A stove-brush made of fir-twigs.

29. It opens wide its hairy mouth, it thrusts in its bald head, they press their breasts together and spread their feet. — Linen weaving

30. A pen full of sheep and a tail. — Baking bread.

31. A pen full of sheep, each of them with iron feet. — A stove and embers.

32. A cave, a cave beneath the earth, a black-currant in the river valley, in the river valley, bread made of bran in the bend of the river. — The bear lives beneath the earth, it eats blackcurreants, and lives in the bend of the river.

33. It opens wide its hairy mouth, it thrusts in its bald head. — Dressing.

34. It is black for the width of a hand, there is a slit in the middle of the black, a tongue in the middle of the slit, smooth Thomas comes in. — A lock and key.

35. Cock-a-doodle-doo: a prayer in the barn. — A rooster.

36. A cave, a cave beneath the earth, in the river-valley, in the river-valley black-currants, a tasty morsel for hen beside the willow-tree, heart-holder beside the shelf. — Radish, bear, berry and salt.

37. Wild service-trees on both sides, a calfskin in the middle. — A flail.

38. A handsome lad stands in the middle of a black wood. — A red hat.

39. A black strap on every house. — Mortise.

40. Something in every house that cannot be seen. — Warmth.

41. Itself it is one fathom long, its paw is a span long. — A kneading-trough.

42. Thirty brothers under one head. — The ceiling.

43. There is a wingless magpie in every house. — A wash-bowl.

44. Crooked and hooked, where are you going? Sh, mistaken monstruosity, you are carved and planed. — A scythe.

45. *ju šer̮in̮ utka pukale̮, be̮ži̮s bere̮gi̮n. — ke̮š.*

46. *ki̮k vok da jorta-jorte̮s oz aǯǯi̮ni̮. — śin.*

47. *ćikľa ćože̮ gozja, i̮ǯi̮d jura obe̮ gozja, ľas ni̮ra ić-ińe̮ gozja, śo śinma ve-žańe̮ e̮tnas. — stan, sve̮le̮k, taľan, kiś.*

48. *pu kar, pu kar pi̮čkas iǯas kar, iǯas kar pi̮čkas de̮ra kar, a de̮ra kar vi̮las ńeme̮ja voda kujle̮. — potan, iǯas voľ-paś, de̮ra ruzum, kaga.*

49. *kopraśas, kopraśas, śťenlań bane̮n vodas. — ćer.*

50. *tū ji̮le̮ mi̮j oz e̮šji̮? — koľk.*

51. *aji̮s ćukľa, mami̮s ge̮na, pii̮s bergale̮. — pećkan.*

52. *mića, mića ić-mоń, viǯe̮dli̮ni̮ on li̮śti̮, bi̮de̮ne̮s be̮rde̮de̮. — luk.*

53. *mića, mića ić-moń da de̮re̮m-gaći̮s pi̮če̮gas. — śiś.*

54. *ti̮ vojti̮šte̮, ta vojti̮šte̮ da ńe-kor oz vojti̮š. — iśerga.*

55. *jaščik pi̮čke̮ mi̮j oz tomnaśśi̮? — šondi̮.*

56. *mui̮s dona, dona, da borji̮s ne̮šna (ne̮šta) dona. — e̮šun, e̮ke̮ńća.*

57. *pu sodje̮d kaan, jaj laviće̮ pukśan. — vē vi̮li̮se̮ pukśan.*

58. *vī̮lań šor vizī̮te̮, ūlań pomeľ tue̮. — vē jue̮ da be̮ži̮s e̮šale̮.*

59. *bi śe̮le̮ma da ge̮ge̮r čuč-ku. — same̮var.*

60. *końe̮r pe̮riś starik rotli̮śe̮, rotli̮śe̮ da ǯońe̮-bure̮ oz i voli̮, vek ruźa. — pī̮śan-gor.*

61. *veś kuźa peki̮ľ da śiźim ruź. — śinjas, ni̮r, peľ, vom.*

62. *i̮ǯi̮d, i̮ǯi̮d e̮dďala da veśi̮s ruź. — ńebesa.*

63. *pi̮de̮ste̮m be̮ćkae̮ jaj solale̮ni̮ da oz i solaśśi̮. — ćuń-ki̮č.*

64. *mića, mića ić-moń da ge̮rd koloćkaa. — kure̮g.*

65. *mića, mića molođeć vek jurblale. — lajkan.*

45. A duck sits in the middle of a river with its tail on the bank. — A ladle.

46. Two brothers who never see each other. — Eyes.

47. My mother's crooked brother and his wife, my father's big-headed sister and her husband, my mother's snub-nosed sister and her husband, my godmother with a hundred eyes alone. — A loom, yarn-beam, tradle and reed.

48. Wood-town, straw-town in the wood-town, linen-town in the straw-town, a mute voivode lies in the linen-town. — A cradle, straw-mattress, linen swathing-clothes and child.

49. It bows and bows, and turns its face to the wall when it is resting. — An axe.

50. What is it you cannot hang on a peg? — An egg.

51. The father is crooked, the mother is hairy, their son goes round and round. — A spindle.

52. A beautiful, beautiful young wife, you do not dare to look at her, she makes everybody cry. — An onion.

53. A beautiful, beautiful young wife with her underclothes in her lap. — A candle.

54. It drops here and it drops there but it never drops down. — An earring.

55. What can't be shut up in a chest? — The sun.

56. Its earth is dear, so dear, its ridge is even dearer. — A window and window-pane.

57. You go up a wooden ladder and sit on a bench of flesh. — Mounting a horse.

58. A brook flows upwards, and a spruce grows downwards. — A horse is drinking with its tail hanging down.

59. Its heart is fire and its belly is all round it. — A samovar.

60. Poor old grand-dad patches it and patches it, but it will not be any better, it is always full of holes. — A besom for the bath-house.

61. A stump a span long and seven holes. — Eyes, nose, ears and mouth.

62. A great big coverlet full of holes. — The sky.

63. Meat is salted in a bottomless barrel yet it is not fully salted. — A ring.

64. A beautiful, beautiful young wife with a red crest. — A hen.

65. A handsome, handsome lad who is always bowing. — A cradle-pole.

(c) Proverbs, idioms

13. *Proverbs*

1. *kačale̮n ge̮ni̮s oz vežśi̮.*
2. *ľok baba dori̮n i bur muži̮ki̮s ľok.*
3. *bur vejt uli̮n i kerkàd bur.*
4. *kań kojd di̮š, pon kojd gorš.*
5. *kodi ge̮ľ, sija i di̮š.*
6. *porśli̮ šegje̮ǯ́, a kure̮gli̮ gaďďe̮ǯ́.*
7. *ozi̮rli̮ una ďeńga, a ge̮ľli̮ una ćeľaď.*
8. *viǯ́ kare̮me̮n mića, a nī̮ mune̮me̮n mića.*
9. *kuče̮m aći̮s mića, seče̮m ćumaľii̮s mića.*
10. *kuče̮m aći̮s miśte̮m, seče̮m i ćumaľii̮s.*
11. *jiki̮i̮ś pe̮ gez in ki̮j!*
12. *oški̮s kośale̮, oški̮s že̮ gorze̮.*
13. *ge̮ra ge̮ra voćća oz voli̮ni̮, a mort mort voććaaśni̮ vek vermas.*
14. *šom ve̮ji, iz ki̮pti.*
15. *va vī̮tii̮s iz ki̮lale̮, a mu berde̮di̮s šom ki̮lale̮.*
16. *kujim are̮sa da pe̮ri̮s e̮t-kojd.*

14. *Idioms*

1. *sija agas-piń vi̮le̮ uśke̮ććas [seče̮m gorš].*
2. *si̮li̮ vomas oz e̮šji̮ [veśse̮ viśtollas].*
3. *sija śura me̮s moz lukalas.*
4. *si̮le̮n śinmi̮s vurzale̮ [bi̮dlai̮ś aǯ́ǯ́e̮].*
5. *ši̮r-bi kojd lampa e̮zte̮ma [ńi-ne̮m oz ti̮dō].*
6. *pur vi̮li̮ś koje̮m.*
7. *meam juri̮s oz uǯō [ńi-ne̮m og pe̮mńit].*
8. *je̮je̮ lejćće̮ma.*
9. *mi̮j-ne̮ paććerse̮ ľićkalan?*
10. *mori̮s vojis, pińe̮ uśke̮ććis.*
11. *ke̮ť pe̮ śira gezje̮n ki̮skasni̮, og pe̮ i mun.*
12. *śira pi̮ža kolasas śujśe̮.*
13. *śira pi̮ža kolasas in śujśi̮!*
14. *ki̮k śin kolasśi̮d ni̮rte̮ pe̮ guasni, oz i te̮dli̮.*
15. *je̮zse̮ ǯ́ugni̮ ńi-ne̮m vi̮le̮.*
16. *ši̮ń pukō!*
17. *jurte̮ pe̮ orōta.*

13.

1. The magpie's feathers are never changed.
2. Beside a bad wife even a good man will become bad.
3. Under a good roof a house is also good.
4. Lazy as a cat and hungry as a dog.
5. He who is poor is also lazy.
6. It is as high as the knuckle of a pig and the bladder of a hen.
7. The rich have much money, the poor have many children.
8. The meadow is beautiful when it is worked, a girl is beautiful when she is walking.
9. As she is beautiful, so beautiful are her stooks.
10. As he is ugly, so ugly are her stooks.
11. Do not make a rope of chaff!
12. The bear tears things to pieces and the bear roars.
13. A hill will not come to a hill, but man can always meet men.
14. The coal has sunk, and the stone has lifted it.
15. Stone swims in the water, coal swims on the land.
16. A three-year-old child and an old man are just the same.

14.

1. He even pitches into the tines of a harrow (so hungry is he).
2. Nothing will stick in his mouth (he lets out every secret).
3. He butts like a cow with horns.
4. His eyes howl (he sees in every direction).
5. She lit a lamp like a glowworm (nothing can be seen).
6. It is like bailing water from a raft.
7. My head does not work (I do not understand anything).
8. He has gone mad.
9. Why do you burden the top of the stove? (Why are you lying idle?)
10. The devil came and dashed at his teeth (quarrelled).
11. I will not go even if they drag me with a tarred rope.
12. He squeezes his way in between two boats coated with pitch.
13. Do not squeeze your way between two boats coated with pitch.
14. They'll even steal his nose from between his two eyes, and he wouldn't notice it.
15. To disturb people for nothing.
16. Sit silently!
17. I'll break your head in pieces.

18. *bija ľok viśe̮m śe̮le̮m še̮rad.*
19. *mije̮n pe̮ sija vi̮ja?*
20. *ku pi̮ri̮s jaji̮s ti̮dalis, jaj pi̮ri̮s li̮is, li̮ pi̮ri̮s vemi̮s.*
21. *ki̮is pećke̮, vomśi̮s ke̮rt kernale̮.*
22. *sija seče̮m ram, ńańte̮ vomi̮ś oz vošši̮.*
23. *pać kojd ki̮me̮si̮s, a vi̮li̮si̮s (porś-kojd) če̮g [ske̮ťinali̮, ke̮ť mortli̮ poże̮ šuni̮].*

(d) Songs

15.

a n a t o ľ e j daj o ľ g i n ase̮ pi̮š-ti̮e̮ śujlam,
ti̮alam i pońtalam,
ešge̮dlam i vožge̮dlam,
ćuške̮dlam i ćaške̮dlam.
paśibe̮-ke̮ viśtalas:
gi̮n-i-je̮n i dodďe̮n,
pe̮ganeje̮n ve̮le̮n,
juś-ni̮r-i sape̮g,*
ke̮ne̮vatne̮j patka
štopne̮j-i sborńik
ki̮ź-vit šajta že̮ńik,
das-vit šajta ńevesta.
paśibe̮-ke̮j oz viśtō.
gi̮r-i ve̮le̮n
tojin-i vožje̮n
šerdi̮n-i dodďe̮n
ši̮beľi̮ś da ši̮beľe̮,
dokjani̮ś da dokjane̮.

16.

munis ved sija pe̮ zej-zej i̮le̮,
vois ved sija daj as mile̮j dore̮,
vois ved sija pe̮ as mile̮j doras.
zdrastvuj že̮, zdrastvuj, aslam mile̮je̮,

* *[joś ni̮r]*

18. May a fiery, evil disease seize the middle of your heart!

19. How much more buttery is he (or she) (how much better is he (or she) than I)?

20. Her flesh showed through her skin, her bones through her flesh, her marrow through her bones (said of beautiful women).

21. Her hands weave, and iron pops out of her mouth (she is so diligent that her teeth like iron can be seen in her mouth which is open while she is working).

22. She is so modest that her mouth does not touch bread.

23. A forehead like a stove, an exterior like bacon (can be applied to beasts as well as to humans).

15.

We push Anatolij and Olgina into the retting-pit,
We soak and work them,
We press them together and separate them,
We pierce them and cleave them apart.
If he gives thanks for it:
A felt-sledge,
A pagan-horse,
Boots with pointed toes,
A linen-kerchief,
A figured head-scarf (be theirs);
A bridegroom worth twenty-five roubles
A bride worth fifteen roubles (shall they be).
If he does not give thanks for it:
With a horse fat as a mortar,
And a shaft like a pestle
And a sledge like a shovel
From hole to hole,
From rut to rut (let them go).

16.

He went far, far away,
He came to his beloved,
He came to his beloved.
Hail to thee, hail to thee, my beloved,

zdrastvuj žę, zdrastvuj, aslam milęję!
zdrastvuj žę, zdrastvuj, ľubeznęję,
zdrastvuj žę, zdrastvuj ľubeznęję!
vęli ved si̯lęn da zęlętnęj ćuń-ki̯č,
vęli ved si̯lęn pę zęlętnęj ćuń-ki̯č.
luna ved sija daj vož ćuńi̯n nōlis,
luna ved sija pę vož ćuńas nōlis.
voji̯n ved sija da jur ulas puktis,
voji̯n ved sija pę jur ulas puktis.
vęli ved si̯lęn ki̯k pukęvej pęduška,
vęli ved si̯lęn ki̯k pukęvej pęduška.
bi̯dsęn ved sija śin-va banęn kętaśis
bi̯dsęn ved si̯lęn śin-va banęn kętaśis.
vęli ved si̯lęn soboľnovęj ęďďala,
vęli ved si̯lęn soboľnovęj ęďďala daj
iz-i ved šonti̯ da moj-i moręsęs,
iz-i ved šonti̯ da moj-i moręsęs da
iz-i ved šonti̯ da i ńež-i-nęj jajęs,
iz-i ved šonti̯ da ńež-i-nęj jajęs.
vęli ved si̯lęn i juś-i da pero,
vęli ved si̯lęn i juś-i da pero.
munis ved sija daj as milęj dorę,
lebis ved sija daj milęj doras.
zdrastvuj žę, zdrastvuj, aslam milęję,
zdrastvuj žę, zdrastvuj, aslam milęję!
zdrastvuj žę, zdrastvuj, ľubeznęję,
zdrastvuj žę, zdrastvuj, ľubeznęję!
ťelo druškaja da ťelo bes mińa,
ťelo druškaja da ťelo bes mińa da
munis ved sija da zej-zej i̯lę.

17.

šu-šu-šu da vić-vić-vić,
kuź šušuna munę.
kod žę munę? da
[ń i n ai̯s] žę munę. da
mi̯j ovna žę munę? da
[i v a n o v n a] munę. da
kodi žę vižędę?

Hail to thee, hail to thee, my beloved!
Hail to thee, hail to thee, my lover,
Hail to thee, hail to thee, my lover!
She had a golden ring,
She had a golden ring.
Early in the day-time she wore it on her finger,
Early in the day-time she wore it on her finger.
At night she put it under her head,
At night she put it under her head.
She had two pillows filled with down,
She had two pillows filled with down.
With her tearful face it became quite wet,
With her tearful face it became quite wet.
She had a coverlet of sable-fur,
She had a coverlet of sable-fur,
(But) it did not warm her beaver-soft breast,
It did not warm her beaver-soft breast.
It did not warm her fragile body,
It did not warm her fragile body.
She had swan's feather,
She had swan's feather.
She went to her beloved,
She flew to her beloved.
Hail to thee, hail to thee, my beloved,
Hail to thee, hail to thee, my beloved!
Hail to thee, hail to thee, my lover,
Hail to thee, hail to thee, my lover!
Our bodies are a pair and your body is without mine,
Our bodies are a pair and your body is without mine.
Far, far distant did he go away.

17.

Shu-shu-shu and *vich-vich-vich*,
Someone in a long sarafan goes by.
Who goes by then?
Nina goes by.
What *-ovna* goes by?
Ivanovna goes by.
Who is watching her?

[i v a ni̯s] da viǯe̯de̯.
mi̯j ović že̯ viǯe̯de̯?
[aľeksandre̯vić].
ki̯ćće̯ že̯ pi̯rte̯das?
[pale̯j roć ki] vi̯le̯. da
ki̯ćće̯ že̯ pukśe̯das?
gi̯rja bašmak vi̯le̯. da
ki̯ćće̯ že̯ votte̯das?
ǯurkja-virkja kre̯vajte̯. da
ki-moǯas vina štop da
kok voǯas kalać-kē̯,
jur voǯas preńik stopa.
vinase̯-ke̯ juvi̯štas da
kuri̯d, kuri̯d. da
kalaćse̯-ke̯ śoji̯štas da
će̯ski̯d, će̯ski̯d. da
preńikse̯-ke̯ śoji̯štas da
jumō, jumō.
paśibe̯, abu?
paśibe̯.
paśibe̯-ke̯ viśtalan da
le̯z gi̯nje̯n dođđe̯n,
pe̯ganeje̯n ve̯le̯n,
juś-ni̯r-i sape̯ge̯n da
štopne̯j sborńike̯n,
ke̯ne̯vatne̯j patkae̯n da
das-vit šajta [ń i n ae̯n] da
komi̯n šajta [i v a n].
ńe paśibe̯.
on-ke̯ viśtō paśibe̯,
ľok re̯zvaľe̯n da
ke̯bi̯laa ve̯le̯n,
ši̯beľiś da ši̯beľe̯
katlaniś da katlane̯,
sle̯be̯da tuj vi̯le̯
koran meše̯k.

18.

me taj, me taj mića zon, ||
m a š u ke̯s viććiśa.

Ivan is watching her.
What *-ovich* is watching her?
Alexandrovich.
Where does he take her?
Into the pen in the clearing (?)
Where does he sit her?
On a mortar-shaped shoe.
Where does he lay her down?
On a squeaking bed.
A bottle of vodka in his hand,
A string of cakes before his feet,
A heap of honey-cakes before his head.
When he drinks vodka
It is bitter, bitter,
When he eats cakes
It is fine, fine.
When he eats honey-cakes
It is sweet, sweet.
You will say: thank you, will you not?
I will say: thank you.
If you say, thank you,
A blue-felt sledge,
A pagan horse,
Boots with pointed toes,
A figured head-scarf,
A linen kerchief,
A Nina worth five roubles (we will present)
To Ivan worth thirty roubles.
I will not say thank you.
If you do not say thank you,
On a rotten peasant sledge
(Drawn) by a mare
From hole to hole,
From rut to rut (may you go),
(And may you reach) the street of the big village
With a beggar's sack.

18.

I indeed, I indeed, a handsome lad, ||
Am waiting for Mašuk. ||

meśa, mi̮j-ke̮ di̮r iz vo,
iz-e̮ mene̮ vune̮d?
vune̮dni̮ me og vune̮d
tače̮m mića zonme̮s.
vune̮dni̮-ke̮ me ke̮sja,
ta-lun ig lok taćće̮.
ta-lun śor ńin, pe̮rai̮s
gorte̮ kole̮ munni̮.
gorti̮n me̮sjas li̮śtōte̮m,
mame̮ mene̮ vidas.
taje̮ vi̮jim je̮ʒi̮d ći̮šjan,
ľoka veśke̮ mića.
ći̮šjan bośtni̮ me bośta,
okaśni̮ og okaś.
okaśni̮-ke̮ te ke̮sjan,
na kole̮-ke̮ ke̮šeľ.
vot i vi̮ʒ̮e̮d nī̮jas vi̮le̮,
mi̮j naja ve̮će̮ni̮.
me taj, me taj mića zon,
m a š u ke̮s viććiśa

19.

gi̮ri̮ś nī̮jas, majbi̮r nī̮jas
voti̮s votni̮ da kaisni̮.
a me ʒe̮ľa nī̮, me šudte̮m nī̮
na be̮rśań i če̮č ve̮ćći.
a gi̮ri̮ś nī̮jas, majbi̮r nī̮jas,
požje̮n-ʒi̮nje̮n daj votisni̮.
a me ʒe̮ľa nī̮, me šudte̮m-i nī̮,
soʒe̮n-ʒi̮nje̮n da če̮č voti.
a gi̮ri̮ś nī̮jas, majbi̮r nī̮jas,
gortani̮s leććalisni̮.
a me ʒe̮ľa nī̮, me šudte̮m-i nī̮,
na be̮rśań i če̮č ve̮ćći.

20.

kiće̮ me ćuń-ki̮če̮s voštali?
ćuń-ki̮č me milojli̮ śeti.

She has not come for some time,
Has she not forgotten me?
As for me, I shall not forget
A handsome lad like you.
If I wanted to forget you,
I should not have come here today.
It is late today, it is time
For me to go home.
At home the cows are unmilked;
Mother will chide me.
This is a white kerchief,
Truly it is very beautiful.
As for the kerchief, I shall accept it,
As for kissing, I shall not kiss you.
If you want to kiss me,
You'll need a purse as well.
So keep an eye on the girls
And see what they are doing.
I indeed, I indeed, a handsome lad,
Am waiting for Mašuk.

19.

The big girls, the happy girls
Were going to pick berries.
Well, I, a little girl, I, an unhappy girl,
Also followed after them.
The big girls, the happy girls
Picked one and a half sieves full.
I, a little girl, I, an unhappy girl,
Picked one and a half handfuls.
The big girls, the happy girls
Went home.
I, a little girl, I, an unhappy girl,
Also followed after them.

20.

Where did I lose my ring?
I gave my ring to my sweetheart.

voʒ́i̮n me-j oli ke̮ʒ́i̮d-ini̮n,
e̮ni me muna kavkaze̮.
stav pe̮drugajas munalini̮,
a me koń e̮r, e̮tnam koľi.
me, końe̮r, muni vere̮s saje̮,
ge̮ge̮r ti̮ri̮s ćeľaď loji.
e̮ťi šue̮: mame̮ ćaj jua.
a me̮d i šue̮: mame̮ śojam.
sete̮n veď menam posńi ćeľaď:
mame̮, me te dine̮ voda.
mužik pukale̮ ďivan vi̮li̮n,
kurite̮ kaľľane̮n tabak:
vajli̮, mame̮, gitarase̮,
me teni̮d śi̮lan-kī̮ śi̮la.

21.

una nī̮jas ćukarććisni̮,
una nī̮jas ćukarććisni̮:
zon, zon, musa nī̮jas,
zon, zon, mića nī̮jas ćukarćći̮sni̮.

e ž - v a dore̮ leććalisni̮,
e ž - v a dore̮ leććalisni̮:
zon, zon, musa nī̮jas,
zon, zon, mića nī̮jas leććalisni̮.

vae̮ naja ćeććalisni̮,
vae̮ naja ćeććalisni̮:
zon, zon, musa nī̮jas,
zon, zon mića nī̮jas ćeććalisni̮.

sete̮n naja śoľke̮ććisni̮,
sete̮n naja śoľke̮ććisni̮:
zon, zon, musa nī̮jas,
zon, zon mića nī̮jas śoľke̮ććisni̮.

v a ś i ľ i s a pre̮studiććis,
v a ś i ľ i s a pre̮studiććis:
zon, zon, musa nī̮jas,
zon, zon mića nī̮jas pre̮studiććis.

Previously I was living in a cold place,
I am going now to the Caucasus.
All my girl friends have departed,
And I, poor soul, have been left by myself.
I, poor soul, got married,
Now I am surrounded with children.
One of them says: Mother, I'd like some tea.
The other says: Mother, let's eat!
And there is a small child too:
Mother, I want to lie beside you.
My husband is sitting on the sofa,
Smoking his pipe:
Give me the guitar, mother,
I will sing a song to you.

21.

Many girls gathered together,
Many girls gathered together:
Zon, zon, dear girls,
Zon, zon, beautiful girls gathered together.

They went down to the bank of the Vyčegda,
They went down to the bank of the Vyčegda:
Zon, zon, dear girls,
Zon, zon, beautiful girls went down.

They jumped into the water,
They jumped into the water.
Zon, zon, dear girls,
Zon, zon, beautiful girls jumped.

They splashed about in the water,
They splashed about in the water:
Zon, zon, dear girls,
Zon, zon, beautiful girls splashed about.

Vasilisa caught a cold,
Vasilisa caught a cold:
Zon, zon, dear girls,
Zon, zon, beautiful girls, she caught a cold.

22.

m e̯ s k u v a ge̯ge̯r saldat ki̯čōtis,
de̯va orde̯ uźni̯ loktis.
de̯vae̯j že̯, de̯vae̯j, a
leǯ mijanni̯me̯s uźni̯,
leǯ mijanni̯me̯s uźni̯!
abu e̯d mi zē unae̯n,
abu e̯d mi zē unae̯n:
se̯mi̯n pe̯ kujim-śo saldat,
se̯mi̯n pe̯ kujim-śo saldat,
śo-veti̯mi̯n ve̯la saldat,
śo-veti̯mi̯n ve̯la saldat.
da oj saldate̯, saldate̯j . . .

(e) Laments

23.

ver-i-dan i verdi̯śe̯j nī̯ ole̯me̯j,
ver-i-dan-i verdi̯ś nī̯ja ole̯me̯j,
i̯ǯi̯d ćine̯j daj nī̯ ole̯me̯j
menam końer-i-le̯n koľi
jen-i bur-i šondi̯e̯j bur-i laća vi̯le̯
jen-i bur-i šondi̯e̯j bur-i laća vi̯le̯
menam-i pe̯ taj da końe̯r-i-le̯n
peľ-i-pom šon-i-di̯ da jansali,
more̯s šondi̯ da otte̯m-i-śis.
ver-i-dan ver-i-di̯ś nī̯ja ole̯me̯j,
i̯ǯi̯d ćinae̯j ver-i-dan ver-i-di̯ś nī̯-j ole̯me̯j
kńaźevskije ver-i-dan ver-i-di̯ś da ži̯ťie̯j
koľi taj menam końe̯r-i-le̯n,
žaľane̯j daj e̯d zej žaľa,
ver-i-dan ge̯śjas, bur šondi̯e̯j daj-i as-i ve̯ľa vi̯le̯-j.

24. *družkali̯ be̯rde̯m*

ver-i-dan-i ver-i-di̯śe̯j
druž-i-ka taj ki̯le̯, lok-i-te̯
śe̯d pe̯ ved daj-i ki̯me̯r-i kojd.

22.

A soldier was walking around Moscow,
He came to a widow's house to sleep.
Widow, widow,
Let us in to go to sleep,
Let us in to go to sleep.
After all, there are not too many of us,
After all, there are not too many of us —
Only three hundred soldiers,
Only three hundred soldiers,
A hundred and fifty mounted soldiers,
A hundred and fifty mounted soldiers.
Oh, soldier, soldier . . .

23.

My dear, precious maiden's life,
My dear, precious maiden's life,
My great treasure, my maiden's life
Has come to an end, poor me.
In my confidence, good as God, good as the sun,
In my confidence, good as God, good as the sun,
For me, poor soul,
My shoulders, my sun, have broken down,
My bosom, my sun, has shrunk.
My dear, my precious maiden's life,
My dearly treasured maiden's life,
My princely, dear life
For me, poor soul, has come to an end.
Oh how I regret, I deeply grieve,
Dear guests, for my freedom, good as the sun.

24.

Mock lament to the best man

My dear sustainer,
The best man can be heard, here he comes
Like a black cloud.
The best man can be heard, here he comes
Like a big cloud.

druž-i-ka taj ki̮le̮, lok-i-te̮
i̮ǯ̮i̮d pe̮ ved daj tuća kojd.
druž-i-ka taj ki̮le, lok-i-te̮
daj śe̮d-i pemi̮d-i ve̮r-i kojd.
druž-i-ka ved ki̮le̮, lok-i-te̮
ʒ́ug iʒ́as-i kojd daj ľok-i mi̮ge̮r-i-nas.
druž-i-ka taj ki̮le̮, lok-i-te̮
ri̮ni̮š-i tupľe̮d kojd jur-i-nas.
druž-i-ka taj ki̮le̮, lok-i-te̮
kosa da nud kojd da sojjasnas.
druž-i-ka taj ki̮le̮, lok-i-te̮
ge̮r-i vož kojd pe̮ daj kokjas-i-nas.
druž-i-ka taj ki̮le̮, lois,
ver-i-dan ver-i-di̮ś nī̮-j ole̮me̮j.
i druž-i-ka taj ki̮le̮, lok-i-tis
roć-i bajar-i kojd da mi̮š-kunas.

25. družkali̮ oškem

aj ver-i-dan verdi̮śe̮j,
druž-i-ka taj ki̮le̮ daj voe̮ma
roć-i bajar-i kojd da mi̮ge̮r-i-nas,
verdan verdi̮śe̮j,
roć preńik kojd da ćuže̮m-i-nas.
družka taj ki̮le̮ daj voe̮ma
roć-akań-i kojd daj mi̮ge̮r-i-nas.
družka taj ki̮le̮ daj voe̮ma
i̮ǯ̮i̮d ge̮śnas daj-i ge̮śťanas,
družka taj ki̮le̮ daj voe̮ma
i̮ǯ̮i̮d ge̮śnas daj-i ge̮śťanas.

26. pili̮ be̮rde̮m (armijae̮ munige̮n)

verdan verdi̮śe̮j menam,
e̮ťi šon-i-die̮, e̮ťi pie̮ menam,
a n a t o ľ e j e̮ da v a ś i ľ e̮ v i ć e̮
menam pe̮ daj mune̮ kuź tuj ʒenōte̮m-ine̮,
paśki̮d tuj vekńōte̮m-ine̮,
vesa ńań pe̮ da śojni̮.
verdi̮śe̮j pe̮ daj pie̮
koľi taj-i tenad as-i ve̮ľai̮d

The best man can be heard, here he comes
Like a black, dark wood.
The best man can be heard, here he comes
With his bad figure like rumpled straw.
The best man can be heard, here he comes
With his head like a bundle of straw used
To block up the window of the corn-loft.
The best man can be heard, here he comes
With his arms like scythe-shafts.
The best man can be heard, here he comes
With his legs like plough-handles.
The best man can be heard, here he comes,
Oh, my dear, precious maiden's life!
The best man can be heard, he has arrived
With his back like a Russian boyar's.

25.

In praise of the best man

Oh, my dear sustainer,
The best man can be heard, he has arrived
With his figure like a Russian boyar's,
My dear sustainer,
With his face like a Russian honey-cake.
The best man can be heard, he has arrived
With his figure like a Russian doll.
The best man can be heard, he has arrived
With great guests, men and women.
The best man can be heard, he has arrived
With great guests, men and women.

26.

Lament for a son called up into the army

My dear sustainer,
My only sun, my only son,
Anatolij Vasilevich
Goes forth to cut short the long road,
To make narrow the broad road,
To live on rationed bread.
My son, my sustainer,
Your freedom is ended

krutne̯j kamańďer dore̯,
te pe̯ ved daj me̯de̯ććan daj bur tuj vi̯le̯.
verdi̯śe̯j pe̯ daj pie̯j
musae̯j pe̯ daj pie̯j
ne̯šta-na ke̯ť me tene̯
końe̯ruško viǯe̯dla,
ješše̯ ke̯ť daj aǯǯi̯la
na-j dona musa pie̯s.
te pe̯ ved-i daj munan da
koľe̯ tenad ve̯ľai̯d,
vesa ńań pe̯ daj śojni̯,
meraa da va juni̯.
teni̯d pe̯ ved e̯ni
ńebi̯d voľ-paśi̯d koľe̯,
šoni̯d voľ-paśi̯d koľe̯.
seni ved pe̯ loe̯ gi̯rǯǯa-pom ji̯lad bergōni̯,
krutne̯j kamańďerjasli̯ś teni̯d loe̯ kī̯zi̯ni̯,
on ne̯ ved daj li̯śti̯
voj-še̯rja krepi̯d unte̯
voj-še̯rja topi̯d unte̯
jonǯi̯ka daj unmōśni̯,
sije̯li̯ loe̯ da kī̯zi̯ni̯,
gi̯rǯǯa-pom ji̯lad bergōni̯.
verdi̯śe̯j menam pie̯j,
musae̯j menam pie̯j
taja pe̯ ved daj bur tuj veś-i-ke̯das,
žaľ meni̯m pe̯ daj te ve̯lin.
kuǯi me tene̯ bi̯tti,
kuǯi me tene̯ viǯi,
e̯tnam pe̯ końe̯ruško?
kuǯi me ńin taje̯
me końe̯ruško daj ťerpita?
zej ved meni̯m pe̯ da žaľ
zej pe̯ meni̯m ved daj šog.
te pe̯ ved daj munan da
krutne̯j kamańďer doras
da iǯi̯d-i puš-i-ka doras
da vostroj sabľa doras
verdi̯śe̯j dona pie̯j,
verdi̯śe̯j musa pie̯j.

Under the stern commander,
But you are starting on the right road.
My son, my sustainer,
My dear son,
If only I could see you again,
My poor son,
If only I could see you once more
My dear, beloved son.
But you are leaving
— Your freedom is ended —
To live on rationed bread,
To drink rationed water.
Now here
Your soft bed you leave behind,
Your warm bed you leave behind.
There you must toss and turn on your elbow,
You must obey stern commanders,
You dare not
Let your true dream at midnight,
Your deep dream at midnight
Come upon you with all its strength,
You must obey him,
You must toss and turn on your elbow.
My son, my sustainer,
My beloved son,
He is starting on the long road.
I am sorry for you.
How have I raised you,
How have I sustained you,
All alone, poor soul!
How shall I endure
All this, poor soul?
I am very sorry for you,
I am very sad.
So you are going away
To the stern commander,
To the big guns,
To the sharp sabres,
My dear son, my sustainer,
My beloved son, my sustainer.

(f) Children's songs, tales in verse

27.

ľeńe̮, ľeńe̮, pi̮šji̮!
śe̮d śi-ke̮ǯi̮d śi̮jad,
palauzji̮d jurad.
ľeń sija oz pi̮šji̮.
gezje̮, gezje̮, ľeńte̮ ǯage̮d!
gez sija oz ǯage̮d.
ši̮re̮, ši̮re̮, gezse̮ kerō!
ši̮r sija oz kerō.
kańe̮, kańe̮, ši̮rte̮ ki̮j!
kań sija oz ki̮j.
či̮ne̮, či̮ne̮, kańte̮ pe̮dti̮!
či̮n sija oz pe̮dti̮.
bije̮, bije̮, či̮nse̮ sot!
bi sija oz sot.
vae̮, vae̮, bise̮ kuse̮d!
vai̮s sija oz kuse̮d.
e̮ške̮, e̮ške̮, vase̮ ju!
e̮ški̮s sija oz ju.
ćere̮, ćere̮, e̮šse̮ naćki̮!
ćer sija oz naćki̮.
(seśśa i zi̮re̮das, seśśa ľeń zi̮re̮das.)

28.

ke̮zae̮ že̮ ke̮zae̮, me ten[e̮] i̮sta tuśla.
ke̮za oz mun tuśla.
ke̮jine̮ že̮ ke̮jine̮, me ten i̮sta ke̮za śojni̮.
ke̮jin oz mun ke̮za śojni̮,
ke̮za oz mun tuśla.
morte̮ že̮, morte̮, me ten i̮sta ke̮jin ki̮jni̮.
mort oz mun ke̮jin ki̮jni̮,
ke̮jin oz mun ke̮za śojni̮,
ke̮za oz mun tuśla.

(g) Rhymes

29.

vina kuri̮d, vina kuri̮d,
abu će̮ski̮d juan-tor.

27.

Snail, snail, run away!
You have your black necklace on your neck,
You have your head-dress on your head.
The snail does not run away.
Rope, rope, choke the snail!
The rope does not choke it.
Mouse, mouse, cut the rope!
The mouse does not cut it.
Cat, cat, catch the mouse!
The cat does not catch it.
Smoke, smoke, choke the cat!
The smoke does not choke it.
Fire, fire, burn the smoke!
The fire does not burn it.
Water, water, put out the fire!
The water does not put it out.
Bull, bull, drink up the water!
The bull does not drink it up.
Axe, axe, chop down the bull!
The axe does not chop it down.
(Then it attacks it, the snail attacks it.)

28.

My goat, my goat, I'm sending you to fetch seed.
The goat does not go to fetch seed.
My wolf, my wolf, I'm sending you to devour the goat.
The wolf does not go to devour the goat,
The goat does not go to fetch seed.
My husband, my husband, I'm sending you to kill the wolf.
The husband does not go to kill the wolf,
The wolf does not go to devour the goat,
The goat does not go to fetch seed.

29.

Brandy is bitter, brandy is bitter,
It is not a sweet drink.

mene̯ mile̯j enōtis,
abu le̯śid šuan-tor.

j e m - v a kuźa purja kī̯te̯,
balalajkae̯n vorse̯.
balalajkae̯n vorse̯
i komi śi̯lan-kī̯ śi̯le̯.

mašina vi̯le̯ me se̯li,
šondi̯ vi̯le̯ viǯe̯dli.
baľ-mame̯ke̯d me prošaćći,
mile̯je̯s me vune̯di.

ńī̯ji̯s-ke̯ pe̯ abu li̯ska,
kozji̯s ved pe̯ zej li̯ska.
menam mile̯je̯-ke̯ ǯe̯ľa,
ćuže̯m vi̯las zej mića.

e̯šun dori̯n nī̯ pukale̯,
drugi̯sli̯ piśme̯ giže̯.
veśki̯d kinas piśme̯ giže̯,
šujganas śin-va ći̯ške̯.

l u gsa ge̯ra, l u gsa ge̯ra,
l u gsa ge̯ra sulale̯.
e̯kajanne̯j l u gsa ge̯ra
menśi̯m śe̯le̯me̯s kośte̯.

oj mame̯j, oj baťe̯j,
kodli̯ gute̯ kodjanni̯d?
ńe-užeľi menśi̯m mile̯j
aste̯ge̯j i ǯebanni̯d?

mile̯j ju, mile̯j ju!
uśte̯ǯi̯d te en ju!
uśte̯ǯi̯d-ke̯ te juan,
me te saje̯ og mun.

gude̯kaśi̯śe̯j zonme̯j,
gude̯kav te ćastuškate̯,

My beloved has forsaken me,
It is not pleasant to talk of it.

A raftsman is going down the Vym,
He is playing the *balalaika.*
He is playing the *balalaika,*
Singing a Zyrian song.

I sat on the machine,
I looked up at the sun.
I took leave of my parents,
I forgot my beloved.

The fir-tree has no needles,
The spruce is full of needles.
Even though my beloved is small,
His face is very beautiful.

A girl sits by the window,
She writes a letter to her belowed.
With her right hand she writes the letter,
With her left hand she wipes away her tears.

The hill of *lug*, the hill of *lug*,
The hill of *lug* stands there.
The cursed hill of *lug*
Withers away my heart.

Oh mother, oh father!
Whose grave are you digging?
Is it my beloved
You will bury without me?

Drink, darling, drink, darling!
Do not drink so much that you'll fall!
If you drink so much that you fall,
I shall not come to you.

My lad with the accordion,
Play a *chastushka?*

med ńin taje̮ vremjajasi̮s
koľľaśas e̮dje̮nǯi̮ka!

vika zore̮d, vika zore̮d,
vika zore̮d sulale̮.
e̮kajanne̮j vika zore̮d
menśi̮m śe̮le̮me̮s kośte̮.

oj tom-lune̮j, tom-lune̮j,
ale̮j ćvet kojd tom-lune̮j!
tome̮n kaji ker doď vi̮le̮
žaľe̮n koľi tom pe̮ra.

das-kvajt are̮se̮j taj menam
ńoľ vo saje̮ koľe̮ma.
musa musuke̮j taj menam
armijae̮ mune̮ma.

mame̮j uźe̮ pać ved dori̮n,
a me uźa pe̮lať dori̮n.
as saji̮n gude̮ka ki̮le̮,
me ki̮vzini̮ petala.

śe̮d gi̮n sape̮g me ke̮mali,
perve̮j ke̮mali, ćegi.
mića zonse̮ me ľubiti,
e̮ťi voj uźi. će̮v ti!

g u - ć e̮ r t kuźai̮s me muna,
kuźa̮la i paśtala.
g u - ć e̮ r t koľe̮, žaľ-žaľ-žaľ,
mile̮j koľe̮, ne̮šta žaľ.

j e m - v a kuźa be̮ćka ki̮vte̮
jona že̮ ńin kaćajćće̮.
g u - ć e̮ r t i̮ n pe̮ ni̮v ole̮,
jona že̮ ńin ǯigľaśe̮.

gude̮kaśi̮śe̮j zonme̮j,
una ćuń-ki̮ča kie̮j!

So that this time may pass
More quickly from us.

A stack of vetch, a stack of vetch,
A stack of vetch stands here.
The cursed stack of vetch
Withers away my heart.

Oh my youth, oh my youth,
My purple-coloured youth!
As a young man I went logging with a sleigh,
Alas, my youth has gone.

My sixteen years
Vanished four years ago.
My dear beloved
Went to join the soldiers.

My mother is sleeping on the ledge by the stove,
While I am sleeping on the edge of the plank-bed.
Behind me an accordion can be heard,
I go out and listen to it.

I put on my black felt boots,
I put them on for the first time and they tore.
I loved a handsome lad,
One night I slept with him. Hush, you!

I walk right through *gu-ćęrt*,
I walk its length and breadth.
gu-ćęrt is left far behind, it's a pity, a pity, a pity.
My beloved is left behind there, and that's still more of a pity.

A barrel is floating down the Vym,
It rocks to and fro.
There lives a girl in *gu-ćęrt*
She flirts to and fro.

My lad with the accordion,
My hand with many rings!

una ćuń-ki̮ča kie̮s,
unae̮s pe̮rje̮dli̮śe̮j!

gude̮kaśi̮śse̮ ľubitli,
aći̮m te̮da, oz lo men.
menam sećće̮ baťe̮le̮n
oz ti̮rmi̮ śe̮mi̮s śetni̮se̮.

gude̮k be̮rśai̮s me vetli,
śi̮li̮ś že̮ ńin me ve̮li,
gude̮kaśi̮ś saje̮ muni,
je̮kti̮ś že̮ ńin me ve̮li.

lokte̮j ni̮vjas, munalame̮j,
gortjase̮j pi̮ralame̮j!
tom zonjasi̮s zańate̮je̮ś,
pe̮ri̮śjasi̮s oz kovni̮.

unme̮j lokte̮-j daj oz uźśi̮,
uź menam poduškae̮j!
og ťerpit, vetla viǯe̮dni̮,
ke̮n guľajte̮ mile̮je̮j.

ge̮le̮se̮j taj bi̮re̮ma
ke̮ǯi̮d vase̮ jue̮mi̮ś.
mile̮je̮j taj le̮gaśe̮ma
me̮d zonke̮d kućći̮śle̮mi̮ś.

šogśi̮ś koke̮j oz novle̮dli̮,
śin-va śľedse̮ og aǯǯi̮l,
ig taj lo mile̮je̮ saje̮,
ńeme̮s taj loi be̮rdni̮.

mene̮ šulisni̮ ľoke̮n,
mene̮ šue̮ni̮ zboje̮n.
ćaśśi̮e̮j-ke̮ menam suǯas,
daške̮ mile̮je̮ vajas.

g u - ć e̮ r t ś a ń i̮ s   k u a - v i ǯ e̮ ǯ
ťeľeponjas ńuže̮dam.

My hand with many rings
And many others he has beguiled.

I fell in love with an accordion-player,
I know he will never be mine.
My father has not got
Enough money for that.

I followed the accordion,
I was a singer already,
I married an accordion-player,
I was a dancer already.

Come on, girls, let us go,
Let us go to my house!
The young lads are occupied,
The old ones are not wanted.

My dream is coming but I cannot sleep,
Sleep, my pillow!
I cannot endure it, I go out and see
Where my sweetheart is roaming.

My voice has been ruined
Because I drank cold water.
My sweetheart has grown angry with me
Because I embraced another lad.

My aching legs will not carry me,
I cannot see traces of tears.
I did not marry my beloved,
So I have nothing to mourn for.

They said I was wicked,
They say I am courageous.
If I have good luck
My beloved will marry me, perhaps.

From *gu-ćęrt* to *kua-viẑ*
We put up telephone wires.

voj-šẹr dorịn pervoj ćasịn
milẹjjasẹs koľľẹdam.

śo ćẹlkẹvẹja-kẹ mijan gudẹkịs,
ez vermị menẹ gažẹdnị.
kịk ćẹlkẹvẹja gudẹkịs
stav milẹjẹs gažẹdis.

mam iz čẹktị zonkẹd uźnị.
ćẹ̄ mamẹ! ńi-nẹm on tẹd.
zonkẹd uźam, kaga vajam,
sẹmịn źep-tịr ďeńga bośt!

rozẹvẹj poduška vịlịn
me bẹrdi, bẹrdi, bẹrdi.
sija rozẹvẹj poduška
oz viśtav ńe-kodlị.

vizị̄ žẹ ńin j ō - v a vaịs,
ẹdjẹ žẹ ńin kịlẹdẹ.
tẹdan žẹ aśśịd paratẹ,
kod te vịlẹ viǯẹdẹ.

About midnight, at one o'clock
We walk out with our beloved ones.

Although our accordion is worth a hundred roubles,
It could not cheer me up,
The accordion worth two roubles
Has cheered up each beloved.

Mother would not let me sleep with a lad.
Be quiet, mother! You know nothing.
I sleep with a lad, I'm going to have a child,
Just give me a pocketful of money!

On my rosy cushion,
I wept and wept and wept.
That rosy cushion
Will not tell anybody about it.

The water of *jō-va* is already swift,
It slows swift already.
You know your partner already,
The one who is looking at you.

II. THE LOWER-VYČEGDA DIALECT

I studied the Lower-Vyčegda dialect in the villages of Ибы (Zyr. *i̮bjas*) and Ляли (Zyr. *ľaj*), both situated along the lower course of the Vym (Zyr. *jemva*). Ибы lies on the right bank of this river and Ляли 15 km to the northeast on the left bank. The Ляли dialect shows several features characteristic of Vym. The texts were taken from the following informants: Ибы: Anna Petrovna B e l o v a (b. 1881), Irina Fëdorovna B y k o v a, Kristina Michajlovna B y k o v a (1925), Marfa Aleksandrovna B y k o v a (b. 1895), Klavdija Iljična Z i n o v e v a, Anna Aleksandrovna K y z j u r o v a, Anna Afanasevna K y z j u r o v a, Anna Pavlovna K y z j u r o v a (b. 1890 Кошки), Elizaveta Michajlovna K y z j u r o v a (b. 1908), Elizaveta Iljinična K y z j u r o v a, Marija Andreevna K y z j u r o v a (b. 1908), Oľga Pankratevna P o p o v c e v a (b. 1896), Roza Pankratevna P o p o v c e v a, Serafima Lukjanovna P o p o v c e v a (b. 1875), Marija Ignatevna S m i r n o v a; Ляли Nadežda Andreevna I g o š i n a (b. 1905), Anna Ivanovna K a r a k č i e v a (b. Шёшки), Anna Stepanovna K i s e l ë v a, Anna Petrovna K y z j u r o v a, Marija Aleksandrovna K y z j u r o v a, Marija Vikentievna P o p o v a.

The dialect has the following main features:

1. As regards the phoneme *l*, *l* ~ *v*, in other words it belongs to the Vyčegda type. For example, *viśtala* 'I relate it' ~ *viśtavni̮* 'to relate'. In certain verbal suffixes (e.g. *-i̮l-* ~ *-il-*) *l* remains unchanged: *ig aǯǯi̮l* 'I did not see it'.

2. In other than initial syllables, *e̮* and *i̮* are replaced by *e* and *i* after palatal consonants. For example: *pukśe* 'he sits down' *e̮dješ̌i̮k* 'more quickly'. *vićkośis* 'from the church', *sajiś* 'from behind'. If preceded by a palatalized consonant in the first syllable, *e̮* and *i̮* often become *e* and *i* respectively: *ńebe̮* 'he buys', *śile̮* 'he sings'.

3. Assimilation at morpheme junctions is characteristic of this dialect, e.g.: *ćań* 'colt' ~ *ćańńas* 'colts' (V *ćańjas*), *peľ* 'ear' ~ *peľľas* 'ears' (V *peľjas*).

4. Instead of palatalized *ś* *js* and *jis* are sometimes found: *jojs* 'spitz, spitzig, scharf' ~ V *jos*, *vojisa* 'offen' ~ V *vośsa*.

5. In the past tense and the imperative mood the negative verb has the same forms as in the Vm dialect: *ig*, *in*, *iz*, etc., *in mun*: 'do not go!' (~ V *eg*, *en*, *ez*, etc.).

6. The dative suffix *-li̯* sometimes assumes an accusative function — e.g. *mužikli̯ oškę* 'she praises her husband'.

(a) Tales and narratives

30.

1. *este̮n, este̮n pe̮ starik gozja ole̮ni̮. | nale̮n vi̮jim e̮ťik me̮s. | starik i šue̮: | "staruka, me pe̮ vetla vićkoe̮." | vićkoe̮ munis | i popi̮s i śile̮: "este̮n, este̮n pe̮ starik gozja ole̮ni̮. | nale̮n pe̮ vi̮jim e̮ťik me̮s. | sije-ke̮ pe̮ śetasni̮ popli̮ | nali̮ pe̮ jen śetas das me̮s." | starik gorte̮ voas, | starukali̮ viśtale̮: | "ta-lun pe̮, | staruka, | mi̮j pe̮ popi̮s śili: | 'este̮n, este̮n pe̮ starik gozja ole̮ni̮, | nale̮n pe̮ vi̮jim e̮ťik me̮s. | sije-ke̮ pe̮ popli̮ śetasni̮, | jen pe̮ śetas nali̮ das me̮s'." | starik gozja ovmisni̮, | pop orde̮ me̮s nue̮disni̮. | ńe e̮ťik poplen, | aslas das | da sija das-e̮ťie̮d me̮s.*

2. *me̮d lun služanka ćeććis, | me̮sjas verdis | vaavni̮ petis. | stariklen me̮s gortas pi̮šje, | a das me̮s sija ćeććale̮ni̮, ve̮ćće̮ni̮. | starik i šue̮: | "vi̮ʒedli̮, | staruka, staruka, | so pe̮ jenmi̮d śete̮ma, | das me̮s lokte̮. | mijan — šue̮ — das e̮ťie̮d. | vaj — šue̮ — e̮djeʒika je̮rtam." | starik gozja petalasni̮, | me̮s je̮rtasni̮, | das-e̮ťi me̮s kartae̮. | viʒede̮-j: | služanka pople̮n pi̮šje̮. | "ti ne̮ taj — šue̮ — me̮sjasse̮ je̮rtalanni̮d." | "mi ne̮ — šue̮ — asśini̮m je̮rtim. | te̮-ri̮t taj — šue̮ — vićko še̮r popi̮d śile̮ma, | ke̮sjema." | "mi — šue̮ — | ke̮sjemae̮s je̮rtim. | mi — šue̮ — | ig guśe̮n nue̮j ńi-ne̮m." | stariklen e̮ťi me̮s | da das-e̮ťik loji, | pople̮n abu koľema.*

31. *ivan sarević*

1. *sar gozjale̮n kujim pi vi̮jim. naja kor-ke̮ — olasni̮, olasni̮ — śorkńi ke̮ʒasni̮, una, repa. śorkńi ke̮ʒasni̮, nale̮n gi̮riśeʒ bi̮dmas i vošni̮ me̮das, e̮tore̮ voše̮, gue̮ni̮. "vaj pe̮ viʒni̮ mun! te pe̮ mun, v a ś i l' i j s a r e v i ć, ta-lun vojnas viʒ!" v a ś i l' i j s a r e v i ć viʒni̮ munas, be̮re̮zdae̮ vodas. voj-še̮r kad ki̮mi̮n lovas i loktas guśaśiś puχ-paχ vojnas. śorkńise̮ me̮das ďergajtni̮ iž-ku paśta da i̮ž-ku paśta mestai̮s. sija vugźiśas. vot pe̮ taj ve̮ri̮d loktis, ve̮ri̮d pe̮ i šedi. "te pe̮ taj lokte̮mi̮d mene̮ i viʒni̮?!" sije bośtas da ne̮jtas da ne̮jtas da ne̮jtas da e̮dva loli̮s koľe v a ś i l' i j s a r e v i ćle̮n. no sija gortas voas. "mi̮j-ke̮ pe̮ aʒʒilin-e̮? kodi guis? kod ve̮li? kod pe̮ ve̮ri̮s?" "a meam pe̮, viśem bośtis da*

30. [The priest's cows]

1. Far, far away there lives an old man with his wife. They have a cow. The old man says: "Mother, I'm going to church." He went to church; the priest sings this: "Over there, over there, lives an old man with his wife. They have a cow. If they give it to the priest, God will give them ten cows." The old man goes home and tells the old woman: "Mother, hear what the priest sang today: 'Over there, over there, lives an old man with his wife. They have a cow. If they give it to the priest, God will give them ten cows'." The old man and his partner set out and took the cow to the priest. The priest has not one cow but ten, and this is his eleventh cow.

2. Next day the maidservant got up and fed the cows. She went out to water them. The old man's cow flees home, and all the ten cows jump up and rush after it. The old man says: "Look, mother, mother, look, God has given us a present, here come the ten cows. Ours is the eleventh" — he says. "Come on now and shut them up quickly!" The old man and his wife go out to shut up the cows in the shed. He sees the priest's maidservant running. "Hey you" — says she — "you have shut up the cows." "As for us" — says he — "we have shut up what belongs to us. Yesterday, after all" — says he — "the priest sang about them in the middle of the church; he promised them to us. We have shut up the promised cows. We have not led away anything in secret." The old man had one cow; he now has eleven, while the priest has not a single one left.

31. Tsarevich Ivan

1. A married couple, the Tsar and his wife, have three sons. Once upon a time — as they live their lives — they sow turnip-seeds, plenty of them. They sow turnip-seeds, and their turnips grow big but from time to time some of them disappear, some of them keep disappearing, they are stolen. "Well, go and guard them! You shall go, Tsarevich Vasily, tonight you shall be on watch!" Tsarevich Vasily goes on watch, lying in the furrow. It is around midnight, and the thief also comes with a great hullabaloo. He begins to pull up the turnips in a patch a lambskin wide and a lambskin long. He (Tsarevich Vasily) dashes at him. See now, the thief has arrived, the thief has turned up. "So you have come here to spy on me?" He takes him, and thrashes and thrashes and thrashes him, till hardly any life was left in Tsarevich Vasily. Well now, he arrives home. "Have you seen anything? Who came to steal? Who was it? Who is the thief?" "I . . . I . . .,

ig pę aǯǯil ńi-nęm." pęrjalis: 'meam pę viśni̯ kućći da ńi-nęm pę ig aǯǯil.' "męd lun mun pę, p e d ę r s a r e v i ć, *te vetli̯!"* p e d ę r s a r e v i ć *munas, bara vodas bęręzdaę. bara voj-šęr kad kįmįn lovas, bara šuχ-paχ voas da mędas i̯ž-ku paśta da i̯ž-ku paśta stav śorkńitę ďergajtni̯. "ak, no taj vęri̯d śuri." "te pę ješšę vi̯ǯni̯ loktin? . . ."*

2. i v a n s a r e v i *ćes seśśa i̯stas.* i v a n s a r e v i ć *kęrt paľić boštas i mune. paľić boštas, munę, bęręzdae vodas. bara voj-šęr kad lovę. puχ-paχ loktas, bara mędas ďergajtni̯, i̯ž-ku paśta da i̯ž-ku paśta mestai̯s koľe. "o — šuę — te menę vi̯ǯni̯ loktin?!" vugźiśas bara sije.* i v a n s a r e v i ć *boštas da nęjtas da nęjtas da nęjtas guśaśistę. "te pę ješšę guśaśan da kįk vokęs ńin nęjtęmi̯d, ti̯dalę."* "*lež pę,* i v a n s a r e v i ć, *koľ pę menśim lov, me pę teni̯d šľapa-ti̯r ďeńga śeta." no ješšę jona nęjtni̯ mędas. "lež pę,* i v a n s a r e v i ć, *me pę ten votluk śeta." ješšę jona nęjtni̯ mędas. "lež pę,* i v a n s a r e v i ć, *lov pę koľ, me pę ten zarńia śura ęš śeta." "ki̯ǯ pę te sije śetalan meni̯m?" —* i v a n s a r e v i ć *šuę. "te pę vęrę ka da sen pę vi̯jim i̯ǯi̯d vad. sećće pę lok, te pę sećće lok!"* i v a n s a r e v i ć *loktas, asi̯v-voǯ ćeććas. mamjas jualęni̯. "mijan pę ńe-kod iz voli̯, ńe-kodęs pę ig aǯǯil." oz viśtav sarli̯. vęrę kaas. suńis motokjas boštas, katuškajas. i̯ǯi̯d va aǯǯas, vad, śed vad. i seni mędas sija suńisjassę bergędli̯ni̯, motajtni̯, taǯi gęgrędli̯ni̯ vasę. bes-pii̯s petas, ǯeľenǯik pii̯s, sija šuę: "ďaďe pę, te nę mi̯j karan? mi̯jla pę taje te krestavlan?" "me pę taje vadsę kęsja śi̯rjovtni̯ da gortę nuni̯." "oj pę, in nu pę, in nu!" da ędje bęr vaas pi̯ras da loktas, mi̯j-kę baťis dorę. "baťe pę, baťe, kučęm-kę pę mort loktis da vadsę pę kęsje śi̯rjovtni̯ da gortas nuni̯, vasę." sija petas ędjeǯik, i̯ǯi̯dǯik. i̯ǯi̯dǯik petas i mędas šuni̯: "no pę loktin?" "lokti pę." "vaj pę, šľapasę lęśed!" sije pę šľapasę ruźedas da sećće mešęk vuras. sija petkędlas da petkędlas da ďeńgasę petkędlas da šľapai̯d ńe-kuǯ oz ti̯r. no kor-kę ti̯rę, puktas . . . si̯li̯ votluk śetas, sećće ęšedas ďeńga-votluk-ľi, mi̯j-ľi. i zarńia śura ęš śetas. "vaj pę, menę koľľi, me pę ętnam og vermi̯ munni̯." sija boštas bi̯dęn i nuas ćes pi̯red, omęľik ľoki̯s, besi̯s. nuas sija. seśśa i munę, munę, jęr vi̯lę voas, etačęm i̯ǯi̯d.*

some illness seized me, and I did not see anything." He lied: 'I began to feel ill and did not see anything.' "Tomorrow you go, Tsarevich Fëdor, you go!" Tsarevich Fëdor goes out and also lies in the furrow. Again about midnight comes, and again he (the thief) comes with a great hullabaloo, and begins to pull up all the turnips in a patch a lambskin wide and a lambskin long. "Aha, so the thief has came into my hands!" "And have you come on guard?!" . . .

2. Then he sends out Tsarevich Ivan. Tsarevich Ivan takes a stick of iron, goes out to the furrow and lies in it. Again it is about midnight. He (the thief) comes again with a great hullabaloo and again he begins to pull up (the turpins), and a patch a lambskin wide and a lambskin long remains (devastated). "Oh" — says he — "you have come here to spy on me?!" Again he rushes on him. Tsarevich Ivan seizes him and thrashes and thrashes and thrashes the thief. "So you are still stealing, and — it seems — you have already beaten up my two brothers." "Let me go, Tsarevich Ivan, spare my life, I'll give you a hatful of money." Well, he begins to beat him all the harder. "Let me go, Tsarevich Ivan, I'll give you a flint and steel in a bag." He begins to beat him all the harder. "Let me go, Tsarevich Ivan, spare my life, I'll give you a golden-horned ox." "How would you give me these things?" — asks Tsarevich Ivan. "Go into the wood, there you'll find a big lake. Go there, you go there!" Tsarevich Ivan goes home and wakes in the morning. His mother and father question him. "Nobody came to us, I have not seen anybody." He does not tell the Tsar the truth. He goes out into the wood. He takes hanks of thread, skeins of yarn with him. He catches a glimpse of the great water, the lake, the dark lake. He starts to unreel the thread, to unwind it, and encircle the water with it. The devil's son, his younger son comes and says: "Uncle, what on earth are you doing here? Why are you putting this crosswise?" "I want to ensnare this lake and take it home." "Oh no, don't take it away!" And he goes back quickly into the water and comes to his father. "Father, father, some man has come here and he wants to ensnare and take home the lake, the water." Quickly the older son goes out. The older one goes out and says: "So you've come, have you?" "Yes, I've come." "Well then, get your hat ready!" He makes a hole in his hat and sews a bag on it. He (the devil) brings more and more and more money out, yet the hat is not filled. Well, at last it is filled; he puts it on (his back). He hands him a bag, he hangs there the money-bag or whatever. And he gives him a golden-horned ox. "See me home, I cannot walk alone." He takes all of them, carrying them along the hunters' track, the feeble devil, the fiend. He carries them, he

seni ge̮re̮ma kod-ke̮ da ge̮ri̮s koľema. “mi̮j pe̮ taja, bur mort, taja tijan?” “taja pe̮ menam perna-ke̮le̮, pernae̮ pe̮ ori da. vaj pe̮ taje če̮č bośt da nu!” sija če̮č bośtas da nuas. mune̮, mune̮, agas aǯǯas. “taja pe̮ mi̮j tijan, bur mort?” “taja pe̮ menam pernae̮.” sije i če̮č bośtas ome̮ľis da nuas. nuas, vajas, kiľće doras ši̮bi̮tas i be̮r bes pi̮šjas vade̮. no i loktas ďaďe, e̮š je̮rtas.

3. “no pe̮ — olasni̮, olasni̮ — me pe̮ guľajtni̮ vetla ki̮ćée-ke̮” — ivan sarević šue̮. ivan sarević ki̮ćće-ke̮ mune̮ guľajtni̮. mune̮, mune̮, mune̮ i̮le̮, ki̮ćće-ke̮ i kuče̮m-ke̮ kerka voas, ľokińǯi. sećće i pi̮ras. “uźni̮, pe̮ mene̮ leǯ, babuška!” e̮tnas babuška ole̮. uźni̮ leǯas. “no kuče̮ma pe̮ tan, babuška, tijan ole̮ni̮, me̮d źemľa·i̮n?” “a mi̮j pe̮ ole̮ni̮?! mijan pe̮ zev ľoka ole̮ni̮. kuče̮m-ke̮ mijan ke̮re̮ľ pe̮ viis stav naro·dse̮. naro·di̮s pe̮ ńin abu. marpa saro·vn ase̮ pe̮ vajni̮ ke̮sje, a stav naro·dse̮ pe̮ ńin viis. a bi̮d lun pe̮ saldat koľe, kokte̮m saldat da vetli̮še e̮šin uvti: ’kod-ke̮ abu-e̮ e̮t-dor mort, kod-ke̮ abu-e̮ vojujti̮s?” “a te pe̮ mene̮ asi̮v vištav, me pe̮ peta — ivan sarević šue̮. no me̮d lun voas. sar tark vartas: “kod-ke̮ abu e̮t-dor mort?” “mijan pe̮ no vi̮jim e̮ťik, uže.” saldat-ľi, mi̮j-ľi vištalas: “te pe̮ sija petav ve̮jujtni̮!” “petala pe̮!” petas, ve̮jna vi̮le̮ munas. “no kuče̮ma pe̮ tijan ole̮ni̮?” “mijan pe̮ ke̮re̮ľ bi̮de̮n stavse̮ li̮jis. ńe-kod pe̮ ve̮jujti̮ś abu.” sija bośtas bed ke̮sti̮ga da i mune̮ ve̮jujtni̮. suvtas poľe vi̮le̮, ke̮sti̮ga vi̮le̮ e̮še̮ććas. no sarle̮n pe̮ i̮ste̮ma ve̮jujti̮ś, e̮ťi mort. “mi̮j pe̮ taje karam, munam pe̮ ta-mi̮danas da taje pe̮ śe̮li̮štam, aľi peľištam, aľi tojištam, aľi mi̮j pe̮ taje kuǯ vijam, e̮ťise̮ eta mi̮dae̮n?” mate̮ lokni̮ me̮dasni̮, vakśeni̮ si̮ vi̮le̮ ve̮jska. sija berge̮ććas da votlukse̮ bośtas da votlukśis biva iz da biva ke̮rt bośtas. e̮t-pi̮r vaćkas: moloďeć ćeććištas; me̮di̮ś vaćkas: moloďeć ćeććištas. “mi̮j pe̮, vi̮ľ ke̮ža·jin, mijan če̮ktan karni̮?” “vaj pe̮, taje stav ve̮jskase̮ e̮vte̮!” e̮tore̮-me̮dore̮ naja e̮vtasni̮, stavse̮ i vijasni̮ ve̮jskase̮. stavi̮s kule̮, e̮ťi saldati̮s koľas, kuče̮m-ke̮ rańine̮jes. “te pe̮ mun da asi̮v ki̮k ta mi̮da med loktasni̮” — sija, ivan sarević šue̮. sija, mi̮j-ke̮ munas, gorte̮ be̮r loktas. sar viǯedlas, a stav ve̮jskase̮ bi̮di̮n vijema. sari̮d i ľube̮ loe̮. sije verdasni̮, ugošša·jtasni̮, kod te̮de̮,

goes on and on until he arrives at a big fenced kitchen-garden like this.* Somebody had been ploughing there, and the plough had been left behind. "What's this, my good man, this thing that belongs to you?" "This is my cross-string, my cross, it has been ripped off. Well now, take it and carry that as well!" He picks it up as well and carries it. He goes on and on, and catches sight of a harrow. "And what's this thing that belongs to you, good man?" "This is my cross." The devil picks this up too and carries it. He carries it, takes it home, throws it beside the porch and the devil flees back into the lake. Tsarevich Ivan arrives and shuts the ox in the shed.

3. They live on and on. "Well, I'm going to take a walk somewhere" — says Tsarevich Ivan. Tsarevich Ivan goes to walk somewhere. He goes on and on, somewhere far away and he arrives at some tumbledown house. He enters. "Let me in, mother, to have a sleep!" The old woman lives alone. She lets him in to sleep. "Well, how do people live here in this place, mother, in this strange land?" "Well, how should they live?! People have a very poor life here. Some king or other has killed the whole population in our land. There are no people left. He wants to marry Tsarevna Marpa, and he has already killed the whole population. Every day one soldier is left behind, a soldier with no legs, and he walks beneath the window in the evening: 'Is there no stranger here, is there no warrior here'?" 'Well, in the morning mention me to him and I shall go out" — says Tsarevich Ivan. Well, the next day arrives. The Tsar knocks: "Is there a stranger here?" "Yes, there is one here; he is asleep." The soldier or whatever says: "Here you, come out and fight!" "I'm coming out!" He goes out and goes to the war. "Well, how are people living in your land?" "In our land the king has shot down the whole population. No warrior has been left alive." He takes the crutch and goes out to fight. He stands in the field leaning on the crutch. Well, the Tsar's forces sent out a warrior, a man. "What shall we do with this one? Shall we all go together and spit him away, or blow him away, or push him away, or what? How shall so many of us kill this one man?" They come near to him and laugh at him, the whole army. He turns round, takes out his bag, and takes the flint and steel out of the bag to strike a light. He strikes once, and a young man springs forth; he strikes a second time and a young man springs forth. "What is your command, our new master, what shall we do?" "Go to it, sweep away this army!" They sweep this way and that way, and kill the whole army. All of them die, only one single soldier remains, a wounded man. "You just go back, and tomorrow twice as many men are to return" — says Tsarevich

* Here my informant pointed through the window to the kitchen-garden.

kuʒ́. "asi̮v pe̮ bara vetli̮ te! me pe̮ teni̮d, asi̮v vetlan, i m a r p a s a r o · v n ae̮s te saje śetam. (ke̮re̮ľ ve̮li vaje). sija me̮d lun bara mune̮, bara poľe vi̮le̮ suvtas i bara sen ke̮sti̮ga ji̮li̮n e̮šjema. i lokte̮ni̮ bara ve̮jska. oj pe̮, sarle̮n ve̮jskate̮ ki̮mi̮n sijes i̮ste̮ma! vakśeni̮ sije. "mi̮j pe̮ tene̮ karam, kuʒ́ pe̮ tene̮ vijni̮ me̮dam?! pe̮ľiš-tam-ke̮ pe̮ stavni̮m, kulan. a śeli̮štam-ke̮ pe̮ i stavi̮d, ńin uśan." bara mate̮ǯi̮k voas. sija votluk ki̮skas, biva iz da biva ke̮rt vaćkas: e̮ťik moloďeć ki̮ś-ke̮ loktas. me̮di̮ś: me̮d moloďeć. "no vaj pe̮, mi̮j, ľube·zne̮j ke̮źa·jin mijan če̮ktan karni̮?" "e̮vte̮ pe̮ stavse̮!" stav ve̮jskase̮ e̮vtasni̮, vijasni̮ bara. no mune̮, bara loktas gorte̮. sar bara vi̮ǯedlas: stavse̮ vijas, vajedas. kod te̮de̮, kuʒ́ sije bara ńin, mi̮j lois-ľi . . . i svaďba karas. m a r p a s a r o · v n ae̮s si̮ saje śetas. veńića·jććasni̮, pirujtasni̮-paruj-tasni̮, bi̮de̮n karasni̮. seśśa sija i votte̮dasni̮ ić-moń gozjae̮s torja kerkae̮. votte̮-dasni̮. sija vodasni̮ da m a r p a s a r o · v n a i šue̮: "i v a · n s a r e · v i ć, ľube·zne̮j mužik pe̮, kuʒ́ pe̮ teni̮d taj jen otsalis ta mi̮dase̮ vijni̮ e̮tnadi̮sli̮? vaj pe̮, te viśtav!" "a kuʒ́-ke̮ pe̮ taj jen otsalis, a mi̮j pe̮ me teni̮d viśtala?" "a mi̮j ne̮ pe̮ as babai̮dli̮ on viśtav? kole̮ pe̮ viśtavni̮." "a vot pe̮ menam vi̮jim votluk, biva iz da biva ke̮rt pe̮ vot vaćka i ćeććištasni̮ ki̮k moloďeć da stavse̮ i vijasni̮." "no vot pe̮ i viśtalin, paśibe̮ pe̮, bur — mužikli̮ oške̮ —. mi̮j ne̮ pe̮ as babai̮dli̮ on viśtav?" no sija koʒʒištas da jona i unmovśas, mužiki̮d. mužiki̮d unmovśas, a babai̮s votlukśid i boštas biva izse̮ da biva ke̮rtse̮. boštas da sećće pre̮ste̮j biva iz da biva, ke̮rt i śujas, m a r p a s a r o v n a babai̮s. sija i asi̮v-voʒ ćeććas, bara kole̮ munni̮ ve̮jska vi̮le̮, ve̮jna vi̮le̮. "asi̮v pe̮ ke̮re̮ľse̮ i bi̮de̮ne̮s ńin vajed!" ke̮re̮ľis ke̮źa·jini̮s, nale̮n sar. lokte̮ni̮. sija ke̮sti̮ga bed ji̮le̮ bara e̮še̮ććema. "kuče̮m pe̮ sari̮dle̮n ve̮js-kai̮s? — ke̮re̮ľis šue̮. — mi̮j pe̮ taje karanni̮d, śe̮li̮štanni̮d, aľi pe̮ľištanni̮d, aľi kuʒ́ pe̮ taje vijam?" "a inli̮ pe̮ — rańenej e̮ťik saldat šue̮ —, taje pe̮ ved ki̮k lun ńin stavse̮ vijis, bara pe̮ vijas." "će̮v pe̮, kuče̮m pe̮ taje vijis, seče̮m mort, e̮ťik mort?!" naja voasni dinad. "no pe̮ vaj, vojujt! te pe̮ ve̮jujte̮mi̮d, vaj pe̮, vij mijane̮s, si̮ mi̮da naro·dse̮!" sija veśke̮ berge̮ććas da biva izse̮ da biva ke̮rtse̮ vaćkas. e̮t-pi̮r vaćkas: bi petalas; me̮di̮ś vaćkas: bi petalas. ńe-kod, ńi-ne̮m abu. vot sija i bed

Ivan. He walks home, and arrives home. The Tsar sees that he has killed the whole army, everyone. The Tsar is delighted. They give him food, feasting him, who knows how. "Go again tomorrow! If you go out tomorrow, we shall give you Tsarevna Marpa in marriage." (That same king wanted to marry her.) Next day he goes out again, again he stands up in the field, and again leans on the crutch. The army comes. "Look, what a big army the Tsar has sent!" they laugh at him. "What shall we do with you? How shall we kill you?! If we give one puff of breath, all of us, you will die. And if we all spit once, you will fall." Again he approaches. He takes out the bag, strikes the flint against the steel: a young man comes along from somewhere or other. He strikes a second time: another young man comes along. "Now, dear master, what is your command, what shall we do?" "Sweep away the whole lot!" They sweep away the whole army, again they kill them. Well, he goes off and arrives home. The Tsar again sees that he has killed the whole lot, he brought them there. Who knows how (they feasted him) again or what happened . . . And he holds a wedding. They give him Tsarevna Marpa in marriage. They are wedded, they feast, and do everything. Then the young wife and her partner are put to bed in a separate house. They lie down, and Tsarevna Marpa says: "Tsarevich Ivan, my dear husband, tell me how God helped you, how you alone were able to kill so many of them! Come on, do tell me!" "Well, God helped me somehow, what else can I tell you?" "Then why will you not tell the tale to your own wife? You must tell me!" "Well, I have a bag with flint and steel in it, and when I strike the flint against the steel, two young men spring out and kill everybody." "Well now, you have told me; thank you, it's all right" — she praises him — "why should you not tell your own wife?" Then he becomes drunk and falls into a deep sleep — that is, the husband. The husband sleeps and his wife takes the flint and steel out of the bag. She takes them and instead puts an ordinary flint and steel in the bag, does Tsarevna Marpa. He wakes in the morning, again he has to go to the army, to war. "Tomorrow bring the king and everybody else here!" The king is their master, their Tsar. They come. He leans on the crutch again. "Which is your Tsar's army?" — asks the king. "What will you do with this man? Will you spit him away or blow him away? How shall we kill this man?" "Just wait" — says a wounded soldier — "for this man has killed everybody for two days past, and he is going to kill everybody again." "Hold your tongue! How could he have killed everybody, such a man, one single man?" They come close to him. "Come on now, fight! You have been fighting before, come on, kill us, as many as we are!" He turns round and strikes the flint against the steel.

ji̮le̮ e̮še̮ććas i sulale̮. "no vij pe̮, te pe̮ vijni̮ loktin, ve̮jujtni̮." "a me pe̮ ig lok ve̮jujtni̮, a me pe̮ ve̮v korśni̮, me pe̮ ve̮v-korśis, me pe̮ ig vij. me pe ve̮v-korśiś vetle̮dla." a saldati̮s i šue̮: "taja pe̮ ve̮li. vaje pe̮, tali̮ ke̮rt asi̮ka be̮ćka kare̮! ńi-ne̮m pe̮ tajeli̮ og vermi̮ vijni̮, taje pe̮ ši̮bi̮tam va vi̮le̮, med pe̮ sen plavajte̮ vai̮n." "no si̮li̮ ke̮rt be̮ćka karasni̮ seni arťeľen i vae̮ i ši̮bi̮tasni̮, i v a n s a r e v i ćse̮.

4. *sija plavajtas sen da plavajtas da ke̮reľ stav ve̮jskanad munas sar dorad. sarse̮ gue̮ śujasni̮, vićkojasse̮, bi̮de̮n śed kue̮n ki̮šasni̮, bi̮de̮n me̮d verae̮ berge̮dasni̮. m a r p a s a r o v n ai̮s i baba ke̮reľli̮ loe̮, ke̮reľli̮ šetasni̮. kor-ke̮ sen i v an s a r e v i ć plavajtas da plavajtas da plavajtas da plavajtas da i kuvni̮ me̮dis. 'atte̮ ďive̮, kole̮ že̮ ńin tan kuvni̮. ke̮n-ke̮ pe̮ eśke̮ menam zarńia śura e̮š ve̮vli, ke̮sjis pe̮ bur karni̮. a ki̮ś ne̮ pe̮ e̮ni sije me korśa sije? ke̮n sija pe̮, kod te̮de̮? me̮d źemľa·i̮n.' a munigas sija šuis: "e̮š-ke̮ pe̮ durmas, ti pe̮ le̮že̮!" mam-baťi̮sli̮ šuis. a sija e̮š durmis. stav pos-ji̮vse̮ bi̮de̮n leptale̮, kerkase̮ leptale̮. naja vośtasni̮ kartase̮ da śviśńitas me̮d źemľae̮ži̮s e̮ški̮d. bi̮de̮n, stav mu i va dre̮žži̮te̮. lokte̮ sija more dorad e̮ški̮d. a i v a n s a r e v i ć i šue̮: "e̮ pe̮, śondi̮-bane̮j daj e̮ške̮j, te pe̮ eśke̮ loktan, ki̮le̮ da mene̮ pe̮ e̮d te vijan." sija buv-bov-bav keras e̮ški̮s da berege̮ vajedas. lukalas da lukalas da lukalas, berege̮ vajedas be̮ćkase̮. berege̮ voas. "da vijan e̮d pe̮ mene̮ te!" sija taj ćapi̮štas e̮ški̮s da źiľ-źoľ mune̮ se̮mi̮n be̮ćkai̮s. pazale̮. i v a n s a r e v i ć i kulas. seśśa sija isalas da isalas da isalas e̮ški̮d da lov-va vajas da pi̮zjas da be̮r lovźas.*

5. *seśśa sija i munas be̮r gortas. be̮r gortas munas e̮ške̮d, e̮ške̮s nue̮das i gorte̮ munasni̮. no munas, gorti̮n, mi̮j-ke̮, oli̮štas i čekte̮ni̮ si̮li̮ ge̮traśni̮. "me pe̮ — šue̮ — og ge̮traś na, me pe̮ ješšę vetla ki̮ćće-ke̮ guľajtni̮." sija guľajtni̮ bara mune̮, bara ki̮ćće-ke̮ guľajtni̮." sija guľajtni̮ bara mune̮, bara me̮d źemľa·e̮ munas. i v a n s a r e v i ć babuška orde̮ sećće pi̮ras. sija oz i te̮d sije. "no pe̮, babuška, kuče̮m ole̮mi̮s?" "će̮v, mi̮j ne̮ pe̮ ńin olasni̮? te kojd že̮ taj volis da ki̮k lun bi̮de̮n vijis ve̮jskase̮, a kojmed lunas pe̮ ki̮ćće-ke̮ voši, vijisni̮ daj!" i oz te̮d sija, babuškai̮d. "no pe̮, babuška, me pe̮, uźam ta-lun, a asi̮v pe̮ me ve̮v loa, tead zarńia ve̮v loa karta vi̮lad. a te pe̮ nue̮d ke̮reľ dortiid vaavni̮! sije da sija pe̮ me̮das korni̮: »vaj pe̮, me tajes bośta, ńe̮ba, vuzav! mi̮j pe̮ ten starukali̮ tače̮m zarńia ve̮v? a-a bur ve̮v sija, jon, i̮ži̮d ve̮v, zarńia.«" no asi̮v-vo̮ž ćeććas, si̮le̮n ve̮v seče̮m loe̮ma karta vi̮las.*

He strikes once: out comes fire, then he strikes a second time: out comes fire. There is nobody there, nothing. He leans on the stick and stands waiting. "Come on, kill us, you have come to kill, to fight!" "Well no, I have not come to fight but to find a horse, I have come here as a horse-dealer." The soldier says: "This was the man. Make an iron-hooped barrel to put him in! We cannot kill him anyhow; let us throw him into the water, let him float in the water!" Well, together they make an iron barrel for him and throw Tsarevich Ivan into the water.

4. There he floats and floats, and the king and the whole of his army go to the Tsar. They put the Tsar into a pit, cover all the churches with black hide, and convert all the people to another faith. Tsarevna Marpa becomes the king's wife, she is given in marriage to the king. Tsarevich Ivan floats on and on and on and he is near his end. "Alas! This is where I must die. But I should have a golden-horned ox somewhere, and that was supposed to do me some good. But where am I to look for it now? Where is it, who knows? In another country." Before leaving (home) he said: "If the ox goes mad, set it free!" So he said to his parents. And the ox did go mad. It lifts up all the barns and the house. They open the stable, and the ox dashes off, like a whirlwind as far as the other country. Everything, the whole earth and waters tremble. The ox arrives at the sea. Tsarevich Ivan says: "Oh, my sun-face, my ox, so you have come here, it seems, you will kill me." The ox gives a bellow and brings the barrel ashore. It butts it and butts it and butts it and brings the barrel ashore. "But you will kill me!" The ox bangs it down and the barrel breaks into splinters. It breaks to pieces. Tsarevich Ivan dies. The ox sniffs at him, and sniffs at him again; it brings life-water, sprinkles it on him, and he comes to life.

5. Then he goes home. He goes home with the ox. He leads the ox, and they go home. For a while he lives at home, and he is ordered to marry. "As for me" — he says — "I will not marry as yet, I am going out again to walk somewhere." Again he sets out on his wandering, again he arrives in the other country. Tsarevich Ivan enters the old woman's house. She does not recognize him. "Now, mother, how is life here?" "Hold your tongue, for how should they live here? A man like you came here and in two days killed the whole of the army and on the third day he disappeared, he must have been killed." The old woman does not recognize him. "Well, mother, I . . ., let us go to sleep today, in the morning I shall turn into a horse, I shall be a golden horse in your stable. And you just lead me past the king's house to where you water me. He will ask you for me: »I'll buy this one, I'll purchase it, sell it to me! What use is such a golden horse to you, an old hag?" Well, this is a good horse, a strong, big golden horse.«" So she

sija i petke̮das, śerme̮dalas vuzavni̮. “te pe̮ vuzav! śo šajt pe̮ śetas, in śet, ki̮ke̮s pe̮ śetas, in śet, kujim-śo pe̮ śetas, śet da śerme̮dte̮ pe̮ in śet!” sija mune̮. ke̮re̮ľ e̮djeǯi̮k petas. “o pe̮, babuška, kuče̮m pe̮ tenad ve̮li̮d bur! kiś ne̮ pe̮ tače̮mi̮s? vaj pe̮, vuzav! mi̮j ne̮ pe̮ ten, etače̮m starukali̮ tače̮m ve̮v kole̮?” “og pe̮, mi̮j ne̮ pe̮ me vuzala?! meam pe̮ etija, aćim bi̮tti, bur ve̮v.” “vaj pe̮ vuzav, śo će̮lke̮vej śeta.” “og, og pe̮.” “ki̮k-śo pe̮ śeta.” “og pe̮ śet.” kujim-śo pe̮ śeta.” no i śetas. “śerme̮dse̮ pe̮ og śet.” śerme̮dse̮ be̮r boštas. “men pe̮ oz i kov śerme̮di̮d.” sija i zev jona ľubite̮ni̮ ke̮re̮ľ gozja, marpa sarovna gozja. bi̮d lun si̮ vi̮le̮ ľubujććeni̮ da vaaleni̮ da verde̮ni̮. da sija seče̮m mića da mi̮j-ľi da! kor-ke̮ ke̮re̮ľ ki̮ćće-ke̮ mune̮ lijśini̮ da mi̮j da. i marpa sarovna petas, sije ve̮ďite̮-babite̮. a ve̮v si̮ vi̮le̮ taj kuź śin-gugnad viǯedlas. a sija povźas da e̮djeǯi̮ka be̮r pi̮ras babai̮d, marpa sarovnai̮d. ke̮re̮ľ loktas. “oj pe̮, ke̮re̮·ľuško, ľube·znej mužik, etija pe̮ mijan ve̮v ve̮re̮g. taja pe̮ mijan važ mužik.” “će̮v pe̮, je̮j, kuče̮m ne̮ važ mužik?!” “da, važ mužik. vaj pe̮, śejćas že̮ palaćjase̮s vajed i tre̮pu-tre̮pu bi̮de̮n sijes keravli̮ i bien sot i pe̮jimse̮ pe̮ te̮le̮d! veľiś pe̮ taiś mi̮nan.” no e̮djeǯi̮ka i śejćas i mune̮ ke̮re̮ľ i palaćjasla. a etija nale̮n ve̮li ďevka-ćerno·vka, prisluga, vek ve̮le̮ma sari̮sle̮n da sija ke̮re̮ľis dori̮n i prislugajća·jte̮. no sija i petas da ve̮lidli̮ kok vi̮las jurbite̮ sija: “oj pe̮, ve̮lej da ve̮lej da šondi̮-banej daj ve̮lej, ńi-ne̮m e̮d te, końer, on te̮d. a tene̮ pe̮ e̮d i palaćjasla munini̮ da palaćjasi̮d pe̮ tene̮ ke̮sjeni̮ tre̮pu-tre̮pu keravni̮ daj bien sotni̮ daj pe̮jimte̮ te̮ledni.” ve̮lis i śi̮aśas: “e̮k pe̮ ďevka-ćernovka da musa ćojilej, te pe̮, voasni̮ pe̮ palaćjasi̮s da mene̮-ke̮ me̮dasni keravli̮ni̮, taćće pe̮ pet vai̮dla da vedrate̮ pe̮ bośt da keri̮štasni̮-ke̮ pervojse̮, ki̮ćće pe̮ pervoj viri̮s ćeććištas, sije pe̮ sije bośt da vedraad pe̮ i pukti̮ da sere̮g-peľesad pe̮ i śuj muas! šu: »bur zarńia ve̮v pe̮ ve̮li, zarńia kiǯ pe̮ te bi̮dmi̮ že̮!« palaćjas, nija, oz na vevjav petni̮ ve̮v dorśid i lokte̮ni̮ ńin, śinni̮s don. bi̮de̮n sije tre̮pu-tre̮pu keravlasni̮, bien sotasni̮, pe̮jimse̮ bi̮de̮n te̮le̮dasni̮. “no vot — marpa sarovna šue̮ — veľiś pe̮ mi važ mužikśid i mi̮nim.”

6. *no kor-ke̮ ovni̮ me̮dasni̮ i zarńia kiǯ bi̮dme̮, seče̮m mića da zarńia. no i ľubujććini̮ oz vermi̮ni̮ ke̮re̮ľ gozja? ’atte̮ pe̮ kuče̮m mijan kiǯ bi̮dmi̮ni̮ me̮dis, atte̮*

gets up early in the morning, and she had got such a horse in the stable. She leads it out and harnesses it for the sale. "Sell me! If he offers a hundred roubles, do not give me to him, if he offers two hundred, do not give me to him, if he offers three hundred, give me to him, but don't give him the bridle!" She goes to the place. The king comes out at once. "Oh, mother, what a good horse you have! Where did you get it? Sell it to me! What use is such a horse to you, old hag that you are!" "No, why should I sell it? It is mine, I have reared it, it is a good horse." "Come now, sell it, I will give a hundred roubles for it." "No, no." "I'll give you two hundred." "I'm not selling it." "I'll give you three hundred." Well, she gives it to him. "I'm not giving you the bridle." She takes the bridle back. "I don't want your bridle anyway." The king and the queen like it very much, the Tsarevna Marpa and his partner. Day by day they take delight in it, they water it and feed it. It is so beautiful! Once the king goes out to hunt somewhere or other. Tsarevna Marpa goes out and tends it. She caresses it. But the horse seems to look somehow askance at her. She is frightened; Tsarevna Marpa returns quickly to the house. The king arrives home. "Oh, my dear king, my beloved husband, this horse of ours is an evil spirit. This is my former husband." "Hush, you fool, how could it be your former husband?!" "But it is my former husband! Order the hangmen to come here at once, and have it cut to pieces, burn it in the fire, and scatter its ashes to the winds! This is the only way we can rid ourselves of it." Well, the king goes at once to fetch the hangmen. They had a black-haired maid-servant, who used to belong to the Tsar, but who now serves the king. Well, she goes out and bows before the horse's feet: "Oh, my horse, my horse, my little sun-face, my horse, surely you do not know, poor soul, that they have gone for the hangmen, and that then the hangmen will cut you to pieces, burn you in the fire and scatter your ashes to the winds." The horse speaks up: "Oh black-haired girl, my dear little sister, when the hangmen come and desire to cut me to pieces, come here for water, take your bucket, and when they make the first cut, take in your bucket the first drop of blood wherever it drops; take it to the clean corner and hide it in the earth! Say this: 'It was a good horse, a golden horse, may a golden birch-tree grow out of you'." She had hardly any time to leave the horse, when the hangmen come along, their eyes are glowing. They cut it to pieces, burn it in the fire, and scatter its ashes, all of them, to the winds. "Well now" — says Tsarevna Marpa — "at last we have rid ourselves of my former husband!"

6. Well, once as they were living on like this, a golden brich-tree grows up, so beautiful and golden. And cannot the king and his wife take delight

ďive̮, kuče̮m bur!' a ďevka-ćernovkali̮ sija ješše̮ ľube̮, sije raďejte̮, kod te̮de̮, kuʒi. no ki̮ćće-ke̮ bara mune̮ ke̮re̮ľ. mi̮j-ke̮, sije e̮tore̮ si̮ ge̮ge̮ri̮n bergale̮, m a r p a s a r o v n a i̮d viʒede̮. kuʒ taj sije zarńija kiʒ si̮ vi̮le̮ šatovćas, vuvźiślas ľok moz. oj sija mi̮j e̮dja pi̮šjas. bara pi̮šjas i bara lokte̮ ke̮re̮ľ. "oj pe̮, ľube·zne̮j mužik ke̮re̮ľ, taja pe̮ mijan zarńija ki̮ʒʒid ve̮re̮g. taja pe̮ važ mužik. vaj, śejćas že̮ pe̮ taje keravli̮, pe̮re̮d i tre̮pu-tre̮pu palaćjase̮s vajed i bie̮n sot i pe̮jimse̮ pe̮ te̮le̮d!" bara sija i pi̮šjas e̮djeʒi̮k, ke̮re̮ľ, babai̮sli̮ ki̮vze̮, mića, eśke̮ žaľ da. bara ki̮vze̮, munas. a ďevka-ćernovka mune̮ da jona be̮rde̮ bara: "oj pe̮, zarńija ki̮ʒʒej da ki̮ʒʒej, me pe̮ ve̮li te vi̮le̮ ľubujćća. e̮ni e̮d pe̮ te ńi-ne̮m on te̮d, a tene̮ keravni̮ da i sotni̮ da i bara pe̮jimse̮ te̮le̮dni̮." ki̮ʒʒid bara si̮li̮ ši̮aśas: "ďevka pe̮ ćernovka da musa ćojile̮j! te pe̮ viʒed, meam me̮dasni̮, palaćjasi̮d voasni̮ da, keravli̮ni̮ da perve̮j ćagse̮ pe̮ keri̮štasni da ki̮ćće ćeććištas, te pe̮ sije bośt da vedraad pukti̮ da moread pe̮ va-dorad i lećći: »zarńia kiʒ pe̮ ve̮li da zarńia utka pe̮ te lov že!«" no sija i bara voas palaćjas, oz vevjav pi̮rni̮, bara ńin lokte̮ni̮. bi̮de̮n keravlasni̮, sotasni, pe̮jimse̮ te̮le̮dasni̮. "vot pe̮ ve̮ľiś pe̮ mi tai̮ś mi̮nim. e̮ni pe̮ ńe-ke̮n ńi-ne̮m abu. taja pe̮ ve̮li važ mužik, mijane̮s pe̮ eśke̮ ki̮knanni̮me̮s vijis." "no tenśid pe̮ ki̮vzim."

7. no i ovni̮ me̮dasni̮. ke̮re̮ľ sija vek vetle̮dle̮, okotńića·jte̮, more dore̮ sija leććas li̮jśini̮, utkajase̮s li̮jle̮. a utka, sija zarńa utka sija di̮r sen gaške̮ ńin lebale̮ vaas. sija i davaj me̮das si̮ be̮rśań ve̮tli̮śni̮. 'atte̮ pe̮, kuče̮m mića, i̮ʒi̮d utka!' li̮jli̮ni̮ me̮das, ve̮tćini̮. vetćas, ve̮tćas. 'gaške̮ me kuľla de̮re̮me̮s da ve̮te̮da tajes. munas, munas, ki̮ćće-ke̮ eśke̮ gać i bi̮de̮n kuľas, berege̮ puktas, utka be̮rśań ve̮tće. šede̮ i šede̮ i, seśśa kvaťitni̮, kvaťitni̮ me̮das. sija vek i̮le̮ʒi̮k da i̮le̮ʒi̮k da beregas kais. pi̮r vi̮le lebas utkai̮s da e̮djeʒi̮ka si̮li̮ś, ke̮re̮ľidli̮ś de̮re̮m-gaćse̮ bośtas da votlukse̮ bośtas e̮djeʒi̮k — votluki̮s si̮ ordi̮n, novle̮dle̮, ke̮re̮ľidli̮ sete̮ma — bośtas ke̮re̮ľidli̮ś. seśśa i biva izse̮ da biva ke̮rtse̮ bośtas votlukśis da e̮t-pi̮r vaćkas, moloďeć ćeććištas, me̮di̮ś vaćkas, moloďeć ćeććištas. "ľube·zne̮j ke̮źa·jin pe̮ važ ke̮źa·jin, mi̮j pe̮ če̮ktan mijan karni̮?" "vaj pe̮, bośte etaje veľmožase̮ da e̮ťi kok vi̮las pe̮ taľište̮, a me̮dse̮ ćašńite̮ da moreas pe̮ ši̮bi̮te̮!" sija naja bośtasni̮ da žive̮ ke̮re̮ľes e̮ťik kok vi̮las taľištasni̮ da me̮dse̮ ćašńitasni̮ da moree̮ ši̮bi̮tasni̮. no vot sija i kae̮ seśśa gortad, i v a n s a r e v i ć. i v a n s a r e v i ć lokte̮, ke̮n-ke̮ vi̮li̮s jatažin m a r p a s a r o v n a

in it? "Look, what a birch-tree has grown for us; look, how beautiful it is!" The black-haired girl is even more pleased with it; she loves it, who knows how? Well, the king again goes off somewhere. She is always around it, Tsarevna Marpa is always looking at it. How that birch-tree bows over her; suddenly it grabs at her in a wicked way. Oh, how quickly she runs away! Again she runs off and the king arrives. "On my beloved king and husband, this birch-tree of ours is an evil spirit. This is my former husband. Cut it down at once, fell it, bring the hangmen, let it burn in the fire, scatter its ashes to the winds!" Again the king runs off in a nurry to obey his wife. She is beautiful, so he is sorry for her. He obeys her and goes off. The little black-haired girl goes that way, weeping bitterly: "Oh, my golden birch-tree, birch-tree, I have taken delight in you, and now — you do not know anything about it — they will cut you down, burn you, and scatter your ashes to the winds." The birch-tree speaks up: "Black-haired little girl, my dear little sister! Listen to me, the hangmen will come and cut me down, and when they cut the first shaving from me, pick it up wherever it may fall, put it in your bucket and go down to the sea, to the seashore. 'It was a golden birch-tree, now turn into a golden duck'." Well, the hangmen come along, she has no time even to go in (the house) before they arrive. They cut it down, burn it and scatter its ashes to the winds. "Well, now at last we have rid ourselves of it. Now it is nowhere to be seen. This was my former husband, he would have killed both of us." "Well, I have obeyed you."

7. Well now, they live on and on. The king always goes out hunting. He goes down to the sea to shoot wild-duck. The golden duck has long been swimming in the water. He starts to chase it. "Look, what a beautiful big duck it is!" He begins to hunt it, to chase it. "Perhaps I can catch it if I take off my shirt." He goes on and on; he takes off his trousers and everything, placing them somewhere on the coast, he goes after the duck. It is already almost within his grasp, he tries to seize it. He goes further and further along the coast. The duck always flies up and away, and it quickly takes away the king's shirt and trousers, it quickly takes the king's bag with the flint and steel — he carries the bag with him, the queen (Tsarevna Marpa) has given it to him. Then it takes the flint and steel out of the bag. It strikes once: a lad springs out; it strikes again: a lad springs out: "Dear master, our old master, what do you command us to do?" "Quick, take this magnate, tread on one of his legs and tear off the other, and throw him into the sea!" They seize him and they tread on the live king's leg, tear off his other leg and throw him into the sea. Well, then Tsarevich Ivan goes home. He arrives at home, somewhere on the upper floor there sits Tsarevna

pukalę: 'u-u, važ mužikid loktę, važ mužikid loktę. taja pę ęni mijanes, stavnimęs vijas važ mužikid.' "eča šud! kiś-kę i v a n s a r e v i ć loktę, ľube·znęj mužik pę loktę. kiś-kę pę uśema da loktę." "lokta pę! mij nę pę og lok, važ mužik?!" bara bergęććilas da biva iz da biva kert vartas. ęt-pir vaćkas: molcďeć, mediś: moloďeć. "mij pę ľube·znęj keźa·jin, ćęktan karni?" "vaj pę, etije boštę da leććedę more doras da ęťi kok-pęlas taľištę, a mędsę pę ćašńitę da goznansę pę vaas śi-bitę!" sije kiknannis sija śibitasni, vijasni da moreas, mij-kę, plavajtę seni ęni sija. seśśa sija bęr kaas, stav sarsvotę, bidęn boštas, bidęnlęn. sar gozjasę guśis šedędas, munas, kęn-kę pędvalin viźeni. stavsę kujassę bidęn kišas vićkośis. mędas ovni i sarę puktasni. i ęni vek oleni-vileni. — pom.

32. *pipiriśťi sokol*

1. *gozja olęni da silęn vijim kujim niv. kor-kę olasni-olasni, mamis munę bazar vilę, a naja, kujim niv pećkęni, pukśemaęś da. bazar vilę munę. "men pę te bošt zarńia plaťťe" — šuę nilis, med iźidis. no sija vetlas, vajas zarńia plaťťe. med lun mędas bazar vilę munni. šer-kosis šuę: "men pę te vaj žemćuga plaťťe!" no med lun mam bara vajas. kojmed lun mędasni munni da med źeľais i šuę: "men pę te — baťmamisli šuas — vaj pipiriśťi sokolliś tivksę-tavksę!" no naja bidęn voćeni, vajasni plaťťejas. i šuęni ćojjasis: "vaj pę tajes kijedam, mij pę tajes kijedam, mij pe taje pipiriśťi sokolliś tivk da tavk koris. mijla pę taja, kićće volivlę, kiti ta dorę, aľi mij pipiriśťi sokolis, mij sija, mort aľi mij? me ęd og tęd." no sija kijedasni da gelbeć ęśińtiid volivlę, gelbeć pirid pipiriśťi sokol niv dorad. no sija i naja sećće bidęn jem čuklalasni, med pipiriśťi sokolis bičlaśas. pipiriśťi sokol ędje mędas pirni da stavid i bičlaśas jemad. "no ęni pę me te doriś pišja kujim ękmis mu saje da kujim ękmis va saje da kujim ękmis more saje. te pę menę taźik izmeńitin, bičlalin." a sija veśkę berdę-karę da oz verit, mij ćojjasis sije izmeńitisni. no sija pipiriśťi sokolis pišjas i niv bęrdas, bęrdas, bęrdas daj munę. kotomka boštas daj munę.*

Marpa: "Alas, here he comes, my former husband, my former husband is coming. Now he is going to kill all of us, my former husband." "What rare fortune! My former husband is coming home from somewhere, he has turned up from somewhere and here he comes." "I am certainly coming! Why should I not come, your former husband?" Again he turns round and strikes the flint and the steel together. He strikes it once: and there is a lad; he strikes it again, and there is a lad. "Dear master, what do you command us to do?" "Quick, seize her and take her down to the seashore, tread on one of her legs and tear off the other, and throw both of them into the water!" They kill her and throw both parts of her body into the sea, they are floating there even now. Then he goes back, conquers the whole of the Tsar's country, everything. He releases the Tsar and his wife from the pit, they have been keeping them somewhere in a cellar. He takes all the hides from the church. He begins to live there, he is elected Tsar. And they are still living to this day. — That is the end of the tale.

32. *pipirišťi* falcon

1. There lives a married couple; they have three daughters. (As they thus) live on and on, their mother goes to the market, and they, the three daughters, sit down and begin to spin. "Bring me a golden dress!" — says the eldest daughter. Well, she goes off and brings her a golden dress. Next day she prepares to go to the market. The middle daughter says: "Bring me a pearly dress!" Well, next day the mother again brings a present. The third day they prepare to go again, and the youngest one says: "Bring me" — says she to her parents — "the *ti̮vk-tavk* of the *pipirišťi* falcon!" Well, they do everything, they bring the dresses. The sisters say: "Let us watch her since she has asked for the *ti̮vk-tavk* of the *pipirišťi* falcon. Why did she ask for that? Where and in what way will it come to her? Or what is this *pipirišťi* falcon? Is it a human being or what? I have no idea." They keep watch on her: it arrives through the cellar window; the *pipirišťi* falcon (comes) through the cellar to the girl. They put pins there for the *pipirišťi* falcon to prick itself. The *pipirišťi* falcon wants to get in quickly and it pricks itself on the pins. "Now I shall escape from you to a place which lies beyond three times nine lands, three times nine waters and three times nine seas. You have betrayed me in this way, you have pricked me." Although she sobs, she does not believe that her sisters have hurt it. The *pipirišťi* falcon escapes, the girl weeps and weeps and weeps, and she goes away. She takes her cloak and leaves.

2. *mune̮ da mune̮ da mune̮ da me̮d źemľa·e̮ǯ ki̮ćće-ke̮. mune̮, mune̮, kor-ke̮ voas seče̮m kerkae̮ že̮, pi̮ras ke̮časas. sen mi kojd že̮ babuška vi̮jim. “atte̮ pe̮ ďive̮, ki̮ćće ne̮ pe̮ te me̮din da ki̮ćće munan da?” “a me pe̮ vot me̮di, ki̮ś-ke̮ pe̮ pipiriśťi sokole̮s in-e̮ aǯǯi̮vle̮, ki̮vli̮vle̮?” “aǯǯi̮vlim pe̮, ki̮vlim. tani pe̮ taćće pe̮ joma vi̮le̮ i pi̮ris, joma ordi̮n pe̮ ole̮. no atte̮ pe̮ ďive̮, sija pe̮ voli̮vle̮ ćaste̮ mi orde̮ pukavni̮. biťťe̮ jomai̮sle̮n ni̮li̮s ić-mońi̮s pipiriśťi sokoli̮sle̮n.” no kor-ke̮ i voas pipiriśťi sokolle̮n ić-moń, joma. no sija i me̮das zarńia si̮nane̮n si̮naśni̮. taja, loktis kodi, seni ole̮ babuška ordas da. “ić-mońe, ić-mońe, zev taj tenad mića ti̮nani̮d!” — si̮le̮n ľok ki̮li̮s jomai̮sle̮n pe̮. — “vaj pe̮ taje meni̮m ti̮nante̮!” “a meni̮m-ke̮ pe̮ mužikte̮ śetlan e̮t-pi̮r uźni̮ i śeta. on-ke̮ pe̮, og.” “śeta pe̮, śeta. lok, voli̮, lok pe̮, lok! mi̮j si̮li̮ ǯagale̮, mi̮j si̮li̮ koćkale̮?! mi̮j sija og śet? lok, lok! be̮rťi lok daj!” no be̮rťi sija i mune̮, be̮r joma. joma sija zev že̮ śuś. vi̮ť kežlad sija lokte̮ ki̮ś-ke̮ ve̮ri̮ś pipiriśťi sokol. no sija voas da si̮li̮ zev jona sije vinae̮n juktalas jomai̮d. joma juktalas da me̮d kerkae̮ i ki̮skas, votte̮das pipiriśťi sokolte̮. loktas sija ić-moń da: “mun pe̮, pi̮r!” si̮ dore̮ i pi̮ras ić-mońid, pipiriśťi sokol dorad. jur voǯas pukśas daj be̮rdni̮ me̮das:*

“pipiriśťi sokole̮j,
akaľiste̮vićej,
važ babai̮d voe̮ma.
važ veńećis i̮ǯi̮dǯi̮k,
vi̮ľ veńećid e̮d ǯe̮ľaǯi̮k.
kujim e̮kmi̮s mu sajiś lokti,
kujim e̮kmi̮s va sajiś lokti.
ki̮lan aľi pe̮ on ki̮v,
aǯǯan aľi on aǯǯi,
aľ pe̮ te narošne̮ on śi̮aś?”

3. *joma petas e̮dje̮ǯi̮k. “ńe pe̮ra uźni̮, a pe̮ra ćeććini̮.” be̮r ńin ćuksale̮. i bara loe̮ petni̮ ić-mońli̮, munni̮, iz ki̮vli̮, mi̮j ne̮ uźśema, kod da. no pipiriśťi sokol ćeććas.*

2. She walks on and on and on somewhere, to another land. As she is thus walking, she arrives at a house like this, enters it and sits down in the corner by the door. There is an old woman like us there. "I say, where did you set off for, where are you going?" "Well I set off to see if I could find the *pipiriśťi* falcon somewhere. Have you not seen it somewhere, have you not heard about it?" "We have seen it, we have heard about it. Here, it has come to a witch here, it is living witch the witch. Why, she often comes to see us and sit here. It is said that the witch's daughter is the *pipiriśťi* falcon's young wife." Now the *pipiriśťi* falcon's wife, the witch once comes to see them. And she begins to comb her hair with a golden comb. She (the girl) who has come there still lives with the old woman. "Young wife, young wife, your comb is very beautiful!" The witch lisps (she has a bad tongue, this witch). "Give me your comb!" "Well if you will lend me your husband just once so that I may sleep with him, I'll give it to you. If you won't, then I won't give it to you either." I'll lend him, I'll lend him. Come on, come, come along, come on! What? Surely he won't choke with it, nor will he have a stitch in the side from it. Why should I not lend him? Come, come on, come then!" So then the witch walks home. The witch is very clever. The *pipiriśťi* falcon returns from somewhere in the wood at meal time. He arrives, and the witch gives him a great deal of vodka to drink. The witch makes him drunk and drags him into another house and puts the *pipiriśťi* falcon to bed. The young woman comes (and she says): "Go in!" The young wive enters the room and goes to *pipiriśťi* falcon. She sits by his head and begins to weep:

"My *pipiriśťi* falcon,
my *akaľistęvić*,
your old wife has come to you.
Your old wedding wreath is larger,
your new wedding wreath is smaller.
I have come from beyond three times nine lands,
I have come from beyond three times nine waters.
Do you hear me or do you not hear me,
do you see me or do you not see me,
or are you deliberately not saying a word?"

3. The witch goes out quickly. "There is no time to sleep, but it is time to get up." She calls her back already. The young wife must leave, she must go away, she did not even realize who the *pipiriśťi* falcon was, she had gone to sleep. Well, the *pipiriśťi* falcon gets up. "Phew, what a deep sleep I have

"uf-uf-uf — šue̯ — kuče̯ma ta-lun uźi da kuče̯ma — šue̯ — važ babae̯s ve̯taśi. bi̯ťťe — šue̯ — jur voǯin be̯rde̯." "ptu, kurva, ptu bľadka, mi̯j te ve̯taśan? koz-li̯ske̯n sitante̯ ći̯ški̯ da karta saje ši̯bi̯t! me̯d lun bara sija mune̯ ki̯ćće-ke̯ uǯ vi̯le̯, ki̯ćće-ke̯ pes keravni̯-ľi, mij-ľi pipiriśťi sokol. ić-moń bara sen pukale̯ i rektaśe. (važe̯n ved ki̯eni̯, rektaśeni̯ ve̯li.) zarńia tupi̯ľ vekse̯ rektale̯ ić-moń. bara loktas da. "ić-mońe, ić mońe, zev taj taja tead mića! meni̯m taje on-e̯ śet?" "a ješše̯-ke̯ pipiriśťi sokolte̯ śetan e̯ťi voj uźni̯ i śeta. on-ke̯ pe̯, og." "śeta, śeta, śeta. ta-lun taj uźin; mi̯j si̯li̯ ǯagale̯, mi̯j si̯li̯ koćkale̯? no mi̯j si̯li̯ loe̯? lok be̯rťi daj!" no i bara pipiriśťi sokol voas. joma bara si̯iś jona juktale̯. bara juktale̯, bara ki̯skas me̯d kerkae̯. bara końer ić-moń voas. lun-ti̯r uźas sen bara. bara be̯rdni̯ me̯das, pukśas jur voǯas da:

"pipiriśťi sokole̯j pe̯ da
akaľiste̯vićej,
važ babai̯d voe̯ma,
važ veńećis i̯ǯi̯dǯi̯k,
vi̯ľ veńećis ǯe̯ľaǯi̯k.
kujim e̯kmi̯s mu sajiś lokti,
kujim e̯kmi̯s va sajiś lokti.
te pe̯ taj on ki̯v,
ki̯lan aľi-j on i ki̯v,
aľi pe̯ narošne̯ i on ši̯as?"

4. *bara ńin joma i pete̯. "ńe pe̯ra uźni̯ a, pe̯ra ćeććini̯." bara loe̯ ćeććini̯, munni̯. no i bara muni. bara pipiriśťi sokol: "atte̯, pe̯ ďive̯, mi̯j pe̯ taja ve̯taśi bara pe̯! bi̯ťťe pe̯ važ baba voe̯ma da jur voǯin be̯rde̯." "ptu, kurva, ptu bľadka, mi̯j ve̯taśan? koz-li̯ske̯n sitante̯ ći̯ški̯ da karta saje ši̯bi̯t! mi̯j sije bi̯d lun ve̯taśan?!" no i mune̯ bara. bara kaas taja pipiriśťi sokol ve̯re̯, ki̯ćće-ke̯ i oz uǯav, lun-ti̯r dumajte̯: 'što da taja? mene̯ bi̯d lun juktale̯. a mijla ve̯taśa vek važ babae̯s? me pe̯ taćće gajd le̯śeda da vinase̯ me̯da sećće kiśtavni̯." pipiriśťi sokoli̯s, sija le̯śedas gajd sećće. a mi̯j-ke̯, joma loktas bara pukavni̯ de̯va orde̯. sija me̯das zarńia koreśen ći̯ški̯śni̯, ić-mońid. "ić-mońe, ić-mońe, zev taj tead mića koreťid — ľok ki̯la —, vaj pe̯ taje meni̯m koreťte̯!" "a ne̯šta ke̯ pe̯ śetlan e̯ťi voj uźni̯ pipiriśťi sokolte̯ i śeta, a on-ke̯ pe̯, og." "śeta, śeta. mi̯j si̯li̯ ǯagale̯, mi̯ć koćkale̯, mi̯j si̯li̯ loas? lok, lok*

had today" — says he — "I have been dreaming of my old wife. She seemed to be weeping by my head." "Ugh, slut, ugh, swine, what are you dreaming about? Wipe your bottom with spruce-needles and throw them behind the stable!" The next day the *pipirišťi* falcon again goes to work somewhere, to fell trees or something. And the young wife sits there, spooling thread. (In former times people wove and spooled thread.) The other young woman arrives. "Young wife, young wife, what a beautiful thing you have there! Won't you give it to me?" "I'll give it to you if you once more lend me *pipirišťi* falcon so that I may sleep with him for one night. If you won't, then I won't either." "I will, I will, I will lend him to you. After all, you have slept with him today: surely he will not choke nor will he have a stitch in the side from it. What trouble can come on him? Come on, then!" Again the *pipirišťi* falcon comes home. The witch makes him still more drunk. She makes him drunk and drags him into another house. The poor young wife comes along. She sleeps there the whole day. She sits by his had and again she begins to weep:

"My *pipirišťi* falcon,
my *akaľistęvić*,
your old wife has come to you.
Your old wedding wreath is larger,
your new wedding wreath is smaller.
I have come from beyond three times nine lands,
I have come from beyond three times nine waters.
Do you hear me or do you not hear me,
or are you deliberately not saying a word?"

4. The witch comes there again. "There is not time to sleep; it is time to get up." Again she has to get up and leave. So off she went. And the *pipirišťi* falcon says: "Just imagine, what I have dreamt again! It was as if my old wife had come here and wept by my head." "Ugh, slut, ugh, swine, what are you dreaming of? Wipe your bottom with spruce-needles and throw them behind the stable! What do you dream about all day long?!" Again the *pipirišťi* falcon goes to the woods. He does not work, he thinks all the day long. "What is this? She makes me drunk every day. Why do I dream of my old wife all the time? I shall put a bladder here, under my arm-pit and pour the vodka into it." The *pipirišťi* falcon puts a bladder there. Well, the witch comes again to sit with the widow. She, the young woman, begins to sweep with a golden broom. "Young woman, young woman, it is a very fine broom you have" — she lisps — "give me your

bęrťi daj!" no i bara loktas. bara joma juktalas da juktalas, sija. sija vek gajdje kiśtę pę, kun-ulad lęśedas da i oz koʒʒi. seśśa kiskas, biťťe bara, koʒʒis, uśi. uśkęććas pipiriśťi sokol da. ić-moń loktas i bara jęrtas. "mun, pįr, uź!" pįras ić-moń, bara jona bęrdnį mędas. "no — śuę — peśľednejiś — śuę — lokti."

"pipiriśťi sokolęj da
akaľistęvićej,
važ babaįd so voęma,
važ veńećid įʒįdʒįk,
vįľ veńećid ʒęľaʒįk.
kujim ękmįs mu sajiś lokti,
kujim ękmįs va sajiś lokti.
te — śuę — taj i on i kįv da
narośnę i on śįaś,
seśśa — śuę — ij og volį."

5. *no sija i bara ńin joma petę. "ńe pęra uźnį, a pęra ćeććinį." a mij-kę, ćeććas pipiriśťi sokol da babasę i kvaťitas i kutas. i kįk peľedįs kutas da i okalas. "oj, leʒ — śuę — menę joma aʒʒas, jomaįd ved vijas. te — śuę — in śįaś voʒʒįktę da on śįaślį da." sija i oz leʒ sije ńe-kuʒ. sija munę, sija oz leʒ. no kįś-kę ić-moń loktis, taj ić-moń loktis. "me keť prisluga vįlę pįra, me keť kagasę męda viʒnį" "no viʒ pę, lok!" no ić-mońes vajedis. petalas pipiriśťi sokol da kįtęn ćań vajedas, doďjavlįtęm ćań da bęžas jomasę kęrtalas. da vaćkas vęvlį da gęńajtas da stavsę i lįjlas jomasę. bįdlaę kįćće-kę koľalas da: kęn ki da kęn kok.*

6. *no vot seśśa i ovnį mędasnį gozja, pipiriśťi sokol gozja. (jomalęn bįdęn vįjim.) kor-kę i mamįs loktę, jomalęn, vidlįnį. mam loktę, įʒįd nopja, vaje bįdśamatę nivlį-źaťlį. aʒʒas ki-pęvsę. "tę taje keť i nua kurnan vįlas pę, taje keť nua nįlęlį." kitę aʒʒas da sije keť kurtnį narman vįlas. "in vęrźed, in vęrźed pę, matuška, sija pę ved nįlįdlęn i kiįs." "ptu, kurva, ptu, bľadka, kod-kę,*

broom!" "I'll give it to you if you once again lend me your *pipirišťi* falcon so that I may sleep with him for one night. If you won't, then I won't either." "I'll lend him, I'll lend him. Surely he will not choke and surely he will not have a stitch in the side from it! What trouble can come to him? Come on, come then!" Again the *pipirišťi* falcon comes home. The witch again makes him drink, again and again. He keeps pouring it into the bladder — he puts it under his armpit — and he does not get drunk. Then the witch drags him into another house, (the *pipirišťi* falcon) seems to have got drunk, he falls down on the ground. The *pipirišťi* falcon falls headlong (on purpose). The young wife arrives and she shuts her in with him. "Go in and sleep with him!" The young wife goes in and again begins to weap greatly: "Well" — says she — "this is the last time I come."

"My *pipirišťi* falcon,
my *akaľistęvić*,
look, your old wife has come to you.
Your old wedding wreath is larger,
your new wedding wreath is smaller.
I have come from beyond three times nine lands,
I have come from beyond three times nine waters.
Perhaps — says she — you do not hear me,
or you are deliberately not saying a word;
after this, says she, I shall never again come to you."

5. Well, again the witch comes there. "This is no time to sleep, it is time to get up." And the *pipirišťi* falcon springs up and clasps and takes hold of his wife. He embraces her with both arms and kisses her. "Oh, let me go" — says she — "the witch will see me and kill me. Earlier you did not say a word, and not even now do you say a word." He will not let her go. The other young wife comes out from somewhere. "And I am ready to go with you as a maidservant, or to nurse a child." "Well, come and serve as a nurse!" He takes the young woman with him. The *pipirišťi* falcon goes out of the house and brings a colt from somewhere, an unbroken colt, and he ties the witch to its tail. He strikes at the colt; it gallops away destroying the witch completely. It leaves her limbs lying all over the place, a hand here and a leg there.

6. Well, the married couple, *pipirišťi* falcon and his wife begin to live together. (The witch has got everything.) Once the witch's mother comes to see them. The mother comes along with a big bag full of all kinds of things for her daughter and son-in-law. She catches a glimpse of the one of the arms:

kučem-kẹ ki nịvlẹn menam olẹ?! rịś-ńań soje da rịś-śu-kẹś śoje da lị-bịd że pẹ olẹ." munẹ, munẹ da koksẹ aǯǯas. "taje pẹ nịlẹlị keť i kľuka vịlas nua." "in vẹrźed, in vẹrźed pẹ, taja nịlịdlẹn i kokịs." bara śẹlaśas, śelaśas, bara šualas sije. seśśa jursẹ aǯǯas. "taje pẹ gịrńić vịlẹ nua." śinsẹ aǯǯas. "rẹmpẹštan vịlẹ nua." seśśa joma voas. loktẹ ťẹšča, strećajtas źať. pịras, bịććama sịlị ńin vajas, mịj ńin kolẹ. bara vajedas ćań da sećće kẹrtalas da "mun pẹ nịlịdkẹd!" bara kitẹ-koktẹ lịjlas. seśśa ovnị mẹdasnị da i pom.

33. *poma jịlịś*

1. *važẹn olẹ-vịlẹ gozja. gozjalẹn ẹťi vẹli pi,* p o m a. *kor-kẹ olisnị-olisnị i* p o m a *sija zev dịš. i baťis-mamịs kulinị. sija zev vek paććerịn kujlis, ńi-nẹm iz karlị, ńi-nẹm iz uǯavlị. ńań bịri, paććer kiśśis i vek* p o m a *siǯ olẹ. kor-kẹ olis-olis* p o m a *i čịglị kulẹ. kor-kẹ loktẹ ruć sećće. ruć loktis. "zdorovo,* p o m a*!" "lok, ruće, viǯa!" "*p o m a*, mịj nẹ kujlan, čịglị kulan!" "ẹ, ruće, ńi-nẹm abu śojnịte." "ćẹvlị, me tenẹ vartnị vẹzja kodlị-kẹ, te vartnị mun!" "ćẹv, kod nẹ menẹ, ruće, bośtas vartnịtẹ?" "ćas vẹzja." ruć munas, ẹťilaẹ tarkńitas: "vartịś oz-ẹ kov?" mẹdlaẹ tarkńitas: vartịś oz-ẹ kov?" mẹdlaẹ vetlas: "vartịś ..?" ẹťi šuẹ: "men kolẹ vartịś. mun, ịstị!" "*p o m a*, mun, vetlị, vart, korisnị tenẹ."* p o m a *vetlas, vartas, sen nalị* p o m a *vartas i sịlị verdasnị, sija śojas. juktalasnị, verdasnị i ďeńga śetasnị sịlị. ďeńga śetasnị, grẹš. "*p o m a*, verdisnị-ẹ?" "verdisnị." "ďeńga śetisnị-ẹ?" "śetisnị." "no vaj men, rućlị!" asịv, uźasnị, bara: "*p o m a*, me tenẹ vetla bara vẹzjịnị vartnị." bara ruć munas. pịšjas, ẹťilị vartịś oz-ẹ kov, mẹdlị? "mijan pẹ kolẹ." "no me ịsta vartịś* p o m a *ẹs."* p o m a *munas, bara vartas. bara ďeńga śetasnị, kẹpejka śetasnị i mịj-kẹ [ruć] loktas bara. "*p o m a*, verdisnị-e?" "verdisnị." "no vot ẹd te čịglị kuvnị mẹdẹmid, a vartin da ı verdisnị, ďeńga śetisnị." "śetisnị kẹpejka." nom unẹ kojmẹd lun bara. bara šuẹ: "me tenẹ bara na vẹzja*

"Well now, I shall take this and use it as a rake, I shall take it to my daughter." She catches a glimpse of the arm: it will do well as a rake, I shall rake with it. "Do not touch it, do not touch it, old woman, for it is your own daughter's hand!" "Ugh, slut, ugh, swine, how can it be my daughter's hand! She eats unleavened bread and she drinks kvas with whey, and she has every one of her bones." She goes on and on, and catches a glimpse of her leg. "I shall take this to poke the fire with, and I shall take it for my daughter." "Do not touch it, do not touch it, for it is your own daughter's leg!" Again she spits and spits, and says, the same as before. Then she catches a glimpse of her head. "I shall take this as a pot." She catches the glimpse of her eye. "I take this as a looking-glass." The witch goes on. The mother-in-law arrives, the son-in-law receives her. She enters the house, bringing all kinds of things for her son-in-law, everything he needs. He again brings a colt, ties her to it and says: "Go along with your daughter!" Again it tears her to pieces, scattering her hands and legs. Then they live happily, and that is the end of the tale.

33. About Poma

1. Once upon a time there lived a married couple. The married couple had a son, Poma. Poma was very lazy; as they lived on and on like this, his parents died suddenly. He was always lying on top of the stove, not doing anything, never doing any work. He ran out of bread, the stove fell apart, yet Poma still lived like this. Poma lived on and on and he was nearly dying of starvation. Once the fox came up to him. The fox arrived. "Good day to you, Poma!" "Hallo, fox, come along!" "Poma, why are you lying there lazily, you will die of starvation!" "Alas, fox, I have nothing to eat." "Just wait; I shall hire you out as a thresher, go and thresh for somebody!" "Don't bother, fox; who would be willing to engage me as a thresher?" "I'll soon hire you out." He knocks at one place: "Do you need a thresher?" He knocks at another place: "Do you need a thresher?" Then he walks to a different place: "A thresher . . . ?" One of them says: "I need a thresher. Go and send him here!" "Poma, go and start threshing! They have engaged you." Poma goes out to thresh. Poma threshes there for them, they give him food to eat, and he eats. They give him to eat and to drink, and they also give him money, a farthing. "Poma, did they give you food to eat?" "Yes, they did." "Did they give you money?" "Yes, they did." "Well, give it to me then, to the fox!" They go to sleep, and in the morning the fox says: "Poma, once more I'm going to get you a job as a thresher." The fox goes out again. He runs about to find a place where one or another

vartnį.'' bara ruć pįšjalas bara: ''vartnį kolę, oz?'' p o m a bara munas, vartas. bara sije verdasnį, bara ďeńga śetasnį. ''no vot ęd, p o m a, śetisnį déńga?'' ''śetisnį.'' ''verdisnį?'' ''verdisnį.'' ''me muna, vetla sar ordę ďeńga merajtnį ćetverikla.'' ''ćęv, jęj ruć'' — p o m a šuę. ''mįjla nę ďeńga ćetverik?'' ''te ćevo, ńi-nęm on tęd'' — p o m alį šuę.

2. *ruć munas. pįras sar ordę. ''viǯa tijan!'' ''lok, viǯa!'' bęž śujas lavić ulę. ''me ęd, sarvennęj ćelovek baťuško, zev iǯid mogęn lokti.'' ''mįj nę tenad mogįs—'' — šuis. ''menam? ďeńga merajtan ćetverikte on-ę śetlį, kęrt ćetveriktę?'' ''no kod nę ńin tijan taćęm ozįrįs?'' ''mijan s k o r o b o g a · t ę j p o m a vijim da silęn ďeńgaįs una da og vermę ščętajtnįsę. ćetveriktę vajlį!'' ''no na, mįj nę ćetverik og śetlį?'' ćetverik śetas. munas, ćetverikę śujas eťi kolasę gręš, mędę kępejka, kojmędę dve kopejki. stavsę końerlįś i śujlas p o m alįś ďeńgasę. i ędjeǯik sarlį bęr pįšjedas ćetverik. voas. ''no, ruće, ďeńgatę merajtin?'' ''merajti.'' ''una-ę loi?'' ''a sarvennęj ćelovek baťuško, lįdtęm-ščęttęm, lįd ńi ščęt abu, eg vermę tędnį.'' ''no attę ďivę, kučęm nę sećęm ozįr vijim tijan, s k o r o b o g a · t e j p o m a! me ig kįvlįvlį.'' ''vijim s k o r o b o g a · t ę j p o m a mijan zev ozįr.'' no ruć bara munas gortas. sar i šuę: ''attę ďivę, mįj nę, kučęm taja ďeńga merajtįś, a pęrjalę-kę a? ćas me pįrkńita, kįćće-kę veśkę kolasas pįris, ďeńga-kę merajtis.'' ęt-pįr pįrkńitas: gręš, mędįś pįrkńitas: kępejka, kojmędįś pįrkńitas: dve kopejki. ''oj, zabiľ pę taj sija ozįr vęlęma, ćetveriknad merajtęma.'' bįdęn ďeńgaįs uśalis. no beda zev ozįr. zev sar ďivujćće.*

3. *ruć i šuę: ''p o m a, me sar ordę koraśnį vetla seśśa.'' ''ćęv, jęj ruć! mįj nę me saje śetasnį m a r p a s a r o · v n aes, sarlęn nįv?!'' ''mi ordę loktas. te ćęv ov, ńi-nęm on tęd. me muna koraśnį.'' ruć bara munę koraśnį. no bara loktas, pįras. ''me iǯid mogęn bara, sarvennęj ćelovek baťuško, lokti.'' ''mįj nę ńin tenad iǯid mogįd bara?'' — šuis. ''a me, m a r p a s a r o v n asę taj s k o r o b o g a · t ę j p o m a įstis koraśnį. attę ďivę, mįj nę taćęm ozįr saje ńin śetan-kę a?'' sar uďivľajćće, sarlį okota śetnį. no sar i: ''lęśeććam, no lęśeććam.''*

needs a thresher. "We need one." "Well, I'll send you Poma who is a thresher." Poma goes out and threshes again. Again they give him money, a kopeck, and the . . . er . . . the fox arrives. "Poma, did they give you food to eat?" "Yes, they did." "Well, you see, you wanted to starve to death, you went to thresh, and they gave you food to eat and gave you money, too." "Yes, they gave me a kopeck." Well, on the third day he goes out again. He says: "Again I shall hire you out as a thresher." The fox runs around again: "Do you need a thresher?" Poma goes out to thresh again. He is entertained and given some money. "Well, Poma, did they give you money?" "Yes, they did." "Did they give you food to eat?" "Yes, they did." "I'm off to the Tsar for his money-counting machine." "Hold your tongue, you stupid fox!" — says Poma. — "What use is a money-counting machine?" "You don' know anything!" — says he to Poma.

2. The fox goes away. He goes in to see the Tsar. "Hail to you!" "Hallo, come in!" He hides his tail under the bench. "All-Highest Father Tsar, I have come on very important business." "And what is this business of yours?" — asked he. "My business? Will you lend me your money-counter, your iron money-counting machine?" "Well, whoever is so rich among you?" "We have a suddenly-enriched Poma; he has a lot of money, and we are unable to count it. Lend us your counting-machined!" "Well, why should I not lend it to you." He lends him the machine. Into one of the slits of the counting-machine the fox slips a farthing, in the second a kopeck, and in the third two kopecks. He thrusts all the coins poor Poma has got into the counting-machine. And he goes and quickly returns the counting-machine to the Tsar. "Well, fox, have you counted the coins?" "Yes, we have." "And were there such a lot?" "Well, All-Highest Father Tsar, they were countless, numberless indeed, there is no way of telling how much there was, we could not find out." "Devil take it! your suddenly-enriched Poma must be a very rich fellow! I have never heard of him." "Yes, our suddenly-enriched Poma is very rich indeed." "Why, what is the matter with this counting-machine? Has it lied? I'll shake it, perhaps the slits are clogged by coins that got in while you were counting." He shakes it once: there is a farthing; he shakes it a second time: a kopeck; he shakes it a third time: two kopecks. "Oh, he must be rich indeed; he did use it!" All the coins dropped out. Yes, he is very rich. The Tsar is very much amazed.

3. The fox says: "Now I am going to ask the hand of the Tsar's daughter for you." "Hold your tongue, stupid fox! how should they give me Tsarevna Marpa? She is the Tsar's daughter!" "She will be married to you! Keep silent, you don't know anything! I am going to ask for her." The fox goes to ask for the girl's hand. He arrives and enters. "Again I have

le̮śeććisni̮. “svaďba kare̮, vaje, mi loktam svaďbae̮n” — ruć voas. “no, p o m a, ge̮to·v svaďba vi̮le̮? sar śete̮ m a r p a s a r o v n ae̮s.” “je̮j ruć, mi̮j ne̮ me saje śetas? plaťťe̮is, ńi-ne̮m abu.” luge̮ leććas da bi̮d ćvet e̮ktas da e̮ktas ruć da si̮le̮n kiśśema plaťťe̮id. sukmani̮dle̮n sećće kolasas śujalas da śujalas, da śujalas da kuz̮ ćvet ćveťite̮ p o m a. no sija aśśe̮ votte̮das vorje (sija staruška paććeri̮n kujle̮ da ńi-ne̮m oz ti̮dav). sije votte̮das, lojlas, lojlas, mi̮śkas sije, bi̮de̮n jez̮i̮d loe̮. no seśśa i “vaj, leććam!” pur karasni̮ va vi̮le̮ da sećće ti̮r ćurkajas suvte̮dlas ruć p o m ali̮ da ćeććas da sećće i pukśasni̮ i ki̮vtasni̮ sar dore̮. voni̮ me̮dasni̮. purte̮, stavse̮ paze̮dlas, ćurkajasse̮ bi̮de̮n je̮tlalas, aćis berege̮. ľok plaťťete̮, ćveta plaťťete̮ kuľas, vae̮ be̮r śi̮bi̮tas ruć i mi̮j-ke̮e̮s i pi̮ž ule̮ i pukśedas, p o m ae̮s paśte̮gi̮s. bara e̮djez̮i̮ka sar orde̮ pi̮šjas, p o m a pi̮ž uli̮n. “atte̮, sarvenne̮j ćelovek baťuško, mi̮j-ke̮ ti on že̮ ćajte̮, mijan stav ke̮liś-pi̮gi̮di̮d ve̮ji, mijan ńe-kod iz koľ, bi̮de̮n ve̮jisni̮. že̮ńiki̮d zev sija śuś da paśte̮g kuľśis da plaťťese̮ śi̮bitis da ujis. a me kuz̮-ke̮ bara uji. a ńe-kod seśśa abu, mijan ke̮liś-pi̮gi̮di̮d, ńe-kod iz lo, bi̮de̮n ve̮jini̮. atte̮ ďive̮, sija pi̮ž uli̮n že̮ńiki̮d pukale̮, paśte̮gi̮d kani̮te̮ oz liśti̮, plaťťete̮ koris.” no sar leććedas, kod te̮de̮, kuče̮m bur plaťťe p o m ali̮. p o m ali̮ vajasni̮, paśte̮dasni̮, p o m ali̮ ľube̮, jona zev. “a ruće, že̮ńiki̮d-ke̮ je̮j-a, ńumjale̮ taj jona!” “ka, mi̮j ne̮ pe̮ — ruć śue̮ — sija oz ńumjav?! taje pe̮ me i ri̮t-pukavmi̮ og paśtavli̮, seče̮m plaťťese̮.” no ješše̮ bure̮s leććedasni̮-karasni̮ da sarle̮n. bara p o m a paśte̮dasni̮, bara ńumjale̮. “ruće, že̮ńiki̮d je̮j!” “će̮v, abu je̮j! kuče̮m?! tae̮n pe̮ me ge̮śťitni̮ og vetli̮vli̮, kuče̮m ne̮ taja, svaďba vi̮le̮ da veńeć dore̮ plaťťe?! atte̮ ďive!” leććedasni̮ i sarske̮j plaťťe. sija i gre̮źitas. “te ke̮ pe̮, p o m a, ńumjalan, smotri, in ńumjav!” no leććedasni̮. paśte̮dasni̮, p o m a oz ńumjav. no i pukśedasni̮, kate̮dasni̮ že̮ńike̮s. pirujtasni̮-parujtasni̮, kod te̮de̮, kuz̮, mi̮j di̮ra. “no p o m a, te vajed svaďbate̮, me muna da le̮śeda pi̮zan, mi̮j vi̮jim, svaďbate̮ teni̮d. gortad muna da ľok kerkaad.”

come on important business, All-Highest Father Tsar." "Well, what is your business?" — asked he. "Well, I have come . . ., the suddenly-enriched Poma has sent me to ask for Tsarevna Marpa's hand. Will you give her to such a rich man?" The Tsar is amazed, he is glad to give her to him in marriage. Well, says the Tsar: "We'll make an agreement, we'll make an agreement." They made an agreement. "Arrange the wedding, we shall come with the wedding-party" — says the fox. "Well, Poma, are you ready for the wedding? The Tsar is willing to give you Tsarevna Marpa." "Stupid fox, why should he give her to me? I have no clothes, I have nothing." The fox goes out into the meadow and collects all kinds of flowers for Poma's clothes are ragged. He pokes the flowers into the holes of Poma's frieze caftan, and Poma blossoms like a flower. He lays Poma in a wash-tub (the old woman lies on the top of the stove and sees nothing). He lays him in it, and kneads and kneads him, washing him until he is completely clean. Then he says: "Let us go!" They make a raft for the water, the fox sets up logs for Poma; he jumps on, and sitting on the raft they travel down the river to see the Tsar. They draw near. The fox breaks the raft into little pieces, pushes away all the logs, and jumps on the bank. The fox tears in pieces the old clothes, the flowery clothes, and throws them back into the water, and makes Poma sit beneath the boat, naked. Again he quickly runs to the Tsar, while Poma stays under the boat. "Alas, All-Highest Father Tsar, imagine, the whole of our wedding-party has drowned, nobody has survived, all of them have drowned. The bridegroom is a very clever man, he undressed himself and threw away all his clothes and swam to the bank. Somehow I managed to swim out too. Now there is nobody, nobody is remained alive, the whole of our wedding party has drowned. And the bridegroom is sitting under the boat, he is shy to go naked and he asks for clothes." Now who knows what fine clothes the Tsar orders to be taken to Poma. They are brought to Poma. They dress him. Poma feels comfortable and has a broad smile on his face. "But fox, the bridegroom is a fool; he does nothing but smile." "Oh, why should he not keep smiling?" — says the fox. "I would not dress up in such clothes even for an evening party!" Well, the Tsar had still better clothes made for him, and brought to him. Poma is dressed again, and again he smiles. "Fox, the bridegroom is a fool!" "Hold your tongue! He is not a fool! Why! I would not go visiting in such clothes, what kind of clothes are these for a wedding feast, a marriage? Devil take it!" They order clothes fit for a Tsar. The fox warns him: "If you smile once more . . . well, just listen, don't smile!" They take him the clothes. They dress him. Poma does not smile. Well, they seat the bridegroom on the boat, and take him away. They feasted and made

4. ruć mune̮. pi̮šjas, pi̮šjas, me̮sjas una zev viǯeni̮. “pijanjase̮, kodli̮ me̮sse̮ viǯanni̮d?” “mi — šue̮ — taje kupećli̮.” “o — šue̮ — lokte̮ g r e̮ m a m a- l a · ń ń a, bite̮g sote̮, vate̮g kuse̮de̮, be̮žnas pe̮ ći̮škovte̮. ti pe̮ viśtale̮, jualasni̮, lokni̮ me̮das sija da ’mi pe̮ taja s k o r o b o g a · t e̮ j p o m ali̮ viǯam me̮s-jasse̮.’ ” mune̮, mune̮, ve̮vjas viǯeni̮ una. bara šue̮: “kodli̮, pijane̮, ve̮vjaste̮ viǯanni̮d?” “mi — šue̮ — taje kupećli̮.” “a lokte̮ — šue̮ — g r e̮ m a m a - l a ń ń a, bite̮g sote̮, vate̮g kuse̮de̮, be̮žnas ći̮škovte̮. ti — šue̮ — viśtale̮, s k o r o- b o g a · t e̮ j p o m ali̮. on-ke̮ šue̮, stavse̮ sotas.” no mune̮, mune̮, ižjas, kod te̮de̮, mi̮j viǯeni̮ bara. “kodli̮, pijane̮, viǯanni̮d?” “mi — šue̮ — taje kupećli̮.” “a ti — šue̮ — viśtale̮, g r e̮ m a m a l a · ń ń a lokte̮, bite̮g sote̮, vate̮g kuse̮de̮, be̮žnas ći̮škovte̮, ti — šue̮ — viśtale̮, s k o r o b o g a · t e̮ j p o m ali̮.” no, no, naja bi̮de̮n povźasni̮. no voas ruć, e̮djeǯi̮k ruć pi̮šjas, kupeć orde̮ pi̮ras, kodli̮ viǯale̮ni̮. “viǯa tijan!” “lok, viǯa!” “oj-oj, ta-lun lokte̮ g r e̮ m a m a l a · ń ń a, bite̮g sote̮, vate̮g kuse̮de̮, be̮žnas ći̮škovte. vaje, e̮djeǯi̮k, svaďba le̮śede̮!” svaď-bujtni̮ kutasni̮ naja. no naja povźasni̮, svaďba le̮śedasni̮, kod te̮de̮, kupećeske̮j kuće̮m bura. “a aśni̮d, med oz vini̮ tijane̮s, pi̮re̮ pi̮vśane̮! me tijan iʒ́as pi̮rta.” iʒ́as sećće pi̮rtas i: “tan kujli̮le̮-ole̮!” kupeć-gozja leććasni̮, pi̮rasni̮ pi̮vśanas. ruć bi čuke̮das da stavi̮s i soććas. kupeć-gozja i oz lo.

5. no kor-ke̮ i p o m a lokte̮ svaďbae̮n. p o m a svaďbae̮n lokte̮, me̮s-viǯiśja-se̮s aʒ́ʒ́as, suvtas: “tijanjase̮, kodli̮, ta mi̮da me̮sjasse̮ viǯanni̮d?” “mi — šue̮ — taja s k o r o b o g a · t e j p o m ali̮.” “no, taje — šue̮ — zev že̮ ozi̮r.” mune̮, mune̮, ve̮v-viǯiśjase̮s aʒ́ʒ́as, zev una viǯeni̮. “tijanjase̮, kodli̮ viǯanni̮d ve̮vse̮?” “mi — šue̮ — taja p o m ali̮, s k o r o b o g a · t e̮ j p o m ali̮.” “no, atte̮ — šue̮ — ozi̮r že̮, zbi̮ľ že̮ — šue̮ — taja ozi̮r ve̮le̮ma, ćetveriknas ďeńgate̮ merajtis da.” mune̮, mune̮, i̮ž-viǯiśjase̮s aʒ́ʒ́as: “kodli̮ viǯanni̮d, tijanjase̮?” “mi — šue̮ — s k o r o b o g a · t e̮ j p o m ali̮.” no i zev bur, bi̮de̮n vi̮jim p o m ale̮n i s k o r o b o g a · t e̮ j p o m a i vi̮jim. mune̮, mune̮ p o m a sija. “no vaj, nue̮d gortad!” — sar šue̮. nue̮de̮ gortad (kuče̮m-ke̮ mi kojd že̮ ľok kerka, stavi̮s kiśśe-

merry, for how long no one knows. "Well, Poma, you fetch the wedding party while I go and lay the table, with what we have got. I shall go home to your rubbishy old house."

4. The fox goes away. He runs and runs. They are grazing many cattle by the road. "Boys, whose cattle are you guarding?" "We" — they say — "are guarding the cattle belonging to this merchant." "Gręma Malańńa is coming" — says he — "and she will burn you up without fire, quench you without water and sweep you away with her tail. She is coming this way, and if she asks you, you must say: 'We are grazing the suddenly-enriched Pomas's cattle'." He goes on and people are herding a large number of horses. He again asks them: "Boys, whose horses are you guarding?" "These" — they say — "belong to this merchant." "Well" — says he — "Gręma Malańńa is coming and she will burn you up without fire, quench you without water, and sweep you away with her tail. You must say that they belong to the suddenly-enriched Poma. If you do not say so, she will burn up everything." Well, he goes on. They are pasturing a flock of sheep or something. "Boys, whose sheep are you guarding?" "They belong to this merchant." — answer they. "Well, you must say, — Gręma Malańńa is coming, and she will burn up everything without fire, quench without water, and sweep away everything with her tail, — that these belong to suddenly-enriched Poma." Well now, they all became scared. The fox comes and runs quickly to the merchant whose beasts they are guarding. "Hallo!" "Hallo, come along!" "Alas, alas, today Gręma Malańńa arrives, she burns everything without fire, quenches without water, and will sweep you away with her tail. Go to it, arrange a wedding at once!" They make preparations for a wedding feast. They were scared, and who knows what a fine merchant wedding they arranged. "And if you do not want to be killed by her, go into the bath-house. I'll take some straw for you." He takes straw there for them: "Stay here and lie down!" The merchant and his wife go into the bath-house. The fox sets fire to the bath-house, and they all burn in it. The merchant and his wife are no longer.

5. Well, Poma comes along sometime with the wedding-party. The Tsar catches sight of the cowboys and stops them. "Whose vast herd of cattle are youg guarding here?" "They belong" — they answer — "to suddenly-enriched Poma." "Well" — says the Tsar — "he is very rich." They go on and on, and the Tsar catches sight of horseherds guarding very many horses. "Whose horses are qou guarding here?" "They are Poma's, suddenly-enriched Poma's" — they answer. "Well then, he is indeed rich, he has counted his money with the counting-machine." They go on and on and on, and the Tsar catches sight of the shepherds. "Whose sheep are you guard-

ma, ʒeľa ęšinjasa) sećće nuędę p o m a *sar-gozjatę, mi̮j-kętę, kęli̮śtę. a ruć aʒʒas, voćća loktę. "*p o m a*, taćće lok,* p o m a*, kupeć ordas,* p o m a, p o m a*!" "a ruće, taje-kę žeńiki̮d jęj a, mi̮j-kę kerkasę taj iz tęd?!" "a mi̮j — šuę — jęj sija. seti — šuę da gęgertę da loktę vęli." no vajedasni̮, pi̮risni̮, pirujtasni̮-parujtasni̮.* m a r p a   s a r o v n aęs *śetasni̮, bi̮dęn loę, bi̮dęn kupećlęn vi̮jim: ďeńgai̮d i, ńańid i, olęmi̮d i. ęni olęni̮ kęn-kę vek* p o m a*-gozja.*

34. *nori̮mę ďaďe*

1. *n o r i̮ m ę   ď a ď e lapťi ki̮jas. "no me lapťięn muna tęrgujtni̮." munę* n o r i̮ m ę   ď a ď e *lapťięn tęrgujtni̮. ʒeľińʒik kerka voas, męs-ťuťiś ʒuʒi̮dʒi̮k, megi̮riś ľapki̮dʒi̮k. "ďida kosa-mesańjasę, on-e leʒe menę uźni̮?" "leʒam, leʒam,* n o r i̮ m ę   ď a ď ę*, uź!" "attę, meam veśkę lapťi vi̮jim da kićće me pukta?" "kurępjas dorę, kurępjas dorę." ďida kosa mesańjas unmovśasni̮,* n o r i̮ m ę   ď a ď e *leććilas, lapťi kośalas. asi̮v-voʒ ćeććas. "no, ďida kosa mesańjas, vaje žę meni̮m lapťitę!" ćeććasni̮. "oj,* n o r i̮ m ę   ď a ď e, *lapťitę kurępjasi̮d i śojemaęś, kośalęmaęś i bi̮dęn." "ęksi̮ pili̮ jurbita, bajar pili̮ śo šajt beda kara." "*n o r i̮ m ę   ď a ď e*, in kar, in kar! tenid med bur kurępsę śetam." ețik kurępen mędęććas. kurep śurę, kurępen munas. munas, bara kerka voas, ʒeľińʒik. "ďida kosa mesańjasę, on-ę leʒe mene uźni̮?" "uź, nori̮mę ďaďe, uź!"* attę, *meam veśkę kurep vi̮jim da kićće nę kurępsę pukta?" "mežjas dore, mežjas dorę." mež dorę puktas. leććilas* n o r i̮ m ę   ď a ď e*, kurep ʒagędas, bęr vodas. asi̮v-voʒ ćeććas i šuę: "no, ďida kosa mesańjas, vaje meni̮m kurępte!" ćeććasni̮. "o-o,* n o r i̮ m ę   ď a ď e*, mežjasi̮d ʒagędęmaęś kurępte tenśi̮d." "ęksi̮ pili̮ jurbi̮ta, bajar pili̮ śo šajt beda kara." "oj,* n o r i̮ m ę   ď a ď e*, in kar, in kar! ten med bur mežsę śetam." mež śetasni̮. mędęććas. munas, bara ʒeľińʒik kerka voas. "ďida kosa mesańjas, leʒe menę uźni̮!" "uź,* n o r i̮ m ę   ď a ď e*, uź!" "attę, meam, veśkę mež vi̮jim da kićće menśim mežsę pukta?" "porśjas dorę, porśjas dorę." porś dorę puktasni̮. leććilas, mežjes, jur ʒigľetas, mež kulę,*

ing?" "We are guarding the sheep of suddenly-enriched Poma" — they answer. "Very good, Poma has everything. It is no surprise that he is the suddenly-enriched Poma." Poma goes on and on. "Take us to your house!" — says the Tsar. He takes them home (the house is an old one like this, tumbledown and small-windowed). Poma takes the Tsar and his wife and the wedding-party there. The fox catches sight of them, and goes to meet them. "Poma, come here, Poma, come to the merchant's, Poma, Poma!" "But fox, this bridegroom is a fool! Doesn't he know his own house?" "How should he be a fool?" — answers he. "He is going that way, taking a turn and here he comes back." Well, they take the wedding-party there, enter the house, feast and make merry. Tsarevna Marpa is wedded to him, they have everything, the merchant had got everything: money, corn and wealth. Even today, Poma and his wife are still alive somewhere.

34. Uncle Norim̦ȩ

1. Uncle Norim̦ȩ is making sandals of bast. "Well, I shall go and trade with these bast sandals." Uncle Norim̦ȩ goes off to trade with the bast sandals. He arrives at a tiny little house: it is taller than a bull's cock but lower than a yoke. "You women cooks with scythes in the stable, will you let me in to sleep?" "We'll let you in, we'll let you in, Uncle Norim̦ȩ. Come and sleep here!" "See here! I have some sandals of bast. Where can I put them?" "By the hens, by the hens." The women cooks with scythes in the stable go to sleep, Uncle Norim̦ȩ gets off the bed and tears the bast sandals to pieces. He gets up early in the morning. "Here, you women cooks with scythes in the stable, give the bast sandals back to me!" They get up. "Oh dear, Uncle Norim̦ȩ, the hens have torn apart and eaten up all the bast sandals." "I bow my head before the prince's son, I cause a hundred roubles' damage to the boyar's son." "Do not do that, Uncle Norim̦ȩ, do not do that! We will give you the best hen we have." He sets out with one hen. He has got a hen, he goes away with the hen. He goes on, again he arrives at a little house. "You women cooks with scythes in the stable, will you let me in to sleep?" "Sleep, Uncle Norim̦ȩ, sleep here!" "See here! I have a hen, where shall I put the hen?" "By the rams, by the rams!" He puts the hen by the rams. Uncle Norim̦ȩ gets off the bed, strangles the hen and goes to bed again. He gets up early in the morning and says: "Come now, women cooks with scythes in the stable, bring me the hen!" They get up. "Oh, Uncle Norim̦ȩ, the rams have strangled your hen." "I bow my head before the prince's son, I cause a hundred roubles' damage to boyar's son." "Oh dear, Uncle Norim̦ȩ, do not do that, do not do that! We will give you

bara vodas. asi̮v-voʒ̇ ćeććas. “ďida kosa mesańjas, vaje meni̮m mežte̮!” ćeććasni̮. “oj-oj-o, n o r i̮ m e̮ ď a ď e, mežte̮ porśjasi̮d kurććale̮mae̮ś, vijemae̮ś.” “e̮ksi̮ pili̮ jurbita, bajar pili̮ śo šajt beda kara.” “o, n o r i̮ m e̮ ď a ď e, in kar, in kar! me ten med bur porśes śeta.” da i porś śetas, porśen me̮de̮ćće. munas, munas, bara kerka, ʒ̇e̮ľińʒ̇ik voas, me̮s-ćupi̮ś ʒ̇uʒ̇i̮dʒ̇ik, megi̮ri̮ś ľapki̮dʒ̇i̮k. “ďida kosa mesańjase̮, on-e̮ mene̮ leʒ̇e uźni̮?” “leʒ̇am, leʒ̇am, n o r i̮ m e̮ ď a ď e, uź!” atte̮, meam veśke̮ porś vi̮jim da ki̮ćće me porśse̮ pukta?” “e̮šjas dore.” no e̮š dore̮ puktas. n o r i̮ m e̮ ď a ď e leććilas. ćer boštas, porśli̮ ki̮me̮sas śetalas, śetalas. porś i kule̮. bara vodas. asi̮v-voʒ̇ ćeććas. “no, ďida kosa mesańjas, vaje ʒ̇e̮ meni̮m porśte̮!” leććasni̮. “oj, n o r i̮ m e̮ ď a ď e, porśte̮ i e̮ški̮d vijema.” “e̮ksi̮ pili̮ jurbita, bajar pili̮ śo šajt beda kara.” “oj, n o r i̮ m e̮ ď a ď e, in kar, in kar! med bur e̮šse̮ śetam.” e̮ške̮s boštas, e̮ške̮s dođđalas; porś puktas, kure̮g puktas, mež puktas. ki̮ske̮. bara kerka voas. “ďida kosa mesańjas, leʒ̇e mene̮ uźni̮!” “uź, n o r i̮ m e̮ ď a ď e, uź!” “atte̮, menam eśke̮ e̮š vi̮jim. da ki̮ćće ne̮ me sije e̮šse̮ pukta?” “ve̮vjas dore̮.” ve̮vjas dore̮ leććas. ćer bara boštas, ćer-ti̮ške̮n e̮šli̮ ne̮šalas ki̮me̮sas. e̮š i bara kule̮. bara vodas. bara ćeććas asi̮v-voʒ̇. “no, vaje meni̮m e̮šte̮!” “oj-oj, n o r i̮ m e̮ ď a ď e, e̮šte̮ ve̮vjasi̮d vijemae̮ś. ćužjale̮mae̮ś.” “e̮ksi̮ pili̮ jurbita, bajar pili̮ śo šajt beda kara.” “in kar, in kar! mi teni̮d i med bur ve̮vse̮ śetam.” no ve̮v śetasni̮. ve̮v dođđalas.

2. vot i n o r i̮ m e̮ ď a ď e me̮de̮ććas gorte̮. e̮š puktas dođđe, porś puktas, mež puktas, kure̮g puktas. munas daj śile̮:

lapťi ki̮jis kure̮ge̮s,
kure̮g ki̮jis mežjes,
mež ki̮jis porśes,

the best ram!" They give him a ram. He sets out. He goes on, and again he arrives at a small house. "Women cooks with scythes in the stable, let me in to sleep!" "Sleep, Uncle Norimę, sleep here!" "See here, I have a ram, where can I put my ram?" "By the pigs, by the pigs." He puts the ram by the pigs. He gets off the bed, wrings the ram's neck, and the ram dies. He goes to bed again. He gets up early in the morning. "Women cooks with scythes in the stable, bring me the ram!" They get up. "Oh dear, oh dear, Uncle Norimę, the ram has been bitten to death by the pigs, they have killed it." "I bow my head before the prince's son, I cause a hundred roubles' damage to the boyar's son." "Oh, Uncle Norimę, do not do that, do not do that! I'll give you the best pig we have." She gives him the pig, and he sets out with the pig. He goes on and on, and again he arrives at a little house: it is taller than a cow's udder but lower than a yoke. "Women cooks with scythes in the stable, will you let me in to sleep?" "We'll let you in, we'll let you in, Uncle Norimę, sleep here!" "Look, I have a pig here, where shall I put it?" "By the oxen." So he puts it by the oxen. Uncle Norimę gets off the bed, takes a hatchet and strikes the pig on the forehead. And the pig dies too. He goes to bed again. Early in the morning he gets up. "Now, women cooks with scythes in the stable, bring me the pig!" They get out of bed. "Oh dear, Uncle Norimę, the pig has been killed by the ox." "I bow my head before the prince's son, I cause a hundred roubles' damage to the boyar's son." "Oh, Uncle Norimę, do not do that, do not do that! We'll give you the best ox." He takes the ox, harnesses it and loads up the pig, the hen and the ram. He pulls them all. Again he arrives at a house. "Women cooks with scythes in the stable, let me in to sleep!" "Sleep, Uncle Norimę, sleep here!" "But see, I have an ox here, so where shall I put this ox?" "By the horses!" He goes down to the horses. Again he takes the axe and hits the ox on the forehead with axe-head. The ox dies too. He goes back to bed. Early in the morning he gets up again. "Now, bring me the ox!" "Oh dear, oh dear, Uncle Norimę, the ox has been killed by the horses, they have kicked it to death." "I bow my head before the Tsar's son, I cause a hundred roubles' damage to the boyar's son." "Do not do that, do not that! We'll give you the best horse." They give him the horse. He harnesses the horse.

2. Well now, Uncle Norimę starts for home. He puts the ox, the pig, the ram, and the hen on the sleigh. He goes along singing:

> The sandal of bast caught the hen,
> The hen caught the ram,
> The ram caught the pig,

porś kịjis ẹškẹs,
ẹš kịjis vẹlẹs.

kẹć loktẹ. "attẹ, n o r ị m ẹ ď a ď e, zev taj mićaa śilan! menẹ on bośt?" "lok, lok, pukśi! mịjla og bośt?" bara śilẹ:

lapťi kịjis kurẹgẹs,
. . . .

vot i ruć pịšje. "oj, n o r ị m ẹ ď a ď e, zev taj mićaa śilan! menẹ on bośt?" "lok, lok! vot i rućes pukśedas." bara śivnị gorẹdas:

lapťi kịjis kurẹgẹs,
. . . .

kẹjin munẹ. "oj, n o r ị m ẹ ď a ď e, zev taj mićaa śilan! menẹ on bośt?" "lok, pukśi!" no i bara śivnị gorẹdas:

lapťi kịjis kurẹgẹs,
. . . .

oš loktẹ. "oj, taj, n o r ị m ẹ ď a ď e zev mićaa śilan! menẹ on bośt?" "lok, pukśi! bośta. mịjla og bośt?" vot oš pukśas. munasnị, bara śivnị gorẹdas:

lapťi kịjis kurẹgẹs,
. . . .

n o r ị m ẹ ď a ď elẹn i zavedkaịs orẹ. "kẹće, mun, vetlị ćerla!" "dịš men." "ruće, mun, te vetlị!" "dịš men." "kẹjin, mun, te vetlị!" "dịš men." "oškẹ, mun, te vetlị!" "dịš men." "oškẹ, mun, te vetlị!" "dịš men." a skẹrmas n o r ị m ẹ ď a ď e. munas ćer korśnị. sek kosta vẹvsẹ kuľasnị, jajsẹ śojasnị i vẹv bịdẹn śojasnị. vẹlas i iẓas śujalasnị. n o r ị m ẹ ď a ď e loktas. oj-oj-oj, porś abu, ẹš abu i kurẹg abu i ńi-nẹm abu, bịdẹn śojemaẹś i munẹmaẹś ńin, ẹtnas koľema. vẹv sulalẹ, vẹv suvtẹdẹmaẹś. vẹvlị žvić vartas, vẹv perẹ. "attẹ, beda, no i

The pig caught the ox,
The ox caught the horse.

The hare comes along. "I say, Uncle Nori̯mę, that's a fine song you are singing! Won't you take me on your sleigh?" "Come on, come and get on it! Why shouldn't I take you?" Again he sings:

The sandals of bast caught the hen.
. . .

See! The fox runs up. "Uncle Nori̯mę, that's a fine song you are singing! Won't you take me on your sleigh?" "Come on, come on!" He lets the fox on to the sleigh too. Again he begins to sing:

The sandal of bast caught the hen.
. . .

There comes the wolf. "Oh, Uncle Nori̯mę, that's a fine song you are singing! Won't you take me too?" "Come on, get on!" Well, then he begins to sing again:

The sandal of bast caught the hen.
. . .

Here comes the bear. "Oh, Uncle Nori̯mę, that's a fine song you are singing! Won't you take me as well?" "Come on, get on! I'll let you on my sleigh. Why shouldn't I take you?" Well, the bear gets on. They go on, and again he starts to sing:

The sandal of bast caught the hen.
. . .

The rope with which the pole of Uncle Nori̯mę's sleigh is fastened breaks. "Hare, go and bring the axe!" "I'm too lazy." "Fox, go on, you go!" "I'm too lazy." "Wolf, you go and fetch it!" "I'm too lazy." "Bear, you go and fetch it!" "I'm too lazy." Uncle Nori̯mę grows angry. He goes to find the axe. While he is away, they flay the horse, eat up all its flesh, they eat up the horse and all. They fill the horse's hide with straw. Uncle Nori̯mę returns. Alas, alas, alas, there is no pig, no ox, no hen, there is nothing left, they have eaten everything and they have gone away; he is alone. The horse stands there, they had made it stand upright. He strikes the horse and the horse falls over. "Oh, what a pity, they have even eaten the horse as well,

vẹvtẹ śojemaẹś no i no!" loktas, bablị i viśtalẹ: "no, staruka, staruka, kịji, kịji da bịdẹnlị śojisnị." "jẹj te, jẹj, mịjla nẹ tuj vịvśis bośtalin, ẹtnad in lok?!" "a vot śili mićaa da vẹzjiśenị da bośti i tịrtẹg i lokta. bẹr lapťisẹ i vaja."

35. *rẹman baťuško*

olisnị-vịlisnị gozja. baťsẹ śuisnị r ẹ m a n ẹn, mamsẹ śuisnị m a r f aẹn. vẹli nalẹn kịk ćoj. viśmis mamịs. lun kujlẹ, kịkẹs, vežavun. kor vorśisnị ćeľaďịs ịvlaịn, mamịs kuli. r ẹ m a n baťis, med iz aǯǯivnị mamsẹ, nuis vẹrẹ i gualis vẹrin, lịskẹn vevťľalis. loktisnị ćeľaďis gortẹ, jualẹnị: "r ẹ m a · n, r ẹ m a · n baťuško, kẹn nẹ mijan matuškaịd?" "sija — śuẹ — leććis kumad pịźsẹ požnavnị, aski kežẹ med pẹžavnị ćẹskịd ńań." ćeľaď pịšjisnị ulịs kumad. a ńe-kod abu vẹlẹma, ńe-kod abu vẹrźedlẹma, ńe-kod abu trẹńitlẹma. kotẹrẹn bẹr pịšjisnị. "r ẹ m a · n, r ẹ m a · n baťuško, kẹn inẹ — śuẹni — mijan matuškaịd?" "sija — śuẹ — kais kumad, mića plaťťesẹ paśtavnị, medịm munnị vićkoẹ." kotẹrẹn kaisnị ćeľaď kumẹ. vịʒedlẹnị, ńe-kod abu jaśśiksẹ vośtlẹma, ńe-kod abu vidlẹma. bẹr leććisnị. "r ẹ m a · n, r ẹ m a · n baťuško, kẹn inẹ — śuẹ — mijan matuškaịd?" "sija — śuẹ — pịris komnataẹ beľilaẹn beľiććinị da kudraẹn kudriććinị." kotẹrtisnị ćeľaď komnataẹ. aǯǯẹnị, ńe-kod abu vẹrźedlẹma ńi beľila, ńi kudra. "r ẹ m a · n, r ẹ m a · n baťuško, kẹni nẹ — śuẹ — mijan matuškaịd?" "uďitis — śuẹ — sije munnị ńin vićkoẹ." kotẹrtisnị vićkoẹ, a vićkoịs naśań vẹli jona ịlịn. viśtavnị regịd, kotẹrtnị ćeľaďlị dịr. voisnị vićkoẹ. kak raz munẹ ẹbedńa. kodi mam koďis ortsiśańis, bịd dorẹ podojďitlisnị, vịʒedisnị, tẹdmalisnị. no mamịs nalẹn ńe-kẹn iz vẹv. i jona bẹrǯǯisnị, petisnị vićkośid i ńežjen kutisnị munnị gortlańis. kịlisnị rakalịś kravzẹmsẹ. ịʒịdʒịk ćojis i śuẹ: "rakaịs mịj-kẹ pẹ nuvẹ.'rakaẹ, rakaẹ, mịj te nuvan? pukśiv žẹ pukśiv, petkẹdlị žẹ, petkẹdlị?" raka pukśis. ćeľaď aǯǯisnị, mịj lebẹdẹ sije ki i tẹdmalisnị, mịj zẹlẹtẹj ćuń-kịčis veśkịd kias mamịslẹn. bośtisnị kisẹ i pịšjisnị gortanịs. "r ẹ m a n, r ẹ m a n baťuško, te — śuẹ — mịjiś mịj-kẹ tajitan? tẹ taj — śuẹ — matuškaịdlẹn mijan kiịd!" seki r ẹ m a · nlị vośtiśnị loi ńe-kịćće. viśtalis sija pravdasẹ, mịj kulis sije i "eg na me śuj guẹ, a ʒebi lịskẹn." kaisnị ćeľaď i baťis

oh dear, oh dear!" He arrives and tells the old wife about it: "Well, old wife, I was spinning and spinning, and they ate everything up." "You fool, you fool, why did you take them up on the road, why didn't you come alone?" "Well, I was singing so beautifully, and they asked me for a lift, so I took them on and now I have returned with an empty sleigh. I'll take some more sandals of bast to sell."

35. Father Ręman

There lived a married couple. The father was called Ręman, the mother Marfa. They had two daughters. The mother grew sick. She lay in bed one day, two days, she lay there for a week. While the children were playing out of doors, their mother died. In order to stop them from catching sight of their mother, father Ręman took her body to the forest; there he hid her, and covered her with pine-needles. The children arrived home and asked: "Ręman, father Ręman, where is mother?" "She has gone down to the food-store to sieve flour in order to bake some tasty bread tomorrow." The children ran down to the lower food-store. But there was nobody there and nobody had touched the flour. "Ręman, father Ręman" — they ask him — "where is mother?" "She has gone to the upper room to put on a beautiful dress to go to church." The children ran up to the upper room. They see that nobody has opened the chest and nobody has looked in it. They went back. "Ręman, father Ręman" — they ask — "where is mother?" "She has gone into the room to put white make-up on her face and curl her hair with curling-tongs." The children rushed off to the room. They see that nobody has touched either the make-up or the curling-tongs. "Ręman, father Ręman, where is mother?" — they ask. "She must have gone to church" — he replies. They ran off to the church, and the church was a very long way off. It takes no time to tell, but it took the children a long time to run there. They arrived at the church. Mass happened to be taking place. They went up to anyone who resembled their mother when seen in profile, looked at them hard and examined them. But their mother was not to be seen anywhere. They began to weep bitterly, went out of the church and started off home slowly. They heard crows cawing. The elder sister spoke up: "The crow is carrying something. 'Crow, my crow, what are you carrying? Fly down, fly down, show it to us, show it to us'!" The crow flew down. The children saw at once that it was carrying a hand and they also perceived that there was a gold ring on the right hand. It was their mother's. They took the hand and ran home. "Ręman, father Ręman, why

vere. aǯǯisni setiś noj-pela mamse, gualisni. berdisni da berdisni, berdisni da gorzisni. kilis ńe tolko aslanis śiksa jezis i kilisni mati-gegersa petkais, mati-gegersa źverjasis.

36.

olis-vilis deva baba. silen veli kik ćelad: m a r f a niv da p a v e l pi. voisni koraśiśjas, ozir jez. m a r p aes koraleni. m a r p ali munni abu eketa, mamis mirden śete. śetisni ile kraje. mamis viśmis, iste p a v e l pise m a r p a dore: "mun pe, p a v e l pije, viśtav m a r p aidli, medim volas, kula me." p a v e l pukśis vev vile, munis. vois ritja vile. m a r p a pelićaen vurśe. "m a r p i d a, musa ćoje — šue — mamid jona viśmis. voli — šue — daške kulas regid." m a r p a ećki piris viǯedlis da šuve: "trepu-trepu-ke pe sije keralan i to pe na lok-gag moz jitliśas." p a v e l petis, pukśis vev vile i munis ber. loktis, mamis ńin kulan vijim. "lokte, oz — šue —, pije, ćojid?" "oz pe." "mij ne pe šuis?" "a sije-ke pe kuligas trepu-trepu keralan i to pe jitliśas lok-gag moz." lun oleni, mamli lokǯik. "mun — šue — jeśše vetli, kula ńin — šue — da oz-ke — šue — lok, te — šue — viśtav: 'taz-dor jugidin med — šue — oz lo oliś i meder jugidin oz lo rediteĺ.' " vev vile pukśis i medeććis. p a v e l vois. ćojis sketes verde, juktale. aǯǯis vokisliś loktemse. "mij mogen — šue — voke?" "a vot — šue — mamid ńin peślednej lunjas ekte, volini — šue — tene koris, a 'oz-ke — šue — voli, te — šue — viśtav, mij medim taz-dor śvetin oz lo oliś, a meder jugidin oz lo rediteĺ.' " "vetla" — šuve. munisni. voisni. pireni berdemen: "mame, mame!" a mamis ńin oz śiaś, kulema. m a r p a berdis da berdis, gorzis da gorzis. no veli ńin śor. ǯebisni, kolledisni mamse. lun-med m a r p a vokisli miśkis, ćiśkis, medis gortas munni. uśkeććisni kejinjas, tor-pirje kośavlisni. vot taǯi sije iz lo ńi meder jugidin rediteĺ, ńi taz-dor śvetin oliś.

are you hiding something from us? Look, this is our mother's hand!" Then Ręman could do nothing more. He told them the truth, that she had died. "I have not yet buried her but I have covered her body with pine-needles." The children and their father went to the forest. They found their mother there with only one hand and buried her. They cried and cried and cried and yelled. They were heard not only by people in their own village, but also by the birds in the forest and even the wild beasts.

36. [The mother curses her daughter]

There lived an old woman. She had two children: Marpa, a girl, and Pavel, a boy. People came to ask for the girl's hand, rich people. Marpa does not feel like going away, her mother forces her to go and gives her away. She was sent on a long journey, to a faraway land. Their mother fell sick; she sends her son Pavel to Marpa: "Go, my son Pavel, and tell Marpa to come here and see me for I am going to die." Pavel mounted a horse and went off. He arrived in the evening. Marpa was sewing a muzzle for the calf. "Marpida, my dear sister" — says he — "mother has become very sick. Come for she may die soon!" Marpa looked at him through her glasses, and said: "If you cut her into very small pieces, even then she will become whole again, like a lizard." Pavel went out, mounted the horse and returned home. He arrived; his mother was dying. "Son, is your sister coming or not?" — she asks — "What did she say?" "Well, if you cut her into very small pieces, even then she will become whole again, like a lizard." They live another day, and the mother grows worse. "Go and see her once more" — rays she — "for I am going to die now, and if she does not come, tell hes: 'may she not be alive in this world, and may she not be a mother in the next'!" He mounted the horse and started off. Pave arrived there. His sister was feeding and watering the cattle. She saw her brother arrive. "What has brought you here, brother?" — she asks. "Well, mother is living her last days and has asked you to come and see her, saying: 'if she does not come, tell her she may not be alive in this world or a mother in the next'!" "I'll come" — says she. They started out. They arrived home. They go in weeping: "Mother, mother!" But their mother does not say a word, she has died. Marpa cried and cried, and yelled and yelled. But it was too late. They buried her, they saw their mother to the grave. Next day Marpa did some washing for her brother, cleaned the house, and started for home. She was attacked by wolves. They tore her to pieces. Well, this is how she did not become a mother in the next world, or alive in this one.

37. *kujim gundi̮r ji̮li̮ś*

(Fragment)

olisni̮-vi̮lisni̮ gozja. nale̮n ve̮li e̮ťi pi. sija munis pastušitni̮. sija munis, munis, seni e̮ťik dom vi̮jim; zev i̮ǯid ki̮me̮r kae̮. i̮ǯid ki̮me̮r kaas, kaas i seče̮m śe̮d loas, pramo ńi-ne̮m oz ti̮dav. kujim jura gundi̮r kae̮. “vot taja gundi̮ri̮d i mene̮ vijas.” sija bośtas i̮ǯid sabľa kojde̮s, e̮ťi jure̮ keri̮štas, me̮d jure̮ keri̮štas, kojme̮d jure̮ keri̮štas. gundi̮r i uśi. bara voǯe munas. “no, tai̮ś mi̮ni me.” voǯe munas. bara zev i̮ǯid ki̮me̮r kaas. kaas, kaas ki̮me̮ri̮s, śe̮d ki̮me̮r i kvajt jura gundi̮r bara li̮be̮ćće. “no ki̮ćće meni̮m vošti̮śni̮?” — zon šue̮. “taja mene̮ — šuas — i vijas gundi̮r.” seśša gundi̮r mati̮śśas. e̮ťi̮ jure̮ śeti̮štas, me̮de̮ śeti̮štas, kojme̮de̮ śetas, ńoľede̮ śetas, vite̮de̮ śetas, kvajte̮de̮ (kvajte̮di̮sli̮), bara gundi̮r uśe. “no, slava bogu, bara mi̮ni, taja izbavićći gundi̮ri̮ś.” munas, munas, zev jona zerme̮. ďaď orde̮ pi̮ras. ďaď vurśe. “no me̮s — šue̮ — vi̮ǯi. me ne̮ ta-lun — šue̮ — kujim jura gundi̮r da kvajt jura gundi̮ri̮ś — šue̮ — izbavićći.” “no — šue̮ — in-ke̮ jurse̮ kerali̮šti̮ ńin, veśke̮ sija gundi̮r vijis. te — šue̮ — na ule̮ in śećći!” seśša i e̮kmi̮s jura gundi̮r bara i li̮be̮ććis, bara śe̮d ki̮me̮r kae̮. bara śe̮d ve̮r kojd loji. “no, taja — šue̮ — mene̮ ńin vijas. e̮ni loktas.” seśša bara sije li̮be̮ććas, gundi̮r i si̮ vi̮le̮ pondas prame̮ vaľiććini̮. bośtas bara, stavse̮ keravlas, keravlas, keravlas, keravlas i bara uśe. “no, tai̮ś izbavićći.” munas i vetlas, gorte̮ voas. “vot, ta-lun — šue̮ (mami̮sli̮-baťisli̮ loktas vištavni̮) — ta-lun — šuas — gundi̮rjas napuśťi·ććisni̮ me vi̮le̮, te̮ke̮ťe — šue̮ — mene̮ iz vini̮. asi̮v — šue̮ — og ńin me̮s vi̮ǯni̮ mun seśša.” me̮d lun bara munas. si̮li̮ i das-ki̮k jura gundi̮r uśke̮ććas. bara śe̮d ki̮me̮r kaas, kaas i das-ki̮k jura gundi̮r. bara sije gundi̮re̮s keralas, keralas i bara mij-ke̮ karas . . .

38.

(Fragment)

kujim ćoj jage̮dla kajisni̮. ki̮k ćojis naberuškase̮ ti̮rtisni̮, a kojme̮di̮s iz ti̮r seśša si̮le̮n jage̮dis. seśša sija i pu sajin naja śorńitisni̮ da e̮ťi ćojse̮ vijasni̮. vužľa ule̮ śujasni da sape̮ge̮n taľalasni̮. gortas voasni̮. “ke̮n ne̮ pe̮ ćojid?” “a iz e̮mij pe̮ voli̮?” “iz pe̮.” seśša voki̮s pesla kaas da i zev mića peľan tače̮m bi̮dmas, peľanse̮ keri̮štas da sen i śivni̮ pondas:

37. About the three dragons

There lived a married couple. They had a son. He set out to guard the cows. He went on and on until he arrived at a house. Here a very big cloud arose. The big cloud came on and on, and it became so dark that he really could not see anything at all. There came a three-headed dragon. "Oh, this dragon is going to kill me." He takes a kind of sword, a big one, and he cuts off one of its heads, he cuts off the second head, and cuts off the third head. The dragon falls. He goes on. "Well, I have got rid of that." He goes on. Again a big cloud arises. The cloud comes on and on, the black cloud, and there arises a six-headed dragon. "Oh, where am I to flee?" — says the lad. "This dragon is going to kill me." Then the dragon approaches. He strikes at one of its heads, at the second, the third, the fourth, the fifth, and the sixth, and the dragon falls down on the ground. Well, thank God, once again I have escaped, I have rid myself of the dragon. He goes on and on, and heavy rain begins to fall. He enters the house of an old man. The old man is sewing. "Well" — says he — "I have been guarding cows. Today I have escaped from the three-headed and the six-headed dragon." "Well, if you had not cut off their heads, they would have killed you to be sure. Do not give in to them!" Then the nine-headed dragon arose, again in the form of a black cloud. Again it grew black as pitch. "Oh, it is going to kill me this time" — says he. "He is coming now." Then the dragon rises higher and higher and starts to attack him. Again he takes the sword and cuts off all its heads. It falls to the ground. "Well, now I have got rid of this one." He goes off and arrives at home. "Well, today" — he says to his parents — "dragons attacked me and they nearly killed me. Tomorrow I am not going to look after the cows." Yet he does go the next day. The twelve-headed dragon attacks him. Again a black cloud arises, and the twelve-headed dragon comes along. He kills this dragon too . . .

38. [The three sisters]

Three sisters went to pick berries. Two sisters filled their baskets, the youngest one's basket was not yet filled. Then the two plotted behind a tree and killed their youngest sister. They hid her body under a tree-stump and trod it down with their boots. They arrive home. "Where is your sister? Why, hasn't she come home?" "No, she hasn't." Then their brother goes to fetch fire-wood, and a very beautiful angelica was growing there; he makes a pipe out of it and begins to play the pipe:

kujim ćoj jagedla kaim da
pu sajin śorńitisni da
vužľa ule śujisni da
sapegen taľalisni.

. . . .

39.

a) svaďba jiliś

1. *žeńik lokte, koraśeni. mam lokte koraśni, ćojjas. źaľ loktis koraśni. samevar suvtedisni, vina vajisni, mij-ke leśeććištisni no seśśa ladmisni, pasjaśisni jenli, seśśa vorsan-in. ladmeććisni, znaćit, lad ńin nalen loi. seśśa vorseni niv-zon, vorseni veža-lun ćež. seśśa lokteni seni vurśiśjas, babajas. to derem vureni, to ki-ćiškan, to višiva·jććeni, to biden sija leśedeni ńevestali. vot to kożinjas vureni. sija veža-lun ćež vurasni. seśśa berdeććasni, berdni pondasni, taźi vaćkivni. seśśa berdasni bara lun kujim kimin. »śondi-banej daj menam daj niv olemej daj stavis taj menam koľi da śondi-banej da olemej daj . . .« me vunedi. biden seni ćukarććasni, jez sija una, ńevesta sija berde, pižesse vaćkile. seśśa si-berťi ńevesta berde, seśśa vaćkileni biden, mam-bať biden seni i stavis. biden berdeni, žaľ aslad nilid.*

2. *no seśśa seni sur pueni, biden vina leśedeni, biden bara. vit pizan leśedeni, biden seni. no seśśa pondasni seni svaďbujććini. pervoj vejpśasni seni, biden bara berdasni. vejpśiśjas pervoj eťi rit vejpśasni, med lun seśśa pivśasni. sećće loktasni biden družkajas, biden ki-ćiškanjas taćće, poloťentsejas eśedemaeś. biden loktasni, unaen. seśśa veńeć ule leśeććeni biden, pivśasni da miśśasni da biden veńeć ule munasni. vot seśśa veńića·jććasni da bara pir. bara sije žeńik ordin ńin seki. seśśa sen pirujteni, bara pizan leśedeni: vina, sur. i jekteni. biden sija etaź paštaśemaeś, śušunaeś, deremaeś. bara med lun seśśa ić-mońpireg-lun, bara na seni praźńićajtasni. bara lun kujim seni biden. ńevesta sija ćiškiśe, asiv-voź ćeććas, ćiškiśe, sili biden jogte koľaleni, sija vek ćiške. vorseni seni. vot svaďbais seśśa i końćiććas.*

b) reštvo vorsem jiliś

reštvois veli voas. lunnas veli mazkaen: ćišjan vevťan da stav ďerevńase j o r e s-d i nse da ź b kuźase vek etare jektam-gimgam. vevtiśam da oz tedni;

We, three sisters, went to pick berries:
They plotted behind a tree
And they hid me under tree-stump
And they trod me down with their boots.

39. Popular customs

About the wedding

1. The bridegroom comes along. They come to ask for the girl in marriage Sometimes the mother or the sisters come. The brother-in-law also came to ask for the girl's hand. They put the samovar on the table, brought vodka and prepared some food quickly. They crossed themselves in front of the icon, then came to an agreement, then played games. They agreed, that is to say there was an agreement made between them. Then the girls and the lads play games for a whole week. Then there arrive the sewing women. They sew blouses, towels, make embroidery, and prepare everything for the bride. They sew gifts. Then they lament for the bride, they begin to weep, slapping their knees like this. They lament for three days or so. "My little sun, my maiden life has gone for ever, my little sun, my life . . ." I forgot the rest. They all gather together there, a lot of people, the bride weeps and beats her knees. Then the bride continues weeping, everybody slaps their knees, parents and all. All of them weep, they are sorry for their own daughter.

2. Then they brew beer and distil vodka. They lay five tables. They hold a wedding-feast. Before the wedding they feast first at the bride's house, and all of them weep. The lamenters feast one night, and bath the next day. The best men arrive, all of them fix the towels here (on their waist). Many people come. Then they prepare for the wedding; they bath and wash, and then they go to the wedding. The wedding ceremony takes place, and again there is a feast. Then another at the bridegroom's. There they eat and drink again, and the table is set out with vodka and beer. And they dance. All of them put on a sarafan, a blouse. The next day is the bride's *pirog*-day, and they go on feasting. For another three days. The bride gets up early in the morning, she cleans the rooms, everybody has left litter behind, and she cleans the house all the time. They play games. Then the wedding is over.

About Nativity plays

Christmas has come. In the daytime we had masks on our faces: you cover your face with a kerchief, and we dance and make a row right through the

kuź sarapanjassę paśtalam, kod med kuźis da viśįvajtęm dęręmjassę. sije oz tędnį: 'taja kodi, taja kodi?' oz tędnį, unaęn voćam. a rįtnas vęli bara vorsęnį, zonjas, medalasnį. seni bara voj-bįd ćasa dvaeʒ juktam da śilam. važęn, važęn sije vot siʒ vęli provoďitam ręštvosę, zev gažaa. — a jęv veža-lunįs vęli voas (jęv veža-lunįs ęni masľeńića), sek vęli k ę z l aas. iʒįd kįr vęli karasnį mijan taćće ďerevńaas. sećće vęli dajd boštasnį da kaam kęzla vįlas. zonjaskęd pukśam da zur-kįlę įskovtam, pol kilometra vęli nuę kįrjis. vot kučęm ińťeresnęja vęli važęn.

c)

iʒįd-lun vęli voas. kaćaj karasnį, ʒuʒįd, bara k ę z l aę. eta kįza snaśťjas i ńužędasnį. sen vęli nįv-zon bara ćukarććam da lun praźńik-kę, lun-tįr kaćajććam, praźńikęn-kę vojin bara. a pręstej lun vęli, oz, sek užalam vęli, pręstej lunas mij-kę aslad kreśťjanskęj . . .

d) kįvzįśem jįlįś

1. *seśśa mi vęli kįvzįśnį petam. mi j o r ę s-d i n į n gęśťitim. kujimęn munim da kuďeľen pećkam vęli. loktisnį eta sudta mužikjas: g ę r ę ś ť e p a n da j o g o r, kuź v a ś g r i š da kod-kę taj zev kuźjasįs loktisnį. naja ki-ćįśkęd, taje kuź pęlęťentsi jialęmaeś da sija ćugaręk bośtęmaeś. (no bi ęztan taj sartasę da kusędan da sije ćugaręk sije.) kujim tuj-vožę munisnį, seni kįvzįśenį, pukśisnį da stavįs. mįj pę kįlam? gętraśan-kę, gętraśem kįlas, a kulan-kę, kulęm kįlan, on-kę, ńi-nęm on kįv, no seśśa loktisnį, mi pukalam. ęťi pukśis gęlbęć sod vįlę, nįv, n a t a ľ ľ a m a t r e n a mijan: viʒędę ręmpęštan pįr. pįzan saje stav pukśedim. pįzan saje stavnįm pukśim, pįzan sajin pukalam. sija viʒędę ręmpęštan pįr: kodi pę kulę, sija uśe pįzan sajas. taśań viʒędam gębećis pįr mi. a kod verės saje munę, sija i śmońaśe. kodi sija mįj-kę lovę, bįdęn sija vot i aʒʒilis. a mijan veď sečęm-žę śmek kojd žę seśśa. ęťi i kįjedę mužįkįs, kęźajinįs pęlaťśańis guśen, kod pę taćće loktas pįzan sajas: viʒędę pę, ńe-kod pę iz lok. a ręmpęštan pįr tįdalę. a me, taje viʒędlįvlim da pravda žę, aʒʒili. ti on veritę daškę?*

village *jorẹs-din* and *ịb* without interruption. We cover ourselves up so that people may not recognize us, we put on long sarafans, the longest ones we have, and embroidered blouses. They do not know who this is, and who that is. They do not know, because lots of people do it. In the evening they play again, the lads hire a house. There we serve drinks to the lads all night long, till two o'clock, and we dance. Well, this is how we spent Christmas in the old days, very happily indeed. — Well, there came butter-week (today *maslica*), then we were in *kẹzla*. They made a big mound of snow here in our village. We take the sleigh there, and we go up the mound of *kẹzla*. Together with the lads we sit on the sleigh and swish down swiftly, the mound sent us even half a kilometer. Oh, how interesting it was in the old days.

Easter games

Easter has come. They make a swing, a high one, similarly in *kẹzla*. They put up ropes as thick as this. Girls and lads gather together there, and if it is a feast-day, we swing all day long, even at night when it is a feast-day. But if it is a weekday, we do not, then we work, on weekdays we do our own peasant work.

About listening

1. We used to go out listening. We were entertained at *jorẹs-dịn*. Three of us went, and spun hemp-fibre. Some very tall men arrived: Gẹrẹ Śťepan and Jogor, the tall Vaś Griš and others, all very tall. They came. Towels, towels as long as this were tied to their waists, and they brought chippings of burnt fir *(ćugarẹk)* with them (you make a torch with fir-chips, then put it out, and that is *ćugarẹk*). They went to the three cross-roads, and sat down there listening. What do you hear? If you are going to marry, you hear about marriage, if you are going to die, you hear about your death. If you are not going to marry or die, you hear nothing. Well, they arrived. We were sitting there. One of the girls, our Natalľa Matrena was sitting at the top of the cellar steps: she looks into a mirror. We sat everybody down at the table. We all sat down at the table; we are sitting at the table. She looks into the mirror: whoever is going to die falls from the table. We look out from here, from the cellar under the house. She who is going to marry is joking. Whatever is to happen to anyone, she can see it. We laugh a good deal. One of the men, the master of the house, lying in the cot spies out in secret who comes to the table here. He watches but nobody comes. Yet a figure can be seen in the mirror. We were watching and I really caught sight of it. Perhaps you don't believe me?

2. *kịvzịśnị żẹ kuććim. me rẹmpẹštan pịr viʒeda. me tan śor ulịń viʒeda rẹmpẹštan pịr, a naja kujim nịv taćće pukśisnị. me naje viʒeda, mịj rẹmpẹštanas loas. kujimẹn mićaa pukalẹnị. (vot ćẹv, lẹń, taʒ, mịj-kẹ ẹnija moz żẹ pukalẹnị.) ẹťik vẹli mekẹd čẹčja żẹ, ńin ńevesta. sija vot bịťťe vot pẹri, pẹri, pẹri bịťťe kịmịn sija uśi. me ẹdjeʒịka bośti rẹmpẹštansẹ. "oj, meśa, uśi g u ś ť aịd" g u ś t vẹli. i seśśa povźim bịdẹn. (seśśa sija i kuli.) a vek pukalẹ, sịịś pẹ oz żẹ tịdav. vot sija vịjim żẹ pravdaịs.*

3. *seśśa kuʒ kužan? mijan mam vẹli pokojńića viśtalẹ: »me pẹ kagaẹn vodi asịv-voʒ, ʒeľa kaga pẹ vẹli. a mam śuẹ: me pẹ kujla a — gẹlbeć vịlịn kaganas — bịťťe-kẹ kẹźajin pịris da gort-pom (kopịrććis, etačẹm ịʒịd mort da) taćće śịbitis. koč-koč-koč, mẹdis keraśnị kerkaịn. me pẹ povźi ẹdjeʒịk śin vośti: ńe-kod, ńi-nẹm abu. kagaịs pịr i kulẹma, gort karẹma i kerkaẹ pịrtẹma. vot sija pravda.*

e)

me taja kerkaas, taś vẹli. me vẹli nịv, das-kẹkjamịs arẹs, das-śiźim-ľi. taja na loktẹm vẹli svaťťaịd, a na ordẹ gẹśťa vois mẹdla-pẹlịś. mi sećće kịk nịv munim, pịśjim da kojmẹd zonmẹs bośťim da ịż kutalim voj-bịd. verẹs saje okota munnị daśkẹ kịk nịvlị? śintẹ kuńam da taʒi pịśjam, pịśjam, etaʒi kvaťitam ịžtẹ. kodlị ịż śedẹ, kodlị mež śedẹ, bịdẹnlị śedali. ńi-nẹm lẹž-kịv abu, vot i pravda.

f) braććina jịlịś

braććina praźńik koľi. no seśśa i "no vaj, babajas, vaje, braććina juam, vaje!" seśśa stavnịm pukśam, nịv-babajas vẹleśtas, kodi vịjim, kodi sẹglasnej. kodi loktas, a kodi i oz. juam lun-tịr, śilam, jẹktam. (kor tomẹś vẹlim, a ẹni ved ńin! . . .) ńań nuam, sur nuam, vina nuam, tačẹm tujisjas. — a kerka sija besplatnẹ leʒalẹnị. etija ved vorsan-insẹ medalẹnị zonjas a, sije besplatnẹ juam braććinasẹ. sija rẹštvo dịrji a.

2. We began to listen. I look into the mirror. Here, under the beam I look into the mirror, while they, the three girls came and sat here. I look at them: what does the mirror show? They are sitting there nicely, the three of them. (Yes, in peace and quiet, just as we are sitting here now.) There was a girl of my age there, already betrothed at that time. She seemed to be falling and falling to one side, then suddenly she fell down on her nose. "Oh dear" — I say — "Guśťa has fallen." It was Guśt. We were all frightened. (And afterwards she did die.) But she sits on and on, though from there (the mirror) she was not to be seen. Well, all this is true as I have told it.

3. And what can you make of this? It was told by my late mother: "Early in the morning I was lying in bed with my child; it was a baby. It was lying in the cellar under the floor, and it seemed as if the master of the house came in (he stooped down, he was as tall as this), and he seemed to throw a small coffin here. Bang, bang, he began to cut and carve in the house. I was frightened and opened my eyes at once: there was nobody there, nothing was to be seen. Soon afterwards the child died. That is why he was making a coffin in my dream and brought it into the house." And this is the truth.

Chasing sheep at night

I was living in this house, this is where I came from. I was a girl of eighteen or seventeen. [She points to one woman]: The bride's mother had come. [She points to another present]: And another woman guest had also arrived from somewhere. We went there, two girls. We ran there bringing a third one, a lad with us, and we were chasing sheep the whole night long. Two girls may feel like marrying, may they not? We close our eyes and run and run and so we grab the sheep. This one takes an ewe, that one a ram, everybody has got one. There is no lie whatever in all this, this is all true.

About the picnic-dance

There is a picnic-dance entertainment. Then we come to an agreement: "Come along, women, we'll have a picnic-dance." Then we all come together, all the women in the district, as many as have agreed. Some come, some don't. We drink, sing and dance all day long. (When we were young, that is, but now . . . !) We take bread, beer and vodka in birch-bark baskets like this. They let us have the house free. (Or) the boys hire a place for the entertainment, but we pay nothing for our drinks at the picnic-dance. It's the same at Christmas too.

g) vo gegerja boštem

stavis vorsan-inas pukaleni: niv da zon da ńin stavis viʒedeni. a tan stavis jekteni da śileni. no gorzeni seśśa: "vaje pe, vo gegerja bośtni!" kole pe enija moz periśʒikjasis śueni, munni, kole pe viʒedni da munni. mijan m i t r e j i v a n e v i ć da kod da etaćće mužikjas miććiśemaeś. gorzeni: "vaje, bośte da semin priś bost!" priś! mijan j o g o r v a ś petis, mene bośtis. kuʒ taj goredisni: 'muža svojevo'. seśśa me bośti med zonmes, m i š s a n d r i kes. m iš s a n d r i k bośtis i kojmedes ńin boštim. j e l' e n a, j e l' e n ais bośtis, petis i bośtis i g ś t' e pes, j e l' e n ais. a i g ś t' e p bośtis d a r j aes vo gegerja vile. bara medisni vetledlini. talen mužikis ćeććis. tan veli geger śiś ezje, kiz śiśjas sal'nej. sija taj medis χrusjedlini. vot stavse biden vezdis, kojis, mijan kovtajasis, doriśeś, piśjinite og ud'ite. no kićće munan? edjeʒika tajeked zvez ule pirim, piśjim. loktim. "i l' l' a i v a n o v i ć, vaj kovtajasse mijan, jen mogiś!" sija stavse vetlalis. kil'će runduksе bośtis da kiʒ taj mijanes lebedis. mi og ud'ite piśjinise. mijan seśśa vo-gegerjajas kovtajasse i vajisni. vot kučem veli! a śileni kiʒ, vaj stav mužikjasis goredisni, vaj stavid śile-viśtale: »muža svojevo«.

(b) Ned-kivjas

40.

1. *borjis dona, dona, mu eśše dona. — eśiń-rama.*
2. *gid-tir iž, et'i bež. — pać-tir ńań.*
3. *ńol' vok et'ik śapka ulin sulaleni. — pizan.*
4. *ʒere-vere va-kuk. — miśśan-doz.*
5. *vojin kalać, a lunin skamja. — pon.*
6. *mića, mića molod'eć da bidenes berdede. — luk.*
7. *kert bereg da dona va. — vij-suka rać.*
8. *želeb dorin teś-taśti. — teliś.*
9. *mića, mića molod'eć da deremis pičegas. — śiś.*
10. *ti vojtište, ta vojtište, ńe-kor oz vojtišt. — iśerga.*
11. *kik ńiź piśje, tevaris vilisas. — śor.*

Choosing a mate for the year

Everybody sits in the place of entertainment, girls and lads; all of them pay attention. Here everybody is dancing and singing. Then they start to shout: "Choice of mates for the year!" As old people say today: you must go and have a look. Our Mitrej Ivanęvić and other men stood up. They shout: "Go on, grab one, grab one!" They say to Jogor Vaś: "Shoo, grab her! Shoo!" Our Jogor Vaś came forward and grabbed me. They shouted: "Her own husband." Then I grabbed another lad, Miš Sandrik, Miš Sandrik also grabbed another, and we grabbed a third one. Jeľena, Jeľena also came forward and grabbed Ig Śťep. And Ig Śťep grabbed Darja for a year. They began to walk about: [she points to someone] her husband jumped up. Candles were burning all round here, thick tallow candles. He wanted to put them out, to be sure. So he pulled everybody about, sprinkled them and our coats — those standing at the side, there was no escape for us. Well where could you flee? We and she [pointing to a woman] rushed to hide under the steps to the barn. (We got there.) "Iľľa Ivanović, give us back our coats for Heaven's sake!" He chased everybody away. He got hold of the bottom of the steps and lifted us all up. We could not escape. Then our mates of the year took away our coats. Oh, what a performance it was! They sang. How all the men roared, how they all sang: "Her own husband!"

(b) Riddles

40.

1. Its ridge is costly, very costly, the land is still more expensive. — A window-frame.
2. A pen full of sheep and a tail. — An oven full of bread.
3. Four brothers standing under one cap. — A table.
4. A wet calf fidgeting. — A hand-bowl.
5. Cake at night, bench in the day-time. — A dog.
6. A handsome, handsome lad that makes everybody shed tears. — An onion.
7. An iron bank and valuable water. — A pan with the remains of butter in it.
8. A bowl of oat-flour by the gutter. — The moon.
9. A handsome, handsome lad with his shirt in his lap. — A candle.
10. It drops here, it drops there, yet does not drop down. — An earring.
11. Two martens run along with their belongings on them. — A cross-beam.

12. *zaloka-ti̯rježi̯d bajdi̯k. — vom-ti̯r piń.*

13. *zaloka-ti̯r ge̯rd bajdi̯k. — pać-ti̯r e̯gi̯r.*

14. *ki̯k akań luna bidlae̯ vetle̯ni̯, vojin kud ule̯ pi̯re̯ni̯. — śin.*

15. *śo śinma, a ńi-ne̯m oz ažži̯. — pož.*

16. *mića, mića ić-moń da ńak-pe̯le̯di̯s ki̯skale̯ni̯. — e̯žes-vug.*

17. *komi̯n mort e̯ťi poduška vi̯li̯n kujle̯ni̯. — pe̯te̯le̯k.*

18. *d a r j a da m a r j a voćća, voćća vi̯žećće̯ni̯. — pe̯te̯le̯k da žož.*

19. *bi̯d kerkai̯n śe̯d tasma. — ńič.*

20. *bi̯d kerkai̯n oš-ki̯me̯s. — pać-vom.*

21. *baťis ćukľa, mami̯s ge̯na. — će̯rs.*

22. *mune̯ i lokte̯, de̯ra voľsale̯. — ľampa.*

23. *kite̯m i kokte̯m, ki̯ne̯m vi̯las ujale̯. — pi̯ž.*

24. *śo de̯masa da rotasa, jema-suńi̯sa abu vole̯ma. — pi̯vśan-gor.*

25. *mića, mića ni̯v da te vi̯le̯ kali̯vle̯. — kore̯ś.*

26. *bi̯d kerkai̯n śiś jukme̯s. — pu-le̯kań.*

27. *bi̯d kerkai̯n śiś jukme̯s. — pu-le̯kań.*

27. *ńoľ ćoj e̯ťi gue̯ kužžaśeni̯. — mes-li̯šte̯m.*

28. *pe̯ri̯ś starik pasjaśas, pasjaśas i paććere̯ me̯das kani̯, sitanas ši̯la pi̯ras. — kań.*

29. *ćuki̯ľ da muki̯ľ ši̯re̯m gogi̯n, mi̯j ten mogi̯s? — šor.*

30. *ki̯k ke̯ć-kok bi̯ń, vit pon-čak žažlań ľas. — zi̯ri̯m-ći̯ške̯m.*

31. *ge̯ra vi̯li̯n ťe̯s da oz kośmi̯vli̯. — ki̯v.*

32. *luna že̯vjaśas, že̯vjaśas da vojin pož ule̯ pi̯ras. — śin.*

33. *ńoľ pi̯šje, ke̯kja·mi̯s ve̯ćće. — ve̯v, ke̯kjami̯s pod.*

34. *kerkai̯n be̯rde̯, a i̯llai̯n śile̯. — ćepńija.*

35. *bi śe̯le̯ma, va ki̯ne̯ma, zarńija plaťťea. — same̯var.*

36. *pu kar, da pu kar, pu kar vi̯las i̯žas kar, i̯žas kar vi̯las de̯ra kar, de̯ra kar vi̯las ńeme̯j sar. — potani̯n kaga.*

37. *žurs-žurs śujis, ľus-ľas ki̯skis. — ćepńija.*

38. *ćaste̯ pi̯rale̯ moľid jura ruže. — de̯ra-ki̯jem.*

12. A long chest full of white partridges. — A mouth full of teeth.

13. A long chest full of red partridges. — A stove full of glowing coals.

14. Two dolls walking everywhere in the day-time and going beneath a basket at night. — The eyes.

15. It has a hundred eyes, yet it sees nothing. — A sieve.

16. A beautiful, beautiful young wife pulled by the nipple. — A latch.

17. Thirty men lying on one cushion. — The ceiling.

18. Darja and Marja look at each other. — The ceiling and the floor.

19. A black strap in every house. — Moss.

20. A bear's forehead in every house. — The mouth of the stove.

21. A crooked father and a hairy mother. — A spindle.

22. It comes and goes, laying out cloth. — Skis.

23. It has neither hands nor feet, and swings on its belly. — A boat.

24. It weighs a hundred pounds and is ragged, yet neither needle nor cotton has ever been in it. — The stove in the bath-house.

25. A beautiful, beautiful girl who creeps on you. — The broom used in the bath-house.

26. A rotten well in every house. — A washbowl made of wood.

27. Four sisters urinating in one pit. — Milking a cow.

28. An old man crosses himself, he crosses himself and wants to climb on to the stove, and an awl pierces his bottom. — A cat.

29. Crooked and hooked shear-knife, what is it to do with you? — A brook.

30. A splash of two hare's legs, five toadstools pressed against shelf. — Wiping one's nose.

31. A plank on the hill that never dries up. — The tongue.

32. It flutters and flutters in the day-time, and goes beneath a sieve at night. — The eye.

33. Four of them run, eight of them are in pursuit. — A horse and eight legs of a sleigh.

34. It cries in the house and sings out of doors. — The dipper for the well.

35. It has a heart of fire, a belly of water, and is clothed in gold. — A samovar.

36. A wooden town and a wooden town, a straw town built on the wooden town, a linen town built on the straw town, and a mute tsar on the linen town. — A suspended swinging cradle.

37. Thrust in fully and drawn out slowly. — The dipper for the well.

38 A smooth head that often goes into the hairy hole. — Weaving cloth.

(c) Proverbs, idioms

41. *(Proverbs)*

1. *be̮rdte̮m kagae̮s oz kaćajtni̮.*
2. *bur baba dori̮n i ľok muži̮ki̮s bur.*
3. *bur muži̮k dori̮n i babai̮d bur.*
4. *bur vevt uli̮n i kerkai̮d bur.*
5. *e̮ťi je̮rš ńeľami̮n vedra ćeri-va kare̮.*
6. *muži̮k jue̮, dom-ǯi̮n soćće, baba jue̮, stavi̮s soćće i teke̮d ole̮mi̮s śir-ju vijede̮m-kojd.*
7. *petukli̮ sorse̮ǯ, porśľi̮ isjane̮ǯ.*
8. *śera ponśid śe̮d pon oz lo.*

42. *Idioms*

1. *agas-piń vi̮le̮ uśi [gorš mort ji̮li̮ś]*
2. *di̮re̮ paććerse̮ ľićkalan.*
3. *ge̮n kojd ńebi̮d, id kojd šuri̮d.*
4. *kań kojd di̮š, pon kojd gorš.*
5. *kiśśem purjiś va kojem kojd.*
6. *koz pu ji̮li̮ś viśtale̮m turi.*
7. *oj pe̮ di̮še̮ daj di̮še̮, ge̮ľe daj ge̮ľe!*
8. *pom ńi pi̮de̮s.*
9. *pruťe ńe baľe ńine̮m abu.*
10. *ri̮ni̮ši̮d soćće [kor žeńiki̮s me̮de̮s vajas].*
11. *śinmi̮s vurdale̮ munni̮.*
12. *ši̮r-bi kojd pe̮ ľampai̮d.*
13. *tag kojd ńebi̮d, id kojd šuri̮d.*

(d) Songs

43.

das-vit are̮ me voji,
guľanka vi̮le̮ peti:
tom zonjas vorsan-ine̮,
tom ni̮vjas śilan-ine̮.
5. *va-dor vi̮las-ke̮ lećći,*
kujim karaba lokte̮.
me še̮r karabas pi̮ri,

41.

1. The child that is not crying is not rocked.
2. Beside a good wife even a bad husband is good.
3. Beside a good man the wife is also good.
4. Under a good roof the house is also good.
5. One perch makes forty buckets of fish soup.
6. If a man drinks, half the house will burn down; if the wife drinks, everything will burn down, and your life will be like a flowing river of pitch.
7. As high as a cock's comb, and as the bottom of a pig.
8. A mottled dog will never have black puppies.

42.

1. He fell against the teeth of the harrow. (Said of a hungry man.)
2. You are propping up the stove a long time.
3. Soft as hair, straight as a barley stalk.
4. Lazy as a cat and greedy as a dog.
5. Drawing water from a raft that has fallen apart.
6. A crane said to have lighted on a spruce.
7. Oh dear, you lazy thing, you lazy thing, you poor thing, you poor thing!
8. It has neither end nor bottom.
9. There is neither cow, nor lamb, there is nothing at all.
10. Your barn is burning. (When the bridegroom brings another fiancée.)
11. His eyes are howling to leave.
12. Your lamp is like a glowworm.
13. Soft as hops and straight as a barley stalk.

43.

I reached my fifteenth year,
I went to a party:
To the place where young lads play,
To the place where young girls sing.
I went down to the river bank,
Three boats come along.
I went aboard the middle boat,

e̮šińedi̮s viǯedli:
k a z a ń ge̮ra ti̮dal'e̮.
'k a z a ń e pe̮ ge̮rae̮,
melań bane̮n berge̮ććiv!"
me sećće i be̮r peti:
posńi šorjas pi̮šjeni̮,
saldatjasle̮n, bedne̮jjasle̮n śin-vani̮s.
me ješšȩ vi̮le̮ kaji:
gi̮riś šorjas pi̮šjeni̮.
me seś ke̮sji mi̮śśini̮,
saldatjasle̮n, bedne̮jjasle̮n virjasi̮s.
me ješšȩ vi̮le̮ kaji:
vež kudri i sulale̮.
me ke̮sji-ke̮ e̮l'i kudri ńečištni̮,
saldatjasle̮n, bedne̮jjasle̮n kudrini̮s.
a me ješše vi̮le̮ kaji:
sakar-jurjas ti̮dale̮.
me ke̮sji e̮l'ike̮s boštni̮,
saldatjasle̮n, bedne̮jjasle̮n jurjasi̮s.

44.

kača-tor vojis e̮šiń voǯe,
kič-kič vartis,
ki̮rni̮š-tor vojis e̮šiń voǯe,
kur-kur vartis.
"[šuanni̮d], uźanni̮d al'i olanni̮d,
ve̮t ve̮tanni̮d,
tun tunanni̮d?
ti vi̮le̮ ved — šuve̮ — vojska li̮beććе,
ćinte̮m i bi̮rte̮m.
l' e v o · ń i ć sar ćeććis,
podzo·rne̮j trubka pi̮r viǯedis:
"važne̮j ge̮ś — šuve̮ — taj ne̮ i pedl'inne̮.
ćećći že̮ — šuve̮ — sluga̮jase̮ da
verne̮j slugajase̮,
ke̮maśe — šuve̮ — da i paśtaśe,
vetle̮ ti — šuve̮ — k i r j a n-v a r j a n dore̮,
roć-mu kuti̮ś, roć-mu krepit'el' bat'uško dore̮!"

And looked out of its window:
The hill of Kazań can be seen.
"Hill of Kazań,
Turn with your face to me!"
I went back there:
Little brooks are flowing,
They were the tears of soldiers, poor things.
I mounted still higher:
Big brooks are flowing.
I wanted to wash there,
They were the blood of soldiers, poor things.
I mounted yet higher:
There was green bunch there,
I wanted to pull off one of the bunches;
They were the locks of soldiers, poor things.
I mounted yet higher:
Sugar-cones could be seen.
I wanted to take one of them,
They were the heads of soldiers, poor things.

44.

A magpie came in front of the window,
kič, *kič*, it croaked;
A raven came in front of the window,
Caw, caw, it croaked.
"Are you asleep or awake?
Are you dreaming,
Or are you practising magic?
Against you" — says he — "an army is coming,
Inexhaustible and untiring."
Tsar Levonić jumped up
And looked at them with his spy-glass:
"An important guest" — says he — "it is true indeed.
Get up" — says he — "my servants,
My faithful servants!
Put on your shoes" — says he — "and put on your clothes,
Go to Kirjan-Varjan,
The protector of the Russian land, to the father
who supports the Russian land!"

naja ke̮maśisni̮, paśtaśini̮ da e̮dje munisni̮.
k i r j a n-v a r j a n ge̮ti̮r i pe̮žaśe.
“ke̮n-ine̮ — šuve̮ — tijan k i r j a n-v a r j a n roć-mu
kuti̮ś, roć-mu krepiťeľ baťuškoi̮d?”
“sija — šuve̮ — mijan i vićkoi̮n,
sulalis — šuve̮ — sija mijan e̮bedńai̮n,
sulalis — šuve̮ — sija mijan dostojnai̮n”.
munisni̮ naja i vićkoe̮,
ge̮ge̮r bi̮de̮n jenjasi̮sli̮ jurbitisni̮,
ge̮ge̮r bi̮de̮n vojti̮ri̮sli̮ lajkjalisni̮ . . .

45.

kar ge̮ge̮ri̮n śe̮d totara sulale̮,
krug ge̮ge̮ri̮n ľok vojti̮ri̮s sulale̮,
krug pi̮čki̮n i mića ni̮v pukale̮,
mića ni̮vle̮n i baťis mune̮.
“baťe pe̮ baťe, vešti̮ že̮, vešti̮!”
“a ni̮le̮ pe̮ ni̮le̮, mi̮j vi̮le̮ vešta?”
“a baťe pe̮ baťe bur ve̮li̮d vi̮le̮.”
“a ni̮le̮ pe̮ ni̮le̮, si̮ don on sulav.”
kar ge̮ge̮ri̮n śe̮d totara sulale̮,
krug ge̮ge̮ri̮n ľok vojti̮ri̮s sulale̮,
krug pi̮čki̮n i mića ni̮v pukale̮,
mića ni̮vle̮n i mami̮s mune̮.
“mame̮ pe̮ mame̮, vešti̮ že̮, vešti̮!”
[“a ni̮le̮ pe̮ ni̮le̮, mi̮j vi̮le̮ vešta?”]
[“a mame̮ pe̮ mame̮,] bur patka vi̮le̮.”
“ni̮le̮ pe̮ ni̮le̮, si̮ don on sulav.”
kar ge̮ge̮ri̮n śe̮d totara sulale̮,
krug ge̮ge̮ri̮n ľok vojti̮ri̮s sulale̮,
krug pi̮čki̮n i mića ni̮v pukale̮,
mića ni̮vle̮n i voki̮s mune̮.
“voke̮ pe̮ voke̮, vešti̮ že̮, vešti̮!”
“ćoje pe̮ ćoje, mi̮j vi̮le̮ vešta?”
“a voke̮ pe̮ voke̮, bur paľto vi̮le̮.”
“ćoje pe̮ ćoje, si̮ don on sulav.”
kar ge̮ge̮ri̮n śe̮d totara sulale̮,
krug ge̮ge̮ri̮n ľok vojti̮ri̮s sulale̮,

They put on their shoes and their clothes and
went off with all speed.
Kirjan-Varjan's wife was baking bread.
"Where" — says he — "is your Kirjan-Varjan, the protector of
the Russian land, the father who supports the
Russian land?"
"He was standing there" — she answers — "at Mass",
"He was standing there" — she answers — "at dostoyna."
They went off to the church.
They prayed to every icon around,
They bowed to every man around . . .

45.

Black Tartars are surrounding the town,
Wicked people are surrounding the circle,
In the middle of the circle there sits a beautiful girl,
The beautiful girl's father comes along.
"Father, father, redeem me, redeem me!"
"Daughter, daughter, with what shall I redeem you?"
"Father, father, with your fine horse!"
"Daughter, daughter, you are not worth that much."
Black Tartars are surrounding the town,
Wicked people are surrounding the circle,
In the middle of the circle there sits a beautiful girl,
The beautiful girl's mother comes along.
"Mother, mother, redeem me, redeem me!"
"Daughter, daughter, with what shall I redeem you?"
"Mother, mother, with you fine silken kerchief."
"Daughter, daughter, your are not worth that much."
Black Tartars are surrounding the town,
Wicked people are surrounding the circle,
In the middle of the circle there sits a beautiful girl,
The beautiful girl's brother comes along.
"Brother, brother, redeem me, redeem me!"
"Sister, sister, with what shall I redeem you?"
"Brother, brother, with your fine overcoat."
"Sister, sister, you are not worth that much."
Black Tartars are surrounding the town,
Wicked people are surrounding the circle,

krug pi̯čki̯n i mića ni̯v pukale̯,
mića ni̯vlen ćojis mune̯.
"ćoje pe̯ ćoje, vešti̯ že̯ vešti̯!"
"a ćoje pe ćoje, mi̯j vi̯le̯ vešta?"
["a ćoje pe̯ ćoje,] bur šal' vi̯le̯."
["ćoje pe̯ ćoje,] si̯ don on sulav."
kar ge̯ge̯ri̯n śe̯d totara sulale̯,
krug ge̯ge̯ri̯n l'ok vojti̯ri̯s sulale̯,
krug pi̯čki̯n i mića ni̯v pukale̯,
mića ni̯vle̯n drugi̯s mune̯.
"druge̯ pe̯ druge̯, vešti̯ že̯, vešti̯!"
"pe̯druga, pe̯druga, mi̯j vi̯le̯ vešta?"
. . . .
"pe̯druga pe̯ pedruga, vešta že̯ vešta."

46.

ge̯ge̯r, ge̯ge̯r ke̯ me viǯedli:
aslam mile̯je abu tan,
aslam mile̯je abu tan.
muna me as gorńićae̯,
muna me as gorńićae̯,
voda me as vol'-paś vi̯le̯,
voda me as vol'-paś vi̯le̯,
i šebraśa as e̯ď'ale̯e̯n,
šebraśa as e̯ď'ale̯e̯n.
kor-ke̯ pe̯ menam mile̯j vove̯ma,
more̯s voǯe ki̯ń uśke̯de̯ma,
uźan-ini̯ś saď'me̯de̯ma,
uźan-ini̯ś saď'me̯de̯ma.
ježel'i te mene̯ on l'ubit,
kuǯ bor-i-jin da turunjas kośme̯ni̯,
siǯ-že̯ te, mile̯je, kośman,
siǯ-že̯ te, mile̯je, kośman.
ježel'i te mene̯, mile̯j, l'ubitan,
kuǯ bor-i-jin da turunjas ćvet'ite̯,
siǯ-že̯ te, mile̯je, ćvet'itan.

47.

paśki̯d, gaža ul'ića, ul'ića,
dol'i-śel'i, nal'i-śel'i govorinske̯j ul'ića.

In the middle of the circle there sits a beautiful girl,
The beautiful girl's sister comes along.
"Sister, sister, redeem me, redeem me!"
"Sister, sister, with what shall I redeem you?
"Sister, sister, with your fine shawl."
"Sister, sister, you are not worth that much."
Black Tartars are surrounding the town,
Wicked people are surrounding the circle,
In the middle of the circle there sits a beautiful girl,
The beautiful girl's lover comes along.
"Sweetheart, sweetheart, redeem me, redeem me!"
"Darling, darling, with what shall I redeem you?"
. . . .
"My darling, my darling, I shall redeem you, I shall redeem you."

46.

I was looking round and round,
My darling is not here,
My darling is not here.
I go into my room,
I go into my room,
I lie down in my bed
I lie down in my bed
And cover myself with my blanket,
I cover myself with my blanket.
All of a sudden my beloved arrived,
He kindled a spark in my bosom,
He woke me from my dream,
He woke me from my dream.
If you do not love me,
As the leaves of grass on the ridge wither away,
So you will wither away, beloved,
So you will wither away, beloved.
If you love me,
As the grass on the ridge flourishes,
So you will flourish, beloved.

47.

Broad, beautiful street, street,
dol'i-šel'i . . . street.

ul'ićaas ni̯v ole̯, ni̯v ole̯,
dol'i-šel'i, nal'i-šel'i govorinske̯j ni̯v ole̯.
ni̯v doras pe̯ zon vole̯, zon vole̯,
dol'i-šel'i, nal'i-šel'i govorinske̯j zon vole̯.
"zonme̯j, zonme̯j, mi̯j volan, mi̯j volan,
dol'i-šel'i, nal'i-šel'i govorinske̯j mi̯j volan?
bat'id tene̯ pińale̯, pińale̯,
dol'i-šel'i, nal'i-šel'i govorinske̯j pińale̯.
mami̯d tene̯ ki̯jede̯, ki̯jede̯,
dol'i-šel'i, nal'i-šel'i govorinske̯j ki̯jede̯."

48.

a)

me taj, me taj, mića zon
m a š u ke̯s viććiša,
me taj, me taj, mića zon
m a š u ke̯s viććiša.
ta-lun mi̯j-ke̯ di̯r iz lok,
iz-e̯ mene̯ vune̯d,
ta-lun mi̯j-ke̯ di̯r iz lok,
iz-e̯ mene̯ vune̯d?
og-že̯, og-že̯ me vune̯d
tače̯m mića zonme̯s,
og-že̯, og-že̯ me vune̯d
tače̯m mića zonme̯s.
ta-lun šor ńiń pe̯rai̯s,
kole̯ gorte̯ munni̯,
ta-lun šor ńin pe̯rai̯s,
kole̯ gorte̯ munni̯.
gorti̯n me̯sjas lišti̯te̯m,
mame̯ mene̯ vidas,
gorti̯n me̯sjas lišti̯te̯m,
mame̯ mene̯ vidas.

b)

me taj, me taj, mića zon
m a š uke̯s viććiša.
mi̯j-ke̯, meša di̯r iz vo,
iz-e̯ sija vune̯d,

In the street there lives a girl, there lives a girl,
doľi-śeľi . . . there lives a girl.
A lad visits the girl, a lad visits the girl,
doľi-śeľi . . . a lad visits her.
"Lad, lad, why do you come, why do you come,
doľi-śeľi . . . why do you come?
Your father will chide you, will chide you,
doľi-śeľi . . . he will chide you.
Your mother will follow you, will follow you,
doľi-śeľi . . . she will follow you."

48.

(a)

I indeed, I indeed, a handsome lad,
Am waiting for Mašuk.
I indeed, I indeed, handsome lad,
Am waiting for Mašuk.
She has not yet come today,
Has she forgotten me?
She has not yet come today,
Has she forgotten me?
No, no, I do not forget
Such a handsome lad.
No, no, I do not forget
Such a handsome lad.
It is late today, it is time
For me to go home,
It is late today, it is time
For me to go home.
The cows are unmilked at home,
Mother will chide me,
The cows are unmilked at home,
Mother will chide me.

(b)

I indeed, I indeed, handsome lad,
Am waiting for Mašuk.
She has not come for some time,
Has she forgotten me?

mi̮j-ke̮, meśa, di̮r iz vo,
iz-e̮ sija vune̮d?
vune̮dni̮ me og vune̮d
tače̮m mića zonme̮s,
vune̮dni̮ me og vune̮d
tače̮m mića zonme̮s.

. . . .

na kole̮-ke̮, ći̮šjan bośt,
ke̮sjan-ke̮, okaśni̮,
na kole̮-ke̮, ći̮šjan bośt,
ke̮sjan-ke̮ okaśni̮ . . .

49.

sad-je̮ri̮n-ke̮ ni̮v guľajte̮,
sećće zon voli̮vle̮.
"zonme̮, zonme̮, moloďeće,
šoća taj voli̮vlan,
zonme̮, zonme̮, moloďeće,
šoća taj voli̮vlan."
"rad pe̮ ved-ke̮ me voli̮vla,
ńi-ne̮me̮n koźnaśni̮,
rad pe̮ ved-ke̮ me voli̮vla,
ńi-ne̮me̮n koźnaśni̮.
p i ť i ras-ke̮ me vetla da
dona koźin vaja,
p i ť iras-ke̮ me vetla da
dona koźin vaja,
dona koźin, ki̮k koźin da
kumać da kitajka,
dona koźin ki̮k koźin da
kumać da kitajka."
"kumaćse̮-ke̮ me-j og paśtav
kitajka og novli̮,
kumaćse̮-ke̮ me-j og paśtav,
kitajka og novli̮.
ki̮ź ľubitan, si̮ź ľubit da
bośt zarńija ćuń-ki̮č,
ki̮ź ľubitan, si̮ź ľubit da
bośt zarńija ćuń-ki̮č,

She has not come for some time,
Has she forgotten me?
Forget you? I shall not forget
Such a handsome lad,
Forget you? I shall not forget
Such a handsome lad.
. . . .
If you need it, take the kerchief,
If you want to kiss me,
If you need it, take the kerchief,
If you want to kiss me . . .

49.

A girl is walking in the garden,
A lad goes that way.
"Lad, lad, young man,
You come here seldom,
Lad, lad, young man,
You come here seldom."
"Why, I come here gladly,
Only I have nothing to give you,
Why, I come here gladly,
Only I have nothing to give you.
If I go to Petersburg,
I shall bring you expensive gifts,
If I go to Petersburg,
I shall bring you dear gifts,
Dear gifts, two gifts,
Red cotton cloth and nankeen,
Dear gifts, two gifts,
Red cotton cloth and nankeen."
"I'll not put on a red cotton dress,
I'll not wear nankeen.
I will never put on a red cotton dress,
I will never wear nankeen.
Love me as you love me now,
Bring me a golden ring,
Love me as you love me now,
Bring me a golden ring,

zarńija ćuń-ki̯č, ki̯k ćuń-ki̯č da
krug ge̯ge̯r ge̯ge̯rtam,
zarńija ćuń-ke̯č, ki̯k ćuń-ki̯č da
krug ge̯ge̯r ge̯ge̯rtam.
krug ge̯ge̯ri̯s-ke̯ ge̯ge̯rtam,
kujimi̯ś okaśam.

50.

ge̯ti̯re̯j mene̯ oz lubit,
kre̯vať vi̯li̯ś mene̯ je̯tkis,
kre̯vať vi̯li̯ś mene̯ je̯tkis da
kije-koke̯ menam ve̯rźis,
kije-koke̯ menam ve̯rźis da.
vetla že̯ me v o l g a vi̯le̯,
vetla že̯ me v o l g a vi̯le̯ da
bośta že̯ me lećid britva,
bośta že̯ me lećid britva da
brita že̯ me vež kudrijas,
brita že̯ me vež kudrijas da
šondi̯-bane̯j vež kudrijej!

51.

a)

ćiži̯ke̯s kole̯ kutni̯ da
sadoke̯ kole̯ je̯rtni̯,
sadoke̯ kole̯ je̯rtni̯ da
ke̯jdi̯se̯n kole̯ verdni̯.
ke̯jdi̯si̯s pe̯ vesjite̯m da
vesjiśi̯s pe̯ bi̯dmi̯te̯m.
k e̯ r t-k e r e̯ s i̯ n bi̯dme̯ma da
ke̯rt pos kuźta lokte̯ma . . .

b)

ćiži̯ke̯s kole̯ kutni̯ da
sadoke̯ kole̯ je̯rtni̯,
sadoke̯ kole̯ je̯rtni̯ da
ke̯jdi̯se̯n kole̯ verdni̯.
ke̯jdi̯se̯n kole̯ verdni̯ da
ke̯jdi̯si̯s pe̯ vesjite̯m.

A golden ring, two rings,
And we shall walk round,
A golden ring, two rings,
And we shall walk round,
We'll kiss each other three times.

50.

My wife does not love me,
She pushed me out of bed,
She pushed me out of bed,
My hands and legs were sprained,
My hands and legs were sprained.
I'll go as far as the Volga,
I'll go as far as the Volga, and
I'll bring a sharp razor,
I'll bring a sharp razor, and
I'll shave off her blonde locks,
I'll shave off her blonde locks.
My little sun, my blonde locks!

51.

(a)

You must catch a siskin and
Shut it in a cage,
Shut it in a cage and
Give it seed to eat.
The seed is unwashed, and
The one to wash it has not yet grown up.
She has grown up in Kẹrt-kerẹs and
Arrived across an iron bridge.

(b)

You must catch a siskin and
Shut it in a cage,
Shut it in a cage and
Given seed to eat, and
The seed is unwashed.
The seed is unwashed, and

ke̮jdi̮si̮s pe̮ vesjite̮m da
mića ni̮vle̮n ki ki̮nme̮,
mića ni̮vle̮n ki ki̮nme̮ da
li̮mjen kole̮ mi̮śki̮ni̮,
li̮mjen kole̮ mi̮śki̮ni̮ da
pać bi dori̮n kośti̮ni̮.

52.

asja pe̮ ki̮a, ki̮a voǯ lebale̮,
voǯ lebale̮ da ri̮t-i-ja pe ki̮a,
ri̮tja ki̮a, ki̮a śor lebale̮,
śor lebale̮ da vi̮vśań pe̮ pi̮ža,
vi̮vśań pi̮ža, pi̮žajas ki̮vte̮ni̮,
ki̮vte̮ni̮ da si̮ni̮śjasi̮s,
tom ni̮vjasi̮s da be̮žali̮śjasi̮s,
be̮žali̮śjasi̮s tom mića zonjasi̮s,
tom zonjasi̮s da še̮ras pukali̮śjas,
še̮ras pukali̮śjasi̮s tom ić-mońjasi̮s,
tom ić-mońjasi̮s da naja śile̮ni̮,
naja śile̮ni̮ zev-i šoga, šoga,
šoga, šoga da va-dor-i kuźa,
va-dor kuźa ni̮v-i daj guľajte̮,
ni̮v guľajte̮ da kokas pe̮ tupeľ,
kokas tupeľ be̮r vi̮las taľale̮,
taľale̮ da juras pe̮ ći̮š-i-jan,
juras ći̮šjan, ći̮šjanse̮ voštale̮,
voštale̮ da taja pe̮ ći̮šjan,
taja ći̮šjan, či̮šjan men abu žaľ,
men abu žaľ da te̮ľ-i-ke̮ pe̮ men-i žaľ,
te̮ľke̮ men žaľ aslam musa druge̮j.

53.

more dori̮n tuman li̮be̮ćće, ok
me dumajti tumane̮n da
ve̮le̮m juś-ǯoǯeg lebe̮-j,
ve̮le̮m juś-ǯoǯeg lebe̮, ok
juś-ǯoǯeg be̮rśań da
pe̮ri̮ś kuč ve̮ćće-j,
pe̮ri̮ś kuč ve̮ćće. ok

The fair girl's hand is frozen,
The fair girl's hand is frozen, and
It must be washed with snow.
It must be washed with snow, and
Dried by the fire in the stove.

52.

The morning twilight, the morning twilight rises early,
It rises early, and the evening twilight,
The evening twilight, the evening twilight comes down late,
It comes down late, and boatmen from upstream,
Boatmen from upstream float downstream,
Oarsmen float downstream,
Young girls and steersmen;
The steersmen are young, handsome lads,
Young lads, and sitting in the middle,
Sitting in the middle are young wives,
Young wives, and they are singing,
They sing very sadly, so sadly,
So sadly, so sadly, and along the bank,
Along the bank a girl is walking,
A girl is walking with slippers on her feet,
The slippers on her feet are worn down,
They are worn down, and she has a kerchief on her head,
She has a kerchief on her had, and she loses her kerchief,
She loses it and for this kerchief,
For this kerchief, for this kerchief I am not sorry,
I am not sorry for it; only,
Only for my dear sweetheart am I sorry.

53.

Fog is rising on the shore of the sea; oh,
I thought it was fog, and
A swan flies there,
A swan flies there, oh.
The swan
Is chased by an old eagle,
It is chased by an old eagle. Oh.

kuče̯j pe̯ kuče̯j daj
ke̯n vetlin-munin?
ke̯n vetlin-munin? ok
me vetli-muni daj
s a r a t o v ai̯n,
s a r a t o v ai̯n. ok
s a r a t o v ai̯n da
mi̯j ki̯vlin-aǯǯin?
mi̯j ki̯vlin-aǯǯin? ok
me ki̯vli-aǯǯi da
more dori̯n jeǯi̯d jaj kujle̯-j,
more dori̯n jeǯi̯d jaj kujle̯. ok
ne-kod sećće-j oz voli̯v da
kujim ćiki̯ć voli̯vle̯-j,
kujim ćiki̯ć voli̯vle̯. ok
e̯ťi-ke̯ pe̯ ćiki̯ćis daj
re̯ďime̯j mami̯s,
re̯ďime̯j mami̯s, ok
me̯d-e̯-ke̯ ćiki̯ćis daj
re̯ďime̯j ćojis, ok
kojme̯d-e̯-ke̯ ćiki̯ćis daj
aslas babai̯s,
aslas babai̯s. ok
mami̯s-ke̯ si̯le̯n be̯rǯǯas daj
si̯le̯n śin-vai̯s,
si̯le̯n śin-vai̯s, ok
vizi̯v-i ju moz vizi̯vte̯ daj
ćojis-ke̯ si̯le̯n be̯rǯǯas,
ćojis-ke̯ si̯le̯n be̯rǯǯas, ok
si̯le̯n śin-vai̯s daj
asja li̯s-va moz uśe-j,
asja li̯s-va moz uśe. ok
aslas babai̯s be̯rǯǯas daj
si̯le̯n śin-vai̯s,
si̯le̯n śin-vai̯s, ok
si̯le̯n śin-vai̯s daj
vizi̯v šor moz vizi̯vte̯.

My eagle, my eagle,
Where have you beeen roaming,
Where have you been roaming? Oh.
I have been roaming
In Saratov,
In Saratov. Oh.
In Saratov
What have you heard and seen,
What have you heard and seen? Oh,
I have heard and seen:
A white corpse lying on the shore of the sea,
A white corpse lying on the shore of the sea. Oh
Nobody goes there.
Three swallows come,
Three swallows come. Oh
One of the swallows
Is his mother,
His mother. Oh,
The second swallow
Is his dear sister, oh,
The third swallow
Is his own wife,
His own wife. Oh,
When his mother begins to weep
Her tears,
Hear tears, oh,
Well up like a swift stream.
If his sister begins to weep,
If his sister begins to weep,
Her tears
Drop like the morning dew,
Drop like the morning dew. Oh
His wife begins to weep,
Her tears,
Her tears, oh
Her tears
Gush forth like a swift brook.

54.

kudrija mića kiǯǯej,
di̯re̯n ńin te sulalan!
oj, ki̯ǯǯej, ki̯ǯǯej, ki̯ǯǯej,
di̯re̯n ńin te sulalan!
mi ved tene̯ pe̯re̯dam,
seśśa tene̯ ćeglalam.
oj, ki̯ǯǯej, ki̯ǯǯej, ki̯ǯǯej,
seśśa tene̯ ćeglalam.
tene̯ i gorte̯ nuam,
seśśa kore̯śe karam.
oj, ki̯ǯǯej, ki̯ǯǯej, ki̯ǯǯej,
seśśa kore̯śe karam.
te̯e̯n ǯoǯni̯me̯s ći̯škam,
seśśa musuke̯s viććam.
oj, ki̯ǯǯej, ki̯ǯǯej, ki̯ǯǯej,
seśśa musuke̯s viććam.

55.

mame̯ mene̯ pińale̯,
kode̯s me ľubita:
kuče̯m-ke̯ ved i ľok mort
vakśema me vi̯le̯,
kuće̯m-ke̯ ved i ľok mort
vakśema me vi̯le̯.
in vakśi te ľok morte̯ . . .

56.

śondi̯-bane̯j, ole̯me̯j da
tom pe̯ra koľľale̯me̯j,
tom pe̯rae̯-j, tom gaže̯j da
ki̯ćće kole̯, vetle̯me̯j,
ki̯ćće kole̯, vetle̯me̯j,
kode̯s kole̯, ľubite̯me̯j da
mi̯j kole̯, śorńite̯me̯j.
. . . .
viǯe pe̯rni̯ vi̯j abu.
p a ľe munni̯ tuj lojis, da
viǯe pi̯rni̯ vi̯j lojis.

54.

My beautiful, spreading birch-tree,
How long you have been standing!
Oh, my birch-tree, my birch-tree, my birch-tree,
How long you have been standing!
We are going to fell you,
Then we shall break you to pieces.
Oh, my birch-tree, my birch-tree, my birch-tree,
Then we shall break you to pieces.
We shall take you home,
Then we shall make a bath-broom of you.
Oh, my birch-tree, my birch-tree, my birch-tree,
Then we shall make a bath-broom of you.
We shall sweep our floor with you,
Then we shall wait for our beloved to come.
Oh, my birch-tree, my birch-tree, my birch-tree,
Then we shall wait for our beloved to come.

55.

Mother you are chiding me
For the man I am in love with:
Some wicked man
Has laughed at me,
Some wicked man
Has laughed at me.
Do not laugh at me, you wicked man . . .

56.

My little sun, my life,
The passing away of my youthful days,
My youthful days, my youthful joys,
I walked where I had to,
I walked where I had to,
I loved whom I had to,
I said what I had to.

. . . .

To begin Lent, we have no butter.
To go to Paľ, a road was made,
To begin Lent, butter was made.

57.

e̯ k ś i ń ń a k r a s a,
mami̯d sur puve̯ma da
sur juni̯ koris.
og ešti̯ pe̯, og ešti̯:
jur-vi̯le̯ vevte̯m,
kok-ule̯-j poste̯m . . .

58.

šondi̯e̯j-mame̯j pe̯ di̯r-i novle̯dlin,
di̯r-i novle̯dlin da ćase̯n re̯ďitin,
di̯r-i novle̯dlin da ćase̯n re̯ďitin.
re̯ďitin, matuška, mićae̯s, bure̯s,
re̯ďitin, matuška, mićae̯s, bure̯s,
bi̯ttin, matuška, verbai̯ś ǯuǯi̯d . . .

(e) Laments

59. *ni̯vle̯n perve̯j be̯rde̯m*

ke̯n-i-ke̯ pe̯ taj lok-i-te̯mae̯ś daj
na ber ľok-i taj re̯d-i-vužjis,
sećće e̯mi̯j me ve̯li ke̯sja da me munni̯.
abu ved menam roć bajari̯s daj baťuškoi̯s,
sija-ke̯-j eśke̯ ve̯li menam da daške̯ med bur sajas śetis.
e̯ni taj ľok-i mužik dore̯ loi men końerli̯ daj munni̯.
ľok raka-ćukar kojde̯ś taj loktisni̯ da mene̯ nuisni̯.
kužli̯vli veśke̯ me aśśim mi̯v-ki̯de̯s kutli̯vli̯ni̯ daj loi munni̯,
šondi̯-bane̯j-ke̯ menam daj ole̯me̯j,
taćće me ve̯li ke̯sjili daj-i munni̯se̯,
ig ved me kužli̯vli̯ sije taǯi daj dumi̯štli̯ni̯se̯.

60. *ke̯sali̯ be̯rde̯m*

i šondi̯e̯-bane̯j-ke̯ menam-i taj ni̯v-i da ke̯sae̯j, ďevjej krasae̯j,
koľ-i-ni̯ taj menam końerle̯n daj pondis daj ni̯v-i ke̯sae̯j, ďev-i-jej krasae̯j,

57.

Beautiful Ekśińńa,
Your mother has brewed beer and
Invited you to drink beer.
I have no time, I have no time:
There is no roof above my head,
There is no floor beneath my feet . . .

58.

My little sun, mother, you carried me for a long time,
Your carried me for a long time, and you gave birth to me in a single hour,
Your carried me for a long time, and you gave birth to me in a single hour.
My pretty mother, you bore me to be fair and kind,
My pretty mother, you bore me to be fair and kind,
My pretty mother, you have reared me to be taller than the willow . . .

59.

The bride's first lament

There arrived from somewhere
A vast number of wicked relatives,
I have to go there.
I have no Russian boyar for a father,
For he would have given me to the finest man.
Now I, poor thing, had to marry a wicked man.
People like an evil flock of crows came to carry me off.
Perhaps I could have lived sensibly, but I had to go away,
My little sun, my life,
Here I had to come,
For I could not have thought it to be like this.

60.

Lament for her plait

My little sun, my maiden plait, my virgin beauty,
I, poor thing, have left behind my maiden plait, my virgin beauty,

i voši taj menam końere̯jlen daj ni̯v daj ni̯v-i ke̯sae̯j,
kor-i-śni̯ e̯d sije kole̯ menśim konere̯jli̯ś daj ni̯v-i ke̯sae̯j.
kor-i̯-śe že̯ musa vokjase̯j menśim zarńi daj ni̯v-i ke̯sae̯s,
vetli̯le̯ že̯ ti daj gaža vićko doras-i daj musa da vok-i-jase̯j,
kor-i̯-śe že̯ vićko dori̯ś-i daj vićko daj vićko ge̯ge̯r-i-śi̯s . . .

61. *baťli̯ be̯rde̯m*

śondi̯-bane̯j pe̯ menam daj baťuš-i-koe̯j,
munin že te me dini̯ś da końere̯j dini̯ś.
ki̯ćće ne̯ mene̯ te me̯din da tojišt-i-ni̯se̯?
kužin taj ne̯šna bi̯tti̯ni̯se̯ daj,
kužin taj mene̯ daj śet-i-ni̯se̯.
paśibe̯ že̯ ten, baťuš-i-koe̯j,
lećid kosanad teni̯d daj i̯čke̯te̯mi̯d vi̯le̯,
paśibe̯ že̯ ten, baťuš-i-koe̯j,
kokńi narmannad mene̯ kurte̯de̯mi̯d vi̯le̯.
in-i taj mene̯ ube̯ľitli̯ ke̯ǯid vi̯las pet-i-ni̯se̯.
e̯ni ved me sećće muna da og kuž vi̯ǯedli̯ni̯se̯,
bi̯de̯nli̯ ved sen lova kovte̯m-i-tor . . .

62. *mamli̯ be̯rde̯m*

lun-i šon-i-di̯e̯j-ke̯ menam daj matuškae̯j,
roć akań-i-jase̯j-ke̯ menam daj musa ćojjase̯j,
roć-i bajarjase̯j-i-ke̯ menam daj musa vokjase̯j,
mi̯rde̯n taj-i ti lok-i-te̯mi̯d daj me dine̯,
końere̯j dine̯ daj me dine̯ . . .

63. *batli̯, kule̯mali̯*

śondi̯-bane̯j-ke̯ menam daj baťuškoe̯j,
ke̯rmiľećej-ke̯ menam daj baťuškoe̯j,
ki̯ćće ne̯ ńin te daj me̯de̯ććin?
ki̯ćće ne̯ ńin mi tene̯ me̯dim daj me̯de̯dni̯?
lun-śondi̯e̯j-ke̯ daj baťuškoe̯j,
bi̯ttin taj mijane̯s da te ki̯mine̯s da jui̯štin.
e̯ni taj ne̯ ki̯ćće-ke̯ te mijane̯s daj bi̯de̯s daj koľan?

I, poor thing, have lost my maiden plait,
I, poor thing, have to find it, my maiden plait.
Search for it, dear brothers, search for my golden maiden plait,
Go to the beautiful church, dear brothers,
Search for it by the church, around the church . . .

61.

Lament to the father

My little sun, my father,
You have gone from me, poor thing,
Where have you thrust me?
Surely you could have reared me a little longer.
Surely you could have given me away.
Thank you, father,
That you gave me a sharp scythe to mow with,
Thank you, father,
That you gave me a light rake to rake with.
You could not bear me to go out in the cold weather.
Now that I am going there, I dare not raise my eyes,
I shall be a burden to everybody . . .

62.

Lament to the mother

My little sun, my pretty mother,
My Russian doll, my dear sisters,
My Russian boyars, my dear brothers,
You have come with might to see me,
Poor thing, to see me . . .

63.

Lament for a dead father

My little sun, my dear father,
My sustainer, my dear father,
Where have you taken your way?
Where shall we accompany you?
My little sun, my dear father,
You have raised us, and how much you have drunk.
Are you now to leave us all?

ok, šondi̮ej-ke̮ menam daj baťuškoe̮j;
ke̮rmi̮ľećej-ke̮ menam daj baťuškoe̮j,
ta regi̮da e̮mi̮j te mijan daj mijan daj me̮de̮ććin!
ki̮ćće ne̮ te mijane̮s daj koľan?
kod vi̮le̮ naďejae̮n ne̮ te baťuškoe̮j daj koľan?
peski̮sla ved te mijane̮s daj nuve̮dlin,
turuni̮sla ved te mijane̮s daj nuve̮dlin,
ke̮ǯid už vi̮las e̮d mijane̮s ńe-ki̮ćće daj en petke̮dli̮v.
e̮ni e̮d mijanli̮ loe, baťuškoe̮j, daj bi̮de̮n asli̮ni̮m karni̮.
ke̮rmi̮ľećej-ke̮ daj lun-šondi̮ej da baťej,
mi̮j ńin taja daj loi?
ki̮ćće ne̮ ńin tene̮ daj me̮de̮dam?
taje e̮me̮j mi tene̮ daj dumajtlim,
ta regidae̮n daj ta kostie̮n daj kulin.
lun-šondi̮ej-ke̮ ke̮rmi̮ľećej daj baťuškoe̮j,
in kuž e̮d taj mijane̮s na daj bi̮tti̮ni̮te̮,
. . . daj koľi e̮d mijane̮s da vere̮s saje daj śetni̮se̮.
pijante̮ e̮d koľi mijan da ge̮travni̮te̮,
veľiś e̮d kole̮ munni̮ da ešte̮ććini̮te̮,
ke̮rmi̮ľećej-ke̮ da baťuškoe̮j,
tome̮n-bure̮n na te taj me̮de̮ććin,
lun-šondi̮ej menam da baťej.

64. *mamli̮, kule̮mali̮*

lun-šondi̮ej-i-ke̮ menam-i daj matuš-i-kae̮j,
ki̮ćće ne̮ te daj na-j me̮de̮ććin?
ki̮ćće ne̮ te mi daj tene̮ me̮de̮dam?
lun-i-šondi̮ej daj matuškae̮j,
ta regi̮dae̮n te taj daj ešte̮ććin,
kužin taj mijane̮s daj bi̮tti̮ni̮se̮,
in na vevjavli̮ te mijane̮s daj ne̮ śet-i-ni̮se̮,
mića plaťťese̮ mijan daj karni̮s,
mića ke̮mse̮ mijan daj le̮śedni̮s,
aćid ve̮d te in ube̮ľitli̮ daj junise̮ daj śojni̮se̮.
e̮ni taj bi̮de̮n i tenad daj-i koľi,
lun-šondi̮ej-i-ke̮ menam da matuškae̮j,
bi̮de̮n gaža kerka-kartai̮d daj koľi,
veśt kuźaśań-ke̮ bi̮ttin mijane̮s daj ćuń kuźaśań,
stavse̮ taj mijane̮s da vele̮din daj ke̮medin daj paśte̮din,

Oh, my little sun, my dear father,
My sustainer, my dear father,
How soon you have set out on your way!
Where, to what fate do you leave us?
To whom do you leave us, dear father, in trust?
You took us when you went for firewood,
You took us when you went for hay,
You never took us to work in cold weather.
Now, dear father, we must do everything by ourselves.
My nourishing little sun, my father,
What has happened?
Where have we accompanied you?
Had we ever thought of you
That you would die so soon?
My little sun, my sustainer, dear father,
You could not bring us up,
. . . you could not live to give us away in marriage.
It has been left for us to arrange for the wedding of your sons,
Now we must go and perform our duties.
My sustainer, dear father,
You departed young and healthy,
My little sun, my father.

64.

Lament for a dead mother

My little sun, dear mother,
Where have you taken your way?
Where shall we accompany you?
My little sun, dear mother,
You have finished very soon indeed,
You could hardly raise us,
You did not even have time to give us away in marriage,
To make fine clothes for us,
To make fine shoes for us,
You could not bear to drink and eat alone.
Now you have left everything behind,
My little sun, dear mother,
All your beautiful farm has been left behind,
From our childhood you raised us,
You taught us everything, and you clothed us,

mi raďiś daške̮ te daj una keǯidse̮ ki̮nmalin,
mi raďiś daške̮ daj ki̮nmalin daj či̮gjalin,
mi̮j će̮ski̮di̮s veli, in ubeľitli̮ te daj śojni̮te̮,
sije taj mijan daj ver-i-din.
ki̮će-ke̮ ve̮li taj tə munan daj viǯedam e̮śińe̮di̮s,
e̮ni tene̮ ki̮ś ne̮ me̮dam mi daj viććini̮se̮?
ke̮rmi̮ľećej-ke̮ menam daj matuška̮i̮s abu,
lun-šondi̮i̮s taj menam daj matuška̮i̮s oz lo,
kode̮s ne̮ ve̮d mi viććam da kod vi̮le̮ daj me̮dam daj ľubujććini̮se̮,
lun-šondi̮ej daj matuškae̮j.

65. *be̮rde̮de̮m*

te vi̮le̮-j spase̮j-ke̮ me daj božja da maťere̮j,
bož-i-ja maťerej pe̮ ve̮d ti daj ke̮rmi̮ľećej daj baťuš-i-koe̮j,
ke̮rmi̮ľeć baťuš-i-koe̮j be̮rdi da lun-i-šondi̮ej matuškae̮j,
mi̮j-i ne̮ taje mene̮ końere̮s pondinni̮d daj-i karni̮se̮,
janse̮d-i-ni̮ taj końere̮s mene̮ ti daj pon-i-dinni̮d,
kov-i-te̮m-i-tor e̮mi̮j me końere̮j tijan daj tijan-i loi?
e̮ťi god keť eś-i-ke̮ mene̮ ješše̮ ti daj viǯinni̮d,
ješše̮ keť eśke̮ me ti dori̮n e̮ťi god-i-se̮, godse̮ da krasujćći!
šondi̮-bane̮j-ke̮ menam daj mame̮ dori̮n da ole̮mej
koľni̮ taj menam końere̮jle̮n da bi̮de̮n daj bi̮de̮n-i pondis.

(f) Children's songs, tales in verse

66.

a)

dude̮, bobe̮, ki̮ćće vetlin?
šegjes pome̮.
mi̮j vajin?
vi̮ja ńań vaji.
ki̮ćće puktin?
šegjes pome̮.
ši̮r-i-bľaď i vole̮ma,
tūke̮ma da jōke̮ma,
be̮žnas kojōte̮ma.
śera pon pi̮šjede̮ma,
śe̮d pon ve̮te̮de̮ma,
poči̮se̮ i śibde̮mae̮ś.

You endured much cold for us,
You endured much cold and hunger for us,
If you had a tasty morsel, you could not bear to eat it alone,
You nourished us with it.
When you left the house, we watched you through the window,
Now from where do we await your return?
I have no mother to sustain me,
I shall have no little sun, no dear mother
For whom to wait, in whom to take pleasure,
My pretty sun, my dear mother.

65.

Lament

I have been crying to you, my redeeming god-mother,
My god-mother, and my sustaining father,
My sustaining father and my pretty sun, mother,
What have you begun to do to me, poor thing,
You began to part from me, poor thing,
And have I, poor thing, become a burden to you?
If only you could have kept me yet one more year,
If only for one year I could have been growing more beautiful with you!
My pretty sun, mother, the life I had with you
Has all been left on me, poor as I am.

66.

(a)

dudȩ, bobȩ, where have you been?
To the end of the bench by the wall.
What have you brought?
I have brought bread and butter.
Where have you put it?
On the end of the bench by the wall.
There came a nasty mouse,
It jogged it and moved it,
It turned it over with its tail.
A spotted dog chased it away,
A black dog chased it away,
They were held up by the fence.

ke̮ni poči̮si̮s?
bi sote̮ma.
ke̮ni bii̮s?
va kuse̮de̮ma.
ke̮ni vai̮s?
e̮ška-me̮ška jue̮ma.
ke̮ni e̮ška-me̮škai̮s?
i̮be̮ ćeććema.
ke̮ni i̮bi̮s?
ćer kerale̮ma.
ke̮ni ćeri̮s?
dudi̮ ľame̮ma.
ke̮ni dudi̮?
pečer pe̮vse̮ uśema.
ke̮ni peče̮r pe̮vsi̮s?
śo ve̮la-ćańa taľale̮mae̮ś da ľok kartae̮ pi̮re̮mae̮ś,
da e̮ťi kača re̮ma,
da stav kartai̮s kiśśema vi̮li̮sas.
śa e̮ťi śin-pe̮la,
me̮d pete̮ peľ-pe̮la,
kojme̮d pete̮ be̮ž-pe̮la,
e̮ťi pete̮ śivko da burko, meščanne̮j voronko.

b)

dude̮, bobe̮, ki̮ćće vetlin?
ćože̮ gue̮.
mi̮j ne̮ vajin?
vi̮ja ńań vaji.
ki̮ćće puktin?
šegjes pome̮ pukti.
abu taj da ve̮vle̮ma.
śe̮d pon pi̮šjede̮ma, śera pon ve̮te̮de̮ma, poči̮s kolase̮ i śibde̮ma.
ke̮n ine̮ poči̮si̮s?
bi sote̮ma.
ke̮n ine̮ bii̮s?
va kuse̮de̮ma.
ke̮n ine̮ vai̮s?
e̮ška-me̮ška jue̮ma.

Where is the fence?
Fire has burnt it up.
Where is the fire?
The water has put it out.
Where is the water?
The rainbow has drunk it up.
Where is the rainbow?
It has jumped on the hill.
Where is the hill?
The axe has chopped it in pieces.
where is the axe?
dudi̯ has made it blunt.
Where is *dudi̯?*
He has fallen into the nettles.
Where are the nettles?
A hundred horses and colts trod on them and went to a tumbledown stable,
One of them was magpie-coloured,
And the whole stable collapsed.
Then one of them comes out with one eye,
The second with one ear,
The third one with half a tail,
A grey, black and brown magic steed comes out.

(b)

dude̯, bobe̯, where have you been?
In my uncle's cellar.
What have you brought?
I have brought bread and butter.
Where have you put it?
On the end of the bench by the wall.
It was not there.
A black dog chased it, a spotted dog drove it away, it stuck in a hole in the fence.
Well, where is the fence?
Fire has burnt it.
Well, where is the fire?
Water has put it out.
Well, where is the water?
The rainbow has drunk it up.

ke̯n ine̯ da e̯ška-me̯škai̯s?
i̯be̯ ćeććema.
ke̯n ine̯ i̯bi̯s?
ćer keraḷe̯ma.
ke̯n ine̯ ćeri̯s?
zud ľame̯ma.
ke̯n ine̯ zudjis?
peče̯r pe̯vste̯ uśema.
ke̯n ine̯ peče̯ri̯s?
śo ve̯la-ćaňa ǯuge̯mae̯ś da ľake̯mae̯ś bi̯de̯n da ľok kartae̯ i pi̯re̯mae̯ś.
e̯ťik ve̯v surtte̯ma jona, stav kartai̯s kiśśema da:
kodi pete̯ śin-pe̯la,
kodi pete̯ peľ-pe̯la,
kodi pete̯ kok-pe̯la.
e̯ťi pete̯ śivko da burko, meščane̯j voronko,
sije vengrijae̯ nue̯dni̯.
me̯d pete̯ śivko da burko,
sije kare̯ nue̯dni̯.

67.

a)

śe̯d ve̯r še̯ri̯n ve̯v ge̯rdle̯,
da ve̯v vi̯las že̯ zon be̯rde̯.
zonme̯, zonme̯, mi̯j be̯rdan?
mi̯j ne̯ me-j og-i be̯rd?!
mame̯-baťe ki̯vte̯m-vorte̯m,
voke̯ ve̯li, stre̯je pe̯ri,
ćoje ve̯li, veśe pe̯ri.
jag-tuj vi̯li̯n śuź bukse̯.
śuźe, śuźe, mi̯j buksan?
mi̯j ne̯ me-j og buksi̯?!
oš-u-mu gue̯s ge̯risni̯,
jur-uv viǯes i̯čkisni̯.

b)

śe̯d ve̯r še̯ri̯n ve̯v ge̯rdle̯,
ve̯v vi̯las i zon be̯rde̯.
zonme̯, zonme̯, mi̯j be̯rdan?
ajid-mami̯d čak votas,

Well, where is the rainbow?
It has jumped on the hill.
Well, where is the hill?
The axe has chopped it in pieces.
Well, where is the axe?
The grindstone has made it blunt.
Well, where is the grindstone?
It has fallen into the nettles.
Where, where are the nettles?
A hundred horses and colts have trampled them about, covered them all with dirt, and gone into a tumbledown stable.
One of the horses gave a big fart, and the whole stable collapsed:
One comes out with one eye,
Another with one ear,
Another with one leg.
A grey, black and brown magic steed comes out,
That they will take to Hungary,
Another grey, black and brown one comes out,
That they will take to Syktyvkar.

67.

(a)

A horse is neighing in the middle of a dark wood,
A boy is crying on the horse.
My boy, my boy, why are you crying?
Why should I not cry?
My parents are dumb,
I had a brother; he became a cripple,
I had a sister; she got a bad name.
An owl is hooting on the path in the fir-wood.
Owl, owl, why are you hooting?
Why should I not hoot?
They have ploughed up the moles' burrow,
They have mown the field with its haystocks.

(b)

A horse is neighing in the middle of a dark wood,
A boy is crying on the horse.
My boy, my boy, why are you crying?
Your father and mother are picking mushrooms,

vedra rok puas,
roć latkai̮n vi̮j si̮vdas.

c)

śe̮d ve̮r še̮ri̮n ve̮v ge̮rdle̮,
ve̮v vi̮las i zon be̮rde̮.
zonme̮, zonme̮, mi̮j be̮rdan?
ajid-mami̮d ćas voas.
ajid-mami̮d ćas voas,
roć ladkai̮n vi̮j si̮vdas.
bajdu pe̮ľanu, streću varvaru,
vaśka vokle̮n vajema
kurka da re . . .

d)

śe̮d ve̮r še̮ri̮n ve̮v ge̮rdle̮,
ve̮v vi̮li̮n pe̮ zon be̮rde̮.
zonme̮, zonme̮, mi̮j be̮rdan?
mami̮d-baťid ćas voas,
kalać, preńik vajasni̮.
kalaćse̮-ke̮ kurććištan,
preńikse̮-ke̮ ćegi̮štan,
vićkoas-ke̮ piran,
teś pop sulale̮:
vi̮j jura, maa pľeša,
e̮labi̮š peľa, si̮ći̮ śinma,
kos ńań beďďa, ri̮ś ńebe̮g li̮ďďe.

e)

śe̮d ve̮r še̮ri̮n ve̮v ge̮rdle̮ da
ve̮v vi̮li̮si̮n zon be̮rde̮.
zonme̮, zonme̮, mi̮j be̮rdan? da
mami̮d-ajid ćas volas.
mami̮d-ajid ćas volas da
końi-veńi rok pue̮,
końi-veńi rok pue̮ da
roć ladkai̮n vi̮j si̮vde̮,
vi̮ľ ťe̮ś pomi̮n ke̮m vure̮ da
ń i k i t a pi ge̮traśe.

They are cooking a bucketful of porridge,
Melting butter in a Russian pan.

(c)

A horse is neighing in the middle of a dark wood,
A boy is crying on the horse.
My boy, my boy, why are you crying?
Your father and mother will soon return.
Your father and mother will soon return,
They are melting butter in a Russian pan.
I am going out into the clearing to meet Barbara,
Vaśka's brother has carried me over
kurka da re . . .

(d)

A horse is neighing in the middle of a dark wood,
A boy is crying on the horse.
My boy, my boy, why are you crying?
Your father and mother will soon come,
They will bring cake and honey-cake.
When you bite into the cake,
When you break off a piece of the honey-cake,
When you enter the church,
An oatmeal priest stands there,
His head is butter, his forehead is honey,
His ears are doughnuts, his eyes are rendered lard,
With a stick of dry bread, and he reads a book of curds.

(e)

A horse is neighing in the middle of a dark wood,
A boy is crying on the horse.
My boy, my boy, why are you crying?
Your father and mother will soon be here.
Your father and mother will soon be here,
They are cooking *końi-veńi* mush,
They are cooking *końi-veńi* mush and
Melting butter in a Russian pan,
Making shoes at the end of a new plank,
Nikita's son is about to marry.

majeg loas svaťťa,
megi̮r sija družka,
sartas pijan bi viźiśjas,
p o m e̮ s dori̮n tuśaśiśjas,
šor dorin kojtaš.
kojtašas-ke̮ me pi̮ri da:
luk kuzov da ńań padjan,
luk kuzov da ńań padjan da
de̮ra beľitan kre̮vať.
vala lećće, śuź bukse̮ da
śuźe, śuźe, mi̮j buksan?
śuźe, śuźe, mij buksan? da
p a ľsa ni̮vjas bľaďjas,
piž vi̮le̮ kavjaśiśjas da
pi̮ž i potke̮dli̮śjas,
ge̮rd ku e̮kti̮śjas.

68.

re̮ttam, ge̮ńitam
ďed orde̮ da bab orde̮
sur juni̮, vina juni̮ da
pire̮g-šańga śojni̮.
pire̮g-šańga śojni̮ da
ďedi̮d strećajte̮,
ďedi̮d strećajte̮ da
vina štope̮n,
babi̮d strećajte̮ da
šańgi-bľudjen.

69.

koke̮, koke̮, pi̮šji da
će̮dja, puvja jag vi̮le̮,
će̮dja, puvja jag vi̮le̮ da
mi̮r-i-poma ńur vi̮le̮,
mi̮r-i-poma ńur vi̮le̮ da
oz-i-tuśa ve̮r vi̮le̮,
oz-i-tuśa ve̮r vi̮le̮ da
maľina pe̮vste̮,
maľina pe̮vste̮ da
sete̮ra kuste̮.

The stake will be the woman who asks for the girl's hand in marriage,
The bent yoke will be the best man,
The sons of the torch will be the guardians of the fire,
Mating by *pome̮s*,
A dance on the banks of the brook.
I have gone to the dancing party:
The wicker onion-basket and the bread-basket,
The wicker onion-basket and the bread-basket, and
The linen-bleaching vat.
She goes to fetch water; and an owl hoots.
Owl, owl, why are you hooting?
Owl, owl, why are you hooting?
The girls of *pal'* are whores,
Creepers in to boats,
Breakers of boats,
Collectors of red leather.

68.

We are trotting, we are galloping,
To grandfather and grandmother,
To drink beer, to drink vodka, and
To eat pirogi and pie.
To eat pirogi and pie.
Grandfather receives us,
Grandfather receives us
With a bottle of vodka.
Grandmother receives us
With a plate of pie.

69.

My feet, my feet, make haste and run
Into the pine-wood where bilberries and cranberries grow,
Into the pine-wood where bilberries and cranberries grow,
To the peat-bog where brambles grow,
To the peat-bog where brambles grow,
To the woods where wild strawberries grow,
To the woods where wild strawberries grow,
Into the raspberries,
Into the raspberries and
Into the black currant bush.

70.

końere̯j da ratńike̯j,
mi̯jen bara ošjiśan?
ruźa pińa babanad,
joś ćepeľa pijannad,
joś ćepeľa pijannad,
ore̯m koska sumkanad.

71.

ši̯r ki̯vte̯, kate̯
kača-ke̯ja pi̯žnas,
ur-be̯ž zibnas,
moj-be̯ž peli̯snas,
kurjai̯ś da kurjae̯.
priluki̯ś da priluke̯.

72.

ki̯siľej, kańiľej,
ǯaǯ-dor kuźta in vetli̯,
popadďali̯ś ne̯k in śoj,
pre̯skurńali̯ś pre̯skur in śoj,
kańe, bri̯ś, bri̯ś bri̯ś!

73.

p a š a pije, ćećći!
ćećća da e̯d og že̯ mi̯śśi.
p a š a pije, mi̯śśi!
mi̯śśa da e̯d og že̯ paśtaś.
p a š a pije paśtaś!
paśtaśa da e̯d og že̯ śojni̯ pukśi.
p a š a pije, pukśi!
śoja da e̯d og že̯ uǯ vi̯lad mun.
p a š a pije, mun!
muna da e̯d og že̯ uǯav.

74.

kača, kača, kič-koč,
turi pomeće kore̯.
vurdi̯ś ker pe̯re̯de̯,
oš kerka lepte̯,

70.

My poor warrior,
What are you boasting about again?
Your wife with her decayed teeth,
Your sons like sharp pincers
Your sons like sharp pincers,
Your hipshot daughters.

71.

The mouse tows down and down the river
In a boat made of the breastbone of a magpie,
With a rudder made of a squirrel's tail,
With an oar made of a beaver's tail,
From inlet to inlet,
From the bend to bend.

72.

My pussy, my tabby,
Do not walk all along the shelf,
Do not lick up the cream of the priest's wife,
Do not eat the sacrificial bread of the wafer-baking woman!
Cat, shoo, shoo, shoo!

73.

Paša, my son, get up!
I'll get up but I won't wash myself.
Paša my son, wash yourself!
I'll wash but I won't dress.
Paša my son, get dressed!
I'll get dressed but I won't sit down to eat.
Paša my son, sit down!
I'll eat, but I won't go to work.
Paša my son, go along!
I'll go along but I won't work.

74.

Magpie, magpie, *kič-koč*,
The crane asks you for a helping hand:
The mole is felling trees,
The bear is building a house,

ke̮jin ker ki̮skale̮,
ke̮ć ke̮vdum pe̮žale̮,
ur bi viʒe,
ruć de̮ra ki̮e̮.

75.

m u r j a-m a r j a, ćećći-že̮, ćećći!
asja koraśid vois,
ri̮tja nui̮śid vois.
m a r j a ćeććis.
e̮te̮re̮-ke̮ gur-gar,
me̮de̮re̮-ke̮ gir-gar,
vedrase̮-ke̮ kvaťitis,
vedrai̮s pi̮de̮ste̮m,
ke̮šse̮-ke̮ kvaťitis,
ke̮šis nudte̮m,
karnanse̮-ke̮ kvaťitis,
karnani̮s čupe̮dte̮m.
vala me̮de̮ććis,
pop voćća̮ loi,
turun-vevt ćužjištis,
jur-śii̮s ľoźmis.
ni̮le̮, ni̮le̮, mi̮j či̮nale̮?
mi̮j či̮n? k i̮ r e̮ d či̮n.
m i̮ j k i̮ r e̮ d? ćade̮ ki̮re̮d.
mi̮j ćade̮? bur ćade̮.
mi̮j bur? ńiki̮ľ bur.
mi̮j ńiki̮ľ? i̮b ńiki̮ľ.
i̮b šeri̮n pe̮ perenose̮n pi̮re̮ni̮ i pete̮ni̮.

76.

ľeńe, ľeńe, pi̮šji!
śe̮d śi-ke̮ʒi̮d śi̮jad,
palauzi̮d jurad.
ľeń sija oz pi̮šji.
gezje, gezje, ľeńli̮ ʒage̮d!
gez sija oz ʒage̮d.

The wolf is dragging logs,
The hare is baking round loaves,
The squirrel watches the fire,
The fox is weaving linen.

75.

Murja-Marja, get up, get up!
Your morning suitor has arrived,
Your evening suitor has arrived.
Marja got up.
In one direction: click-clack,
In the other direction: crack-bang,
She seized the bucket,
The bucket has no bottom,
She grabbed at the ladle,
The ladle has no handle,
She grasped the water-carrying pole,
The water-carrying pole is not fashioned.
She went to fetch water,
The priest came from the opposite direction,
He kicked at the grass,
His hair became tousled.
Daughter, daughter, what sort of smoke is that smoke there?
What sort of smoke? The smoke of *Kı̮re̮d*.
What *Kı̮re̮d*? *Ćade̮ Kı̮re̮d*.
What *Ćade̮*? *Bur Ćade̮*.
What *Bur*? *Ńikiľ Bur*.
What *Ńikiľ*? *Ńikiľ* from the hill.
In the middle of the hill they go in and out with a pyx.*

76.

Snail, snail, run away!
With your black necklace round your neck,
And your head-dress on your head.
The snail does not run away.
Rope, rope, strangle the snail!
The rope does not strangle it.

* Perhaps: an amulet.

ši̯re̯, ši̯re̯, ľeńľi̯ kerav!
ši̯r sija oz kerav.
kańe, kańe ši̯rli̯ ki̯j!
kań sija oz ki̯j.
či̯ne̯, či̯ne̯, kańli̯ pe̯dti̯!
či̯n sija oz pe̯dti̯.
bije, bije, či̯nli̯ sot!
bi sija oz sot.
vae̯, vae̯, bili̯ kuse̯d!
va sija oz kuse̯d.
e̯ške̯, e̯ške̯, vali̯ ju!
e̯š sija oz ju.
ćere̯, ćere̯, e̯šli̯ naćki̯!
ćer sija oz naćki̯.
zudje, zudje, ćerli̯ ľam!
zud sija oz ľam.
zud zi̯re̯das ćer vi̯le̯,
ćer zi̯re̯das e̯š vi̯le̯,
e̯š zi̯re̯das va vi̯le̯,
va zi̯re̯das bi vi̯le̯,
bi zi̯re̯das či̯n vi̯le̯,
či̯n zi̯re̯das kań vi̯le̯,
kań zi̯re̯das ši̯r vi̯le̯,
ši̯r zi̯re̯das gez vi̯le̯,
gez zi̯re̯das ľeń vi̯le̯,
ľeń zi̯re̯das, kod te̯das, ki̯ćće,
iz-ki pom vi̯las i mića le̯žkai̯s koľema.

77.

t u t u r u t u ś e m e̯
ke̯ć ki̯jni̯ kais,
ge̯ra vi̯vti ćeććištis,
koľkjis poti,
śi̯de̯si̯s kiśśis:
e̯ g r e̯ m a r p a kuri̯štis,
ǯe̯ľa k u ź m a koki̯štis.
vićko vi̯li̯n guľu,
ke̯le̯ke̯ľńa vi̯li̯n galka.
guľu, guľu mića gaž gaže̯de̯,

Mouse, mouse, cut the rope!
The mouse does not cut it.
Cat, cat, catch the mouse!
The cat does not catch it.
Smoke, smoke, stifle the cat!
The smoke does not stifle it.
Fire, fire, burn up the smoke!
The fire does not burn it up.
Water, water, quench the fire!
The water does not quench it.
Bull, bull, drink up the water!
The bull does not drink it up.
Axe, axe, slaughter the bull!
The axe does not slaughter it.
Grindstone, grindstone, blunt the axe!
The grindstone does not blunt it.
The grindstone dashes at the axe,
The axe dashes at the bull,
The bull dashes at the water,
The water dashes at the fire,
The fire dashes at the smoke,
The smoke dashes at the cat,
The cat dashes at the mouse,
The mouse dashes at the rope,
The rope dashes at the snail,
The snail dashes at who knows what,
At the millstone, and there remains a beautiful ladle.

77.

Tuturutu Śemę,
Went out to hunt a hare.
He jumped over the hill,
The eggs were smashed to pieces,
The porridge poured over:
E̮grę Marpa scraped it up,
Little Kuźma picked it up.
There is a pigeon on the church,
There is a jackdaw on the bell-tower.
The pigeon, the pigeon cheers us up,

galka, galka mića śer śere̮de̮,
koľk viʒ́an-e̮ dozje,
kiśkaśan-e̮ šore̮,
paśtaśam mi mi̮ľk vi̮li̮n.

78.

ľoľe, ľoľe
surte̮, peľte̮ mi̮ćći,
aćid veś kuźaa ńuže̮ćći!

79.

r u j, r u j, ki̮ćće vetlin?
r u j, r u j, me̮ske̮s korśni̮.
r u j, r u j, kuče̮m ne̮ r u j e me̮ski̮d?
r u j, r u j, da biľkja ki̮me̮sa.
r u j, r u j . . . .

80.

a)

baj-baj-i-baj-i-baj
ezi̮ś pi menam uźe,
sokol pi menam uźe,
zarńi pie̮j uźe,
ʒ́e̮ľa pie̮j uźe.
ruj-ruj-ruj-ruj,
baj-baj-baj-baj-baj-baj-baj,
dorogoj da śerďešne̮j,

b) bajeććem

baj-baj da ʒ́e̮ľa ni̮v uźe,
baj-baj da tuśka ni̮v uźe
e̮vve̮-e̮vve̮-e̮vve̮,
baju-baj da bajuški,
ľuľu-ľuľu da ľuľuški,
mijan tuśkai̮s uźe,
mijan jage̮d ni̮v uźe,
jage̮d vajali̮ś uźe . . .

The jackdaw, the jackdaw draws beautiful patterns,
Into the vessel where eggs are kept,
Into the brook that pours out.
We dress on the hill.

78.

Snail,
Put out your horns and ears,
Stretch yourself out the length of a span!

79.

ruj, *ruj*, where have you been?
ruj, *ruj*, looking a cow.
ruj, *ruj*, what kind of *ruj* is your cow?
ruj, *ruj*, her forehead is white,
ruj, *ruj* . . .

80.

(a)

baj-baj-baj-baj,
My silver son is sleeping,
My falcon son is sleeping,
My golden son is sleeping,
My little son is sleeping.
ruj-ruj-ruj-ruj,
baj-baj-baj-baj-baj-baj-baj:
My darling, my beloved.

(b) Lullaby

baj-baj, the little girl is sleeping,
baj-baj, the little-seed of a girl is sleeping,
ẹ̮vvẹ̮-ẹ̮vvẹ̮-ẹ̮vvẹ̮,
baju-baj da bajuški,
ľuľu-ľuľu da ľuľuški,
Our little seed is sleeping,
Our berry-girl is sleeping,
The berry-bearer is sleeping . . .

c)

baj-baj da e̮ťi pi uźe,
vode̮ma daj uźište̮,
bi̮dmas i̮ǯi̮d da men . . .

d)

baj-baj da zarńi pi uźe,
mijan dorogoj uźe,
regi̮d ve̮jna vi̮le̮ sije me̮de̮dni̮ kole̮ viʒ́ni̮,
kole̮ i ćeľaďse̮, ni̮vjasse̮ jage̮d vajavni̮ viʒ́ni̮.

(g) Rhymes

81.

regi̮d, regi̮d voasni̮ da
mića śili̮ś kajjas,
parakodi̮s e ž-v a kuźa
leććilas da kajlas.

mile̮je mene̮ koľľedis
gude̮ke̮n da gort dore̮ʒ́,
seśśa di̮r og aźźiśle̮ da
p e t i̮ r lun ge̮ge̮rjase̮ʒ́.

ar das-ki̮ka kuʒ́ me ve̮li,
sek me tene̮ ľubiti,
te mene̮ šuin »milaja«,
a me tene̮ »mile̮jen«.

ńe-kor, ńe-kor me-j og vune̮d
tenśid me ńežne̮j ki̮vjas.
voj i lun ponda kaźti̮vni̮,
ńe-kor, ńe-kor og vune̮d.

mame̮ uź i mame̮ uź i
me tene̮ i šebrala.
šor sajin gude̮ka ki̮le̮,
me ki̮vzi̮ni̮ petavla.

(c)

baj-baj, the only son is sleeping,
Ha has gone to bed and sleeps a little,
He is growing big . . .

(d)

baj-baj, the golden boy is sleeping,
Our darling is sleeping,
We raise him to send him to war soon,
We have to raise sons and daughters to pick berries . . .

81.

Soon, soon will they arrive,
The beautiful singing birds,
On the Vyčegda the boat
Is going up and down.

My beloved escorted me
Home with his accordion,
Then we shall not meet for a long time,
Not until St. Peter's day, or so.

When I was twelve years old,
I fell in love with you.
You called me your sweetheart,
And I called you my sweetheart.

Never, never shall I forget
Your gentle words.
I shall remember you night and day,
Never, never shall I forget you.

Mother, sleep, mother, sleep,
I will cover you;
An accordion-player is playing over the brook,
I shall go out and listen to him.

ke̮ni te, ke̮ni te,
ke̮ni te guľajtan?
ke̮ni te, e̮kajanne̮je,
me̮dse̮ zavľekajtan?
tani me, tani me,
tani me guľajta.
tani me, śo ze̮le̮teja,
me̮dse̮ zavľekajta.

mile̮jele̮n kuź tušai̮s
se̮mi̮n kore̮ś ćeglavni̮,
koľľedis mene̮ gort dore̮ʒ́,
iz kuž e̮ććid okavni̮.

mame̮, viǯedli̮ va vi̮las!
so kod-ke̮ vaas ve̮je:
vi̮ši̮vajte̮ma de̮re̮ma,
gude̮kse̮ kias kute̮.

mi̮jla taja ke̮ǯidi̮s, a
mi̮jla taja šoni̮di̮s?
mi̮jla taja e̮kajanne̮j,
ľubov ule̮ zańati̮s?

i̮ b ge̮rai̮s, i̮ b ge̮rai̮s,
i̮ b ge̮rai̮s ti̮dale̮.
ok, prokľate̮j ib ge̮rai̮s
menśim śe̮le̮me̮s kośte̮.

li̮a kuźta ki̮ke̮n lokte̮n:
naverne̮ tenad da menam.
tenad ale̮j de̮re̮ma,
menam nave·rne̮ gude̮ka.

gude̮kse̮-ke̮ paśke̮dam da
śivni̮se̮-ke̮ gore̮dam.
gude̮kse̮-ke̮ paśke̮dim da
śivni̮se̮-ke̮ gore̮dim.

oj, mi̮j že bara gore̮dim da:
oj, pod ľipoj pod ľipoj,
oj, pod ľipoj, pod ľipoj da
pod kudravoj źeľenoj,

Where, where
Are you walking?
You cursed one,
Where are you enticing another girl?
Here, here
I am valking.
I, a hundredfold golden,
Here I am enticing another girl.

The tall figure of my sweetheart
Is good for nothing but breaking brushwood besoms,
He escorted me home,
Yet not once could he give me a kiss.

Mother, look at the water,
See, somebody is drowning.
He has an embroidered shirt,
He holds an accordion in his hands.

Why this cold?
Why this warmth?
Why is this cursed one
Bound by love?

The hill of *Ĭb*, the hill of *Ĭb*,
The hill of *Ĭb* can be seen.
Oh, the cursed hill of *Ĭb*
Is withering my heart away.

Two men are coming along the sand:
Probably yours and mine.
Yours has a purple shirt on,
Mine is probably with an accordion.

We take the accordion in our hands
And begin to sing.
We took the accordion in our hands
And began to sing.

Oh, what did we sing:
Oh, under the lime-tree, under the lime-tree,
Oh, under the lime-tree, under the lime-tree
And under the fringe of green leaves,

pod kudravoj źeľenoj da
śiďit moloďeć takoj,
śiďit moloďeć takoj da
kudrivaťeńkoj baskoj.

bere̮gi̮n sulale̮n ki̮ke̮n:
naverne̮ tenad, menam.
e̮ľiki̮s jeǯi̮d de̮re̮ma,
me̮di̮s ale̮j saťina.

oj, vizi̮v vai̮s vove̮ma,
meľńićase̮, ki̮le̮de̮ma.
ni̮vśis, końer, voše̮ma,
babaas abu voe̮ma.

tea-mea ćoja-voka:
pemi̮d voj da gi̮ri̮ś jag;
te gude̮kse̮ paśke̮dan, a
me si̮ kuźta je̮kti̮šta.

oj, gude̮ke̮j pe̮ lećid ge̮le̮s,
gažed menśim śe̮le̮me̮s!
śili̮šta me ćastuškajas,
e̮nija guľajte̮me̮s.

śerbijanka viśme̮ma,
ńi-ne̮m abu śojle̮ma.
kise̮-kokse̮ krestale̮ma,
vek raďia ki̮vze̮ma.

mame̮, uź, mame̮ uź i
me tene̮ i šebrala.
ve̮r dori̮n gude̮ka ki̮le̮,
me petala, ki̮vzi̮šta.

aľi mi kodi̮ś-ke̮ polam,
aľi kodi̮ś-ke̮ rodam?
ki̮ćće kole̮, sećće munam,
kode̮s kole̮, raďejtam.

ti babajas, in pińaśe!
mi e̮d tii̮ś og pole̮.
tïjan saje, pijan sajas
vere̮s saje og mune̮.

Under the fringe of green leaves
There sits a lad,
There sits a lad,
He is so curly, so handsome.

Two folk are standing on the bank:
Probably yours and mine.
One of them in a white shirt,
The other in purple sateen.

Oh, the rushing water came
And it swept away the mill.
The poor girl lost her maidenhood,
But she did not become a wife.

You and I are brothers,
Dark night and tall fir-wood;
You play the accordion,
And I dance to it.

Oh, sharp sound of my accordion,
Make my heart merry!
I am singing a *chastushka*
About this walk we are taking.

The little gypsy girl fell ill,
She did not eat anything,
She crossed her hands and feet
And always listened to the wireless.

Mother, sleep, mother, sleep,
I'll cover you up.
An accordion can be heard by the wood,
I'll go out and listen to it.

Are we afraid of somebody?
Are we scared of somebody?
We'll go where we have to,
We'll love whom we want to.

You women, do not curse us!
After all, we are not afraid of you.
To lads like you
We shall never get married.

je̮kti̮, je̮kti̮, menam kok,
in žaľit sape̮gte̮!
śo se̮tana menam kok
žaľite̮ sape̮gse̮.

m e̮ s k v a a s-ke̮ mi vetlim da
una bur tor aʒ́ʒ́ilim,
re̮ďinali̮ś śe̮ľe̮m-še̮rse̮,
zarńi mić-lun viʒ́edlim.

vizi̮v j e m-v a kuźta ki̮vte̮
asi̮v voʒ́in jeǯi̮d ru.
vizi̮v j e m-v ae̮j, te, śe̮rśid
parťijali̮ aťťe nu!

Dance my feet, dance,
Do not worry about the boots!
My feet are like a hundred devils,
They worry about the boots.

We have been up to Moscow
Where we have seen many nice things,
The heart of the homeland,
We have looked on its golden beauty.

Down the swift Vym
White fog floats early in the morning.
Swift Vym, take
Our greetings to the Party!

III. THE MIDDLE-VYČEGDA (SYKTYVKAR REGION) DIALECT

The two following narratives were related by the linguist Gennadij Grigorjevič Baraksanov, a native of Šoška (Zyr. *śośka*), a village situated 20 km south of Syktyvkar. He was born in 1934. The dialect spoken by him agrees in essence with that of the Syktyvkar region (Middle Vyčegda) which serves as the basis of literary usage, but apart from this, his style of performance is markedly influenced by the literary taste of an educated person. Minor deviations from the literary norm can be observed in his language: 1. in all syllables apart from the first, *e̮* and *i̮*, preceded by a palatal consonant are replaced by *e* and *i* respectively, e.g. *ćojes* 'my sister (acc.)', *vi̮jeǯ* 'indeed', *pi̮šjini̮* 'to run away', *kujimi̮ś* 'three times'; 2. *śeśa*, *śa* 'then' (∼lit. *seśśa*), *tulus* 'spring' (∼lit. *tuli̮s*). For other characteristic features of the dialect, see: *Т. И. Жилина—В. А. Сорвачева*, Образцы коми-зырянской речи. Syktyvkar, 1971. pp. 42—44.

Narratives

82. *ćel̓ad̓-di̮rśa vojasiś*

1. *me ćužli ś o ś k a śikti̮n, stе̮ć komi̮n vo sajin. mam-bat̓ menam uǯalisni̮ seki kari̮n, si̮ ve̮sna me ńe-una oli̮šti kari̮n, a śeśa bi̮dmi vek ś o ś k ai̮n. ś o ś k a sikt i̮ǯi̮d-kod̓. pomjasas kerkajasi̮s jonǯi̮kase̮ e̮t̓i rade̮n mune̮ni̮. še̮ras śikti̮s paśki̮dǯi̮k, vi̮jeǯ ńe-ki̮mi̮n ul̓ića em. mijan kerkani̮m sulale̮ karla-dor pomas. kerka abu zev i̮ǯi̮d, važi̮ńik ńin. e̮ni seni e̮tnas mam ole̮, a kor-ke̮ ovlim unae̮n. d̓ed na ješše̮ lovja ve̮li menam ćužige̮n da ješše̮ vok daj ćoj ćužisni̮ me beri̮n. bat̓ mijan kuli zev tome̮n, mem ješše̮ ńol̓ are̮s na ez ve̮v. bi̮dtis mijane̮s mam. bi̮dmim mi śe̮ki̮d-kod̓ kade̮. školae̮ pi̮rige̮n vojna bure̮č zavod̓iććis. školai̮n me vele̮ćći śiźim vo. te̮vnas, arnas da tulusnas ve̮li vele̮ććam, a gože̮mnas me̮s viǯam, pastukalam.*

2. *mestajas mijan sete̮n zev gažae̮ś. śiktśań ńe-i̮li̮n vizuvte̮ si̮kti̮v-ju. kerkajasśańis-ke̮ ńe-una keži̮štan boke̮, ve̮r ńin zavod̓ićće. me̮sjas mijan ve̮li ćaste̮-kod̓*

82. About my childhood

1. I was born in a village called *Śośka*, exactly thirty years ago. My parents were then working in Syktyvkar (in the town), so I too lived in a town for a short time, but later I was brought up entirely in *Śośka*. The village of *Śośka* is quite large. In general, the houses are built in a line at both ends, while in the middle the village is wider; indeed, it even has a few streets. Our home is towards the town end. The house is not large, and it is old now. Mother lives in it alone now, but once upon a time there were a lot of us living there. When I was born grandmother was still alive, and after me a brother and a sister were born. Father died very young; I was not yet four years old. We were brought up by mother. They were hard times when we were brought up. Just when I went to school the war began. I attended school for seven years. We studied in winter, autumn and spring, but in the summer we looked after cows, and pastured them.

2. The land is very beautiful round about here. Not far from the village there flows the River Sysola. If you turn a little to one side from the houses, you reach the edge of the forest. Quite often our cows ran into the forest. Sometimes you look for them and go on looking, and they will not turn up. They even sleep in the forest. At that time there were still bears in these parts. Hardly any clearing was done in the forest, and you came across a bear fairly often. Walking in the forest, we found bear-droppings; we stuck our fingers into the droppings: to see whether they were hot? If they were hot, it meant that the bear was near. We had to run, and drive the cows. Once we saw a bear from close to. We were sitting on the bank of the river, beside a fire. All of a sudden something crackled in the forest; at first we did not think anything of it. Then we saw a bear coming out of the forest. Our feet froze to the spot. We did not know what to do: whether to run off or drive the cows away? But probably the bear was not hungry, it did not even look at us. It went down to the river, clattered into the water and swam to the other side. The far bank was very steep, but this did not worry the bear. It hung on with its sharp claws, and climbed up quickly. We had not quite recovered from our fright, when the bear went into the forest. The cows gave a bellow, then became silent again. In that year four cows were torn to pieces by the bear. Perhaps it would have torn some more to pieces, but it was caught. In the winter wolves came as far as the village and seized dogs. Once mother and I were going to Syktyvkar with a horse and cart, and we had to return by night. We were very frightened that wolves might attack us. We deliberately took ropes to scare them off in case the wolves would attack us. You see, wolves were very much afraid

pi̯šjivle̯ni̯ ve̯re̯. muke̯d-di̯rji korśan, korśan, oz i śurni̯. siʒ ńin i uźasni̯ ve̯ras. mijan seki ośke̯ś na ve̯li. ve̯rse̯ omeľa na pe̯re̯disni̯, ośki̯d ćaste̯-koď na pani̯-daśli̯vlis. mi ve̯li aʒʒam ve̯re̯d vetli̯ge̯n oš-sit, ćuńni̯me̯s śujlam sitas: pe̯ś, abu? pe̯ś-ke̯, siʒ-ke̯ oš mati̯n. kole̯ pi̯šjini̯, me̯sjase̯s ve̯tli̯ni̯. e̯ććid aʒʒilim ošse̯ zev mati̯ś. pukalam ve̯li ju-bere̯g dori̯n, bi dori̯n. i drug ve̯ras mi̯j-ke̯ trać-muni. mi pervojse̯ ege̯ i dumi̯š(t)le̯j ńem-tor. a śa viʒedam da ve̯rśis oš pete̯. siʒi mesta vi̯le̯ ki̯nmim. ńi-ne̯m oge̯ puťme̯j ve̯ćni̯: pi̯šjini̯ aľi me̯sjase̯s ve̯tli̯ni̯? no ośki̯d bura-ke̯ abu či̯g ve̯le̯ma, mijan vi̯le̯ ez viʒedli̯. leććis ju doras, pi̯ris vaas i̯zbaz da varććis me̯daras. me̯dar bere̯gi̯s zev krut ve̯li, no ośli̯ taje ez mešajt. šašariććis još giʒjasnas da zev e̯dje kajis. mijan veśig povźemnim na e̯z bi̯r, a oš ve̯ras ńin pi̯ris. me̯sjas buali̯štisni̯ daj lańtisni̯. sije vonas ośki̯d ńoľ me̯s kośavlis. gaške̯ eśke̯ unʒike̯s na kośavlis, no ki̯jisni. te̯vnas ke̯jinjas ve̯li voli̯vle̯ni̯ śikte̯ʒis, ponjase̯s guśavle̯ni̯. e̯ććid mi mame̯ke̯d kare̯ leććilim ve̯le̯n da be̯rse̯ lokni̯ kovmis vojnas. jona polim ke̯jinjas uśke̯ććemi̯ś. naro·šne̯ gez le̯śedlim, med povźedni̯, uśke̯ććasni̯-ke̯ ke̯jinjasi̯s. kuź gezśis pe̯ taj ke̯jinjasi̯s zev jona pole̯ni̯, važ je̯z siʒi viśtavle̯maś. a mijan vi̯le̯ naje ez uśke̯ććini̯, omľale̯mse̯ toľke̯ ki̯vlim. gorte̯ voim bura.

3. *teli̯s mijan sete̯n voʒ zavoďićće da kuźa pukale̯. jona i ve̯li islavlam te̯v-bi̯dnad, una gi̯n-sape̯g da gać kiśtlam. islalam ve̯li li̯źen, daďďen, muke̯d-di̯rjis ve̯li końušńaiś i̯ʒi̯d doď bośli̯vlam. doďnas zev gaža islavni̯s. ćaste̯-koď ve̯li ki̯ćće-śure̯ krukaślam: to pi̯vśan-peľese̯, to kerka-peľese̯. unale̯n-koď pľeški̯s potli̯vlis. islalam ve̯li muke̯d-di̯rjis asi̯vśań da śor ri̯te̯ʒ, śojni̯ oz kov ńi. pem-de̯m be̯ras ve̯li ćag-torjas e̯ztavlam muke̯d-di̯rjis da soććiś ćag-torse̯ vome̯ bośte̯-me̯n islalam: gažaʒik siʒse̯. gortad loktan ʒik li̯m-juž-koď, ďert e̯djeʒi̯k paććerad kajan. le̯śida i uźśe tače̯m guľajte̯m be̯rad.*

83. *svaďba ji̯li̯ś*

mi ńe-važe̯n ćojes śetim vere̯s saje. mame šue̯: "važe̯n pe̯ ńin svaďbase̯ važ nogi̯s ez većli̯ni̯, kole̯ pe̯ ve̯ćni̯." vot i ve̯ćisni̯. svaďba di̯rjis pirujte̯ni̯ ki̯k lun: pervej lunse̯ ńevesta ordas, me̯d lunse̯ žeńik ordas. giʒśem be̯ras mijane̯ ćuke̯rć-ćisni zev una je̯z. kujim pi̯zan saje pukśalisni̯. pervoj śojištisni̯-jui̯štisni̯, śeśa družkai̯s žeńiki̯sle̯n »gorko« gore̯dis. ńevestaa-žeńikaa okaśisni̯, a źaťis mijan zev ińťeresne̯j: ez kut viććiśni̯, kod ješše̯ »gorkose̯« kutas gorzi̯ni̯, aćis juaśe: "kodli̯ ješše̯ »gorko«? e̯ťi sajin pe̯ ńin okaśni̯s." śeśa be̯r-vi̯las omeľa i gorzisni̯ »gorkose̯«. śojisni̯-juisni̯ stavi̯s dundi̯te̯ʒis, kiʒ šuasni̯: be̯re̯n pette̯ʒis. kod-śure̯ uśte̯ʒis juisni̯, jona je̯ktisni̯, śilisni̯, gaže̯ććisni̯.

aski asi̯vnas žeńiki̯s družkai̯ske̯d loktisni̯ para ve̯le̯n ńevestai̯sla da pridan-nejisla. vežajis najes kerkaas ez le̯ʒ: kali̯m pe̯ kole̯. družkai̯s pervoj kali̯m mestaas same̯kur ste̯kan ve̯li ve̯zje, no vežajis kore̯ śpirt suľa. seki družkai̯s

of long ropes, or so old people said. But they did not attack us, we only heard them howling. We arrived at home undisturbed.

3. Winter sets in early here and lasts a long time. Throughout the winter we did a lot of sliding, and wore out lots of felt-boots and trousers. We went in for skiing and sleighing; sometimes we even brought the big sleigh out of the stable. It is very pleasant to slide along in a sleigh. Quite often we bumped into something: now the corner of the bath-house, now the corner of the house. Many of us had their foreheads broken. Sometimes we went on sleighing from morning to late in the evening without eating anything. When it grew dark, we sometimes lit wood-chips and putting them into our mouths we went on sleighing. It was more fun that way. We arrive home frozen hard like crusts of snow, and of course we immediately climb on top of the stove. How good it is to sleep after such an excursion.

83. About the wedding

Not long ago we married off our sister. Mother said: "It is a long time since a wedding was held in the old style, so it would be nice to have one." And so they did indeed. At weddings people feast for two days: on the first day at the bride's home, on the second day at the bridegroom's. After they had been to the registor's, many people gathered together in our house. They sat at three tables. First they had food and drink, then the bridegroom's best man gave a great shout: "It is bitter!" The bride and the bridegroom kissed each other. But our brother-in-law is a very interesting man: he could not wait until anyone else shouted: "It is bitter!", but he himself asks: "Who else finds it bitter? They must kiss again!" Later they shouted "bitter" less frequently. All ate and drank fit to burst, as they say — until it comes out of them again. Some drank so much that they fell down on the floor; they danced hard, sang and had a good time.

Next day the bride and his best man came along with a couple of horses for the bride and the dowry. Godfather did not let them into the house: first a bridal ransom has to be paid. As the first ransom, the best man offers a glass of home-made spirits. But godfather asks for a bottle of methylated spirit. Then the best man said: "I'll give you a bottle of St. John's wort spirits." Godfather says: "Well, let me see it!" The best man showed it to him, while godfather opened the porch door a little and then snatched the bottle. Then he closed the door. "This isn't enough!" The best man had to produce another bottle of St. John's wort spirits. Only then were they let in the house. We drank up the St. John's wort spirits, in other words we drank away the bride. Then the brother-in-law took the young

šuis: "źveroboj suľa pe̮ śeta." vežaj viśtale̮: "no ko pe̮ petke̮dli̮!" družkai̮s petke̮dlis, a vežaj sek-kosti kiľće-e̮ʒ́esse̮ ćuť-ćuť vośti̮šlis da i kvaťitis suľase̮. śa e̮ʒ́esse̮ be̮r ignalis: "eča pe̮ taje!" kovmis družkai̮dli̮ me̮d źveroboj suľa śetni̮. seki toľke̮ najes le̮ʒ́isni̮ kerkaas. źverobojte̮ mi juim, bi̮ťťe-ke̮ ńevestase̮ juim. śa źaťis bośtis tom ge̮ti̮rse̮ da uźlan-ke̮lujse̮ i pukśedis para-ve̮v doďďe i munisni̮. a mijanli̮ viśtalisni̮: "loktad-ke̮, lokte̮j, a me̮di̮ś korni̮ og vole̮j." a aśse̮ źaťse̮ korni̮ ńevesta ordas ge̮śťitni̮, ńevestai̮sle̮n pe̮drugaa̮jasi̮s kujimi̮ś vetlisni̮. mi munim bara. sete̮n jona gaže̮ććim, oke̮dim gozjae̮s. no oke̮dim ńe toľke̮ ić-moń gozjae̮s, no i stav gozjase̮, kodjas ve̮lini svaďba vi̮las. taǯi svaďba koľi zev gažaa.

wife and the bedding and piled them all on the sleigh which was drawn by two horses. So they left, and they spoke to us as follows: "Come if you want to; we shall not come to invite you a second time!" But to invite the brother-in-law to the bride's party, the bridesmaids went to see him three times. We also went along to see him. There we had a good time, making the young couple to kiss each other. But not only the young couple were made to kiss each other, but every married couple present at the wedding. The wedding feast went off like this very happily.

IV. THE UPPER-VYČEGDA DIALECT

I visited three villages to study this dialect, which is spoken in an extensive area but which cannot be regarded as uniform owing to differences in the behaviour of the *l* phoneme. These were Ручь (Zyr. *ruć*), Деревянск (Zyr. *ďerevannej*) and Усть-кулом (Zyr. *kulem-din*, *kulęm-din*). In addition, while in Usť-Kulom I noted down a song from a woman from the village of Носим (Zyr. *nośim*) (see below). Носим is situated 6 km from Usť-Kulom on the left bank of the Vyčegda. The following were my informants: Ручь: Agrafena Andreevna J u d i n a (aged 64), Matrena Iljinična U ľ n y r o v a (aged 69), Elizaveta Semënovna U ľ n y r o v a (aged 75), Agrafena Semënovna Z e z e g o v a (aged 71); Деревянск: Marija Dmitrievna A n t o n o v s k a y a (aged 80), Boris Ivanovič A n t o n o v s k i j (aged 37), Evgenij Semënović G u l j a e v (in 1957 when I noted down three of his narratives, he was 29 years of age and a linguist-aspirant; he was a scientific researcher, died in 1977) Jurij Semënovič G u l j a e v (aged 32, younger brother of E. S. Guljaev), Marija Andreevna G u l j a e v a (aged 73), Pavla Michajlovna G u l j a e v a (aged 58), Anastasija Ivanovna K i p r u š ë v a (aged 60), Agrafena Michajlovna R a k i n a (aged 73); Усть-кулом: Anna Nikolaevna Č a l a n o v a (aged 54), Irina Egorjevna K i p r u š ë v a (aged 68), Anna Petrovna K o č a n o v a (aged 55 from Nośim), Ekaterina Michajlovna L i p i n a (aged 50), Lidija Dadovna T i m u š e v a (aged 62).

The main characteristics of the dialect are as follows:

1. As for the *l* phoneme, the dialect area of the villages Ruć and Derevjansk is characterized by *l* ~ *v*-, and therefore belongs to the Middle-Vyčegda type. In contrast, in Usť-Kulom we encounter a symbiosis of two dialect types (*l* ~ *v* and *l* ~ Ø). Occasionally these two types are mixed in the usage of one and the same person. For example: A. N. Čalanova: *kī̮* 'word', but: *ki̯vzis* 'he obeyed', *nī̮ked* ~ *ni̯vked* 'with a girl', *zē* ~ *zev* 'very', etc. The phoneme *l* remains unchanged in certain verbal suffixes (*-il-*, *-lill-*,

-oll-) : *eg aǯǯil* 'I did not see', *predupreďitlillis* 'he warned him', *petolla* 'I go out'.

2. In Usť-Kulom the phonemes *e̮* and *i̮* if in an absolute initial position in the first syllable, or if preceded by *p*, *b*, *k*, and *g*, frequently have labial allophones *(ȯ, u̇)* : *kȯsji* 'I wanted', *u̇sta* 'I send', *kū̇* 'word', etc. For Zyr. labial *ȯ* and *u̇* phonemes see LYTKIN, IstVok. 118—9, VJa. 1968/1:88; RÉDEI, SLW 41, 44.

3. In other syllables than the first *e̮* and *i̮* are replaced by *e̮* and *i̮* formed more to the back in the area of Ruć and Derevjansk, e.g. *pi̮de̮* 'deeply', *kok-śi̮* 'stamping'. In my texts these two phonemes are shown as *e* and *i*. In certain instances we find *i̮* in secondarily accented third syllable: *a·rja-vi̮:vnas* 'in the autumn', *mu·ked-di̮:rji* 'sometimes'. The non-first syllabic *e̮* and *i̮* in the Middle-Vyčegda dialect become *e* and *i*, respectively, in the Usť-Kulom dialect. For example, *ve̮re* 'into the forest', *či̮nis* 'its smoke, the smoke'. But in songs I often heard *e̮* and *i̮* in non-initial syllables as well, obviously affected by the melodic stress. The same holds true sometimes in prose texts. As a result of the melodic stress, occasionally *e* and *i* become *e̮* and *i̮*, respectively, in the first syllable. For example, *e̮śke* ~ VC *eśke̮* 'Partikel zur Bildung des Konditionals u. a.'; *mi̮gajćće* 'he keeps winking' ~ SR *migajćći̮ni̮*, id.; *šľapa pi̮jas* (instead of *šľapa pijas*) 'in the hat'. See in this connection my notes to the Usť-Kulom songs.

4. In Ruć and Derevjansk, velar vowels in the first syllable of words with mixed vowels are followed by *i̮* instead of palatal *i*. For example, *ve̮li̮* 'I was', *ki̮vli̮* 'I heard', *povźi̮li̮* 'I was frightened'. Palatal *i* and *e* occur exclusively in words with palatal vowels (*seki* 'then') or in the first syllable of words with mixed vowels (*vite̮d* 'fifth', *eśśa* 'later').

5. Nouns ending in a vowel (mainly in rapid speech) drop the linking vowel of suffixes, i.e. the second vowel of the sequence is omitted: *kerkan* (~ VC *kerkain*) 'in the house', *kerkaś* (~VC *kerkai̮ś*) 'out of the house', *kerka* (~VC *kerkae̮*) 'into the house', *kerkas* (~VC *kerkai̮s*) 'his house', *kerkas* (~VC *kerkaas*) 'into his house', *unas* (~VC *unae̮s*) 'much' (acc.).

6. Sometimes *č* is replaced by *šč*, e.g. *kuščem* (~VC *kuče̮m*) 'what sort of', *seščem* (~VC *seče̮m*) 'such'.

7. Where velar or velar and palatal vowels are juxtaposed, the hiatus is filled by *v* (for example, *nuvas* 'he carries it' *šuve* 'he says it', *love* 'it will be'), while in the case of palatal vowels the hiatus is filled by *j* (*pije* 'my son', *kije* 'my hand').

8. In the final position the *t* phoneme of the *śt* sequence is preserved: *bośt:* 'take it !'.

For the development of the Upper-Vyčegda dialect, see LAŠUK, Очерки этнической истории печорского края. Syktyvkar, 1958:95—111; ŽEREBCOV—LAŠUK: Sborn. 1960:53 ff. VÁSZOLYI: NyK 68:75—7; Верхне-вычегодский диалект коми языка. Sborn. 1966; RÉDEI, SLW 71—2.

(a) Tales and narratives

84.

1. *olis-vi̮lis ge̮ľinik kresťa·ńin. si̮len ve̮li kujim pi : v a ś, p e d e r da i v a n. olisni, olisni daj kor-ke bať ij šuve: "pijane, vaj-že śorkńi ke̮ʒam!" śorkńi ke̮ʒisni. a śorkńi bi̮dmis da baťis i šuve: "kole pe pijane, śorkńite viǯni, kod-ke pe pakeśťite. talun pe e̮ćered i̮ǯid vok p e d e rli, aski pe v a śli, a kojmed ri̮tse pe i v a nli kovmas." vot e̮ťik ri̮te baťis šuve: "no, talun, p e d e r pije kaj śorkńite viǯni!" p e d e r kajis. kajis da śorkńi viǯedlis, ge̮ger ki̮čōtis, da bergeććis. loktis da śiktin uźis. aski baťli i šuve. bať juvale: "p e d e r, volis, ez kod-ke?" "ńe-kod ez voli, baťe". "no, ez-ke, ladne." aski kajis bara, pre̮verite. "kod-ke, p e d e r, volema, te abu volemid mu dorad. talun kovmas kajni v a śli i viǯed bura!" i v a ś k ais bara-že je̮r ge̮ger ki̮čōtis. loktis daj bara de̮va dine pi̮ris da uźis. bara bať juvale: "pije, śorkńi mu dinad kod-ke volis, ez?" "ez pe voli, baťe, ńe-kod." bať kajis da pre̮veritis. bara pili šuve: "ki̮ś pe abu volema? volema pe, pije, abu viǯemid." "viǯi pe." "no pe, i v a n pije, te pe omeľik da og te̮d pe, te pomiś love, oz śorkńi viǯem." i v a n šogśe, paććer seregin sija pi̮r ole, gi̮riś vokjas zbojeś. i i v a n me̮dećće di̮šińik pi̮riś. i bať šuve: "piej, en enōt, viǯ!" i v a n kajis, ki̮čōtis je̮rjas ge̮ger i ʒebśis. ʒebśis da ćas das-kikin ki̮min, śoreńiken ki̮t-ke tē-ni̮r moz kutis ki̮ptini. lokte i v a n i poškedis peľse: "kod-ke lokte, taja kodi bara lokte?" kīʒe, loktis śorkńi je̮r dore tē-ni̮ren, pi̮ris i kutis śorkńi ńečkini. i v a n "śećas, ćas me taje pi̮r i kija" — šuve. — "taje kijni ki̮ǯi kole?" — šuve. i v a n kijis, kijis daj šuve: "leǯ pe, bur morte, leǯ! a leǯan-ke pe, me ted tabak-paćka śeta." seśśa i v a n šuve: "tabak-paćka vi̮le pe og milujćći." "bośt, bośt — šuve — zge̮ďiććas. tabak-paćkate̮, pike-ke voan, tabak-paćkase vojćća vart, me pe tani lova." no ladne, sije leǯas. i v a n muǯema lokte. baťis šuve: no, pije i v a n, kod-ke volis, ez?" i v a n ez "viśtō: ez pe, baťe, ńe-kod voli." ij askinas bať kajis daj pre̮verite: śorkńi dore abu volemaeś. "i v a n, te pe abu ae̮ǯilemid" — bať šuve.*

84. [Lazy Ivan]

1. Once there lived a poor peasant. He had three sons: Vaś, Peder and Ivan. They lived on and on, and then once their father says: "Sons, let us sow turnips!" They sowed turnips. The beets grew, and the father says: "Sons, the turnips must be guarded in case somebody ruins them. Today is the eldest brother Peder's turn, tomorrow Vaś's, and the day after tomorrow Ivan's." One evening the father says: "Well, Peder, my son, go and watch over the turnips!" Peder went off. He went to the field, took a look at the turnips, walked round and then returned. He returned and slept in the village. Next day he reports to his father. The father asks: "Did anyone come there, Peder?" "Nobody came father." "Well, if nobody came, that's all right." Next day he went to the field to check. "Peder, somebody was there, and you did not go to the field. Today Vaś must go there. Watch it carefully!" Vaśka also walked round the vegetable plot, then returned to the widow's and slept there. The father asks: "Son, somebody came to the turnip-field, didn't they?" "No, father, nobody came." The father went to the field to check. He says to his son: "How can you say there was nobody there? Someone must have been there, son; you were not on guard." "Yes, I was!" "Well, Ivan, my son, you are unimportant, and I do not know what sort of turnip-guardian you will prove." Ivan is gloomy, he spends his time lying lazily in the back corner of the top of the stove; his brothers are bold. And Ivan sets out lazily. The father warns him: "Son, don't leave the field, just watch!" Ivan went there, walked round the vegetable-plot and hid. He hid, and about twelve o'clock, rather late, a whirlwind arose from somewhere. Ivan comes out, pricking up his ears: "Somebody is coming. Who is coming?" He listens; somebody came like a whirlwind to the turnip-field, went into it and began to tear up the turnips. "I'll grab him immediately" — says he. "But how can I catch him?" Ivan caught hold of him, and he says: "Let me go, my friend, let me go! If you let me free, I'll give you a tobacco-pouch." Then Ivan answers: "I'll not be satisfied with a tobacco-pouch." "Take it, take it" — says he — "for it will be to your advantage! If you get into trouble and hit the tobacco-pouch, I'll be there immediately." Well, that's all right; he lets him go free. Ivan arrives home tired. The father asks him: "Well Ivan, my son, did anybody come there?" Ivan did not tell him. "No, father, nobody came." Next day the father went out to check. Nobody had been in the turnip-field. "Well, Ivan, you didn't see anybody" — says the father.

2. *bať seśśa pijanli šuve: "vole-že pe, pijane, me dine, menam pe olem eštini kutis i me pe tijanli śeta nakaz gętraśni." i olisni, olisni da bať kuli. bańes uberitisni. i p e d e r gętraśis i p e d e r bęrin v a ś i ľ e j gętraśis. vokjas i šuveni: "a jęj i v a n, ted kõmas — šuve — śęla-sit purkedni paććer seregad."*

3. *vot seśśa olisni-olisni da męd gosudarstvoin kutis kı̄śini, mıj pe sar aslis korśe nılisli žęńik. i kole pe suǯedni zęletej ćuń-kič tęrelka vıliś. kod pe suǯedas, sija pe love sılen žeńik-puis. vot męde ććisni stav jęz. stavis mićaa kęmaśisni-paśtaśisni i męde ććisni. i v a n ętnas koľi paććer-serege. i v a n i dumajte: 'ćas me petolla.' eśśa i v a n munis, munis da munis da vęr dorę̌ vojis daj tabak-paćka švaćkis vojćća. i petisni kujim bagatir. "mıj, ivanuško, ted kole?" "men kole sećće munni i sečem jon vę̄ pe men kole." "en śogśi, i v a n!" i v a n vę̄ vıle sęlis i munis. i jęzis stavis šenźeni: ez mun tuj vı̄ti, a sija pramo vozduktiis munis. vıliti, vıliti kıčõtis da veśtas mıjen vovis balkon veśte i kıpeć-ćilis da bľud dorśis, mıj-ke ćuń-kičse inmedlis bľud doras. i sarlen nılis sajd-tegis pı̌šjis, pıris: "bańe, bańe, kod-ke volis da tęrelka dorśid, bľud dorśis kod-ke ćuń-kište bośtalis da." ez, ez-na pe, oz.* i askinas pe bara sar objavitis, mıj ćuń-kič ez-na nı̄liś bośtni vermini bľud vıliś. i vokjas loktemaeś. a i v a n termaśis gorte, med naiś voǯ vois. i v a n loktis, vokjas i šuveni: "atte pe kuśčem, mıj-ke volis, mort vęlen pe vıle ććććilis." jęj i v a n kı̄ze paććer seregin, oz ju, ńe oz śoj, muǯema daj śojćće. i naja šuveni, kık vok: "aski pe bara na kõmas munni." aski bara na vokjas i v a nes zaďeńejteni: "i v a n, te ńe-kićće on mun. te śęla-sitte purked paććer seregad!" i bara munas kık vok, kęma-śasni da paśtaśasni. i v a n bara dumajte. i v a n dumajtas da munas daj bara mıj-ke kere, mu pome vovis da bara tabak-paćka vojćća vaćkis. vaćkis da šuve: "mıj, i v a n u š k o, tenid kole?" "menim vot bara kole munni, seščem-te vę̄, vę̄!" "en śogśi, i v a n u š k o!" vę̄ bara loktis, i v a n sęlis. bara i v a n munis jęzjas dine, ćukaras. voemen vıliti, vıliti kaćeććilis i ćuń-kičse vęrźędlis nin. bara sarlen nılis sajdtegis ćepesjis balkon vıliś bańli viśtõnı: "bańe, bańe, ta-lun ćuń-kičse nin vęrźedlis seščem-te, seščem-te mort." ij rad, mıj nı̄li love. i bara i v a n starajćće, med ędjeǯik eśke vokjasśis gortas vovis. i bara vokjas lokteni da šue: "atte pe tavun ćuť nin ez ćuń-kičse mıj-keśis bośt, tęrelka vı̄śis." a i v a n bıťťe sija oz i tęd. i v a nes zaďevajteni vokjas: "i v a n, sija ńi-nem oz i tęd, paććer seregin śęla-sit purkede." a i v a n śojćće muǯemisla. vot*

* Having made an error, the informant added, by way of correction: "No, not yet [this will come later]".

2. Later the father says to his sons: "Sons, come here, the end of my life is near, and I order you to get married." They lived on and on, and their father died. They buried their father. Peder married, and after Peder Vasilej also married. The brothers say: "Foolish Ivan, you must beat the hazel-hen's droppings in the back corner of the top of the stove."

3. Well, they lived on and on, and in the next state the rumour spread that the Tsar was looking for a bridegroom for his daughter. The bridegroom has to obtain the golden ring from the plate. He who gets it will be the bridegroom. Well, all the people began to stir. All put on fine clothes. Ivan alone stayed on the back corner of the top of the stove. Ivan just thinks. "I'll go out." Then Ivan went on and on and on; he arrived at the edge of the forest and struck the tobacco-pouch. Three heroes appeared. "What do you want, Ivanuška, what do you want?" "I've got to go that way, and I need such a strong horse." "Do not grieve, Ivan!" Ivan mounted the horse and started off. People all wondered at the sight: he did not ride along the road but flew straight through the air. High in the air, high in the air he circled and got right above her on the horse, right above the balcony he rose and touched the ring on the edge of the plate. The Tsar's daughter, quite out of mind, ran away and went in: "Father, father, somebody has come and taken the ring from the edge of the plate!" (No, not yet, no.) Next day the Tsar proclaimed that nobody had yet been able to take his daughter's ring from the plate. The brothers arrived home. Ivan also dashed home so that he might get there before them. Ivan reached the house, and his brothers say: "Hey, what man was that who came there, leaping high on his horse." Foolish Ivan just listens in the back corner of the top of the stove; he neither drinks nor eats anything, he is tired out and rests. The two brothers say: "We must go again in the morning." Next day the brothers begin to insult Ivan again: "Ivan, you're not going anywhere. Beat the hazel-hen's droppings in the back corner of the top of the stove!" The two brothers put on their clothes and go off. Ivan ponders. Ivan ponders and again goes to the end of the ploughed field. There he struck the tobacco-pouch. He struck at it, and the hero spoke: "What do you want, Ivanuško?" I have to go again; give me a horse, a horse of the same kind." "Do not grieve, Ivanuško!" The horse came and Ivan mounted it. Ivan went out among the people, the crowds. High, high in the air he arrived, rose and touched the ring. Again the Tsar's daughter, out of her mind, dashed away from the balcony to tell her father: "Father, father, such and such a man has touched the ring today." He is glad that his daughter's bridegroom has arrived. Again Ivan hurries to reach home before his brothers. The brothers arrive and one of them says: "Hey, today he almost snatched the

aski keže i v a *nid sogśe nin. aski pęśľednej lun sarlen. vot bara vokjas šuveni: "vaj, mędeććamej, munamej, a* i v a n, *te bara na, końer, koľ paććer serege!" — šuve. a* i v a n *oz vokjasli ętvećajt. munisni vokjas.* i v a n *bara ńe-dįr-miśľi nęrevitis da jęzis mįjen munisni, bara vęććis daj bara mu-pome vovis vęr dore. da bara tabak-paćka vojćća vaćkis. bara šuveni kujim bagatir: "mįj ted,* i v a n u š k o, *kole?" "vot, vot-te, menim kole sećći munni sarliś nįliś ćuń-kič mįj kerni, vaj menim vę!" bara vę śetis ij munis. i jęzjas ćukerććemaeś sį-minda. i* i v a n *jęz dorjas voteʒ kaćeććis i ćuń-kište boštis. i nįlis sajdtegis pįris: "baťe, baťe, ćuń-kište, seščem-te, seščem-te mįj-ke keris, mort boštis ćuń-kište. i seščem rad lovi sarli.*

4. *i sar objavitis stav narodes ćukarććini, kod orde veśkalis sija ćuń-kič. vot bara* i v a n *starajććis gortas lokni, med eśke kįk vokiś voʒʒik vois.* i v a n *paććer seregin nin, vokjas lokteni. "no pe tavun, druge, ćuń-kište boštisni nin. i bara na pe sar objavitis, mįj kod orde sija ćuń-kičis lovi." ďivujććeni, kod eśke seščem mortis.* i v a n *bara molćite, ńi-nem oz śiećći. seśśa naja šogśeni, bara mędeććeni munni sarliś śojni, śojem-juvem vįle. "i kodli śuris mįj-ke, ćuń-kič boštis, sija menam pe źať love." vot munisni, aski ćukarććasni. sar jona verćće. juktaśe i pręverite stav jęzse. a* i v a *nli vokjas munigas šuveni: "śo rovno,* i v a n, *ted kōmas taun munni. on-ke mun, tene sarid lįjlas, vijas pe." a* i v a n *šuve: "me kįćće muna, me ńe-kįćće og mun." a* i v a n *aćis dumajte eśke. vokjas munisni nin,* i v a·n*es mįrden kįskeni. i* i v a n *vek oz šećći (šedśi). mijen munalisni, bęrinnas* i v a n *bara petis, naʒeńiken-ľokińiken kęm-paśtalis. śik kuźa dōge-mune. "jęj* i v a n *pe jęj* i v a n *ij em" — jęzis šuveni. munis* i v a n *čęč i sije stav jęzis nin pręjďitisni mįj-ke pįris, sar verdem pįr, pręverka pįr, a* i v a n *porog ulin sulale ľokińik šabur-jasa, zįrimis gęg, mįj-keeʒis ęśeććema, čękaeʒis.* i v a n*es mįrden kįskeni pįzan saje,* i v a n *oz pįr. a jęzis veśigte vękteni sį vile. ij* i v a n*len ćuńis kęrteda vęli. ćuńis kęrteda vęli da* i v a n*liś ćuńse raźeni.* i v a n *oz śet. "taja pe menam dojmema ćuńej da og, og pe śet raźni." i aʒʒisni i kaźalisni, mįj sar-nįlen ćuń-kičis* i v a n *ordin. stav jęz šemese uśini. i sar-nįked orććen pukśedisni. sarlen nįlis mića,* i v a n *mištem. vot bįť ōmećći. znaćit, sar*

ring from the plate." Ivan pretended not to know about it. The brothers begin to insult Ivan: "Ivan knows nothing, he beats the hazel-hen's droppings in the back corner of the top of the stove." Ivan, tired, takes a rest. Ivan grows sad because of the next day. Tomorrow is the last day for the Tsar. The brothers say: "Let us set out and go; poor Ivan, you stay in the back corner of the top of the stove!" — they say. Ivan does not answer his brothers. The brothers went off. Ivan waited a while, and soon after they had left he set out after them, and again he went to the end of the ploughed field, to the edge of the forest. He struck the tobacco-pouch. The three heroes spoke: "What do you want, Ivanuško?" "Well now, I have to go there, to take the ring of the Tsar's daughter, bring me a horse!" Again they gave him a horse, and he went away. A great crowd of people gathered together. Before reaching the crowd, Ivan rose high into the air and took the ring. Out of her mind, the girl went in. "Father, father, such and such a man has snatched the ring!" And the Tsar was very glad.

4. The Tsar proclaimed that all the people should be assembled to find out who has got the ring. Well, Ivan again hurried to reach home before his two brothers. Ivan is lying in the back corner of the top of the stove when the brothers arrive. "Well, friend, today the ring was taken. And the Tsar proclaimed whose hand the ring had got to." They wonder who the man may be. Ivan is silent again, not saying a word. They are filled with grief and so they go to the Tsar's feast. "He who has got the ring will be my son-in-law." They went there, and next day they all assemble. The Tsar gives them much to eat and drink, checking the whole people. As they go off, the brothers say to Ivan: "It's all the same, Ivan, today you have to go as well. If you do not go, the Tsar will shoot you and kill you!" Ivan answers: "Where should I go? I'm not going anywhere." Ivan thinks hard. The brothers started off already, dragging Ivan by force. Ivan always slips out of their hands. As they left, Ivan also went out, slowly and dressed in slovenly fashion. He wanders along, right through the village. "Foolish Ivan will always remain a fool" — people say. Ivan also went there. The whole people have gone through the Tsar's feast and inspection. And Ivan stands at the doorstep in his shappy hacket, his snot hanging down to his belly-button or what, down to his chin. They drag Ivan forcibly to the table. Ivan will not go. People are even disgusted with him. Ivan's finger is all tied up. His finger is wrapped up and they tear at the bandage on his finger. "This finger of mine has got hurt, no, I will not let you untie the bandage." They noticed and perceived that the ring of the Tsar's daughter was with Ivan. All the people were amazed. The Tsar's daughter is beautiful, Ivan is ugly. Well, you must arrange to live here. The Tsar says: "You have the

šuve no, znaćit: "te ordin ćuń-kič, i menam nī̮ te sajin love i ted ʒońnas sarstvo love."

5. *no kor-ke, ńe-kor-ke ōmeććisni i vokjas šenźeni: taja ne ki̮ʒi je̮j i v a n i sli ćuń-kičis lovi da i v a nes i̮ledleni. "ted ki̮ʒ love?" i v a n ďert oz viśtō pravda, sije. vot naja, kujim vok kutisni ōni da kor-ke, ńe-kor-ke eśśa-j vojna me̮d sarstvośań objavitisni. sija sarisli ve̮li kole si̮len ni̮lis, ki̮k sarlen vojćća ge̮traśem vi̮le. i ke̮n mi̮j bara je̮z, stavis petisni vojujtni. vot vojujtni petisni da poľe vi̮le pe̮šťi, što ʒi̮n je̮zse uśkedisni. a i v a n bara na tabak-paćkanad spaśiććis. ge̮teris si̮liś pravda oz ted. i bara sija i̮ʒid vēnad ti̮škaśis ij unas vijis. i bara i v a n loktis i bara ge̮tiris oz te̮d. i v a n vek uźe. i ge̮tir šenźe: "ke̮n taʒi taja muʒema?" — šuve, oz te̮d. "te ne, te ne pe, ki̮ćće munan — ge̮tir juaśe — te ki̮ʒi vojujtan? tene pe pi̮r vijasni." vot i bara me̮d lun-že munisni vojujtem vi̮le. me̮d lun vojujtem vi̮le munisni da siʒ-že bara zē jona mi̮j-ke keris i v a n, mu pome vojis da bara tabak-paćkate švaćkis ki-pi̮desnas. da bara petisni kujim bagatir: "i v a n u š k o — šuve — mi̮j kole?" "taun — šuve — me̮d lun vojujtni muna." "en šogśi pe, i v a n!" i v a n bara munis, vojujtis zē jona, ti̮škaśis je̮zked. i bara pomalisni da loktis gorte. a ge̮tiris vek uďivľa·jćće: "te, i v a n, ki̮ćći vetlan da ke̮n taʒ muʒtiśan?" i ge̮tiris kor-ke si̮liś kaźalis, si̮len ve̮lema śe̮rśis, tabak-paćka ve̮lema. i uďivľa·jćće ge̮tiris: 'taja pe mi̮jla talen?' a i v a n zē krepida uźe. 'taja pe kuščem talen tabak-paćka'? vot eśśa ge̮tiris sije-j tabak-paćkate kaźalis da sije pre̮stej tabak-paćkan vežis, ge̮tiris. ge̮tiris vežis da askinas bara munni kutisni, kojmed lun nin. seki ge̮tirisli šuve, znaćit, i vokjasisli: "taun-ke pe me og vermi gorte bergeććini da kutas-ke pe jeʒid e̮škid karta-e̮ʒeste žugedni, ti pe leʒej!" vot vok-mońli viśtale. vot ij i v a n munis. sija ďert oz te̮d, mi̮j ge̮tiris si̮liś vežis tabak-paćkase. munis da tabak-paćkate vojćća švaćkis kinas. toľko purk mune i i v a n uďivľa·jćće: 'mi̮j pe taja lovi menam? znaćit, menim ez nin kut služitni tabak-paćka.' kujimiś ki̮min vaćkis i vek . . . i śo rovno munni kole. munis i v a n pront vi̮le. i i v a nes regidja kaden ij mi̮j, mi̮j kerisni, vijisni. vijisni, a i v a nes predupreďitlillis. sije e̮škis, kor i v a nis kuli i kutis gorzini, kartase pramo . . . i vokjas šuveni: "oge pe leʒej!" śo rovno stav e̮zesse žugedlemen e̮škis petis.*

ring with you, I will give you my daughter and the whole of my empire will be yours."

5. Well, as they were living like this, the brothers began to wonder how foolish Ivan had got the ring. They begin to tempt Ivan. "How did it get into your hands?" Ivan of course does not tell the truth. Well, the three brothers began to live together, and at some time the next empire declared war upon them. The Tsar of that country wanted to have the other Tsar's daughter for the sake of intermarriage between the two Tsars. All the people they had went out to battle. They went to battle, and almost half of the people were lost on the battlefield. Ivan managed to escape with this tobacco-pouch. His wife does not know the truth. He had been fighting on the big horse, killing many people. Ivan came home, his wife still knew nothing. Ivan sleeps on and on. His wife wonders: "Where has he grown so tired?" — says she. She has no idea. "Well you, well you, where are you going?" — asks his wife. "How should you fight? They will kill you!" Next day they went off to fight again. Next day they go to fight, and in great haste Ivan went to the end of the ploughed field and struck the tobacco-pouch with his hand. Once again three warriors appeared: "What do you want, Ivanuško?" "This is the second day that I am fighting." "Do not grieve, Ivan!" Ivan went there and fought bravely together with all the people. When they had finished, he returned home. His wife was more and more amazed: "I say, Ivan, where do you keep going, where do you grow so tired?" Once his wife noticed that he had a tobacco-pouch with him. His wife wonders: "What use is this to him?" Ivan is lying in a deep sleep. "What tobacco-pouch is this he has got?" Then his wife exchanged this tobacco-pouch for an ordinary one. His wife exchanged it, and they went to fight the next day again; it was now the third day. Then he said to his wife and his brothers: "If I do not happen to return today, and if the white ox starts to break up the door of the stall, then let it out!" He says the same to his sisters-in-law as well. Ivan leaves. Of course he is not aware that his wife has exchanged the tobacco-pouch. He went there and struck the tobacco-pouch. Only a spark comes out, and Ivan wonders: "What is the matter with this? The tobacco-pouch is no use to me any longer." Three times or so he struck it, and it was always the same ... Anyhow, he must go. Ivan went to the front. And in a short time Ivan was killed. He was killed, although he had been warned. And the ox began to bellow as Ivan died, it was about to break the stall-door ... The brothers say: "We will not let it out." Yet the ox broke the whole door to pieces and went out.

6. *e̮škis petis daj loktis daj* i v a *nes pol'e vi̮l'iś korśis.* i v a *nlen tor-pi̮rigaen nin li̮-śe̮mis. e̮š ćukartis daj nuvis mi̮j-ke dore, va dore. va dore nuvis da e̮škis bi̮kestas da stav ćeriis vaśis gi̮źasni: "mi̮j ne tenid bi̮kej kole?" "menim pe kole lō burdan źel'l'a." "lō burdan źel'l'as pe zē pi̮din. sija pe kole na munni ju kuźa daj šor kuźa na kole kajni daj ke̮n-ke pe ješši vićkoin daj vićko ǯoǯ ulas na pe. sećći pe og te̮d, kodes mi vermam me̮dedlini. ćas pe ne̮revitli pe eśke! mi pe bara ćukarććilam." bara ćerijas ćukarććeni, kodes me̮dedni lō burdan źel'l'ala. i bara e̮škid bi̮kestis. i bara ćerijas loktisni: "mi̮j ne — šuve — kole ten?" "lō burdan źel'l'ala kole vetlini." "ćas, ćas — šuve — ćukarććilam da i̮stam." vot me̮diś ćukarććisni da ćerijas i šuveni: "ćas pe mi i̮stam nal'imes. nal'imli pe ki̮k bordas ki̮s ke̮rtalam. nal'im pe sija mi̮j-keǯik, etije ńin ńil'egǯik, sija pe t'ikejaǯik vettedle." vot ki̮s ke̮rtalisni mi̮j-keli, nal'imli da nal'im šor kuźa kaje daj sije mi̮j-ke pi̮ris na ješče pi̮ris. lō burdan źel'l'ase guvis vićko ǯoǯ uliś. vićko ǯoǯ uliś guvis daj kutis nal'imid petni da seśśa kaźalisni daj i ki̮s-pē̮te, e̮l'ise-j oredisni. a śo rovno me̮dnas, me̮d ki̮s-pē̮nas nuvis. nuvis da i vajis. vajis, e̮škid sijen e̮ććid pi̮zjis, juvištis da me̮diś pi̮zjis i kojmediś. kojmediś pi̮zjis da seśśa* i v a n u s k o-*j šuve: "uf pe, mi̮j di̮ra uźśema!" "da* i v a n u š k o, *pe, ńe bur e̮škid pe, te važen nin uže tenad ve̮li pom olemidli. a e̮śnad pe vot bara na lōźin." seśśa gortas munis i ge̮tirisked ladmisni da e̮ni oleni-vi̮leni, sarstvoen sarstvujteni.*

85. *ši̮r kī̮te, kate*

olisni-vi̮lisni ši̮r da kača. kor-ke kajisni naje vartni. kajisni vartni da i ši̮r i šue: "atte, kača, menam ǯikeǯ vunema ši̮d ćugunes ki̮skini. vaj, lećći, kača, ši̮d ćugunte ki̮ski, a me kol'tajaste ši̮blala." kača leććis gorte, ši̮d-ćugun ki̮skis daj kača ij ši̮d-ćugune špavgiśis. šir mi̮j sije? kača ez lok. 'atte d'ive, mi̮jla taja kača ez lok?!' leććis pre̮veritni kačaes. kača jignaśema. ńe-ki̮t oz pi̮rni piśt. ki̮člalis da ki̮člalis e̮ǯes dorin daj ši̮r šuve: "ki̮ti pi̮rni?" ruź śuris daj

6. The ox went out and arrived there to look for Ivan on the battlefield. Ivan's bones had been all broken to pieces by now. The ox collected them and took them to the shore. It took them to the shore, and there the ox bellowed loudly, and all the fish stirred up waves in the water. "What do you want, ox?" "I want medicine that heals the spirit and restores life." "The medicine that restores life is very deep down. You must walk right along the river and up the brook, it is somewhere in the church beneath the church. I do not know whom we can send there. Just a moment, wait! We'll have an assembly once again." The fish assemble to find out whom to send for the medicine that restores life. Again the ox starts to bellow. Again the fish come there. "What do you need?" — they ask. "You must go and fetch the medicine that restores life." "Immediately, immediately" — they answer — "we'll assemble and send someone out." For a second time the fish gather together. "Let us send the burbot. To the two fins of the burbot we'll fasten the hide from a reindeer's leg. The burbot is rather slimy and it goes along quietly." Well, they fastened the hide of the reindeer's leg to the burbot. The burbot swims up the brook, and went out. It stole the medicine that restores life from beneath the floor of the church. It stole it from beneath the floor of the church, and was just about to leave, but it was seen, and the hide of one of the reindeer's legs was torn off. But with the other, the other hide of the reindeer's leg it carried the medicine and brought it back. Then the ox sprinkled him with it once, then he drank; it sprinkled him a second time, and even a third time. It sprinkled him a third time, then Ivanuško speaks up: "Phew, what a long time I have been asleep!" "Well, Ivanuško, had you not got such a fine ox, your life would have ended long ago. With the help of your ox you have come to life again." Then he went home, and made peace with his wife. They are still alive, and govern their empire.

85. The mouse travels down and up the river

There lived a mouse and a magpie. One day they went out to thresh. They went to thresh, and the mouse says: "Oh dear magpie, I quite forgot to take the soup-pot off the stove. Go along, magpie, take the soup-pot off the stove, while I go on tessing the sheaves." The magpie went home, took the soup-pot off the fire and fell into the soup-pot. So what can the mouse do now? The magpie did not return. "Well now, why doesn't the magpie come back?" It went to check on the magpie. The magpie is shut up, and there is no hole to get in. The mouse turned round and round by the door and said: "Where can I get in?" It found a hole and got in. It went in and

pi̮ris. pi̮ris da pać-pe̮dan vośsa. vižedlis, kača ši̮d-ćugune špavgiśema. ši̮r pukśis da śojis da kējase i ši̮bitis šegjas pomas. vot seśśa be̮rinnas ši̮r leććis va-dore gul'ajtni kača-ke̮ja pi̮žen.

ši̮r kīte, kate
kača-ke̮ja pi̮ža,
moj-lopta pelisa
vurd-be̮ž zibja.

ki̮lis ke̮ć. "ši̮rul'ej, ćojil'ej, zē taj le̮śida śi̮lan da bośt-že mene če̮č pi̮žad!" "og, te ved ve̮jtan ićet pi̮žej menam da. og, og!" "me ved ńiki̮l'ćišta daj." "no ne lok, ki̮ken kutam katni."

ši̮r kīte, kate,
kača-ke̮ja pi̮ža,
moj-lopta pelisa,
vurd-be̮ž zibja.
ki̮r-keč-dorse si̮ništam
li̮va-dorse zibjištam.

ruć ki̮lema. "a kuščem le̮śida, ši̮ril'ej, ćojil'ej, śi̮lan! bośt vaj mene če̮č!" "og, te ved l'apńitan paśkid be̮žnad da mene ve̮jtan. pi̮žnim ićet da og, og". "me pi̮ž-ni̮rad ńiki̮l'ćišta daj." no ne lok!" me̮deććisnì kujimen.

ši̮r kīte, kate
kača-ke̮ja pi̮ža,
moj-lopta pelisa,
vurd-be̮ž zibja.
ki̮r-keč-dorse si̮ništam,
li̮va-dorse zibjištam.

oš ki̮lema daj lokte. "ši̮rul'ej, ćoje, zē taj le̮śida śi̮lan da bośt-že mene!" "og, og me tene, m i k a j l e i v a n e v i ć, og, og, og. te ved i̮ži̮d da mijanes, pi̮žnimes putkil'tan." "on-ke pe, on-ke pe bośt, ži̮k pe srazu-j putkil'ta." "no ne, lok!" se̮lisni ńol'en.

ši̮r kīte, kate,
kača-ke̮ja pi̮ža,

found the door of the stove open. It realized that the magpie had fallen into the soup-pot. The mouse sat down, ate it up, and tossed the breast-bones onto the end of the bench by the wall. Then later the mouse went down to the shore to sail in the boat made from the breast-bone of the magpie.

The mouse travels down and up the river,
In a boat made from the breast-bone of the magpie,
With an oar made from the beaver's paw,
With a punt-pole made from the otter's tail.

The hare overheard it. "Little mouse, dear sister, you sing very beautifully, take me in your boat as well!" "No, you will sink my little boat. No, no!" "But I shall roll into a ball." "Well, come on then, and the two of us shall travel up the river."

The mouse travels up and down the river,
In a boat made from the breast-bone of the magpie,
With an oar made from the beaver's paw,
With a punt-pole made from the otter's tail.
We row past the steep bank,
We punt the boat forward with the pole past the sandy shore.

The fox overheard it. "How beautifully you sing, little mouse, my dear sister! Take me as well!" "No, for a beat of your broad tail is enough to sink me. Our boat is small; no, no!" "I shall roll into a ball in the prow of your boat." "Well, come on then!" The three of them set out.

The mouse travels up and down the river,
In a boat made from the brest-bone of the magpie,
With an oar made from the beaver's paw,
With a punt-pole made from the otter's tail,
We row past the steep banks,
We punt the boat forward with the pole past the sandy shore.

The bear overheard it and comes along. "Little mouse, dear sister, you sing very beautifully, take me along!" "Not you, no, no, *Mikaile Ivanević*, no, no, no! For you are too big and you will turn us over, turn our boat over." "If you won't take me along, I'll turn you over at once." "Well, come on then!" The four of them got in.

The mouse travels up and down the river,
In a boat made from the breast-bone of the magpie,

moj-lopta pelisa,
vurd-bež zibja.
kir-keč-dorse siništam,
liva-bežse zibjištam.

oš taj kiʒi putkiľćis i vejini. šir piris ošli mij-ke sitanas. ij oš pegibe vovis i śorōno kōmis šires petkedni berege. petkedis i minis veľiśt oš. i šir petis mu vile.

86. *kiʒi me povźili?*

1. *me veli ićet-na, vited klassin veli veleďća. menim zev okota veli kajlini vere čak votni. seki me kivli, mij petema jeľdeg, zev una. lun nin veli, śor nin veli. i me eg aʒʒi aslim jortjases vere munni i lovi kajni vere etnamli. bośti ćuman da peśťer, a koske ešedi purtes. purtesse aćim i vurli kućikiś. pervojse veli zev leśid. me muni jered, miľk vivti. vereʒis pervojse veli ilin-na. eśśa piri vere. veli ar. pujas viliś korjis veli gilalema nin. veli zev leń i men lovi šuštem, no me vek muni voʒe.*

2. *med-berin vovis sečem mesta, keni veli jeľdeg. me stavse ekti, no peśťerej ez tir. lovi munni voʒe vere pide. vuʒi ʒoľańik joľ i seśśa kiʒa ras, kučem-ke tila (važen velema tila). eśśa so mij aʒʒi: tuj bokas stav koʒuv-kot-karjis puzuvtema, žugedema, paś-vartema. taiś kińʒi aʒʒi važ siś mirjas, kodjas siʒ-že veli perlaśemaeś mu-vilas. me povźi-koď. keť i ʒoľa-na veli, kivli nin, mij ośjas raďejteni lukjiśni koʒuv-kot-kar pijin, a siʒ-že važ siś kolodajasiś korśni pu-ćejjases. voʒe muništi da ješče eťi tor aʒʒi: stav ežase kod-ke kuľema, parsalema, tidale: vettedlema oš da korśema śojan. kok-tujjasis da giž-tujjasis velini ʒik-na viľeś. menim ez lo leśid. bergeďći i dumajta: čaknas i stavnas, a me lećća gorte. muna ńežjeńiken da et-medarla dore viʒedlivla.*

3. *eśśa kili beriś una vevliś korskem da kok-ši. kežišti ńe-una tuj-boke, med mene oz taľavni. zev iʒid eden naje skaćitisni me dinti. me zev iona povźi i dumajta: tidale, vevjaste suvede oš, a naje pišjeni. siʒ-že dumajta: menam kokjas abu sečem teribeś, kučem vevjaslen. dumajta, mene oškid suvedas. a me*

With an oar made from the beaver's paw,
With a punt-pole made from the otter's tail.
We row past the steep banks,
We punt the boat forward with the pole past the sandy shore.

The bear tumbled off and they sank. The mouse crept into the bear's bottom. The bear got into trouble and he had to land the mouse anyway. He landed it, and this was the only way the bear could escape. And the mouse went into the ploughed field.

86. How I was frightened

1. I was still a small boy at the time in the fifth class. I badly wanted to collect mushrooms in the forest. Just then I heard that parasol mushrooms grew there in plenty. It was already daytime and too late to go. And I did not see my friends go into the forest, so I had to go by myself into the forest. I took the birch-bask basket and a rucksack made of birch bask, and hung my sheath on my waist. I myself had sewn the sheath for my knife out of leather. At first it was very pleasant. I crossed a fenced vegetable garden on a hill. First of all it seemed a long way to the forest. Then I entered the forest. It was autumn. Leaves were already falling from the trees. It was very quiet, and I grew uneasy, but I kept walking onwards.

2. At last I reached a place where I found parasol mushrooms. I collected all of them, but my birch-bask rucksack was not full. I had to go deeper into the forest. I crossed a little river, and then through a birch-wood, and then through a clearing. And whatever did I see? The whole ant-hill by the road was turned upside down, scattered, and dug up. Besides I also saw old stumps of rotten trees also lying on the ground. I was frightened a little. Although I was still young, I had heard that bears are fond of poking about in ant-hills, as well as searching for insects in rotten tree-stamps. I went on a little further and saw something else. Somebody had torn up and stripped all the grass. Apparently a bear has been looking for food. The marks of its feet and claws were quite fresh. The sight was not pleasant at all. I turned round and thought: "To hell with mushrooms and everything, I shall go home." I walked slowly, and kept watch in every direction.

3. Later I heard many horses snorting and galloping behind me. I moved a little aside from the road so that they should not trample me down. They passed me at a fast gallop. I was very scared: It looks, I thought, as if the horses were being chased by a bear, and were in full flight. And at the time, I also thought: My feet are not as swift as those of the horses.

tedi, mij taje ver-tujisked orććen em paśkid ťeľega-tuj. sija tuježis, me dumiś, veli vers-žin. og ted, dir-e koterti taje tuježis, no regid me lovi taje tuj vilas. as vile vižedli i ažža: deremej kośaśema kujimlati, purtej purtesnas i stavnas vošema, peśťer-kevjej, eťiis orema, me veli rad, keť i koterti rasked i voštiśi mij-śure, no mini oškiś. pom.

87. *kiži me liji pervojiś utka?*

1. *me veli seki a b j a ć e jin. vetli sećće (sećći) šojććini. veli ar. samej veli lebe utka lun-vile. ritnas me daśti (leśedi) porok, puľa i vož asivnas, remid-na veli, mededći eťi ti dore, z i ľ a ti dore. z i ľ a tiis a b j a ć e jśań śiźim vers sajin. muni ćas ćež. ti pomas vižedli da eťi utka abu. vože kuti munni ti pelen. og-na veli kuž šiteg vettedlini i utkajas menam kok-šiiś veli lebźeni. me, semin muked-dirji kivlivli naliś šporeććemse.*

2. *seśśa vovi ti pomlańis. ažža: lebźe staja ti veśttiis. me leśedi ružje, okti kurekjas i viććiśa. seśśa naje kutisni žik me veśtti lebźini, biťťe narešne. biťťe naje tedisni, mij tačem kijśiśiś povni ńi-nem. me seśśa peźdedi ružje, vižeda vivlań: čin, gumaga-torjas i utka-stajaiś torjalis eťi śed jokmiľ i uśi sije jokmiľis me saje. taje veli utka, pervoj menam utka. peś-vivśis menam utkaid ješče šporeććištis-na va-verkes vilas, a me dumajti, mij sija kesje pišjini da peś-vivśim ješče sili kikiś liji. a kiś nin pišjas? berinnas śojigen me tedmali, mij eťi dreb-tuś veśkalema śelemas. pom.*

88. *kiži mi kijim eťi śir?*

1. *mi munim vokked ćeri kijni pižen, podoľńikaśni. podoľńik sije kuź šert, kićće pisavlema una vugir: muked-dirji ovle kiź-komin vugir, vetiminež. veli šede śir. arja-vivnas nin taje veli. medim kijni śir, kole korśni sam, lovja ćeri. mi vugraśim vokked i kijim goz-med keľći da pedďazek (sin-pi). seśśa mi ležim podoľńnik vae, žužid jire. śormim. pemdis.*

I thought: The bear would catch up with me. But I was aware that near to that forest path there was a wide cart-track as well. In my opinion it was half a verst to that track. I do not know how long it took me to run that far, but soon I was on that track. I looked at myself and saw that my shirt was torn in three different places, I had lost my knife and sheath and everything, one of the shoulder-straps of my rucksack of birch-bask was torn. I was glad to have escaped from the bear, even though I had had to run in the forest and lost one or two things. That is the end of the story.

87. How I first shot wild-duck

1. At that time I was in *abjaćej.* I went there to have a rest. It was autumn. The wild-duck were just flying southwards. In the evening I prepared gun-powder and bullets, and early in the morning, when it was still half dark I left for a lake called *zil'a.* The *zil'a* lake was seven versts away from *abjaćej.* It took me an hour to reach it. At the end of the lake I looked around, but not a single duck was to be seen. I began to go along the shore of the lake. Then I did not yet know how to walk noiselessly, and the ducks flew away at the noise of my footsteps. I only could hear their wings beating at intervals.

2. Then I reached the other end of the lake. I saw a flock of them flying over the lake. I made ready the gun, cocked the triggers, and waited. Then they began to fly just above me, as though deliberately. They seemed to know that they need not fear such a hunter. Then I fired the gun, and looked up: there were smoke, bits of paper, and a black ball separated from the flock, and that ball fell behind me. It was a duck, my first duck. The duck beat once more with its wings on the surface of the water, and I, thinking it was about to escape, fired furiously at it twice. But how could it escape? Later when I was eating it, I realized that a piece of shot had hit it in the heart. That is the end of the tale.

88. How we caught a pike

1. My brother and I went fishing in a boat, to catch pike with a *podol'ńik.* The *podol'ńik* is a long string to which many hooks are fastened: sometimes there are as many as twenty or thirty, up to fifty. There were pike about then. It was in the autumn. If you want to catch pike, you have to use bait, live fish. My brother and I angled for fish, and we caught a few sturgeon and red-finned carp. Then we cant the *podol'ńik* into the water, into a deep whirlpool. It was already late. It grew dark.

2. *seśśa le̮śeďćim ki̮jni. me pukśi pi̮ž be̮že si̮nni (be̮žavni), a vok le̮śedis aźlas da kutis kaťťini podoľńik-śures, vidlavni vugirjas. seśśa šuvis: "kod-ke pe em, ďerkjedle i le̮ńʒika, pe si̮n!" seśśa vovim sije vugireʒ, ki̮ćće šedema śir. a pemid-koď nin. vok e̮ććid sučkis aźlasen da ez veśkav, me̮diś sučkis, ez-že. seśśa viʒeda-da, mortid suvtis pi̮ž še̮re. šeništis e̮ććid aźlasen da boľsńitis vaas. lovi le̮ń. seśśa žugiľ-pi̮riś mortid šuvis menam: "pi̮šjis, mi̮nteććis. eśśa pe ńe-kor og kut vojin ćeri ki̮jni." pom.*

89. *ve̮ralem ji̮liś*

1. *ke̮ć ki̮jni mijan zavodiťeni li̮m uśem be̮rin. ke̮ʒdedas, kajeni ve̮re. kodi ki̮ʒi kuže ki̮jni: kodi vetliśeni ponjen, me aćim kaja puktavni petľajas. puktala, kor ľapkidʒik-na li̮mjis, li̮ź-petľajas. korśala mesta, ke̮niʒik ke̮ćjas ovmeććemaeś i tre̮pa vi̮las pukta petľa. petľa ve̮ćema ńebiďik provolokaś. ńe-iʒid ki̮č ve̮ća petľaśis i tre̮pa vomenis i petľase sije pukta. petľa puktigen kole te̮dni, medim mort-dukis ez ve̮v i ve̮reʒis voteʒ-na kijes stavse zi̮rala śiren, i provolokase tože zi̮rišta iľi-že ńi̮v-li̮sken, koz-pu-li̮sken. pukta, krepita iľi-ze kučem-ke ve̮sińik baďďe, iľi ve̮sińik ki̮ʒʒe, med ve̮li ńebid, šedas-ke, med oz orećći. no ovle, mi̮j me̮d lunas vi̮ʒedan, a ke̮ć volema, petľaas matiśćilema i bergeććema, oz pre̮jďit. si̮li mi̮j-ke oz kažićći. dukis ki̮le, iľi-že puktemis ľok loema i kapkanen siʒ-že. kapkanes jona ćiśťitan, puktilan kapkan ke̮ć vile. volas ʒik kapkan doreʒis, dukaśas, ni̮r-tujis veśig sija te̮ćće kapkan doras i bergeććas iľi-že boke ʒi̮biććas. śa ke̮ć ji̮vśis stavis, mi̮jen ki̮jeni.*

2. *kapkanse eśke pukteni mukedis koj-beďďen. me pervoj vo-na ki̮jśi, pukti pre̮ste siʒi: kepiśa, kušeńća-kepiśen suʒećća metra ki̮min. śa kepiśen li̮mse śujišta pi̮deʒik, guran-tor ve̮ća i guranas pukta kapkanse; kapkan vi̮las jeʒid bumaga-ľist i bumaga-ľistse ve̮sńińik sle̮jen li̮mnas ti̮rtišta. seśśa bergećća da aśśim kok-tujes tože ti̮rtišta i tre̮pa dorśis kok-tujis menam ńeťi oz te̮ćći.*

3. *še̮d-be̮ž ki̮jeni, ve̮ćeni ʒugjas. a n d r e j e v k a ś aʒʒili, tatiś me̮dla pe̮liś aʒʒili. pukteni sečem zored-dorjase. ve̮ćema kučem-ke tačem pe̮vjiś, sečem*

2. Then we prepared to fish. It sat in the stern of the boat to steer it, while my brother held the gaff, and started to pull the string of the *podoľńik*, to examine the hooks. Then he said: "There's something here, it's pulling at the hook, row more gently!" Then we got to the hook on which the pike was caught. But now it was almost dark. My brother struck once with the gaff but missed it, he struck a second time and missed again. Then I looked up and saw my brother standing in the middle of the boat. He struck once more with the gaff, and hit the water with a lot of noise. There was silence. Then he said disheartened: "It has escaped, it has got away, we are never going to fish again at night." That is the end of the story.

89. About hunting

1. People where we live begin to hunt here after snow has fallen. It grows cold, and they go to the forest. One hunts as one can. Some prefer to hunt with dogs, I myself put down snares. If the snow is thin, I set winter-snares. I look for places where hare generally prefer to stay and lay the snares on the path. The snares are made of soft wire. I make a little loop and put the snare across the path. When setting snares you have to see that there is no human scent, and before arriving in the forest I smear my hands with pitch, and I also tub the wire with fir or pine-needles. I fasten the snare to a slender willow-tree or birch so that it may be springy and soft and not break if a hare is caught. Well, it occurs fairly often that next day when you go to look at it you see that the hare has come there, right up to the snare but then turned back without touching it. It must have been suspicious of something. Either it sensed the scent or the snare was badly set. You have to deal in the same way with the trap. You clean the trap thoroughly, and set the trap for a hare. It goes right up to the trap, smells it, even putting its nose to it, then it turns back or jumps to one side. Well, that is all there is about hares and how they catch them.

2. Some people set traps with the aid of a shovel. When I first went hunting, I set the trap in a simple way like this: Putting on my outer fur-gloves, I reach down to the depth of a meter or so. Then pressing deeper into the snow with the gloves, I make a hole and place the trap in the pit, put a white sheet of paper on the trap and spread a thin layer of snow on the paper. Then I turn tound, and cover my footprints with snow. My footsteps cannot be seen at all by the path.

3. Ermine are hunted by making snares. I saw it done at Andrejevka, I saw it in a place on the other side. The snare is set by the hay-stacks. It is made of some kind of planking in the shape of a chest. They place about

jaščik modaa. jaščikas puktalemaś vẹv-śiiś sečem petľa, kẹkjamises kịmin, vịlas kẹkjamis, ulas kẹkjamis i zorod doras puktasni. śẹd-bẹžis zev raďejte zorod dorśis šịrjases kutavni i ʒug dorse počištasni. metra kịk kịmin. no seti prẹjďitigas, sija ʒugjas šede i garćće. sijen kịjeni. me kịjlivli posńi kapkanen trẹpajas vịlas-že. sija raďejte vot pịravni roźjas, sečem ʒoľańik roźjas, šịr-roźjase. počis uvjasti, zorod bokti vučjas boke pịras i kịt-ke pete, sịlen petan i pịran ruź vịjim. ruźas pukta ʒoľańik kapkan, tože godjišta. godjištem-inas, kịv vilas tože bumaga vevťťišta ʒik roź doras. no sija iľi pịrigas, roźas pịrigen śẹd-bẹžis šede, iľi-že petigas. no pervoj voas ďert ovlivlis, mịj oz šed. prẹjďitas, kokis veśkavlas, a uďitas kapkanis ẹtlaśni i śẹd-bežis oz šed. lokta da stavis ẹtlaśema. sije unʒik lịmse vẹlem puktiśśe, kiʒʒika da i kịvse, kapkan-kịvse abu sečem ćutkej (og tẹd, kịʒi kominas šuleni). a siʒ-že kapkanas zev že bura šede. eśśa tateni eśśe vidlim, etija vedraiś kịntam ji. jias seteni . . . jise perjam vedraiś, ji-pịčkis koľe kuš. jise kịntan, on ʒik, on stavse kịnti, sečem slẹj vedra gẹgeris kịnmas, a vais pičkesas koľe. seśśa ed on vịvti kịza kịnti, a viʒedlan, kịnmema sańťimetra kịk kịmin. seśśa kerkad pịrtan, sịvdištan, śa vịlias roź vẹćan, setiś vase kištan, a jiis koľe vedra doras. i ji sečem loe forma, vedra formaa ji. seśśa vịlas roź, ʒoľańik. śa puktan, śẹd-bežis kẹni ole, vevťťan, med vẹli rẹvnej, vịlas eśśe lap, lịs-lap puktan, med roźis oz tupkiś. lịs-laptis kute. eśśa vetlig-munigas sija roźas pịre, sećće šịr-sam puktan, šịres iľi śẹd-bežes.

4. *vot śẹlajas vịle kajlivli aslam leć-tujed. vidlala seteni, purtike me puktivla. sečem sija, zev raďejte vot avgust-śeńťabrasas purtikaśni kuregid-moz že. sija seśśa korśan sečem keres-bokjas, jag-bokjas, śa šondia lunjasad sija jona purtikaśe, sećće korśan iľi aćid vẹćan purtik-mestase. me žịlkaiś vẹli sečem mịj-ke vẹća, vẹśńińik žịlkaiś lećjas. kịk beď, tačem ʒoľańik beď sačkan, vẹćan sečem vorota-koď i bokas kịk poneľ keričtan da puktan. tačemes vẹćan i seti śẹlais loktas purtikaśni, pịras i kak raz sịli goľas i šede. — a poneľis, med bokiti ozʒik mun, bokśań oz pịr, med vomenis pịras, leć vomenis pịras. ẹtar-mẹdar-śańis iľi vịliśańis iľi uliśańis — šuam — lokte, a bokśańis oz med sećći purtikaśnis lok. — no sečem mićańik mesta, kuš-injas vẹrśis aʒʒan, jagjas. seśśa*

eight nooses made of horsehair in the chest, eight above and eight below, and place it by the hay-stack. Ermine are fond of chasing mice around hay-stacks, and they make a ring of snares two metres away. When the ermine crosses this, it gets caught in the snare and tangled up. This is the way they are hunted. I often hunted with small traps as well, also along the paths. It likes to craw into holes, little tiny holes, mouse-holes. Under the fence, along the side of the hay-stack, along the side of small heaps of earth it goes in and gets out somehow; it has both an etrance and an exit. I place a little trap in the hole, digging it in likewise. In the place where I dig, on the tongue of the trap, I spread a sheet of paper too, quite close to the hole. Well, when the ermine comes, it is caught in the snare entering the hole or coming out of it. It went over it touching it with its leg, the trap closed up properly, though it failed to catch the ermine. I go to it and see it is fully closed. Either the layer of snow was too thick or the tongue of the trap was not sensitive enough. (I do not know how to put it in Zyrian.) But it may well be caught in the trap. Then we tried another method too: We freeze water in a bucket, and catch the ermine in ice. You take the ice out of the bucket, leaving the inside of the ice empty. You freeze ice, though not the whole of it, you do not freeze the whole of the water completely, a layer of ice is frozen round the sides of the bucket, and water is left in the middle of it. You do not freeze it too thickly, you see whether it is frozen about two centimetres thick. Then you take it into the house, melt it and drill a hole in the top of it and pour the water out through it. The ice is left round the sides of the bucket. The ice will have the shape of the bucket. Then you drill a small hole in the top of it, and then put it where there are ermine, cover it to make it level, putting a fir-twig on top of it so as to keep the hole open. The fir-twig holds the snow. Then the ermine comes along and enters the hole in which you put bait, a mouse or an ermine.

4. I hunted hazel-hen by making my own snare-paths. Examining the snare, I put it in a sandy clearing. The hazel-hen is a bird that likes to take a sand-bath in August and September, like hens. You go and look for hill-slopes with fir-woods on the sides, where they like to bath on sunny days; there you either find a place for sand-bath or you make one. I made snares of sinews, thin sinews. You drive two sticks, as little as this, into the ground, make a kind of gate, fell two young spruces, one on each side, and set up the snare. You make a snare like this and wait for the hazel-hen to come to the sand bath; it goes in and it is immediately snared by its neck. The young spruce are needed to prevent it from approaching from the side, to prevent it from walking sideways, to make it enter through the snare. It may come from this side or that side — say, from above or from below, —

pre̮ste me purten mi̮j-kese kuľišta, ńičse, jalase-ľi. śa kijen ši̮ľedišta da śa kośmas da, sečemse taj korśeni, aǯǯe zev e̮dje. li̮va sečem gaľkija, sečem, no li̮va, no med toľko ve̮li ńebid, kos mu ve̮li, iľi-že koloda, iľi-že koʒuv-kot-kar, seś puzuvtan. koʒuv-kot-karjas sećće vot dozmer jonʒika lokte, a śe̮lad ozʒik.

5. *dozmeris, tože purtiken ki̮ja. koľan vo dozmerse me ki̮ji lećken že, no ʒik te̮dteg, og ve̮li te̮d, mi̮j taje ve̮li petavli ʒik tuj vile. tačem traktorjas vetleni, mašinajas vetleni. a e̮ććid muni ružjen me ki̮jśini. lebźisni tuj vivśis. me̮diś muni, lebźeni, śa-j dumišti, miśa, mi̮jes tateni tuj vilas dozmerjasis. śa vi̮ʒedi bura kok-tujaśni, a seten ve̮lem vajalemaś kor-ke li̮va mašinaen. li̮vase kiś-temaś, a li̮va pias zev posińik iz-tor vi̮jim. vot sija ve̮lem izjasse, na petaleni ve̮rśid, i e̮kteni. śa me pukti vomenis tože dozmer-leć, ʒi̮lkaśid že pukti. me̮d lunas kaji, a e̮ťi šedema, e̮ťiis śin voʒin oreććis. a juaśi da sija pe taj kurćće ʒi̮lkase a. seśśa sutugaś puktili, mednej sutugaiś, tože oreććilis. kujimes taj ki̮jli a. seśśa enovti, li̮m uśis da śa eg kajli.*

6. *a tar kuźa. me tar vilas kojt vile vetlivla. bi̮d vo, bi̮d tulis. m i ć a j a g šuśe, taśań e̮kmis kilometra, zev sečem ćistej, no mića požemjas bi̮dme, jagis zev mića že. seten bi̮d vo e̮ťi mestan tar kojte. menam seten ve̮ćema sečem ćom-koď. ćomjas muna ve̮li ritśańis-na, ri̮tnas ćas ke̮kjamisin ki̮min pukśa. mića-ke ri̮tis, kojteni, ri̮tnas lokteni, šondi kutas leććini da, a ľokʒik-ke, asivnas. no si̮ʒi, mi̮j-ke, viʒedalan mestase, ke̮ni le̮śidʒik i ćomje pi̮ra šondi leććigas ki̮min. i pukalan ši̮-ńi-te̮v, on kurićći ńi, si̮ʒi viććiśan. eśśa bokiś ki̮lan, seteni iľi-že taris lebźe, a bord šuťlalemis ki̮lište. šuťlale iľi-že ki̮ćće-ke pu vilas pukśas da ki̮lište, znaćit loktaleni kojt vilas. seteni ešše pukalan, ešše-na viććiśan. seśśa pemdištni kutas, śa re̮mdini, śa drug loktas iľi-že kojt vilas, srazu mesta vi̮las, iľi-že boke loktas da srazu i goredas sija: pš-š-š. stav jag paštalais zev gora sija ki̮le matiad da. bara goredas kod-ke, kojmed goredas, vopšem sečem šum kutas loni, bi̮ťťe stavis lovźas. seśśa i kojt-še̮r vi̮jim nalen, ke̮ni menam ćomjis. śa sećći lokteni muked-di̮rjis kujimen, muked-di̮rjis e̮ťi, muked-di̮rjis das-viten srazu loktasni. ritśańis li̮jnis pemid, da on, onʒik vermi li̮jnis. asileʒis og li̮j. daške, miśa, asivnas unʒik loktasni da poźe e̮ťien-e̮ťien unʒik li̮jni. ri̮tśańid seśśa kojt vilas loktasni. vojin, vojnas ʒońnas pukala. asivnas vot seśśa i ki̮k ćase murtsa oz vo, srazu zavoďitas seteni. pervoj e̮ťi zev gora ćušńitas, lańtištlasni. eśśa e̮ťik kutas ćuškini, me̮d ćuške, śa e̮tlaśasni. śa zev*

but it must not come from the side to bath in the sand. Well you find such nice places, clearings in the forest, you find woods of spruce. With a knife I simply strip off the green moss, and white moss. Then I smooth it with my hands. They look for such places, and they are quick to find them. It should be gravelly sand, soft sand, dry earth, a tree-stump or an anthill; there you make a little mound. As for the anthill black grouse will usually come there, hazel-hens less frequently.

5. I also catch capercaillie, while they are bathing in the sand. Last year I trapped capercaillie although it was by accident for I did not know they liked to walk as far as the road. Tractors and things go there, machines. Once I went hunting with a gun. They flew up from the road. Next time I went, they also flew away. Then I began to ponder why capercaillie were there on the road. Then I followed their tracks attentively; sand was once carried there by trucks. The sand was poured out, and the sand contains tiny bits of gravel. The fowl come out of the forest and pick out the stones. Then I set up a trap for the capercaillie across the road; I made it of sinews. Next day I walked there, one was caught, another escaped before my eyes. I was intrigued to know why; I saw it had bitten the sinew. Then I made a snare of wire, copper wire, and that too snapped. I caught perhaps three fowl, but later I abandoned it, the snow fell, and I did not go hunting again.

6. About black-grouse. I go hunting black-grouse at mating-time. In spring every year. The place is called *beautiful fir-wood,* nine kilometres away, it such a clearing, with fine firs growing in it, a beautiful wood it is. Year by year the black grouse goes there to mate in the same place. I went there in the evening; at about eight o'clock I settle down. If it is a nice evening, they come in the evening as the sun sets. If not, then in the morning. Well then, you take a look at the place, find out where it is best and about sunset you go into the hut. You sit in silence, you do not even smoke, that is how you wait. Soon you hear from one side the black-grouse fly up in the air, only the noise of its wings can be heard. Then it grows dark, dusk begins to fall and it comes either directly to the mating-place, or it turns aside and suddenly begins to call: psh-sh-sh. Nearby, and all through the breadth of the fir-wood their loud cries are heard. Again one of them emits a cry, then a third one, in general they make as much noise as if all of them were coming to life. It is the centre of their mating-place where my hut stands. Sometimes three of them come, sometimes only one, occasionally as many as fifteen at a time. It is too dark in the evening to shoot, no, you cannot shoot, I do not shoot till morning. Perhaps — I think — more of them will come in the morning, and you can shoot them more successfully one by one. I sit all through the night, throughout the whole night.

iń'eresneja kiken panidaśasni, voća kutasni bordjišni. petukjas moz ćeććištlasni, mij-ke, bordnas šenaśeni. śa mukedis tomʒikis kajemaś, il'i abu kajemaś, a pukaleni pu vilin. naja kurgeni kučem-ke vot: kurr-kurr. etija gelub modaad kurgeni. a giriśʒikis seteni tiškaśeni, kotraleni. zev edje kotertas seśśa. no jugdan-doris seśśa matin — menam medśa ilinis daške metra komin kimin — stavis da stavis geger tidale. das-viten kimin sija unais, kiźiś una eg aʒʒiv, pravda, ez volini, kiźen kimin medśa unais. eśśa kodi matinʒik da kodi kažićće tenid, sije lijan, oz-ke ud'itni lebźini, medes lijan. a medas lijan da lebźeni, kik, kikes. jugdas nin, kujim ćasin pomaśe, boštan tar gorte. kojtemse seśśa torka me, lija da. kujim ćasin seśśa jugde nin, tećće nin. seśśa lija da lebźasni pujas vile, eśśa-j enovteni. asivnas seśśa oz kutni kojtni. a med lunnas seśśa bara lokteni. da stavis menam.

90. *gožśa lun*

leśid že nin śiktin ovni; vot mi olam d'erevannej śiktin, osobenna gožemin, turun puktan kade. ćeććan, mesjas muneni lud vile, ćuksaśeni petukjas. brigad'er lokte, iste viʒ vile. śojištan, ćeććan, leććan ež-va dore, sen perevozčik, sen kolχozńikjas una ćukarććemaś, kodi kosaa, kodi kurana. i vot vuʒan medla pele i bid brigadaś ćukarććeni seći jez. kor-ke kekjamis ćasjasin razeććeni aslanis brigadajase. i vot munan, jukleni jezes: kodi kurte, kodi ičke, kodi ćevte, kodi jur kiskale. vot lun-tir ćevtan, ćasov śiźim-kekjamisin ritnas ber loktan, vuʒan ež-vas, stavis jajid lude, peśalema, turun-korobid vilad uśema. loktan, periś mam pivśan lomtema. vot sija dobra! kiʒ piran, peś vaen miśśan, gorjad kujim keš va kojištan, peś koreśen kiʒ švaćedan aśśid ludem bokjaste. ot sija da!

Then in the morning, a little before two o'clock, it starts all of a sudden. First one of them begins to pant loudly, then silence follows. Then another begins to pant, then still another, and finally they start fighting. It is interesting, the way two of them clash, beating at each other with their wings. They spring and clap their wings like cocks. Later a few young fowl came there or else they did not come, but sat in the trees. They coo somehow like this: kurr-kurr. They coo like pigeons. The bigger ones fight and run to and fro. They can run fast. At dawn everything is visible around the place — the farthest fowl is perhaps thirty metres away from me. There are about fifteen of them; truth to tell, I did not see more than twenty of them, they did not come in greater numbers, twenty was the most. Then you shoot the one nearest to you, whichever you like, and if they fail to fly away in time, you shoot another one as well! If you fire at the second one and they fly away, then you have bagged two fowl. It gets higher now; at three o'clock the mating is over, you take home the black-grouse. At three o'clock I disturb the mating with the firing. At three o'clock it is getting light. I fire my gun, they fly on to-the trees and leave. Then they will not mate in the morning. Next day they come again. This is all I can say.

90. A summer day

It is pleasant to live in a village: you see we are living in *ďerevannej* village; especially is it pleasant in summer, during hay-making. You get up, the cow go to the pasture, the cocks are crowing. The leader of the brigade arrives and sends you to work in the meadow. You get up and eat a little, walk down to the banks of the Vyčegda, there is the ferryman, several members of the kolkhoz have assembled, one with a sycthe, another with a rake. You cross over to the other side, people have come from every brigade. At about eight o'clock they split up, each of them going to his own brigade. You go there, and they divide the folk: this one works with the rake, that one with the scythe, another one spreads hay, still another pulls the stooks. Well, all day long you are pitching hay, at seven or eight o'clock you return, cross the Vyčegda; your whole body itches, your are sweating, you are covered in dust from the hay. You arrive home, your old mother has heated the bath-house. That's really good! You go in and wash in hot water, throwing three ladles full of water onto the stove. You beat your itching sides with a hot bathing-broom. It's just the thing!

(b) Ned-kījas

91.

1. *mu-gu, mu-gu mu ulin, va-gu, va-gu va ulin, ćeskid, kurid bad' jilin, śelem-vižan žaž dorin. — kušman, ćeri, tag, sō.*

2. *bid kerka geger siteś gez. — ńič.*

3. *et'i jurles vilin komin ćoja-voka kujleni. — petelek.*

4. *iži-iži kik ćoj, aži-aži ńol' ćoj, tila vilin das ćoj. — iž-ńak, mes-ńak, porś-ńak.*

5. *ćukl'a ćož-ińe gozja, l'as-nir un-ińe gozja, t'ūgun vežań. — stan, tal'an, ćēnek.*

6. *kitem-koktem bid tor veće. — tē-nir.*

7. *śed ver šerin jurtem kerka. — pes-ćipas.*

8. *śed ver šerin gerd gaća molod'eć sulale. — kiž-pu.*

9. *ćukil'-mukil' kićće vetlin, širem buriś, mij ted mogis. — ju da viž.*

10. *bid želeb dorin kos taśti. — teliś.*

11. *kud-tir šeg da et'i l'išnej. — kožū da teliś.*

12. *kiken indeni, viten kuteni, nilis omel'ik, ruźis ićet'ik, kiken śujeni. — jem-pisalem.*

13. *kiz, kiz ić-moń da ńak-peledis kiskaleni. — ežes-vug.*

14. *kik m i k e l a vojćća jurbiteni. — gebeć-ežes da kerka-ežes.*

15. *bid kerkain śveńi-gered. — bad'-ules.*

16. *kok-pēnas sulale, śin-pēnas vižede, poč vītiis zeletej d'eńga mune. — peša-bi.*

17. *ńol' koka, va ruška, bija śelema. — samevar.*

18. *tom, tom ić-moń da ćipanli sorsežis porśli l'ekježis. — tuj.*

19. *tom, tom molod'eć da bid bež uliś ažžile. — porog.*

20. *ilin, ilin vē gerektas da taććež donis uśe. — piśme.*

21. *more vomen kert megir. — vedra-vug.*

22. *more šerin utka da beregas bežis. — keš.*

23. *more vomen šńari ji kutema. — šid-keń.*

(b) Riddles

91.

1. A cave, a cave under the ground, a cavern in the water, a water-cavern under the water, it is tasty, bitter on the willow-tree, heart-holder by the shelf. — Radish, fish, hops, salt.

2. A mucky string round each house. — Moss.

3. Thirty brothers are lying on one pillow. — The ceiling.

4. *iẑi-iẑi* two sisters, *aẑi-aẑi* four sisters, there are ten sisters in the clearing. — Udders of ewe, cow and pig.

5. Crooked aunt on my mother's side together with her husband, snub-nosed aunt on my father's side together with her husband, nimble god-mother. — The loom, its treadle and shuttle.

6. It has neither hands nor feet, still it can do anything. — A blast of wind.

7. A roofless house in the middle of a dark wood. — A pile of wood.

8. A young lad with red trousers standing in the middle of a dark wood. — A birch-tree.

9. Twisting and turning, where have you been? Shorn hedge, what does it matter to you? — A river and meadow.

10. A dry cup by every gutter. — The moon.

11. A basket full of shavings and something else into the bargain. — The stars and moon.

12. Two of them show it, five of them hold it, the girl is lean, her slit is narrow, two of them poke it in. — Threading a needle.

13. A fat, fat young wife yanked by her breasts. — Handle of the door.

14. Two St. Nicolases praying opposite each other. — The door of the cellar and the door of the house.

15. There is a *Ẑveńi-gorod* in each house. — A chair made of wicker.

16. It stand on one leg, looks with one eye, gold coins pass through the pole. — The flame of a pine-torch.

17. It has four legs, a watery belly and a fiery heart. — A samovar.

18. A young, young wife, it reaches up to the chicken's crest and the pig's ankle. — A road.

19. A young, young lad who sees under every tail. — Threshold.

20. Far away, far away a horse neighs, and its price reaches this place. — A leaf.

21. An iron yoke over the sea. — The handle of the bucket.

22. A duck in the middle of the sea with its tail on the shores. — A ladle.

23. A thin sheet of ice covering the sea. — The skin on the soup.

24. *śo koka da peľesteg oz vermi sūtni. — ros*
25. *lunnas skamja, vojnas kemuťina. — pon*
26. *ti vojtište, ta vojtište, vek oz vojtišt. — iśerga.*
27. *gid-tir iž da eťi bež. — ńań-zir.*
28. *munigen voľsale, loktigen voľsale. — ľampa-tuj.*

(c) A proverb

92.

śintem una aǯǯe, koktem una vetle, peľtem una kile.

(d) Charms, curses

93.

a) iž širigen

eśt-eśt!
širan-kad ted,
joma-babali en śećći,
ber gorte lok,
en śećći!

b) iž širigen

gospoďi blageslevi kristo·s!
širan-kad ted,
joma-babali en śećći,
śiźim počis vomen ćeććišt
da ber gorte lok!

ć) vomiǯiś

śir-piń goršad,
kert-neš pľešad,
poma jokiš sitanad!
sitan-gente kurćći da
veľiśt mene vomǯō!

d) koken (ćeľaď pīśedigen)

en berd, ďiťa, en, en! ćas kekeńte pīśedam da kokeńte da kokeńte, kokeńte, kekeńte, med edje kokeń kotredlas, kekeńid med edje kutas vorsni. en berd, ďiťa, en!

24. It has a hundred legs, yet it cannot stand without a corner. — A broom.

25. Bench in the daytime, hames by night. — A dog.

26. It drops here and drops there, but never drops down. — An earring.

27. A pen full of sheep and a tail. — A bread-shovel.

28. On the way out it lays out, on the way back, it lays out. — A ski-trace.

92.

The blind see a lot, the lame walk a lot, the deaf hear a lot.

93.

(a) At the sheep-shearing

Lamb, lamb!
You must know when shearing is due,
Yield not to the witch,
Come home,
Do not surrender!

(b) At the sheep-shearing

Our Lord Jesus Christ, bless it!
You must know when shearing is due,
Do not yield to the witch,
Jump over seven fences
And come home!

(c) Against the evil eye

Pike's teeth in your throat,
Iron mallet on your forehead,
A Kama perch in your bottom!
Bite the hair of your arse,
And only then bewitch me!

(d) Pretty feet (to children when they are bathed)

Don't cry, child, no, don't cry! We'll bathe your little hands and your little feet at once, your little feet, your little hands, so that your little feet can run fast, your little hands can play fast! Don't cry, child, no, don't cry!

e)

kod vomʒalis, śir-piń goršanis, ke̯rt ne̯š pľesanis, koma jokiš papaľanis.

f)

ši̯rli jaj-piń, a menim li̯-piń.

g)

porśli pe ludem, ośli viśem, men zdorovje (kupaľńića di̯rji šueni, viľ koreśen pī̯śigen.)

h)

joma-babali en śećći, śiźim poč vī̯ti ćeććišt da pi̯šji! (i̯žse ši̯rigen šueni, ši̯rannas ve̯ćeni.)

(e) Songs

94.

"mamej, matuškaj, daj di̯r-i ved novledlin,
di̯r-i ved novledlin da ćasen re̯ďitin,
ćasen re̯ďitin daj i̯ʒida-j bi̯ttin,
i̯ʒida-j bi̯ttin da ber-i-ba sudnaeʒ.
mate ved ke̯sjin da mati źemľae,
i̯le ved śetin da i̯li źemľae,
i̯li źemľae daj una śemjae,
una śemjae da das-ki̯ked tuje,
das-i ki̯ked tuje daj ńoľ aja-ni̯le.
mamej, matuškaj, daj ćaste ved ke̯sjin,
ćas-i-te ved ke̯sjin da mene vidlini.
e̯ťi vo-j oli da mene-j en vidli,
me̯d-i vo me-j oli da bara-j en vidli,
kojmed vo-j oli da aćim me̯dećći,
aćim me̯dećći da paśkid poľeśań,
paśkid poľeśań da kuź-i ve̯ra inti."
kuź-i ve̯ra inti da mam-i panid lokte,
mam panid lokte de mam-i ni̯les ez te̯d.
"šondiej mamej da en emej ne te̯d?"
"ďiťaej, ni̯lej da ke̯ni jugid virid,
ke̯ni jugid virid da ke̯ni jeʒid jajid?"
"mamej, matuškaj daj pľeťen ne̯jtisni,

(e)

To those who bewitched me, a pike's tooth in their throat, an iron mallet in their forehead, a perch from the Kama in their cunt!

(f)

Flesh-teeth to the mouse, bone-teeth to me!

(g)

Itching to the hog, sickness to the bear, health to me. (Recited on St. John the Baptist's day, when bathing with a new bath-broom.)

(h)

Do not yield to the witch, jump over seven poles and run away! (Recited at sheep-shearing while making a † with the scissors.)

94.

"Mother, my dear mother, you carried me a long time,
You carried me a long time and gave me birth in an hour.
You gave me birth in an hour and raised me tall,
Your raised me tall, as tall as a willow-tree.
You promised me to one nearby, to a land nearby,
And you have given me away far off to a distant land,
To a distant land, to a large family,
To a large family, to be the twelfth in it,
To be the twelfth, with four sisters-in-law.
Mother, my dear mother, how often you wanted,
How often you wanted to visit me.
I lived a year and you did not come to visit me,
I lived two years, again you did not come to visit me,
In the third year I myself started out,
I myself started from the broad field,
From the broad field in the long forest."
In the long forest the mother comes to meet her,
The mother comes to meet her, and she does not recognize her daughter.
"My pretty sun, mother, did you not recognize me!"
"My child, my daughter, where is your light blood,
Where is your light blood, where is your white body?"
"Mother, my dear mother, they lashed me with whip,

pľeťen nẹjtisni da pľeť-śer nuvisni,
pľeť-i-śer nuvisni da kulak-śer nuvisni.”

95.

“šondiej mamej daj verdemej ďiťaj,
dịr ved nōledlin daj ćas ved rẹďitin.
rẹďitin, matuška, mićaja, bura,
bịttin, matuška, berbaiś ǯuǯid,
veledin, matuška, školńej mańere,
en kẹsjil, matuška, ịleje śetni.
śetin, matuska, ịle źemľaje,
ịle źemľae daj una śemjae,
una śemjae daj das-kịked tuje
das-kịked tuje daj śiźim ľevere,
śiźim ľevere daj ńoľ aja-nịle,
ńoľ aja-nịle daj ịli źemľae.
ẹťi vo oli daj mames eg kịlli,
mẹd vo oli daj mames eg aǯǯil,
kojmed vo oli daj gẹśťitni mẹdi,
ťom-i-ńom ľesu da paś-i-kid poľed,
paśkid pole da ǯuǯid vẹre,
ǯuǯid vẹre daj mamked vojććaśi.”
“šondiej mamej, daj verdemej ďiťaj,
kẹn ne tenad daj alej virid?”
“šondiej mamej daj verdemej ďiťaj,
alej virid-i pľeť-i-śer muni.”
“šondiej mamej daj verdemej ďiťaj,
kẹn ne tenad-i kẹć-gen ńebid jajid?”
“šondiej mamej daj verdemej ďiťaj,
sija ved menam-i kulak-śer muni.”
“šondiej mamej daj verdemej ďiťaj,
kẹn ne tenad-i mića ćuvkiid?”
“sija ved menam daj pi-verej kokin.”
“šondiej mamej daj verdemej ďiťaj,
kẹn ne tenad-i alej šẹvk ćịšjanid?”
“sija ved menam daj aja-nī jurin”
“šondiej menam daj verdemej ďiťaj,
kuščem ne tenad daj kẹźajinid?”

They lashed me with whip, they took it away with the whip,
They took it away with the whip, they took it away with their fists."

95.

"My pretty sun, my dear mother,
You carried me a long time and gave me birth in an hour,
Dear mother, you bore me to be beautiful, to be kind,
Dear mother, you raised me taller than the willow-tree,
Dear mother, you taught me school-manners,
You did not want, dear mother, to give me far away.
Dear mother, you have given me far away,
To a far land, to a large family,
To a large family, to be the twelfth in it,
To be the twelfth with seven brothers-in-law,
With seven brothers-in-law, with four sisters-in-law,
With four sisters-in-law, to a far land.
I lived a year and heard nothing from mother,
I lived two years and did not see mother,
I lived three years, I started off to a party,
In the dark wood, in the wide field,
In the wide field, in the deep forest,
In the deep forest, and I met mother."
"My pretty sun, my dear child,
Where is your purple blood?"
"My pretty sun, dear mother, my darling,
My purple blood has been lashed out of me."
"My pretty sun, my dear child,
Where is your body that used to be soft as hare's fur?"
"My pretty sun, dear mother, my darling,
They beat my body with their fists."
"My pretty sun, my dear child,
Where are your fine stockings?"
"They are on my brother-in-law's feet."
"My pretty sun, my dear child,
Where is your purple silken kerchief?"
"It is on my sister-in-law's head."
"My pretty sun, my dear child,
What is your husband like?"

"sija menam daj ľutaja źmeja."
be̮rdisni da be̮rdisni ińa-ni̮la,
ǯoń ći̮šjan-i ke̮tedisni.

96.

le̮z more vi̮v-i-ti da se̮kel lebale,
lebale, lebale.
o-o-o-oj daj se̮kel lebale.
se̮kelis vi̮v-i-ti (vi̮liti) daj jeǯid juś vetle,
vetle, vetle, vetle.
o-o-o-oj da jeǯid juś vetle.
juśej pe juśej da ki̮t vetlin, munin,
munin, munin, munin?
o-o-o-oj daj ki̮t vetlin, munin?
me pe vetli, se̮kelej, le̮z more vi̮vti,
vi̮vti, vi̮vti, vi̮vti.
o-o-o-oj da le̮z more vi̮vti.
more vi̮las, se̮kelej, karabjas vetle,
vetle, vetle, vetle.
o-o-o-oj daj karabjas vetle.
karab pi̮čkas, se̮kelej, gaža gorńića,
gorńića, gorńića.
o-o-o-oj daj gaža gorńića.
gorńićas pe, se̮kelej, de̮va pukale,
pukale, pukale.
o-o-o-oj daj de̮va pukale.
de̮vaslen pe, se̮kelej, mića ni̮v vijim,
vijim, vijim, vijim.
o-o-o-oj daj mića ni̮v vijim.
mića ni̮lislen, se̮kelej, k a ť e ń k o j ńimis,
ńimis, ńimis, ńimis.
o-o-o-oj daj k a ť e ń k o j ńimis.
k a ť e ń k o j vetlis daj ki̮va petteǯis,
petteǯis, petteǯis.
o-o-o-oj daj ki̮va petteǯis.
k a ť e ń k o j pe ćeććis da šondi petteǯis,
petteǯis, petteǯis.
o-o-o-oj da šondi petteǯis.
k a ť e ń k o j pe ćećći da morskej vanas mi̮śśi,

"He is a bloodthirsty snake."
The mother and her daughter wept and wept;
They soaked with tears an entire kerchief.

96.

Over the blue sea a falcon is flying,
Flying, flying.
O-o-o-oj, a falcon is flying.
Above the falcon a white swan is soaring,
Soaring, soaring, soaring.
O-o-o-oj, a white swan is soaring.
My swan, my swan, where have you been roaming,
Roaming, roaming, roaming?
O-o-o-oj, where have you been roaming?
My falcon, I have been roaming over the blue sea,
Above, above, above.
O-o-o-oj, over the blue sea.
On the sea, my falcon, boats are sailing,
Sailing, sailing, sailing.
O-o-o-oj, boats are sailing.
Inside the boat, my falcon, there is a beautiful chamber,
There is a chamber, a chamber.
O-o-o-oj, there is a beautiful chamber.
In the chamber, my falcon, a widow is sitting,
Sitting, sitting.
O-o-o-oj, a widow is sitting.
The widow, my falcon, has a beautiful daughter,
She has, she has, she has.
O-o-o-oj, she has a beautiful daughter.
The beautiful daughter, my falcon, is called *Kaťeńkoj*,
That is her name, her name, her name,
O-o-o-oj, her name is *Kaťeńkoj*.
Kaťeńkoj walked till dawn,
Till dawn, till dawn.
O-o-o-oj, till dawn.
Kaťeńkoj got up before the sun rose,
Before the sun rose, before the sun rose.
O-o-o-oj, before the sun rose.
Kaťeńkoj, get up and wash yourself in sea-water.

mi̯śśi, mi̯śśi, mi̯śśi!
o-o-o-oj daj vanas mi̯śśi!
k a ť e ń k o j pe ćećći da kuź ći̯šjanas ći̯škiś,
ći̯škiś, ći̯škiś, ći̯škiś!
o-o-o-oj daj ći̯šjanas ći̯škiś!
k a ť e ń k o j pe cećći daj korašiś vovis,
vovis, vovis, vovis.
o-o-o-oj daj korašiś vovis.
k a ť e ń k o j pe ćećći da kite kutni suvt,
suvt, suvt, suvt, suvt, suvt, suvt!
o-o-o-oj daj kite kutni suvt!
k a ť e ń k o j pe ćećći da bazarad kajli,
kajli, kajli, kajli!
o-o-o-oj daj bazarad kajli!
k a ť e ń k o j pe ćećći da med donase bośt,
bośt, bośt, bośt, bośt, bośt, bośt!
o-o-o-oj daj med donase bośt!

97.

poľeiś či̯n pete da
moreiś tuman kaje.
aľi ńe tuman daj
juś-ǯoǯeg lebźe,
juś-ǯoǯeg be̯rśa da
pe̯riś kuč ve̯ćće.
kučej pe kučej da
ki̯t-i vetlin-i daj munin!
me vetli, muni da
s a l a t u l ati.
mi̯j ki̯ś ki̯vlin, aǯǯilin daj?
me ki̯vli, aǯǯili:
s a l a t u l ain daj
jeǯid jaj kujle,
jeǯid jaj doras da
kujim ćikiš volivleni.
med-voǯǯa ćikišis daj
re̯ďimej daj mamis,
še̯r-kost ćikišis daj
re̯ďimej ćojis,

Wash yourself, wash yourself, wash yourself!
O-o-o-oj, wash yourself in water!
Kaťeńkoj, get up and dry yourself with a long kerchief,
Dry yourself, dry yourself, dry yourself!
O-o-o-oj, dry yourself with a kerchief!
Kaťeńkoj, get up, a suitor has come!
Come, come, come.
O-o-o-oj, a suitor has come.
Kaťeńkoj, get up and stand up for the betrothal,
Get up, get up, get up!
O-o-o-oj, stand up for the betrothal.
Kaťeńkoj, get up and go to market,
Go, go, go!
O-o-o-oj, go to market.
Kaťeńkoj, get up and buy the dearest wedding-kerchief,
Buy, buy, buy, buy, buy, buy!
O-o-o-oj, buy the dearest wedding-kerchief!

97.

From the field smoke is rising,
From the sea fog is rising.
Maybe, it is not fog
But a swan that flies up;
In the wake of the swan
An old eagle follows.
My eagle, my eagle,
Where have you been roaming?
I have been roaming
In Salatula.
What have you heard and seen there?
I have heard and seen:
In Salatula
A white corpse is lying,
To the white corpse
Three swallows come.
The first swallow is
His loving mother,
The next swallow is
His loving sister,

be̮rja ćikišis daj
ľubeznej babas.
mamis-i-ke-j be̮rǯǯas da
tuvsov ju moz śin-vas vizuvtas,
ćojis-i-ke-j be̮rǯǯas da
tuvsov šor moz śin-vas vizuvtas,
babais-ke-j be̮rǯǯas daj
arśa li̮s-va mi̮nda uśe.
mamislen oz vun da
guvas-gortjas pi̮rteǯis.
ćojislen oz vun daj
veres sajas munteǯis,
babaislen oz vun da
vi̮ľiś naževitteǯis.

98.

moreś tuman kaje,
aľi ńe tuman,
juś-ǯoǯeg lebźe.
juś-ǯoǯeg be̮rśas daj
gi̮riś kuč ve̮ćće,
pe̮riś kuč ve̮ćće.
pe̮riś kuč be̮rśa
tom ťitsa lebźe,
tom ťitsa lebźe.
tom ťitsa pe dumajte
kučes panotni,
kučes panotni daj
"kučej, pe kučej,
kučej pe kučej daj
ki̮t vetlin, munin?
ki̮t vetlin, munin daj
mi̮j kiś aǯǯilin?
mi̮j kiś aǯǯilin daj"
"me vetli, muni
me vetli, muni daj
s a r a p u l ati.
s a r a p u l ati da
me kīli-j aǯǯili,
me kīli-j aǯǯili daj:

The last swallow is
His loving spouse.
When his mother begins to weep,
Her tears well up like a stream in the spring,
When his sister begins to weep,
Her tears well up like a brook in the spring,
When his spouse begins to weep,
Like the autumn dew her tears are falling.
His mother will not forget him
Until he is laid in the grave,
His sister will not forget him
Until she is married,
His spouse will not forget him
Until she marries again.

98.

From the sea fog is rising,
Maybe, it is not fog
But a swan that flies up.
In the wake of the swan
A big eagle follows,
An old eagle follows.
In the wake of the old eagle
A young bird is flying,
A young bird is flying.
The young bird thinks
That it will catch up the eagle,
That it will catch up the eagle.
"My eagle, my eagle,
My eagle, my eagle,
Where have you been roaming?
Where have you been roaming,
Where and what have you seen?
Where and what have you seen?"
"I have been roaming,
I have been roaming
In Sarapula,
In Sarapula.
I have heard and seen,
I have heard and seen:

s a r a p u l aas,
s a r a p u l aas daj
ježid jaj kuǰle,
ježid jaj kuǰle.
ježid jaj doras daj
kujim ćikiš vole,
kujim ćikiš vole.
per-i-voja ćikišis
re̯ďinej mamis.
re̯ďinej mamis daj
toraja ćikišis,
toraja ćikišis daj
re̯ďinej ćojis.
re̯ďinej ćojis da
treťťaja ćikišis,
treťťaja ćikišis daj
as̯las babais.
re̯ďinej mamis-ke be̯rǯ́ǯas da
tūšõ ju moz śin-vas mune.
tūšõ ju moz śin-vas mune daj
re̯ďinej ćojis-ke be̯rǯ́ǯas,
tūšõ šor moz śin-vas mune.
re̯ďinej ćojis-i-ke-j be̯rǯ́ǯas daj
tūšõ šor moz śin-vas mune.
aslas babais-i-ke be̯rǯ́ǯas daj
arśa li̯s-va moz kiśśe.
re̯ďimej mamislen oz vun daj
guas-gortjas pi̯rteǯ,
guas-gortjas pi̯rteǯ.
re̯ďimej ćojislen oz vun,
re̯ďimej ćojislen oz vun daj
veres sajas munteǯ.
aslas babais-i-len oz vun daj
me̯d-i-ked panidaśteǯ.

99.

poleiś, pe či̯n pete daj
moreś toman kaje,
aľi ńe toman da,
juś-ǯoǯeg lebźe.

In Sarapula,
In Sarapula
A white corpse is lying,
A white corpse is lying.
To the white corpse
There come three swallows,
There come three swallows.
The first swallow is
The mother that bore him,
The mother that bore him,
The second swallow,
The second swallow
Is his dear sister,
Is his dear sister.
The third swallow,
The third swallow
Is his own wife.
When his dear mother begins to weep,
Her tears flow like a stream in spring,
Her tears flow like a stream in spring.
When his dear sister begins to weep,
Her tears flow like a brook in spring.
When his dear sister begins to weep,
Her tears flow like a brook in spring.
When his own wife begins to weep,
Her tears flow like autumn dew.
His dear mother will not forget him
Until he is laid in the grave.
Until he is laid in the grave.
His dear sister will not forget him,
His dear sister will not forget him,
Until she is married.
His own wife will not forget him,
Until she meets another.

99.

From the field smoke is rising,
From the sea fog is rising,
Maybe, it is not fog
But a swan that flies up.

juś-ʒoʒ́eg be̮rśis daj
pe̮riś kuč ve̮tće.
"kučej, te kučej daj
ki̮t vetlin, munin,
ki̮t vetlin, munin daj?"
"s a r a p u l aed."
"mi̮j kī̮lin, aʒ́ʒilin daj?"
"me kī̮li, aʒ́ʒili:
ďikej mu vilin daj
jeǯid jaj kujle;
jeǯid jaj doras daj
kujim ćikiš vole.
med-i-voʒa ćikišis daj
re̮ďimej-i ved mamis,
še̮r-kost ćikišis daj
re̮ďimej ćojis,
be̮rja ćikišis daj
zakonnej babas.
mamis pe be̮rʒ́ʒas daj
śin-i-vais si̮len petas,
tūsō e ž - v a s moz daj
śin-i-vais vizūtas.
ćojis pe ved be̮rʒ́ʒas daj
śin-i-vais si̮len petas,
tūsō juis-i moz-i
śin-i-vais vizūtas.
zakonnej babas be̮rʒ́ʒas da
ar-i-śa li̮s-vas moz śin-vas petas.
mamukej pe mamukej da
radeś-ke-j lokta:
jur-vile vejttem daj
bokej sti̮ntem daj
kok-ulej pod-ūtem."

100.

i̮lin, i̮lin, va sajin
vi̮ľ sle̮beda ti̮dale.
vi̮ľ sle̮bedas tom-tom de̮va,
tōm de̮vaslen tom-že-j ni̮v vi̮jim.

In the wake of the swan
An old eagle follows.
"My eagle, I say, my eagle,
Where have you been roaming?
Where have you been roaming?"
"In Sarapula."
"What have you heard and seen?"
"I have heard and seen:
On the rough (? silent) ground
A white corpse is lying.
To the white corpse
There come three swallows.
The first swallow
Is his dear mother.
The next swallow
Is his dear sister.
The last swallow
Is his lawful wedded wife.
When his mother begins to weep,
Her tears well up,
Like the Vyčegda in spring
Her tears flow forth.
When his sister begins to weep,
Her tears well up,
Like a stream in spring
Her tears flow forth.
When his lawful wedded wife begins to weep,
Her tears fall like autumn dew.
Dear mother, dear mother,
I would gladly come,
Only there is no roof above my head,
There is no fence by my side,
There is no floor under my feet."

100.

Far, far away, over the water
A new free village can be seen.
In the new free village there lives a young widow.
The young widow has a young daughter.

tom ni̯lislen roža vi̯las
alej viris vorsećće.
ńe-dekmi̯-šte roža vi̯las,
śinjasnas ved vor-vorsećće,
ńe-dekmi̯-šte śin-i-jasnas
gižeden gižni-j on kuž,
ńe-dekmi̯-šte gižeden gižni,
še̯k plaťťese paśtalas da
poľe vi̯las petas da
te̯vźiśas daj te̯vźiśas,
bi̯tsen kutas pujas ńukľaśni.
ki̯ǯ etija puis ńukľaśe,
siǯ-že menim slava lokte.
etija slava ve̯sna love,
starik saje love munni.
"starikej pe da starikej,
leǯli-že mene pos-pomeǯid!"
ńe-dekmi̯-šte pos-pomeǯ,
kerka-ge̯ger ki̯čovtas,
važ drugisked panid lovasni.
kuććiśasni da naja-j be̯rdasni,
će̯lej ći̯šjan ke̯tedasni,
ćuń-kič naja vežśasni.
"starikej pe da starikej,
leǯli-že da mene kiľće vi̯leǯid!"
"ńe-dekmi̯-šte kiľći vi̯leǯ."
kujim voža moľľa poma pľeť.
"starikej pe da starikej,
leǯli-že mene porog uleǯid!"
"ńe-dekmi̯-šte porog uleǯ."
kvajt voža moľľa, moľľa poma pľeť.
"starikej pe starikej,
leǯli-že mene e̯šiń doreǯid!"
"ńe-dekmi̯-šte e̯šiń doreǯ."
e̯kmis voža moľľa poma pľeť.
"starikej pe starikej
leǯli-že mene voľ-paś vi̯leǯid!"
"ńe-dekmi̯-šte voľ-paś vi̯leǯ."
das-ki̯k voža moľľa poma pľeť.
kujim vožanas var-i-tas da

In the cheeks of the young girl
Purple blood can be seen.
Not only does blood appear in her cheeks
But she winks mischievously with her eyes.
Not only does she wink mischievously with her eyes.
It is beyond description.
It is not only beyond description:
She puts on a silken dress
And walks out into the field.
The wind is blowing, the wind is blowing,
All the trees begin to sway.
As this tree is swaying,
So does my shame arise.
Because of my ill-fame
I have to marry an old man.
"Old man, old man,
Let me go as far as the porch!"
Not only to the porch does she go
But she walks round the house.
She meets her former lover.
They embrace each other and weep,
Their tears soak a whole kerchief,
They exchange rings.
"Old man, old man,
Let me go as far as the porch!"
"Not even to the porch will I let you go!"
Knobbly scourge with three tails.
"Old man, old man,
Let me go as far as the threshold!"
"Not even to the threshold will I let you go!"
Knobbly scourge with six tails.
"Old man, old man,
Let me go as far as the window!"
"Not even to the window will I let you go!"
Knobbly scourge with nine tails.
"Old man, old man,
Let me go as far as the bed!"
"Not even to the bed will I let you go!"
Knobbly scourge with twelve tails.
He beats her with the three-tailed scourge:

peľ-pom vi̯jenis alej viris i̯skovtas,
kvajt vožanas var-i-tas da
kos vijenis alej viris i̯skovtas,
e̯kmis vožanas var-i-tas da
piʒes vijenis alej viris i̯skovtas,
das-ki̯k vožanas var-i-tas da
kok-ćuń ji̯vtis alej viris i̯skovtas,
tuvsov te̯len te̯ledas,
arśa bi̯gen końerejes bi̯gedas.

101.

i̯lin muin va sajin
vi̯ľ sle̯beda ti̯dale daj
vi̯ľ sle̯bedaas daj
gaža kerka sulale.
gaža pe-j kerkaas
tom-i de̯va-j ole daj
tom-i de̯vaislen daj
mića tom-i ni̯v bi̯dme.
mića pe-j ni̯lislen daj
alej viris vorsećće,
gižeden veśig on kuž gižni,
ve̯ten on kuž ve̯tavni.
"mamukej da mamukej daj
etija puis mi̯jla, daj
lun i voj, daj ʒurte?"
"taja puis ʒurte da
starik saje munem voʒe."
starikis taj loktis da
starik sajas śetisni.
starik saje munis da
starikked oleni.
"starikej pe da starikej da
leʒ-že pe mene-j, leʒli
kiľ-i-ći daj vi̯leʒid!"
starikid i leʒis daj
kerka ge̯geris-i ki̯čovtis;
važ drugse pe aǯǯis-i da
be̯rdisni da be̯rdisni da
će̯lej ćišjan ke̯taśis da

Her purple blood runs down to her shoulders.
He beats her with the six-tailed scourge:
Her purple blood runs down to her waist.
He beats her with the nine-tailed scourge:
Her purple blood runs down to her knees.
He beats her with the twelve-tailed scourge:
Her purple blood runs down her toes.
Winds of spring blow at her,
Winds of autumn dry her, poor thing.

101.

Far away, far away over the water
A new free village is to be seen.
In the new free village
There is a beautiful house.
In the beautiful house
There lives a young widow.
The young widow's
Beautiful young daughter is growing up.
The beautiful girl's
Purple blood can be seen.
It is beyond description.
Not even in your dreams can you dream of it.
"Dear mother, dear mother,
What is the reason that this tree
Creaks night and day?"
"This tree is cracking
Because you must marry an old man."
The old man arrived,
She was married to the old man.
She married the old man,
She lives with the old man.
"Old man, old man,
Let me out, let me out
As far as the porch!"
The old man let her out,
And she walked round the house.
She saw her former lover.
They wept and wept,
A kerchief was soaked through.

e̮tnas gortas pi̮ris da
starik si̮li le̮śedema
kujim voža moľľa poma pľeť.
sije taj vartis daj
alej viris i̮skovtis
peľ-i-pom vi̮jenis.
bara taj sija ve̮z-i-jiśis da
"starikej pe starikej
mene pe vaj že-j leǯli
pos-pom plaka vi̮leǯid!"
starik pe sije leǯis da
je̮r ge̮ger sija ge̮ger ki̮čovtis.
bara panidaśisni da
be̮rdisni da be̮rdisni da
će̮lej ći̮šjan ke̮taśis.
gor-i-tas taj pi̮ris daj
starik ve̮li le̮śedema
kvai̮-i-t voža moľľa poma pľeť.
sijen var-i-tis daj
alej viris i̮skovtis
kos-i vi̮jenis.
olisni daj vi̮lisni da*
starikiś bara-j ve̮zjiśis:
"leǯli starikej da
kerka ge̮gerid-i ki̮čovtni!"
seki sija ki̮čovtis da
bara drugse pe aǯǯis da
be̮rdisni da be̮rdisni da
će̮lej ći̮šjan ke̮taśis.
kerkad-i pi̮ris da
starik ve̮li le̮śedema
e̮kmis voža moľľa poma pľeť.
sije var-i-tis, vartis da
alej viris i̮skovtis
kok-i-ćuń vi̮jenis.
e̮šin doras taj pukśis da
i̮llaas-i viǯedlis,
aćis sija-j koľema
viž ke̮k-akań koď.

* Some of them said: *olisni.*

She went home alone,
The old man prepared for her
A knobbly scourge with three tails.
He beat her.
Her purple blood ran
Down to her shoulders.
Again she entreated him.
"Old man, old man,
Let me go
As far as the rail of the porch!"
The old man let her go:
She walked round the vegetable garden.
Again they met.
They wept and wept,
Their tears entirely soaked a kerchief.
She went home,
The old man prepared
A knobbly scourge with six tails.
With that he beat her.
Her purple blood ran
Down to her waist.
They lived on and on,
Again she asks the old man to let her out:
"Let me out, old man,
To walk round the house!"
Then she walked round,
And again she caught sight of her lover.
They wept and wept,
And their tears entirely soaked a kerchief.
She entered the house,
The old man prepared
A knobbly scourge with nine tails.
He struck her and beat her
Her purple blood ran
Down to her toes.
She sat by the window,
And looked out of the window:
She was left all by herself
Like a Christmas rose.

102.

i̮lin, i̮lin poľe vi̮lin
vi̮ľ sle̮beda ti̮dale.
vi̮ľ sle̮beda doras daj
gaža, gaža gorńića.
gaža, gaža gorńićas daj
tom-i že-j de̮va ole.
tom-i že-ji de̮vaslen
tom-i že-ji nī̮ vi̮jim.
tom-i že-ji ni̮lislen
veśkid roža-ban vi̮las daj
alej viris vorse.
e̮šin ulas pu ńugľaśe daj
esija puis ńugľaśe,
siʒ́-že men slava lokte.
esija ved slava pondas
daj love pe̮riś saje munni.
ńe-de̮kmi-šte pe̮riś saje daj
starik saje love munni.
starik sajad munan da:
"starikej pe starikej daj
lok že-j vi̮lis gorńićas kajlam!"
vi̮lis gorńićas kajasni daj
ić-moń pos-voʒe koľććas.
kiľće vi̮las petas daj
e̮tar-me̮dar viʒ́edlas:
ńe-kod ńe-ke̮n ij abu.
karta sajas munas daj
kujim tuj-vež vove.
kujim tuj-vež vove daj:
"etati-ke me muna,
mameked panidaśa daj,
etati-ke-j me muna daj
baťeked panidaśa daj,
etati-ke-j me muna daj
važ drugejked panidaśa."
sija tujedis munas daj
važ drugisked panidaśas daj
be̮rdasni daj be̮rdasni,

102.

Far, far away in the field
A new free village is to be seen.
In the outskirts of the new free village
There is a beautiful, beautiful room.
In the beautiful, beautiful room
There lives a young widow.
The young widow
Has a young daughter.
On the young girl's
Right cheek
The purple blood can be seen.
There is a tree swaying by the window,
As this tree is swaying,
So does my shame come.
Because of this shame of mine
I must marry an old man.
Not only an old man,
But a very old man she has to marry.
She marries the old man.
"Old man, old man,
Let us go to the upper room!"
They go to the upper room,
The young wife stays in the porch.
She walks to the outside stairs.
She looks to the right and to the left:
There is nobody to be seen.
She walks behind the stable,
And reaches the three crossroads.
She reaches the three crossroads:
If I go this way
I shall meet mother,
If I go that way
I shall meet father,
If I go that way
I shall meet my former lover.
She sets out that way,
And she meets her former lover:
They weep and weep;

će̯lej ći̯šjan ke̯tedasni
še̯ri kośalasni daj
veśkid źeptanis śujasni,
veśkid źeptanis śujasni daj
e̯tar-me̯dar munasni.
ić-moń gortas loktas da
starikislen ńimale
kujim voža moľľa poma pľeť ńimale daj
ńe-de̯kmi-šte kujim voža,
kvajt voža moľľa poma pľeť ńimale,
ńe-de̯kmi-šte kvajt voža,
e̯kmis voža moľľa poma pľeť ńimale.

. . . .

103.

kvajt suda pe̯lata pi̯ri da
jen-uvlańis viʒ̯edli,
jev-uvlańis viʒ̯edli da
seni vi̯jim ge̯rd pi̯zan,
seni vi̯jim ge̯rd pi̯zan da
pi̯zan vi̯las samevar.
pi̯zan vi̯las samevar da
samevar doras sakar,
samevar doras sakar da
sakar doras moloďeć.
sakar doras moloďeć da
moloďećis migajćće,
moloďećis migajćće da
šujga śinnas makajćće,
šujga śinnas makajćće da
me si̯ vile-j le̯gaśi,
me si̯ vile-j le̯gaśi da
me setiś i be̯r peti,
me setiś i be̯r peti da
e̯śiń uvtiis muni,
e̯śiń uvtiis muni da
e̯śińas i śarkńiti,
e̯śińas i śarkńiti da
menam śe̯lem bergeććis,
menam śe̯lem bergeććis da

Their tears soak a whole kerchief.
They tear it in two and
Put it into their right pocket,
Put it into their right pocket,
And part, the one this way, the other that way.
The young wife arrives home.
The old man, they say,
Has a knobbed scourge with three tails.
Not only a scourge with three tails,
They talk of a knobbed scourge with six tails,
Not only a scourge with six tails,
They talk of a knobbed scourge with nine tails.
. . . .

103.

I entered a six-storeyed palace,
I looked towards the corner where the ikons stand,
I looked towards the corner where the ikons stand,
There is a red table there,
There is a red table there,
On the table a samovar,
On the table a samovar.
Sugar beside the samovar,
Sugar beside the samovar.
Beside the sugar there stands a lad.
Beside the sugar there stands a lad.
The lad is winking,
The lad is winking and
Beckons with his eyes.
He beckons with his left eye.
I grew angry with him,
I grew angry with him
And left the place.
I left the place and
I passed by the window,
I passed by the windows
I knocked at the window, and
I knocked at the window,
My heart turned back,
My heart turned back and

me sećći i be̯r pi̯ri.
me sećći i be̯r pi̯ri da
iń-pe̯vlańis viǯedli,
iń-pe̯vlańis viǯedli da
seni vi̯jim viž škap,
seni vi̯jim viž škap da
viž skap pomas kľuć vi̯jim
viž škap pomas kľuć vi̯jim da
kľućse me-jej berkńovti,
kľućse me-jej berkńovti da
seni vi̯jim ze̯letej perśťeń.
seni vi̯jim ze̯letej perśťen da
og te̯d šondi-j, og te̯d, te̯liś,
seščem sija-j ǯirdale,
seščem sija-j ǯirdale da
veśkid ćaľ-ćuńe śuji,
veśkid ćaľ-ćuńe śuji da
bazar vi̯le leććedi,
bazar vi̯le leććedi da
ti̯śećaiś vuzali,
ti̯śećaiś vuzali da
vit-śose-j aslim bośti.
vit-śose-j aslim bośti da
i̯rgen kerka karedi,
i̯rgen kerka karedi da
bekar-ložka bośtali,
bekar-ložka bośtali da
viććiśi da viććiśi,
viććisi da viććiśi da
menam te̯variš ez lok.
menam te̯variš ez lok da
lećća, vae ši̯bitća,
lećća, vae ši̯bitća da
aslam sadje veśkala,
aslam sadje veśkala da
menam te̯variš lokte,
menam te̯variš lokte da
vi̯ťažnej sapeg kokas,
vi̯ťažnej sapeg kokas da
ľistevej gaćis kokas,

I went back there.
I went back there and
Glanced towards the kitchen,
I glanced towards the kitchen.
There is a yellow chest there,
There is a yellow chest there,
In the yellow chest there is a key,
In the yellow chest there is a key;
I turned the key,
I turned the key,
There was a jewelled golden ring there.
There was a jewelled golden ring there:
I cannot tell whether it is the sun or the moon,
It sparkles so brightly,
It sparkles so brightly.
I put it on my right little finger,
I put it on my right little finger and
I went to the market,
I went to the market.
I sold it for a thousand,
I sold it for a thousand,
I took five hundred for myself,
I took five hundred for myself,
And built a house of copper.
I built a hose of copper,
I bought a cup and a spoon,
I bought a cup and a spoon,
I waited and waited,
I waited and waited.
My beloved did not come.
My beloved did not come,
I shall go and throw myself into the water,
I shall go and throw myself into the water.
I arrive in my own garden,
I arrive in my own garden:
My beloved is coming,
My beloved is coming,
With creased boots on his feet,
With creased boots on his feet,
With velvet trousers on his legs,

ľistevej gaćis kokas da
roćnej aźamis vi̯las,
roćnej aźamis vi̯las da
vina-štopa pičegas.
vina-štopa pičegas da
vina-štopa pićegas da,
"sulav, sulav, moloďeć,
sulav, sulav, moloďeć da
menam teked śorńi em,
menam teked śorńi em da
vuǯed mene me̯daras,
vuǯed mene me̯daras da"
pi̯žis doresas abu,
pi̯žis doresas abu da
pi̯žse naja-j leǯisni,
pi̯žse naja-j leǯisni da
d u n a j-reka vuǯisni,
d u n a j-reka vuǯisni da
"pre̯ščaj, pre̯ščaj, m i k a j l e-j!
pre̯ščaj, pre̯ščaj, m i k a j l e-j da"
"pre̯ščaj, pre̯ščaj t a ť ť a n e j !"

104.

sad-je̯rin pe ni̯v guľajte,
mića zon volivle.
"mića zonmej daj moloďećej,
šoća taj volivlan,
šoća taj volivlan."
"me pe veśke rad vola da
ńi-nemen koźnavnis,
ńi-nemen koźnavnis.
p i ť e r e-ke me vetla da
dona koźin vaja,
dona koźin vaja,
dona koźin, ki̯k koźin da
kumać da kitajka,
kumać da kitajka."
"kumaćse pe-j og novli da
kitajkase-j og paśtav.

With velvet trousers on his legs,
He wears a kaftan of Russian cloth,
He wears a kaftan of Russian cloth,
A bottle of vodka in his arms,
A bottle of vodka in his arms,
A bottle of vodka in his arms.
Stop, stop, lad,
Stop, stop, lad!
I have something to say to you,
I have something to say to you.
Take me to the other side,
Take me to the other side!
There is no boat on the bank,
There is no boat on the bank,
The boat has been launched on the water,
The boat has been launched on the water,
And they crossed the River Danube,
They crossed the River Danube.
Good-bye, good-bye, *Mikajle*,
Good-bye, good-bye, *Mikajle*,
Good-bye, good-bye, *Tatyana*.

104.

A girl is walking in the garden,
A handsome lad goes that way.
Handsome lad, young man,
You seldom come here,
You seldom come here.
But I'll gladly come here,
Only I have nothing to give you,
Only I have nothing to give you.
If I go to Petersburg,
I shall bring you expensive gifts,
I shall bring you expensive gifts,
Expensive gifts, two gifts:
Cloth of red cotton and nankeen,
Cloth of red cotton and nankeen.
I will never put on red cotton,
I will never wear a nankeen,

ki̯ž ľubitan, si̯ž raďejtan,
bośt men zarńa ćuń-kič!
zarńa ćuń-kičse-ke boštan,
krug ge̯ger ge̯gertam,
krug ge̯ger ge̯gertam.
krug ge̯geris ge̯gertam da
kujimiś okaśam,
kujimiś okaśam.
kujimiś pe-j okaśam da
vosadoľies bośtam,
vosadoľies bośtam."
vo sado ľi da v ogoroďi
ďevitsi guľala.

105.

sad-je̯rin pe ni̯v gulajte,
mića zon volivle da
"zonmej, zonmej, moloďećej
šoća taj volivlan,
zonmej, zonmej, moloďećej
šoća taj volivlan."
"rad pe veśke me vola da
ńi-nemen koźnõni,
rad pe veśke me vola da
ńi-nemen koźnõni.
p i ť e ras-ke me vetla da
dona koźin vaja,
p i ť e ras-ke me vetla da
dona koźin vaja,
dona koźin, ki̯k koźin da
kumać da kitajka, da
dona koźin, ki̯k koźin da
kumać da kitajka."
"kumaćse pe-j og paśtõ da
kitajka og nõli,
kumaćse pe-j og paśtõ da
kitajka og nõli.
ki̯ž raďejtan, si̯ž raďejt da
bośt men ćerevićki, da
ki̯ž raďejtan, si̯ž raďejt da

Love me as you love me now,
Bring me a golden ring!
If you bring me a golden ring,
We shall walk round,
We shall walk round.
We shall walk round and
Kiss each other three times,
Kiss each other three times.
We shall kiss each other three times and
Buy an accordion,
Buy an accordion.
In the garden and in the vegetable garden
Girls were walking.

105.

A girl is walking in the garden,
A handsome lad passes that way
"Lad, lad, young man,
You seldom come here,
Lad, lad, young man,
You seldom come here."
"I'll gladly come here,
Only I have nothing to give you,
I'll gladly come here,
Only I have nothing to give you.
If I go to Petersburg,
I'll bring expensive gifts,
If I go to Petersburg,
I'll bring expensive gifts:
Expensive gifts, two gifts:
Cloth of red cotton and nankeen.
Dear gifts, two gifts,
Cloth of red cotton and nankeen."
"I'll not put on red cotton,
I'll not wear nankeen.
I'll not put on red cotton,
I'll not wear nankeen.
Love me as you love me now,
Bring me a pair of high-heeled boots,
Love me as you love me now,

bośt men ćerevićki!
ježeľi ke̮sjan raďejtni,
bośt zarnija ćuń-kič,
ježeľi ke̮sjan raďejtni,
bośt zarńija ćuń-kič!
zarńija ćuń-kič, ki̮k ćuń-kič da
krug ge̮ger ge̮gertam,
zarńija ćuń-kič, ki̮k ćuń-kič da
krug ge̮ger ge̮gertam.
krug ge̮geris-ke-j ge̮gertam,
kujimiś okaśam,
krug ge̮geris-ke-j ge̮gertam,
kujimiś okaśam.
kujimiśse-j okaśam da
vo sadoľes bośtam,
kujimiśse-j okaśam da
vosadoľes bośtam."

106.

e ž - v a ju kuźa terib gi̮ vivti
lebźe i̮ǯid pi̮ž, jeǯid parusa,
lebźe i̮ǯid pi̮ž, jeǯid parusa.
pi̮žas pukaleni das-vit udal-i zon,
pi̮žas pukaleni das-vit udal-i zon.
naja śi̮leni das-ńoľ ge̮lesen,
naja śi̮leni das-ńoľ ge̮lesen.
naja vorseni kujim gudeken,
naja vorseni kujim gudeken.
e̮ťi burlak-i mort mića ćužema,
e̮ťi burlak-i mort mića ćužema.
jurse-j e̮šedema daj ij leptištli,
jurse-j e̮šedema ij leptištli,
vomse tupkema, oz ij goredli,
vomse tupkema, oz ij goredli.
"*mi̮jla burlak mort taǯi žugiľćin,*
mi̮jla burlak mort taǯi žugiľćin,
mi̮jla jortjasked te-j on gažećći,
mi̮jla jortjasked te-j on gažećći?"
šuvis, goredis šogśiś burlak mort,
šuvis, goredis šogśiś burlak mort:

Bring me a pair of high-heeled boots!
If you want to love me,
Bring me a golden ring,
If you want to love me,
Bring me a golden ring!
A golden ring, two rings, and
We shall walk round and round,
A golden ring, two rings, and
We shall walk round and round.
We shall walk round and round,
And kiss each other three times,
We shall walk round and round,
And kiss each other three times.
We shall kiss each other three times and
Buy an accordion,
We shall kiss each other three times and
Buy an accordion."

106.

On the Vyčegda, on swift waves
A big, white-sailed boat slips past,
A big, white-sailed boat slips past.
There are fifteen brave lads sitting in the boat,
There are fifteen brave lads sitting in the boat.
They are singing a song in fourteen parts,
They are singing a song in fourteen parts,
They are playing three accordions,
They are playing three accordions.
One of the brave lads has a fine face,
One of the brave lads has a fine face,
He hung his head, then raised it,
He hung his head, then raised it,
He shut his mouth, he does not sing,
He shut his mouth, he does not sing
"Brave lad, why have you grown so sad,
Brave lad, why have you grown so sad,
Why are you not rejoicing with your companions,
Why are you not rejoicing with your companions?"
The sorrowful lad spoke up,
The sorrowful lad spoke up, saying:

"ene ďivitej daj ene le̯gaśej,
ene ďivitej daj ene le̯gaśej!
menam śe̯lemej šogen ti̯rema,
menam śe̯lemej šogen ti̯rema . . ."

107.

jagin bi̯dmis zev mića požem,
si̯len e̯t-koď ji̯v i din.
śiktin bi̯dmis ge̯gres ćužema,
mića, mića-j e̯tka ni̯v,
śiktin bi̯dmis ge̯gres ćužema,
mića,mića-j e̯tka ni̯v.
aski kaja pues pe̯redni,
med-bur jagśis ki̯skala.
ri̯tnas muna ni̯les koravni,
śemja pi̯čśis ńečišta,
ri̯tnas muna ni̯les koravni,
śemja pi̯čśis ńečišta.
aski kaji pues pe̯redni,
puid menim di̯r ez pe̯r.
ri̯tnas muni ni̯les koravni,
ni̯lid me saje ez mun,
ri̯tnas muni ni̯les koravni,
ni̯lid me saje ez mun.
di̯rnad eśke-j puid pe̯ri da
śiś na ve̯lem śe̯mesis.
di̯rnad eśke ni̯lid munis da
viśe ve̯lem śe̯lemis.

108.

kor me ve̯li da ki̯ź aresa,
sek ve̯li da vi̯v-i-ti zboj.
ľok kerkae da važ kerkae
me vetlivli bi̯d voj,
važ kerkae da ľok kerkae
me vetlivli bi̯d voj.
mijla si̯t-i-ćći vetlivli?
sen ovlis mića ni̯v.
mijla si̯t-i-ćći vetlivli?

"Do not wonder, do not be angry,
Do not wonder, do not be angry,
My heart is full of sorrow.
My heart is full of sorrow."

107.

A very fine pine-tree grew up in the woods,
Its crown and roots are fine too.
Only one fair girl has grown up in the village,
She is round of face,
Only one fair girls has grown up in the village,
She is round of face.
Tomorrow I shall go to fell trees,
I shall bring it from the best pinewood.
In the evening I shall go and ask for a girl's hand,
I shall pluck her out of her family,
In the evening I shall go and ask for a girl's hand,
I shall pluck her out of her family.
In the morning I went to fell trees,
The tree did not come down.
In the evening I went and asked for the girl's hand,
The girl did not come to me,
In the evening I went and asked for the girl's hand,
The girl did not come to me.
In time the tree came down,
It was decayed inside,
In time the girl came, but
Her heart was sick.

108.

When I was twenty years old,
I was very resourceful.
A tumbledown house, an old house
I visited every night,
An old house, a tumbledown house
I visited every night.
Why did I visit it?
A beautiful girl was living there.
Why did I visit it?

sen ovlis mića ni̯v.
pi̯r pukalis, pi̯r dumajtis;
mi̯j dumajtis, og te̯d.
pi̯r pukalis, pi̯r dumajtis;
mi̯j dumajtis, og te̯d.
sije menćim juvalis:
"te tuje-j on-e me̯d?"
sije menćim juvalis:
"te tuje-j on-e me̯d?
en dumajt tatiś pi̯šjini
da lutše gor-i-tad ov,
en dumajt tatiś pi̯šjini
da lutše gor-i-tad ov!
en vi̯ǯed te ľok je̯z vile,
ľok je̯zli kuščem mog,
en vi̯ǯed te ľok je̯z vile
ľok je̯zli kuščem mog.
ki̯ǯ mene vojdar raďejtlin
da ne-kodiś en pov,
ki̯ǯ vojdar mene raďejtlin
da ńe-kodiś en pov!"

109.

paśkid gaža-j uľića-j, uľića-j,
paśkid gaža daj uľića da
gi̯riś stolba tuj kuźa,
gi̯riś stolba tuj kuźa,
gi̯riś stolba tuj kuźa da
niv gortśań vala lećće,
ni̯v gortśań vala lećće,
ni̯v gortśań vala lećće daj
ni̯v be̯rśańid zon ve̯tće,
ni̯v be̯rśańid zon ve̯tće,
ni̯v be̯rśańid zon ve̯tće da
"ni̯le, ni̯le, sulavli,
ni̯le, ni̯le, sulavli,
ni̯le, ni̯le, sulavli da
teked menam śorńi-j em,
teked menam śorńi-j em."
"će̯vli pe će̯vli je̯j zonmej da

A beautiful girl was living there.
She set there all the time, pondered all the time,
What she was pondering about I do not know,
She sat there all the time, pondered all the time,
What she was pondering about I do not know.
She asked me:
"Are you not going to leave?"
She asked me:
"Are you not going to leave?"
Have you never thought of running away?
Would it not be better to live at home?
Have you never thought of running away?
Would it not be better to live at home?
Do not pay heed to evil people,
What have we to do with evil people?
Do not pay heed to evil people,
What have we to do with evil people?
How dearly you used to love me,
And you were not afraid of anyone.
How dearly you used to love me,
And you were not afraid of anyone.

109.

Wide, beautiful road, road,
Wide, beautiful road, road,
All along the big road with the verst-stones,
All along the big road with the verst-stones,
All along the big road with the verst-stones
The girl goes out of her home to fetch water,
The girl goes out of her home to fetch water,
The girl goes out of her home to fetch water.
A lad sets out after the girl,
A lad sets out after the girl,
A lad sets out after the girl.
"Lass, lass, stop,
Lass, lass, stop,
Lass, lass, stop,
I have something to say to you,
I have something to say to you!"
"Hush, lad, hush,

tone baťe viǯede,
tone baťe viǯede,
tone baťe viǯede-j, a
tone mame luk-je̯rin."

110.

"e̯kśińa pekrasa,
ivanovna pekrasa,
ćojid koris sur juni,
će̯skid sur-i-se juni."
"oj, og mun, og mun, og mun,
jur-ulej vevttem,
kok-ulej postem,
arśa li̯s-vais ke̯ǯid,
arśa vojis pemid."
"ek-i-śińa pekrasa da
ivanovna pekrasa,
vokid koris sur juni,
će̯skid sur-i-se juni."
"oj, og mun, og mun, og mun,
jur-ulej vevttem,
kok-ulej postem,
arśa li̯s-vais ke̯ǯid,
arśa vojis pemid."
"e̯k-i-śińa pekrasa,
ivanovna pekrasa,
mamid koris ge̯śťitni,
će̯skid ne̯k-i-se śojni.
"oj, og mun, og mun, og mun,
jur-ulej vevttem,
kok-ulej postem,
arśa li̯s-vais ke̯ǯid,
arśa vojis pemid."
"e̯k-i-śińa pekrasa,
ivanovna pekrasa,
baťid koris sur juni."
"oj, og mun, og mun, og mun,
jur-ulej vevttem,
kok-ulej postem,

Look, father is watching,
Look, father is watching,
Look, father is watching,
Look, mother is in the onion-patch.

110.

"Fairest *Ekśińa*,
Fairest *Ivanovna*,
Your sister has called you to drink ale,
To drink sweet ale."
"Alas, I cannot come, I cannot come, I cannot come,
There is no roof above my head,
There is no floor under my feet,
The autumn dew is cold,
The autumn night is dark."
"Fairest *Ekśińa*,
Fairest *Ivanovna*,
Your brother has called you to drink ale,
To drink sweet ale."
"Alas, I cannot come, I cannot come, I cannot come,
There is no roof above my head,
There is no floor beneath my feet,
The autumn dew is cold,
The autumn night is dark."
"Fairest *Ekśińa*,
Fairest *Ivanovna*,
Your mother has called you to a feast,
To drink fine cream."
"Alas, I cannot come, I cannot come, I cannot come,
There is no roof above my head,
There is no floor beneath my feet,
The autumn dew is cold,
The autumn night is dark."
"Fairest *Ekśińa*,
Fairest *Ivanovna*,
Your father has called you to drink ale."
"Alas, I cannot come, I cannot come, I cannot come,
There is no roof above my head,
There is no floor beneath my feet,

arśa-li̯s-vais ke̯ʒid,
arśa vojis pemid."
"e̯ k - i - ś i ń a   p e k r a s a,
i v a n o v n a   p e k r a s a,
drugid koris sur juni."
"oj, muna, muna, muna,
jur-ulej vevta,
kok-ulej poska,
arśa vojis jugid daj
arśa li̯s-vais šonid."

111.

uźi daj oli da
rumjańićći da beľićći da
rumjanjasse boś-i-tali da
ćas-že-j va dore leććila,
oz-e kod-ke pi̯ža lok?
viʒedi da viʒedi da
ńe-ke̯n ńe-kod daj oz lok i
med že eśke-j me lova
pop-pi saje daj
ńe že menim siś-i-mini daj
esija siś kolodais moz.
uźi daj oli da
rumjańićći da beľićći da
rumjanjasse boś-i-tali daj
ćas-že-j va-dore leććila,
oz-e kod-ke pi̯ža lok daj?
viʒedi da viʒedi da
ńe-ke̯n ńe-kod ij oz ti̯dav daj
med že eśke-j me lova
kupeć-i-pi saje daj
ńe že menim siś-i-mini
etija siś kolodais moz.
uźi daj oli da
rumjańićći da beľićći da
rumjanjasse boś-i-tali da
ćas-že pe me va-dore leććila daj
oz-e kod-ke pi̯ža lok?

The autumn dew is cold,
The autumn night is dark."
"Fairest *Ekśińa*,
Fairest *Ivanovna*,
Your beloved has called you to drink ale."
"Oh, I'm coming, I'm coming, I'm coming.
There is a roof above my head,
Ther is a floor beneath my feet,
The autumn night is light,
The autumn dew is warm."

111.

I had been sleeping and I lay for a while,
I rouged my face and painted it white,
I took the rouge,
I am going down at once to the river bank,
To see whether a boatman is coming,
I looked around, I looked around,
There was nobody anywhere, nobody coming.
Let me be loved
By the priest's son!
Let me not rot away
Like this rotten tree-stump.
I had been sleeping and I lay for a while,
I rouged my face and painted it white.
I took the rouge,
I am going down at once to the river bank.
To see whether a boatman is coming.
I looked around, I looked around,
There was nobody to be seen anywhere.
Let me be loved
By the merchant's son.
Let me not rot away
Like this rotten tree-stump.
I had been sleeping and I lay for a while,
I rouged my face and painted it white.
I took the rouge
I am going down at once to the river bank.
To see whether a boatman is coming.

viʒ́edi da viʒ́edi da
ńe-ke̮n ńe-kod daj oz ti̮dav.
med že p-eś-kej me lova da
kreś-i-ťańin-pi saje daj
ńe že menim siś-i-mini
etija siś kolodais moz.
uźi daj oli da
rumjańićći da beľićći da
rumjanjasse boś-i-tali da
ćas-že me va-dore leććila daj
oz-e kod-ke-j pi̮ža lok?
viʒ́edi da viʒ́edi da
ńe-ke̮n ńe-kod daj oz lok da
med že eśke me lova da
koriś-i-pi saje.
ńe že menim siś-i-mini daj
etija siś kolodais moz.
uźi daj oli da
rumjańićći da beľićći daj
rumjanjasse bośtali da
ćas-že pe va-dore leććila daj
oz-e kod-ke pi̮ža lok daj?
viʒ́edi da viʒ́edi da
pi̮ža daj lokte da
med že eśke me lova
i̮ʒ́id śirli sam pi̮ďďi da
ńe že menim siś-i-mini da
etija siś kolodais moz.
pi̮žaej daj pi̮žaej da
lok, mene me̮daras vuʒ́ed!
pi̮ža si̮li loktis da
še̮r vijeʒ́is nuvis daj
i̮ʒ́id śir ij ńi̮lištis.

112.

ki̮ź-vit areʒ́ me-j oli,
vek-i na me-jej ge̮tirtem.
e̮ťi nī̮ked te̮dmaśi,
nī̮ked te̮dmaśi,

I looked around, I looked around,
Nobody was to be seen anywhere.
Let me be loved
By the peasant's son.
Let me not rot away
Like this rotten tree-stump.
I had been sleeping and I lay for a while,
I rouged my face and painted it white.
I took the rouge,
I am going down at once to the river bank.
To see whether a boatman is coming
I looked around, I looked around.
Nobody was coming anywhere.
Let me be loved
By the beggar's son.
Let me not rot away
Like this rotten tree-stump.
I had been sleeping and I lay for a while,
I rouged my face and painted it white.
I took the rouge,
I am going down at once to the river bank.
To see whether a boatman is coming?
I looked around, I looked around,
A boatman was coming.
Let me be used
As a bait for the big pike!
Let me not rot away
Like this rotten tree-stump
Boatman, boatman,
Come and take me across to the far side!
The boatman came to her
And took her to the middle of the river.
And the big pike swallowed her up.

112.

I am twenty-five years old,
I'm still a single man.
I made a girl's acquaintance,
  Acquaintance,

me sije ke̯sji vajni.
eg kuž kodliś juvōni,
kuž kodliś juvōni,
je̯zis taj veledisni.
"te pe baťidliś juvō,
baťidliś juvō!"
baťisliś taj juvali.
baťis piliś ez verit,
piliś ez verit,
mi̯j ve̯ľ-nej śvetin ľubov,
ve̯ľnej śvetin ľubov em,
mi̯j śvetin ľubov em,
kodi e̯ťies raďejte.
baťis veśig kī̯ ez šu,
veśig kī̯ ez šu.
pijis bergeććis, be̯rǯis,
pemidin ve̯re kajis,
pemidin ve̯re kajis
aslas s a š e ń k as dine.
e̯šińedis starkńitis,
e̯šinedis starkńitis.
"s a š a, s a š a da petō,
s a š a, petō ćas kežle,
š a petō ćas kežle!
vajli, vajli da kite,
vajli, vajli da veśkidse̯
vajli veśkidse,
veśkid kiśid ćuń-kičse,
vajli, vajli da sabľase,
vajli, vajli sabľase!
aśśim jures kerišta,
bi̯dsen s a š e ń k a ve̯sna."

113.

ge̯tirej mene oz raďejt,
ge̯tirej mene oz raďejt.
ki̯ćći-j i̯sta, sećći-j oz mun,
ki̯ćći-j i̯sta, sećći-j oz mun.
ke̯ť-kor-ke sija i munas,

I wanted to marry her,
I did not know whom to ask,
  Whom to ask,
People informed me.
"Ask your father,
Ask him!"
He asked his father.
The father did not believe his son,
  did not believe his son
That love existed anywhere in this wide world,
That in this wide world love existed,
  In the world love existed,
That someone could love another.
Not a word did the father say,
  Not a word did he say.
The son turned and began to weep,
He walked into the dark forest,
He walked into the dark forest
To see his Sashenka.
He knocked at the window,
He knocked at the window.
"Sasha, Sasha, come out,
Sasha, come out for an hour,
  come out for an hour!
Here give me, give me your hand,
Here give me, give me your right hand,
  give me your right hand,
Give me the ring from your right hand,
Bring here, bring here the sabre,
  bring the sabre!
I sever my own head
Because of Sashenka."

113.

My wife does not love me,
My wife does not love me.
She does not go where I send her,
She does not go where I send her.
If she goes.

ke̯ť-kor-ke sija i munas,
di̯r-di̯r ved sija i vetlas,
di̯r-di̯r ved sija i vetlas.
ke̯ť-kor-ke sija i loktas,
ke̯ť-kor-ke sija i loktas,
drug-drug ved sija-j goredas,
drug-drug ved sija-j goredas.
kre̯vať vomen . . .

114.

"vošti pe me-jej daj ćuń-kičes,
vošti me-jej ľuboves.
ki̯ćće menam ćuń-kič voši,
seti sija kraśite,
ki̯ćće menam ćuń-kič voši,
seti sija kraśite.
ke̯ni menam daj musukej?
kī̯nas sija ke̯sjiśis.
ke̯ni menam daj musukej?
kī̯nas sija ke̯sjiśis.
ke̯sjiśis menam musukej
i verićći vek keže,
ke̯sjiśis menam musukej,
i verićći vek keže.
musuk munis, musuk koľis
menim soj vi̯lam kaga,
musuk munis, musuk koľis
menim soj vi̯lam kaga.
ki̯ǯ viǯedla kaga vi̯le,
siǯ śin-va-j menam petas,
ki̯ǯ viǯedla kaga vi̯le,
siǯ śin-va-j menam petas.
a te ponda-j aslam ďiťaj
lećća, moreje pi̯ra,
a te ponda-j aslam ďiťaj
lećća, moreje pi̯ra.
a tene me zloj mućiťeľ,
vek keže-j prokľinajta,
a tene me zloj mućiťeľ
vek keže-j prokľinajta."

If she goes,
She is away for a long, long time,
She is away for a long, long time.
If she returns,
If she returns
At once she starts shouting,
At once she starts shouting.
Across the bed . . .

114.

"I have lost my ring,
I have lost my beloved.
Where my ring was lost
There it gleams,
Where my ring was lost
There it gleams.
Where is my beloved?
He made a promise with his hand.
Where is my beloved?
He made a promise with his hand.
My beloved made a promise,
And I believed it was for good,
My beloved made a promise,
And I believed it was for good.
My beloved has departed,
And he has left me with a child in my arms.
My beloved has departed
And she has left me with a child in my arms.
As I look at the child,
My tears begin to flow,
As I look at the child,
My tears begin to flow.
Because of you, my child,
I shall go out and drown myself in the sea.
Because of you, my child,
I shall go out and drown myself in the sea.
And as for you, my wicked tormenter,
I curse you eternally,
And as for you, my wicked tormenter,
I curse you eternally."

kudra jurnas, kuź ke̮sanas
gi̮iś-gi̮e plavajte.
veśkid kinas i makajte:
"pre̮ššaj, ďiťaej, pre̮ššaj!"
veśkid kinas i makajtis:
"pre̮ššaj, ďiťaej, pre̮ššaj!
ńe-kod ponda eg stradajtli,
ki̮ǯ i musukej ponda,
ńe-kod ponda eg stradajtli,
ki̮ǯ i musukej ponda."

115.

me-je ri̮tjiśni peti da
menam ri̮tjanej abu.
menam ri̮tjanej abu da
ki̮ćći sija munema?
kićći sija munema da?
b o g o s l o v e munema.
b o g o s l o v e munema da
mi̮jes sija munema?
mi̮jes sija munema da?
brukila, kološila.
brukila, kološila da
men ke̮sjis ge̮śťin vajni.
men ke̮sjis ge̮śťin vajni da
kašimerevej ći̮šjan.
kašimerevej ći̮šjan daj
menśim panidse koris.
menśim panidse koris daj
kašimerevej ke̮šeľ.
kašimerevej ke̮šeľ da
śo majbirej olemej.
śo majbirej olemej da
p i d a š ge̮ra ti̮dale.
b i d a š ge̮ra ti̮dale da
seten menam milojej.
seten menam milojej da
maćen, paľićen vorse.
maćen, paľićen vorse-j daj

With her curly hair, and long plaits
She swims from wave to wave.
With her right hand she waves:
"Good-bye, my child, good-bye!"
With her right hand she waved:
"Good bye, my child, good bye!
For no one have I suffered so much
As through my own sweethart,
For no one have I suffered so much
As through my own sweetheart."

115.

I went to spend the evening outside,
But I have no companion for the evening.
I have no companion for the evening,
Where has he gone?
Where has he gone?
He went to Bogoslov.
He went to Bogoslov.
Why did he go there?
Why did he go there?
For trousers, for galoshes.
For trousers, for galoshes,
He promised to bring me gifts,
He promised to bring me gifts:
A cashmere kerchief.
A cashmere kerchief,
He asked me for a gift in exchange,
He asked me for a gift in exchange
A cashmere purse,
A cashmere purse.
My hundredfold happy life,
My hundredfold happy life,
The hill of *Pidaš* can be seen,
The hill of *Bidaš* can be seen,
That is where my beloved is.
That is where my beloved is,
He is playing with ball and stick.
He is playing with ball and stick.

ke̯n menam pi̯žej, poskej?
ke̯n menam pi̯žej, poskej daj
b i d a š ge̯rajas vuǯni.
b i d a š ge̯rajas vuǯi da
te taj, v a ń u k, taten-že?!
te taj, v a ń u k, taten-že daj
mi̯j dorińō vettedlan?
mi̯j dorińō vettedlan da
mi̯j bukišen viǯedlan?
mi̯j bukišen viǯedlan da
mi̯j vom-dorte kurććalan?
mi̯j vom-dorte kurććalan da
pe̯ra ńin miriććini.
pe̯ra ńin miriććini da
beśtam-ke-j parta vina!
beśtam-ke-j parta vina da
še̯rien-že juvištam!
še̯rien-že juvištam da
l'ubovse sotvoritam.
l'ubovse sotvoritam da
śo majbirej olemej.
śo majbirej olemej da
l'ubov sotvoritemej.

116.

ke̯n olam mi, sen sulalis
zē važśań pemid ve̯r.
sen kotravlis, sen gul'ajtis
kuź śura, jeǯid ke̯r;
sen kotravlis, sen gul'ajtis
kuź śura, jeǯid ke̯r.
sen oš da ke̯jin še̯jtisni,
ur ćeććalis, ez muǯ.
sen li̯dtem ve̯li pe̯tkais
ez bi̯rli keć da ruć;
sen li̯dtem ve̯li pe̯tkais,
ez bi̯rli keć da ruć.
ǯor kozjas ule lažińćis
l'ok kerjiś ve̯ćem ćom.

Where is my boat, my bridge,
Where is my boat, my bridge,
To cross over to the hill of *Bidaš?*
I crossed over to the hill of *Bidaš*
Vanyuk, are you here?!
Vanyuk, are you here?!
Why do you shun me?
Why do you shun me,
Why do you look cross?
Why do you look cross,
Why do you bite your lips?
Why do you bite your lips,
It is time for us to make peace,
It is time for us to make peace.
Let us buy a bottle of vodka!
Let us buy a bottle of vodka
And drink it, half each!
Let us drink it, half each,
And let us make love,
Let us make love.
My hundredfold happy life!
My hundredfold happy life,
And my love-making!

116.

Where we are living, there
A dark wood has long been standing,
There was running, there was walking
A long-horned, white reindeer,
There was running, there was walking
A long-horned, white reindeer.
Bears and wolves were roaming about,
The squirrels leapt and never grew tired.
There were numberless wild fowl,
There were hares and foxes always in plenty,
There were numberless wild fowl,
There were hares and foxes always in plenty.
Under hoary spruces they lurked
The hut knocked up out of rotten timber.

ez pe̯dlaś si̯len e̯ʒesis,
ki̯ʒ pe̯riś pećlen vom;
ez pe̯dlaś si̯len e̯ʒesis,
ki̯ʒ pe̯riś pećlen vom.
ľok plakajasen veťťema,
mu-ʒoʒa, śťenjas śe̯d,
ki̯k ićet vośsa e̯šińa,
či̯n seti petas med;
ki̯k ićet vośsa e̯šińa,
či̯n seti petas med!
ri̯t-gor-uv taja ćom dore
tom ćukerććasni je̯z.
tom vojtir pi̯r na gažeććej,
ke̯ť pe̯tema, ke̯ť en;
tom vojtir pi̯r na gažeććej,
ke̯ť pe̯tema, ke̯ť en.

117.

kerka śťene ke̯ʒid švaćkis,
zev ed sija ľok.
te̯liś-juger śinme vaćke,
menam un oz lok.
pukala me-j e̯šin dorin
kɨ̯za mamliś mojd.
"mamej, mamej, te̯liś vi̯las
kodi, kod ne sen?"
"kor-ke pie zev ńin važen
ovlis mića nɨ̯.
olem si̯len ez ve̯v gaža,
ve̯li ić-iń-vo̯ʒ.
ić-iń vi̯ʒis i ponjes moz,
ez kɨ̯li sija bur kɨ̯.
ni̯les i̯stis ić-iń vala:
mun pe leććiv da va vaj!
ni̯lid leććis jukmes dore,
ni̯les boštis šog."
"te̯liś vi̯las-ke me verma,
og-e me-j ne kaj?
te̯liś, te̯liś, ted me kevma,

Its door would not close,
Like an old woman's mouth,
Its door would not close,
Like an old woman's mouth.
It is roofed with rotten planks,
It is earth-floored, its walls are black,
It has two small, open windows,
For the smoke to escape,
It has two small, open windows,
For the smoke to escape.
Towards evening, by this hut
The young folk would gather together.
Young folk, keep rejoicing
Whether you have eaten your fill or not,
Young folk, keep rejoicing
Whether you have eaten your fill or not!

117.

Cold weather is beating against the walls of the house,
It is very cruel.
The moonbeams shine into my eyes,
I cannot sleep.
I sit by the window,
I listen to mother's tales.
"Mother, mother, there in the moon
Who can it be?"
"Once upon a time, son, long, long ago,
There lived a beautiful girl.
Her life was not happy,
She was a step-child.
Her stepmother kept her like a dog,
She never heard a kind word.
The stepmother sent the girl to fetch water:
Go, hurry up and fetch water!
The girl went down to the well,
The girl was overcome by grief."
"If only I could go up to the moon!
Shall I not go?
Moon, moon, I beg you,

bośt as vi̮lad vaj!"
te̮liś ki̮vzis, ni̮les bośtis,
e̮ni na vek sen.
ješče karnan peľ-pom vi̮las,
bi̮ťťe katle va.

118.

moski vī̮ti me vetledla,
oj tom de̮vaes e̮ťvedajta,
tom de̮vaes e̮ťvedajta.
oj de̮vais ved kiľće vi̮las,
de̮vais ved kiľće vi̮las.
"oj, de̮vaej pe daj de̮vuškaj,
de̮vaej pe daj de̮vuškaj,
oj, lež-že mijanes šojććini,
lež šojććini, lež šontiśni!"
"oj, rad pe eśke-j me leža da
rad pe eśke-j me-j leža da
oj, žoľa ved menam kerkaej,
žoľa ved menam kerkaej.
oj, ićet ved menam gorńićaj,
ićet ved menam gorńićaj."
"oj, abu e̮d mi zē unaneś,
abu ved mi zē unaneś.
oj, ve̮la je̮zis ved śo-vetimin,
ve̮la je̮zis ved śo-vetimin,
oj, poda je̮zis ki̮k-śo vetimin,
poda je̮zis ki̮k-śo vetimin."
oj, naja ved i mi̮rden pi̮risni,
naja ved i mi̮rden pi̮risni,
oj, pi̮risni daj poklon śetisni,
pi̮risni daj poklon śetisni.
oj, pukśalisni labić ge̮ger,
pukśalisni labić ge̮ger,
oj, labić ge̮ger, pi̮zan ge̮ger,
labić ge̮ger, pi̮zan ge̮ger,
oj, med bur ge̮śtis e̮šin še̮ras,
med bur ge̮śtis e̮šin še̮ras,
oj, de̮vais ved pać-vož doras,

Take me up to you!"
The moon listened to her, it took up the girl,
And now she is there for ever.
The yoke for the water buckets is always on her shoulders,
As if she were carrying water.

118.

I am walking along the path,
Oh, I am looking for a young widow,
I am looking for a young widow.
Oh, the widow is in the porch,
The widow is in the porch.
"Oh, my widow, my pretty little widow,
My widow, my pretty little widow,
Oh, let us in to have a rest,
Let us in to have a rest, let us in to warm ourselves!"
"Oh, I would gladly let you in,
I would gladly let you all in,
Oh, my house is small,
My house is small,
Oh, my room is small,
My room is small."
"Oh, we are not too many,
We are not too many,
Oh, we are cavalrymen, a hundred and fifty of us,
We are cavalrymen, a hundred and fifty of us.
Oh, we are foot-soldiers, two hundred and fifty of us,
Foot-soldiers, two hundred and fifty of us."
Oh, they entered by force,
They entered by force,
Oh, they entered and bowed,
They entered and bowed,
Oh, they sat round on the bench,
They sat round on the bench,
Oh, round the bench, round the table,
Round the bench, round the table.
Oh, the guest of honour in the middle of the window,
The guest of honour in the middle of the window,
Oh, the widow in front of the stove,

de̯vais ved pać-voʒ doras.
"oj, de̯vaej pe daj de̯vuškaj,
de̯vaej pe daj de̯vuškaj,
oj, ki̯min vo-že te de̯vujtin,
ki̯min vo-že te de̯vujtin?
oj, ki̯min vo-žej śiretujtin,
ki̯min vo-žej śiretujtin?"
"oj, das-kvajt vo me-jej de̯vujti,
das-kvajt vo me-jej de̯vujti,
oj, das-śiźim vo śiretujti,
das-śiźim vo śiretujti."
"oj, de̯vaej pe daj de̯vuškaj,
de̯vaej pe daj de̯vuškaj,
oj, lok-že, juriś śľapaes bośt,
lok-že, juriś śľapaes bośt!
oj, śľapa pijas ći̯šjan vi̯jim,
śľapa pijas ći̯šjan vi̯jim,
oj, ći̯šjan pomas ge̯red vi̯jim,
ći̯šjan pomas ge̯red vi̯jim,
oj, ge̯red pi̯čkas ćuń-kič vi̯jim,
ge̯red pi̯čkas ćuń-ki̯č vi̯jim."
"oj, korśa-že taja ćuń-kičis,
korśa-že taja ćuń-kičis?"
"oj, kor ki kutim, kor veńćajććim,
kor ki kutim, kor veńćajććim,
oj, śekśa-že taja ćuń-kičis."

119.

"ajgigla pe śialam, śialam."
[źeľonej roščića alaja ćvetela ćvet.]
"mi pe ved-i brosa ke̯ʒam, ke̯ʒam,
ajgigla da brosa ke̯ʒam, ke̯ʒam."
"me pe ved-i taľalam, taľalam,
ajgigla da taľalam, taľalam"
"mi̯jen ješče taľalan, taľalan,
ajgigla da taľalan, taľalan?"
"mi aśnimes leʒalam, leʒalam,
ajgigla da leʒalam, leʒalam."
"mi pe ved-i kutalam, kutalam,

The widow in front of the stove.
"Oh, my widow, my pretty little widow,
My widow, my pretty little widow,
Oh, how many years have you been a widow,
How many years have you been a widow,
Oh, how many years have you been an orphan,
How many years have you been an orphan?"
"Oh, I have been a widow for sixteen years,
I have been a widow for sixteen years,
Oh, I have been an orphan for seventeen years,
I have been an orphan for seventeen years."
"Oh, my widow, my pretty little widow,
My widow, my pretty little widow,
Oh, come and take the hat off my head,
Come and take the hat off my head!
Oh, there is a kerchief in the hat,
There is a kerchief in the hat,
Oh, there is a knot at the end of the kerchief,
There is a knot at the end of the kerchief,
Oh, there is a ring in the knot,
There is a ring in the knot."
"Oh, when did you get this ring,
When did you get this ring?
Oh, when we joined hands, when we were wedded,
When we joined hands, when we were wedded
Oh, that's when I got this ring."

119.

Ajgigla, we are going to set a trap, set a trap,
[źeľonej roščica alaja ćvetala ćvet.]
"We are going to sow millet, sow
a. sow, sow millet."
"We are going to trample it down, trample it down,
a. We are going to trample it down, trample it down."
"With what are you going to trample it down, trample it down?
a. Trample it down, trample it down?"
"We ourselves are going there, going there,
a. Going there, going there."
"We shall catch you, catch you,

ajgigla da kutalam, kutalam.”
“mi̮jen ješče kutalan, kutalan,
ajgigla da kutalan, kutalan?”
“še̮k-i tī̮jen-že tī̮jištam, tī̮jištam,
ajgigla da tī̮jištam, da tī̮jištam.”
“ki̮tiś tijanli še̮k tī̮jis, še̮k tī̮jis,
ajgigla da še̮k tī̮jis, šek tī̮jis?”
“še̮k-i tī̮jis ved zakladin, zakladin,
ajgigla da zakladin, zakladin.”
“mi ped ved-i veštam, veštam, veštam,
ajgigla da veštam, veštam, veštam.”
“mi̮jen ješče veštan, veštan,
ajgigla da veštan, veštan?”
“śo šajt-že pe śetam, śetam, śetam,
ajgigla da śetam, śetam, śetam.”
“mijanli śo šajtid oz kov, oz kov, oz kov,
ajgigla da oz kov, oz kov, oz kov.”
“mi̮j-že tijanli kole, kole, kole,
ajgigla da kole, kole, kole?”
“mijanli kole mića ni̮v, mića ni̮v,
ajgigla da mića ni̮v, mića ni̮v.”
“ki̮tiś-že pe kole, kole, kole,
ajgigla da kole, kole, kole?”
“med dorśis-že kole, kole, kole,
ajgigla da kole, kole, kole.”
“sija ved mijan zarńija, zarńija,
“ajgigla da zarńija, zarńija.”
“vośtej že pe e̮ǯeste-j, e̮ǯeste,
ajgigla daj e̮ǯeste-j, e̮ǯeste!”
“mijan polke sodi, sodi, sodi,
ajgigla da sodi, sodi, sodi”
“mijan polkis ćini, ćini, ćini,
ajgigla da ćini, ćini, ćini.”
“mi pe ved-i je̮ktam, je̮ktam, je̮ktam,
ajgigla da je̮ktam, je̮ktam, je̮ktam.”
“mi pe ved-i be̮rdam, be̮rdam, be̮rdam,
ajgigla da be̮rdam, be̮rdam, be̮rdam.”

a. We shall catch you, catch you."
"With what will you catch us, catch us,
a. Catch us, catch us?"
"With a silken drag-net we shall catch you, catch you,
a. Catch you, catch you."
"Where will you get your silken drag-net, your silken drag-net?
a. Your silken drag-net, silken drag-net?"
"Our silken drag-net is in pawn, in pawn,
a. In pawn, in pawn."
"We shall get it out, get it out, get it out,
a. Get it out, get it out, get it out."
"With what will you get it out, get it out,
a. Get it out, get it out?"
"A hundred roubles we'll give, we'll give, we'll give,
a. We'll give, we'll give, we'll give."
"The hundred roubles we do not want, we do not want,
a. We do not want, we do not want, we do not want."
"What do you want, what do you want, what do you want,
a. Want, want, want?"
"We want a beautiful girl, a beautiful girl,
a. A beautiful girl, a beautiful girl."
"Which do you want, do you want, do you want,
a. Want, want, want?"
"The one we want at the end, want, want, want,
a. Want, want, want."
"She is our golden darling, golden darling,
a. Golden darling, golden darling."
"Open your door, your door, your door,
a. Your door, your door."
"Our group has increased, increased, increased,
a. Increased, increased, increased."
"Our group has decreased, decreased, decreased,
a. Decreased, decreased, decreased."
"We are dancing, dancing, dancing,
a. Dancing, dancing, dancing."
"We are weeping, weeping, weeping,
a. Weeping, weeping, weeping."

120.

e̮šiń dorin nī̯ pukale:
zē korošoj, mića.
e̮šiń ūti tom zon vetle:
mi̯jes borjed vetlan?
e̮šiń ūti tom zon vetle:
mijes borjed vetlan?
je̮z nī̯jaslen peľ-pom paśtad
baťistevej ći̯šjan,
je̮z nī̯jaslen peľ-pom paśtad
baťistevej ći̯šjan.
baťej ordin ge̮ś, ge̮śťajas,
mamelen ge̮śťajas;
baťej ordin ge̮ś, ge̮śťajas,
mamelen ge̮śťajas.
vokej ordin śo kompańe,
aslam pe̮drugajas;
vokej ordin śo kompańe,
aslam pe̮drugajas.
alej ćveťik, ki-pom ćaća,
ńe-kodli og śetli,
alej ćveťik, ki-pom ćaća,
ńe-kodli og śetli.
voj-šer be̮rin pervoj ćasin
ď e m i n v a śli śľopka.

121.

ki̯ʒ-puś ve̮ći balalajka,
ki̯ʒ-puś ve̮ći balalajka,
ľaľi-ľaľi balalajka,
ľaľi-ľaľi balalajka.
pe̮riś mužukej, ćećći, ćećći,
pe̮riś mužukej, ćećći, ćećći,
ľaľi-ľaľiu ćećći,
ľaľi-ľaľiu ćećći!
pomejen te mi̯śśi,
pomejen te mi̯śśi,
ľaľi-ľaľiu mi̯śśi,

120.

A girl is sitting by the window:
She is very good and beautiful.
A young lad is walking beneath the window:
Why are you walking in the furrow?
A young lad is walking beneath the window:
Why are you walking in the furrow?
The alien girls' shoulders
Are covered with batiste kerchiefs,
The alien girls' shoulders
Are covered with batiste kerchiefs.
My father has male guests, female guests,
Mother's female guests,
My father has male guests, female guests,
Mother's female guests.
My brother has a party of a hundred,
My girl friends,
My brother has a party of a hundred,
My girl friends.
Purple flower, small toy,
I shall not give it to anybody.
Purple flower, small toy,
I shall not give it to any body.
After midnight, at one o'clock
I shall throw it to *D́emin Vaś*.

121.

I made a balalaika of birch,
I made a balalaika of birch,
ľaľi-ľaľi balalaika,
ľaľi-ľaľi balalaika.
My old husband, get up, get up,
My old husband, get up, get up,
ľaľi-ľaľiu get up, get-up,
ľaľi-ľaľiu get up, get up,
Wash yourself in the pig-wash,
Wash yourself in the pig-wash
ľaľi-ľaľiu wash yourself,

ľaľi-ľaľiu mi̯śśi!
ńamede te ći̯škiś,
ńamede te ći̯škiś,
ľaľi-ľaľiu ći̯škiś,
ľaľi-ľaľiu ći̯škiś!
zi̯r vile te jurbit,
zi̯r vile te jurbit,
ľaľi-ľaľiu jurbit,
ľaľi-ľaľiu jurbit!
izse te pokušajt,
izse te pokušajt,
ľaľi-ľaľi pokušajt,
ľaľi-ľaľi pokušajt!
tom mužukej, ćećći, ćećći,
tom mužukej, ćećći, ćećći,
ľaľi-ľaľiu ćećći,
ľaľi-ľaľiu ćećći!
kľućevej vaen te mi̯śśi,
kľućevej vaen te mi̯śśi,
ľaľi-ľaľiu mi̯śśi,
ľaľi-ľaľiu mi̯śśi!
pe̯leťentsije ći̯škiś,
pe̯leťentsije ći̯škiś,
ľaľi-ľaľiu ći̯škiś,
ľaľi-ľaľiu ći̯škiś!
m i k e l ali jurbit,
m i k e l ali jurbit,
ľaľi-ľaľiu jurbit,
ľaľi-ľaľiu jurbit!
ke̯laćse te kušajt,
ke̯laćse te kušajt,
ľaľi-ľaľiu kušajt,
ľaľi-ľaľiu kušajt!

122.

šondi-banej olemej,
tom olemej, tom gažej.
tom olemej, tom gažej,
tom pe̯ra koľľalemej.

ľaľi-ľaľiu wash yourself!
Dry yourself with the foot-cloth,
Dry yourself with the foot-cloth,
ľaľi-ľaľiu dry yourself
ľaľi-ľaľiu dry yourself!
Pray to the shovel,
Pray to the shovel,
ľaľi-ľaľiu pray,
ľaľi-ľaľiu pray!
Breakfast as stones,
Breakfast as stones!
ľaľi-ľaľiu breakfast,
ľaľi-ľaľiu breakfast!
My young husband, get up, get up,
My young husband, get up, get up,
ľaľi-ľaľiu get up,
ľaľi-ľaľiu get up!
Wash yourself with water from the spring,
Wash yourself with water from the spring,
ľaľi-ľaľiu wash yourself,
ľaľi-ľaľiu wash yourself!
Dry yourself with the towel,
Dry yourself with the towel,
ľaľi-ľaľiu dry yourself,
ľaľi-ľaľiu dry yourself!
Pray to St. Nicholas,
Pray to St. Nicholas,
ľaľi-ľaľiu pray,
ľaľi-ľaľiu pray!
Eat cake,
Eat cake,
ľaľi-ľaľiu eat,
ľaľi-ľaľiu eat!

122.

My pretty sun-face life,
My young life, my young joys.
My young life, my young joys
My youthful days are spent,

tom pe̮ra koľľalemej,
das-kvajt ares-i ti̮rtemej.
das-kvajt ares ti̮rtemej,
ki̮ź ares viććiśemej.
kiź ares viććiśemej daj
tom zonmes raďejtemej.
tom zonmes raďejtemej da
ki̮ćći bara koľema.
ki̮ćći bara koľema da
v i ć k o - š o r e koľema.
v i ć k o - š o re koľema da
ni̮vjasli drug koľľini.
ni̮vjasli drug koľľini da
ić-mońjasli gorzini.

123.

das-vit areǯ me-j oli
da guľba vi̮le-j eg petō.
das-śiźim areǯ oli
da guľba vi̮le me peti.
guľba vi̮le me peti da
voj-pukan-ine pi̮ri.
voj-pukan-ine pi̮ri daj
e̮šin doras pukale.
e̮šin doras pukale daj
jeǯid kuďeľse pećke.
jeǯid kuďeľse pećke da
me dumajti ge̮traśni.
me dumajti ge̮traśni da
baťej veśke-j ge̮trale.
baťej veśke-j ge̮trale da
mamej oz mun koraśni.
mamej oz mun koraśni da
saldat-pu pi̮ďďi viǯe.
saldat-pu pi̮ďďi viǯe da
prijem vi̮las-ke kaja.
prijem vi̮las-ke kaja da
źerkala vi̮le viǯedla.
zerkala vi̮le viǯedla da
me koď ǯe̮ľais abu.

My youthful days are spent,
I turned sixteen.
I turned sixteen,
I was nearing twenty.
I was nearing twenty,
I loved a young man,
I loved a young man,
Where has he got to?
Where has he got to?
He has stayed at *Vićko-šor*.
He has stayed at *Vićko-šor*,
Girls must accompany their beloved,
Girls must accompany their beloved,
Young wives must weep.

123.

I turned fifteen
And I had not been to a party.
I turned seventeen
And I went to a party.
I went to a party,
I went to the spinnery.
I went to the spinnery:
She was sitting by the window.
She was sitting by the window
Spinning white flax,
Spinning white flax.
I thought, I'll marry her.
I thought, I'll marry her,
Perhaps father would arrange the wedding.
Perhaps father would arrange the wedding,
But mother will not go to ask for the girl's hand,
Mother will not go to ask for the girl's hand,
She regards me a would-be soldier,
She regards me a would-be soldier.
I go to enlist,
I go to enlist
And look in the mirror.
I look in the mirror:
There is nobody as short as I am.

me koď ǯeľais abu da
me koď ićetis abu.
me koď ićetis abu da
kvaťićći-ke boštemaś.
kvaťićći-ke boštemaś da
prijem vī̯śis me peti.
prijem vī̯śis me peti da
gortlań banen bergećći.
gortlań banen bergećći da
be̯r gorte me-jej lokti.
be̯r gorte me-jej lokti da
para vē̯se doďďali.
para vē̯se doďďali da
v i ź i n kuźa guľajti.
v i ź i n kuźa guľajti da
v i ź i n kabake pi̯ri.
v i ź i n kabake pi̯ri da
štop vina pe me juvi da
voj-pukan-ine pi̯ri.
voj-pukan-ine pi̯ri da
śor dorśis vorsan bośti.
śor dorśis vorsan bośti da
oj, ni̯vjasej, ni̯vjasej,
oj, ni̯vjasej, ni̯vjasej da
meteg ved gažtem love,
meteg ved gažtem love da
šor dorin požjaśemej,
šor dorin požjaśemej da
ńur dorin pū śojemej,
ńur dorin pul śojemej da
lud vi̯lin me̯s viǯemej,
lud vi̯lin me̯s viǯemej da
meteg ved gažtem love.

124.

mi̯jla pe talun, musa kajej,
zev žugiľa pukalan?
asi̯ vovis, stavis śi̯le,
a te ši̯-ńi-te̯v olan.

There is nobody as short as I am,
There is nobody as little as I am,
There is nobody as little as I am,
While I was musing, they enlisted me,
While I was musing, they enlisted me.
I left the recruiting office,
I left the recruiting office,
I turned my face towards home.
I turned my face towards home,
Back I went, I arrived home.
Back I went, I arrived home,
I harncssed a couple of horses.
I harnessed a couple of horses,
Rode through the village of *Viźin*.
I rode through the village of *Viźin*,
And entered the inn of *Viźin*.
I entered the inn of *Viźin*,
I drank a bottle of vodka,
Then I went to the spinning-house.
I went to the spinning-house,
I took the accordion from the rafters,
I took the accordion from the rafters.
Oh, girls, girls,
Oh, girls, girls,
Without me it will be sad for you,
Without me it will be sad for you
To do the rinsing on the bank of the brook,
To do the rinsing on the bank of the brook,
To eat cowberries at the edge of the marsh,
To eat cowberries at the edge of the marsh,
To graze the cattle on the pasture,
To graze the cattle on the pasture
Without me will be sad for you.

124.

Dear little bird, today
Why do you sit so sad?
Morning has come, everybody is singing,
But you are silent.

asi̯ vovis, stavis śi̯le,
a te śi̯-ńi-te̯v olan.
ve̯vlis pe̯ra i me śi̯vli,
zē dolid da le̯ń ve̯li.
ve̯rjas vī̯ti, viǯjas vomen
med-voǯ bi̯d lun lebavli.
ve̯rjas vī̯ti, viǯjas vomen
med-voǯ bi̯d lun lebavli.
kujim pi menam sek ve̯li,
zē me najes raďejtli;
śonid, ńebid naliś pozse
ǯuǯid pu vi̯le ve̯ćli.
śonid, ńebid naliś pozse
ǯuǯid pu vi̯le ve̯ćli.
će̯skid śojan nali korśli,
lunin na dinin śi̯vli,
a vojjasnas ke̯ǯid di̯rji
as bordjasen śebravli,
a vojjasnas ke̯ǯid di̯rji
as bordjasen śebravli.
no ľok mortlen iz śe̯lemis
ńe-ki̯ǯ abu mileśta.
menćim pijanes i poznas
ľok ćeľaďjas nuvisni,
menćim pijanes i poznas
ľok ćeľaďjas nuvisni.
si̯ be̯rin me dugdi śi̯vṇi,
eśtis dolid olemej.
e̯ni ola, e̯dva lovja,
regid pote śe̯lemej,
e̯ni ola, e̯dva lovja,
regid pote śe̯lemej.

125.

ke̯n-ke kar sajin, pe̯dval kerkain
mene ćužtema ge̯ľińik mam.
das-kvajt aresen końera ni̯lej
kirpić-zavode medaśi me.
das-kvajt aresen końera ni̯lej

Morning has come, everybody is singing,
But you are silent.
There was a time when I too liked to sing,
I was so gay and serene.
Above the woods and over the meadows
I was the earliest to flutter every day,
Above the woods and over the meadows
I was the earliest to flutter every day.
At that time I had three fledglings,
And I loved them dearly.
Their warm, soft nest
I built in a tall tree.
Their warm, soft nest
I built in a tall tree.
I gathered delicate morsels for them,
I sang beside them in the daytime,
And at night, when it was cold,
I covered them with my own wings.
At night, when it was cold,
I covered them with my own wings.
But the stony hearts of wicked people
Know no mercy in any way
Together with their nest, my fledglings
Were carried away by wicked children.
Together with their nest
Were carried away by wicked children.
Then I stopped singing,
My merrey life came to an end.
Hardly do I live now,
Soon my heart will break.
Hardly do I live now,
Soon my heart will break.

125.

Somewhere beyond the town, in a cellar,
My poor mother gave birth to me.
At the age of sixteen, poor girl that I was,
I went to work at the brick-factory.
At the age of sixteen, poor girl that I was,

kirpić-zavode medaśi me.
śe̯kid ve̯li zē voǯǯa pe̯rais,
no e̯ťi vo uǯōmiśti sen
gora gažisla kirpić-torjasis,
musmis zavodsa olemis men.
gora gažisla kirpić-torjasis,
musmis zavodsa olemis men.
seni zavodas zonked te̯dmaśi.
mi̯jen ćukesćas śvistokis u-uk,
kijas mi̯śkišta, ve̯li koterta,
ći̯šjan jur vi̯le šlavgišta čuk.
kijas mi̯śkišta, ve̯li koterta,
ći̯šjan jur vi̯le šlavgišta čuk.
bi̯d ri̯t si̯ked mi ve̯li aǯǯiślam,
asja vojeǯis on te̯dli un.
ś e m e zon kuźa kirpić-ćipasjas,
lovi musa men bi̯d peľes sen.
ś e m e zon kuźa kirpić-ćipasjas,
lovi musa men bi̯d peľes sen.
di̯r-e regid-e lovi taǯ nogen,
zabastoka-ke seki ez tork?
ortse ve̯tlisni mene ś e m eked,
ne̯šta čeč ki̯k-śo śiźim-das mort.
ortse ve̯tlisni mene ś e m eked,
ne̯šta čeč ki̯k-śo śiźim-das mort.
seśśa si̯ be̯rin sar vojna di̯rji
de̯zmis laśt vi̯le uǯaliś je̯z.
puź-paź žuglisni stavse tor-pi̯rig,
i̯ǯid zavodiś iz-tor ez koľ.
puź-paź žuglisni stavse tor-pi̯rig,
i̯ǯid zavodiś iz-tor ez koľ.
veľa šedmiśťi se̯vet laśt di̯rji
gaža ōmeććis uǯaliś je̯z.
zavod be̯r ki̯ptis, lovi važśis bur,
lun-lun gi̯male, mune sen uǯ.
zavod be̯r ki̯ptis, lovi važśis bur,
lun-lun gi̯male, mune sen uǯ.
seki bara me pi̯ri zavode,
šudes sek aćim aǯǯi be̯r.
bara me̯dećći seni uǯavni,

I went to work at the brick-factory.
At first it was very hard,
But after a year's work there,
In the loud cheerful atmosphere, the bricks
And the factory life pleased me.
In the loud and cheerful atmosphere, the bricks
And the factory life pleased me.
There in the factory I became acquainted with a young man.
As the factory's whistle blow: *u-uk*,
I wash my hands and run,
In a flash I put on my head-scarf.
I wash my hands and run,
In a flash I put on my head-scarf.
We meet each night,
Until morning comes you know no dreams.
Because of the lad *Śeme*, the heaps of bricks
And every corner were lovely to me there.
Because of the lad *Śeme*, the heaps of bricks
And every corner were lovely to me there.
Would this have lasted a long or a short time,
Had the strike not disturbed it?
They drove me away together with *Śeme*,
And another two hundred and seventy people with us.
They drove me away together with *Śeme*,
And another two hundred and seventy people with us.
Then, at the time of the tsarist war,
The working people grew angry with the authorities.
They smashed everything to pieces,
Not a stone remained of the big factory.
They smashed everything to pieces,
Not a stone remained of the big factory.
Gaining freedom, under the Soviet rule,
The working people started to live happily.
The factory was rebuilt, it was better than the old one,
Day by day it is loud with noise of work in progress.
The factory was rebuilt, it was better than the old one,
Day by day it is loud with noise of work in progress.
Then again I joined the factory,
And again I found my happiness.
I started to work there,

ś e m e n jort lovi juraliś mort.
bara me̯dećći seni uǯavni,
ś e m e n jort lovi juraliś mort.
tani śuś-lunej, tani mus-lunej,
ďeľegatkae be̯rjeni pi̯r.
važ moz og ńin pō, guśen og ńin ō,
vi̯ľ nog olemen śe̯lemej ti̯r.
važ moz og ńin pō, guśen og ńin ō,
vi̯ľ nog olemen śe̯lemej ti̯r.

126.

ǯuǯid keresin, gaža ne̯risin
e̯tnas jon kerka sulalis di̯r.
juśań zev i̯lin, śikśań zev i̯lin,
se̯min ti̯dale ve̯r da śe̯d mi̯r.
juśań zev i̯lin, śikśan zev i̯lin,
se̯min ti̯dale ve̯r da se̯d mi̯r.
kerka berdedis, ǯoľa erdedis
ǯoľge vizi̯vte ićeťik šor.
pulen šuvgemis, te̯vlen uvgemis
e̯tka kerkae ki̯le ke̯ť-kor.
pulen šuvgemis, te̯vlen uvgemis
e̯tka kerkae ki̯le ke̯ť-kor.
ri̯tin volivle, śoreǯ ovlivle
vizi̯v šor dorin tom mića ni̯v.
nora śi̯vlivle, i̯leǯ ki̯vlivle,
se̯min v a ń u šis sijes oz kı̯̄.
nora śi̯vlivle, i̯leǯ ki̯vlivle,
se̯min v a ń u šis sijes oz kı̯̄.
v a ń a na ordin, ki̯ǯi as gortin
ovlis kazakin una ńin vo.
prizi̯v vośtisni, v a ń es bośtisni
ge̯rd saldate služitni ki̯k vo.
prizi̯v vośtisni, v a ńes bośtisni
ge̯rd saldate služitni ki̯k vo.
olem-vi̯lemnas, gora śi̯lemnas
tom ni̯v paľedis aśśis jon šog.
bi̯d voj ve̯tale, ćaste me̯vpale:
di̯r-e v a ń u šis be̯rse ez lok?

Comrade *Śemen* became a leading man there.
I started to work there,
Comrade *Śemen* became a leading man there.
Here is my reason, here is my love.
I am always appointed a delegate.
I do not live as before, I am not living hidden away,
My heart is filled with the new life.
I do not live as before, I am not living hidden away,
My heart is filled with the new life.

126.

On a high hill, on a beautiful plateau in the woods,
A strong house had been standing alone for a long time.
Far away from the river, far away from the village,
Only the woods and the black tree-stump can be seen.
Far away from the river, far away from the village,
Only the woods and the black tree-stump can be seen.
Beside the house, in a little clearing,
There purls and flows a little brook.
The whispering of trees, the roaring of winds
Can always be heard in the solitary house.
The whispering of trees, the roaring of winds
Can always be heard in the solitary house.
Arriving late at night, the beautiful, young girl stays long there
On the banks of the swift brook.
She sings sadly, she is heard afar off,
Only *Vańuš* does not hear her.
She sings sadly, she can be heard afar off,
Only *Vańuš* does not hear her.
Vańuš has lived with them as if at home,
As a farm-hand for many years.
They sent a conscription-order and *Vań* was enlisted
To serve as a red soldier for two years.
They sent a conscription-order and *Vań* was enlisted
To serve as a red soldier for two years.
With life and with loud songs
The girl cheered up her great sorrow.
She dreams every night, often she muses:
Will *Vańuš* not return soon?

bi̯d voj ve̯tale, ćaste me̯vpale,
di̯r-e v a ń u šis be̯rse ez lok.
arśa pe̯rain, ǯuǯid ge̯rain
e̯ććid ti̯dōćis ši̯ńeľa mort.
aǯǯis a ń u šis: lokta v a ń u šis,
lokte tom ni̯vli ńem-kežas jort.
aǯǯis a ń u šis, lokte v a ń u šis,
lokte tom ni̯vli ńem-kežas jort.
v a ń e volema, te̯lka lovema,
ni̯ga vajema ǯik mešek-ti̯r.
e̯ni voema, te̯lka lovema,
ni̯ga vajema ǯik mešek-ti̯r.

(f) Children's songs, tales in verse

127.

ćože-bobe, ki̯ćći vetlin?
ćože gue vetli.
mi̯j-i vajin?
mavtem ńań vaji.
ki̯ćći-že puktin?
šegjas pome pukti.
abu taj ne seni.
śe̯d pon śojema.
ke̯ni śe̯d ponjis?
počes koste śibdema.
ke̯ni počesis?
bi sotema.
ke̯ni biis?
va kusedema.
ke̯ni vais?
i̯be kajema.
ke̯ni i̯bis?
ši̯r ki̯redema.
ke̯ni ši̯ris?
naľkje šedema.
ke̯ni naľkjis?
pečer koste ši̯bitim.
das-ki̯k ćańa-ve̯la,
śivko-burko, veščannej voronko,
vićko vomen ćeććištas veščannej voronkos,

She dreams every night, often she muses:
Will *Vaňuš* not return soon?
In autumn-tide, on the high hill
There suddenly appeared a man in a great coat.
Aňuš caught a glimpse of him: *Vaňuš* is coming.
The young girl's mate for life is coming.
Aňuš caught a glimpse of him; *Vaňuš* is coming,
The young girl's mate for life is coming.
Vaňa has arrived, he has become educated,
He has brought a bagful of books.
He has arrived now, he has become educated,
He has brought a bagful of books.

127.

Brother *bobe*, where have you been?
I have been in my uncle's cellar.
What have you brought?
I have brought bread smeared with butter.
Where have you put it?
I have put it on the end of the bench by the wall.
It is not there.
The black dog has eaten it up.
Where is the black dog?
It has been caught in the fence.
Where is the fence?
It has been burnt by the fire.
Where is the fire?
It has been quenched by the water.
Where is the water?
It has climbed the hill.
Where is the hill?
It has been bored through by the mouse.
Where is the mouse?
It has got into a trap.
Where is the trap?
We have thrown it in the nettles.
Twelve colts and a horse,
A grey, black and brown magic steed.
The magic steed jumps over the church,

kodes omeľteni: tenid pe iǯas koka,
śoj jura, pe̯v-boka,
vomedis či̯n pete,
sitanedis e̯gir kiśśe.

128.

bobe, bobe ki̯ćći vetlin?
ćože gue vetli.
mi̯j ne vajin?
vi̯ja ńań vaji.
ki̯ćći ne puktin?
pos-voǯ ǯaǯje pukti.
abu taj ne!
śe̯d pon nuvema.
ke̯n-že śe̯d ponjis?
počis koste śibdema.
ke̯n-že počisis?
bi taj sotema.
ke̯n-že biis?
va kusedema.
ke̯n-že vais?
e̯ška-me̯ška juvema.
ke̯n-že e̯ška-me̯škas?
i̯be kajema.
ke̯n-že i̯bis?
ši̯r taj ki̯redlema.
ke̯n ne ši̯ris?
naľkje šedema.
ke̯n ne naľkjis?
ćer taj keralema.
ke̯n-že ćeris?
zud taj naľema.
ke̯n ne zudjis?
ǯuǯid pečer pije ši̯biti da
das-ki̯k ćańa-ve̯la pi̯ź-pe̯jime petisni:
śivko-burko, vešša·nej voro·nko;
a eme̯ś sečem vējas:

Whom they chide* is straw-legged,
Clay-headed, plank-sided,
May smoke come out of your mouth,
May live coals come out of your bottom.

128.

bobe, bobe, where have you been?
I have been in my uncle's cellar.
What have you brought?
I have brought bread and butter.
Where have you put it?
I have put it on the shelf in the porch.
It is not there.
The black dog has carried it away.
Well, where is the black dog?
It has been caught in the fence.
Well, where is the fence?
It has been burnt by the fire.
Well, where is the fire?
It has been quenched by the water.
Well, where is the water?
It has been drunk up by the rainbow.
Well, where is the rainbow?
It has climbed the hill.
Well, where is the hill?
It has been bored through by the mouse.
Well, where is the mouse?
It was caught in a trap.
Well, where is the trap?
It has been cut in two by the axe.
Well, where is the axe?
It has been blunted by the grindstone.
Well, where is the grindstone?
I have thrown it in the tall nettles.
Twelve colts and a horse came out in a cloud of flour and ash:
Grey, black and brown magic steeds:
But such horses do exist.

* For example: a child.

i̯ʒas-kokaś, siś kartupeľ juraś,
sitantis či̯nis pete, vomtis e̯gir kiśśe.

129.

r u j, r u j, ki̯ćće vetlin?
kosa dorni vetli.
mi̯jes pe kosase?
turun i̯čkištni.
mi̯jes turunse?
kuk-tor bi̯dtištni.
mi̯jes pe kuk-torse?
je̯v-tor li̯śtištni.
mi̯jes je̯v-torse?
pi-tor verdištni.

130.

r o j, r o j, ki̯ćći-že vetlin?
ve̯les korśni vetli.
kuščem tenad ve̯lid?
zarńi buriśa.
r o j, r o j, ki̯ćći-že vetlin?
me̯skes korśni vetli.
kuščem tenad me̯skid?
kaľa jura.
r o j, r o j, ki̯t-i-ći-že vetlin?
mežes korśni vetli.
kuščem tenad mežid?
zarńi śura.
r o j, r o j, ki̯ćći-že vetlin?
porśes korśni vetli.
kuščem-že tenad porśid?
zarńia šče̯ľa.
r o j, r o j, ki̯t-i-ći-že vetlin?
ćipanes korśni vetli.
kuščem tenad ćipanid?
zarńi sorsa.
r o j, r o j, ki̯tći-že vetlin?
petukes korśni vetli.

They are straw-legged, rotten potato-headed,
Smoke comes out of their bottoms and live coal comes out of their mouths.

129.

ruj, ruj, where have you been?
I have been whetting the scythe.
What is the scythe for?
To mow grass.
What is the grass for?
To raise a little calf.
What is the little calf for?
To get a little milk.
What is the little milk for?
To raise the little boy.

130.

roj, roj, where have you been?
I have been looking for a horse.
What is your horse like?
It is golden-maned.
roj, roj, where have you been?
I have been looking for a cow.
What is your cow like?
It is white-headed.
roj, roj, where have you been?
I have been looking for a ram.
What is your ram like?
It is golden-horned.
roj, roj, where have you been?
I have been looking for a pig.
What is your pig like?
It is golden-bristled.
roj, roj, where have you been?
I have been looking for a chicken.
What is your chicken like?
It is golden-crested.
roj, roj, where have you been?
I have been looking for a rooster.

kuščem tenad petukid?
zarńi sorsa.
r o j, r o j, ki̯tći-že vetlin?
ponjes korśni vetli.
kuščem tenad ponjid?
kači̯sa śi̯vja.
r o j, r o j, ki̯tći-že vetlin?
kańes korśni vetli.
kuščem tenad kańid?
naľim śera.

131

r u j, r u j, ki̯tći ne vetlin?
kosa dorni vetli.
mi̯jes ne kosase?
turun-tor i̯čkištni.
mi̯jes ne turun-torse?
kukań viʒ́ni.
mi̯jes-že kuk-torse?
ľeľ-tor li̯śtini.
mi̯jes-že ľe̯ľ-torse?
pi-tor verdištni.
mi̯jes-že pi-torse?
aslim verdiś vi̯le.

132

r u j, r u j, ki̯ćći vetlin?
ve̯les korśni vetli.
kuščem tenad ve̯lid?
čaja koka.
r u j, r u j, ki̯ćći vetlin?
me̯skes korśni vetli.
kuščem tenad me̯skid?
mi̯ľkja pľeša.
r u j, r u j, ki̯ćći vetlin?
i̯žes korśni vetli.
kuščem tenad i̯žid?
kača jura.

What is your rooster like?
It is golden-crested.
roj, *roj*, where have you been?
I have been looking for a dog.
What is your dog like?
It has a white stripe round its neck.
roj, *roj*, where have you been?
I have been looking for a cat.
What is your cat like?
It is spotted like a ling from the river.

131.

ruj, *ruj*, where have you been?
I have been whetting my scythe.
What is the scythe for?
To mow grass with.
What is the grass for?
To feed the calf.
What is the calf for?
To get milk from.
What is the milk for?
To nourish the little boy with.
What is the little boy for?
To nourish myself.

132.

ruj, *ruj*, where have you been?
I have been looking for a horse.
What is your horse like?
It has a white stripe on its ankle.
ruj, *ruj*, where have you been?
I have been looking for a cow.
What is your cow like?
It has a white forehead.
ruj, *ruj*, where have you been?
I have been looking for a sheep
What is your sheep like?
It is magpie-headed.

r u j, r u j, ki̯ćći vetlin?
porśes korśni vetli.
kuščem tenad porśid?
zarńi šče̯ťa.
r u j, r u j, ki̯ćći vetlin?
mežes korśni vetli.
kuščem tenad mežid?
zarńi śura.
r u j, r u j, ki̯ćći vetlin?
petukes korśni vetli.
kuščem tenad petukid?
zarńi sorsa.
r u j, r u j, ki̯ćći vetlin?
ćipanes korśni vetli.
kuščem tenad ćipanid?
ke̯n-tuś śera.
r u j, r u j, ki̯ćći vetlin?
kańes korśni vetli.
kuščem tenad kańid?
naľim śera.

133.

veťeľej pe veťeľej da
mi̯jla bara ki̯lalin?
mi̯jla bara ki̯lalin da
će̯skid ćerien verdiśej?
će̯skid ćerien verdiśej da
śerebrannej śertugej?
śerebrannej śertugej da
k u l e m - d i nin krepki,
k u l e m - d i nin krepki da
bazar vi̯lin "vosado",
bazar vi̯lin "vosado" da
kikilulu petuk,
kikilulu petuk da
da zavoronka śiďot.

134.

ti̯ vivti ge̯na koka vettedle,
va-vužľa da sobanćik,

ruj, ruj, where have you been?
I have been looking for a pig.
What is your pig like?
It is golden-bristled.
ruj, ruj, where have you been?
I have been looking for a ram.
What is your ram like?
It is golden-horned.
ruj, ruj, where have you been?
I have been looking for a rooster.
What is your rooster like?
It is golden-crested.
ruj, ruj, where have you been?
I have been looking for a chicken.
What is your chicken like?
It is speckled.
ruj, ruj, where have you been?
I have been looking for a cat.
What is your cat like?
It is spotted like a ling from the river.

133.

My fish weir, my fish weir,
Why did you float down the river?
Why did you float down again
You who nourish me with a tasty fish?
You who nourish me with a tasty fish,
My silver coat,
My silver coat.
A game of draughts (?) in *Kulem-din,*
A game of draughts (?) in *Kulem-din* and
An accordion at the fair,
An accordion at the fair and
A cock-a-doodle-doo
A cock-a-doodle-doo and
A skylark are sitting there.

134.

On the surface of the lake a hairy-legged one goes by,
A trunk in the water and a dog-dealer.

miľeńkoj pe̯dem ni̯r,
počitsa da ďevitsa,
milij starik.
počitsa da ďevitsa,
kulem-dinin krebitki,
bazar vi̯lin "vosadoľ",
kikilullu petuk,
za voroni koś iďot,
ťe̯t-i-ka pe ve̯taśe,
oponaśej gudekaśe,
gut-i-jur, ćerep-jur,
ćirem ni̯ra vaśka,
eziś ni̯ra giľ da goľ,
ľek-i ni̯ra e̯ďa.

135. *ćeľaďes buredem*

kuč-kuč kočanej,
mučkir-mačkir makarej,
je̯la-vi̯ja totara
jenli ke̯sjis kvajt-śo ur,
kvajt-śo urli lopi-ćań,
lopi-ćańli e̯stap,
e̯stapli pe̯stap,
vi̯j-ćuńaliś e̯ďa.
vi̯j-ćuńaliś e̯ďa,
ri̯niš-tupjed malań,
sapeg-koka pedeś,
śiźim ura jogor.

136.

ke̯ć je̯kte, je̯kte
mića tabjan koka,
šabdi-kuďeľ be̯ža,
vi̯j-tupiľ jurnas,
aslas "dona" kunas,
"si̯la-gosa" kīnas,
śe̯d seter śinnas
ľe̯m-pu kor peľnas.

A charming, fuggy nose
počitsa da ďevitsa,
A pious old man,
počitsa da ďevitsa
A game of draughts in *Kulem-din,*
A gramophone in the bazaar,
A cock-a-doodle-doo
Za voroni koś iďot,
The aunt is dreaming,
Oponaśej is playing the accordion,
Fly's head, tile-head,
Vaśka with the stinking nose,
Silver-nosed tinkling,
Ankle-bone-nosed *E̮ďa.*

135.

Curing the child

kuč-koč kočanej,
mučkir-mačkir Makarej,
Milk-and-butter Tartar,
He promised six hundred kopecks (squirrels) for the icon.
For the six hundred kopecks (squirrels) a *lopi*-colt,
For the *lopi*-colt *E̮stap,*
For *E̮stap Pęstap,*
E̮ďa licking butter from his fingers.
E̮ďa licking butter with his fingers,
Malań with the straw-hair shock-head for plugging the window of the barn.
Boot-legged *Pedeś,*
Jogor with seven kopecks.

136.

The hare is dancing, dancing
With its fine, broad soles,
Its flax-tow tail,
Its butter-pat head,
Its own "valuable" skin,
Its "fat" tongue,
Its blackcurrant eyes,
Wild-service leaves of ears.

a n e - k a n e, ki̮ćće vetlin?
jenme kajli.
mi̮j ne vajin?
eziś ćas.
ke̮n ne eziś ćasid?
vaj pe ve̮len vežam!
vaj vežam!
me̮deććis voʒ́e.
a n e - k a n e, ki̮ćće vetlin?
jenme kajli.
mi̮j ne vajin?
eziś ćas.
ke̮n ne eziś ćasid?
vē̮ked veži.
vaj ve̮len-me̮sken vežam!
vaj vežam!
bara voʒ́e me̮deććis.
a n e - k a n e, ki̮ćće vetlin?
jenme kajli.
mi̮j ne vajin?
eziś ćas.
ke̮n ne eziś ćasid?
vē̮ked veži.
ke̮n ne ve̮lid?
me̮sked veži.
vaj me̮sken-porśken vežam!
vaj vežam!
bara voʒ́e me̮deććis.
a n e - k a n e, ki̮ćće vetlin?
jenme kajli.
mi̮j ne vajan?
eziś ćas.
ke̮n ne eziś ćasid?
vē̮ked veži.
ke̮n ne ve̮lid?
me̮sked veži
ke̮n ne me̮skid?
porśked veži.

137.

Ane-Kane, where have you been?
I went up to the sky.
What have you brought?
A silver plate.
Where is your silver plate?
Let us exchange it for a horse!
Let us exchange it.
He started off again.
Ane-Kane, where have you been?
I went up to the sky.
What have you brought?
A silver plate.
Where is your silver plate?
I have exchanged it for a horse.
Well, let us exchange the horse for a cow!
Let us exchange it!
Again he started off.
Ane-Kane, where have you been?
I went up to the sky.
What have you brought?
I have brought a silver plate.
Where is your silver plate?
I have exchanged it for a horse.
Where is your horse?
I have exchanged it for a cow.
Well, let us exchange the cow for a pig!
Let us exchange it!
Again he started off.
Ane-Kane, where have you been?
I went up to the sky.
What have you brought?
A silver plate.
Where is your silver plate?
I have exchanged it for a horse.
Where is your horse?
I have exchanged it for a cow.
Where is your cow?
I have exchanged it for a pig.

vaj porśken-mežen vežam!
vaj vežam!
a n e - k a n e, ki̮ćće vetlin?
jenme kajli.
mi̮j ne vajin?
eziś ćas.
ke̮n ne eziś ćasid?
vē̮ked veži.
ke̮n ne ve̮lid?
me̮sked veži.
ke̮n ne me̮skid?
porśked veži.
ke̮n ne porśid?
i̮žked veži.
vaj i̮žen-mežen vežam!
vaj vežam!
a n e - k a n e, ki̮ćće vetlin?
jenme kajli.
mi̮j ne vajan?
. . . .
vaj mežen-petuken vežam!
vaj vežam!
a n e - k a n e, ki̮ćće vetlin?
. . . .
vaj petuken-ćipanen vežam!
vaj vežam!
a n e - k a n e, ki̮ćće vetlin?
. . . .
vaj ćipanen-kańen vežam!
vaj vežam!
a n e - k a n e me̮deććis gortas. baťis juvale.
ke̮n ne eziś ćasid?
vē̮ked veži.
ke̮n ne ve̮lid?
me̮sken veži.
ke̮n ne me̮skid?
porśken veži.
ke̮n ne porśid?

Well, let us exchange the pig for a ram!
Let us exchange it!
Ane-Kane, where have you been?
I went up to the sky.
What have you brought?
A silver plate.
Where is your silver plate?
I have exchanged it for a horse.
Where is your horse?
I have exchanged it for a cow.
Where is your cow?
I have exchanged it for a pig.
Where is your pig?
I have exchanged it for a sheep.*
Well, let us exchange it for a ram!
Let us exchange it!
Ane-Kane, where have you been?
I went up to the sky.
What have you brought?
. . . .
Well, let us exchange the ram for a cock!
Let us exchange it!
Ane-Kane, where have you been?
. . . .
Come on, let us exchange the cock for a chicken!
Let us exchange it!
Ane-Kane, where have you been?
. . . .
Come on, let us exchange the chicken for a cat!
Let us exchange it!
Ane-Kane went home. His father asks him:
Where is your silver plate?
I exchanged it for a horse.
Where is your horse?
I exchanged it for a cow.
Where is your cow?
I exchanged it for a pig.
Where is your pig?

* The informant made a mistake: she had previously said "ram".

i̯žked veži.
kẹn ne i̯žid?
mežked veži.
kẹn ne mežid?
petukked veži.
kẹn ne petukid?
ćipanked veži.
kẹn ne ćipanid?
kańked veži.
kẹn ne kańid?

bať šuve: "mun-że, pie, nažetkate en vaj, mun-że gortiś!" baťis ortse seśśa vẹtlas.

138

ťẹs kuźa kortertis.
kodis-że kotertis?
k a ť a-że kotertis.
ki̯ćće-że sūtis?
ś ť e p a n ẹ ń e pos-pome.
kodis-że petis?
j o g o r-że petis.
ki̯ti-że kvaťitis?
kos-šẹredis kvaťitis.
ki̯ćće-że pi̯rtis?
krẹvaťas pi̯rtis.

139.

važen olis ińka,
važen olis ajka
strẹj kaga-babka,
puli̯soližanka,
veś veśelanka.
kureg-tor vẹli,
koľk-tor vajištis,
iz-ki pome puktema.
ši̯r loktis, tuvkis,
ši̯r loktis, tavkis,
bẹžnas ševkńitis.

I exchanged it for a sheep.
Where is your sheep?
I exchanged it for a ram.
Where is your ram?
I exchanged it for a cock.
Where is your cock?
I exchanged it for a chicken.
Where is your chicken?
I exchanged it for a cat.
Where is your cat?

The father says: "Go, son, you have brought in nothing, get out of the house!" And then his father chases him away.

138.

Someone was running along the fence.
Who was running?
Kaťa was running.
Where did she stop?
On *Sťepan Eńe*'s porch.
Who came out?
Jogor came out.
Where did he grab her?
He grabbed her by the waist.
Where did he take her?
He took her to the bed.

139.

Long ago there lived a mother-in-law,
Long ago there lived a father-in-law,
A crippled midwife,
Half a maidservant,
A useless joker.
There was a little hen,
It laid eggs,
It put them by the millstone.
There came a mouse, it kicked it,
There came a mouse, it tossed it,
It touched it with its tail.

uśi, žugali,
uśi da pazali.
ińkais be̮rde,
ajkais te̮žde.
e̮šiń, e̮ǯes klupka-klopka ki̮le,
e̮ǯes ǯirki da virki ki̮le.

140.

turururururu,
ke̮bilali vi̮ľ megir
aslim vi̮ľ ćer-pu,
babali vi̮ľ žaket,
n a s t ali parnij,
i z o ś i mli ge̮rd paś,
samevar, samevar,
ki̮ǯ kužan da razńićći!

141.

ki̮suľej, kańuľej,
śe̮d śor kuźad en vettedli!
kok-pi̮desid śe̮daśas, śe̮daśas.
popaďďadliś vi̮jte, ne̮kte en kurt, en kurt!
paććer-seregad kaj da bri̮zńit!

(g) Rhymes

142.

e̮šiń vi̮lin kań pukale,
zev ićeťik pijana.
mene pe milojej enovtis
zev ǯoľańik kagaen.

e̮šiń dorin ni̮v pukale,
me pi̮ra da okala.
e̮šin ulin pu sulale,
*me peta da kerala.**

ki̮mer lokte, ki̮mer lokte,
og te̮d, zeras, aľi oz.

*Or: *pe̮reda.*

It fell down and broke to pieces
It fell down and smashed in pieces.
The mother-in-law is weeping,
The father-in-law is sad.
The door and the window are rattling,
The door is squeaking and creaking.

140.

tururururururu,
A new yoke to the mare,
A new axe-handle for me,
A new costume-coat for the wife,
A bridegroom for *Nasta*,
A red furcloak for *Izośim*,
A samovar, a samovar,
Tell the difference if you can!

141.

My pussy, my kitty,
Don't walk on the rafter!
Your pads will get black, get black.
Do not skim the milk of the priest's wife!
Climb up to the hind corner of the stove's top and splash it!

142.

The cat is sitting in the window,
It has very young kittens.
My lover has left me
With a very young child.

A girl is sitting in the window,
I go in and kiss her.
A tree is standing beneath the window,
I go out and fell it.

The cloud is coming, the cloud is coming,
I do not know if it is going to rain or not.

milej lokte milej lokte,
og te̮d, pi̮ralas, ij oz.
ki̮mer loktis, ki̮mer loktis,
ki̮mer loktis daj ez zer.
milej loktis, milej loktis,
milej loktis daj ez pi̮r.

b a ď - j e̮ l ji̮lin em ńevesta:
i s a k - j o g o r - j e ľ i s a.
sija munis veres saje,
i v a n ď e m i t pi saje.
sija ez uǯollivli da
toľko śojlis da julis.
śojlis, śojlis da julis da
e̮statki pe̮denćaǯis.

una śe̮d e̮šale tuvjin,
se̮min ježid oz e̮šō.
una zonjas voj-pukin,
abu k o ľ a, ši̮ľid jur.

šondi-banej, tom olemej,
šogśa jona aćim.
menćim emej pe̮ś śe̮lem,
ćajtan ke̮ća-maćen.

zbi̮ľiś raďejććemid je̮zlen
med voǯa med musa.
tom pe̮ś śe̮lemad-ke e̮zjas,
regiden on kused.

menam ve̮li śe̮lem kośtiś,
ćajti, miśa, vajas.
p e ć e r ae vetlig kosti
munema me̮d saje.

My lover is coming, my lover is coming,
I do not know if he will come in or not.
The cloud came, the cloud came,
The cloud came, and it did not rain.
My lover came, my lover came,
My lover came, but he did not come in.

A bride lives at the end of *Bad'-jel':*
Isak-Jogor-Jel'isa.
She married
Ivan Ďemit's son.
She did not work,
She only ate and drank.
She ate and ate and drank,
To the last milking pail.

A lot of black things are hanging on the peg,
Only white things do not hang there.
There are many lads in the spinning room,
Only *Kol'a*, the bald-headed one, is missing.

My pretty sun face, my young life,
I am very sad.
Maybe my heart is hot,
Yet I think it is a puff-ball.

One's real love is
The first one, the dearest one,
If your young heart is set aflame,
You will not quench it easily.

I had a lover who dried up my heart,
I thought he would marry me.
When he went to Pečora,
He married someone else.

V. THE VIŠERA DIALECT

In my collection the Višera area is covered by the dialect of the Bogorodsk (Zyr. *viśer śikt*) and Nivšera (Zyr. *od-ib*) villages. The material from the former, representing a much smaller proportion than that of the latter, comes from college students from whom I recorded texts in Syktyvkar in 1964. My informants were aged between 20 and 22; they no longer spoke their dialect clearly, owing to their education. Their speech was characterized by a mixture of folk and literary usage. My Bogorodsk informants were: Nina Andreevna G a b o v a, Ija Michajlovna I v a š ë v a, Lija Vasiljevna I v a š ë v a, Lija Aleksandrovna M i š a r i n a, Dmitrij Vasiljevič P o d o r o v.

Compared with the dialect of Bogorodsk, that of Nivšera displays minimal deviations. Here I had the opportunity of collecting material for five days; my informants were: Egor Archipovič Ž i ž e v (aged 74), Evdokija Germogievna M i c h a j l o v a (aged 72), Ivan Kornilovič M i c h a j l o v (aged 77), Kirill Vasiljevič M i c h a j l o v (aged 55).

The Višera dialect belongs to the Upper-Vyčegda dialect area. But separate treatment of the Višera material is justified, because it is comparatively uniform within the fairly heterogeneous Upper-Vyčegda dialect area.

The Nivšera dialect displays the following main characteristics:

1. The phoneme *l* belongs to the *l* ~ Ø type. For example, *vę̄* 'horse' ~ *vęlen* 'with a horse', *tūsō* (~S *tulsol*) 'spring (adj.)', *zē* 'very', *julīlim* (~V *julįvlim*) 'we kept drinking', *og vetlī* (~V *og vetlįv*) 'I do not walk'. From the evidence of the last two examples, contrary to the practice of the Vm and the VL dialects, *l* is not preserved in the verbal suffixes *-įl-*/*-il-*, *-lįl-*/*-lil-*, *-lįll-*/*-lill-*, etc., but cf. *viśtollas* ~ V *viśtavlas* 'he relates it', *kośollini* ~ V *kośavlįnį* 'to tear to pieces'. If preceded by *a*, *l* disappears — probably owing to an *āC* > *aC* (C = consonant) development: *matni* 'to smear' ~ S *maltnį*.

2. In the absolute initial position, and if preceded by *m, p, b, k, g*, the phonemes *e̯* and *i̯* often become *ȯ* and *u̇*: *u̇ž* 'sheep', *mȯd* 'other, second', *pȯžal-* 'bake', *pu̇šji-* 'run, escape'.

3. In syllables other than first, *e̯* and *i̯* are replaced by *e̯* and *i̯* respectively. Palatal consonants are followed by *e* and *i*. In songs, the melodic stress often induces *e̯* and *i̯*, e.g. *trubaśi̯s* 'from the chimney', *tumani̯s* 'fog'. Sometimes, through mistaken analogy, under the impact of melodic stress, the original *e* in the first syllable is replaced by *e̯*, e.g. *i śe̯redlig-i-ti̯r-i-ja* (see Song 177, Line 11).

4. Mainly in rapid speech nouns ending in vowels drop the linking vowel of suffixes, which means that the second vowel is omitted. For example, *sarapula* (~*sarapulae*) 'to Sarapul', *ti̯la* (~*ti̯lae*) 'to the clearing', *oblavan* 'by hunting', *sle̯bedas* (~*sle̯bedaas*), 'in the village of free peasants', *de̯vaslen* (~*de̯vaislen*) 'of the widow, the widow's'; but: *vae* 'into the water', *vedraen* 'with a bucket', *taiś* 'therefore'. The kind of assimilation typical of the Bogorodsk dialect (e.g. *unaan* ~ V *unae̯n* 'many', *babaas* ~ V *babai̯s* 'his wife', *muus* ~ V *mui̯s* 'his land', cf. SrSlK 460), was not observed by me in Nivšera.

5. Assimilation of consonants may also occur. For example, *ke̯ććas* (~*ke̯ćjas*) 'hares', *begľeććas* (~V *begľećjas*) 'fugitives'.

6. Where velar vowels or velar and palatal ones are juxtaposed, the hiatus is filled by *v* (e.g., *nuvas* 'he carries', *lovi* 'it came into being', but also *nuas* 'he carries'), while in the case of palatal vowels the hiatus is filled by *j* (*kije* 'into the hand'; sometimes similarly in the case of a velar + palatal vowel: *šujim* 'we said', *śin-vajen* 'with tears').

7. In the final position the *t* of *śt* sequence is not omitted: *bośt*: 'take it !', *ez kiśt* 'he did not pour it out'.

(a) Tales and narratives

143.

olis-vi̯lis starik gozja. si̯len kujim pi ćužis: eťik v a ń a ; *me̯d* v a ś e ·, *kojmed* p e t r u š. *no naja šueni: "ćas pe, mi, baťe, munam ve̯raśni." "no, mune, mune!" no sē̯tasni, naja ve̯raśni muneni. no naja munasni, munasni, munasni, zē gaža olan-in vovas. sen bi̯dśamase puśeni da pe̯žaśeni da kodjas-ke sećći volasni. no sećći vovasni naja, kajasni naja suske. zē i̯ǯid sus seni, nalen puśan-inanis. sen špiontjas-že puśeni, pe̯žaśeni. seśśa naja kajasni suske. no loktasni seśśa begľeććas, naja. "up, jona-že mi̯ǯim." nop ši̯blalasni naja. kujimen loktasni. a sija suskin* p e t r u š. *naja pondasni puśini da pe̯žaśni seni, žariććini, te̯ľke žargeni raćen.* p e t r u š *seśśa sija pondas mi̯j-ke kerni, kuǯōni sećće: sija i̯z da i̯z! "vot taja suslen vais kiśśe" — naja šueni, begľeććasid. seśśa pondas i sitōni. "taja sus-koľľis gi̯lale." seśśa ćań-kok (naja muniganis bośtasni tuj vi̯liś da seni nopjas), ćań-kokse seśśa ćē̯tasni pu vi̯śańid nali. gri̯m! raćanis, žariććan-inas. naja pōžasni daj pi̯šjasni. stavnis nali koľe, bi̯dśama seśśa. seśśa naja nopje sē̯tasni, gorte loktasni. baťisli śuasni: "vot, baťe, mijanli śuris." bi̯dśamase vajisni seśśa.*

144.

1. *vot* v*e̯li* š u d b a l a k i r o v. *naja te̯ľke olisni, ćoja-voka. gožemin turin ez puktini, a me̯s viǯeni. sija seśśa turin puktini munis ji vi̯le. a pe̯śalema sije seteni. pop lokte, zonme, ve̯la, tulupa. sūtis si̯ dine: "tenad pe, druge, pe̯ś pete, a me ki̯nma, tulupa da." "paś-kemnad vaj pe vežšilam i te pe pe̯śalan." pop ćeććis. vežšis, probujtasni. sija dođďe se̯lis da popađďa dore ge̯ńitis, vē̯nas i stavnas turinnas. "no, baťuško, pe koris tenśid vit-śo će̯lkevej ďeńga, e̯dje me̯ded, mi̯j-ke ke̯sje ńe̯bni." vot pe ve̯lis i turunis, stavis si̯ ordin. sija śetas i sija gorte munas. śa pop sije: "mi̯j si̯liś boštan? davaj sije kazake boštni!" a poplen kujim nī̯ vijim. "kazake bośta; sije užalas, med mi̯j nuis, nuis, a seśśa mijanli užalas." sija pop orde loktis nī̯te baba vi̯le korōni, bogatej. a sije, druge, proverite, koľća pi̯r kuǯaśni med eśke ve̯li, mi̯j-ke, verme. ńe-kod nin oz vermi koľća pi̯r kuǯōni. sija seśśa nī̯ paś-kemen paštaśis: "menam pe ved — šue — vi̯jim mi̯j-ke . . ." da sije nī̯ paś-kemen i pervojse loktis, prisluga, možet pe, sija šogmas. a sija "nī̯" koľća pi̯r kuǯalis. "vot taje mi boštam."*

143. [Petruš and the fugitives]

There lived an old man and his mate. Three sons were born to them. The first was Vańa, the second Vaśe, and the third Petruš. They say: "Father, we are going out hunting." "Well, go on then, go!" They pack up and set out to hunt. They go on and on, and arrive at a very beautiful place. There were already folk cooking and frying all kinds of food there; somebody had arrived. They arrive there and climb a yellow pine. There is a very tall yellow pine where they are cooking. Spies are cooking and frying. Anyhow they climb up the yellow pine. The fugitives arrive. "Oh, how tired we have become!" They throw down their bags. Three of them have come along. In that yellow pine sits Petruš. They start cooking there, they have only one frying-pan. Then Petruš starts pissing there: piss, piss! "This yellow is leaving sap" — the fugitives say. Then he starts to shit there. "The cones of the yellow pine are falling" — the fugitives say. Then one throws a colt's leg from the tree (they had picked it up from the road as they came and it is in their bag). Bang! into the frying-pan, in the place where they are cooking! They are scared and flee. All their things remain behind for them, all kinds of things. Then they put them in their bags and come home. They say to their father: "Look, father, what we have found!" They brought all sorts of things.

144. [Stupid Balakirov]

1. There lived a man called Šud Balakirov. He lived alone with his sister. They did not mow in the summer, but they keep a cow. Then he went to mow on the ice. He sweated there. The priest comes along with a horse and a fur coat. He stops by him. "Friend, you are sweating while I am cold even though I have a fur coat!" "Well, let us change clothes, then you too will sweat!" The priest jumped down. They changed clothes, and try them on. He got on the sleigh and drove to the priest's wife, horse and hay and all. "The reverend priest asks you for five hundred roubles; send the money at once for he wants to buy something!" He has the horse and hay and everything. She gives him the money, and he starts for home. Then the priest says: "What can I take from him? I'll hire him as a servant!" The priest has three daughters. "I'll engage him as a servant. Whatever he has taken from me, from now on he will work for us." A rich man came to the priest to ask for his daughter in marriage. Well, he wants to see whether she can piss through a ring. None of them can piss through a ring. Then he (Balakirov) put on a woman's dress. "Well, I have" — says he — "a some-

seśśa gortas nuisni, ćulane jignalisni, uźni etďeľne. sije śa: "menam pe sit pete." "vaj pe, eśiń pirid leẑli gez jilin!" no vśo-taki illae pe kole sitaśni. leẑas. sen velini kezajas. sije kezate domalis, leptis, śura lokte. sije petis da sije pišjema nin bara. vot! kezaiś põźis; taje pe svaďba vilad, vot mij-ke, voľšo·bńik čikedema, kezae većis. naja pońaťije bara seś ez imejtni, mij taja š u d b a l a-k i r o v *većis. seśśa kor-ke kaźalisni, sija pe taj taja velema.*

2. *silen eťi iž veli. sija naćkas, virte śujas gaď pičkas. gaď pičke śujas, ćojte veledas: "te pe — šue — mij-ke mene viśtõ, me pe purten tojišta gaďďad, te uś sećće, mij-kee! a varta pe pľeťen, te ćećći!" voasni,* i v a n e s *kesjeni vini ćojis seteni kujle. "ken pe* i v a n i d*?" "sen pe" — viśtalas. a sija dezmas, purten tojištas gaďďad, sije uśe. vir kõ-kile, petas. "menam pe taje pľeťis tačem, tajen pe kodli vartan, sije lõźas, keť kulem." naja probujtasni i gorte nuni bara koľasni* i v a n e s. *gorte voan lunnas probujtasni mamte. tojište-ke purten, uśe, pľeťen vaćke, ez ćećći. oz ćećći. eni pe bespośśa·dne taje munam i vijam,* i v a n e s. *seśśa sije leććasni jukmes dore, vae śujni: "vot taje pe vae śujam." jukmes dorin sije kujle da vuremaeś kućike. kod-ke pe bara bogatej kupeć lokte. "mij pe ne tani?" "a mene pe vot care pukteni da og pukśi da taćće vae śujni kesjeni." "a me pe pukśa." raźas i sija sećće piras. a vot, druge, voasni, sije śujasni vaad.* š u d b a l a k i r o v *veleśte kajis.*

3. *śa kor-ke i carskej mij-kee veśkale, gut car. vot gutjas dinin car pe. bal vile loktasni geńeraljas. gut pukśas, sijes i kõ, meleten vartas. "tijan vilin me iẑid. mijla sećće pukśemid pe?" car sije pereśiľitas. "menam mu viliś pe mun te." sije gorte loktas. aslas ľokińik kebila vijim da ťeľega vile mu sẽtema. bara car dinti mune. "me pe aslam mu vilin. tead mued pe og vetlį. ťeľegaas menam aslam muid pe." seśśa car sili śetas zadaća: vot merajtni šondi, una-e pe loe šondieẑ. sija boštas śem vile stavse: "śem miľľion śemsot śemďeśat śem pe." "ńepraviľne pe!" "vetli pe da preverit!"*

thing or other . . ." Dressed as a woman, he arrives first, a maid-servant, perhaps she will do. Well, this "girl" pissed through the ring. "Well, we'll take this one." Then they took him home and locked him in the pantry to sleep by himself. Then he says: "I must shit !" "Let her down by a rope through the window !" After all, she must shit outdoors. They let her out. There were some goats there. He tied up a goat and drew it up, there comes the horned beast ! He pulled it up and ran away. The bridegroom was frightened by the goat: look, the wizard had bewitched the bride before the wedding, changing it into a goat. They had no idea that it was Balakirov's work. Later they realized that he had done it.

2. He had a sheep. He cuts it down and lets its blood into a bladder. He lets the blood into a bladder and says to his sister: "You tell me something, then I'll stab the bladder with a knife, and then you fall down ! When I strike at you with my whip, get up !" They come along and want to kill Ivan. His sister is lying there. "Where is Ivan?" "He is there" — she answers. At this he grows angry, stabs the bladder with the dagger, and she falls down. The blood spurts out. "This whip of mine is such that if I strike at somebody with it, dead though he is, will be restored to life." They test it and take the wip home. On the day they arrive they try it on their mother. They stab her with a knife and she falls down; they strike at her with the wip, but she would not get up. She does not get up. Now we will go now and kill Ivan without mercy ! Then they go down to the ice-hole to throw Ivan into the water. He is lying by the ice-hole, they had sewn him up in skins. A rich merchant arrives. "What is going on here?" "They want to make me a Tsar, but I am not willing to be one, and therefore they want to throw me into the water." "Well, I'll undertake it." He unwraps him and conceals himself inside. Well, my friend, they arrive there and throw him into the water. Šud Balakirov went back to his village.

3. Some time later he arrives at the Tsar's court, the court of the Tsar of the flies. Well, anyway, the Tsar of the flies. The generals come to the ball. The fly sits on the throne and hits him (Balakirov) with a hammer. "I am your lord. Why did you sit there?" The Tsar sends him into exile. "Get out of my land !" He arrives home. He has a bad mare and he put earth on the cart. Again he passes the Tsar. "I am on my own land, not yours. I have my own earth on my cart." Then the Tsar sets him a task: he must measure the sun: how many kilometres is the sun from here. He does everything in sevens: "Seven million seven hundred and seventy-seven !" "You are wrong !" "Go and check it yourself !"

145. *pop jịliś*

1. *pop služitis bura komin vo. popes vẹli ľubiteni stav arkireja i bịden. seśśa loktis mijan kojd saldat, pop orde pịris. "te pe on menim medaś kazake?" "medaśa pe" — šue. "me pe — šue — ten śeta dveśťi rubľej vonas." no saldat služite. poplen vẹli nī, ľ i ď a ńima. sịked poznakomiććis, nịlisked. i poplen vẹli kujim mẹs. pop tẹľke nẹk vịlin i ole vẹli. seśśa ńi-nem oz śoj, tẹľke nẹk śoje. i popes i kutisni i uǯedni. i popaďďaid nẹkse kutis źaťli verdni. popli taje ďive kažiććis: 'mịjla taje nẹk oz śur?' popaďďali i noraśe. seśśa, druge, saldat petalis (samej vẹli m i k e l a lun), m i k e l a śīteǯis. petis da m i k e l a ẹbraz ǯońen sije nẹkjen matis. pop vośtis vićko: stavis m i k e l a ẹbraz nẹkja. "vot taja kod vẹlem nẹkte śoje" — pop šue. vićkos tupkis i pịšjis. "vaj menim nop!" i pop pịšjis. śịlem dugdis i davaj mẹdeććis tuje.*

2. *munis kilometra dva iľi tri. vois starikked voćća. starik tože nopja. "te kịćće munan?" pop sịli šue: "a me pe — šue — seććen sị mịda vo služiti i nẹk pe — šue — menśim śojema m i k e l a ẹbraz. ta-lun pe eg i śī, siǯ pe enōti i muni seśśa. me pe śa kịćći voa, sećće i mẹdećći. muna aslam tujed. mene pe on tẹvariše bośt?" "bośta pe" — šue. vot munini kịken. munisni, munisni, pukśisni šoććini ju boke. soććisni, uźisni-kerisni, śojisni seteni. starik śojis prẹskur, a pop śojis sija tože aśśis mịj-ke, ľepjo·śki. aski voǯ ćeććisni, starik leććilis, mịśśis (ńet, pop!) i starik leććis, mịśśis. i pop, druge, nopte vidlis i prẹskurte guis, kịk prẹskur vẹlema da mịj-keidliś, starikidliś. no seśśa starik loktis, ćịškiśis-keris, prẹskur vidlis. abu. "te pe guin?!" "eg, druge, me eg prẹskurse gu." "no, en-ke, davaj, munam!" vot sije lun-tịr munisni ju pẹlen. no pemdini kutis, mẹdla pẹlas ďerevńa. pịž abu, no kịǯ vuǯni? starik šue: vẹćći me bẹrśa!" "no vẹćća." starik oz vẹj i pop tože nin metrov dvaćeť munis, tože oz vẹj. i kutis vẹjni. "me pe — šue — en pe koľ, vẹjni kuti." "prẹskurte pe taj guin?" "eg pe, kẹť pe — šue — goľaeǯ vẹja." "no lok, vẹćći*

145. About the priest

1. The priest served well for thirty years. All the bishops and all the people loved him. Then a soldier of some our sort came and entered the priest's house. "Will you engage yourself to be my servant?" "I will" — answers he. "I'll pay you two hundred roubles a year." Well, the soldier serves him. The priest had a daughter, Lidia by name. He became acquainted with her, the girl. The priest has three cows. The priest lived only on cream. He does not eat anything but the cream of the milk. They began to keep the priest on scanty rations. The priest's wife began to feed her son-in-law with the cream. The priest wondered: "Why don't I get any cream?" He complained to his wife. Then, my friend, the soldier went out before the service for Saint Nicholas began. (It happened to be Saint Nicholas's day.) He went out and smeared the icon of Saint Nicholas all over with cream. The priest opened the church: the whole of the icon of Saint Nicholas was smeared with cream. "So this is who eats the cream" — says the priest. He shut up the church and fled. "Give me my bag!" And the priest ran away. The service did not take place and he set out on his way.

2. He covered some two or three kilometres. He met an old man. The old man also has a bag. "Where are you going?" The priest answers: "Well, I have served so many years there, and the icon of Saint Nicholas has eaten up the cream before me. So I did not hold a service today, I just left and came along. The place I arrive at is where I started for. I'm going my own way. Will you take me to be your companion?" "I will" — says he. They set out, the two of them. They went on and on, and sat down to rest on the river bank. They rested, slept and ate there. The old man ate sacrificial bread, the priest also ate his own pie. Early in the morning they got up, the old man went to wash in the water. (No, it was the priest!) The old man went down and washed himself. The priest searched bis bag and stole the sacrificial bread. The old man had two sacrificial loaves. The old man returned and dried himself, then took a look at the sacrificial bread. It was not there. "Have you stolen it?" "No, friend, I have not stolen the sacrificial bread." "Well, if you have not, then let us go!" Well, all day long they continued their way along the river. It was getting dark; there was a village over the river. There is no boat about, so how to cross the river? The old man speaks up: "Come and follow me!" "All right, I'll follow you." The old man does not sink, and the priest also went twenty metres and did not sink either. Then he began to sink. "Look" — he says — "don't leave me here; I've began to sink!" "Perhaps you did steal the sacrificial bread?" "No" — he answers — "not even if I sink up to the neck."

ine!" vot bara munis, munis, vižed-te, pidežik kutis pop vejni. bara juale: "te preskurse guin?" "eg pe" — šue. "no bara, no ladne, veććí!" no vot i goľaež kutis vejni, pir ez viśtō. nu vot vśo-taki vovisni. berege voisni. med pervej bia kerkaas vezjiśisni. petis kežajka: "ležam pe eśke da, mijan pe kiź-vit vo nin viśe nī, stavis pe lem — šue — oz pe spraviććí. oz pe poź uźnis — šue. — spokoj pe tijanli, oz śet tijanli, vśo rovno." "ńićevo" — starik śue. starik sen etvećajte, pop oz. "ńićevo pe — šue —, mi pe vižedlam sije." no ladne, kežajka ležis. śojisni-juvisni, uźis spoko·jne. aski-vož starik i vižedlis, verne lemeś i em. zē, ta sudta, das-kekjamis aresa nin sija. "vajli pe — šue — menim ćer da vor da kiśtej vedraen va!" kaga puktis vorje, sije trepikežse keralis, starik. va kiśtis med tazje, miśkis-ćiśkis, etlaalis. ber lōźis i ćeććiśtis. druge, vorjiś ćeććiśtis. "baťe da mame" — kutis viśtōni. "mij pe taiś boštan?" dveśťi rubľej ne vaj!" — šuis. a popidli ez śet, starik źepte śujis da munisni bara vože. vot muneni, muneni, bara kučem-ke kerkae voisni. med kaga, sečem-že bara viśe. bara sije lećitis. taži-že lećitis, keralis vorjin. no starik śue: "tajen śa pe torjeććam!" "torjeććam pe!" — šue. no pop etnas seśśa munis. starik tože.

3. *pop vetlis vežon, ľibe kikes vetlis, siž, druge, vois, bara ďerevńa vovis. i bara vezjiśe. pemdis, vezjiśe. "oz pe ed poźležni, mijan — šue — kaga viśe." "ńićevo pe, vižedlam" — pop šue. "me pe vižedla." ležisni. sije, druge, ez i uź, ńe-kučem ritnas, koris bara vor. sije vate koris, ćerte koris. keralis bura, bura i keralis pop. miśkalis-keris, kaga oz ćeććí. no zonme seśśa i: "mortte davaj — kežajka, kežajin šue — tažte pe mij, śa kićće voštam? kerōni śojse oz poź! žagedam pe!" — šue. no vot mortte śa davaj matićae eśedisni. vot teľke nin ules vile sūtedisni, teľke tojiśtni. vot i vois starikid kamgini-zereććini da spokoj ez śet žagedni nali. a nali ved teľke tojiśtni ules viliś i vot getov eśke. vot mortes ležisni. "no ladne pe — šue — vižedlam." starik jeśśe na sije keralis, jeśśe buržika mij-kete, šujte jitis. kaga ćeććis bara vorjiś. bara baťte da mam kutis viśtōni. "mij pe — šue — taiś boštan?" "sto rubľej pe teľke bośta." nalen lovi, vožnad śetisni sen trista rubľej, nalen šeśťsot rubľej lovi deńgaid. no vot naja*

"All right, come on and follow me!" Again he went on and on, and look, the priest began to sink deeper. Again he asks: "Did you steal the sacrificial bread?" "No!" — he answers. "Well, all right, follow me!" Well now, he sank up to the neck yet he still did not own up. Anyway, they got across the river all the same. They came out on the bank. They asked to be let into the first house that was lit up. The lady of the house came out: "I would let you in, but our daughter has been ill for twenty-five years now, she is a mass of scabs" — says she — "she cannot be cured. You can't sleep. She would not let you be quiet." "Never mind" — says the old man. The old man answers, the priest does not say a word. "Never mind" — he answers — "we'll take a look at her." Well, all right, the lady of the house let them in. They had food and drink; the girl slept quietly. Early in the morning the old man examined her, she was indeed a mass of scabs. She was as big as this, eighteen years old already. "Bring me an axe and a wash-bowl" — says he — "and also a bucket of water!" He placed the child in the wash-bowl and cut her into small pieces. He poured water into another wash-bowl, washed and dried her, and then made her whole again. She revived and got up. My friend, she jumped out of the bowl. "Father and mother" — she started saying. "What do you want for this?" "Give me two hundred roubles!" — said he. But he gave nothing to the priest. The old man put the money in his pocket, and they started off again. They went on and on, again they turned into a house. There was another child suffering there from the same sickness. He cured this child too. Well, the old man says: "After this we'll go our own ways." "Well, let us part then!" — answers the priest. The priest started out by himself. So did the old man.

3. The priest went on for a week or two. So he arrived at another village. He asks to be let in. It was getting dark, so he asked to be let in. "We can't let you in, our child is sick." "It doesn't matter, we'll examine the child" — says the priest. They let him in. My friend, even before he went to sleep he asked for a wash-bowl. He asked for water and an axe. He cut the child into pieces, and he did it thoroughly, did the priest. He washed the child, but it did not revive. Well, son, then they say: "This man" — say the man and his wife — "must be killed, but how and where? You must not cut a dead body into pieces. Let us stifle him" — they say. Well, they hanged him on the main beam. Well, they stood him on a chair, they only had to give him a push. Well, the old man arrived and began to knock at the door — he banged the door, not giving them time to hang him. All they had to do was to give him a push and that would have done it. They let the man free. "Well, all right" — says the old man — "let us see!" Once more the old man cut the body to pieces, and once more he put the pieces together.

pop da starik, mȩdeććisni munni. munisni, munisni, munisni i pukśisni. "vaj pe, druge, jukśam ďeńganad!" pop šue: "jukśam pe! mi̮jla pe og jukše?!" davaj pukśisni jukśini. starik i juke: "dveśťi rubľej taje menim, taje tenid, a etije prȩskur guiśli, kojmed dveśťise." "a me pe — šue — gui prȩskurte." vot sek vȩľiśt viśtalis. "no guin-ke pe i na" — šue. vśo-taki ez pe starik bośt bȩr. "no mun pe seśśa, śi̮ bura! me pe m i k e l a *ugodńikid i em.*

146.

1. *olisni-vi̮lisni starik gozja. nalen ćužis pi,* i v a n. *sija mijan moz-že sije bi̮dme, ez i jona i̮ʒid tuśaa vē. kor-ke nalen kūśis mam. bať gȩtraśis vi̮ľiś i kutis* i v a n *es žegdini. no oleni vo, ki̮kes, kujimes,* i v a n *vȩli nin ar dasśiźim. i vśo-taki ťȩtkais šue: "kȩť pe — šue — śinmen pe viʒedni og vermi, vaj pe, ki̮ćće-ke vȩtlam tajes." "no ladne, mi̮j sija sȩgla·śiććis. seśśa baťid i katedisni vȩre mortte. pes keralisni, bura zē.* i v a *nes koľisni seten pes potkedlini. "a mi pe — šue — tati loktam." naja, gozja, munisni voʒe, bať da ťȩtka. naja ȩšedisni nȩ! sije ki̮k pu koste. vot nȩš kōge, keraśe-potkećće.* i v a *nlen peskis potkedśis i tećśis. seśśa lun-ti̮rśa uʒ i vek ez voni bať da ťȩtka. mi̮jla ne, ki̮ʒi mi̮j? pemid daj vek oz voni daj?* i v a *nid seśśa munis, kȩni kōge. seśśa vȩli, sen nȩš ȩšale. vot bȩrdis da bȩrdis da mi̮j śa, ki̮ćće voštiśan? i vot pemid. voj-bi̮d sija munis i vovis ju boke. ju pȩlen leććis, vovis zored. zored ule pi̮ris, uźis zored ulin.*

2. *aski voʒ paľalis, ćeććis, druge, seni zored počis vi̮lin, mi̮j-ke, kapka*n. *ćasli kȩććas olemaeś, kȩć trȩpae puktis. ćas ki̮k-kujim olis, ruć kēgini kutis.* i v a n *gȩńitis, zonme, ruć šedema. ruć šue: "mene pe — šue — en vi! me vot tenid kuta kȩćtȩ kutōni." rućes i leʒis seśśa. ruć ki̮ćće-ke ez di̮r vetli, vajis ki̮k kȩć mortidli.* i v a n, *sija davaj žaritis bi dorin sija, beď vi̮le ȩšedemen. kȩn pe pȩrtjis sija?! "ćas pe — šue,* i v a *nli šue ruć —, me pe vetla — šue —* g r i̮ m *car orde." tēźis-munis sija* g r i̮ m *car orde.* g r i̮ m *carliś i juale: "tenad pe — šue — abu mi̮j-ke, pudovńa,* i v a n *pe kȩsje ďeńga merajtni."*

The child jumped out of the wash-bowl. He started to call his father and mother. "What do you want for this?" "I only want a hundred roubles." So now, for they had received three hundred roubles before, well, they had six hundred in all. Well, the priest and the old man set out once again. They went on and on and on, and finally they sat down. "Friend, let us share the money!" The priest answers: "Let us share it! Why should we not share it?" They sat down to share it out. The old man portions out the shares: "Two hundred roubles to me, this to you, and the third two hundred is due to him who stole the sacrificial bread." "I stole it" — says the priest — "the sacrificial bread." Not until then did he own up. "So you did steal it after all" — says the old man. Yet the old man did not take it back. "Go on then and sing the service well! I am Saint Nicholas, the man of holy life."

146. [Ivan and Tsar Grim]

1. Once there lived an old man and his wife. A son was born to them, Ivan. He is raised in the same way as we are, he was not of very tall build. One day the mother died. The father married again, and the wife began to treat Ivan badly. They lived for a year, two years, three years, Ivan was already seventeen. In spite of this, the stepmother keeps saying: "I cannot bear to see him. Let us chase him away!" Well, all right, the father agreed, and they took him to the woods. They chopped firewood, and they did it very well. They left Ivan there to chop up wood. "And we" — they say — "will come soon." They, the married couple, the father and the mother went away. They hang a mallet between two trees. The mallet clatters, chops and cleaves by itself. Ivan chopped all the wood and piled it up. He worked the whole day, yet his father and stepmother do not come. Why, how? It is dark, still do they not come? Somewhere there is a clatter. The mallet was hanging there. He wept and wept, not knowing what to do or where to go. It is dark. He walked the whole night and arrived at the bank of a river. He walked down the river, and reached a haystack. He crept under the haystack and slept under the haystack.

2. He woke early in the morning. He got up. My friend, there is a trap on the pole of the haystack. Wait a minute! there were hare nearby; he put it on the hares' track. He waited for two or three hours. A fox began to cry somewhere. Ivan ran up to it, a fox had got into the trap. The fox says: "Do not kill me! I shall hunt hares for you." Then he let the fox free. For a short time the fox disappeared, and returned to the man with two hares. Ivan quickly roasted them by the fire, on a spit. Where could he have got a pot from?" "Wait a moment" — says the fox to Ivan — "I'll go

"što za pudovńa pe, ďeńga merajtni?!" g r i̯ m car slavnej car da pudovńa ďenga merajtnis abu si̯len. "ki̯ś-ke vot korś pe!" — šue. no śetis, mi̯j ne oz śet g r i̯ m car, sije?! ńe-una poskeʒ pudovńa ki̯skis ruć i pos ule koľis. i ivanliś juale, loktis da: "tenad pe — šue — abu ďeńga?" og te̯d pe" — šue. ki̯ś-ke kuš, druge, śuri ʒik tri kopejki ďeńga. ak, rućli ńim-kojd lovi sije. ki̯ćće-ke pudovńa koste śujis, kučem-ke čeľ koste i nuvis g r i̯ m carli. i ruć be̯r bergeććis. g r i̯ m car tarkedis i uśi setiś, mi̯j-ke, ďeńga. 'zbi̯ľ pe taje merajtema! što za i v a n, taje tačemis, sečem bogat?!' no ladne, bara vetlis, bara ki̯k keć kutis i v a nli. ruć bara tēźis-munis g r i̯ m car orde. g r i̯ m car dine vovis: "i v a n pe i̯stis koraśni." "ńićevo, śetam pe sečem ozir mortli." i lokte, viśtale ruć i v a n li: "no munam, lok! me tenid baba-pu korśi, g r i̯ m carliś. lok, munam si̯ orde!" no i v a nli — te̯dad, on — paś-kemis omeľik, sija ťe̯tka voʒin bi̯dmis, ki̯ś seśśa bur paś-kem? mijan vojder ez vē bur paś-kem. no vot, voisni sija pos ulas. "te pe tan viććiśli, me pe vetla g r i̯ m car orde." ruć tēźis, bara munis, sije beʒ ćurgedema da. no vot vove. "i v a nte pe — šue — mi̯j-kejas ʒikeʒ pe — šue — kuľisni paś-kemse, re̯zeritisni, ʒik pe paśtem koľi. bańďitjas pe pe̯rććedisni." a car, druge, davaj, mića medede źaťli; paś-kem me̯dedis, śetis rućli. i vot i v a n paśtaśis. nastaja·śśej lovi mužik sije. no vot i lokteni be̯r, ruć voʒin mune. ke̯ni mi̯j, caris, i v a n oz te̯d kerkase. no vot vovisni. car primitis sije, srazu pīśane, vannae. mi̯śkisni-ći̯śkisni. i vot veńićajććis. vežon sen ge̯śťitisni, śojisni-juisni.

3. *no kole ved i i v a n orde munni. i v a nlen kerkaid zored-ū, ki̯ćće śa munan? ńe-ke̯n abu. ruć: "ńićevo pe" — šue. a car oz te̯d ńem-tor. me be̯rśa pe ve̯ćće!" — šue. no ladne. vot ruć voʒe petis, śa i v a n gozja i g r i̯ m car gozja. g r i̯ m car gozja be̯rin, a i v a n voʒin mune. ruć tujed i mune, si̯ kod tujed. munisni verst-ľi, ki̯kes-ľi, daške i dases munisni. volis me̯s-stada. atte beda i̯ʒid, daške ki̯k-śo-ľi, kujim-śo me̯s seni. vot šue, ruć šue: "g r i̯ m car pe lokte." kićće pe voštiśni?" "ńe-ki̯ćće pe en voštiśe! tan mi̯j-ke, stadase pe teľke viśtale i v a nlen me̯s-stada!" i ruć bara voʒe mune. i v a n toľke si̯ be̯rśa ve̯ćće. i vovis g r i̯ m car. "taje kodlen me̯s-stadais?" — šue. "o — šue*

and see Tsar Gri̮m." He bolted off to Tsar Gri̮m. He asked Tsar Gri̮m: "Have you got a pood-scale, for Ivan wants to measure money." "What kind of pood-scale to measure money?" Tsar Gri̮m is a glorious tsar, but he has no pood-scale to measure money with. "Go and find one somewhere!" Well, he gave him one, why should Tsar Gri̮m not give him one? The fox pulled the pood-scale a little below the stairs and left there it under the stairs. He returns and asks Ivan: "You have no money, have you?" "I do not know" — answers he. Altogether three kopecks turned up from somewhere. Oh, the fox was very glad. He put the coins somewhere in the pood-scale, in some slit, and took it to Tsar Gri̮m. The fox returned. Tsar Gri̮m shook the pood-scale, and coins fell out of it. "So it is money that he measured! What kind of man is this Ivan? He must be very rich!" Well, all right, the fox went off and again he caught hares for Ivan. Again the fox bolted off to Tsar Gri̮m. He arrived at Tsar Gri̮m. "Ivan has sent me for a girl to marry." "No matter, we'll marry her to such a rich man." The fox comes along and tells Ivan about it all. "Come on, let us go! I have found a bride for you, from Tsar Gri̮m. Come and see her!" Ivan — as you know — had no . . ., well, his clothes are worn out. He was brought up by his stepmother, where could he have got fine clothes? Well then, they arrived at the foot of the steps. "Wait here while I go to Tsar Gri̮m!" The fox rushed off, ran away and threw up his tail. He arrives. "Ivan" — says he — "has been robbed, his clothes have all been stipped off and he is left naked. He was stripped naked by bandits." At once the Tsar sends fine clothes for his son-in-law, he sent clothes and gave them to the fox. Ivan put on the clothes. He turned into a real man. Well, they return, the fox showing the way. Where does the Tsar live? Ivan does not know the house. The Tsar received him, and showed him in at once, to the bathroom right to the bathtub. They washed and dried themselves. They got married. For a week they feasted, eating and drinking.

3. Well, it is time to see Ivan's house. But Ivan's home is under the haystack, where should they go? He has no house anywhere. "Never mind" — says the fox — "the Tsar knows nothing. Come and follow me!" Well, all right. The fox showed the way, followed by Ivan and his wife, then by Tsar Gri̮m and his wife. Tsar Gri̮m and his wife were at the back, Ivan went in front of them. He walks behind the fox, in his footsteps. They went on for one or two, perhaps ten versts. They reached a herd of cows. Devil take it, the herd was a big one indeed, perhaps there were two or three hundred cows there. The fox says: "Tsar Gri̮m is coming." "Where shall we hide?" "Don't hide at all! Just say that the herd belongs to Ivan!" The fox goes on. Ivan follows him. Tsar Gri̮m came to the place. "Whom

— kučem ozir źaťnim. siʒ-že munisni seśśa kilametrov ďeśeť-ľi, petna·ćeť. vē-stada vovis. ruć bara šue: "g r i m car pe to lokte." "kiććе pe voštiśni?" "ńe-kiććе en voštiśe!" ďert sije vējas seni una i końuk abu eča. "teľke pe i v a nliś viśtale! seśśa pe — šue — g r i m car ńi-nem oz već" no vot i vovis g r i m car i juale: "kodlen pe taja?" "i v a nlen pe taja." no ladne, voʒe, mij-ke, medeććisni. no, vovis sečem carstvo (car ńimse vunedi), med gosudarstvo. ruć i lokte i viśtale: "vot pe g r i m car pe lokte." "kiććе voštiśam?" "ńe-kiććе pe en — šue — voštiśe! vot tan pe dub vijim, dub ulas pe i pire!" — car gozjali šue. a služa·nkajasli viśtale: "i v a nliś pe viśtale!" (piralis dvorećas da viśtalis.) i ruć voćća nin lokte, bež ľegede. i v a n volis, sūtis; rućlen voʒe tuj ez mun. i rućis šue: "što za pe! g r i m car, te, vot dubjas pe — šue — rezišt, lij!" dubje reziśtis, ńem koľi dub. sećće car gozja i koľini, vot i v a n seśśa ōmeććis i eni ole-vile.

147.

1. *olisni-vilisni starik gozja. nalen ćuži pi, tože i v a n. (vek taj mojd-kījasin i v a n gižśe-a, kokńiʒik i v a nse šunis-ľi, mij-ľi.) so oleni sije. ďert, i v a n ez nin vē ʒoľa sije, ćuže, ed taj mojd-kilin edje i bidme. seśśa i nalen kūśis bať. ez ozira ōni geľińik kerkain, lokińik kerka veli nalen. bať tože ez ozira ōli. i vot mamked oleni sije. mij veli, stavse vuzalisni. i v a n tože mi vok kojd diš-že veli sije, pjańńik kojd, mij-ke juište da mij-že sije. juemid tože veli putajte sije mortte. no vśo-taki verin vetle, petkate lijište. eťi petkanad, ďert, on ōmeććі. i bid-tor biri i kiś? stavse vuzalisni.*

2. *kor-ke ne śa gebećis śuri sili simem lampa. kiskis, petkedis, sije zē jona simema, kutis vesōni. kik molođeć drug setiś ćeććištisni simem lampaiś: "mij ne — šue (daj stavis veli derem geredeś), mij ne tenid kole" — šue. "a mij ne, vot, śojni-juištni, seśśa pe ńi-nem eśken da." "no ladne pe, vod, buď spokojen pe, loe." ćeććis, pizan vilin śojan-juan, druge, stavis ruale. "traśića, taje bur*

does this herd of cattle belong to?" "It belongs to Ivan" — answers he. "Oh" — says he — "how rich our son-in-law is!" Thus they went on another ten or fifteen kilometres. They reached a herd of horses. The fox says: "Tsar Grim is coming." "Where shall we hide?" "Don't hide at all!" There were really lots of horses there, and the horseherds were more than a few too! "Just say they belong to Ivan! Then Tsar Grim will not do you harm." Well, Tsar Grim arrived and asks: "Whom does this belong to?" "It belongs to Ivan." Well, all right, they went on. They arrived in another Tsar's land, I forgot the name of that tsar, well, it was another country. The fox comes and says: "Well, Tsar Grim is coming." "Where shall we hide?" "Don't hide anywhere! Here is an oak, creep under the oak!" So he offers it to the Tsar and his wife. At the same time he tells the maid-servants: "Say this belongs to Ivan!" (He entered the castle and said all this there.) The fox comes along wagging his tail. Ivan arrived from the other direction and stopped because the fox's way did not lead any further. The fox says: "What's that? Tsar Grim, spray it, shoot at the oak there!" He fired at the oak and nothing remained. Only the Tsar and his wife remained there dead. Then Ivan grew rich and he is still alive today.

147. [The miraculous lamp]

1. There lived an old man and his wife. A son was born to them, also called Ivan. (In tales it is always Ivan, it is easier to say, or what.) Well, they live on, of course Ivan was no longer a small child, he is born and, you see, in tales he grows up quickly. Then his father died. They did not live like rich people in the poor house, — for they had a tumbledown house. His father was not rich either. They sold everything they had. Ivan was lazy like us, a drunkard. Drinking upset this man. Yet he goes to the woods hunting wild-fowls. Of course, one wild-fowl does not make you rich. They ran out of everything. Where from? They sold up everything.

2. One day he found a rusty lamp in the cellar. He pulled it out and took it out; it was all covered with rust and he began to clean it. Two lads suddenly jumped out of the rusty lamp: "What" — ask they (his shirt was nothing but patches) — "what do you want then?" "What indeed? To eat and drink and nothing more!" "All right then, go to sleep and be sure you will have what you need!" He got up and found steaming food and drink on the table. "The deuce! This is a fine meal!" — thinks Ivan. His mother? No, he does not tell his mother. Again he went into the woods. Again he brought down two or three hazel-hens. He comes along and brings them home. Just cook and eat them. In what way do you cook them? They are

štuka!" — i v a n dumajte. mames, mamli oz viśtõ sije. vot vetlis bara vere, bara kik-ľi kujim śela lijis. lokte sije, vajis sijes. śojnise, punise, kiži sijes puan, stavis puemaeś nin. vot seśśa i dumajte: getraśni kole. ďert da, a sen veli kiź kilometrain śed koroľlen nī. sije šue: "mam, vetli pe, mun koraśni!" bara lampae kutis nešni. ńe-dir ćas miśťi bara kik moloďeć ćeććištisni. "no mij pe, mij kole?" — šueni. "mij pe eśke kole? geśńeć koroľli. mame pe kesje vetlini koraśni da." "ladne pe, vod, buď spokojen pe, loe." ďert i v a nidlen jona dir ez uźśi. sija kiž ne sek uźśas?! ćeććis, sečem, kučem-ke sije? voobše abu zeleta, abu mij-ke, ńe-ižid komok i em. sija pir-že śetis mamli. "te, mame, vetli koroľ orde koraśni!" "da kiži ne te koraśni sije? — mam šue. — tenad kerkaid na abu da, te kićće koraśni? — mam šue: te saje ne kod munas? so ed i paś-kemid nin tenad stavis gered — šue — daj geržžilema pe stavse, latka vurištni abu ńi-nem ńi." no ladne, sije bara pukśis i lampae kuććisis. ńe-dir mišt petis bara kik maľćik. "no mij kole?" "med veli menam kem-kot, paśkem i veli med menam kerka, med koroľliś buržik — šue — veli!" no ladne, ľibe vod pe — šuve — buď spokojen, loe." naja bara šuisni. ćeććis, druge, paśkemid ed jugdale. i krustaľnej dom strejitema. "ak, eni — šue — mames istila ta-lun." vot i mam munis. no ladne, koroľ orde vovis. vezjiśis, no piris, no kiži taje: "perććiś, babuška!" "vot — šue — i v a n istis koraśni, menam piej: so lokti koraśni tijane." a koroľ veli tede sije, mij geľińika naja olisni. "a ńićevo pe — šue — taja, mij-ke, med pe krustaľnej pos meśań da aslas poska pomež strejitas da pos bokas pe med veli ju, sečem ju, ti, ti bokas pe med veli vićko, vićkoas pe med sijen, mij-ke veńćajććasni." o-o, druge, sija mamlen, srazu-že i seśśa pańikae uśi? 'kiž taje mijan śa strejitas sije vojen?' loktis i viśtale: "da-a, kiž pe — šue — tenad, sije mij-ke karasni, koroľ nījases — šue — te kesjan mij-ke kerni, vot te ažžan, mij čektis strejitni." "no ladne, mame." kīziśis, bara lampae kuććiśis. mam oz ted lampa, sije mamiś guśen viže. no śa, druge, nali viśtalis: "vot pe — šue — mames istili, čektemaeś pe strejitni krustaľnej pos, poska pomśańis aslanis mijan poska pomež, a pos bokas pe med veli ti, ti bokas med veli vićko." šuisni: "buď spokojen, loe pe." no ďert, sija jona dir ez mortid uź, daške i uźis, ćas-ľi, dva-ľi, tri-ľi. daške dases uźis. ćeććis, vižede: krustaľnej pos strejitemaeś. i veli ješše, me vunedi, sadjas sen pos bokas. 'no, ľibe bara ista mames'. "mun, ćećći, vetli koraśni!" "no,

all cooked already. Then he thinks: I must marry! You see, the black king's daughter lives twenty kilometres off. He says: "Mother, go and ask for the girl's hand!" Again he began to strike the lamp. Two lads sprang forth in no time. "Well now, what do you want?" — they ask. "What should I want?" Gifts for the king! My mother wants to ask for the girl's hand." "All right, go to sleep, be sure you will get what you want!" Of course, it took Ivan some time to fall asleep. How could he sleep then? He got up, well, what is it like? On the whole it is not gold, nor is it a big parcel. At once he gave it to his mother. "Mother, go to the king to ask for his daughter's hand!" "What, to ask for her hand? How?" — says his mother. "You have not got a house, how do you want to ask for the girl's hand?" His mother says: "Who will marry you? Look, your clothes are nothing but patches, worn away, and we have no patches to mend it." Well, all right, he sat down again and seized the lamp. In a short while again two young men appeared. "What do you want?" "I want to have shoes, clothes and a house better than that of the king!" "All right, go to sleep" — they say — "be sure you will get what you want!" They said it again. He got up, his clothes were glittering. And they had built a crystal house. "Ah, now" — says he — "I am going to send my mother today." Well, his mother went off and came to the king. She asked to be let in; she went in. "How then?" — says the king. "Take off your coat, old woman!" "Well" — says she — "Ivan has sent me to ask for your daughter, — he is my son. Well, you see, I have come to you." The king knew that they were badly off. "Never mind" — says he — "let him build a crystal bridge reaching from here to his own stairs, let there be a river by the bridge, a lake, a church by the lake, and then he may wed her in the church!" Oh, my friend, at this the mother was seized by panic. "How can he, our son, build all this in a night?" She came home and said: "Well, how can they do it for you? You want to ask the king's daughter in marriage, and, you see what you have been ordered to build!" "It's all right, mother." She gave in. Again he took the lamp in his hand. His mother knows nothing about the lamp. He kept it a secret from his mother. Well, then he told them: "I sent my mother, they commanded me to build a crystal bridge reaching from their stairs to our stairs, a lake by the bridge, and a church by the lake." "Be sure all this will be done!" Of course, the man could hardly sleep, perhaps an hour, or two or three he slept. He may have slept ten. He got up and saw that they had built a crystal bridge. And there was in the garden, by the bridge, well, I forget what. "Well then, I'll send mother again." "Get up and go to ask for the girl!" "Well, all right" — says the king — "let him come!" The mother went there. "Tomorrow

ladne pe, — šue — med loktas — mamis munis, viśtale — med loktas aski dvena·ćeť ćaso·vin das-ki̮k ke̮reta ve̮len i med pe menam poska pomin ve̮li sūtedema das-ki̮k ke̮reta vē̮!" druge, mamli bara šog bośtis. 'ki̮ǯi ne, mi̮j taje, ki̮ś ne mijan ve̮lis taje? kodli, mi̮j ne če̮ktisni śetni?' no, lokte, bara si̮li viśtale: "vot, sija pe eśke ke̮sjis śetni, no če̮ktis le̮śedni das-ki̮k ke̮reta vē̮ aslis daj te pe med loktin aski dvena·ćeť ćaso·vin! sek pe ke̮sjis śetni." no mam bara mi̮ǯis. ďert, sije ki̮ź kilometra abu matin sija, be̮ra-voǯe ńeľamin kilometra. i v a n sije lampa perjis, bara ki̮k moloďeć ćeććištisni. "no, mi̮j — šue — kole, i v a n?" "vot pe — šue — aski pe ke̮sja munni koroľ orde ge̮traśni, med pe eśke menam ve̮li menim aslim vi̮le das-ki̮k ke̮reta vē̮ i med koroľ poska pomas das-ki̮k ke̮reta vē̮!" "no, ladne, vod, buď spokojen, loe." no, druge, jona mortlen ez uźśi. stavis ľentaa, ke̮lekala vējasse le̮śedemaeś sije. i v a n ćeććis. ďert, sije stavse le̮śedis i davaj, das-ki̮k ćas kežle i leććis, munis koroľ orde. ďert sen veńćajććisni. sija lovis kod, seten śa svaďbujtisni. i vot i v a n ordin ge̮śťitisni.

3. no, sije vot pi̮r že ve̮rte ľubite, mortid. ta-lun ve̮re petalis, ńe-kod ez šed, aski petalis ve̮re, ńe-kod ez šed. i vettedlisni. vovisni, kerkate matiś bura eśke oškisni: "bur kerka, no abu pe pańikaďile." i v a nliś kuľitisni kerkase. ki̮ken vovisni, ki̮k moloďeć da. no, lokte, ge̮tir si̮li i viśtale: "vot pe eśke i kerka pe oškeni bi̮dlaed, no vot pańikaďile pe abu — šue —, seś pe kuľitisni." a ge̮tir oz te̮d, a ge̮tirli ez viśtō i lampate puktis mi̮j-kee, ćardakas nuvis vi̮le. munis, bara lampaad jirk-tark keris. vot sije viśtale: "no taje pe oge — šue — taje pe izmena." ez ke̮sjiśni ve̮ćni voj kežlas. no ladne, bara ve̮re petis i v a n, kojmed lun. no ki̮ken, druge, ve̮len loktisni. simen lampa mića lampa vi̮le vežlaleni. a sije ge̮tirid mi̮j-keśis te̮de ve̮li lampase. lampase sije vežis, śetis. i vot sije ve̮rśid loktis: ge̮tir abu ńi, aslas važ kerkae i koľi. aslas be̮r de̮remis si̮len koľis. no vot i koreľ kore mortte. "te̮liś pe srok, ki̮ǯ kužan, ge̮tires vaj, ni̮les menśim vaj! on vaj, jurte kerišta." ki̮ćće voštiśan?! "vaj pe — šue —, ke̮ť kujim te̮liś kežle śet srok daj vē̮ — šue — vaj! daške aǯǯa — šue —." ez eśke śet da ge̮tiris če̮ktis koroľlen: "śetam pe — šue —, daške pe ki̮ś-ke korśas." no ladne, kujim te̮liś srok śetisni i i v a n me̮deććis munni.

at twelve o'clock he must come in a coach with twelve horses, and let him also put a coach and twelve in front of my stairs as well!" My friend! The mother was again seized with grief. How and where can we get horses? What orders can be given to whom? She comes and tells him about it again: "Well, he promised to give you his daughter, but he has commanded you to order a coach and twelve horses for him and that you should come by twelve o'clock tomorrow! Then he promised to give her to you." The mother grew tired again. You see, twenty kilometres is not a short walk, there and back it is forty kilometres. Ivan took the lamp, again two lads sprang forth: "Well, what do you want, Ivan?" "Tomorrow I want to go and ask for the king's daughter, let me have a coach and twelve horses myself, and let there be another coach and twelve horses at the bottom of the king's stairs!" "All right, go to sleep and be sure all this will be done!" Well, my friend, the man did not sleep very much. They ordered horses to come there, all decorated with ribbons and bells. Ivan got up. Everything was certainly made ready, and by twelve o'clock he had come to the king. There they got married. He got drunk, and they had a great feast. They were guests at Ivan's house.

3. Well, the man still loves the woods more and more. One day he walked into the woods, there was nothing to catch, the next day he walked into the woods, there was nothing to catch. People passed that way, they came near to praise the house. "It is a fine house, but it has no chandeliers." They found fault with Ivan's house. Two lads arrived. Ivan arrives home, his wife tells him: "Although the house is certainly praised everywhere, there are no chandeliers in it, therefore they find fault with it." The wife does not know, he did not tell his wife that he had taken the lamp to the loft. Again he knocked on the lamp. They say: "This we shall not do, this is treason." They did not promise to do it by night-time. All right, again Ivan went into the woods on the third day. Two folk arrived there on horseback. They replaced the rusty lamp with a beautiful new one. The wife did not know anything about the lamp. She exchanged the lamp, she gave it away. He came home from the woods: there was no wife, so he stayed in his own old house. He was left with his own shirt. The king calls the man. "Within a month, in some way or other, you must bring back your wife who is my daughter! If you do not bring her back, I will cut off your head." Where can you flee? "Give me a time-limit of three months and a horse as well! Perhaps I can find her." The king was not willing to give him these, but the king's wife ordered him to: "We will grant him what he asks for, perhaps he can find her somewhere." Well, all right, Ivan was granted a time-limit of three months, and Ivan set off on the way.

4. munis, munis, lun kujim, ńoľes munis, vežon, vois ju-pos. ju-pos še̮re voćća vois: "no, ki̮ćće pe, veža-pi, munan?" veža-pien šuis, druge. "ki̮ćće?! vot, siǯ i taǯ vot — šue — muna, tuje vot — šue — me̮dećći, babaes korśni pe, babaes pi̮šjedisni pe. ve̮re petali da si̮ kosti pe nuvisni — šue — da." "o-o, ďiťa-pije — šue — on aǯǯi pe, og-ke pe me veled — šue —. sije pe nuvis ľešej: ve̮lem ki̮ź-vit vo nin korśeni sije lampase, baťis pi̮šjedlema nin sijes. ki̮ź-vit vo korśeni ve̮lem lampase, toľke śurema lampais. će̮rtlen ve̮lema sije lampais, a će̮rtiś pi̮šjedlema baťis. no, ladne pe — šue — no pe vot ten tupiľ, ta be̮rśa ve̮ćći!" i śetis bulo·vka. "taje — šue — bulo·vka, babaidli pe śetan, voan da, sija pe kužas, ki̮ǯi mi̮j ve̮ćni. a taje pe tupiľis ki̮ćće munas, te pe sećće i mun! śa voǯe ńe-ki̮ćće en vośkōt. ten ki̮ǯ okota kole, te e̮dje munan, e̮dje ťuras, pukśan, tože oz ťur." vot, siǯi śa mort tupiľ be̮rśa ve̮ććis, lun, me̮des daj vežon daj ki̮ź lun. daj vovis, tupiľ ostanoviććis, ki̮ǯi ćurs pi̮ris, vśo. no, ki̮ćće śa voślōni? tupiľ vošis. voǯe munni ńe-ki̮ćće. da korśis da korśis, ńe-ki̮ś kod oz aǯǯi. sije ki̮ǯ korśis, da ńič ńe-una ve̮ržištema. ńičte sije lukjištis. śuri e̮ǯes, veťťištema će̮rtid. śuris, pi̮ris sećće. vośśis i pi̮ris, mi̮j-ke, ki̮ǯi taj pe̮dvalas pi̮ran, ge̮lbećas, ǯoǯśańis ve̮ćemaeś sije. pi̮ris. ge̮tir sen pukale, mi̮j-ke sen viši̮vajćće. "o-o — šue —, ki̮ǯi te — šue — taćće vovin?" "vot, taǯi — viśtalis — vovi pe — šue —." "no, će̮rt pe — šue —, me pe — šue — eg na si̮ked śorńitli. vot so te̮liś da kujim lun pe nin tani ola, eg na pe ši̮aśli — šue —. a tene pe sije loktas i śojas." "ńićevo, vež-ajid pe bulovka tenid me̮dedis." no bulovka seni babali śuri. "no, ńićevo — šue —, ōmeććam pe — šue —." vot sija bulovkae mi̮j-ke keris, id-tuśe pe̮rtis sije mužikes. "a me pe ta-lun si̮li guśa pe̮žaśa i vroďe pe pir da bal ve̮ća si̮ked ta-lun. no voǯe pe me og leǯ ńe-ki̮ćće sije munni, ke̮sja si̮ked ōmeććini. a lampate pe boštis sije śe̮ras. a seśśa pe sije unmōśas. śa seki i pi̮šjam." id-tuśe pe̮rtis. vot, će̮rt loktis. "uf — šue — roć du̮k ki̮le." "te pe — šue — roć muin vetlin da as pomśid, možet, tenad ki̮le. "kod pe taćće loktas guad pe, guad, taćće?" a mužikidli, sije, će̮rtli ńi̮m-kojd lovi, mi̮j pe taje ez na ši̮aśli, ta-lun śorńitis. śojan-juan ruale pi̮zan vi̮lin, zonme, sije. "no, nadoje-ďitis pe — šue mi̮j-ke, ge̮tir-puid. si̮len — ōnise pe taǯi e̮tnamlise śorńitteg. no, mi̮j, e̮ni ed ńe-ki̮ćće menim voštiśni. no me rešiti ta-lun teked ōmeććini.

4. He went on and on for three or four days, for a week, and he arrived at a bridge over a river. In the middle of the bridge someone met him: "Where are you going, my godson?" He called Ivan his godson. "Where? Well, I am just walking, I set out on the way" — says he — "to find my wife, my wife has been carried off. I went into the forest and she was carried away while I was there." "Oh, my child, my son" — he answers — "you will never find her unless I teach you. It is the devil who has taken her away. They have been looking for twenty-five years for that lamp; her father took it off in secret. For twenty-five years they have been searching for that lamp, and it has just turned up. The lamp was the devil's, and it was stolen from the devil by her father. All right, here is a reel of thread for you, follow this!" And he gave him a pin too. "You will give this pin to your wife" — says he — "and she will know what to do with it. Whenever this reel goes you must go too! Do not take a step further! Wherever the fancy takes you: if you go fast, it will roll fast, if you sit down, it will not roll." Well, the man followed the reel as he was told to: one day, two days, a week, twenty days. And he arrived. The reel stopped and went right in somewhere. Now what direction should he follow? The reel was lost. He does not know which way to go now. He looked and looked for it, but he could not see where it had gone. As he was searching, the moss stirred a little. He scratched the moss aside a little, and hit upon a door, it had been covered by the devil. He entered. It opened, and he went in as you go into a pit or a cellar; it was all built down under the ground. He stepped in. His wife was sitting there, embroidering something. "Oh" — says she — "how did you come here?" "Well, I came like this" — answers he. "The devil" — says she — "I have not yet talked to him. Look, I have been living here for one month and three days, and I have not spoken a word yet. He will come here and devour you." "Never mind, your godfather has sent you a pin." The pin was passed to the woman. "Never mind, we shall be all right" — says she. She hid him in the pin, she changed her husband into a barley corn. "Today I shall bake something for him in secret and pretend to arrange a feast and a ball. I will not let him go anywhere but stay with him. He has got the lamp with him. Then he will fall asleep, and we can escape." She changed him into a barley corn. The devil arrived. "Pooh" — says he — "I smell the smell of a Russian." "You have been walking on Russian land and you can smell it on yourself" — she answers. "Who is coming here, to this pit?" The husband, the devil was glad that his wife, who had not spoken a word so far, was talking that day. Food and drink were steaming on the table. "Well, the young wife has grown tired of living alone, with no-one to speak to. Look, I have nowhere to go now. Today I

vśo-taki pir da bal lęśediśtam, kęť i ńe-kod abu da.'' ''da, da, da — śue, ćęrt śue — sije pe — śue — poźe.'' no vot, ćaj juisni. sije stękanen vežlaśisni, aslas stękane, ďert, ez kiśt sije, mędarse, kodes juis sije. i sećće kir unmōśis. źepśis lampa kįskis i i v a n *es bulovkaiś pęrtis i lovi,* i v a n *lovi sije. ęni že vovisni aslanis kerkae i seni ōmeććisni.*

148.

a)

ošked panidaślem gežeda vęli. ošked panidaślem vęli sęvśem malo ōle, potomu što oškis ed jonase ez vę̄. no a mortśis ed sije tože pole ed. viććiśe, kor kįle mortse, seki i sije keže boke, potomu śte sije ved tože samoja źver, źverid i em aslas jur vęli tože dona. vot sija śa pįšje, sija mortśid. mortśid sija pįšje. em i pįšjitem źverjas, em i ľokǥikjas. emeś! em, śuam, enli, śataj, śatunjas nazvańije. śatun, kodi, znaćit, gue oz i pįr, tę̄-bįd śatajćće. sije vot sečemid i ępasnej, potomu što sija vot i kerkaad, znaćit, vęralan kerkaad loktas, pįrni kutas. ęććid slućiććis i sečem slućiććem. ęććid vot mijan įǥid ďed vęli viśtollas: ''pukśema pe vęli pać dorin guśa, a pon mįj-ke kere, kręvaťin pe pukale. mįj-ke pe śį kutis pe, mįj-ke śorok-śį kįni. pon pe peľľas ńužedis, lańtis pe taǥi. ęǥesed pe mįććiśis eta paśta pľeśis, oś mįććiśis ęǥesed. a me seteni bľin pęžala pać dorin da sup pua. ńi-nem pe eg dumajt, me eg dumajt, kvaťiti pe sija sup ćugunte da sįli juras puan vanad. oś pe seśśa goredis da pįšjis, śa pe ez voli mate.''

b)

męd ďaďeli mijan tože siǥi slućiććis. oškid, sija tūsō vęrin; kor sija tulisnas ur kįjeni, mįj-kein, ćarem vįti kor kįjśeni. sija petas, znaćit, vęrōni lunnas. seśśa śila vomen vośkōtas, śila vomen. a sija vęlem śila ulas kujle oškid. śila ulas kujle daj sįlen lįź-bęžid, śila vįti vośkōtas da i śľapkeććas sećće. sįli mįš-kuad inmas. sija taj zįredas sećće da mortid eśke i ćepesjas pįšjini da i oz uďit. seśśa sija oškid i lįź-bežse kvaťitas. kvaťitas seśśa da sija mortes i taskajtas do śmerťi. kujimen vęlem ęťi vęralan kerkain oleni. rįt pe loktis, mort pe ez vo. kįćći mort pe lovi?! pemdi pe i vek abu. aski voǥ petim, korśni munim. loktim pe, stavis majdan tapkedema, ńe-kįten tuj ńi ńę̄ ńi. stavis pe oś-tuj da vir da bįdsen stavis krov i bidsen. śa pe śa kįćće-ke gualema, bįdsen seśśa ńič-źe,

decided to live with you. We shall hold a feast and a ball, although there is nobody here." "Yes, yes, yes" — says the devil — "this can be done." They drank tea. They exchanged glasses, of course she did not pour tea in her own glass, only in the one of the devil drank from. Then there was a snort and he fell asleep. She took the lamp out of his pocket, and recharmed Ivan out of the pin. It became Ivan again. Now they came home to their own house and began to live there.

148. [Hunters' stories]

(a)

It was rarely that we met a bear. Very few meetings did we have with bears, since there weren't many bears about. After all, it is afraid of man too. It lies in waiting and when it perceives a man, it goes aside, for it is a wild beast, and wild beasts also love their own heads dearly. It escapes from man. But there are beasts that will not escape, there are more evil ones too. There are! There are, say, wait a minute, wandering beasts. This is what you call them. A wandering beast will not go into its den, it roams about throughout the winter. These are dangerous, because they even come into houses and into the hunters' hut. Once such a thing occurred. Grandfather once told this story. "I was sitting peacefully by the stove, and the dog was sitting on the bed. All of a sudden a noise, a swishing sound was heard. The dog pricked up its ears, it remained silent. In the doorway there appeared a broad forehead; a bear loomed up in the doorway. And I was frying pancakes and cooking soup in front of the stove. I did not think of anything, I had no thoughts in my mind, I took the soup-pot and tipped the boiling water on its head. The bear gave a howl and ran away, then it never came near again.

(b)

This is what happened to another old man here. There was a bear in the woods in spring, at a time when they hunt for squirrels, when they go hunting on frozen snow. He comes out to hunt in the day. He was stepping over a fallen tree-trunk. The bear was lying under that trunk. The bear was lying under the trunk, and as he is stepping over the trunk, the end of his ski hits the bear. It struck the bear on the back. It dashes at the man, he tries to escape, but without success. Then the bear seizes the end of the ski. It seizes it and drags the man along until he dies. Three of them were living in the hunters' hut. Evening came, and the man did not come home. Early in the morning we went out to look for him. We arrived, all

śujema. śa zē i̮ǯid mesta pe sija taľalema bi̮dsen, med pe og aǯǯe. mi pe kutim lokni da am-am-am pe mijan vile zi̮redis. sije pe srazu ki̮k piššaľen ǯenebtimli̮jim. sija uśi sećće. mortte pe mi lun-ǯi̮n korśim. setiś mu pijas pe śa ti̮rtema da. vot ed ki̮ǯ ʒ́ebema! vot sečem slućajis vē̮li.

c)

kojmed slućaj vot tačemid vot ve̮li, sečem. eťik oχo·tńik mijan, ve̮li tatiś, koľan vo kuli. sije mune ve̮lem ve̮r vī̮ti. goredas ponjis, a bergeććas, oškid vi̮las ćeććište. a sija etaǯi, mi̮j-ke sije ćeććištig-moz gi̮rǯǯase le̮śedas. gi̮rǯǯas vomas pi̮ras da seśśa sija kvaťitas gi̮rǯǯate etatise da jurse seśśa si̮li pińnad stavse ńečkas, jajti etati. śa ćuť lōja koľema ve̮li, ńečkema da. seśśa ponjid pe seśśa ske̮rmis da volis pe da vi̮lad oškidli kajis da kutis kośollini peľedis da ve̮ľiśťi leǯema ve̮li. vot kučem slućajjasid vē̮lini vojder-že.

d)

kor-ke tateni eťik voe mijan ve̮li ke̮jin. gožemnas kujim-śo i̮ž śojis. oz śoj, a etati bośtas, ruźedas goľase, virse jue da leǯas. seśśa tē̮ lois da okotńikjaslen — te̮dan — bi̮dsenlen pon vi̮jim. śa ve̮leśtśid kutis sija pon nōlini. śiźim-das pon tē̮-bi̮den śojis ve̮leśtiś. seśśa oblavan petisni stav naśeľeńie. vojnas ve̮li pon śojema, seśśa ve̮ľďďalema. śa tateni sije das ki̮min vers saje kajema ke̮jinid da śa oglavaen petisni. bi̮d tuj-veže, bi̮dlae sūtisni, kole ke̮jines ki̮jni. ponte eśke śojas nin da ćeľaďes kutas śojni. seśśa arťeľnad petisni daj ki̮jisni.

149.

1. *mijan kolko·znim (kolχo·znim) zē ozir. pervojse tože ve̮li koľććiś kolkoz (kolχoz). ńeľ vo sajin be̮rjisni viľ predśeda·ťeľes i kolkoznim te̮dćimenja burmis. me gortin og ńin ō ńe̮ľ vo i og te̮d, ki̮ǯi je̮zis uǯaleni kolko·zas. a gožemnas me aćim tože uǯala turun puktigen viǯ vi̮lin. babajas mijan i̮čkeni kosān, ge̮rbušen. i̮čkinise śe̮kid babajasli i turun puktan kadis medśa śe̮kid pe̮ra. šoććiteg uǯaleni bi̮d lun.*

the ground was trampled down, there was no way in or out. Bear's tracks and blood were everywhere, the whole place was covered with blood. It must have hidden him away. In a very large area it had trodden down everything, so that we could not find him. Then we began to approach: *am-am-am*, it dashed out upon us. At once we fired two guns at it. It collapsed. We looked for the man for half a day. It had buried him there in the ground. How deeply it had hidden him! Well, such an event occurred.

(c)

The third story ran like this. One of our hunters, who came from here, died last year. He was walking through the forest. His dog began to yelp, he turned round: a bear rushed at him. And he jumped up holding his elbow like this. His elbow got into the bear's mouth, then it seized his elbow here and his head, and tore off all the flesh with his teeth. He was hardly alive after it had torn him. Then the dog grew angry, came there and attacked the bear, but no sooner had it begun to tear off its ears than the bear let the man free. Well, such things happened in the old days.

(d)

Some time ago, one year there was a wolf here. That summer it killed three hundred sheep. It does not devour them, but seizes them and bites through their throats, then sucks their blood; then it leaves them there. Winter came, the hunters — as you know — all have dogs. Then it began to haul off the dogs in the district. It killed seventy dogs in the district each winter. Then all the inhabitants went out on a hunt. At night it devoured the dog, then fresh snow fell. The wolf had gone about ten versts away when people started for the hunt. They stopped at each crossroad everywhere; the wolf had to be killed. If it starts to devour dogs, it will soon begin to eat children too. They went out in a crowd and killed it.

149. [Our village]

1. Our kolkhoz is very rich. First it was backward, like the other ones. Four years ago a new president was elected, and our kolkhoz has visibly improved since. For four years I have not been living at home and so I do not know how people are working in the kolkhoz. I myself used to work in summer mowing hay in the meadow. Our women cut grass with scythes and sickles. It is hard for women to mow, and haymaking is the hardest time. They work without resting every day.

2. *eni mijan śiktin,* *v i ś e r* *ju dorin strejiteni eľektrostanćija, kutas stav v i ś e r-vožisli bi śetni. eni toľke na zavoďitisni strejitnise. śikte loktisni viľ jez. tom jezli gažagik love. mijan śiktin vtoroj apre·ľa praznujteni i ľ ľ a-lun. keť i lunjasis mićaeś i ľ ľ a-lun dirji, ńe-kod oz ugō. tagi veli važen, a eni stav tom jezis ugaleni, toľke periśjas praźńićajteni. (praźńik kežle pueni igid ćugun jaja śid, žariteni ćeri-ńań, śańga da kēdim pežaleni). no ritnas ug berin śoravna juśeni i med lunnas ńe-kod oz ugav.*

150.

ta-vo gožemnas asivśańis kesji votćini vetlini. dir uźśema (uśśema) i ńe-kod-ked munnise: votćinise vog muneni jezis veras. vedra bośti da kotrali, ńe-kod tevariś ez śur (eś śur). mame śue: "etnad pe kaj veras, seni ved jezis ver tiris, uva-ava kileni." me pervojse poli, etnam eg liśt kajnise, no śor nin lovi i ńe-kićće voštinise da biť lovi kajni vere. jez kok-tuj śerťiis kaji veras, a voge og ted, kićće munnise. kesji pū votni, a kor veras vovi, dumajta, keť ńin mij śure, vota. jezis, tidale, zē ile munemaś, veśig ńe-kodes eg aggil i eg kili. polig-tirji ektiśtali, mij śuris daj. veras sečem leń, ńi eťi śum (śi) abu, no drug-ke kok ulin trać mune ū-tor. dregńita da i daś gorte geńitni, kotertni. berinnas aćim śenźi, kigi sečem dirse veras ovśema. gorte munigen ńin tuj vilas panidaśi votćiśjasked. stavislen vedranis (dozjasnis) tir, a menam toľke ginjis. jezis veśig ez veritni, mij me etnam votći. me toľke vovi gorte da kuti pōni. (drug-ke mij-ke lovi, iľi aggi kodes-ke veras.)

151. *viśer śikt*

v i ś e r *ś i k t* *kujle* *ś o j n a* *tiśań ńeľamin-ńoľ verst sajin. voan da kole vugni* *v i ś e r* *ju. viśer ju zē vizi. ćojed kajan i zavoďiććasni kerkajas. kerkajas igideś, giriś eśińaaś.* *v i ś e r* *ś i k tin średnej śkola, kićće lokteni veleććini ćeľaď mati gegerśa śiktjasiś. kolkoz* *d r u ž b a* *ozir da vina. kolkozin bidteni kartupeľ da muked ovoščijas. kolkozin em una mesjas, vējas. no mujas eni*

2. At present a power plant is being built in our village on the banks of the Višera. It is to supply current for the whole Višera region. Construction has just begun. New people came to the village. Young people are beginning to lead a merrier life. In our village people celebrate Elijah's day on the second of April. Although the weather is fine on those days, nobody goes to work. So it was in times of old, now the young people work, only the old ones keep the festival. (For the feast they cook a big pot of broth, and bake *pirogi* with fish, pie and round loaves.) Still, in the evening, when they have done day's work, they have a drink, and next day nobody is at work.

150. [Picking berries]

This summer I wanted to go picking berries one morning. I slept late and found nobody to go with. They go early in the morning to gather berries in the woods. I took the bucket and ran after them, but I had nobody to keep me company. Mother said: "Go by yourself to the woods; after all, the woods are full of people. You can hear 'hoho, hoho' everywhere." At first I was afraid, I had no courage to go alone, but it was already late, there was nothing else to be done, by all means I had to go to the woods. I went into the forest after the people. But then I did not know where to go. I wanted to pick cowberries, but when I arrived in the woods I thought I would gather whatever I found. It seemed people had gone a long way off, I could not see or hear anybody. In great fear I picked what I found. There was such silence in the woods, no noise at all, but suddenly a twig cracked under my feet. Trembling, I was ready to dash home, to run away. Later I myself was amazed that I could stay in the forest so long. On the way home I met the people who had been picking berries. All their buckets were full of berries, but mine was only half-filled. People did not even believe that I had been picking berries alone in the forest. Only when I arrived home did I begin to worry. (All of a sudden something happened or I caught a glimpse of somebody in the forest.)

151. Bogorodsk

Bogorodsk lies forty-four kilometres from the Šojna lake. You arrive, you have to cross the Višera. The Višera is very swift. You walk up the hill, and there the row of houses begins. The houses are big, with large windows. There is a secondary school in Bogorodsk, children of the neighbouring villages come to study there. The kolkhoz named Druzhba is very rich and strong. Potatoes and other vegetables are grown in the kolkhoz. There are

gereni traktorjasen, ičkeni mašinajasen. śikt šerin sulale iǯid klub, kik sudta kirpićnej kerkān. požema jagin zē iǯid boľńića. — eni leśedćeni gera-keǯa keže. gozemnas kutasni ičkini; viďjasis mijan zē ilineś, v i ś e r *jilin. sećće muneni pižjasen, vējasen munni oz poź. arnas vundeni, kartupeľ kereni, śilośiććeni tulisnas i arnas. liva kiskaleni vējasen tuj vecigen. tēnas mijan zē una lim, veśig eni na kujle limjis, osobenno verjasin. sećće eni ńe-kučem tuj abu. ji munem beras kikiś-kimin parakod kajlas. seśśa* v i ś e r *jūs zē edje kośme, ju šeras liva kesajas loveni; daže pižen mukedlatīs on vermi projďitni.*

152. *vevlem-tor*

taje veli v i ś e r ś i k *tin. kik pośńi ďeťinka munisni vere pū votni. kiknannisli veli ar kvajt-śiźim. naje vetledlisni veredis lun-tir i vošisni. med lunnas śiktsa jez i siǯ-že ćeľaď munisni korśni najes. me i siǯ-že ńoľ mort munim najes korśni traktoren ju saje. veli uže (ńin) rit, pemid. mi vetledlim veredis voj-bid i eg aǯǯe ćeľaďse. śiktsa jez taje ćeľaďse korśisni lun-vit i ez aǯǯini. vežon-miśťi najes aǯǯisni ker-leǯiśjas i naje uśkedćisni piśjini voǯe. ker-leǯiśjasis kutisni ćeľaďse i vajisni gortas. na piiś eťik ďeťinkais viśtalis, mij naje kilisni gorzemse, no ez liśtni javiććini. polisni. eťik ďeťinkais viśtalis, mij naje aǯǯilisni ponjes i zavoďitisni ćuksavni sijes. zbiľiśse taje ez vev pon, a oš. tajes naje ez tedni. si vesna, mij oškis ez vev čig i ez uśkedći ćeľaďis vile.*

153. *vevlem-tor*

mi ďedked kajim gožemnas l i m - v a *ju kuźa ńeľamin verst saje; śerśinim čeč boštim* b u s k o *ńima pon. mi kajigen kisnaśim i siǯ-že kijim utka. mi ju kuźa kajim kik lun. eťik asile ďed mene ćukestis. me ćećći i peti ivlae: i kila ponliś uvtem-śi. i ďedked medeććim munni uvtem-śi vile pon dore. kor mi vojim pon dore i aǯǯim, mij* b u s k o *uvte pu vile ćatertćemen zev ľokiś. mi ďedked kaźalim mij-ke pu jivśis śed tor. si-berin geger-vojim, mij pu vilas kajema oš-pi. velem-ke, ponjis zavoďitema vetćini oš-pi berśais, i oškis povźemisla*

many cows and horses in the kolkhoz. Lands are ploughed by tractor and mowed by machines nowadays. A big club-building stands in the middle of the village, a three-storeyed building of brick. In the pine-forest there is a very large hospital. — Now they are preparing for ploughing and sowing. In summer they will do mowing: our meadows are a long way off, at the upper end of the Višera. They get there by boat, it is impossible for horses. In autumn they reap and harvest potatoes, in spring and autumn they deal with silage. When they are road-building they transport sand with horses. In the winter we have much snow, especially in the forests. There is no road leading there today. After the ice has gone, steamers come twice a day. Then the Višera river dries very soon, sandbanks develop in the middle of the river; not even a small boat can get through certain stretches.

152. Something that happened

It happened in Bogorodsk. Two small children went to pick cowberries in the woods. Both of them were six or seven years old. All day long they were walking in the woods and they lost their way. Next day the villagers and the children in the village started out to find them. I and three of my friends also went to search for them by tractor, over the river. It was evening, it had grown dark already. The whole night we were searching the woods, but we could not find the children. The villagers were looking for them for five days, yet they did not find the children. A week went by, and finally they were found by rafters. The rafters caught the children and brought them home. One of the children related later that he had heard the shouting, but they were afraid to come out. They were afraid. One of the children said that they had seen a dog and that they tried to call it. In point of fact, it was no dog but a bear. They did not know. As the bear was not hungry, it did not attack the children.

153. Something that happened

In summer grandfather and I went forty kilometres up the river *Lįm-va*; we took our dog named *Busko* with us. On our way up the river we fished with a pike-hook, and we shot wild-duck. For two days we travelled up the river. One morning grandfather called me. I sprang up and went out: I heard dogs barking. Following the direction of the barking, grandfather and I started off to find the dog. When we arrived at the dog, we saw that *Busko*, with his head thrown back, was furiously barking at a tree. We perceived a black thing in the tree. Then we realized that a bear-cub had

kajema pu vile. seśśa ďed li̮jis oškisli piššaľiś i oškis uśi mue. siǯi mi ďedked ki̮jim oškes i vajim ve̮ralan kerkae. leććigen mi ďedked botajććim i vejtalim kulemjas ti̮e. mijanli šedi kujim-ńoľ vedra ćeri. i ki̮jim para utka.

154.

mijan śiktin ćeľaď vorseni jonǯikase voľibolen, maćen, futbo·len, ǯebśaśemiś: e̮t-kimin ćeľaď ǯebśasni, a mukedjas korśeni najes. siǯ-že vorseni śarjasenis. krug pi̮čke suvtedaleni beďjas, a ćeľaď li̮jleni, starajććeni taje beďjasse krug pi̮čśis ve̮tlini. maćen vorsem ji̮liś: ćeľaď pudjaśemen jukśeni ki̮k juken vi̮le. e̮ťi gruppais vaćkile maćse beďďen i srazu-že pi̮šje voǯe. a mukedjas starajććeni maćnas li̮jni pi̮šjiśisli. jeśľi-ke maćis veśkalas taje mortisli, to maćse vaćkini zavoďitasni me̮d gruppais. voľibolen vorsem: voľibolen vorseni das mort. vit mortis suvtaleni śetkaśańis veśkidla-bokas, e̮staľnej vit mortis šujgala-dor bokas. maćse ši̮blaleni śetka vomenis i starajććeni ńe uśkedni muas. jeśľi-ke maćis uśe muas, to sije gruppaisli, kodlen maćis oz uś, pasjeni e̮ťik oćko.

(b) Songs

155.

truba, truba, truba, mu truba,
trubaśis pe či̮n-i kaje.
trubaśis pe či̮n-i kaje,
more vomen tuman pukśe.
tumanis pe ńe tuman,
juś-ǯoǯegjas lebeni.
juś-ǯoǯegjas be̮r-i-śańis
pe̮riś-pe̮riś kuč-i ve̮će.
kučiľej da ćojiľej
ki̮tjasti ne vetlin da munin?
s a r a p u l a vetli da muni.
kiś mi̮j ki̮lin adǯilin?
me ki̮li daj adǯili:
ťikeja mu vilin
kujim jeǯid jaj-i kujle.
kujim jeǯid jaj-i dine

climbed the tree. Obviously the dog had gone after the bear-cub, and the frightened bear had climbed the tree. Then grandfather fired his gun at the bear, and it fell to the ground. Thus grandfather and I brought down the bear, and took it to the hunters' hut. As we were going down the river, with a pole we drove fish into the net and laid wicker fish-nets in the lake. We caught three or four buckets of fish. And we shot two wild-ducks as well.

154. [About games]

The children in our village mainly play volley-ball, a ball-game, football and hide-and-seek. Some of the children hide and the rest find them. Likewise they play ball as well. They stand sticks in the middle of a circle, the children throw balls at it, trying to knock these sticks from the middle of the circle. As for the ball-game: the children draw lots and stand in two groups. One group hits the ball with sticks and runs away quickly. The others at the same time strive to hit the runners with a ball. If one of them is hit by the ball, the other group begins to strike. Volley-ball: ten men play volley-ball. Five of them stand on the right side of the net, the other five on the left side. The ball is thrown over the net, the players strive to do it so as not to drop the ball to the ground. If the ball falls to the ground, then the group that does not drop it gets a point.

155.

Chimney, chimney, chimney, chimney on the earth,
Smoke rises from the chimney.
Smoke rises from the chimney,
Fog has settled over the sea.
The fog is no fog,
Swans are flying,
The swan
Is chased by an old, old eagle.
My eagle, my little sister,
Where have you been wandering?
I have been wandering in Sarapul.
Where and what have you heard and seen?
I have heard and seen:
In peaceful ground
Three white corpses are lying.
To the three white corpses

kujim že daj ćikiš volīle.
per-i-vojja ćikišislen
re̮ďimeja baťis ve̮lema,
toroja ćikišislen
re̮ďimeja mamis ve̮lema,
treťťeja ćikišlislen
re̮ďimeja ćojis ve̮lema.
per-i-vojja ćikišislen
śin-i-vais uśe
tūsōja i̮t-i-va mi̮da.
toroja ćikišislen
śin-i-vais uśe
tūsōja šor-i-va mi̮da.
i treť-i-ťeja ćikišislen
i śin-i-vais uśe
ar-i-śa li̮s-i-va mi̮da.

156.

i̮lin, i̮lin va sajin
vi̮ľ sle̮beda ti̮dale,
vi̮ľ sle̮bedas tom de̮va-j ole,
tom de̮vaslen tom že nī vi̮jim.
ićeťik da ʒ̮eľańik,
ge̮gres ćužema, śe̮d śin-tasjasa.
ge̮gres ćužema, śe̮d śin-tasjasa,
roža vi̮las alej vir vorse,
da śin-i-jas-i-nas pe da vom-i-jas-i-nas da
čeč-že sija vorsećće-j.
daj etija slava kuźa
starik saje love munni.
ki̮ʒ̮ pe ved taj uľ pu ńukľaśe,
si̮ʒ̮-že menim slava lokte.
ki̮ʒ̮ pe ved da kos pu ćegjaśe,
si̮ʒ̮-že menim slava lokte.
"starikej da musa starikej,
le̮ʒ̮ te mene guľajtni!"
"ić-mońej da musa ić-mońej,
važen jona guľajt-i-lin."
"starikej da musa starikej,

Three swallows arrive.
The first swallow
Was the father,
The second swallow
Was the mother,
The third swallow
Was the dear sister.
The first swallow
Sheds tears
Profusely like the spring flood.
The second swallow
Sheds tears
Profusely like a brook in spring.
The third swallow
Sheds tears
Profusely like the autumn dew.

156.

Far, far away, over the water
A new, free village is seen,
In the new, free village there lives a young widow,
The young widow has a young daughter.
She is small, has a tiny figure,
A round face and black eyebrows.
A round face and black eyebrows,
Purple blood shines playfully on her cheek,
With her eyes and mouth
She also gestures playfully.
For the shame of it
She must marry an old man.
As this verdant tree is swaying
So shame comes upon me.
As the dry tree breaks
So shame comes upon me.
"Old man, dear old man,
Let me out to have a walk!"
"Young wife, dear young wife,
Formerly you walked very often."
"Old man, dear old man,

leǯ te mene braććina juni!"
"ić-mońej da musa ić-mońej,
važen jona julīlin."
"starikej da musa starikej,
leǯ te mene e̮g-i-radajad!"
"ić-mońej da musa ić-mońej,
on ed šogmi e̮šiń ulad."
"starikej da musa starikej,
leǯ te mene kil'će pomad!"
"ić-mońej da musa ić-mońej,
ki̮ś nin eśke kil'-i-će pome?
on ed šogmi e̮šiń ulad."
"starikej da musa starikej,
leǯ te mene porog ulad!"
"ić-mońej da musa ić-mońej,
on ed šogmi kil'će vi̮lad."
"starikej da musa starikej,
leǯ te mene ge̮beć dorad!"
"ić-mońej da musa ić-mońej,
on ed šogmi porog ulad."
"starikej da musa starikej,
leǯ te mene pe̮lat' dorad!"
"ić-mońej da musa ić-mońej,
on ed šogmi ge̮beć dorad."
"starikej da musa starikej,
leǯ te mene vol'-i-paś vi̮lad!"
"ić-mońej da musa ić-mońej,
ki̮ś nin eśke vol'-i-paś vi̮le?
on ed šogmi pe̮lat' dorad."
"starikej da musa starikej,
leǯ te mene veśkid soj vi̮lad!"
. . . .

157.

nī vala lećće da čaj vala lećće.
zon voj juktale da mića pukale,
zē ved sija i las-i-kov,
zē ved sija da primet'it.
i̮le da kare me̮de da

Let me have a drink at the picnic-ball!"
"Young wife, dear young wife,
Formerly you drank very much!"
"Old man, dear old man,
Let me go to the fence!"
"Young wife, dear young wife,
Look, it is not fitting for you to stand beneath the window!"
"Old man, dear old man,
Let me go to the end of the porch!"
"Young wife, dear young wife,
Why to the end of the porch?
Look, it is not fitting for you to stand beneath the window!"
"Old man, dear old man,
Let me go to the threshold!"
"Young wife, dear young wife,
Look, it is not fitting for you to stand in the porch!"
"Old man, dear old man,
Let me go to the cellar!"
"Young wife, dear young wife,
Look, it is not fitting for you to stand on the threshold!"
"Old man, dear old man,
Let me climb up to the hammock-bed!"
"Young wife, dear young wife,
Look, it is not fitting for you to stay in the cellar!"
"Old man, dear old man,
Let me into your bed!"
"Young wife, dear young wife,
Why in my bed?
Look, it is not fitting for you to climb up to the hammock-bed!"
"Old man, dear old man,
Let me onto your right arm!"
. . . .

157.

The girl is going to fetch water, to fetch water for tea.
She gives the lad to drink at night, and he is sitting so nicely,
He is very gentle,
He is very remarkable,
He sets off for a distant city,

oz i̯le kare me̯d,
kazań-i kare da
kazań-ju pe vizīte-j.
ge̯ra ji̯las-ke viʒedlam da
stavis seni sakar-jur,
ge̯ra gor-ulas-ke viʒedlam da
stavis seten saldat-jur,
stavis seni kok-pe̯la saldat.
gi̯riś šorjas-ke vizīteni,
stavis seni saldat-i-vir.
ʒe̯ľa šor-i-jas-ke vizīteni,
stavis seni aj-mamlen śin-va.

158.

šondi-banej olemej da
ki̯ćći bara koľema?
ki̯ćći bara koľema da
dašk̆e-j abu-j ve̯lema.
šondi-banej od-ib śiktej,
ki̯rja dora kerkaej.
mi̯jen bara-j od-ib ozir?
kuranen da vilaen.
ješše bara mi̯jen ozir?
trepać, bakval zonjasen.
kerka vi̯lin pe una ťe̯s da
kije bośtni ńe-kodes,
od-ib śiktin pe una zon da
druge bośtni ńe-kodes.

159.

šondi-bane̯j ole̯me̯j,
tom ole̯me̯j, tom gažej!
tom ole̯me̯j, tom gaže̯j,
tom pe̯ra koľľale̯me̯j!
ki̯ćće̯ bara koľe̯ma?
abu-ke̯ i ve̯vle̯ma-j.
ji moz sije̯ si̯le̯ma,
va moz pe̯ i uśe̯ma,
ćag moz pe̯ ki̯lale̯ma.

Not for a distant city,
(But) for the city of Kazań.
The River Kazań is flowing.
If we look at the hill,
We see it is nothing but a sugar cone,
If we look at the foot of the hill,
We see it is nothing but soldiers' heads,
Nothing but one-legged soldiers.
If big rivers are flowing,
They are nothing but soldiers' blood.
If small rivers are flowing,
They are nothing but parent's tears.

158.

My pretty sun-faced life,
Where has it disappeared?
Where has it disappeared?
Perhaps I have never had
My pretty sun-faced village of *Odib*,
My house on the steep river-bank.
What has *Odib* in plenty?
Rakes and forks.
And what else has it in plenty?
Gossiping, bragging lads.
There are many planks on the house,
But none of them can you take in the hand
There are many lads in the village of *Odib*,
But none of them can you take as a lover.

159.

My pretty sun-faced life,
My young life, my youthful joys!
My young life, my youthful joys,
My early years have passed away.
Where have they gone?
It is as if they had never been.
Like ice, they have melted,
Like rain, they have fallen,
Like shavings, they floated down the river.

ki̮ćće̮ sije̮ ľase̮ma?
li̮a be̮žas ľase̮ma,
sećće nasi̮pajte̮ma
ńeććid aǯǯivte̮m vi̮le̮
ńeććid perji̮vte̮m vi̮le̮.
šondi-bane̮j ole̮me̮j,
tom ole̮me̮j, tom gaže̮j,
je̮ktig-ti̮rji tuvćće̮me̮j,
tuvććig-ti̮rji je̮kte̮me̮j.
ki̮ćće bara koľe̮ma?
koľe̮ma i bi̮re̮ma.

160.

ćikišes kole ki̮jni da
sadege kole je̮rtni.
sadege kole je̮rtni da
ke̮jdisis na vesōtem.
ke̮jdisis na vesōtem da
verdiśis na bi̮ttitem.
verdiśis na bi̮ttitem da
ke̮ǯ pos kuźa loktema.
ke̮ǯ pos kuźa loktema da
ke̮rt-keresin bi̮dmema.

161.

kozje̮, kozje̮, mi̮j sulalan?
me e̮d tene̮ pe̮re̮da.
kozje̮, kozje̮, mi̮j sulalan,
me e̮d tene̮ pe̮re̮da.
peske̮ kerala da
paće lomta,
peske̮ kerala da
paće lomta.
ki̮z e̮gire̮ uśke̮da da
śo bľin pe̮žala,
ki̮z e̮gire̮ uśke̮da da
śo bľin pe̮žala.
ve̮sńi e̮gire̮ uśke̮da da

Against what were they dashed?
They were dashed against a sandy bank.
They were scattered there,
So that I may not see them again,
So that I may not recover them again.
My young life,
My young life, my youthful joys,
Dancing, I walked,
Walking, I danced.
Where has all this gone?
It has disappeared, it has come to an end.

160.

You must catch a swallow,
And shut it in the garden.
You must shut it in the garden,
The seeds are unwashed as yet.
The seeds are unwashed as yet,
The feeder is unraised as yet.
The feeder is unraised as yet,
He has come over the bridge at the river-bend,
He has come over the bridge at the river-bend,
He has been raised in *Kẹrt-keres*.

161.

Spruce, spruce, why are you standing?
Look, I am going to fell you!
Spruce, spruce, why are you standing?
Look, I am going to fell you!
I am going to chop you up for firewood,
I am going to heat the stove,
I am going to chop you up for firewood,
I am going to heat the stove.
I will drop you on thick glowing ashes
And fry a hundred pancakes.
I will drop you on thick glowing ashes
And fry a hundred pancakes.
I will drop you on thin glowing ashes

śo peće·ńka pe̯žala,
ve̯sńi e̯gi̯re̯ uśke̯da da
śo peće·ńka pe̯žala.

162.

ve̯ri̯n bi̯dmis zev mića pože̯m,
e̯t-koď si̯le̯n ji̯v iľi din.
śikti̯n bi̯dmis ge̯gre̯s-ge̯gre̯s ćuže̯ma
mića, mića, e̯tka ni̯v.
śikti̯n bi̯dmis ge̯gre̯s ćuže̯ma
mi̯ća, mića e̯tka ni̯v.

aski kajim puse̯ pe̯re̯dni̯,
puid menim ez i pe̯r.
ri̯tnas muni ni̯le̯s, ni̯le̯s koravni̯,
ni̯li̯d me saje̯ ez pet.
ri̯tnas muni ni̯le̯s, ni̯le̯s koravni̯,
ni̯li̯d me saje̯ ez pet.

kor-ke̯ eśke̯ pui̯d pe̯ris da
śiśme̯ ve̯le̯m śe̯vme̯si̯s.
kor-ke̯ eśke̯ ni̯li̯d, ni̯li̯d munis da
viśe̯ ve̯le̯m śe̯le̯mi̯d.
kor-ke̯ eśke̯ ni̯li̯d, ni̯li̯d munis da
viśe̯ ve̯le̯m śe̯le̯mid.

kor-ke̯ eśke̯ pui̯d pe̯ris daj
eksport vi̯le̯ ez šogmi.
kor-ke̯ eśke̯ ni̯li̯d, ni̯li̯d munis da
ge̯ti̯r vi̯le̯ ez šogmi̯.
kor-ke̯ eśke̯ ni̯li̯d, ni̯li̯d munis da
ge̯ti̯r vi̯le̯ ez šogmi̯.

163.

pukala ke̯ť vetle̯dla,
uǯala ke̯ť og,
ke̯ť me vorse̯m viǯe̯da,
pi̯r men mi̯j-ke̯ šog.
ke̯ť me vorse̯m viǯe̯da,
pi̯r men mi̯j-ke̯ šog.

And bake a hundred potatoes.
I will drop you on thin glowing ashes
And bake a hundred potatoes.

162.

In the forest there grew a very beautiful pine-tree,
Its crown and roots are beautiful too.
In the village only one round, round-faced,
Beautiful, beautiful girl has been raised.
In the village only one round, round-faced,
Beautiful, beautiful girl has been raised.

In the morning we went out to fell a tree;
I could not fell the tree.
In the evening I went to ask for a girl, to ask for a girl,
The girl did not marry me,
In the evening I went to ask for a girl, to ask for a girl,
The girl did not marry me.

Some time the tree fell down,
Its inside was decayed.
Some time the girl, the girl came, but
Her heart was sick.
Some time the girl, the girl came, but
Her heart was sick.

Some time the tree fell down,
It was unsuitable for export,
Some time the girl, the girl came, but
She was unsuitable for a wife.
Some time the girl, the girl came, but
She was unsuitable for a wife.

163.

Whether sitting, whether walking,
Whether working, whether not,
Whether watching the game,
I always have a kind of sorrow.
Whether watching the game,
I always have a kind of sorrow.

muke̮d-di̮rji ki̮la me:
ki̮le̮ śi̮lan-ki̮v.
ve̮te̮n kod-ke̮ ćuksale̮:
saďmi̮, musa ni̮v!
ve̮te̮n kod-ke̮ ćuksale̮:
saďmi̮, musa ni̮v!

mi̮jla ne̮ men, mamuke̮j,
loi tače̮m šog?
taje̮ šogśe̮m-viśe̮mśi̮s
kor-ke̮ mi̮jla og?
taje̮ šogśe̮m-viśe̮mśi̮s
kor-ke̮ mi̮jla og?

taje̮ viśe̮m, diťuke̮j,
regi̮de̮n oz bi̮r,
saďmis tenad śe̮le̮mi̮d,
puźis tenad vir.
saďmis tenad śe̮le̮mi̮d,
puźis tenad vir.

164.

ve̮li šonid gaža tulis,
ovni ve̮li same̮j lad.
pomaśisni šonid, gaža lunjas,
janseďćini vois kad.
en mene koľ, men jona šog,
oz śur men teteg olan-nog.
en mene koľ, men jona šog,
oz śur men teteg olan-nog.
kodli te̮lin ovni doli̮d,
musa si̮li aslas lad,
meni̮m teteg ovni jona śe̮kid,
musa ǯoriǯ, musa ni̮v.
en jona be̮rd [2x], śi̮v śi̮lan-ki̮v [2x]
en jona šogśi, musa ni̮v!
en jona be̮rd [2x], śi̮v śi̮lan-ki̮v [2x]
en jona šogśi, musa ni̮v!
ne̮šta med-be̮rjaiś okišt,
okišt, okišt menśim vom,

Sometimes I listen:
A singing voice is heard.
Someone is calling me in my dreams:
Wake up, you lovely girl!
Someone is calling me in my dreams:
Wake up, you lovely girl!

Why, mother, have I got
Such a sorrow?
From this sorrow, from this sickness
Why can I not be cured some day?
From this sorrow, from this sickness
Why can I not be cured some day?

This sickness, child,
Will not pass soon,
Your heart has woken,
Your blood has boiled,
Your heart has woken,
Your blood has boiled.

164.

It was a beautiful warm spring,
That was the real life.
The warm, beautiful days came to an end,
The time to part came.
Do not leave me, I am very sad,
I shall have no life without you.
Do not leave me, I am very sad,
I shall have no life without you.
He who leads a merry life in winter
Likes his own ways.
For me it is very hard to live without you,
Dear flower, dear girl.
Do not weep bitterly, do not weep bitterly, sing a song, sing a song,
Do not grieve bitterly, dear girl!
Do not weep bitterly, do not weep bitterly, sing a song, sing a song,
Do not grieve bitterly, dear girl!
Once more, for the last time kiss me,
Kiss, kiss my lips,

topidʒika mores berdad toped,
okaśemli vois pom.
taje bur lun [2x] oz ńe-kor vun [2x],
oz ńe-kor vun ta-lunja lun.
taje bur lun [2x] oz ńe-kor vun [2x],
oz ńe-kor vun ta-lunja lun.

165.

kor mi aʒʒiślam teke̯d,
menam kusli̯te̯m koʒuv,
seki jugdi̯vle̯ jen-ež,
vi̯ľ-nog ve̯ćći̯vle̯ sad.
kor mi aʒʒislam teke̯d,
menam ʒirdalan koʒuv,
pe̯śa ťipke̯ sek śe̯le̯m
i mićme̯ tan kad.
zarńie̯n e̯zje̯ ki̯ale̯n re̯m,
ri̯ti̯s zev šoni̯d da le̯ń.
śe̯le̯me̯j menam viććiśe tene̯
sećće̯, ke̯n še̯pke̯ vež ľe̯m.
paśki̯d e ž - v a ju dori̯n
mijan ge̯rʒaśis mus-lun;
doli̯d uʒ vi̯li̯n se̯vmis,
ki̯ʒi viʒ-vi̯v ćveto·k.
sije̯ mijane̯s kore̯
aśse̯ se̯ste̯ma viʒni̯,
medi̯m more̯se̯ ńe-kor
ez pi̯ravli̯ šog.
zarńie̯n e̯zje̯ . . .
jugi̯d mus-lun em rad-lun:
lepte̯ mijanli̯ś se̯le̯m,
i pi̯r nue̯de̯ voʒe̯
ve̯ćni̯ mićae̯n nem,
medi̯m ʒorʒalis sije
ki̯ʒi mijane̯ʒ ez na,
i ki̯ʒ tuvsovja ʒoriʒ
pi̯r ʒorʒalan te.
zarńie̯n e̯zje̯ . . .

Press me more closely to your bosom,
Kissing has come to an end.
This lovely day, this lovely day will never be forgotten, never be forgotten,
This day will never be forgotten.
This lovely day, this lovely day will never be forgotten, never be forgotten,
This day will never be forgotten.

165.

When we meet,
My never-fading star,
The vault of the sky is bright,
And the garden is beautified in a new way.
When we meet,
My glittering star,
My heart beats with fire,
And time is beautified here.
The heart of dawn glows like gold,
The evening is very warm and calm,
My heart is waiting for you to come
Where green wild service tree is rustling.
On the banks of the wide Vyčegda
Our love began to be woven.
It grew as we worked happily,
Like the flower of the meadow.
It asks us
To keep ourselves chaste,
So that our bosom should
Never be filled with sorrow.
The heart of dawn glows like gold . . .
Bright love is happiness:
It raises our hearts
And carries us ever forward
To make our life beautiful,
To make it flourish
As never before us.
And like a spring flower
You are flourishing.
The heart of dawn glows like gold . . .

166.

me̮dla-pe̮li̮n gude̮k ki̮le̮,
ľivkńitlas da lańtlas suč;
a me ki̮vza kere̮s ji̮lin,
oz-e̮ mijane̮ ńin vuǯ,
oz-e̮ mijane̮ ńin vuǯ?
kodi bara seni vorse̮,
e̮tnas paľe̮de̮ bur un?
mi̮j sen bereg dorśis korśe̮,
mi̮jla ve̮le̮śte̮ oz mun,
mi̮jla ve̮le̮śte̮ oz mun?

167.

śe̮d ki̮r-ke̮či̮n i̮ǯi̮d pośoľok,
sen ole̮ rud śinjasa ni̮v.
daś si̮ ve̮sna śetni̮ stav ole̮m,
me si̮ di̮rji gažte̮m og ki̮v.
si̮ke̮d men
lomźe̮ šondie̮n mu,
e̮zjis ǯoriǯa šud.
kor zapańe uǯavni̮ petas,
le̮ń e ž - v a li̮n śile̮ stav erd.
i radle̮ stav i̮vla-vi̮v petas,
i kokńia purjaśe ker.
si̮ked men . . .
a ńumjovtas-soti̮štas, śe̮le̮m,
on aǯǯi̮ te mićaǯi̮k ćve̮t
i e̮vti̮šte̮ ńebi̮d lun te̮le̮n,
le̮z e ž - v a berd i̮vlai̮s ted.
si̮ke̮d men . . .
śe̮d ki̮r-ke̮či̮n i̮ǯi̮d posoľok,
sen ole̮ rud śi̮njasa ni̮v.
daś si̮ ve̮sna śetni̮ stav ole̮m,
me si̮ di̮rji gažte̮m og ki̮v.
si̮ke̮d men . . .

168.

jugi̮d koǯuv, petav, petav,
eziś koǯuv petav!

166.

From the far bank an accordion is heard,
Someone is playing songs and falls silent for a moment;
I listen on the hill-top,
Will he not come over to see us,
Will he not come over to see us?
Who, then, is playing there,
Alone awaking good dreams?
What has he to do on the bank there,
Why does he not go to the village,
Why does he not go to the village?

167.

On the dark, steep bank, there is a large settlement,
Over there lives a grey-eyed girl.
I am ready to give my life for her,
By her side I know no sadness.
With her, for me
Like the sun, the earth blazes up,
Flowers of happiness blaze up.
When she goes to work in the inlet,
The whole surface of the calm Vyčegda is singing.
And all nature is glad, unfolding,
And she puts the logs together easily to make a raft.
With her, for me . . .
She smiles, and my heart burns,
You cannot see a flower fairer than she.
And with a soft southerly wind
Nature around the blue Vyčegda fans you.
With her, for me . . .
On the dark, steep bank there is a large settlement,
Over there lives a grey-eyed girl.
I am ready to give my life for her,
By her side I know no sadness.
With her, for me . . .

168.

Bright star, come forth, come forth,
Silver star, come forth!

ǯirdav, pe̮rtmaś vi̮liśań,
ǯirdav ri̮tja ki̮a be̮ri̮n!

musa ni̮le̮j, petav, petav,
zarńi ni̮le̮j, petav!
gažed mene̮, śe̮le̮m-še̮r,
petav ri̮tja ki̮a be̮re̮!

petas eśke̮ jugi̮d koǯuv,
ǯirdale̮me̮n vorsas.
gudi̮r ki̮me̮r taj oz leǯ,
vevťe pemi̮d eže̮s ule̮.

petas eśke̮ musa ni̮le̮j
ki̮a be̮ri̮n me di̮ne̮.
mami̮s taj sijes oz leǯ,
viďće̮, ni̮vli̮ś veľa kute̮.

169.

bur baťke̮d-mamke̮d ole̮m
oz ńe-ke̮r menam vun,
me seki šog eg ki̮vli̮,
eg aǯǯi̮v gažte̮m-lun.
me seki šog eg ki̮vli̮,
eg aǯǯi̮v gažte̮m-lun.

kor guľajtni̮ me peta,
kor śi̮la śilan-ki̮v,
stav je̮zi̮s ve̮li šue̮ni̮,
zev šuda taje ni̮v.
stav je̮zi̮s ve̮li šue̮ni
zev šuda taje ni̮v.

me zbiľi̮ś šuda ve̮li
daj vošti aśśim šud,
me, końe̮r, taje̮ šudjase̮
eg krepi̮d kie̮n kut.
me, końe̮r, taje̮ šudjase̮
eg krepi̮d kie̮n kut.

ez viďći̮v-ske̮rmi̮v baťe̮j,
zev ve̮li sije šań,

Shine, sparkle from above,
Shine after evening twilight has come!

Dear girl, come out, come out,
Bonny girl, come out!
Cheer up my heart, my darling,
Come out after evening twilight has come!

The bright star would come forth,
It would play, glittering bright,
Gloomy clouds do not let it out,
They hide it under a dark coverlet.

The dear girl would come
To me after evening twilight.
Her mother will not let her out,
She chains the girl's freedom.

169.

My life with my kind parents
Will never be forgotten.
Then I heard of no sorrow,
I saw no sadness.
Then I heard of no sorrow,
I saw no sadness.

When I go out walking,
When I sing a song,
All the people say,
This girl is very happy.
All the people say,
This girl is very happy.

And really I was happy,
But I lost my happiness.
I, poor soul, could not cling to this happiness
With a firm hand.
I, poor soul, could not cling to this happiness
With a firm hand.

Father did not chide me, he was not angry with me,
Mother was very kind to me,

pi̯r oškis mene̯ mame̯j:
te mijan roć akań.
pi̯r oškis mene̯ mame̯j:
te mijan roć akań.

170.

je̯ǯi̯d tugje̯n paśke̯de̯
ľe̯m-pu asśi̯s si̯v.
ezi̯ś ri̯te̯ guľajtni̯
petis mića ni̯v.
jen-ež-koď le̯z śinjasa,
strojne̯j, meli, zboj;
gude̯kaśiś si̯ vi̯le̯
viǯe̯de̯ kuź voj.

ni̯vle̯n i̯ǯi̯d slavai̯s
kičovte̯ stav mu.
te̯vnas murtsa e̯tnase̯n
kerje̯n ez ti̯rt ju.
jen-ež-koď . . .
i kolko·zne̯j uǯ vi̯li̯n
abu ni̯v, a bi.
ľube̯j uǯe̯ śibale̯
si̯le̯n varov ki.
jen-ež-koď . . .

kruge̯ petas je̯kti̯ni̯,
siǯ oz je̯kti̯ me̯d.
donse̯ taje̯ ni̯vkali̯
ńe-kod oz i te̯d.
jen-ež-koď . . .

171.

leǯale̯j ǯe̯ tom je̯z ve̯vte̯,
i̯rke̯di̯šte̯j, juktale̯j!
a me peta gaža sadje̯,
sadji̯n struba kodji̯ni̯.
a me peta gaža sadje̯,
sadji̯n struba kodji̯ni̯.

She always praised me:
Your are our beauty (our Russian doll).
She always praised me:
Your are our beauty (our Russian doll).

170.

With white tassels
The wild-service decorates its lap.
On a silvery night
The girl went out walking.
    She has sky-blue eyes,
    She is slender, tender and courageous;
    The accordion-player
    Looks at her throughout the long nigh⁺.

The girl's fame has spread wide,
It encircles the whole earth.
In winter, almost by herself
She fills the river with logs.
    She has sky-blue eyes . . .
When working in the kolkhoz
She is no girl but fire.
Whatever work she takes up,
She has a skilful hand.
    She has sky-blue eyes . . .

She goes out to dance in the circle,
Nobody else can dance like her.
The value of this girl
Nobody knows.
    She has sky-blue eyes . . .

171.

Young men, let out the horse,
Give it air, give it to drink!
While I go to a beautiful garden
To dig a well in the garden.
While I go to a beautiful garden
To dig a well in the garden.

kodja, kodja me va-struba
daj višńe·ve̯j sad-je̯ri̯n.
oz taj ne̯ pet mi̯ća ni̯li̯s
truba dore̯ va boštni̯.
oz taj ne̯ pet mi̯ća ni̯li̯s
truba dore̯ va boštni̯.

petis, petis mića ni̯li̯s
struba dore̯ van boštni̯,
a be̯ršańi̯s tom moloďeć
vajis ve̯vse̯ juktavni̯.
a be̯ršańi̯s tom moloďeć
vajis ve̯vse̯ juktavni̯.

koris, koris ni̯vli̯ś vedra,
ni̯li̯s vedrase̯ ez śet.
śetis, śetis zoni̯s ćuń-ki̯č,
ni̯li̯s ćuń-ki̯čse̯ ez bośt.
śetis, śetis zoni̯s ćuń-ki̯č,
ni̯li̯s ćuń-ki̯čse̯ ez bośt.

te̯da, te̯da, mi̯jla, ni̯le̯j,
mi̯j me tene̯ de̯zme̯di,
te̯-ri̯t ri̯tnas voj-puk be̯ri̯n
me̯d ni̯le̯s me koľľe̯di.
te̯-ri̯t ri̯tnas voj-puk be̯ri̯n
me̯d ni̯le̯s me koľľe̯di.

sije̯ tušanas ńe-i̯ǯi̯d,
i ar-li̯dnas zev na tom,
rud ke̯sai̯s kos śe̯re̯ǯi̯s,
ke̯saas ľentai̯s ge̯lubej.
rud ke̯sai̯s kos śe̯re̯ǯi̯s,
ke̯saas ľentai̯s ge̯lube̯j.

(c) Laments

172.

menam ve̯li śe̯d-i še̯k-i ľentoćka,
voši sija śe̯d-i ve̯r še̯re.
menam ve̯li le̯z-i še̯k-i ľentoćka,
voši sija će̯d-i-ja jage.

I am digging, digging the well
In the morello-cherry garden.
Will the beautiful girl come out, I wonder,
To draw water from the well?
Will the beautiful girl come out, I wonder,
To draw water from the well?

The beautiful girl came out, came out
To draw water from the well.
After her a young man
Brought his horse to water.
After her, a young man
Brought his horse to water.

He asked, for the girl's pail,
The girl did not give him the pail.
The young man offered, offered her a ring,
The girl did not accept the ring.
The young man offered, offered her a ring,
The girl did not accept the ring.

I know, I know why not, little girl,
It is because I have hurt you.
Last night, leaving the spinnery,
I saw home another girl.
Last night, leaving the spinnery,
I saw home another girl.

As to her figure, she is short,
As to her age, she is very young,
Her blond plait reaches down to her waist,
She has a blue ribbon in her hair.
Her blond plait reaches down to her waist,
She has a blue ribbon in her hair.

172.

I used to have a ribbon of black silk,
It was lost in the middle of the dark forest.
I used to have a ribbon of blue silk,
It was lost in the black bilberry forest.

menam ve̯li ge̯rd-i še̯k-i ľentoćka,
voši sija oz-i-ja ti̯la.
menam ve̯li ježid še̯k-i ľentoćka,
voši sija jala jage.
menam ve̯li alej še̯k-i ľento̯ćka,
voši sija-j e̯miǯa kuste.
menam ve̯li viž-i še̯k-i ľentoćka,
voši sija ni̯r-poma ńure.
menam ve̯li ge̯lubej-i še̯k-i ľentoćka,
voši sija će̯d-laća kuste.
menam ve̯li vež-i še̯k-i ľentoćka,
voši sija vež turin pije.
menam ve̯li ze̯leta pijej,
voši sija-j armijaje.

173.

i ri̯t-i-ja pe voje matuška,
mene da re̯ďitin,
da voj-i-še̯r-i kade, matuška,
karab ij eštedin.
da jug-i-dan-i-dore, matuška,
mene da me̯dedin.
i pre̯š-i-šaj pe pre̯ššaj, ďiťotka,
rad-i pe me pre̯šajćća.
ćer-i-ńeć-i pe-j oz-i če̯kti da
karab ij oz-i sūtili.
da ki̯nta pe ki̯nta da, matuška,
voj-i-še̯r-i morozen,
i si̯da pe si̯da, matuška,
as-i-ja da šondien,
i koś-i-ta da koś-i-ta da, matuška,
lun-i-še̯r-i šondien,
da kerišta, kerišta matuška-j
as-i-lam sab-i-ľajen,
da be̯rd-i-ǯa pe be̯rd-i-ǯa da, matuškaj,
as-i-lam śin-vajen,
i ke̯kišta, ke̯kišta, matuška,
poz-i-tem-i ke̯k-i moz,
i puk-i-śa pe puk-i-śa da, matuška,

I used to have a ribbon of red silk,
It was lost in the strawberry-clearing.
I used to have a ribbon of white silk,
It was lost in the pine-forest full of reindeer-moss.
I used to have a ribbon of purple silk,
It was lost in the raspberry bush.
I used to have a ribbon of yellow silk,
It was lost in the marsh full of brambles.
I used to have a ribbon of blue silk,
It was lost in the dewberry-bush.
I used to have a ribbon of green silk,
It was lost in the green grass.
I used to have a son of gold,
He was lost in the war.

173.

My dear mother, early in the night
You gave me birth,
And at midnight, mother dear,
You prepared the ship.
At daybreak, mother dear,
You sent me away.
Good-bye, good-bye, my child,
I take leave gladly.
The bridegroom does not give orders
And he does not set up a ship.
I shall freeze, freeze myself, mother dear,
With the midnight frost,
I shall melt, melt myself, mother dear,
With the morning sun,
And I shall dry, dry myself, mother dear,
Wit the noonday sun,
And I shall cut, off my head, mother dear,
With my own sword,
And I shall weep, weep, mother dear,
Pouring out my tears,
And I shall cuckoo, cuckoo, mother dear,
Like a cuckoo that has no nest,
And I shall sit, sit, mother dear,

še̮r e̮šiń vi̮le̮,
i be̮rd-i-ʒ́a pe be̮rd-i-ʒ́a da, matuška,
as-i-lam śin-vajen.
ve̮ľiś pe ve̮ľiś-i, matuška,
tom-i voj-i-tir gažmim.

174.

i jugid šondiej da menam
i śvetnej śveťitemej.
i v a n-lun di̮rśa ved ve̮li
kupaľńića-śvetej,
i ve̮źńeśeńńe di̮rśa ved ve̮li
je̮n-ʒoriʒ́ śvetej.
jugid šondiej da menam
śvetnej śveťitemej.
prokopej di̮rśa ved ve̮li
ľežneg-ʒ́oriʒ́ śvetej.
i i ľ ľ a-lun di̮rśa ved ve̮li
vež turin-i śvetej.
jugid šondiej da menam
śvetnej śveťitemej,
koľi ved koľi menam
stavis-i koľi.
i trojća di̮rśa ved menam ve̮li
i koreś-i kor-i śvetej.
jugid šondiej da menam
śvetnej śveťitemej.
i e̮ni ved me, końerej, koľi
i arśa turin-i kojd.

175.

[ni̮ pukśas be̮rdni. ni̮ pukśas jurles
vi̮le da pondas be̮rdni.]

i spas-i daj-i prićistaja
i jenśań pe ved menim burśiin.
eta lunja da lunis kuźa,
i burśi že daj blagos-i-levit
eta lunja lunis kuźa!

In the middle window,
And I shall weep, weep, mother dear,
Pouring out my tears,
Not long ago, not long ago, mother dear,
We young folk were making merry.

174.

My bright day,
My flowery blossoming.
On midsummer-day
I had a buttercup flower,
On Ascension-Day
I had a sowthistle.
My bright day,
My flowery blossoming.
On Procopius' day
I had a wild-rose.
On Elijah's day
I had a green grass-flower.
My bright day,
My flowery blossoming.
It has gone, it has gone,
It has gone for good.
And on Holy Trinity day
I had a broom-leaf flower.
My bright day,
My flowery blossoming.
Now, I, poor soul, have been left
Like the autumn grass.

175.

(The girl sits down to weep.
The girl sits on a cushion and begins to weep.)

Reedemer and Holy Virgin,
From Heaven you have blessed me.
For this day
Bless me,
For this day!

i jenśań pe ved menim burśi
i jen koʒulis mi̯da-j,
i vaśań pe ved menim burśi
va ćeriis mi̯da-j,
i muśań pe ved menim burśi
vež turinis mi̯da-j.
i burśi že daj menim końerejli
i blagos-i-levit!
i taśań pe ved menim burśi
i petan-i e̯ʒes,
i setći pe ved menim burśi
i pi̯ran-i e̯ʒes!
i burśi že daj menim końerejli
i blagos-i-levit!

176.

i jugid šondiej da menam
i nī̯ veľaej da
i nī̯ veľaej pe da menam
i i̯ʒid-i ve̯ľaj
i koľi ved koľi menam
i końerejlen.
i jugid šondiej da menam
i vetlem-munemej.
i tuj kuźa ved me-jej vetli
i tujse da śeredlig-ti̯rja,
i tuj kuźa ved me vetli̯
i tujse da moľedig-ti̯rja.
i ćuń-pom pe ved me-jej vetli
i čulki daj čol-i-ki,
i śinmen pe ved me-jej vetli
i migajććig-ti̯r-i-ja-j.
jugid šondiej da menam
i vetlem-munemej.

177.

[nī̯ pondas be̯rdni]

i vetla me že vetla me
i ze̯letajasej daj pe̯d-i-rugajasej,

From Heaven send blessings on me,
As many times as there are stars in the sky,
From the water send blessings on me
As many times as there are fish in the water,
From the earth send blessing on me
As many times as there are blades of green grass.
Bless me, poor as I am,
Bless me!
Bless here
The door through which I go out,
Bless there
The door through which I go in!
Bless me, poor as I am,
Bless me!

176.

My bright day,
My maiden's freedom,
My own maiden's freedom,
My great freedom
Has been taken away from me,
Poor soul.
My bright day,
My coming and going.
I walked along the road,
Leaving tracks on the road,
I walked along the road,
Treading smooth the road.
I walked on tiptoe:
Tip-tap, tip-tap.
I walked with my eyes
Winking.
My bright sun,
My coming and going.

177.

(The girl begins to weep.)

I am going away, I am going away,
My dear girl-friends,

i nule že, nule mene
i med-i-be̯rjaśis!
i ze̯letajasej da menam
i bur-i zonjasej,
nule že mene gora daj gudeknanid!
i vetlame že vet-i-lame
i mića daj ar-i-ťeľnanim,
tujse moľedlig-i-ti̯rja da
i śe̯redlig-i-ti̯r-i-ja.

[śa že̯ńike vovasni.]

i ćećći že pe mi̯ś-i-śi!

[mužikes pondasni ćuksōni, žergini, kľongini.]

ćećći že mi̯śśi!
ńe-pe̯ra uźni,
pe̯ra ćeććini.
on-ke ved ćećći,
girjam da garjam,
girjam da garjam.
ri̯niš-tup-i-jed jurej,
ćećći že, mi̯śśi,
ćećći že, mi̯śśi!
re̯veśńik-puej,
ćećći že, mi̯śśi!

[da seśśa pondasni petni, śojasni, juasni da.]

paśibe da pomeśibe,
śojim da juvim,
śojim da juvim
roć tagja surse
roć tagja surse,
i̯b-vī̯ da ruǯeg-ńańse,
keres-še̯r pirogse.
paśibe da pomeśibe.

178.

[be̯rdni pondas nī̯, asi-voǯnas pukśas da.]

i vešti že te, veš-i-ti mene.
i baťuš-i-koej!
i gidńa-še̯r med ľubej vē̯nad
i vešti te, vešti!

Take me, take me,
For the last time!
And you, dear,
Kind lads,
Accompany me with your loud accordion.
Let us go, let us go
With our fine group,
Treading the way smooth
And leaving tracks behind.
(At this point they arrive at the bridegroom's.)
Get up and wash yourself!
(They begin to call the lad with much noise and ringing.)
Get up and wash yourself!
There is no time to sleep.
It is time to get up.
If you will not get up,
We shall tickle you and scratch you,
We shall tickle you and scratch you.
You have a head like the straw-plug in a barn window,
Get up and wash yourself,
Get up and wash yourself!
You would-be bridegroom,
Get up and wash yourself!
(Then they begin to go out to eat and drink.)
Thanks and gratitude,
We have eaten and drunk,
We have eaten and drunk,
Beer brewed from Russian hops,
Beer brewed from Russian hops,
Bread baked from oats grown on the heights.
Pirogi made of flour from the hills.
Thanks and gratitude.

178.

(The girl begins to weep, sitting down early in the morning.)

Redeem me, redeem me,
Father dear!
With the favourite horse from your stable
Redeem me, redeem me!

[taja asi-voʒnas be̯rdeni, nī̯ bośtni loktasni da.]
i vešti že, vešti ke̯rmića
i matuš-i-kaj-i daj
i karta-še̯r daj ľubej me̯snad!
vešti že, veš-i-ti,
i ke̯rmićaj da menam
mamej, matuš-i-kaj!
i śo sī̯ja pe ved menam ve̯li
še̯k-i povodej,
i vit-śo sī̯ja ved menam ve̯li
i še̯k-i povodej.
i śo sī̯ja ved menam pondis
menam i uś-i-ni.
i jugid šondiej da menam
še̯k-i povodej,
[taje jur si̯naleni nī̯li seki.]
i vetimin sī̯ja ved menam
i uś-i-ni pon-i-dis.
jugid šondiej da menam
še̯k-i povodej,
ki̯ź-vit sī̯ja ved menam
i menam ij uśi daj.
i ke̯rmiľićaj da menam
i matuš-i-kaej
i raka-pozje ved menam
i menam ij uśi.
i ke̯rmiľićaj daj menam
i matuš-i-kaej,
mi̯j ne te ta-lun pać-i-te lomtin daj
pes-i-te śujin?
i menam ed sija ve̯li-j
li̯ej da śe̯mej.
i mi̯j te̯len ne, ke̯rmića matuškaej
či̯n-i-te leʒin?
i sija ved menam ve̯li
jugid vir-jajej.
i lun-te̯len-ke ved ke̯rmića matuškaj
leʒin men-i-śim daj
i sija ved voj-more menam,

(This is recited in the early morning, in a mournful tone, when the bridegroom's relatives are come to carry away the bride.)

Redeem me, redeem me, you who nursed me,
Mother dear,
With the favourite cow from your shed!
Redeem me, redeem me,
You who nursed me,
Mother, mother dear!
A hundred fathoms long
Was my silken hair,
Five hundred fathoms long
Was my silken hair.
And what was a hundred fathoms long, look, has begun
To fall.
My bright sun,
My silken hair,

(At this point they comb the bride's hair.)

And what was fifty fathoms long, look,
Has begun to fall.
My bright sun,
My silken hair,
What was twenty-five fathoms long, look,
Has fallen.
You who nursed and raised me,
Mother dear,
My crow's nest, look,
Has fallen.
You who nursed and raised me,
Mother dear,
Why have you lit your stove today,
And why have you filled it with firewood?
Why, it was,
My bones and my skin.
Mother dear who raised me, with what wind
Will you let out the smoke?
Why, it was
My light body.
Mother dear who raised me, with the southerly wind
You have let out my body,
And it has fallen into the northern sea.

menam ij uśi.
i voj-te̯len-ke ved matuškaj leʒin,
lun-more ij uśi.
sija ved ke̯rmiľićaj matuška,
menam ve̯li jugid virej-jajej.

(d) Rhymes

179.

požem jagin le̯śid ōni,
kor te̯la da nom abu.
kor mene milej ľubite,
sek men dolid ij ōnise.

ti̯rmas, miloj, ti̯rmas, miloj,
ti̯rmas vinate juni.
ti̯rmas, miloj, ti̯rmas, miloj,
ti̯rmas i̯ledlinite.

oz kō menim ki̯k miloj da
ke̯ť ij e̯ťik ge̯tirtem.
oz kō menim ki̯k ćuń-ki̯č,
ke̯ť ij e̯ťik ze̯letej.

og mun, og mun veres saje,
ke̯ni viten da kvajten;
lučče muna veres saje
ke̯ni lova da ke̯źajka.

Mother dear who raised me, with the northerly wind
You have let it out,
It has fallen into the southern sea.
It was, mother dear who nursed me,
My light body.

179.

It is pleasant to live in the woods of forest-pines,
When the wind blows and there are no gnats.
When my lover loves me,
Then life is gay.

Enough, dear, enough, dear,
Enough of your drinking vodka.
Enough, dear, enough, dear,
Enough of your cheating me.

I do not want two lovers,
Only one who is single.
I do not want two rings,
Only one made of gold.

I will not marry, I will not marry a man
In whose house five or six people live.
I would rather marry a man
In whose house I shall be mistress.

VI. THE IŽMA (LOWER OB) DIALECT

The next four narratives and tales, I took down from Jurij Gerasimovič Ročev, scientific researcher and his younger brother, Valerij Gerasimovič Ročev. Both of them were born in the village of Мужи (Zyr. *mi̯ži*) on the lower reaches of the Ob (Tjumen region, Šuryškar district). Apart from Zyrians, this village is inhabited by Ostyaks and Russians. In 1964 J. G. Ročev was 28, V. G. Ročev 21 years of age.

The limited amount of material does not permit an analysis of the characteristic features of this dialect (for more abundant data, see Vászolyi: NyK 67:24—7). I merely note that J. G. Ročev, following the norms of literary usage, substituted *ǯ* for I *d́* (∼V, SR, etc. *ǯ*), while his brother pronounced I *d́*. According to Erik Vászolyi (loc. cit. 25), in 1959 J. G. Ročev's pronunciation was characterized by *d́*. This apparent contradiction has a simple explanation in the fact that in the meantime our informant had acquired the use of *ǯ* from the literary idiom of Syktyvkar. In other respects he had preserved the typical features of his dialect area, and I can state this not only on the evidence of the two tales he told me, but also from the style of speech he used in the course of friendly conversations we had together.

(a) Tales and narratives

180. e̮ťik li̮kjedli̮ś starik pomlaś

1. *taje mojdse men viśtōlis e̮ťi starik, z e̮ ś i m f i l. og te̮d, bi̮gjalis sija, iľi zabi̮ľ ve̮li stavis, no aći̮s viśtalis, mi̮j stavi̮s si̮ked vē̮lema kor-ke.*

e̮t-pi̮r kor-ke me ve̮li i̮čki̮śa. ri̮t ńin re̮mde, a me — bi̮d oho·tńiklen ved piśaľi̮s pi̮r ordas — me pi̮r viʒedla da viʒedla ńebesa vi̮las, oz-em utkajas lebźi̮ni̮s mati ge̮ger. a kor pemdas, sek pi̮r naja uleʒi̮k leććeni̮s. bergećći, a mať si̮li̮ kantuk, ʒe̮m me vi̮lam lebe. no me e̮djeʒi̮k kosaes ćē̮ti, ćapki piśaľes, buh-gri̮m varti, daže ig imećći. lebi utkai̮s, iz i uś, a i̮ʒi̮d zej ve̮li, gaške ʒoľa kukań-koď. no iz śur, iz śur, me bara i̮čki̮śni̮ vošji. seśśa pi̮r-pi̮r kor pemdis, će̮tśi i̮čki̮śemśi̮s. a kerkaam ve̮li bi pestiśe. va-tor ve̮li me̮da puźedi̮štni̮. čan-koď i ve̮li ćuguni̮s. vase ki̮ski, voji da viʒeda: vi̮j plavajte. no mi̮j sečemi̮s? merajti: ki̮k ćuń soda. isi̮šti: utka-ši̮d. a sije ve̮lema, utkase kor me li̮ji, si̮li̮ śurema ki̮ćće-ge da pi̮m vī̮śańi̮s lebema ećińʒik i uśema samej pać-trubaas i uśema vaas. bura di̮r i śoji će̮ski̮d ši̮dse. vot ed kuʒ ōle.

2. *me̮di̮ś, kor-ke tuli̮si̮n dor-va petema ńin ve̮li, munim ki̮ken jortked važ k i j e v a t sojime. no i li̮jśam sen. utka una si̮-si̮ vi̮le ij ľake. a ji ve̮rźis, munni̮ oz poź. stavse ti̮rtis dor-vase, ki̮k vežō-lun ćež li̮jśim. ośenćik ve̮li kujle mu vi̮las. sećće mi karim sklad i zej una utkase tećim. kor-ke asi̮le paľalim, viʒedam, a jii̮s ńin stavi̮s munema. mijan ośenćiknum bara-že ki̮ćće-ge ki̮lalema. puk-śim pi̮že, ve̮teććam, m i̮ ž i bereg dore kućim mati̮śśi̮ni̮. a seten beregas narodi̮s vojlaleni̮s vedrajasen, ušatjasen be̮re-voʒe. mi̮j taja sečemi̮s, mi̮j? a sija ve̮-lema ośinćiki̮s mijan si̮lema, utkai̮s stavi̮s vaas lōma, te̮li̮s beregas ľićkema sije. seśśa stavi̮s vot i e̮kteni̮s utkase, kaźalemaś da. ʒoń tē̮ mijanćunumi̮ś utkase śojisni̮s.*

3. *ćeri ki̮jni̮ vetli mašeńolnam. muna protohaed, a ćerii̮s śerśis vejśen pete. vaj pukta taćće kulem. kulem pukti, aćum muni me̮dlae. śa kor-ke kulemjas viźlōni̮ muni; voji protohaas puktem kulem doras, a sen zej i̮ʒi̮d śir. čukema kulem śinjasas da be̮re ńi vode oz vermi̮, i̮ʒi̮d da, a protohai̮s kos ńin, a śiri̮s*

180. About a lying old man

1. This was related to me by an old man called *Zęśim Fil.* I do not know if he was telling tales or the whole thing was the truth, but he himself said that it all happened to him once upon a time.

Once upon a time I was mowing. It was growing dark, but I — for every hunter always has his gun at hand — I keep looking up the sky all the time to see if there are any ducks flying nearby. When it grows dark, they always fly lower. I turned round, and damn it! There's one flying just above me. At once I flung away the scythe, seized the gun and, crack, fired it without aiming. The duck flew away; it did not fall down, it was very big, perhaps the size of a little calf. So I failed to bring it down, I failed to bring it down; I began to mow again. Later on, when it was quite dark, I stopped mowing. The fire began to burn in my house. I wanted to boil water. The pot was the size of a tub. I fetched water, and came back; and I see that fat is floating on the surface. What on earth is this? I measured it: it was two fingers thick. I smelt it: it was duck soup. It was the same duck I had fired at, I must have hit it somewhere, although it flew off somewhat hurriedly. It had fallen right down the chimney and into the water. For a long time I was eating the tasty duck soup. You see, curious things happen.

2. On another occasion, when the banks had already been flooded, I and my companion, the two of us, walked out to the old spruce-woods at Kijevat. We went hunting there. There are many ducks there, one sticks to another. The ice began to form, it was impossible to proceed. The waters on the bank were completely covered, we hunted for two weeks. The ground was covered with ice. We made a storage-place there and piled up lots of ducks. When we awoke in the morning we noticed that the ice had already gone completely. Our ice had floated away somewhere. We got into a boat and followed it, and we began to draw near to the bank at Mi̭ži. People were running to and fro on the bank there carrying buckets and pails of wood. What on earth is this? Well, our ice had melted, all the ducks had got into the water, and the wind had driven them to the shore. Then they gathered all the ducks together, when they noticed them. Throughout the whole winter they were feeding on our ducks.

3. I went to fish with an Ostyak boat. I make my way along a side-stream, and fish come along in swarms. I cast the net here. I cast the net, while I myself went in another direction. Later on I returned to take a look at the net. I arrived at the net I had set in the side-stream, well, there was a huge pike there. It had become entangled in the mesh of the net and could not struggle either forward or backward, so huge it was, the side-

mašeńolśis i̮ǯidǯik. ńi-nem og vermi̮ si̮ked karni̮. e̮ďďen taj vetli kerkae da bośti seti̮ś kolhozli̮ś ńeodńik. ńeodńiknas e̮dva vajim. či̮čjase kerōlim da. śa bara tē-bi̮d śir-jaj śojim.

181. *be̮ža-ku parka*

olis-vi̮lis b e̮ ž a - k u p a r k a. sija ottore nōlis b e̮ ž a - k u p a r k a i sijen si̮li̮ ńimse puktisni̮s b e̮ ž a - k u p a r k a. b e̮ ž a - k u p a r k a ve̮li pastuh. si̮len aslas ke̮rjas iz vēnis i sija re̮bitis ozi̮r ke̮r viǯiś dori̮n, j e ǯ i̮ d k u p a r k a dori̮n. kor-ke nija ve̮rźisni̮s, b e̮ ž a - k u p a r k aes i̮stisni̮s je̮raśni̮. je̮raśis, kutalis bi̮kjases, seśśa sija dađūaśis, śetis dađūjasse he̮źa·jini̮sli̮, raźis ćomjasse, tećis utića vi̮le stav ľesse i nija munisni voǯe. a b e̮ ž a - k u p a r k a daže iz ešti̮ asli̮s domaśni̮, si̮li̮ bara loi kutōni̮ ke̮rjas. no kutalis bara, dađūaśis asli̮s ńin i kućis ve̮tli̮ni̮ ke̮rjasse vi̮ľ mestae. no ki̮ćće munisni̮s j e ǯ i̮ d k u p a r k a da si̮len babai̮s? j e ǯ i̮ d k u p a r k alen ve̮li das ti̮śeća ke̮r. stavse sije kole ve̮li ve̮tli̮ni̮, a vošti̮ni̮ oz poź, hoźa·jin kućas pińaśni̮. no vot ve̮tle ke̮rjasse b e̮ ž a - k u p a r k a i ki̮le be̮rśańi̮s kučem-ke śi̮jas, kok-śi̮jas. be̮ras bergeććis:

be̮ras bergeććis,
be̮ras bergeććis,
ki̮k dađđa lokte,
ki̮k dađđa lokte.
e̮ťikis taj i̮rgen dađđa,
me̮di̮s taj že ńin eziś dađđa
i̮rgen dađđai̮s voďlas dortii̮s garōtis,
sa vi̮ti šagajtis.
b e̮ ž a - k u p a r k a,
b e̮ ž a - k u p a r k a.
e̮ťikes jualam,
e̮ťikes jualam,
ki̮num oz bergō,
ki̮num oz bergō.
eziś dađđai̮s voďlas dortii̮s garōtis,
sa vi̮ti šagajtis
b e̮ ž a - k u p a r k a,
b e̮ ž a - k u p a r k a.

stream was already dried up, and the pike was bigger than the Ostyak boat. I could not do anything with it. I went quickly to the house and took out the fishing boat belonging to the kolkhoz. Even with the fishing boat I was hardly able to carry it home. We cut it into pieces. Throughout the whole winter we were eating pike.

181. Ermine-coat

There lived once a man called Ermine-coat. He always wore an ermine-coat, therefore he was given the name Ermine-coat. Ermine-coat was a shepherd. He had no reindeer of his own, he worked with the rich reindeer-keeper called White-leather-coat. One day they set out; they sent Ermine-coat to catch some of the reindeer from the herd. He caught the bulls, then harnessed them, handed the sleighs over to his master, took down the tents, placed everything on the tent-carrying sleigh, and they started off. But Ermine-coat had no time to harness for himself, his duty was to tie the reindeer one after another. So he tied them together, then harnessed and started to drive the reindeer to the new place. But where did White-leather-coat and his wife go? White-leather-coat had ten thousand reindeer. He had to drive all of them, none of them might be lost, or the master would curse him. Ermine-coat drives the reindeer and hears some sound coming from behind, the sound of hooves. He turns back:

He turned back,
He turned back,
Two carriages are coming,
Two carriages are coming.
One of them is a carriage of copper,
The other is a carriage of silver.
In front of the carriage of copper he turned round,
There stepped over the traces
Ermine-coat,
Ermine-coat.
We question one of them,
We question one of them,
Our tongue does not move,
Our tongue does not move.
In front of the carriage of silver he turned round,
Here stepped over the traces
Ermine-coat,
Ermine-coat.

e̯ťikes jualam,
e̯ťikes jualam,
kı̯num oz bergō,
kı̯num oz bergō.
b e̯ ž a - k u p a r k a,
b e̯ ž a - k u p a r k a,
kod ne̯ tenad he̯źa·jini̯d,
kod ne̯ tenad he̯źa·jkai̯d?
me vi̯lam das ćom pi̯čkas
stavi̯s he̯źa·jin, stavi̯s he̯źajka.
b e̯ ž a - k u p a r k a,
b e̯ ž a - k u p a r k a.

seśśa i̯rgen daďďa vi̯las mortjasi̯s da eziś daďďa vi̯las vi̯śtaleni̯s b e̯ ž a - k u p a r k ali̯, mi̯j sija aći̯s oz te̯d, kod si̯ vi̯li̯n he̯źa·jini̯s, kod si̯len he̯źajkai̯s. i nija si̯li̯ viśtaleni̯s:

b e̯ ž a - k u p a r k a,
b e̯ ž a - k u p a r k a,
ted vi̯lad he̯źa·jini̯s
j e ʒ i̯ d k u p a r k a,
he̯źa·jkai̯s ved
j e ʒ i̯ d k u p a r k a ge̯ti̯r.

viśtalisni̯s i ki̯ćće-ge vošisni̯s. b e̯ ž a - k u p a r k a bara e̯tnas koľi ke̯rjasi̯sked. seśśa b e̯ ž a - k u p a r k a tojištis stav ke̯rjasse vi̯ľ mestae, loktis ćom dore i pukśis utića vi̯le šojććini̯. sek mime peti hoźa·jkai̯s, j e ʒ i̯ d k u p a r k a ge̯ti̯r i kućis pińaśni̯:

b e̯ ž a - k u p a r k a,
peste vajin-em,
ke̯rjaste da viʒlin-em?

no mi̯j seśśa karan? b e̯ ž a - k u p a r k ali̯ bara loi munni̯ re̯bitni̯. b e̯ ž a - k u p a r k a vase katlis, di pesse pi̯rtlis di ke̯rjasse viʒlis. seśśa bara loktis da utića vi̯le pukśis. i kı̯ʒi̯śe, a ńi-kučem zi̯k oz kı̯ ćomśi̯s. i. dumaćće b e̯ ž a - k u p a r k a, mi̯j ne̯ nali̯ lōma, ki̯ćće ne̯ naja lōmaś? seśśa b e̯ ž a - k u p a r k a ki̯k kepiśse voćća tarkńitas i lebźas, p i̯ n o - s t a r i k ćom dore voas. pukale bara utića vi̯li̯n p i̯ n o - s t a r i k ćom vo̯ʒi̯n. i. ćomśi̯s sečem i̯ʒid zi̯k ki̯le i bara dumaćće: 'mi̯j ne̯ sečemi̯s? mi̯j seten kareni̯s?' i ćomśi̯s peti p i n o - s t a r i k i viśtale b e̯ ž a - k u p a r k ali̯:

We question one of them,
We question one of them,
Our tongue does not move,
Our tongue does not move.
Ermine-coat,
Ermine-coat,
Who is your master,
Who is your mistress?
Above me in ten tents
Everyone is master, everyone is mistress.
Ermine-coat,
Ermine-coat.

At this people sitting in the carriage of copper and in the carriage of silver say to Ermine-coat that he himself does not know who his master is, who his mistress is. They say to him:

Ermine-coat,
Ermine-coat,
Your master is
White-leather-coat,
While your mistress is
White-leather-coat's wife.

They gave him this information and vanished somewhere. Again Ermine-coat was left alone with his reindeer. Then Ermine-coat drove all the reindeer to a new place, came to the tent and sat down to rest in the tent-carrying sleigh. Then his mistress passed by, White-leather-coat's wife, and began to curse him:

Ermine-coat,
Have you brought firewood,
Have you guarded the reindeer?

What could he do? Again Ermine-coat had to go to work. Ermine-coat fetched water and brought firewood and guarded the reindeer. Then he returned and sat in the tent-carrying sleigh. He listens, but no noise is to be heard from the tent. Ermine-coat tries to think out what has happened to them. Where had they gone? Then Ermine-coat strikes two gloves together and flies off; he arrives at the tent of old *Pi̮no*. Again he sits on the tent-carrying sleigh in front of old *Pi̮no*'s tent. Such a great noise is heard from the tent, and he thinks again: "What is this? What are they doing there?" Old *Pi̮no* comes out of the tent and says to Ermine-coat:

be̮ža-ku parka,
be̮ža-ku parka,
mi̮jla ne̮ on ćomjas pi̮r?
mi̮jla ne̮ on ćomjas pi̮r?
be̮ža-ku parka
pino-starikli̮ viśtale:
mi̮jla ne̮ me ćomjas pi̮ra?
mi̮jla ne̮ me ćomjas pi̮ra?
pi̮no-starik taj viśtale:
menam ćomji̮n,
menam ćomji̮n
una mort taj ćukarććis,
una mort taj ćukarććis
da ńe-kod taj menćum ńē̮-vuǯjes ve̮rźedni̮ oz vermi̮.
be̮ža-ku parka ćomjas taj pi̮ris di
ki̮k kusiń taj ńuki̮ľćis di
ńē̮se bośtis di
vuǯse bośtis di
mukota-ruźedis taj i̮skōtedis,
pījasśi̮s ūtiǯik,
pu-jī̮jasśi̮s vī̮tiǯi̮k taj lebi.

182.

ćeri ki̮jeni̮s kulemen. kulemi̮s ćistej, kośmema. kulemse sije ke̮rtalema, kulemnas mune pi̮ž dore. kor sija voas se̮r vi̮le, kulemse le̮śede siǯ, medum si̮li̮ bur ve̮li le̮dni̮ vaas. med voď ke̮rtale uli̮s śuresse kulem pu pomas, kodi̮s loe vai̮n. seśśa kulem-puse sija śurkńitas muas. med voď pui̮s dolžen pukōni̮ topta. seśśa sija ke̮rtale vi̮li̮s śuresse. e̮tik kinas tojlaśe bereg dorśi̮s, a me̮dnas leďe kulemse, medum ńe-kićći iz je̮rmi̮. pu-kolasti̮s dolžen vē̮śi̮ni̮ metra ńoľ, no i siď-že sije kulemse ńužede, poka sija oz ešti̮ me̮dike sija ńužedni̮ ki̮mi̮n-ke pom sija kuď i med vodďa puas ke̮rtale uli̮s śuresse. no i seśśa stavi̮s siď-že. muked-di̮rjas da i ćaste siǯ ōle: ćeri-ki̮jśiś na pukte kulemse, a me̮dar pomas ńin varte ćeri. kor ńin eštedas pukti̮ni̮ kulemse, sija kulem-gezjedi̮s ki̮ski̮śe ćeri doras. kor sija voas sećće, eča ki̮pedas kulemse e̮tik kinas, me̮dnas kute ćerise i šedede ćerise kulem-śinśi̮s. unǯiki̮s seten šede (se̮r vi̮li̮n): sin, si̮rok, pi̮žjan. si̮rokse li̮ďďeni̮s med se̮stem ćerien i sije śojeni̮s ńarhulen. sija, znaćit, kor svežij ki̮jema ćerise, kod na ve̮re, ćiśťiteni̮s śe̮mse, śe̮mjeni̮s. si̮ be̮ri̮n sije vundeni̮s plastjas vi̮le.

Ermine-coat,
Ermine-coat,
Why do you not enter the tent?
Why do you not enter the tent?
Ermine-coat
Says to old *Pino:*
Why should I enter the tent?
Why should I enter the tent?
Old *Pino* answers:
In my tent,
In my tent
Many people have gathered together,
Many people have gathered together,
And nobody is able to lift my bow.
Ermine-coat entered the tent and
Bending double, down to the ground
He took the arrow and
He took the bow and
Sent it out through the smoke-hole:
Below the clouds,
Higher than the tops of the trees it flew.

182. [About fishing]

Fishing is done with a fishing-net. The net is clean and dry. He ties the net up, takes the net to the boat. When he reaches the flood-land, he arranges the net in such a way that casting is easy. First the bottom-string is tied to the end of the pole that will stand in the water. Then the net-pole is thrown down upon the ground. The first pole has to be set firmly. Then he fastens the top string. He pushes himself off the bank with one hand, while lowering the net with the other so that it may not be caught up anywhere. The distance between the poles must be four metres; he stretches the net until he can fasten some of the ends of it to the other pole, in the same way that he fixed the bottom string to the first pole. Well then, the whole thing is done in this manner. Sometimes, indeed, rather often it happens that no sooner does the fisherman set the net than fish start leaping at the other end of it. As he casts the net, he pulls himself close to the fish by the rope of the net. When he gets there, he lifts the net a little, grasps the fish with the other hand and frees it from the mesh. The most frequently founded fish are white fish, *sirok* and *pižjan. Sirok* is considered the cleanest fish, and it is eaten raw. When they have caught a fresh fish,

ni̮i̮ś pete ńoľ plast: be̮kjasi̮s, mi̮ški̮s i pupkai̮s. sije śojeni̮s siď: e̮tik pomse plasti̮sli̮ś bośteni̮s vomani̮s i e̮tik kinas ńužedeni̮s, me̮d kias si̮len purt, koden sija mati̮n ľe̮b doras vunde či̮čse, ūśań vi̮le. koľem li̮jasse da jurse komijas ši̮bi-teni̮s a e̮sľakjas sije kośteni̮s bi vi̮li̮n, śūjasśi̮s nija ďoľa bi vi̮li̮n kareni̮s ćeri-vi̮j. ćeri-vi̮jse śojeni̮s ńańen, varkaen i sija mune pre̮sti̮j vi̮j meste. si̮rokse ne̮šta-na śojeni̮s malo solen. sije potkedeni̮s šagľa-dorśi̮s i ruźedi̮s kiškajasi̮s (iľi śūjasi̮s) muneni̮s ćeri-vi̮j karni̮, a ćerise aśse pukteni̮s sole. seten sija kujle ćas ki̮k-kujim. si̮ be̮ri̮n ńin sije poźe śojni̮.

183.

tuli̮snas, kor ńin vošjeni̮s vośśi̮ni̮ jujasi̮s, ke̮r-dorśa mortjas lokteni̮s m i̮ ž i e i bośteni̮s śojan stav gožemi̮s keže. si̮ be̮ri̮n ni̮a kaslajteni̮ ńežen more dore. sećće ni̮a muneni̮s si̮ śerti: gožemnas una nom i ke̮rjasi̮s oz vermi̮ni̮s bura śojni̮, a more be̮ki̮n ečaǯik nomji̮s. i naja seten bura oleni̮s, ťelajasi̮s tuli̮snas bura aś-ni̮sse ćustvujteni̮s. gožemnas ke̮r-dorśa narodlen sulaleni̮s kokńid ćomjas, kod-jas karemaś ve̮śnid pujasi̮ś i vi̮li̮stii̮s gartemeś śumeden. sečemeś gožśa ćomjasi̮s. kor ńin voas ari̮s, ni̮a kaslajteni̮ pi̮čkeǯik maťerikas. sije ni̮a kareni̮s si̮ śerti, medum ke̮rjasi̮sli̮ kokńidǯik ve̮li suďedni̮ aslanis śojanse, ńič. tēnas more be̮ki̮n zej ke̮ďi̮d i ottorńi voj-vī te̮li̮s dujte. a li̮mji̮s si̮ śerti korkaaśe i ke̮rjasi̮sli̮ śe̮ki̮d suďedni̮ śojanse. korka śertii̮s že ni̮a undeni̮s kokjasni̮sse, kor kojśeni̮s korśigen ńič. tēnas-že, kor ke̮rjasi̮s śe̮kaeś, kolho·zjasi̮n nije vajedeni̮s pośelok dore i vije-ni̮s jaj vi̮le. bi̮kjasse ni̮a viďeni si̮ vi̮le, medum nōledli̮ni̮ śe̮ki̮d gruzjas. ni̮a med i̮ǯideś stav ke̮rjasśi̮s. tēnas, bi̮d tē, rajonnij śelei̮n le̮śedeni̮s ke̮rjas vi̮li̮n gonkijas, seten viďeni̮s med e̮ďďe vojlan ke̮rjas. kod vi̮igrajte ni̮je, si̮li̮ śeteni̮s i̮ǯi̮d priz i si̮len brigadai̮s li̮ďďiśe med buren stav kolhozas. ke̮rjasse pregiteni̮s kokńid, as karem daďjase. bi̮d atďeľnej sečem ṕagitema daďjasse šueni̮s doď-ulen. tēnas ke̮r-dorśa mortjaslen ćomjasni̮s vi̮li̮stii̮s gartemaś ke̮r-kuen, medum ve̮li šoni̮dǯik, a pi̮čkesas važenǯik karisni̮s bi mu vi̮li̮n, a e̮ni kolhozjas śeteni̮s ni̮li̮ ke̮rt-paćjas. seten, te̮d-ńin, abu kre̮vaťjas, no ni̮a pać ge̮geras kareni̮s iľi le̮śede-ni̮s ke̮r-kujasi̮ś bur šoni̮d uźan mesta. pastukjasi̮s karauľiteni̮s ke̮rjasse siď: vojnas-ke ki̮mi̮n-ke mort, a bi̮denlen vi̮ji̮m, med ečai̮s kujim veledem ponmen karauľiteni̮s stadese (stadse). a med ki̮mi̮n-ke mortjas si̮ kosti uźeni̮s, šoćceni̮s.

which is still moving, they clean off its scales. Then they cut it into slices. It makes four slices: the sides, the back and the belly. They eat it like this: they put one end of the slice into their mouth, stretching the slice with the one hand and holding a knife in the other hand, with which they cut a piece of fish, making the cut near the mouth from below upwards. Zyrians usually throw away the remaining bones and head, but the Ostyaks will dry them above the fire, making fish-fat of the gut at a small fire. They eat fish-fat with bread or dried fish, and use it like ordinary fat. They eat *si̮rok* too, with a little salt. They cut it open at the gills and pull out the gut to prepare fish-fat from it; at the same time they put the fish in salt. There it stands two or three hours. Then it may be eaten.

183. [About reindeer-breeding]

In spring-time when rivers begin to open, reindeer-breeders come to *Mi̮ži* to acquire their supply of food for the whole summer. Then they move slowly towards the sea-coast. They move there because there are too many gnats in summer, and the reindeer cannot feed well, while by the sea there are fewer gnats. They live well there. The calves do well in the spring. In summer the reindeer-breeders have light tents made of thin poles and covered with bark of birch. Such are the summer tents. When the autumn comes, they go deeper into the dry land. They do so to make it easier for the reindeer to get their food which is moss. In winter it is very cold by the sea, and the north wind blows incessantly. Therefore the snow is covered by a crust of ice, and the reindeer can hardly reach their food. They cut their feet in the crust of ice as they dig in search of moss. In winter when reindeer are fat they are taken to the kolkhoz to be slaughtered for meat. The bulls are kept because they are used to carry heavy loads. They are biggest of all the reindeer. In winter, every winter, a reindeer race is held in the district centre. The fastest-running reindeer are brought there. The winner is given a big prize, and the brigade to which it belongs is regarded as the best in the whole kolkhoz. Reindeer are harnessed to light sleighs which people make for themselves. Each harnessed sleigh is called a carriage. In winter the tents of the reindeer-breeders are covered with reindeer hide outside to keep them warmer, in times of old people laid fires on the ground inside the tents, but today they received iron stoves from the kolkhoz. As is known, there are no beds in them, instead they prepare fine, warm sleeping quarters from reindeer skins round the stoves. The herdsmen guard the reindeer like this: At night, a few men, each having at least three well-trained dogs, guard the herd while the rest are sleeping and resting.

VII. NORTHERN PERMYAK DIALECT

The following texts are not resulting from field-work in the Komi-Permyak National District. They were recorded from young people studying in Syktyvkar during my stay there, namely from the folklorist Ľubov Stepanovna G r i b o v a then aspirant to Candidate's degree (aged 30, Петухова, Kočevo district); Marija Makedonovna P y s t o g o v a (aged 22, Кочево), Anna Andreevna M i n i n a (aged 21, Большая Коча, Kočevo District); Larisa Nikolaevna S n i g y r o v a (aged 20, Коса, Kosa District). Essentially all of them had preserved their original dialect, although their speech showed occasionally influences of the Syktyvkar dialect, as well as of Komi-Permyak and Komi-Zyrian literary usage. The material supplied by Gribova is the most valuable from the point of view of both linguistics and ethnography. The texts recorded from the other three informants are of a lesser importance for folklore but are still interesting for the linguist studying the present usage of the young Komi-Permyak generation.

In the following we list certain characteristic features of the Northern Permyak dialect which distinguish them from Southern Permyak. Naturally we have not enumerated all those features of phonetics, accentuation, morphology and syntax, which distinguish Permyak (including Northern Permyak) dialects from Northern Zyrian (Komi-Zyrian).

1. As regards the phoneme *l*, Northern Permyak is one of the group of dialects which use it in all positions. From the phonetic aspect, *l* has more of a velar character than the Russian *л*, and shows an acoustic affinity with the bilabial *w* (<*l*) occurring in Southern Permyak.

2. Before consonants the labiodental *v* is sometimes replaced by bilabial *w*, e.g. *ľawgȩ* 'barks', *tarowćȩ* 'rolls' (verb.). See further *goto·w* 'ready' < Russian *готов* 'ready'.

3. The spirantization of *j* is weaker than in the Syktyvkar dialect and other Zyrian dialects in general. For example, *kai̯ȩtli̯-* 'to carry', *ki̯i̯ə* 'he weaves', *sii̯a* 'he'.

4. Under the influence of more recently borrowed Russian loanwords the following phonemes have come into use: (*f*), (*c*), (*χ*). Certain vacillations may be observed between the borrowed forms and the original phonemes: *cep* ~ *ćep*, 'chain', *dvore·c* ~ *dvore·ć* 'palace', *kolχo·z* ~ *kolko·z* 'kolhoz'. I also noted, sporadically palatalized consonants in Russian loanwords (*ḿ, ṕ, b́, ŕ*): *ḿać* 'ball', *ṕerḿak* 'permyak', *ŕad* 'line', *stŕapńa* 'food'. In certain instances palatalized consonants precede palatal vowels even in original Zyrian words: *ḿenam* 'mine', *ṕetni̯* 'to go out', *ṕećki̯ni̯* 'to spin', *b́eď* 'stick', *ŕeźśi̯ni̯* 'to sprinkle' *ŕekti̯ni̯* 'to evacuate'. Since the consonants mentioned here cannot be regarded — at least for the present — as real phonemes, I have indicated their palatalized character only in Russian loanwords and even then only when I found convincing evidence of their palatalization.

5. In Russian loanwords the phonemes *ś* and *ź* correspond phonetically to the Russian *ś* and *ź* and not to the *ś*, *ź* (= *ś*, *ź*) phonemes in original words.

6. In the absolute final position the *e̜* phoneme has a reduced *ə̂* allophone. For example *ki̯i̯ə̂* 'he weaves', *kodilə̂* 'to whom', *me̜də̂* 'he wants', *ultə̂* 'to under'. Uotila (SyrjChr. 30—1) also gives *ə̂* in an identical position in a song collected in the Kosa dialect (= PK): *śe̜d ve̜r śe̜rə̂* 'to the middle of the dark wood', *pukalə̂* 'he sits' etc. I have also observed some cases of the reduction of *e̜* in other than initial syllables: *vermə̂m* 'he could'.

7. Substantives ending in a vowel drop the linking vowels of suffixes mainly in rapid speech, so that the sequence of vowels merge into a long or half-long phoneme. For example, *ińkà* (< *ińkae̜*) 'my wife', *bańān* (< *bańai̯n*) 'in the bath-house', *garmo·ńńān* (< *garmo·ńńae̜n*) 'with the accordion', *kerkūs* (< *kerkui̯s*) 'the house', *vān* (< *vai̯n*) 'in water', *vān* (< *vae̜n*) 'with water'. In the case of Pystogova the merger of two vowels results rather in a half-long phoneme: *carstvòn* (< *carstvoi̯n*) 'in a kingdom', *gosudarstvòn* (< *gosudarstvoi̯n*) 'in a state'. The double forms which occur fairly often in my texts (*vān* ~ *vai̯n* 'in water', etc.) are due to the circumstance that I noted these texts not from the tape-recorder but from my informants' dictation. The fuller forms appeared when the informants were asked to repeat what they had said more slowly, in more articulated speech.

8. While dictating her texts, my informant L. S. Gribova, repeatedly enumerated the variants of certain words in the forms they are used in her village. Such are, e.g.: *kuče̜m* ~ *kuče̜·m* ~ *ki̯če̜·m* 'what kind of, which one', *mi̯mda* ~ *mi̯nda* ~ *munda* 'as much as', *śorkńi* ~ *śe̜rkńi* ~ *śortńi* 'turnip', *sośe·ddese̜* ~ *suśe·ddese̜* ~ *se̜śe·ddese̜* 'the neighbours (acc.)'.

9. In the Northern Permyak dialect the postposition *vi̯l*-(*vi̯li̯n*, *vi̯liś*, *vi̯le̜*) exists in its original postpositional form (*ve̜llez vi̯li̯n* 'on horses' etc.), while

in Southern Permyak the same postposition has become a suffix (*pi̮zan-vi̮n* < *pi̮zan vi̮wi̮n* 'on the table').

10. Occasionally the allative-dative suffix (*-le̮*) fulfils an accusative function: *aǯǯim mi ke̮r-ke̮ zonkao·kle̮* 'at some time we found a little boy'.

11. The egressive suffix (*-śań*) has very occasionally a *-śiń* allomorph: *gortśińi̮s* 'from home'. This variant occurs more frequently in the Southern Permyak dialect.

12. As compared with Southern Permyak, stress is less dynamic, and shows some vacillation. In general, the main stress is transferred from the root-vowel to certain deverbal formative suffixes (*-al-*, *-an*, *-aś-*, *-e̮m*, *-e̮rt-*, *-e̮t-*, *-i̮l-*, *-iś*) (that is, the accent is morphologized), although not consistently. For example, *ćapka·le̮ni̮* 'they cut', but: *juktale̮* 'he gives to drink', *si̮na·las* 'he combs', but: *si̮·nalas* 'he combs', *nue̮·te̮ni̮* 'they carry', *li̮ďďi̮·lise̮* 'they regarded it as . . .', *vugra·śe̮ni̮* 'they fish', *ďi̮ťťaśa·n* 'swinging'. Vacillation of this kind is frequent especially when the word contains a suffix-cluster, e.g.: *ćeria·liśśez* ~ *ćeriali·śśez* 'fishermen'. According to my observations, the place of the stress may depend on the momentary disposition of the speaker that is, whether he intends to stress the root syllable or some suffix. In the speech of my informants Pystogova, Minina and Snigyrova, the stress often falls on the first syllable of the word (Syktyvkar influence?). This feature is mainly characteristic of Gribova's style of accentuation. Naturally only stress placed on other than initial syllables is indicated in my texts.

(a) Tales and narratives

184. *aľo·nuška ji̯liś*

1. *ole̯maś-ve̯le̯maś starik da staru·ka. ni̯le̯n ve̯le̯maś kujim ni̯l. loktas go-že̯m, starik koras ni̯lni̯se̯ di̯nas i šue̯: “pe̯riś ńi me loi, i̯be̯ og vermi̯ vetle̯·tni̯. mune̯-že̯ ti, ćeľaď ve̯re̯ da vaje̯ meni̯m jage̯·d! ke̯da med bur jage̯·d e̯ktas, si̯le̯ ńe̯ba me base̯k je̯rne̯·s.”*

2. *munase̯ kujimnan ni̯li̯s ve̯re̯. ki̯ki̯s pe̯riśži̯kkes eča·ži̯k (ječa·ži̯k) e̯kte̯ni̯, una·ži̯k śoje̯ni̯. med ućeti̯s med una e̯ktas. si̯le̯n jage̯·di̯s med base̯k da med će̯ski̯t. loktase̯ nija gortani̯s. ajni̯s ośke̯ med ućetse̯ i ke̯sje̯ bośni̯ si̯le̯ base̯k je̯rne̯·s. me̯dik lune̯ be̯ra· nije̯ ińde̯ ve̯re̯ jage̯·dla. be̯ra· med uće̯·ti̯s med una da med bur jage̯·d e̯ktas. ke̯sjas si̯le̯ aji̯s ńe̯bni̯ base̯k ći̯šjan (ći̯ššan). kujme̯dćid be̯ra· med uće̯·ti̯s e̯ktas med una i med bur jage̯·d. e̯kśase̯ ni̯lles ve̯ras i viǯe̯·te̯ni̯, kinle̯n med una i med bur jage̯·d. aǯǯe̯ni̯ be̯ra·: a l' o · n u š k ale̯n. le̯ga·śase̯ i̯ǯi̯tǯi̯kkes uće̯·tik ni̯lkao·ki̯s (ni̯lećkai̯s) vi̯le̯. vijase sije̯, śuji·štase̯ mue̯, ti̯rtase̯ pese̯·ke̯n. jage̯·dse̯ si̯liś juka·lase̯ e̯ta-me̯d kolasi̯n, a beke̯rse̯ žugdase da ćapkase̯ kustteze̯. loktase̯ gortani̯s, aj-mami̯s jua·le̯ni̯: “ki̯te̯·n ne̯ a l' o · n u š k ai̯s (a l' o · n u š-k à s)?” ni̯lles i šue̯ni̯: “i̯ksim, korim mi sije̯. kićće̯· i lois, ez lok.” kerni̯ ńem, gorzase̯, gorzase̯ stari·k da staru·ka i śetase̯ koži·nnese̯ i̯ǯi̯tǯi̯k ni̯llezni̯sle̯.*

3. *vot mune̯ e̯ććid ve̯re̯t pastu·k (pastu·χ). aǯǯe̯, bi̯dme̯ pese̯·k vi̯li̯n base̯kśa base̯k pe̯ľa·n. vundi̯·štas sija pe̯ľa·nse, keras pe̯ľa·n i pondas orsni̯. no kiče̯·m eta ćude̯?! pe̯ľa·ni̯s aći̯s pondas śi̯lni̯: “menam ajińe̯j, menam mamńe̯j, mije̯ sojjeze̯ke̯t jage̯·dalime̯. nija jage̯·dse̯ meńćim juka·llise̯ i beke̯·ri̯s meńćim žug-dise̯. mene̯ uľ mue̯ nija ǯebise̯, vež pese̯·ke̯n mene̯ ti̯rtise̯.” polźas pastu·k, kote̯·rte̯ ďere·vńae̯ǯ, pondas ďere·vńa vi̯li̯n orsni̯. pe̯ľa·ni̯s be̯ra· aći̯s śi̯le̯: “me-nam ajińe̯j, menam mamńe̯j . . .” każa·lase oťiri̯s, kinle̯n ni̯li̯s śi̯le̯. ińdase̯ pastu·kse̯ stari·k da staru·ka orde̯. pondas sija pe̯ľa·śni̯, pe̯ľa·ni̯s aći̯s śi̯le̯: “menam ajińe̯j, menam mamńe̯j . . .” le̯ga·śase̯ stari·k da staru·ka pe̯ri·śži̯k (pe̯ri·źži̯k) ni̯llezni̯s vi̯le̯ i ve̯tlase̯ nije̯ gortśińi̯s. boštas staru·ka pe̯ľa·nse̯ kias, pondas pe̯ľa·śni̯, pe̯ľa·ni̯s aći̯s śi̯le̯: “menam ajińe̯j, menam mamńe̯j . . .” ćapkas staru·kai̯s pe̯ľa·nse̯ porog ulte̯, potas pe̯ľa·ni̯s i ćećće̯·ltas si̯ pi̯čkiś ni̯le̯n uće̯·ťik ni̯lni̯s. — bi̯de̯·s.*

184. About Aľonuška

1. Once upon a time there lived an old man and an old woman. They had three daughters. Summer came, the old man called his daughters to him, saying: "I have grown old now, I cannot walk to the field. Go, children, go to the forest and bring me some berries! For the one who picks most berries I shall buy a beautiful blouse."

2. The three girls go into the forest. The two older ones gather fewer berries, and eat more. The youngest collects the most. The berries she has picked are most beautiful, most tasty. They come home. The father praises the youngest daughter and is ready to buy her a beautiful blouse. Next day he again sends them out to pick berries in the forest. Again the youngest one picks the most and the best berries. The father promises to buy her a beautiful kerchief. The third time again the youngest girl collects the most and the best berries. The girls come together in the forest to see who has the most and the best berries. Again they see that it is Aľonuška. The older ones grow angry with the youngest girl, kill her, and bury her body, covering it with sand. They share her berries between them, while they break her bowl and throw it into the bushes. They go home, their parents ask them: "Where is Aľonuška?" The girls answer: "We shouted and called her. Where is she gone; she has not come." There is nothing to be done? The old man and the old woman weep, and they give the gifts to the older daughters.

3. Once a shepherd goes through the forest. He notices that a very beautiful wild angelica is growing in the sand. He cuts the angelica, makes a pipe from it and begins to blow it. Oh, the marvel of it! The pipe starts singing all by himself far: "Father, mother, we were collecting berries, I and my sisters. They shared my berries, and broke my bowl. They buried me in wet ground and covered me with yellow sand." Frightened, the shepherd runs as far as the village and starts playing: again the pipe sings by himself: "Father, mother . . ." People soon discover whose daughter is singing. They send the shepherd to the old man and the old woman. He starts piping and the pipe sings by himself: "Father, mother . . ." The old woman grew angry with their older daughters and chased them out of the house. The old woman takes the pipe in her hands and starts to blow it. The pipe sings by himself: "Father, mother . . ." The old woman hurls the pipe under the threshold, the pipe falls to pieces and the youngest daughter springs out of it. — That is the end of the tale.

185. *m a r k o b o g a · t e̮ j ji̮liś*

1. *e̮tik (e̮ti) gore̮di̮n ole̮m eďďe̮n boga·te̮j mort, m a r k o. a orćće̮n si̮ ker-kuke̮t sula·le̮m uće̮·ťik, ume̮·ľik kerkuo·k. si̮i̮n ole̮m eďďe̮n bedne̮j mort. m a r k o b o g a · t e̮ ji̮s viććiśe̮m pia·n, ińkai̮s śe̮ki̮t ve̮le̮m. i vot kin-ke̮ viśta·las si̮le̮, bi̮ťťe̮ pe̮ eta lunneze̮ ki̮me̮·rśań lećći·śas jen i loktas ge̮śľi·tni̮ eta gorode. m a r k o b o g a · t e̮ j e̮ďďe̮n loas rad i če̮ktas vićkuśań gorte̮ʒas tujse̮ velťťi̮ni̮ barχate̮n. jeni̮s pe̮ ed vićkuśań-že̮ petas, aś pe̮ me di̮ne̮ (me orde̮) lokte̮. vićći·śas, vićći·śas, ńe-kin oz lok. sija če̮ktas barχatse̮ ʒimľa·lni̮.*

2. *seśśa śore̮n ńi ri̮tnas kin-ke̮ ni̮ orde̮ stuke̮·ćće̮. ośtase̮: koriś. pe̮riś, ume̮ľik starićo·k, bi̮re̮m paś-ke̮me̮n (paś-ke̮ma). šue̮: "leǯ mene̮ uźni̮!" kin te i seče·mi̮s em da? mun tatiś, oge̮ leʒe̮." seśśa sija stuke̮·ććas bedne̮j kerkuo·kas. ke̮źa·jka i šue̮: "leʒi-bi̮ da kerkue̮ uće̮t, ćeľaďi̮s una, verdni̮ tene̮ ńeme̮n." "a meni̮m pe̮ ńem oz kol, labi·ćni̮t pe̮ ke pros, sete̮n i uźa." leʒase̮. a ke̮źa·jkai̮s uźni̮ oz vermi̮, oj-bi̮t ve̮re̮ća·ćće̮. sija śe̮ki̮t ve̮le̮m, ćužtan vote̮ʒ ńi da ojnas i ćužte̮m. seśśa ki̮le̮, sija e̮šine̮, ke̮da veśti̮n stari·ki̮s uźe, kin-ke̮ švatke̮·tni̮ pondis. "mi̮j — šue̮ — teni̮t kole̮?" "a ta-lun ćužise̮ ki̮k kaga: e̮ti̮s pe̮ eta kerkuiś: zonkao·k, a me̮di̮s orćća kerkuiś boga·teji̮sle̮n: ni̮lkao·k." "mi̮j pe̮ ni̮ke̮t kerni̮?" stari·ki̮s pe̮ i šue̮: "kor nija bi̮dmase̮, ni̮je̮ ge̮tra·lni̮." stari·ki̮s pe̮ aći̮s jeni̮s ve̮le̮m. asi̮lnas sija mune̮m, a ke̮źa·jka sek-že̮ veśka·le̮m.*

3. *pondase̮ ćeľaďi̮s bi̮dmi̮ni̮. m a r k o b o g a · t e̮ j l e̮ ki̮lśas, bi̮ďte̮ jeni̮s volle̮m pe̮ i če̮kte̮m ge̮tra·lni̮ kaga·ese̮. si̮le̮ žaľ loas ni̮li̮s. sija pondas korni̮ zon-kase̮ bedne̮jjei̮sliś (bedne̮jjezi̮sliś): "ti pe̮ śete̮ meni̮m, me pe sije̮ bi̮dta." duma·j-tase̮, duma·jtase̮, kerni̮ ńem. "ńe śojni̮, ńe juni̮ abu, ńe paśtalni̮ ńem, śetame̮ pe." śetase̮. a m a r k o b o g a · t e̮ j toľko sije̮ (si̮ ji̮liś) i duma·jte̮, kiʒ-bi̮ śvet vi̮lśis zonkase̮ vošti̮ni̮. pondas sija munni̮ me̮di·k (me̮di·) goroddeze̮ te̮rgu·jte̮m ďeloeze̮n. bośtas śe̮ras zonkase̮. loktas ju de̮re̮ʒ. doras sije jaššike̮ i leʒas vaas, aći̮s munas.*

4. *di̮r-ľi, ńe-di̮r-ľi kuče·m-ke̮ monasti̮·r (manasti̮·r) di̮ni̮n mona·kkes va kaje̮·tni̮. aʒʒe̮ni̮, bereg doras jaššik lokte̮m. "dava·jťe̮ pe̮ ki̮skam, viʒe̮·tam, mi̮j sete̮n." ki̮skase̮, raźase̮. pi̮čkas aʒʒe̮ni̮, kagao·k kujle̮, ćvettezen orse̮. "viʒe̮·t-že̮ pe̮, ki̮če̮·m basek kagao·k! ki̮če̮·m pe̮ eta ćude̮?! ćvettezen pe̮ orse̮, abu pe̮de̮ma.*

185. About Rich Marko

1. There lived a very rich man, Marko, in a city. Next to his house there stood a small tumbledown hut. A very poor man lived in it. Rich Marko was expecting a child, his wife was pregnant. Well, someone tells him that God is to descend at this time from the clouds and will come to this city and stay there as a guest. Rich Marko is very glad and orders the road from the church to his home to be covered with velvet. Thus when he comes out of the church, God shall come to me. He waits and waits, but nobody comes. He orders the velvet to be cleared away.

2. Then late one night someone knocks at their door. They open it; it is a beggar. An old, crippled man in worn clothes. He says: "Let me in to have a sleep!" "What sort of a man are you? Get out of here, we will not let you in!" Then he knocks at the poor man's house. The wife says: "I would gladly let you come in, only our home is small, there are many children, and I have nothing to offer you." "But I do not want anything, and if your bench is unoccupied, I will sleep on that." The wife cannot sleep, she tosses and turns throughout the night. She was pregnant, her time was due, and indeed she gave birth to a child that night. Then she hears somebody knock at the window facing where the old man was lying. "What do you want?" — she asks. "Today two children have been born: one in this house, a boy, the other in the neighbour's house, a girl." "What am I to do with them?" The old man answers: "When they are grown big, they must be married." The old man was God himself. He left in the morning, and at the same time the wife was cured.

3. The children begin to grow up. Rich Marko learns that God had been there and had commanded that the children be married. He takes pity on his daughter. He asks the poor couple for the little boy. "Give him to me and I shall raise him." They think and think; there is nothing to be done. "We have nothing to eat or to drink; nor have we clothes to put on, we will give him to you." Rich Marko ponders all the time how to get rid of the little boy. He begins to visit other cities on business. He takes the little boy with him. He reaches a river. He nails him up in a chest and drops it into the water and goes away.

4. Some time later friars were carrying water past some monastery. They notice that a chest had come to the bank. "Let us go and pull it out and see what is in it!" They pull it out and break it up. Inside, they see, a child is lying, playing with flowers. "Look, how beautiful the child is! What a miracle! He is playing with flowers, he has not drowned. We will take him and bring him up!" They take him and start to bring him up.

mi pe̮ sije̮ kaje̮·tam i bi̮dti̮ni̮ pondam." kaje̮·tase̮, pondase̮ bi̮dti̮ni̮ i aǯǯe̮ni̮: ki̮ni̮·m i̮ǯi̮tǯi̮k sija loe̮, si̮ni̮·m boga·tǯi̮k loe̮ ni̮le̮n monasti̮·ri̮s. vot i i̮ǯi̮t ńi bi̮dmas. mune̮ e̮ććid monasti̮·ri̮s pi̮r m a r k o b o g a · t e̮ j *i ďivu·će̮: "mi̮j pe̮ tijanke̮t sečе̮mi̮s lois? ti pe̮ meśśa ńi ćoža boga·tǯi̮ke̮ś loat." "a mijan pe̮ vot mi̮j lois. aǯǯim mi ke̮r-ke̮ zonkao·kle̮ (zonkao·ke̮s). ki̮ni̮·m mi sije̮ bi̮dtam, si̮ni̮·m burži̮ka olam." i viśta·śase̮ ki̮ǯ i ki̮ti·ś aǯǯase̮ nija ete̮ zonkase̮.* m a r k o b o g a · - t e̮ j *dogada·ććas: 'sija pe̮ ed menam.' "me pe̮ sije̮ e̮šti, guśa·lise̮. śete̮ pe̮ meni̮m be̮r!" nija bi̮ oze̮ śete̮, me̮di̮s korni̮. a nija oze̮ śete̮. "me pe̮ tijanle̮ si̮mda ďeńga śeta, tije̮ kujim ečče̮m monasti̮·r stre̮ji·tate̮." me̮ddes i śetase̮. sija i šue̮ zonkai̮sle̮: "vot tenit giže̮·t, nu sije̮ gorte̮! tene̮ ińkà (ińkae̮) bura panta·las." bośtas sija giže̮·t i munas.*

5. *munas, munas, loktas ve̮r de̮re̮ǯ. pukśas šoććiši̮·šni̮. petas sećće̮ starik. jua·śe̮: "ki̮ćće̮ munan, kin te?" zonkàs (zonkai̮s) viśta·śas, me̮di̮s i šue̮:"mi̮j tejat (tenat) karma·nat?" me̮di̮s šue̮: "ńań-korka, seśśa ńem abu. a košši̮, noko mi̮j-ke̮, može̮t, aǯǯan." me̮di̮s šuji̮·štas kise̮ karma·nas i ki̮skas piśmo. "vot, i̮šše̮· mi̮j em!" "me vune̮·ti." i viśta·śas bi̮de̮·s. stari·kis i šue̮: "vajli̮ noko sije̮ meni̮m!" me̮di̮s śetas. stari·k guśe̮n liďďe̮·tas: piśmō·as gižе̮m: ki̮ǯ (kić) pe̮ eta tom morti̮s loktas, tije̮ kuji·m lun vi̮ǯe̮ ponnese̮ čigje̮n, seśśa ni̮ diṅe̮ le̮ǯa sije̮. me pe̮ lokta, med-bi̮ bi̮de̮·s ve̮li keram. stari·k ši̮ oz śet (oś‿śet), śetas zonkai̮sle̮ piśmo·se̮ be̮r. a stari·ki̮s aći̮s jeni̮s ve̮le̮m i piśmo·se̮ veže̮m. loktas zonkai̮s* m a r k o b o g a · t e̮ j *orde̮, śetas piśmo·se̮. piśmo·as gižе̮m: ke̮r eta zonkai̮s loktas, ti sije̮ ge̮tra·le ni̮le̮ vi̮le̮ (vi̮li̮n)! kuji·m lun be̮ri̮n (be̮rti) me lokta, med-bi̮ bi̮de̮·s ve̮li keram. ińkàs si̮ǯi keras. ge̮tra·las zonkase̮ ni̮li̮s vi̮le̮. loktas* m a r k o b o g a · t e̮ j i̮ s *gorte̮, a ni̮li̮s si̮le̮n ajka saji̮n. "mi̮j ti — šue̮ — kere̮maś? miľa nije̮ ge̮tra·lite̮ (ge̮tra·le̮maś)?" "a vot — šue̮ ińkai̮s — tenat piśmo. bide̮·s giže̮m." liďďe̮·te̮* m a r k o *i biľ si̮le̮n kii̮s. "vidne̮ pe̮ kod-ja, mi̮j-ja ve̮li gižšem (giššem) ńe siǯ. mi̮j keran?"*

186.

1. *ole̮maś-vele̮maś stari·k da staru·ka. stari·kisle̮n ve̮le̮m nil i staru·kai̮sle̮n. staru·kai̮s e̮ďďe̮n ńe-re̮dne̮·j ni̮lse̮ abu raďe̮·jtle̮m. med śeki̮t, med umeľ, med ńaťe̮ś uǯ vi̮le̮ šo ńe-re̮dne̮·j ni̮lse̮ ińdi̮·lle̮m. vot ińde̮m sije̮ e̮ććid sija mottez miśkal-*

And they notice: the bigger the child grows the richer their monastery becomes. Well, he has grown big now. Once Rich Marko passes by the monastery and wonders: "What has happened to you? You will soon be richer than I am." "Well, this is what has happened to us. One day we found a little boy. As we bring him up and he gets bigger, so we grow all the richer." They relate how and where they found the little boy. Rich Marko soon discovers — "The boy is mine!" "I lost him, he was stolen. Give him back to me!" They refuse to give him back, but the man insists. They still refuse to give him back. "I shall give you money enough to build three monasteries like this one." Then the friars give the boy to him. He says to the little boy: "Here is the document; take it home. My wife will receive you well." He takes the document and goes off.

5. He goes on and on, and arrives at a wood. He sits down to have a rest. An old man goes up to him. "Where are you going, who are you?" The boy tells him, and the man says: "What is it you have in your pocket?" The boy answers: "A crust of bread, nothing else. Search it, perhaps you can find something else." He thrusts his hand into his pocket and draws out the letter. "Look what else you have!" "I forgot about that." And then he tells the whole story. The old man says: "Give it to me!" The boy hands it over. The old man reads it in secret. This is what is written in the document: "When this young man arrives, you must starve the dogs for three days, then I will set them on him. By the time I arrive, let everything be ready!" The old man does not say a word, but gives the letter back to the boy. The old man was God and he changed the letter. The boy arrives at Rich Marko's and hands over the letter. This is what is written in the letter: "When this boy arrives, you must marry my daughter to him! In three days I shall arrive, let everything be arranged by that time!" The wife acts accordingly. She marries the boy to the girl. Rich Marko arrives at home, and his daughter has been married. "What have you done?" — says he — "why have you married them?" "Here" — answers the wife — "is your own letter. Everything is written in it." Marko reads it, and it really is in his hand. "It seems I was drunk or something when I wrote it. What can be done?"

186. [The witch and the two girls]

1. Once there lived an old man and an old woman. The old man and the old woman each had a daughter. The old woman did not like her stepdaughter at all. She always sent the stepdaughter to do the hardest, worst and dirtiest work. Well, one day she sent her to wash skeins of yarn. The

ni̯. munas nilkao·ki̯s va-de̯re̯, pondas miśkalni̯ mottez (mottese̯) da uśke̯·tas vaas. ki̯lte̯ moti̯s vaeťťas, beregeťťas, ni̯lkao·ki̯s ve̯će̯ si̯ śe̯ri̯n. kote̯·rtas, kote̯·rtas, ažže̯, kerku sula·le̯. pi̯ras, baba-jaga puka·le̯. tojjeste̯ aśśis e̯kte̯ da śoje̯. " o — šue̯ — di̯r viććiśi me tene̯, kiž-ke̯ te i loktin? kužan — šue̯ — uža·lni̯ meni̯m, me tene̯ leža da i koźi·n seta, a on kuž, gori̯n pe̯žala i śoja. na teni̯t ćer, šedti̯ pes i lont baňa, pože̯n va kaje̯·tli̯ (kae̯·tli̯), da kuž mene̯ miśśe̯·tni̯!" ni̯lka boštas ćer, ćeri̯s gi̯ne̯ve̯j, oz potke̯·tli̯. pondas gorzi̯ni̯: "mi̯j — šue̯ — ponda kerni̯?" sećće̯ kajo·k loktas. "mi̯ľa — šue̯ — gorzan?" "a vot če̯ktis pe̯ baba-jagai̯s meni̯m pes potke·tli̯ni̯, a ćeri̯s pe̯ gi̯ne̯ve̯j." kajo·ki̯s i šue̯: "a te sije̯ vai̯n (vān) kete̯·t i ki̯nt!" siži keras. šedtas pes, bi̯de̯·s ćaggese̯ e̯ktas, lontas baňa, boštas śi-po·ž, leććas vala. gumi̯·štas vase̯ požnas, sija kiśśe̯. pete̯ be̯r. be̯ra gorze̯. be̯ra loktas kajo·k da šue̯: "mi̯j gorzan?" me̯di̯s višta·las. "a te — šue̯ kajo·ki̯s — gľinae̯n malt!" ni̯lkao·k (ni̯lo̯ćka) siž i keras. kaje̯·tlas va, šontas, baba-jaga šue̯: "vaj miśśe̯·ta ćeľaďte̯ i tene̯." baba-jaga leććas baňā (baňae̯), ćuman-ti̯r ćeľaď boštas: i že̯ži·li̯s i ńiži·li̯s i ľagu·šai̯s i śake̯j strami̯s. ni̯loćka nije̯ pi̯lśe̯·tas, šoni̯t vān (vae̯n) miśśe̯·tas, ruši̯·ťik vān kiśka·las, baba-jagaliś zi̯ri̯m, duľse̯ ćiškas, jur-śise̯ si̯na·las (si̯·nalas) i gortas kaje̯·tas. baba-jaga dovo·ľne̯j koľććas. śetas aši̯nas si̯le̯ mot i jašši·k. "te pe̯ gorte̯žat kićće̯ž on lok, jašši·kse en oś!" ni̯lka siži keras. loktas gortas, vajas mot, oštas jašši·kse̯ sete̯n bi̯d-be̯rśai̯s: šolki̯s, ľentai̯s, donnes, ćuń-kiččes, peľ-kiččes i śake̯j paške̯m. sije̯ pondase̯ ćoža kora·śni̯ i sija že̯ńi·k saje̯ munas.

2. *staru·kale̯ ni̯li̯ske̯t zavid kutas. "kiś pe̯ te ete̯ si̯mda dobro·se̯ vajin?" ni̯lkao·k višta·śas. staru·ka śetas aslas ni̯lle̯ mottez i i̯stas miśka·lni̯. siž-že̯ ni̯li̯s uśke̯·tas nare̯·šne̯ motse̯ i dava·j ve̯ćći̯ni̯ si̯ śe̯ri̯n. kote̯·rtas, kote̯·rtas, loktas kerku di̯ne̯, pi̯ras baba-jaga orde̯. baba-jagai̯s siž-že̯ če̯kte̯m sije̯ baňa lontni̯ i ćeľaďse̯ pi̯lśe̯·tni̯. śetas si̯le̯ siž-že̯ gi̯ne̯ve̯j ćer i śi-po·ž. pondas ni̯lkao·k pesse̯ potke̯·tli̯ni̯ da oz vermi̯. sećće̯ kajo·k loktas da šue̯: "te vān (vae̯n) kiškal da ki̯nt!" "te̯dan pe̯ te mi̯j-ke̯?! kičče̯·m pe̯ teni̯t ďela me di̯ne̯ž? mun, lebal!" potke̯·tli̯ni̯ oz vermi̯, baňaas ćurka·ese̯ siž kaje̯·tas, lontas, munas vala, vai̯s poššiś (ɔ: požsiś) kiśśe̯.*

little girl goes off to the river bank and starts washing the skeins. She lets them fall into the water. The skeins float in the water, the little girl sets out after them along the bank. She runs and runs and sees a house standing there. She goes in; a witch is sitting inside. She is collecting her own lice and eating them. "Oh" — says she — "I've been waiting for you a long time! Now you've arrived somehow or other, haven't you? If you can work for me" — says she — "I will let you free and give you gifts; if you cannot, I will fry you in the oven and eat you. Here, take this axe and cut wood, and heat the bath-house, then bring water with a sieve and see how you can wash me!" The girl takes the axe; the axe is made of felt. She begins to weep: "What shall I do?" — says she. A little bird comes to her. "Why are you weeping?" — asks the bird. "Well, the witch has commanded me to cut wood, but the axe is made of felt." The little bird says: "Soak it in water and freeze it!" She does so. She cuts wood, collects all the shavings, heats the bath-house, takes the sieve made of thick horse's hair and goes to fetch water. She draws water with the sieve and it runs through. She goes back. She weeps again. Again the little bird comes and asks: "Why are you crying?" The girl tells her. "Smear it with clay!" — says the bird. The little girl acts accordingly. She fetches water, makes a fire and says to the witch: "Now I will wash your children as well as you." The witch goes down to the bath-house, taking her children in a basket of birch-bark: lizards, earthworms, toads and all kinds of nasty creatures. The little girl baths them, washes them with warm water, rinses them with lukewarm water, wipes away the witch's snot and spit, combs her hair and takes them home. In the morning the witch gives her skeins and a chest: "Don't open the chest before you arrive home!" The girl acts accordingly. She walks home, bringing the skeins, and opens the chest. It contains all sort of things: silk, ribbons, precious jewels, rings, earrings and all kinds of clothes. Soon suitors come, and she marries.

2. The old woman grew envious of her (step)daughter. "Where have you brought all this treasure from?" The little girl tells her about it. The old woman gives some skeins to her own daughter and sends her to wash them. The girl drops the skeins into the water intentionally and see, she sets out after them. She runs and runs, reaches the house and goes in to the witch. As before, the witch ordered her to heat the bath-house and bath her children. As before, she gives her an axe of felt and a thick sieve of horse-hair. The little girl starts cutting wood but cannot do it. The little bird comes to her saying: "Pour water on it and freeze it!" "You don't know how to do it! And what have you to do with me? Go and fly away!" She cannot cleave the wood, she just carries the stumps into the bath-house,

kajo·k loktas. "te — šue — gľinaen malt!" "mij-ke tedan te, arttem, ilestem?! mun tatiś!" va oz vermi kaje·tlini. leććetas sija baba-jagase ćeľaďnas bańā (bańae), kes rosen kuľas, kuľas i oz ćiški: "aćit pe abu uće·ťik, kolas pe dak ćiškan." ašinas baba-jaga sile śetas mot i jašši·k. "te pe kićće·ž on lok gortat, en oś jaššikse!" nilkao·k siž i keras. loktas gortas, kikna·nnis mamisket kińi·ć-ćase jašši·kis dine, ośtase. jašši·kśis kiśśas žirit šom da reśśas (ɔ: rezśas) kerku omeńńas. kerkūs (kerkuis) ezzas i nija bide·nnis soććase.

187.

1. *olemaś-velemaś stari·k da staru·ka. nilen velem nil. staru·kās (staru·kais) šoga·lni pondem da i kulem. stari·k getra·śas, medi·k ińka vaje·tas. ińkàslen (ińkaislen) tože nil velem, stari·kis nilkase abu pondem raďe·jtni. "mun — šue — kićće-ke nuet nilte, ok (ɔ: og) siket vermi olni." stari·kle žaľ nilse, no kerni ńem. "leśe·ćći — šue — nil, muname vere, pećkini seććin pondam." bośtas nilka pećka·n, ćerssez, tork, puktas sile ńe-redne·j mamis kejićà· (ke-jića·e) ńań tuje gaľa, piź tuje pejim, sol tuje pese·k. duma·jte, aś čigjen kule seććin. pukśe·tas ajis nilse rozva·ľe i nue·tas. loktase nija ver šere, izbu·ška sua·le (sula·le). sećće stari·kis i koľas nilse. "en pol — šue — ritnas me lokta." nilka lontas gor, pondas puni kaša, peji·mśis piź loas. sećće šir petas. "nil-kao·k, nilkao·k, verd mene kašanat!" nilka verdas. ažže: izśis ńań lòm (loem), pese·kśis sol lòm (loem). śojas, pukśas pećkini. śor ritnas dir mijiś ńi ajis śo oz lok. duma·jte: "etnam-ja, mij-ja ponda uźni?" drug kile, kite·n-ke śilka·nnez kileni. duma·jte, ajis lokte. pire mort, tošis kok ultež, zirim-duľľis lećće, juris pož paśta, śeras jašši·k. "miśśe·t — šue — nilka, mene, ćiški zirim-duľes!" sija ćiškas, miśśe·tas (miśśe·tas), vodas kaľa·nis pela·ť dore. "te — šue —, nilka, kićće — vodan?" "me — šue — gor vil dore." ojnas kile nilka, kaľa·nis si dine lokte, mala·śe, kutni ńi toľke. "te — šue —, kiten, nilka?" sećće šir petas da šue guśe·ńik* nilkaisle: "te pe gor-vil-śordas žepśiś (ɔ: žebśiś), a me sije*

* *guśen, guśena*

makes a fire and goes to fetch water, but the water flows out of the sieve. The little bird comes, and says: "Smear it with clay!" "How shared you know, you stupid creature, you fool! Away with you!" She cannot fetch water. She takes the witch and her daughters down to the bath-house, uses dry brooms to beat them and does not dry them. "You're not an infant; if you need a towel, there it is!" In the morning the witch gives her some skeins and a chest. "Don't open the chest before you arrive home!" The girl does as she is told. She comes home, her mother and she, the two of them, hurl themselves on the chest and open it. Live coal pours out of the chest, spreading all over the house. The house catches fire, and they are all burnt up.

187. [The ghost and the two girls]

1. There lived an old man and an old woman. They had a daughter. The old woman fell ill and died. The old man marries again; he brings home another wife. His wife also had a daughter, and disliked that of her husband. "Go" — says she — "take your daughter somewhere else; I can't live with her!" The old man is sorry for his daughter, but he has no other choice. "Get ready, daughter" — says he — "let us go into the forest and do some spinning there." The girl takes the spinning wheel and the spindles, also some rough oakum, her stepmother puts stone instead of bread in a little bag, ash instead of flour, sand instead of salt. She thinks, 'let her starve to death there'. The father sets his daughter on a peasant sleigh and takes her away. They arrive in the middle of the forest. A small hut is standing there. The old man leaves his daughter there. "Never fear" — says he — "I shall be back by nightfall." The girl lights the stove, starts to cook porridge, and the ash turn into flour. A mouse comes along. "Little girl, little girl, give me something to eat!" The girl feeds it. She sees that the stone has turned into bread, the sand into salt. She finishes eating, then sits down to spin. It is late at night yet her father does not come. She thinks: "Shall I have to sleep alone?" Suddenly she hears bells ringing somewhere. She thinks her father is coming. There enters a man with a beard reaching down to his feet, with snot and spit coming out of his nose and mouth; his head is as broad as a sieve, and there is a chest in his hands. "Wash me, little girl" — says he — "wipe the snot and spit off my face!" She wipes his face, washes him, and the ghost lies on the hanging bed. "And you, little girl" — asks he — "where are you going to sleep?" "On top of the stove." During the night the little girl hears the ghost coming over to her, feeling his way, until he well-nigh seizes her. "Where are you, little girl?" — asks he. The

i̮le̮ta." sećće̮ śilka·n bośte̮m i dava·j kotraśni̮ gor-vi̮lśań ʒoʒe̮, ʒoʒśań pe̮la·t́e̮. kaľa·ni̮s si̮ śe̮ri̮n ve̮tli̮śe̮, oj-bi̮t ve̮tli̮śas, kutni̮ oz vermi̮. petu·k ki̮tse̮·ltas, kaľa·n pi̮ššas. jašši·kse̮ koľas. viʒe̮·tas ni̮lkai̮s jašši·k: ti̮r dobro: aši̮nas siʒ́-že̮ loas i me̮d lunas tože̮. koľććas ni̮lkale̮ kujim jašši·k.

2. *ńe̮le̮t lunas stari·k lokte̮ ni̮lla. pukśe̮·tas sije̮ dobro·nas rozva·ľ vi̮le̮ i śi̮le̮ni̮, mune̮ni̮. a gortas ńe-re̮dne̮·j mami̮s tupe̮·ššez pe̮ža·le̮. sete̮n uće̮·t́ik pon (ki̮ća·n, pon-pijan) ľawge̮: "stari·ki̮sle̮n ni̮lse̮ dobro·e̮n vaje̮·te̮ni̮." "aχ, te i̮le̮ste̮m, te, kole̮ šuni̮: 'stari·k ni̮lliś koskaese̮ vaje̮ni̮' " a ki̮ća·n śojas tupe̮·ś da be̮ra aśśis: "stari·k ni̮lse̮ dobro·en vaje̮·te̮ni̮." i bi̮ľ loktas stari·k, doď-ti̮r dobro· ni̮li̮sliś vajas. e̮dva kerkue̮ pi̮rtlase̮.*

3. *zavid loas staru·kale̮, šue̮: "seki meńćim ni̮le̮s nue̮·tli̮! aś tože̮ dobro·e̮n lokte̮!" pukśe̮·tas stari·k staru·kai̮sliś ni̮lse̮ i nue̮·tas. staru·ka si̮le̮ ke̮ji·ćaas tećas šogdi̮e̮vej ńań, id-piź da sol. śetas be̮rśase̮ a pećki̮ni̮ puktas se̮ʒ. loktase̮ ve̮r še̮re̮, stari·ki̮s šue̮: "en pol, me ri̮tnas te di̮ne̮ lokta." a ni̮lka pani̮t: "kin tene̮ taćće̮ kore̮, me e̮tnam ola." lontas sija gor, pondas puśi̮ni̮. ńańi̮s ize̮ pe̮ras, piźi̮s pe̮ji·me̮ pe̮ras, soli̮s pese̮·ke̮. puas kaša, śojni̮ oz tuj. sećće̮ ši̮ro·k petas. "verd-že̮ — šue̮ —, ni̮lka, mene̮!" "mun tatiś, asli̮m śojni̮ ńem, ńe-te̮-lište̮ tene̮ verdni̮." le̮ga·śas ši̮r, ši̮ seśśa oz śet. śore̮n ri̮tnas pi̮ras kerkue̮ kaľa·n. toši̮s kok ulte̮ʒ, zi̮ri̮m-duľi̮s lećće̮, juri̮s pož paśta. "mi̮śśe̮·t — šue̮ —, ni̮lka, mene̮!" "aći̮t mi̮śśan, kolas dak." me̮di̮s ši̮ oz śet. seśśa jua·le̮: "ki̮te̮n te, ni̮lka, uźan?" "me gor-vi̮l dore̮ voda." vodas kaľa·ni̮s pe̮la·ť dore̮, ojnas leććas ni̮lkàs (ni̮lkai̮s) di̮ne̮ da i śojas sije̮. kujim sutki ćula·las. staru·ka me̮de̮·te̮ (ińde̮) stari·kse̮ ni̮li̮sla: "mun — šue̮ —, vaje̮·t sije̮ dobro·nas!" stari·k munas.*

4. *staru·ka tupe̮·ššez pe̮ža·le̮, a ki̮ća·n bokas ćećća·le̮, ľawge̮: "stari·k lokte̮, meše̮·k-ti̮r koskaez vaje̮." "ak, te i̮le̮ste̮m, te, na śoj da šu: 'stari·k lokte̮, staru·ka-*

mouse comes out and whispers: "Hide at the back of the stove, and I'll mislead him." Then it took the bell and began to run about, from the stove to the floor, from the floor up to the hanging bed. The ghost pursues it, chasing it all through the night but he cannot catch it. The cock crows, and the ghost flees. He leaves the chest behind. The girl takes a look at the chest: it is full of treasures. Next morning it happens again, and also the day after. The girl has three chests left to her.

2. On the fourth day the old man comes to bring home the girl. Together with her treasures he puts her on the sleigh, and they leave, singing. At home the stepmother is baking rolls. The little dog barks: "The old man's daughter is brought home with all her treasures." "Oh, you stupid dog, what you should say is this: 'The bones of the old man's daughter are brought home'." The little dog eats the rolls and continues: "The old man's daughter is brought home with all her treasures." And the old man really comes, carrying the girl's valuables that fill the sleigh. They are hardly able to carry them into the house.

3. The old woman grows envious of the girl, and says: "Take my own daughter there as well! Let her come home with treasures!" The old man seats the old woman's daughter on the sleigh and takes her to the place. The old woman puts wheat-bread, barley-flour and salt in her bag. She gives her all sorts of things, the best kind of oakum to spin. They arrive in the middle of the forest. The old man says: "Never fear, I shall be back by nightfall!" The girl answers: "Who's asking you to come here? I'll live alone!" She lights the stove and begins to cook. The bread turns into stone, the flour into ash, and the salt into sand. She cooks porridge, but it is uneatable. A little mouse comes out. "Give me something to eat, little girl!" — it says. "Get out of here for I myself have nothing to eat! How could I feed you as well?" The mouse grows angry but says nothing. Late at night the ghost enters the house. His beard reaches down to his feet, snot and spit come out of his nose and mouth, his head is the breadth of a sieve. "Wash me, little girl!" — says he. "Wash yourself if you need a wash!" The ghost does not say a word. Then he asks: "Where are you going to sleep, little girl?" "I shall sleep on top of the stove." The ghost lies in the hanging bed; he comes down that night and devours the girl. Three days pass by. The old woman sends the old man for her daughter: "Go and bring her home with all her wealth!" The old man goes off.

4. The old woman bakes rolls. The little dog jumps about and barks: "The old man is coming, bringing a sack full of bones." "Oh, shameless dog, here you are, eat and say: 'The old man is coming, bringing the old woman's daughter and a sleigh full of valuables'!" The little dog eats it

liś nilkasę vajeꞏtę doď-tir dobroꞏen'." *a kićaꞏn śojas da bera aśśis:* "*stariꞏk loktę, mešęꞏk-tir koskaez vaję.*" *i biľ loktas stariꞏk, pirtas mešęꞏk ǯoǯ šeras giľ-goľ kištas koskaesę.*

188.

1. *ker-kę etik carstvòn, etik gosudarstvòn olis car. silen veli kujim nil. nillez velisę eďďen basekeś i car nijes eďďen ľubiꞏtis. vot et-pir nija korśisę carliś, med-bi sijaležis nijes guľaꞏjtni sadin. car čektis munni guľaꞏjtni sad kuźa, no aćis zakaźiꞏtis služaꞏnkajasli, med-bi silen nillez ez pidę pirę sadas. vot nillez guľaꞏjteni sad kuźa, ľubuꞏjććeni priroꞏdanas, kileni kajjezliś ǯulźem. no drug leptiꞏśis iǯit vina tel i nuis kiććęꞏkę nillesę. služaꞏnkaes gorzeni ni ponda. nija polemen viśtalisę carlę, mij siliś nillesę nuis kiććę-kę tel. car śetis prikaꞏz, aǯǯini carskej nillesę i kin aǯǯas nijes, to car śetas etik nilsę žeńiꞏk saję i śetas nagraꞏda.*

2. *i vot tom oťir pondisę koššini carskej nillesę, no ńe-kin oz vermi aǯǯini nijes. carlen veli soldaꞏt, i v a ꞏ n u š k a d u r a č o ꞏ k. vot sija loktis car dinę i šuę:* "*me aǯǯa teńćit nillestę.*" *car śetis silę eššęꞏ kik soldaꞏtes. i v a ꞏ n medis munni koššini nillesę oǯ asilnas. ritnas sija pukśis pos-eǯ vilę i pondis orsni garmoꞏška vilin. kiǯ toľko sija pondis orsni, drug kitiꞏś-kę lois si oǯin ućeꞏťik ǯor stariꞏk, kuź toša i pondis jektini. stariꞏk jektis, jektis i miǯis ńi, a i v a ꞏ n śo orsę i orsę. vot i pondis kelmiśni stariꞏk i v a ꞏ nlę, med-bi sija dugdis orsni. jeśľi sija dugdas, to stariꞏkis medis silę mij-kę viśtalni. i v a ꞏ n dugdis orsni. stariꞏk viśtalis silę: carskej nillez oleni źmejjez ordin. seśśa stariꞏk ńem ez viśtal i medis piššini, no i v a ꞏ n vermis siję kutni. i v a ꞏ n boštis ćurka, vaćkis siję ćeren, ćurkaiś artmis šeľ. i artmem šeľas i v a ꞏ n śujiꞏštis stariꞏkliś kuź tošsę i aćis munis uźni. oǯ asilnas sija ćeććis i aǯǯilis, mij stariꞏkis abu, a toľko koľććema ńe-una tošis. i v a ꞏ n koris aśśis jorttesę munni. i drug sija kaźalis vir, keda veli mu vilin. i v a ꞏ n dogadaꞏjććis, mij viris stariꞏkislen. nija rešiꞏtisę munni stariꞏk vir kuźa. munisę, munisę i drug sľedis ešis. aǯǯeni,*

up and again continues: "The old man is coming, bringing a sack full of bones." And the old man really comes, brings the sack to the middle of the floor and shakes out the rattling bones.

188. [How Ivan rescued the Tsar's daughters from the dragons]

1. Once upon a time there lived a Tsar in some tsardom, in some state. He had three daughters. The girls were very beautiful, and the Tsar loved them dearly. One day they asked the Tsar to let them out for a walk in the garden. The Tsar permitted them to walk in the garden, but commanded his servants not to let the girls go far into the garden. Well, the girls walk in the garden, enjoying the beauties of nature, listening to the twittering birds. All of a sudden, a powerful wind arose and carried the girls off somewhere. The maidservants weep for them. All in a fright, they report to the Tsar that the girls were carried off by the wind to some unknown place. The Tsar gave orders that the girls must be found, and that the one who finds them would be given one of his daughters in marriage, and a great distinction besides.

2. The young men began to search for the girls, but none of them succeeded in finding them. The Tsar had a soldier, called Stupid Ivanuška. He came to the Tsar, and said: "I shall find your daughters." The Tsar ordered another two soldiers to keep him company. Early in the morning Ivan set out to search for the girls. In the evening he sat outside in the porch and began to play the accordion. Suddenly an old man of small stature and with a long beard sprang out, and began to dance. The old man danced and danced, and he had grown tired already, but Ivan went on playing and playing. The old man began to beg Ivan to stop playing the accordion. If he stopped, the old man would have say something to him. Ivan stopped playing. The old man says: "The Tsar's daughters are living with the dragons." After this the old man did not say anything, but began to run; Ivan, however, was able to grab him. Ivan took a stump of wood, and drove a hatchet into it so that a cleft remained. Into that cleft Ivan stuck the old man's beard to hold it tight, and then went to bed. Early in the morning he got up and saw the old man had disappeared, only a little of his beard had remained behind. Ivan called his companions to set out. Suddenly he noticed a spot of blood on the ground. Ivan soon discovered that the blood belonged to the old man. They decided to proceed along the track of blood the old man left behind. They walked on and on, until the track suddenly vanished. They found a pit in the earth. They tried to measure the depth of the pit with a rope, but the rope did not reach down

muas em jama. nija pondise̮ merajtni̮ jamaliś pi̮di̮nse̮ geze̮n, no gez ez suǯ. sečče̮m pi̮di̮n ve̮li jamàs. domalise̮ ešše̮ e̮tik gez eta gez berde̮ i toľko sek vermise̮ mera·jtni̮ jama pi̮de̮·sse̮. i v a · n šue̮ jorttezle̮: "kinle̮-ke̮ kolas lećći̮ni̮ geze̮n jamaas i viʒe̮·tni̮, mi̮j em seććin." jorttezi̮s ši̮ oz śete̮, pole̮ni̮. sek i v a · n ni̮le̮ šue̮: "ti mene̮ ležete̮ geze̮n jamaas! a ke̮r me loa jama pi̮de̮·si̮n, sek me gezse̮ ve̮ŕźe̮ta, tijanle̮ loe̮ znak, mi̮j me seććin. me loa seććin sećće̮·ʒ, ki̮ćće̮·ʒ og aʒʒi̮ ni̮llezes; a ke̮r aʒʒa, to vokta [sic!] *be̮r eta jama pi̮de̮·sas i ve̮ŕźe̮ta gezse̮. sek tije̮ pondat lepti̮ni̮ mijane̮s." ke̮r ležise̮ pervo i v a · nes, ve̮li pemi̮t, a si̮ be̮ri̮n, ke̮r sija lois jama pi̮de̮·si̮n, lois e̮ďďe̮n jugi̮t. bi̮dlàn bi̮dmise̮ base̮k pujez, ʒul-źisni̮ kajjez, kote̮·rtis ju. i v a · n munis oʒlań, ľubu·jććis priro·danas. drug sija każa·lis base̮k ni̮le̮s, ke̮da gi̮lja·śis ju doras. i v a · n pondis si̮ke̮t baji·tni̮. ni̮l viśtaśis si̮le̮: "me carske̮j ni̮l, mijane̮s guśalis ďeveťigla·ve̮j źmej. me ola tŕoχ-glave̮j źmejke̮t. sija samej uće̮t von ďeveťigla·ve̮j źmejle̮n. a me̮d sojjeze̮ ole̮ni̮ i̮li̮nʒi̮k." i v a · n viśtalis, mi̮j loktis osvoboďi·tni̮ nije̮s. carske̮j nue̮tis sije̮ gortas. vaje̮·tis e̮tik boćka di̮ne̮ i šue̮: "eta boćkaas em śiľne̮j va, ke̮da sotte̮ śila, jeśľi sije̮s juan. te ju sije̮ ćoʒʒi̮k i boćkaese̮ kole̮ vežni̮ mestaeznas. źmej će̮ktas juni̮ teni̮t sija boćkaiś, ke̮dai̮n vai̮s besśiľne̮j, a aći̮s juas śiľne̮jse̮. a jeśľi mestanas veža, sek loas me̮d-ńož." i v a · n toľko ještis juni̮ i boćkaesse̮ vežni̮ mestaeznas, ki̮ʒ pondis ki̮lni̮ i̮ʒi̮t šum. ete̮ lokte̮ źmej. care·vna ʒebis i v a · ne̮s me̮d komnatae̮. źmej loktis i šuis, mi̮j paχńite̮ ruske̮j duke̮n. care·vna viśtalis, mi̮j em ruske̮j mort i sija me̮de̮ źmejke̮t vojujtni̮. i v a · n petis, a źmej si̮le̮ će̮ktis juni̮ vase̮ boćkaśis. i v a · nle̮n lois una śila, a źmejle̮n śilai̮s e̮śis. vot ponde̮·ććise̮ nija vojujtni̮. i v a · nle̮n ve̮li lećit meć, a źmej paritis bie̮n. sotis ·i v a · ne̮s, no i v a · n vermis keralni̮ kujimnan jurse̮. care·vna lois e̮ďďe̮n rad i pe̮dari·tis aslas osvoboďi·ťeľle̮ śťekla·nne̮j dvore·ć. i v a · n će̮ktis vićći·śni̮ sije̮, ke̮r sija loktas me̮d ni̮llesk̮e̮t.*

3. *i v a · n munis oʒlań. aʒʒe̮ me̮d carske̮j ni̮le̮s ju dori̮n. ni̮l viśtalis si̮le̮, mi̮j sija ole̮ šeśťigla·ve̮j źmej ordi̮n, še̮r von ďeveťiglave̮j źmejle̮n. ni̮l će̮ktis vežni̮ boćkaesse̮ mestaeznas, će̮ktis juni̮ śiľne̮j vase̮. i v a · n vermis i ete̮ źmejse̮, ore̮tis źmejliś ki̮llese̮ mećen i puktis aslas sumkae̮. ni̮l koźnalis si̮le̮ śere·branne̮j dvore·c.*

to the bottom. So deep was the pit. They tied another rope to the first one, and only then were they able to measure the depth of the pit. Ivan says to his companions: "One of us must drop down the pit on the rope and see what is there." His companions say nothing, they are afraid. Then Ivan says: "Let me down the pit on this rope! When I reach the bottom of the pit, I shall jerk the rope, and that will tell you that I am there. I shall stay until I find the girls; when I have found them, I shall return to the bottom of this pit, and jerk the rope again. Then you will pull us up!" When Ivan was let down, at first it was dark, but later when he was at the bottom of the pit it became very bright. Beautiful trees were growing everywhere, and birds were twittering, and a river was flowing there. Ivan went on enjoying the delights of nature. Suddenly he perceived a beautiful girl rinsing some clothes by the river. Ivan began to talk to her. The girl told him: "I am the Tsar's daughter, and it is the nine-headed dragon that kidnapped us. I am living with the three-headed dragon. He is the youngest brother of the nine-headed dragon. My sisters are living farther off." Ivan told her that he had come to rescue them. The Tsar's daughter led him home. She took him to a barrel, saying: "There is strong water in this barrel that increases strength if you drink of it. Be quick and drink, then the barrels will have to be changed. The dragon will command you to drink from that barrel in which the water has no strength, while he will drink from the strong one. But if I change their places, everything will turn out differently." Ivan had hardly enough time to drink and change the barrels before a great noise was heard. The dragon is coming. The Tsar's daughter hid Ivan in another room. The dragon arrived and said that there was a Russian smell there. The Tsar's daughter said there was a Russian there who wanted to fight the dragon. Ivan came out, and the dragon ordered him to drink water from the barrel. Ivan acquired great strength while the dragon ran out of strength. They started fighting. Ivan had a sharp sword, and the dragon breathed burning fire. He burnt Ivan but Ivan was able to cut off all his three heads. The Tsar's daughter was very glad, presenting her saviour with the palace of glass. Ivan told her to wait until he returned with the other girls.

3. Ivan went on his way. He finds the next girl on the banks of the river. The girl said that she was living with the six-headed dragon who was the middle brother of the nine-headed dragon. The girl ordered him to change the barrels, and also told him to drink strong water. Ivan defeated this dragon too, cut out his tongues and put them in his bag. The girl presented him with a palace of silver.

4. *i v a · n mune̮ oǯlań. aǯǯe̮ kujme̮·t ni̮lse̮ ju dori̮n. vištaśisni e̮ta-me̮d-ni̮sle̮. i v a · n keris siǯ, ki̮ǯ če̮ktis ni̮li̮s. dvenaćeťiglave̮j źmejke̮t ve̮li i̮ǯi̮t kośa-śe̮m, no i v a · n i sije̮s vermis. solda·t i care·vna e̮ta-me̮di̮sle̮ gľeńi·ććise̮. nija dogovori·ććise̮ e̮tlaaśni̮, ke̮r loktase̮ aslani̮s carstvoe̮. ni̮l podari·tis si̮le̮ zolote̮j dvoreć.*

5. *i v a · n boštis carske̮j ni̮llese̮ i loktise̮ jama pi̮de̮·s di̮ne̮. pe̮ri·śži̮k soji̮s višta·lis i v a · nle̮, mi̮j jeśľi sije̮s, i v a · ne̮s oz lepte̮, to ke̮r vermas petni̮ ja-maśis, med kerkuezi̮n pešli̮lle̮, pe̮jim pi̮m iľi abu sija. jeśľi pi̮m, to ve̮lise̮ sete̮n ńe-važe̮n. i v a · n ve̮ržetis gezse̮. si̮le̮n jorttez pondise̮ lepti̮ni̮ perve̮j ni̮lse̮. i ke̮r kaźalise̮ ni̮lse̮, solda·ttez pondise̮ sporitni̮ ni̮l ponda. e̮tik šue̮: "sija menam. me̮dik šue̮: "ńet, menam." vot leptise̮ i me̮d ni̮le̮s. be̮ra· sporite̮ni̮. a ke̮r leptise̮ kujme̮·t ni̮le̮s, nija ćuť ez kośaśe̮ si̮ ponda. i v a · ne̮s siǯ ez i lepte̮, a aśni̮s mu-nise̮ oǯlań. i v a · n sula·li̮štis i reši·tis munni̮ oǯlań. loktis ki̮če̮·m-ke̮ kerkue̮, pukśis pi̮zan dore̮ i pondis orsni̮ garmo·ška vi̮li̮n. drug lois si̮ śin oǯi̮n toštе̮m stari·ki̮s, ke̮da pi̮ššis si̮ di̮niś. i v a · n orse̮, orse̮, a stari·k je̮kte̮, oz vermi̮ sultni̮. i pondis stari·k kelmiśni̮. i v a · n vištalis si̮le̮: "jeśľi te mene̮ leptan mu vi̮le̮, to dugda orsni̮." stari·k leptis i v a · nse̮ mu vi̮le̮. eta kade̮ solda·ttez loktise̮ ni̮llеske̮t car di̮ne̮ i vištalise, mi̮j nija mezdise̮ care·vnaesse̮ i e̮ni med car śetas ni̮ saje̮ aśśis ni̮llesse̮. car śetis aśśis soglaśi·ese̮ svaďba vi̮le̮. eta di̮rńi i v a · n loktis kerku di̮ne̮. pešlis pe̮jimse̮, sija ve̮li šoni̮t, sić-ke̮ [ɔ: siǯ-ke̮] nija ńe-i̮li̮neś. i v a · n loktis gorode̮. ki̮lis, mi̮j oťiri̮s cari̮sle̮n ge̮tevi·ćće̮ni̮ svaďba keže̮. ni̮llez vištalise ajni̮sle̮: "mi munam žeńik saje̮ sek, ke̮r nija solda·ttez vajase̮ mijanle̮ me̮d carstvoiś narja·ddez, dvore·ććez." i v a · n ki̮lis eta ji̮liś. ojnas petis pos-e̮ǯ vi̮le̮ i pondis orsni̮ garmo·ška vi̮li̮n. loktis tošte̮m stari·k. je̮ktis, je̮ktis i ke̮r mi̮ǯis, jualis, mi̮j kole̮ i v a · nli̮. i v a · n vištalis stari·kle̮: "vaj meni̮m me̮d carstvoiś dvore·ććez i dvore·ććese̮ sulte̮t carske̮j dvore·c oǯe̮! vaj i care·vnaesliś narja·ddese̮!" stari·k siǯ keris. asilnas car sajmis i aǯǯi̮lis: sula-le̮ni̮ i̮ǯi̮t base̮k dvore·ccez, ke̮dna daže̮ guśale̮ni̮ śinnez, siǯ nija jugjale̮ni̮. ni̮llez vištalise̮ ajni̮sle̮, mi̮j eta dvore·ccezi̮s me̮d carstvoiś. nija dogada·jććise̮, mi̮j i v a · ni̮s lovja i e̮ni ole̮ gorodas.*

6. *i v a · n d u r a · k boštis care·vnaezliś narja·ddese̮ i sumka, ki̮te̮·n ve̮-lise̮, ki̮te̮·n olise̮ źmejjezle̮n ore̮te̮m ki̮llez. i v a · n loktis car di̮ne̮ i vištalis,*

4. Ivan went on his way. He found the third girl on the banks of the river. They told each other everything. Ivan did what the girl told him to do. There was a big fight with the twelve-headed dragon, but Ivan conquered him as well. The soldier and the Tsar's daughter took a liking for each other. They agreed to marry when they returned to their own country. The girl presented him with a palace of gold.

5. Ivan took the tsar's daughters to the bottom of the pit. The eldest sister told Ivan that if they refused to lift him up now, at some time when he could get out of the pit he should examine if the ash is hot or not in the house. If it was hot, they would have left not long before. Ivan gave a jerk to the rope. His companions started to pull up the first girl. When they caught sight of the girl, they started to quarrel over her. One of them says: "She is mine!" The other says: "No, she is mine!" They pulled up the second girl too. Again they quarrelled. When they pulled up the third girl, they nearly started a fight over her. So they did not even pull Ivan up, but went on their way. Iven stopped there and decided to continue his way. He arrived at some house, sat down at the table and began to play his accordion. Suddenly the bearless old man appeared before his eyes, the one who had fled from him. Ivan plays while the old man dances and cannot stop. The old man began to beseech him. Ivan said to him: "If you will pull me up to the surface of the earth, I will stop playing." The old man pulled Ivan up to the surface of the earth. Meanwhile the soldiers arrived at the Tsar's and said that they were the ones who had rescued the Tsar's daughters and that the Tsar must marry the daughters to them. The Tsar gave his consent to the weddings. In the meantime Ivan arrived at the house. He examined the ash, it was hot, so they could not be far away. Ivan arrived at the city. He heard news that the Tsar's people were preparing for a wedding. The girls said to their father: "We will marry when the soldiers bring us dresses and palaces from the other tsardom." Ivan also heard of this. At night he went out to the porch and began to play on the accordion. The beardless old man came. He danced and danced and when he grew tired, he asked what Ivan wanted. Ivan said to the old man: "Bring me palaces from the other tsardom and stand those palaces in front of the Tsar's palace!" The old man acted accordingly. In the morning the Tsar awoke and saw beautiful palaces standing there, and they were so bright that they blinded the eyes. The girls told their father that those palaces came from another tsardom. They realized that Ivan was alive and living in the city.

6. Stupid Ivan took the robes of the Tsar's daughters, as well as the bag containing the severed tongues of the dragons. Then Ivan went to the Tsar,

mij sija mezdis nillesę i miććalis źmejjezliś killez i narja·ddessę. nillez viśta·śisę bide·s i v a · n jiliś ajnislę. car eďďen legaśis solda·ttez vilę, kedna bebetisę carsę i čektis pukśetni nijes ťurmaę. med lunas veli svaďba. i v a · n getraśis peri·źźik [ɔ: peri·śźik] soj vilas. (me setən veli, sur, braga jui, a emam ńem ez śur.)

189.

olis eďďen umnej jorš aslas norà·n sto godśa una·źik. nora·s veli pemid i ʒeskit. ńe šondi juge·ris seććin ez śurli, ńe šonit duk ez kil. silen ńe-kin ez vel i si ordę ńe-kin ez volli. toľko pukalę nora·s, ńe-kinlę oz kol, pir dreźźitę. nora· oʒet švirkjeni medi·k ćerijez i etik ez ińťeresu·jććí sien, eťiklę ted vilę oz uś jualni joršliś, kiʒ sija kužis sto god olni, ńe šuka sije ez ńiliśt, ńe rak ez ľet, ńe ćeri-kijiś ez kij vugiren. dosto·jnej graždanaen oz vermę liďďiśni jorššez, kedna po-lem uvja pukaleni nora·in da dreźźiteni. ńe ena, ńe graždana, a bespoľeznej jorššez, ńe-kinlę niśań ńe šonit, ńe keʒit. i uśis ted vilas kulem oʒas aslas olanis i jualis, kinę·s sija burę·tis, kinlę kil viśtalis, kin kilis si jiliś. i bidę·s ena vo-prossez vilę kolśis silę śetni otve·t: ńe-kines, ńe-kinlę,, ńe-kin. i ńe-kin siję eďďen umnejen ez šu.

190.

ker-kę ńe-važen olis etik mort. silen veli iʒit śemja· i olis šuć umeľa. sija so-vetu·ććis aslas ińisket, mij kolę kerni, med-bi petkę·tni śemja·sę ńuždaiś. bed-ńa·k reši·tis munni uʒa·lni boga·tej ordę. boštis koto·mka da petis oʒ asilnas tuję. munis siʒ sija bidsa lun. pondis śormini ńi i bedńa·k pondis munni ćoź-źik, med-bi ojeʒ lokni med ďerevńaę, kitę·n sija medis uʒalni. drug sija kilis kiče·m-kę šutńa·lem. sija leptis jursę i kaźalis, tuj boket munę eďďen iʒit mort, keda veli et-koď giriś puezket kuźanas. eta veľika·nis i šutńalis. bedńa·k polźis i medis munni eššę ćoźźika. i eta kuź tušaa mortis tožę pondis munni ćoźźika, šo gorę·nʒika i gorę·nʒika šutńa·lemen. iʒit mortis loktis matę·ʒik bedńa·k dorę. sek bedńa·k siję burʒika viʒę·tis. juris silen veli kiʒ paravoznej koťol, kiezis kiʒ kura·nnez, a paś-kemis veli źelo·nej ńičiś. giriś bija śinnez siʒ i soć-ćisę. bedńa·k uśis saďteg, a veľika·n šo sula·lę. ńe-ilin si dinśań da šutńa·lę. ńeuna kujlem berin bedńa·k saďaśis da pondis liďďini moľi·tvaes, kednes sija ker-kę velę·tlis. i mij-žę lois? iʒit mortis verźę·ććis mesta vilśis i pondis munni

saying that it was he who had rescued the girls; he also showed him the dragons' tongues and the dresses. The girls told their father all about Ivan. The Tsar grew very angry with the soldiers who had cheated him, and ordered them to be thrown into prison. Next day the wedding feast was held. Ivan married the eldest sister. (I was present, drinking beer, home-brewed beer, although not a drop of it got into my mouth.)

189. [The clever perch]

There lived a very clever perch in its own hole, and it was more than a hundred years old. The hole was dark and narrow. Neither sunbeam could get there nor warmth could ever be felt there. It had no dependants, and nobody came to see it. It just sits in its hole, not wanted by anybody, trembling all the time. Other fish swim swiftly past the opening of the hole, and none of them takes any interest in it. It never occurs to any of them to ask the perch how it was able to live for a hundred years without being swallowed by a pike , seized by a crab or caught by a fisherman. By no means can one regard as honourable citizens the perches which in their fear sit and tremble in their holes. No, they are not citizens but useless perches, neither warm nor cold to anybody. As it was nearing its death it reviewed its life, asking whom had it treated well, whom had it addressed kindly, who had heard about it. To all these questions it had to give the following answers: nobody, nobody, nobody. And nobody said it was very clever.

190. [The poor man and the forest ghost]

In olden times there once lived a man. He had a big family and always lived badly. He took counsel with his wife as to the ways and means of relieving his family of misery. The poor man made up his mind to go to work with the rich man. He took his cloak and started on his way early in the morning. All day long he walked like this. It was growing late now, and the poor man began to walk faster, so that he should reach the next village of whistling. He raised his head and saw a huge man walking at the side of the road; he was as tall as the trees. It was this giant that was whistling. The poor man was frightened and began to walk faster. And this man of tall stature also began to walk fast, whistling louder and louder. The giant came closer to the poor man. Then the poor man took a closer look at him. His head was as big as the boiler of a steamer, his hands as large as rakes, while his clothes were made of green moss. His big, fiery eyes were burning. The poor man collapsed in a swoon, while the giant just stood by. Having

me̮dla-pe̮le̮. i drug sovśe·m e̮šis. bedńa·k tulis śinnesse̮, ez-ľi si̮le̮ kažićći̮, mi̮j ve̮rśa morti̮s ki̮ćće̮·-ke̮ e̮šis. bedńa·k ubeďi·ććis, mi̮j veľika·ni̮s bi̮ľiś e̮šis. sija ćeććis da ćoža·ži̮k munis ďere·vńae̮ǯ. loktis sećće̮ da meda·śis uǯa·lni̮ boga·te̮j orde̮.

191. *ge̮traśe̮·m ji̮liś*

1. *mijan ni̮lkaez da zonkaez te̮dsa·śilse̮ oďži̮k [ɔ: oǯǯi̮k] orsanneze̮n iľi, ki̮ǯ šuśe̮, pukala·nneze̮n. kuče̮m-ke̮ kerkūn iľi bańan ri̮tnas ni̮lkaez e̮kśi̮·llise̮ pećki̮ni̮. śerani̮s nija vaja·llise̮ śoja·n da jua·n: sur iľi jua·n, tuji·ssezi̮n koľťťez, bľinnez i me̮di·k strepńa· (bi̮d-be̮rśa). ni̮lkaez pećkise̮ ri̮ti̮l-bi̮t da śi̮lise̮ peśńaez, a zonkaez orsise̮ bara·nneze̮n, koľťťeze̮n. puktase̮ ki̮ni̮m-ke̮ koľť ǯoǯe̮, porog ultas, a seśśa eta-me̮d veže̮n (eta-me̮d be̮rśań) ćapka·le̮ni̮ gi̮ne̮ve̮j mać (šar). kin inmas, sija ki̮je̮ koľťse̮. kin kužis, orsis garmo·ńńān (garmo·ńńa vi̮li̮n). muke̮d ni̮lkaes orsise̮ pe̮ľa·nnez vi̮li̮n i piksa·nnez vi̮li̮n. nija je̮ktise̮. ni̮lkaes geśťite̮·tise̮ zonkaese̮ geśťińe·ććeze̮n. di̮r mi̮jiś pi̮d oje̮ ni̮lkaez i zonkaez munise̮ aslani̮s gortteze̮. zonkaez stara·ććise̮ me̮de̮·tni̮ ni̮lkaese̮, bi̮di̮s aśśis. ge̮traśe̮·m vote̮ǯ ni̮lkaez i zonkaez dogova·rivaćći̮li̮se̮.*

2. *si-be̮ri̮n zonkai̮s baji·tlis aj-ma·mi̮ske̮t, kine̮s sija me̮de̮ bośni̮. seśśa ježeľi aj-ma·mi̮s se̮glaśi·ćći̮llise̮, to arśań-že̮ ińdi̮·llise̮ koraśi·śśeze̮s. sek pervo ińdi̮·llise̮ kine̮s-ke̮ je̮ze̮s jue̮re̮n, śetase̮, oze̮ nija ni̮lni̮se̮ nija zon saje̮. jeśľi ni̮lkai̮sle̮n aj-mami̮s ez e̮tka·ži̮tle̮, to ińde̮·tlise̮ svatteze̮s kora·śni̮. kora·śni̮ vetli̮·llise̮ muke̮·dćid (muke̮·ććid) ďaď, kor veža·j, kor je̮z suśe·ddez, kor zonkai̮sle̮n aji̮s kinke̮·t-ńibuď, a muke̮ććid ni̮ke̮t munlis i aći̮s že̮ńi̮·ki̮s. koraśi·ssez pi̮rase̮ kerkue̮, sultase̮ porog ulte̮ i sula·lle̮ni̮, oz pukśe̮. ke̮źaji·ni̮s če̮kte̮ nije̮ pukśi̮ni̮. nija śoronno· oz pukśe̮. koda-ke̮ koraśi·śśez kola·siś ponde̮ baji·tni̮. pervo sija ponde̮·te̮ pogo·ďďa ji̮liś, si̮ be̮ri̮n ponde̮ juaśni̮, ki̮ǯ olśe̮, seśśa veľ di̮r mi̮jiś ponde̮ kora·śni̮. baji·te̮: mijan pe̮ em zel bur zonka, kodile̮ loktis kad ńi ge̮tra·śni̮, a tijan pe em ni̮lka i pondis ośki̮ni̮ že̮ńi·kse̮. sija pe̮ mijan i̮ǯi̮t, bi̮če̮m, uǯa i boga·te̮j: mi̮lki̮d si̮le̮ bur, oz ju, ńe oz kurit, kośa·śni̮ oz kuž, olni̮ si̮ke̮t bur loas. mijan pe̮ śemja abu i̮ǯi̮t, uǯa·lni̮ oz kol una, ńań, poda em, tommesle̮ ti̮rmas. jeśľi ni̮lkai̮sle̮n*

lain there for a while, the poor man came and started to recite prayers which he had learned at some time. And what happened? The huge man stirred from his place and began to go in a different direction. And then he suddenly disappeared. The poor man rubbed his eyes to make sure that he was not merely imagining that the forest man had disappeared. The poor man was really convinced that the giant had indeed vanished. He got up and went all the faster to the village. He arrived and hired himself out to work for the rich man.

191. About getting married

1. Our daughters and sons, in earlier times, made each other's acquaintance through games or, as they say, at meetings. The girls gathered together to spin in some house or bath-house in the evening. They brought food and drink with them: beer, kvas, eggs in birch-bark vessels, and pancakes and all sorts of food. The girls would spin all night and sing songs, while the lads were playing like rams butting each other, or played with eggs. They place a few eggs on the floor under the threshold, and then one after another start throwing balls at them. He who hits it wins the egg. Those who could, played the accordion. Other girls played the bagpipes or pipe. They also danced. The girls presented the boys with gifts. After a while, late at night, they started for home. The lads were eager to see the girls home, each his own girl. Before marrying, the girls and the boys made an agreement.

2. Then the boy discussed with his parents the girl he wanted to marry. Then, if the parents agreed, they sent suitors from autumn onwards, to ask for the girl's hand. First of all someone was sent to ask if they were willing to give their daughter in marriage to the lad. If the girl's parents did not object, suitors were sent. Sometimes an uncle, sometimes the godfather, neighbours who were not related, sometimes the young man's father in the company of someone else went to ask for the girl's hand, and sometimes the bridegroom himself went with them. The suitors entered the house and stop on the threshold; they stand, they do not sit down. The master of the house asks them to take a seat. All the same they will not sit down. One of the suitors begins to speak. First he speaks about the weather, then he puts questions as to how the people in the house are faring, and only then does he begin to ask for the girl in marriage. He speaks like this: "We have a very good son for whom it is time to marry, and you have a daughter . . .", and he starts praising the bridegroom: "He has a fine figure, he is handsome, industrious and wealthy, quick of mind, he is neither a drunkard nor a

aj-mami̮s eze̮ me̮de̮ e̮tkaži̮·tni̮, to pukše̮·tlise̮ ge̮ššese̮ pi̮za·n saje̮ ńań-sol dore̮. toľko sek koraśi·śśes pukśi̮·llise̮. jeśľi nija me̮dise̮ e̮tkaži̮·tni̮, to baji·tise̮, što ni̮lni̮s ešše̮· uće̮t, tom, ńem oz kuž kerni̮ i abu kad ešše̮· si̮le̮ munni̮ že̮ńi̮·k saje̮. kuče̮·m pe̮ si̮le̮ ešše̮· že̮ńi·k, aś ke̮ť mi̮gse̮ vela·las vurni̮. pondi̮·llise̮ spori·tni̮ i svattez munlise̮. a jeśľi aj-ma·mis se̮glaśi·ćći̮llise̮, nija ge̮śťite̮·tlise̮ svattese̮, a si̮ be̮ri̮n korise̮ di̮nani̮s ni̮lni̮se̮. vot tene̮ pe kora·śe̮ni̮, viśtal, munan, on. jeśľi ni̮lkai̮sle̮ že̮ńi̮·ki̮s gľeńi·ćći̮llis, sija śi̮ ez śetli̮ iľi šullis, što munas. pi̮za·n saji̮n jullise̮ vina, kode̮ vajlise̮ (vajli̮·llise̮) svattes. ni̮lkai̮s ez julli, i daže̮ ez puka·lli̮ pi̮za·n saji̮n.

3. *seśśa dogova·rivaćći̮lli̮se̮ ki-kutan ji̮liś. ki-kutan vi̮le̮ e̮tlan svatteske̮t voli̮·llis aći̮s že̮ńi̮·ki̮s. ki-kutan kosta ni̮lkai̮s, zonkai̮s, aj-ma·mmeznas (aj-ma·mmeznani̮s) bi̮de̮·nni̮s puka·llise pi̮za·n saji̮n i le̮śe̮ććise̮ svaďba keže̮. dogova·rivaćći̮llise̮, kuče̮·m kade̮, kor loas svaďbai̮s, ki̮če̮·m loas ńeve·stale̮n prida·nej i mi̮j le̮śe̮·tase̮ pir keže̮. ki-kuta·n be̮ri̮n ńe že̮ńi̮·k, ńe ńeve·sta e̮tkaži̮·ćći̮ni̮ ez ńi vermi̮lle̮. ńeve·sta ge̮te̮vi·ććis že̮ńi̮k saje̮. si̮le̮ otsa·llise̮ ni̮lkaez, podruškaez. nija ge̮rʒʒise̮ ćulkiez, kepiśśez, ćuńa kepiśśez, noski·ez, ge̮rʒʒise̮ śeran, bi̮d-re̮ma še̮rtiś. ki̮jise̮ pe̮kre̮·mmez da kuša·kkez garusiś i mi̮će̮·te̮m noje̮vej suńi·śśeziś. nija vurlise̮ že̮ńi̮·k-je̮rne̮·s, veššan (vešjan), vi̮ši̮va·jtlise̮ ni̮lkai̮sliś i zonkai̮sliś je̮rne̮·sse̮.*

4. *svaďba vote̮ʒ ńeve·stase̮ miśśe̮·tlise̮ (miśśe̮·tli̮llise̮, pi̮lśe̮tlise̮) bańai̮n. oʒ asi̮lnas že̮ńi̮·ki̮s druškaeske̮t i kinke̮·t-ke̮ rodńa·śiś ve̮llez vi̮li̮n mune̮ni̮ ńeve·stala. muke̮·ććid ve̮li̮llise̮ ńe e̮tik, ki̮k ve̮l, a kuji·m, vit, śiźi·m, e̮kmi̮s i daže̮ das-e̮tik; pi̮r ve̮li ńićo·tne̮j ćislo: ve̮lle̮se̮ i sbrujase̮ baśi·tlise̮ ľentaeze̮n, kuša·kkeze̮n, pe̮kre̮·mmeze̮n, mića ći̮šja·nneze̮n. duga· berde̮ doma·llise̮ śiľka·nnez. ni̮lka ordi̮n piru·jtlise̮. ni̮ orde̮ e̮kśi̮·llise̮ una ge̮śśez: re̮dńa·iś, podru·škaez, suśeddez. vermis lokni̮ bi̮dsa ďere·vńa. i bi̮de̮·nni̮se̮ ge̮śťite̮·tise̮. že̮ńi·k, ńeve·sta, re̮dńa·i̮s i kore̮m ge̮śśes puka·llise̮ pi̮za·n saji̮n. kin pi̮za·n sajas oz te̮r, puka·llise̮ labi·ććez vi̮li̮n, zapadńa· vi̮li̮n. bi̮de̮·nnise̮ jukta·llise̮ sure̮n, i̮re̮·še̮n, ćeľaď-pe̮le̮sle̮ (ćeľaď-pe̮le̮sse̮) verdise̮ šańgaeze̮n, pire̮·ggeze̮n, koľťťeze̮n. e̮tik mort ez koľćći̮lli̮ siʒ.*

smoker, he cannot even be said to be quarrelsome, it will be fine to live with him. Our family is not large, she will not have to work much, there are bread and cattle, enough for the young people." If the girl's parents did not wish to object, they bade the guests sit at table with bread and salt on it. Only then did the suitors sit down. If they wanted to refuse, they spoke in a way to bring out that their daughter was small, young, did not know how to do anything, and that it was not yet time for her to marry. What sort of a bridegroom would be suitable for her? First she must learn how to hem her blouse. A debate ensued, after which the suitors left. But if the parents agreed, they entertained the suitors and then called out their daughter. Look now, they want you to marry; tell them if you are willing to marry the young man. If the girl liked the young man, she did not say a word, or said she would marry him. At the table they drank vodka which the suitors had brought with them. The girl did not drink at all, indeed she did not even sit at the table.

3. Following this, they agreed upon the betrothal. For the betrothal the bridegroom himself appeared with the suitors. During the betrothal both the girl and the young man, as well as the parents and all present were sat at the table discussing the preparations for the wedding. They agreed on the time of the wedding, what dowry the bride would bring and what food they should prepare for the wedding. After the betrothal, neither the bridegroom nor the bride could retreat. The bride was made ready for the wedding. The girls, her friends assisted her. They knitted stockings, gloves, ankle-socks and socks, gaudy ones, knitted from yarn of every colour. They knitted narrow and broad belts of wool and dyed cloth. They sewed the bridegroom's shirt and trousers, and embroidered the bride's blouse and the bridegroom's shirt.

4. Before the wedding ceremony the bride was washed and bathed in the bath-house. Early in the morning the bridegroom, the best man and some relative(s) mounted on horseback went to fetch the bride. Sometimes it was not one or two horses, but three, five, seven, nine and eleven, always odd numbers. The horses and their harness were decorated with ribbons, broad and narrow straps and beautiful kerchiefs. To the arched yokes small bells were fastened. They feasted at the bride's home. Many guests gathered together at their house: relations, girl-friends and neighbours. The whole village might come as well. And everybody was entertained. The bridegroom. the bride and the invited guests sat at the table. Those who could not get to the table were seated on benches, in the upper part of the cellar by the stove. Everybody was given beer and kvas to drink, and the children were given pies, pirogi and eggs to eat. Not one single person was left hungry

ńeve·sta ordśań munli̯·llise̯ vićkue̯ veńća·ćći̯ni̯. vićkuśań tommese̯ nue̯·tlise̯ že̯ńi̯·k orde̯. este̯n e̯kśi̯·llise̯ una ge̯ššez. pi̯d oje̯ ńeve·stase̯ že̯ńi̯·kke̯t nue̯·tlise̯ śeńi·ke̯ uźni̯. jeśl'i ve̯li e̯d'd'e̯n ke̯ǯi̯t, tommese̯ pi̯rtlise̯ ǯoǯi̯·le̯. asi̯lnas eššе̯· e̯kśi̯·llise̯ ge̯ššez. ni̯lkase̯ provera·jtlise̯: proka-l'i sija. ǯoǯas ve̯li pi̯rte̯m ti̯r iǯa·s. ge̯šśes nare̯·šne̯ sije̯ re̯źńi·tase̯ i če̯kte̯ni̯ ći̯ški̯ni̯ ǯoǯse̯. ni̯lkai̯s siǯ-že̯ asi̯l-bi̯t jukta·se̯. sija-že̯ lune̯ sija kaje̯·tle̯ va, otsa·lle̯ strepa·jtni̯, verdni̯ poda i siśań sija ponde̯ olni̯ kiǯ tomǯi̯k ke̯źa·jka.

192. *ćužte̯·m ji̯liś*

kagaez e̯ni ćužte̯ni̯ re̯d'i·l'ne̯j domi̯n, a od'ǯi̯k [ɔ: oǯǯi̯k] ćužti̯·llise̯, ki̯te̯·n šedas. śe̯ki̯t ińka med-be̯rja lunneze̯ǯ uǯa·llis. vetlis i̯be̯ vundi̯ni̯, i̯čkiśni̯, kurtni̯, kaje·tlis (kaje̯·tli̯llis) va, jukta·llis poda, ćil'ke̯·tlis me̯s, kerlis bi̯d-be̯rśa. muke̯·ććid kagai̯s i̯bi̯n i ćužli̯llis. stara·ććise̯ kerni̯ siǯ: med-bi̯ ńe-kin ez te̯d kaga ćužan ji̯liś, sije̯n ińkai̯s ćužtni̯te̯ peta·llis gide̯, munlis bańā il'i śeńike̯ i seććin ćužti̯·llis. ińka di̯ni̯n vermis loni̯ si̯ kosta tol'ko babi·ććiś. sija ore̯·tlis i doma·llis kagai̯sliś ge̯gse̯, sija mišše̯·tlis (mišše̯·tli̯llis) kagase̯ i ćužti·šse. ni̯ ponda nare̯·šne̯ lontli̯·llis baña. od'ǯi̯k bi̯d šog veśke̯·tlise̯ aśni̯s, kin kiǯ kužis.

193. *ǯebśe̯·m ji̯liś i kaśtiśe̯·m ji̯liś*

1. *ke̯r morti̯s pondas jona šoga·lni̯ i aǯǯe̯ni̯ ńi, sija ćoža kulas, sije̯ votte̯·de̯ni̯ torja ol'pa·ś vi̯le̯. ke̯r morti̯s pondas kulni̯ ńi, si̯le̯ stara·ćće̯ni̯ otsa·lni̯. kin-ke̯ rodńa·i̯s kola·siś: zon, ni̯l il'i mam lepte̯ni̯ si̯liś jurse̯ ki-soj vi̯lani̯s. sek pe̯ lolis ćožaǯi̯k (ćoǯǯi̯k) pete̯. od'ǯi̯k (odǯi̯k) veriti·šses baji·tlise̯, bi̯t't'e̯ (bi̯d'te̯) loli̯s pete̯ pe̯ par moz. ke̯r morti̯s kulas, sije̯ mišše̯·te̯ni̯, kore̯ni̯ nare̯·šne̯ (nare̯·šne̯j) mišše̯ti·šseze̯s. paśta·le̯ni̯ sije̯ vi̯l' paś-ke̯me̯, sina·le̯ni̯ si̯na·ne̯n, vodte̯·te̯ni̯ (votte̯·te̯ni̯) gre̯be̯. gre̯bas ol'sa·le̯ni̯ pervo kore̯ś l'is, sešša velt't'e̯ni̯ sije̯ kiče̯·m-ke̯ trepi·ćeze̯. sešša velt't'e̯ni̯ de̯rān (de̯raen), jure̯·ǯas pukte̯ni̯ ńe-iǯi̯t podu·ška, si̯ vi̯le̯ votte̯·te̯ni̯ kule̯m mortse̯. kijese̯ teće̯ni̯ si̯liś moro·s vi̯las. moro·s vi̯las-že̯ pukte̯ni̯ jen i masiś. sešša lokte̯ni̯ re̯dne̯·jjes proša·ćći̯ni̯. bi̯dis lokte̯ kule̯mis di̯ne̯, oka·le̯ sije̯ i mi̯j-ńi-bud' viśta·le̯, naprime·r: 'kujli̯ bura, tate̯n kužin olni̯ i seććin kuž!' nare̯·šne̯j gorziśi·šsez gorze̯ni̯ i med-matiś rodne̯·jjez d'erja·le̯ni̯, šue̯ni̯: 'kin vi̯le̯ te mene̯ kol'in e̯tname̯s? mi̯l'a te kol'in mene̯ ćel'ad'iske̯t, mi̯j me ponda kerni̯ te-*

From the bride's home they went to the church to the wedding. From the church the young couple were led to the bridegroom's home. Many guests gathered there. Late at night the bride and the bridegroom were led up to the hay-loft to sleep. If it was very cold, they led the young folk to the cellar under the floor. In the morning the guests came together once more. They wanted to see for themselves if the young wife was clever. The ground was covered with straw. It was strewn intentionally by the guests who ordered the young wife to sweep the floor. Throughout the morning the girl gives them drinks as on the previous night. On the same day she brings water, helps to cook, feed the animals, and from that time onwards she starts to live like a younger mistress of the house.

192. About childbirth

Today babies are born in the maternity home; earlier they were born wherever fate dictated. The pregnant woman worked till the very last days. She went to the fields to reap, mow and rake, she carried water, watered the animals, milked the cow, and did all kinds of work. Sometimes the baby was born in the field. They tried to follow this procedure: nobody was supposed to know about the childbirth, therefore the woman went to give birth to the child in the stable, or the bath-house or up in the hay-loft and there she gave birth. Nobody except the midwife was allowed to stay by her meanwhile. She cut and bound the infant's umbilical cord, and she washed the child as well as the mother. It was just on their account that the bath-house was heated. In times of old people cured all kinds of sickness by themselves, to the best of their ability.

193. About burial and commemoration of the dead

1. When someone begins to become very sick and people see that he will soon die, he is laid in a separate bed. When the person begins to die, they try to do everything to help him. Some relative — a son, daughter or mother — lifts his head on his arm. Then the soul will depart all the sooner. In earlier days, believers thought that the soul departed in the form of vapour. When a man dies he is washed, special folk are called in to wash him. They dress him in new clothes, comb his hair with a comb, and lay him in the coffin. First leafy twigs are spread in the coffin, then it is covered with rags. Then it is covered with canvas, a small pillow being placed in to support the head, and then the dead body is laid on it. His hands are laid across his chest. Icons and candles are also put on his chest. Then relatives come to take leave of him. Everybody comes to the dead body, to kiss it and say something to it, for example: "Have a good rest, you were able to live here,

tęg? kįʒ me ponda olnį tetęg? kęr bįdę·nnįs proša·ććasę, kulęmsę velťťęnį dęraęn iľi boštęnį koľinko·ręn, puktęnį grębas kulęmįsliś veššes (kolan torrez): sįna·n, kńiga, očki, buma·ga (gižę·t), karanda·š, kias śetęnį ďeńga. seśśa velťťęnį grębpelęn i dorenį ker-tu·llezęn. seśśa petkę·tęnį ętęrę, puktęnį grębsę doď vįlę i kįnį·m-kę mort nuę·tęnį šojna· vįlę. kęr kulęmsę petkę·tasę, ʒoʒsę brįzga·jtęnį vān (vaęn). ʒoʒas, poso·ʒas i tuj vįlas, kįt nuę·tisę poko·jńiksę, ćapka·lęnį kęzullez. šojna·-gusę garjęnį odźįk. ćišę·ttez vįlįn grębsę leʒęnį guas. seśśa siję tįrtęnį. bįd mort ćapkę muas kęť ętik mu-komo·k. kęr ʒebśiśi·śśez loktasę gortanįs, kęźa·jka (χoźa·jka) verdę niję i juktalę. ʒoʒsę rįtnas miśka·lęnį i stara·ććęnį pįlśinį bańān. siję oľ-paśsę, kęda vįlįn kulis mortįs, ćapkęnį ętęrę (ętę·rę).

2. *kujmęt lunas kulęmsę kaśtįllisę. korlįllisę (korlisę) niję-žę kaśtiśi·śśesę i gęśťitę·tisę. seśśa kaśti·ślisę kvať lun bęrįn, śiźimęt lunas. sį bęrįn kaśtįllisę šeśť ńeďeľ i kęr loas god (gęd). sį bęrįn kaśtįllęnį bįd god kįkiś: sija lunę, kęr sija kulis i kaśtiśa·n lunę, tulįsnas, streća votęʒ. jeśľi kaśtį·llęnį gortanįs, to jurbį·tęnį jen oʒįn, śojęnį i voššę·tęnį kulęmsę. jeśľi kaśtį·llęnį šojna· vįlįn, to munęnį kįnį·m-kę mort bįd kerkuśań, každij (bįdįs) aslas kulęmmez dįnę. loktasę šojna· vįlę, tećasę śoja·n-pelęs, každęj aslas šojna· vįlę. pukśęnį gęgęrę·ńńas, pervoj jurbį·tęnį. kin-kę ďerjalį·štas, seśśa pondęnį śojnį i junį. mukę·dtorsę puktęnį šojna· vįlas i čęktęnį kulęmsę voššįnį. gęśťitę·tęnį sośe·ddesę (suśe·ddesę, sęśe·ddesę). odźįk una śeta·llisę kori·śśezlę. kęda śoja·nįs koľććas, siję nębę·tlisę gortanįs bęr i seććin śojlįllisę ćeľaď. šojna· vįlę nullisę ńe toľko śoja·n, no i sur: ćasto·žįk ćęskįt sur i gęrd vina·.*

194. *ďiťťaśa·n jįliś*

1. *miję ęďďęn ľubi·tam ďiťťa·śnį. pervo me viśta·śa kaga-ďiťťętę·m jįliś. ućę·tśań vež kagasę (kagalę) ďiťťę·tęnį zįbkaįn (zįbkàn). zįbka keršę bįd-koď pellezįś. kįʒ jašši·k, ńe-vįlįn dora kerenį; sįʒ-žę śimę·tęvejsę (śimę·tiś) iľi ban-pala·k-*

know how to live there as well!" Specially skilled lamenters came to weep, and the nearest relatives say, sobbing with tears: "Who have you left me to, all by myself? Why have you left me here with the children? What am I to do without you? How shall I live without you?" When everyone has said farewell, the dead body is covered with a sheet of linen or calico. The most necessary belongings of the dead man are placed in the coffin: comb, book, spectacles, paper, pencil, — and money is put in his hand. Then they cover him with the coffin-lid which is nailed down. Then it is brought out of the house, the coffin is put on a sleigh, and escorted by a few men to the graveyard. When the dead body is taken out, the floor is sprinkled with water. Twigs of spruce are scattered on to the floor, the porch and the road, wherever the deceased one has been carried. The grave is dug in advance. The coffin is lowered into the grave by means of a sheet. Then it is buried. Everybody throws at least one handful of earth into the grave. When the people return from the graveyard, the housewife gives them food and drink. In the evening they wash the floor and try to take a bath in the bath-house. The bedclothes in which the man died are thrown away.

2. The third day is passed in commemoration of the dead man. They invite to the commemorative feast those people who were present at the burial. Then the next commemoration takes place six days later, that is on the seventh day. Then again after six weeks, and again on the first anniversary. Then they devote two days each year to commemoration of the deceased person: one being the anniversary of his death, the other All Souls' Day (Commemoration Day) in spring, before Whitsun. When the commemoration takes place at home, they say prayers in front of the icon, arrange a feast and feast the dead man too. If the commemoration is held in the graveyard, a few people from each house visit their own departed ones. Arriving at the graveyard, they place kinds of food on the graves, each on their own relative's. They sit round the grave, and first they pray. Someone breaks out in sobs, then they begin to eat and drink. They place some things on the grave, telling the dead man to eat. They entertain the neighbours. Earlier, the beggars were given much food. What remained of the food was taken home and given to the children, who ate it up. They took not only food to the graveyard but also beer: mostly sweet beer and red wine.

194. About swinging

1. We love to swing very much. First I shall talk about rocking children. From its early days the baby is rocked in a cradle. The cradle is made of all sorts of boards. Shaped in the form of a chest, its sides are not made too

keziś iľi ki̯je̯ni̯ šuľľeziś. olle̯ni̯ i ńine̯ve̯je̯ś. zi̯bkase̯ e̯še̯·te̯ni̯ gezo·k vi̯le̯, ke̯de̯ ke̯r-ta·le̯ni̯ laťťan śor berde̯. zi̯bka e̯ša·le̯ iľi komi̯n, iľi i̯ǯi̯t ži̯ri̯n (ži̯rji̯n). e̯ni kere̯ni̯ iľi ńe̯be̯ni̯ uće̯·ťik kre̯va·tkaez, no ďere·vńaezi̯n una·žikse̯ giće̯·te̯ni̯ ešše̯ zi̯bkaeze̯n.

2. *ćeľaď i gi̯ri·ššez jona raďe·jte̯ni̯ ďiťťa·śni̯. tuli̯snas, i̯ǯi̯t lun kosta bi̯dsa ńeďe·ľa ďiťťa·śe̯ni̯. kere̯ni̯ e̯tik iľi ki̯ni̯-·m-ke̯ obše̯j (e̯tla·asa) ďiťťa·n i e̯kśe̯ni̯ si̯ di̯ne̯ bi̯d ri̯t una oťir: una·ži̯ki̯s tom-pe̯le̯s. i̯ǯi̯t ďiťťa·n kerśe̯ iľi ki̯ǯǯez kolase̯, iľi nare̯·šne̯j kozlaez vi̯le̯. e̯še̯·te̯ni̯ gez iľi cep (ćep), ke̯da ul-de̯re̯ doma·le̯ni̯ pe̯l. pukśe̯ni̯ pe̯l vi̯las una, mi̯mda (mi̯nda, munda) te̯ras, a dorrezas sulte̯ni̯ ďiť-ťeti·ššez. ućet ćeľaďle̯ ďiťťa·nese̯ kere̯ni̯ i gortani̯s. e̯še̯·te̯ni̯ e̯šin ulte̯, karta· vi̯le̯, pos-o·ǯe̯ (pos-e̯·ǯe̯) i daže̯ kerku ži̯re̯ (ži̯rje̯) iľi kome̯.*

195. *polźe̯ćće̯·mmez ji̯liś*

1. *mijan una viśta·śe̯ni̯ bi̯d-kod polźe̯ćće̯·mmez ji̯liś. polźe̯·ćće̯ni̯ pe̯ ćuddez i bi̯d-koď mesta·ez. e̯tik stari·k meni̯m viśta·śis: mune̯m sija e̯ććid ve̯re̯ śerme̯·te̯n ve̯l kutni̯. panta·śe̯m ńuro·k i kiś-ke̯ o̯ǯas pete̯m ki̯z, paśki̯t plakaeziś pos. sija ni̯ kuźa vuže̯m ńurse̯, aǯǯe̯, o̯ǯas ki̯ǯo·k vi̯li̯n puka·le̯ i̯ǯi̯t śed kań. śinnese̯ ba-re̯·te̯m si̯ vi̯le̯, śinne̯s pe̯ i̯ǯi̯teś, veǯeś. sija polźas i me̯das pi̯šši̯ni̯ be̯r (berge̯ćći̯ni̯ be̯r). viǯe̯·te̯ be̯ras, posi̯s abu ńi. e̯dva-e̯dva petas ńurśis i sek ve̯lse̯ abu verme̯m kutni̯.*

2. *mune̯m e̯ććid zonka karau·le̯ ve̯llez deźira·jtni̯. mune̯ sija veršne̯je̯n ve̯-reťťas (ve̯reťťis). panta·śe̯ si̯le̯ me̯di·k mort, toźe̯ veršne̯j, ćoćkom (ćoćke̯m) ve̯l vi̯li̯n. zēť-viǯe̯ i ve̯li̯s i morti̯s. munas, tujse̯ popere̯ga·las si̯liś, zonka oz polźi̯ ńe-mi̯j-ńe, a ojnas ki̯le̯, ćańńez ḱiwzi̯ni̯ pondise̯. ni̯ vi̯le̯ ke̯ji·nnez uśke̯·ćće̯maś. zonkai̯s ńem abu verme̯m kerni̯, vit ćań śoje̯maś. sija pe̯ ve̯r-ďa·ďi̯s i panta·śe̯m ri̯tnas zonkai̯sle̯.*

3. *e̯tik muži·k ve̯le̯m e̯ďďe̯n bojok ve̯raliś i ćeri-ki̯jiś. arśa ojjeze̯ sija meľńi·-ćai̯n śu ize̯m. mej-ke̯ vidne̯ ve̯ras di̯r ole̯m, kote̯·rtas, loktas gortas, ińisle̯ šue̯: „vaj-že̯ meni̯m śojni̯! meľńi·ćae̯ naťte̯ proste̯n ńi ize̯." ińkai̯s śetas si̯le̯ ńań-ja-*

high; others make it of birch-bark, weaving it of strips of birch-bark or bast. Some are made of lime. The cradle is hung on a rope the end of which is fastened to a flexible rod. The cradle hangs either in the kitchen or in the room. Nowadays people make or buy little beds, though in the villages children are mostly rocked in cradles even today.

2. Both children and adults are fond of swinging. In the spring, around Easter, they swing throughout a whole week. They make one or several swings to be used in common, and every night many people gather together — young people for the most part. The big swing is hung either from birch-trees or a special stand. A rope or a chain is tied to it, and a piece of board is fastened to the lower end. Lots of them sit on the seat, as many as can find room, while the swingers stand on both sides. For small children swings are made at home also. They are hung under the window, in the stable, on the porch, indeed even in the room or the kitchen of the house.

195. About frightening things

1. Among us many tales are told about frightening things. Devils and all sorts of places are frightening. An old man told me the following tale: once he was going to the forest in order to harness his horse. He arrived at a small swamp, and all of a sudden a thick bridge made of broad planks appeared in front of him. He crossed the swamp on it and saw that a big black cat was sitting on a small birch-tree in front of him. It was staring at him; its eyes were big and yellow. He was frightened and started to run back. Looking back he did not see the bridge standing there. He was hardly able to get out of the swamp, and when he was out he could not harness his horse.

2. Once a boy went to serve as a horseherd, grazing horses. He goes through the forest on horseback. He meets a man, also on horseback, mounted on a white horse. The horse glows with light and so does the man. He goes along; the other tries to block his way, but the boy is not afraid of anything; at night he hears the colts beginning to neigh. Wolves attacked them. The boy could not do anything; they devoured five colts. What the boy had met the previous night was the forest spirit.

3. There was a peasant who was very clever at hunting and fishing. On autumn nights he was grinding rye at the mill. Obviously he had lived a long time in the forest, he ran home and said to his wife: "Give me something to eat! The mill is running empty in all likelihood." His wife gives him barley bread and potatoes, he sticks them into his bag of birch-bark and leaves. He arrives at the mill, and indeed, only empty rattling can be heard.

ru·śńik da karto·škaez, śuji̮·štas peššo·rkà i sija munas. loktas siję meľńićaę i biľ goľętę pę toko ki̮lę. kiśtas sija babaas śu, leśę·tas bi̮dę·s, mi̮j kolę i munas šoććiši̮ni̮. pi̮ras izbuškà (izbuškaę), keras ęćag, pęža·las karto·škaez. śojas, seśśa oǯiś labi·ć vi̮las pondas sunaśni̮. śeras si̮lęn vęlęm ćer, piššaľ, ki̮k pon. ki̮knan poni̮s šoni̮t-inas ńiskęni̮, uźęni̮ pę. a i̮bę·si̮s ńewna (ńe-una) ośta-koď (ośtęm) vęlęm. drug mi̮j-kę sija sajmi̮štas. aǯǯę, veśki̮ta si̮ oǯi̮n ośta i̮bę·s veśtas (i̮bę·sas) mort keke·rkai̮n (keke·rkān) pukalę i riz-viǯę, śera·lę pę. morti̮s siję tędęm: kujim gęd ńi pę, ki̮ǯ siję ǯebęmaś. sečę·m-žę pę gęrd tošo·ka, sečę·m-žę gi̮nęvej šľapaęn, źipu·nęn, ćoćkom vešša·nęn i sapo·ga (sapo·gęn). nęręvi·tas, oz tęd, mi̮j šuni̮. duma·jtas i šuę: „te pę, j a k ę · l i v a · n, raz kulin, to menim tęva·rišas on kol." mędi̮s ki̮ǯ ćeććęltas da i̮kę·stas: „me pę tenę eššę· śoja." seććę ponnes sajmasę, kińi·ććasę i dava·j ćećća·lni̮ kęźa·jinislę moŗosas. męd morti̮s ęšęm, ńe-kin pę abu, muži·ki̮s eššę· abu na polźęm. vidnę, vorrez pę polźę·ććęni̮ iľi kin-kę narę·šnę śera·lę. boštas pišša·ľ, ęztas sarta·ssez, petas, krugęn izbu·škasę munas. gęgę·rtas, ńe-kin ńe-ki̮tę·n abu. kak raz li̮m-poro·ška uśęm i ńe-kučę·m śľed pę abu. tęžnę· sija polźęm. pi̮ras izbu·škaas, pędna·śas, pukśas, kias ćer boštas i oj-bi̮t puka·las (pu·kalas), oz i vęrźi̮. jur-śies ki̮šęn sultęmaś. meľńićaas abu i peta·lęm. ǯuz-viǯni̮, jugdi̮ni̮ pondęm, sija gortas loktęm. dręž-źi·tę pę, ćistę śedętęm. ińi̮s abu i tędęm siję. mi̮j-kę pę ińka loas i biľ sija gędę ni̮lęn pę bur vęl torkśęm, ni̮l kulęm, kerku soććęm i aći̮s kęźa·jini̮s kulęm. vot sija siję i śojęm.

196. *śoja·n-jua·n ji̮liś*

1. *komi-perḿakkezlęn śoja·n bi̮d-koď. ńań pęžalisę zęręveję, idęveję, ruǯę·gę-veję, šogdieveję, una·žiksę ruǯę·gęveję. kerlisę iǯi̮t gęgresa ćelpa·nnez. idiś i zęriś kerlisę ńe-iǯi̮t jaru·śńikkez. niję kerlisę lun kežę, śojlisę ńebi̮tęn, ćasto·žik jęlęn.*

2. *strepńa· (strapńa·) vęli tožę raznej. ińka bi̮d asi̮l pęža·llis tupę·śśez (šog-diiś, zęri̮s, idiś), pirę·ggez ruǯę·gęvej sećę·nneziś (kęriššeziś) pirę·ggesę kerlisę jajiś, kapu·staiś, karto·škaiś, čakiś, jagędiś, ľęmiś, riśis i bi̮d-bęrśaiś. jagę·dis mijan šuśęni̮ siǯ: ćed, pul-jagęd, ńur-meľ, śęla-jagę·d, oz-jagę·d, maľi·na, setę·r. šańgaez kerlisę šęma ťestaiś. ęďďęn perḿakkez ľubi·tęni̮ bľinnez i peľ-ńa·ńńez. bľinnez kerlisę oďǯi̮k zęręvej piźiś, a ęni ćastę·žik šogdievejiś i kraχma·l sorę̈n. bľi̮nnesę pęža·lęni̮ vi vi̮li̮n i śojęni̮ vijęn. peľ-ńa·ńńez ćasto·ži̮k kerę̈ni̮ jajiś. kerasę ućę·ťik kęriššez (kęldę·msę torję·tlasę ućę·ťik torrez vi̮lę), bigrę·tasę big-*

He pours rye into the hopper and arranges everything, and then goes to rest. He goes into the hut, lays a fire and cooks potatoes. He eats and then starts slumbering on the bench next to the door. He has an axe, a gun and two dogs with him. The dogs are snoring in the warm place, sleeping. The door stood a little open. Suddenly he wakes up. He sees a man squatting right in front of him facing the door, showing his teeth and laughing. The man recognized him: three years previously he had been buried. As in life he was red-bearded, with a felt hat, a frieze caftan and white trousers and boots. He waits, not knowing what to say. He thinks and finally he speaks: "I say, Ivan Jakel̦, you have died once already, and I do not want you as a companion." Jumping up, the other man shouts: "And I shall devour you!" At that, the dogs awoke and sprang to the side of their master. The other man vanished, there was nobody present and the peasant was not even frightened. Obviously thieves are scaring him, or someone deliberately wants to make a fool of him. He takes his gun, kindles some pine-shavings and goes out round the hut. He walks round and sees nobody about. Only then did he feel frightened. He enters the hut and locks himself in. He sits down with the axe in his hand, and remains motionless, sitting there throughout the whole night. His hair stands on end. He did not go out of the mill. It was dawning at daybreak, he walked home. He trembles, indeed, he has turned black. Even his wife did not recognize him. He found another woman, and indeed, their good horse died that year, their house burnt down, and the master himself died. So you see, he did eat him up.

196. About food and drink

1. There is a great variety of food among the Komi-Permyaks. They mostly baked bread of oats, barley, rye and wheat, but mainly of rye. They made large, round loaves of bread. They also baked small loaves from barley and oats. These they made for one day, they ate it fresh, mainly with milk.
2. The method of preparing food also varied. The housewife baked round loaves every morning (of wheat, oats, barley), pirogi from rye-pastry, never from leavened pastry. The pirogi were stuffed with meat, cabbage, potatoes, mushrooms, berries, wild-service berries, curds and the like. The berries that we have are called: blackberry, cowberry, cranberry, mulberry, wild strawberry, raspberry, and black currant. Pastry was made of leavened dough. The Permyak are very fond of pancakes and meat turnovers. Earlier pancakes were made of oat flour, but today mostly of wheat flour with dried yeast. Pancakes are fried in butter and eaten with butter. Meat turnovers are mostly stuffed with meat. They make small

re̮·ććane̮n se̮će̮·nnez. bi̮d se̮će̮·ne̮ pukte̮ni̮ maśte̮m jaj i ke̮ri̮šse̮ kusi·ńte̮ni̮. peľ-ńa·ńńese̮ ćapke̮ni̮ seśśa piźe̮m vae̮ (vā). ke̮r peľ-ńa· ńńes lebase̮, va vi̮las palja·le̮ni̮, sek nije̮ ki̮ska·le̮ni̮. nija ge̮te̮·veś śojni̮. śoje̮ni̮ nije̮ śmeta·nae̮n, je̮le̮n, vije̮n uksuse̮n. śoje̮ni̮ nije̮ pi̮mmeze̮n. koľćće̮m peľ-ńa·ńńese̮ (peľ-ńe·ńńese̮, peľ-me·ńńese̮) žarite̮ni̮ vi vi̮li̮n. čake̮ve̮j peľ-ńańńez šuśe̮ni̮ uški·eze̮n. kerśe̮ni̮ nija ke̮s čakiś. čakse̮ vadase̮ pi̮m pi̮m vai̮n (vān), seśśa maśtase̮ luk sore̮n, pukte̮ni̮ ešše̮· pereć, sol i loe̮ čake̮ve̮j ikra. seś i kere̮ni̮ uški·ese̮. uški·ese̮ puase̮ vaas i śoje̮ni̮ se̮vśe·m vanas, ki̮ǯ ši̮dle̮.

3. *ši̮ddez pue̮ni̮: jaje̮ve̮j ši̮d, še̮ma ši̮d, čaka ši̮d, ńańa ši̮d, je̮la ši̮d i me̮di·kkez. jaja ši̮d pue̮ni̮ siǯ: ke̮r gori̮s lonti·śśas, sulte̮·te̮ni̮ i̮ǯi̮t ćugune̮ vae̮n jaj, sola·le̮ni̮ i sija puśe̮. ke̮r jaji̮s puśas, sije̮ ki̮ske̮ni̮ ske̮ve̮re̮da· vi̮le̮ kośti̮ni̮, a jaj-vaas pukte̮ni̮ ši̮de̮·s, a muke̮·ććid karto·ška luke̮n. kušma·n ťe̮ri·tase̮, sola·lase̮, kiśtase̮ sećće̮ še̮ma jua·n, vunda·las pue̮m karto·ška i siǯ pańa·le̮ni̮. oďži̮k (oďǯi̮k) kiślise̮ kušma·nse̮ pue̮ve̮j beke̮·rreze̮, pańa·llise̮ pue̮ve̮j, as-kere̮m pańńeze̮n. ešše̮· me viśta·śa luka-sol ji̮liś. gože̮mnas, ke̮r śojni̮ abu e̮ďďe̮n ńem, ľubi·te̮ni̮ śojni̮ luka sol. źeľo·ne̮j lukliś korse̮ perjase̮, vunda·lase̮ posńi toro·kkez vi̮le̮, tojase̮ sije̮ beke̮·ri̮n, sola·lase̮ jona, kiśte̮ni̮ sećće̮ va, muke̮·ććid kre̮ši·te̮ni̮ pue̮m koľť i siǯ śoje̮ni̮. vai̮s kole̮ ke̮ǯi̮t. je̮l śoje̮ni̮ siǯ, muke̮·ććid piźe̮·te̮ni̮ sećće̮ǯ, što je̮li̮s loe̮ ge̮rd re̮ma, suk i će̮ski̮t. še̮m-je̮l oďži̮k ez i śojle̮. li̮ďďi·lise̮ poda śoja·ne̮n, no muke̮·d še̮m-je̮lse̮ riśti̮llise̮. riś śoje̮ni̮ siǯ: sorase̮ sije̮ ne̮ke̮n, sola·lase̮ i pańa·le̮ni̮. šuśe̮ ne̮kja riś. riśśis ešše̮· kerlise̮ riśa tupe̮·śśez. sodtase̮ ne̮k, će̮ge̮·tase̮ koľť-me̮d, sola·lase̮ i kaťľa·le̮ni̮ ke̮lde̮·mmez. nije̮ kośte̮ni̮ šondi vi̮li̮n. riśa tupe̮·śśese̮ nolje̮·te̮ni̮ še̮rani̮s uǯ vi̮le̮. paži̮·n keže̮ nolje̮·te̮ni̮ pue̮m koľťťez, ńań-jaru·šńikkez, luk-jurrez (grezd) i pe̮ža·le̮m karto·ška. kapu·sta kerale̮ni̮, sola·le̮ni̮ ke̮ńe̮·sseze̮. sola·le̮ni̮ iľi gi̮riś ke̮ća·nneze̮n, iľi posńita vunda·le̮ni̮, ši̮re̮ni̮. ogurći·ez śoje̮ni̮ sveže̮je̮s, ki̮ǯ i pomido·rrez-že̮ iľi sola·le̮ni̮. śorkńi·, kaľe·g pe̮že̮ni̮ iľi pe̮žale̮ni̮. śoje̮ni̮ sije̮ suslo·e̮n. lukse̮ grezzeze̮n ńečkase̮, ši̮rase̮ i viže̮ni̮ ke̮s, šoni̮t-ini̮n. te̮l-bi̮t śoje̮ni̮.*

4. *e̮ďďe̮n raďe·jte̮ni̮ perḿakkez jua·n .suk, ke̮ǯi̮t jua·n oďǯi̮k pi̮r nolje̮·tlise̮ še̮re̮ paži̮·n keže̮. nolje̮·te̮ni̮ i e̮ni. sur e̮ďďe̮n rade·jte̮ni̮, kere̮ni̮ bi̮d prazńik keže̮.*

round pieces of dough, which they roll out into small pies with a rolling-pin. Minced meat is put into each pie which is then folded up. Then the meat pies are thrown into hot water. When the meat pies come up and float on the surface of the water, they take them out of the pot. They are ready to eat. They eat them with sour cream, milk, butter and vinegar. They eat them hot. The meat turnovers which are left are fried in butter. Mushroom turnovers are called 'ears'. They are made with dried mushrooms. The mushrooms are soaked in hot water, then chopped into small pieces with onion, and seasoned with pepper and salt; they make a kind of 'mushroom roe'. The 'ears' are filled with these. The 'ears' are boiled in water, and eaten with the same water like soup.

3. The following kinds of soup are made: meat broth, sour soup, mushroom soup, bread soup, milk soup and so on. Meat broth is made like this: when the oven is hot, they put meat and water into a big iron pot, add salt and cook it. When the meat is cooked, it is placed in a pan to get dry; they put mush into the meat broth, sometimes potato and onion. They shred radishes, salt them and pour in kvas; they chop boiled potatoes into it and eat it with a spoon. In older times radishes were poured into wooden bowls and eaten with home-made wooden spoons. I'll also tell you now about salted onions. In summer when there is not much to eat, people like to eat salted onions. They tear off the green onion leaves, cut them into small pieces, and crush them in a plate, then add a good quantity of salt and pour on water; sometimes they chop up boiled eggs, and eat it like this. Cold water is used for this. Milk is drunk as it is. Sometimes they boil it to make it red in colour, thick and sweet. Sour milk was not drunk in earlier days. It was regarded as kind of feed for animals, but occasionally they made curds of the sour milk. Curds are eaten in the following way: they are mixed with sour cream, salted and eaten with a spoon. It is called curds with sour cream. They also made little loaves with curds. They add sour cream, break a few eggs into it, salt it and roll out small loaves. They dry them in the sun. They take the loaves of curds to work with them. For lunch they also take boiled eggs, small loaves of bread, onions, and baked potatoes. Cabbages are sliced and salted in small barrels. The big heads of cabbage are either salted or cut in pieces and sliced. They eat cucumbers uncooked, and tomatoes too, or they salt them. Turnips and swedes are steamed or fried. They are also eaten with mush. Onions are uprooted complete, sliced and stored in dry warm places. They eat onions throughout the whole winter.

4. The Permyaks are fond of kvas. Earlier they always took thick, cold kvas with them to work for lunch. They still do today. They are very fond of beer and make it for each feast day. Rye is soaked in a trough, which is

ruʒ́e̮·g ke̮te̮·te̮ni̮ e̮rrezi̮n, seśśa pukte̮ni̮ sije̮ šoni̮t-ine̮, med-bi̮ sija pe̮žśis. ke̮r ruʒ́e̮·gi̮s ćužas, sije̮ kośte̮ni̮ i ize̮ni̮. arkme̮ će̮ski̮t (iľi će̮s-viʒ́an) ćuž-piź, ke̮daiś kere̮ni̮ sur. boštase̮ i̮ǯ́i̮t di̮re̮va·tka, tupka·lase̮ ośta·se̮, śuji̮·štase̮ tul, maltase̮ sije̮ uľ ńańe̮n, si̮ be̮ri̮n pi̮čkas pue̮vej ʒ́allez, si̮ vi̮le̮ iʒ́a·siś kere̮m koľća·, bi̮de̮·s eta vi̮le̮ kiśte̮ni̮ ćuž-pi·źiś sore̮m suk massa (gudi̮·r). si̮ be̮ri̮n tupka·lase̮ gi̮rńi·ćse̮ i śuji̮·šte̮ni̮ ješte̮m gore̮. sija sula·le̮ sećći̮n bi̮dsa sutki. ke̮r ki̮skase̮, veltse̮ bośte̮ni̮, kiśte̮ni̮ gi̮rńi·ćas pi̮m va i sija ńewna (ńe-una) sulali̮·šte̮. si̮ be̮ri̮n raźe̮ni̮ tupke̮·ś i ponde̮ lećći̮ni̮ suk, śe̮d, će̮ski̮t ma-koď suslo. suslose̮ ńewna (ńe-una) koľe̮ni̮, torja beke̮re̮ ke̮ʒ́e̮·tni̮. si̮ be̮ri̮n śoje̮ni̮ pe̮ʒ́e̮m kaľeg i še̮rtńi: estaľne̮·j surse̮ sore̮ni̮ vije̮·te̮m kiźer sure̮n, seśśa ke̮ʒ́e̮·te̮ni̮. ruš-koď suras pukte̮ni̮ še̮ma je̮l i še̮me̮·te̮ni̮ a siʒ́-ʒ́e̮ tag. sutki be̮ri̮n arkme̮ kuri̮t, krepi̮t sur. sije̮ viʒ́e̮ni̮ ke̮ʒ́i̮·tini̮n i julle̮ni̮.

197.

1. mijan ve̮rrezi̮n bi̮dme̮ una· čak. oso·benno una em jeľde̮·g, ri̮ži̮·k, masľa·k, śińa·wka, gut-kulan-čak. e̮ktim mi e̮ććid una· jeľde̮·g. sija bi̮dme̮ če̮k ve̮ri̮n, oso·benno ke̮zzez ulti̮n. vajim čakse̮ gorte̮, pervo vese̮·tim joggeziś, a si̮ be̮ri̮n ke̮te̮·tim và, med-bi̮ joggesiś eššе̮· jonʒ́i̮ka vese̮·tni̮. mi̮nda-ke̮ sula·le̮m be̮ri̮n čakkese̮ tećam krinkae̮ i sola·lam. jeľde̮·gi̮s solaśše̮ e̮ďďe̮n di̮r, a kor sija loas gotow, e̮ďďe̮n će̮ski̮t sije̮ śojni̮ pue̮m karto·škae̮n.

2. e̮ďďe̮n una· mijan ki̮je̮ni̮ ćeri. mijan juesni̮m boga·te̮ś bi̮d-koď ćerie̮n: naľi·me̮n, šukae̮n, keľći·e̮n, jorše̮n, are̮n. ćerise̮ pervo vese̮·te̮ni̮ śe̮miś, si̮ be̮ri̮n miśka·le̮ni̮ i pože̮ puni̮ uχa·. pervo pue̮·te̮ni̮ vai̮n karto·ška, a kor karto·škai̮s puśis, pukte̮ni̮ ćeri i luk. ćerii̮s puśe̮ e̮ďďe̮n ćoža. kor će̮ltasni̮ beke̮·re̮, pože̮ pukti̮ni̮ sećće̮ eššе̮ gorći·ća. ćeriiś pože̮ kerni̮ ćeri-ńań. ge̮te̮·vej ťeste̮ vi̮le̮ teće̮ni̮ ćeri i pe̮ža·le̮ni̮ sije̮ gori̮n.

3. śoje̮ni̮ mijan i peľ-ńa·ńńez (peľiez). pervo maśte̮ni̮ jaj, sećće̮ pukte̮ni̮ luk, ge̮te̮·vite̮ni̮ ťesta, a ťestase̮ vundale̮ni̮ uće̮·ťik torrez vi̮le̮ i bi̮gre·te̮ni̮. bigre̮·te̮m be̮ri̮n kere̮ni̮ peľiez. peľiese̮ pue̮ni̮ vàn i si̮ be̮ri̮n nije̮ pože̮ śojni̮.

4. śoje̮ni̮ mijan i luka sol. pervo ćepľa·le̮ni̮ luk-turun, sije̮ ši̮re̮ni̮ i si̮ be̮ri̮n toje̮ni̮. toje̮m be̮ri̮n pukte̮ni̮ va sol i śoje̮ni̮ ńańe̮n.

then placed in a warm corner, where it is kept to steam. When the rye begins to sprout, it is dried and ground. It turns into sweet malt from which beer is brewed. They take a large pottery vessel, plug the mouth of it by thrusting a wooden wedge in it and smearing dough on it. Laths are placed in the vessel, and rings made of straw are put on the laths; on this they pour the thick mass of malt. Then the vessel is plugged and placed in the well-heated stove. There it stands the whole day. When they pull it out, they remove the lid, pour hot water into the pottery vessel and let it stand for a while. Then they take out the plug, and the thick, dark-coloured mash, sweet as honey, begins to settle down. For a short time the mash is kept in a special vessel to cool it down. Stewed swedes and turnips are served with the beer. The rest of the beer already drawn off is mixed with thin beer and put aside to cool down. Sour milk and hops are added to the lukewarm beer to turn it sour. In a day it turns into bitter, strong beer. It is stored in a cool place, and so it is drunk.

197. [About food and drink]

1. Mushrooms grow in plenty in our forests. Especially abundant are bitter mushrooms, the russula, orange-agaric, boletus and fly-agaric. Once we picked a lot of bitter mushrooms. They grow in thick woods, especially under spruce-trees. We brought home the mushrooms, first cleaned them of dirt, then soaked them in water so that they might be still better cleaned. After a short time we put the mushrooms in a pottery jug and salt them. It takes a long time for the bitter mushroom is salted, but when it is ready, it is very tasty with boiled potato.

2. They catch very many fish in our district. Our rivers are rich in all kinds of fish: ling, pike, roach, perch and smelt. The fish is first cleaned of its scales, then washed, and then you can make fish-soup of it. First they cook potatoes in water, and when the potatoes are cooked, the fish and onions are put in the pot. The fish cook very quickly. When it is ladled out into the plate, mustard can be added. You can make fish pirogi as well. Pastry is made, the fish put on it, and put into the oven to bake.

3. With us they eat meat turnovers as well. First the meat is minced, then onion is added, pastry prepared and rolled out and cut up into small pieces. After rolling it the turnovers are made. The turnovers are boiled in water, and then they are ready to eat.

4. People eat also salted onions in our region. First the onion stalks are pinched off, then minced and crushed. When they have been crushed, the water is salted. It is eaten with bread.

5. *pe̮ža·le̮ni̮ i šańgaez. siǯ-že̮ ge̮te̮·vite̮ni̮ ťesta, pue̮ni̮ karto·ška. karto·škase̮ toje̮ni̮ i pukte̮ni̮ sećće̮ koľk, je̮l, sol i ete̮ bi̮de̮·s sore̮ni̮. ťestase̮ siǯ-že̮ kere̮ni̮ uće̮·ťik kruggez i bi̮gre̮·te̮ni̮. ni̮ vi̮le̮ teće̮ni̮ karto·ška, a vel-de̮ras kište̮ni̮ ne̮k koľk-sore̮n. siǯ ge̮te̮·vite̮ni̮ pire̮·gse̮, pe̮ža·le̮ni̮ gori̮n, a ke̮r pe̮ža·śase̮, nije̮ malte̮ni̮ vije̮n.*

6. *śoje̮ni̮ mijan i ne̮kja je̮l. pukte̮ni̮ še̮me̮·tni̮, je̮l vi̮las artme̮ ne̮k. ne̮kse̮ bośte̮ni̮, a koľćće̮m prostokvaša·se̮ pukte̮ni̮ gore̮ riśti̮ni̮. riśse̮ ke̮ǯde̮·te̮ni̮, sećće̮ pukte̮ni̮ sol i ne̮k i siǯ śoje̮ni̮.*

7. *mijan jue̮ni̮ sur. pervo bośte̮ni̮ ruǯe̮·g, ruǯe̮·gse̮, ke̮te̮·te̮ni̮ vai̮n, seśśa kište̮ni̮ e̮rreze̮ i ćužte̮ni̮. si̮ be̮ri̮n gor vi̮li̮n kośte̮ni̮ sije̮ i ize̮ni̮ meľńićai̮n. piźse̮ gudra·le̮ni̮ krinkai̮n, sije̮ pukte̮ni̮ gore̮ a gorse̮ ľaka·le̮ni̮. viǯe̮ni̮ sete̮n asi̮lśań me̮d asi̮le̮ǯ. si̮ be̮ri̮n krinkaezse̮ ośte̮ni̮ i vije̮·te̮ni̮ sur. ke̮r suri̮s ke̮ǯda·las, sećće̮ pukte̮ni̮ tag, a si̮ be̮ri̮n si̮ssa·le̮ni̮. sije̮ poźe̮ uže· juni̮. piźiś kere̮ni̮ braga. pervo piźse̮ gudi̮·rte̮ni̮ vai̮n, seśśa śuji̮šte̮ni̮ gore̮ pe̮žni̮. unaiś sije̮ sorla·le̮ni̮, med-bi̮ ez soćći̮. si̮ be̮ri̮n sije̮ ke̮ǯde̮·te̮ni̮ i si̮ssa·le̮ni̮. pukte̮ni̮ sećće̮ maje̮l i sulte̮·te̮ni̮ gor vi̮le̮ šoni̮tni̮. ńe-una sulale̮m be̮ri̮n sije̮ poźe̮ juni̮.*

8. *žari·te̮m karto·ška: pervo ćiśťite̮ni̮, miśka·le̮ni̮ vai̮n, ske̮re̮·vda vi̮le̮ pukte̮ni̮ vi i vunda·le̮ni̮ uće̮·ťik torrez vi̮le̮: karto·škase̮ pukte̮ni̮ pećka vi̮le̮ žari·tni̮.*

9. *pue̮ni̮ eśše̮· ši̮d. vai̮n pervo pue̮ni̮ karto·ška, sećće̮ pukte̮ni̮ jaj, luk, sol, lavro·ve̮j ľist i sije̮ bi̮de̮·s pue̮ni̮. jeśľi ši̮di̮s loe̮ e̮ďďe̮n gosa, jajse̮ ki̮ske̮ni̮, pukte̮ni̮ tare·ľka vi̮le̮, vunda·le̮ni̮ uće̮·ťik kuso·kkez vi̮le̮ i pukta·le̮ni̮ sije̮ ši̮de̮s śojikas.*

198. *kerku stre̮jite̮·m ji̮liś i gortsa uǯǯez ji̮liś*

1. *ki̮ǯ oďži̮k siǯ i e̮ni kerkuez kere̮ni̮ una·ži̮kse̮ puiś. kera·lase̮ ve̮ri̮n kerrez, voľe̮·tase̮ nije̮, vaja·le̮ni̮ gorte̮. e̮ktase̮ pomeć, čupe̮ni̮. uǯa·le̮ni̮ će̮re̮n, pila·e̮n, e̮zi̮·ne̮n, ge̮gi̮·te̮n, čupase̮, lepte̮ni̮ srubse̮ ńič vi̮le̮. teće̮ni̮ ńičse̮ kerrez kolase̮. ki̮ni̮·m-ke̮ ker ore̮·tase̮, med-bi̮ seśśa e̮ši̮·nnez da i̮be̮·s piśke̮·tni̮. kri̮ša-velt kere̮ni̮ ťosiś, dore̮ni̮ ker-tu·lleze̮n. ke̮r kri̮šase̮ velťťase̮ ńi, oľsa·le̮ni̮ ǯoǯ ki̮z plaka·eziś i leśe̮·te̮ni̮ potolo·g. seśśa varte̮ni̮ gor. gor varte̮ni̮ muiś, gľine̮iś. truba (struba) teće̮ni̮ kirpi·ćiś. kerkuas torje̮·te̮ni̮ zabo·rreze̮n kom i ki̮ni̮·m-ke̮ žir. si̮ be̮ri̮n*

5. They also bake pies. Pastry is made and potatoes are boiled. The potatoes are mashed and eggs, milk, and salt added, then it is all mixed together. Little round pieces are formed of the pastry, and these are rolled. Potatoes are put on them, and sour cream with eggs poured on top of them. Pirogi are made in this manner, baked in the oven, and when they are baked, they are buttered.

6. Among us they also eat sour cream with milk. It is put aside to get sour, sour cream develops on the surface of the milk. The sour cream is skimmed off, and the sour milk placed into the oven so that it turns into curds. The curds are cooled down and eaten with sour cream and salt added.

7. Beer is drunk here. First they take the rye, and the rye is soaked in water, poured into troughs and left to sprout. Then it is dried on the stove. It is ground in the mill. The flour is mixed in a pottery vessel, put into the oven, and the holes in the oven are stopped up with clay. It is kept there from one morning to the next. Then the pottery vessels are opened up, and the beer is drawn off. When the beer is cooled, hops are added, and then it is strained. It can be drunk then. They make kvas from flour. First the flour is mixed with water, then placed into the oven to steam. They keep stirring it so that it may not burn. Then it is cooled and strained. They add yeast and place it on the stove to heat. In a short time it is ready to drink.

8. Fried potatoes: first they are peeled, washed in water, then they put butter in a pan and cut the potatoes in small pieces. The potatoes are put on the stove to fry.

9. They also make soup. First they boil the potatoes in water, then add meat, onions, salt and bay leaves and cook them all together. If the soup happens to contain a lot of fat, they take out the meat, place it on a plate, cut it into small pieces, and serve it when the soup is put on the table.

198. About the building of the house and household work

1. As in the old days, houses even today are mostly built of wood. They fell logs in the woods, stip the bark and take them home. They collect help, and notch the logs. They work with axes, saws, chisels, and sheath-knives; they notch them and lift and place the frame on moss. They also fill the gaps between the logs with moss. Some of the logs are cut in two so that windows and a door can be fitted into them. The roof is made from thin planks and pegged together with wooden pegs. When the roof is covered, they lay down the floor made of thick boards and put up the ceiling. Then they set up a stove. The stove is constructed of earth and clay. The chimney

lęśę·tęnį pos-ęʒ (pos-o·ʒ). ętę·rįn matįn kerku dįnśańas sultę·tęnį karta· iľi įʒįt gid sarajęn turu·n viʒan ponda.

2. *kapu·śńikę garjęnį śortńi gu i sultę·tęnį viręć. gor lontęnį puęvęj pesęn. pes lęśę·tęnį oʒ tulisnas eššo· lįm vįlęt (lįm kuźa). kera·lasę, piľi·tasę, potkę·tlasę, tećęnį poľe·ńićaezę. pesįs gožum-bįtęn kośmę. seśśa śor arnas lįm kuźa-žę vaja·-lęnį pessę gortę i tećęnį iľi karta·vįlę, iľi pes viʒa·n-inę, iľi siʒ ęšį·n ultas. ogo-ro·ďeć jęrtęnį jęręn. sulte·tasę maję·ggez, kaťťasę niję ńęręn, seśśa tećęnį poččez. niję vajęnį vęriś. viʒʒez da mįj jęrtęnį mukę·ććid ęsľa·ďęn. jęrtęnį jęr, med-bį poda ez pįr, med-bį śu da turu·n ez travi·ććį. śu vundasę, doma·lęnį koľta·ezę i tećęnį suslo·nnezę, a seśśa vaja·lęnį guna· vįlę. kośtęnį ęvi·nįn, seśśa vartęnį varta·nęn iľi varta·n-maši·naęn i tęlę·tęnį. ruʒęg-pęlęs snopęn (koľta·ęn) te-ćęnį śoro·mmezę. śu vundęnį ćarla·ęn i vunda·n-maši·naezęn. turu·n įčkęnį ľito·vkaezęn i įčkiśa·n maši·naezęn. turu·n kurtęnį kura·nęn iľi vęla-kura·nęn. keręnį ľoʒʒez, seśśa ęktęnį zoro·dę. ętik mort lepta·lę vila·ęn (vilā·n), mędik zoro·d vįlas tećę. vaja·lęnį turu·nsę gortę vęla-doďęn. turu·nęn verdęnį vęllez, męssez, baľa·ez da kęza·ez. viʒęnį i mędi·k poda: porśśez, kroľikkez; kaj-pęlęsiś viʒęnį ʒoʒo·ggez, kuri·ćaez, utkaez.*

199. *mu uʒalę·m*

1. *kęr vundasę, arśań-ʒę musę gęręnį. seśśa pińa·lęnį, seśśa kęʒęnį ęźi·m. ęźi·mįs-kę bura petalas, śuęnį: 'loam ńańęn, śu bur loas.' tulįsnas, med-bį ęźi·msę ńe kįntnį, kęʒįt asįllezę, kęʒįt ojjezę įbbesę čįnę·tęnį. tulįsnas gęręni i kęʒęnį ośa·ez: id, zęr, šogdi. kęʒęnį siʒ-žę ań-kįč, ľon, piš (pįč). med pervo ještę ruʒę·g. siję vundęnį. ruʒę·gis bįdmę kuź iʒas vįlįn, gįriś šepa. seśśa ještę zęr, sį bęrįn id, sį bęrįn šogdi. vundasę, tećęnį śoro·mmezę, seśśa, kośtęnį i var-tęnį. vartęm śusę tęlę·tęnį. seśśa izęnį. oďʒįk (oďʒik) izlęmaś kia izį·nnezęn. piźśis pęʒa·lęnį ńań, strepa·jtęnį bįd-bęrśa; sijęn verdęnį poda.*

is built of bricks. In the house partitions separate the kitchen and some rooms. Then they construct the porch. In the courtyard the shed for animals is erected near the house, and so are the big stable and the barn for storing hay.

2. In the vegetable-garden they dig the pit for turnips and set up the forcing-frame as well. The stove is heated with firewood. Firewood is chopped in early spring on the snow. Trees are felled, sawn, cut and heaped up in piles. The firewood dries throughout the whole summer. Then late in the autumn they carry the wood home on the snow, and pile it up either in the shed, or the wood-store, or simply under the window. The vegetable-garden is surrounded with a fence. They set up stakes, bind them round with twigs and then lay poles along the fence. They bring them from the woods. The meadows and the like are sometimes fenced with fallen trees. They are fenced in so that domestic animals may not get in to trample on the crops and the grass. The corn is harvested, bound into sheaves and piled into stooks and then carried over to the threshing-yard. It is dried in the drying-shed, then threshed with flails or the threshing machine, and then it is winnowed. Rye and the like is bound into sheaves and heaped in stacks. Corn is harvested with sickles or reapers. Grass is mown with scythes and mowing machines. The hay is raked together with rakes, sometimes drawn by horses. They make lines of them, then pile them up in ricks. One man lifts them with a fork, the other piles them on the rick. Hay is taken home on a horse-drawn sleigh. Hay is used to feed horses, cows, sheep and goats. They also keep other domestic animals—pigs and rabbits; and fowl, geese, hens and ducks.

199. About tilling the land

1. After harvesting, the lands are ploughed while it is still autumn. Then the autumn crops are sown. If the autumn crop comes up well, they say: "We are going to have bread enough, the crop will be good." In the spring, when mornings and nights are cold, they smoke the ploughlands so as to prevent the autumn crop from freezing. In spring they plough and sow the spring crops—barley, oats and wheat; similarly they sow peas, flax and hemp. The rye is first to ripen. It is harvested. Rye has a long stalk and large ears. Next the oats get ripe, then the barley, then the wheat. They are harvested, gathered in ricks, then dried and threshed. The threshed corn is winnowed. Then it is ground. In the old times they used hand-mills for grinding. From the flour they bake bread, and cook all sorts of food. Animals are fed with it.

2. *mije̮ aslani̮m ogoro·ďeććeze̮ saďi·tame̮ karto·ška, kapu·sta, morko·v, tur-ńep, śe̮rkńi, kaľe·g, luk, pomido·rrez, ogurći·ez. pervo garjame̮ muse̮ zi̮rreze̮n, seśśa ńebźe̮·tame̮, sije̮ naźmi·tam (naźmi·tame̮), śujam zi̮r ulte̮ karto·ška. kapu·s-ta-re̮sa·da pervo bi̮dtam vire̮·ć vi̮li̮n. mijan vire̮·ććes šuśe̮ni̮ koka vire̮·ććeze̮n. nija sula·le̮ni̮ ste̮bbez vi̮li̮n, mati̮nǯi̮k šondilań. bi̮d tuli̮s vire̮·ććis [ɔ vire̮·ćśis] muse̮ veže̮ni̮. ultas teće̮ni̮ naźo·m, si̮ vi̮le̮ kiška·le̮ni̮ śed-mu-śin. seśśa ke̮ǯe̮ni̮ ke̮ǯi̮·s, sija petale̮, bid asi̮l i ri̮t sije̮ kiśka·le̮ni̮ vàn (vae̮n). vedrà (vedrae̮) va kaje̮·tase̮, koreś ke̮te̮·tase̮ i sije̮n bri̮zga·jte̮ni̮. kor re̮sa·dai̮s bi̮dmas, lepte̮ni̮ grad-dez (ǵraddez) i saďi·te̮ni̮ sećće̮ šoći·ťik ľoǯǯeze̮n kapu·sta i kaľe̮·g. śorkńi· ke̮ǯe̮ni̮ med śore̮n, sija ćoža bi̮dme̮. ogurći·ez ponda vire̮·ććese̮ kere̮ni̮ mu vi̮las, a po-mido·rrez saďi·te̮ni̮ siǯ muas. karto·ška ťape̮·te̮ni̮ ťapkae̮n. ke̮r pe̮ ve̮re̮·tan, bur-ži̮ka pe̮ bi̮dme̮. si̮ ponda petalte̮ńńas muke̮·ććid pińa·le̮ni̮. kor bi̮dmas, karto·š-kase̮ garje̮ni̮ zi̮rreze̮n, pi̮rtle̮ni̮ ǯoǯi̮·le̮ iľi śorkńi-gue̮.*

200. *ćeri-ki̮ja·n*

ćeri ki̮je̮ni̮ sake̮n, kule̮·me̮n, vugi̮·re̮n, morda·e̮n, aǯla·se̮n. ćeria·liśśez (ćeria-li·śśez) pukśase̮ pi̮žje̮ (pi̮že̮), si̮ne̮ni̮ peli̮·sseze̮n, uje̮ni̮. ojnas vetle̮te̮·ni̮ ki̮bni̮. boštase̮ śime̮·t, kaťťase̮ sije̮ beďo·kkez vi̮le̮, e̮ztase̮ i žage̮·ńik (žag-vi̮l) uje̮ni̮. aǯ-ǯase̮, kujle̮ i̮ǯi̮t šuka. sačke̮ni̮ aǯla·se̮n. kule̮·m ńuže̮·te̮ni̮ bereg vi̮lśań bereg vi̮le̮. kule̮·mse̮ ge̮rǯǯe̮ni̮ aśni̮s pi̮š suńi·siś. śime̮·tiś kere̮ni̮ goľki·ez i kiša·le̮ni̮ sije̮ kule̮·m vel-deras gezo·k vi̮le̮, a mu-goľki·ez kiša·le̮ni̮ kule̮·m ul-de̮ras, morda· ke-re̮ni̮ pu-ǯalleziś. vugi̮·r doma·le̮ni̮ kuź suńi·-se̮n vugi̮·r-šať berde̮ i siǯ vugra·śe̮ni̮. ćerise̮ i̮le̮·tle̮ni̮ gaggeze̮n, gutteze̮n, bobi̮·lleze̮n. e̮ktase̮ nije̮ ćumane̮ iľi bankae̮ i nue̮ni̮ śe̮rani̮s vade̮re̮ (ju de̮re̮).

201. *śime̮·t*

komi-perḿa·kkez jona ki̮je̮ni̮ śime̮·tiś. ki̮je̮ni̮ ńin-ke̮mmez, peśťe·rrez, peš-šo·rkaez, solo·nkaez (solońi·ćaez), ke̮re̮bja·ez, purte̮·ssez i me̮di·ke̮. śime̮·tiś-že̮ kere̮ni̮ tuji·ssez, ćumannez ćumpe·ľľez.

202. *de̮ra-ki̮ja·n ji̮liś*

veďi·te̮ni̮ mijan ľon i pi̮š. pervo ke̮ǯase̮. ke̮r bi̮dmas, ńečke̮ni̮, doma·le̮ni̮ soǯ-ǯeze̮, a soǯǯeze koľta·eze̮ i kośte̮ni̮. kośme̮m ľonse̮ iľi pi̮šse̮ varte̮ni̮, med-bi̮ kiśśis

2. In our vegetable gardens we plant potatoes, cabbages, carrots, mangolds, turnips, beets, onions, tomatoes and cucumbers. First we dig the field over with spades, then break it up, manure it, and set potatoes under the spade. Cabbage plants are first grown in forcing-frames. We call our forcing-frames "legged forcing-frames". They stand on poles, nearer to the sun. Every spring the earth in the forcing-frame is replaced. They put manure at the bottom and spread black soil on the dung. Then they sow the seed. As they sprout, they are watered in the mornings and the evenings. They bring water, soak the bath-broom, and sprinkle the water with it. When the plant grows big enough, they make beds, and sow cabbage and beet in wide rows. Turnips are sown last, they grow quickly. For cucumber, forcing-frames are made on the ground, while tomatoes are simply planted in the ground. Potatoes are earthed up with hoes. They grow better if you break up the ridges. Therefore when they begin to grow up, they are harrowed several times. When they are fully grown, they dig up the potatoes with a spade, and carry them into the cellar or turnip-pit.

200. Fishing

Fish are caught with a drag-net, fixed net, hook and line, fishweirs and gaffs. The fishermen sit in a boat; they row and float along. At night they are fishing with fish-spears by artificial light. They take a piece of birch-bark, fasten it to a stick, kindle it and drift slowly. They catch sight of big pike swimming. They stab it with the gaff. They roll out the fixed net from one bank to the other. They weave the fixed net themselves from hemp-yarn. They make small balls of birch-bark and fix them to the upper part of the net, fastening them with strings, while they fix small balls of earth to the lower part of the net. The fishweir is made from chips of wood. The hook is fastened to fishing-rod by means of a long thread, and so they fish. Fish are lured by insects, flies and butterflies. These are collected in vessels of birch-bark or fruit jars, and so taken down to the river.

201. Birch-bark

The Komi-Permyaks weave many things from birch-bark. They weave sandals, bags, shoulder-bags, salt-boxes, baskets, knife-sheaths and the like. Of birch-bark, they make round baskets, small baskets and dippers.

202. About the weaving of canvas

With us people grow flax and hemp. First they are sown, then torn up when ripe, and bind them into swaths, and the swaths into sheaves, then they

ke̮ǯi·si̮s. ke̮ǯi·ssis toje̮ni̮ vi, kode̮ śoje̮ni̮. ke̮n-tu·śiś strepa·jte̮ni̮ pire̮·ggez. ľonse̮ iľi piśse̮ tie̮·te̮ni̮ i kośte̮ni̮. kośtem ľonse̮ ńarja·le̮ni̮ ńarja·ne̮n, pi̮rke̮·te̮ni̮ pi̮rkeć-ćane̮n (pi̮rke̮ćća·ne̮n), zua·le̮ni̮ zueze̮n. kuďeľse̮ pećke̮ni̮ ćerse̮n i pećka·n vi̮li̮n. muke̮·d suńi·sse̮ (piše̮vej) pučke̮ni̮. seśśa bi̮dmale̮ni̮, pane̮ni̮ i ponde·ćće̮ni̮ ki̮jni̮ de̮ra: ki̮je̮ni̮ stan vi̮li̮n de̮ra; preste̮·ď, se̮ǯ, tork. polovi·kkez ki̮je̮ni̮ iľi torkiś iľi važ kraśi·te̮m (mićе̮·te̮m) trepi·ćaiś. e̮ďďe̮n base̮ka ki̮jli̮·llise̮ kuša·kkez da pe̮-kre̮·mmez: śe̮re̮n, bi̮d re̮me̮n. pe̮kre̮·m kone·ććeze̮ e̮še̮·tlise̮ si̮rrez i goľki·ez.

203. *ćuď ji̮liś*

1. *mijan e̮ďďe̮n una vista·śe̮ni̮ ćuď ji̮liś. ole̮m pe̮ tate̮n ke̮r-ke̮ me̮di·k, je̮z oťir, šuśe̮m ćuťťeze̮n, nija ve̮le̮maś ućе̮·ťikе̮ś, śede̮ś, ke̮ǯle̮maś śu. ni̮le̮n śui̮s ki̮če̮·m-ke̮ me̮d-koď ve̮le̮m: bi̮dme̮ma rozzeze̮n. nija vundi̮·lle̮maś ńe ćarlā·n, a e̮ǯi̮·ne̮n da ši̮la·eze̮n. kor-ke̮ aǯǯe̮maś ćarla· i'dava·jťe̮ pe̮ nuame̮ sije̮ i ve̮je̮·tame̮!' pukśase̮ das-ki̮k mort pi̮žje̮, munase̮ ju še̮re̮, doma·lase̮ ćarla·i̮s berde̮ iz i le̮ǯase̮ sije̮ vaas. ćarla·i̮s ki̮ša·śas pi̮ž doras i berge̮·tas pi̮žse̮. bi̮de̮·nni̮s ve̮jase̮. nija pe̮ śuse̮ vi̮ǯle̮maś uće̮·ťik ke̮ji·ćaezi̮n, kok-i̮ǯ-koďďezi̮n. ni̮ ji̮liś vista·le̮ni̮ bi̮d-be̮r-śase̮. šue̮ni̮, loktase̮ pe̮ e̮ććid ju de̮re̮. aǯǯe̮ni̮, juas ćeri palјale̮. 'dava·jťe̮, puam pe̮ ćeri-va' kišta·se̮ meše̮·-k-ti̮r sol i pańa·le̮ni̮.*

2. *ki̮ćće̮· sija loe̮m oťiri̮s, oze̮ te̮de̮. bi̮ďte̮ ke̮r pe̮ viľ naro·di̮s ponde̮m lokni̮, važi̮s ki̮ćće·-ke̮ vošti·śe̮m; muke̮·di̮s pi̮śśe̮m ve̮rreze̮, muke̮·di̮s torke̮m aśse̮. gar-je̮maś nija guez, ke̮re̮maś muevej velttez ste̮bbez vi̮li̮n. seśśa ke̮rale̮maś ste̮bbese̮, nije̮ sećće̮ i ľićke̮m. nija pe̮ jenle̮ abu veri·tle̮maś, abu ťelmi̮·lle̮maś.*

204. *ćuddez ji̮liś*

1. *ćuddes nija kaľa·nnez. nija polźe̮·ćće̮ni̮. ke̮r pi̮lśase̮ oťiri̮s ki̮k e̮di̮n ńi, kujme̮t e̮das munni̮ pole̮ni̮ ńi. šue̮ni̮, ćas pe̮ pi̮lśe̮ni̮ ćuddez. e̮tik mort lećće̮m pi̮lśi̮ni̮, si̮le̮ ke̮s rose̮n śinnezas koji̮·šte̮maś. me̮di·ke̮s pe̮ ǯage̮·te̮maś, muke̮·di̮s bi̮ďte̮ aǯǯi̮·lle̮maś pe̮ uće̮·ťik śed moto·kkeze̮s baña-pe̮las iľi ni̮liś śleddese̮. nija polźe̮·ćći̮le̮maś jonǯi̮ka (jonži̮ka) kreśśe·ńńo (kreśśe·ńńe̮) lunneze̮. sek ni̮lkaez vetli̮·lle̮maś ki̮lziśni̮, ve̮reǯi·ćći̮ni̮. pukśase̮ ju de̮re̮ (dore̮), tuj-vež vi̮le̮ iľi guna de̮re̮. ćerľi·tase̮ aśnise̮ gor-me̮ćća·ne̮n i puka·le̮ni̮, ki̮lze̮ni̮. ježeľi ki̮lase̮ pe̮ ke-*

are dried. When dried, the flax or hemp is threshed, so that the seeds may fall out. From the seeds oil is pressed, and this is eaten. Of the hemp-seed they bake pirogi. They soak the flax or hemp, then let it dry. The dried flax is broken with the flax-breaker, scutched with the scutcher, and carded with the carder. The tow is spun on the spindle and spinning wheel. Hemp-yarn is twisted by hand. Then they spool it, put the yarn on the loom, and begin to weave linen. The loom is used for weaving linen, checkered linen, and pure and rough tow. Door-mats are made either from rough tow or from old, coloured rags. They used to weave very beautiful belts, broad and narrow alike: they were mottled, of all colours. They fastened tassels and tiny balls to the end of the belts.

203. About the Chuds

1. With us many tales are told about the Chuds. Once upon a time another people, a foreign one used to live here; they were called Chuds. They were short of stature and black-skinned, and they grew corn. Their corn was somehow of a different kind, growing in clusters. They used chisels and punches for harvesting. Once they found a sickle, and said: "Let us go and sink it!" Twelve men got into a boat, went to the middle of the river, tied the sickle to a stone and dropped it in the water. The sickle caught on the boat, and the boat turned upside down. All of them were drowned. They stored corn in small sacks, the size of a stocking. They tell all sorts of tales about them. They say that once they went to the river bank. They see a fish swimming. "Let us make some fish-soup!" They pour a sack of salt into the water and begin to ladle it out.

2. What happened to this people nobody knows. A new people began to arrive, the old one vanished somewhere. Some of them fled to the forest, others destroyed themselves. They dug pits, built roofs of earth on pillars. Then they cut out the pillars, and the roof crushed them to death. They did not believe in God, nor did they pray.

204. About unchaste spirits

1. Unchaste spirits are devils. They frighten people. When people have bathed in two temperatures, they are afraid to go into the third. They say: "Devils are bathing now." A man went down to have a bath; they squirted him in the eyes with a dry broom. They stifted another one. Another man is said to have seen small, black balls in the dressing-room, or traces of them. They mostly come to frighten people on the days around Twelfth

raśe̮·m, mort kulan vote̮ǯ. ježeľi ki̮lase̮ pe̮ śiľka·nnez, svaďba keže̮. e̮ććid pukśe̮maś kuka·ń-kući·k vi̮le̮, be̮ži̮s koľćće̮m ćerta· sajas. kin-ke̮ nije̮ kvaťi·te̮m (ćapale̮m) be̮že̮ććas i dava·j ki̮ski̮ni̮. ki̮ske̮ma jukme̮s dore̮ǯ. sete̮n ke̮da·-ke̮ ni̮lkaes kolasiś ponde̮m li̮ďďe̮·tni̮ moľitva. kućikse̮ le̮ǯe̮maś.

2. *nija ćuddes pe̮ veže̮ni̮ oťirse̮, pukte̮ni̮ pe̮ ni̮ meste̮ pue̮ve̮j (puove̮j) ćurkaez. uće̮·ťik vež kagale̮, ke̮da eśśe̮· abu pi̮rte̮m, sije̮ bańae̮ e̮tnasse̮ pole̮ni̮ koľni̮. sije̮ pe̮ vermase̮ vežni̮. veže̮m kaga una pe̮ śoje̮, no oz bi̮dmi̮. loe̮ i̮ǯi̮t jura, oz kotraś, ńe oz baji·t. a mort-kagase̮ ćuddes pe̮ bi̮dte̮ni̮ aśni̮s. e̮ććid bi̮dte̮maś ni̮loćkae̮s (ni̮loćkale̮) ńeve·stae̮ǯ bańai̮n i ponde̮maś śetni̮ ajka saje̮, aslani̮s ćud saje̮. sija pe̮ e̮ććid lokte̮m gortas i šue̮: "mame̮, vaj meni̮m śi-pož. me pe̮ i̮re̮·š me̮da si̮ssa·lni̮." "kin pe̮ te seče̮·mi̮s mene̮ šuan mame̮n, me pe̮ tene̮ og te̮d." "me pe̮ tenat ni̮l." "abu, te pe̮ ńe menam, menam vot pe̮ ni̮le̮ kujle̮ zi̮bkai̮n." "sija pe̮ ńe ni̮l tenat, a ćurka. me pe̮ ni̮li̮t tenat. mene̮ śete̮ni̮ ńi ajka· saje̮, aslani̮s ćud saje̮. ježeľi pe̮ te mene̮ žaľe·jtan, kor pondam munni̮ e̮tik bańaśań me̮di·ke̮, ki̮lan peśńaez, ćapki̮ sećće̮ perna·!" mami̮s si̮ǯ i keras. kor sija ćapkas perna·se̮, ni̮li̮s lebźas li̮m-purga pi̮čkiś ture̮pe̮n, kurićae̮n. seśśa gortas lokte̮m, ni̮lka ńi, bośtem ćer i kera·le̮m veže̮m kagase̮. kagaśis pes arkme̮n (šogme̮m).*

205.

gožumśa asi̮l. zoloťi·ste̮j šondi juge̮·rrez šonte̮ni̮ muse̮. mijan śelo saji̮n te̮ćće̮ni̮ paśki̮t kolχo·zne̮j i̮bbez. ju saji̮n sulale̮ pemi̮t ve̮r. eta ve̮re̮ mi munim e̮tpi̮r jage̮dla. ve̮ri̮n ve̮li eďďen le̮ń. pujez vi̮li̮n ćuť-ćuť ki̮še̮·tise̮ ľisttez. mi janse̮ććim bi̮de̮·nni̮m i bi̮d mort pondis e̮kti̮ni̮ pu-jage̮dse̮, ke̮da bi̮dmis una ve̮ri̮n. me muni i̮le̮ jorttezśań. aǯǯi una jage̮d i vune̮·ti bi̮de̮·nni̮s ji̮liś. drug me ki̮li ki̮če̮·m-ke̮ ši̮, ke̮da pondis śo sodni̮ i sodni. me sulti, viǯe̮·ti sećće̮, kiśań loktis šumi̮s. i mij-že̮ me aǯǯa? mune̮ aći̮s ve̮rsa χoźa·jin, oš. me ki̮nmi mesta vi̮lam. mij-že̮ meni̮m kerni̮? kote̮·rtni̮ iľi uśni̮ mu vi̮le̮ da pritvori·ćći̮ni̮, mij me kule̮m. eta dumajte̮mi̮s kiśśis e̮tik śeku·nda. me reši·ti kote̮·rtni̮. bośti ćoźa·žik vedra·e̮s i pondi kote̮·rtni̮ si̮lań, ki̮te̮n ve̮lise̮ jortteze̮. ńewna kote̮·rte̮m be̮ri̮n me berge̮ćći viǯe̮·tni̮, ve̮će̮, oz oši̮s me śeri̮n. me aǯǯilli, mij oši̮s munis voǯe̮ pemi̮t ve̮ras.

Night. That was the time the girls used to listen and tell fortunes. They sit down on the river bank, at a crossroad or in the threshing-yard. They draw a circle around themselves with a poker, and keep sitting there listening. If they hear someone chopping wood, a man will die. If they hear bells ringing, a wedding will take place. Once they sat on the skin of a calf its tail stretching over the line. Somebody jerked them, seizing the skin by the tail, and started to pull them away. They were pulled as far as the ice-hole, but there one of the girls began to pray. They let go of the skin.

2. The devils change people, replacing them by tree stumps. They are afraid of leaving babies who are not yet baptized by themselves in the bath-house. They might be changed. A changed child eats very much yet it does not grow. It will have a large head; it cannot walk nor can it speak. Human children are raised by the devils themselves. Once a little girl was brought up in the bath-house, and they (the devils) made arrangements to marry her to their devil of the house. She came home once, saying: "Mother, give me a good, thick sieve of horse hair. I want to strain kvas." "What kind of being are you to call me your mother? I do not know you." "But I am your daughter!" "You are not mine, my daughter is lying there in the cradle." "It is not your daughter but a stump of wood. I am your daughter. I am about to be married to their devil. If you are sorry for me, when we go over from one bath-house to the other, and you hear singing, throw the cross to us!" The mother does as she was told to. When she throws the cross at them, the girl flies away in the form of a hen, a whirlwind in a snowstrom. Later the girl came home, took a hatchet and chopped the changed child to pieces. The child became firewood.

205. [Meeting a bear]

It is a summer morning. The golden rays of the sun warm up the earth. Behind our village broad stretches of kolkhoz fields are to be seen. There is a dark wood over the river. Once we went to gather berries in this wood. Everything was very quiet in the wood. The trees were just beginning to come into leaf. We all parted from each other, and each of us started to pick cowberries of which there grew plenty in the wood. I went far away from my companions. I found berries in abundance and forgot everything. Suddenly I heard a noise which grew louder and louder. I stopped and looked in the direction the noise came from. And what do you think I saw? The lord of the woods himself, a bear was walking there. I froze to the spot. What was I to do? Run away or throw myself down upon the ground pretending to be dead? This thought passed in a second. I decided to run

me lokti jorttez di̮ne̮ da viśtali oš aǯ́ǯ́i̮le̮m ji̮liś. nija uďiviććise̮ eta novośť vi̮le̮ i mi reši·tim e̮kti̮śni̮ bi̮de̮·nni̮m e̮tlai̮n. siǯ i kerim. ćoža ti̮rise̮ mijan dozzez i me̮de̮·ććim munni̮ gorte̮.

206.

med matiś ďere·vnae̮ǯ koľććis eššе̮· das versta mi̮mda, a i̮ǯi̮t pemi̮t ľilo·ve̮j ki̮me̮·r ćoža veššis mijanlań. šoći̮·ńika i̮li̮n e̮zji̮vle ćar-ńe̮l i ki̮le̮ guśa gi̮male̮m, ke̮da žag-vi̮l sode̮, mate̮·ćće̮ da vuǯe̮ orlaśan raska·tteze̮. ve̮llez sulte̮te̮ni̮ peľľezni̮se̮, ki̮ǯ biťťe̮ ńukajte̮ni̮ svežе̮j vozduχse̮, ke̮da ki̮le̮ mate̮·ććan ki̮me̮·r di̮nśań. i brićkai̮s ćožaži̮k tarowće̮ busa tuj kuźa. menam pole̮m pete̮ i me ki̮la, ki̮ǯ vire̮ peri̮tži̮ka vetle̮ žilaezi̮n. i vot ki̮me̮·ri̮s pondis saje̮wtni̮ ńi šondise̮. vot sija viǯe̮ti̮štis med be̮rjaiś jugde̮tiś gorizo·ntliś strašne̮j gažte̮m lade̮rse̮ i sajaśis. ome̮n bi̮de̮·s drug veššis da lois gažte̮m. vot pondis dre̮žžitni̮ pipu ras. i̮ǯi̮t ki̮ǯǯezle̮n ji̮llez ponde̮ni̮ oklaśni̮ i ke̮s turunle̮n pućo·kkez lebźe̮ni̮ ke̮s tuj kuźa. toľko ješti nije̮ ve̮rźe̮·ćći̮ni̮, śinnez guśalana ćar-ńe̮l če̮kte̮ ve̮llese̮ sulćći̮ni̮ i sek-že̮ ki̮le̮ seče̮m ćarkńite̮m, što kažićće̮, biťťe̮ ńeboi̮s kišše̮ mijan vel-de̮ri̮n.

207. *loś*

loś mijan ve̮rrezi̮n šoća pantaślan źver. sija torje̮ćće̮ vi̮ne̮n, a muke̮d-kosta śvirepośťe̮n. loś bura kotraśe̮ i ujale̮. kote̮·rtike̮ sija ćeglale̮ kusta·rńikkez, ullez, ke̮s pujez, ke̮dna pantaśe̮ni̮ si̮le̮ tuj vi̮las. ńur si̮le̮ ńem tuje̮. paśki̮t kopi̮taes viǯe̮ni̮ sije̮ zi̮bu·n vi̮las. ke̮r e̮ďďe̮n ńi ve̮je̮·te̮, sek ľos vode̮ ki̮ne̮·m vi̮las, ńuže̮·te̮ oǯ́ǯ́iś kokkese̮ i siǯ ki̮šše̮ oǯ́lań. ke̮r-ke̮ mijan ve̮rrezi̮n loššes olise̮ e̮ďďe̮n una. ke̮ť i opa·sne̮j ve̮li loššez vi̮le̮ oχo·tai̮s, no ve̮ra·liššez vijilisni̮ nije̮. loššez pondise̮ e̮šni̮. se̮ve·ćke̮j vlaśť di̮rja v l a d i m i r i l j i ć ľ e ń i n podpeši·tis loššez oχra·na ji̮liś ďekre·t: ni̮ vi̮le̮ oχo·tase̮ zapreťi·tise̮. mijan źver ve̮ďiti·ššez reši·tise̮ vele̮tni̮ loššese̮ mort di̮ne̮, med-bi̮ nija uǯalise̮, ki̮ǯ uǯale̮ni̮ me̮di·k gort-poda. god-me̮d ńi ćula·lis, ki̮ǯ mosko·vske̮j oblaśťi̮n orgańizu·jtise̮ miri̮n perve̮j le̮ši·ne̮j ferma. e̮ni loššez vi̮li̮n ki̮skale̮ni̮ pes, kerrez i bi̮de̮·s, mi̮j kole̮ χoźa·jstvoi̮n.

away. Quickly I seized my pail and began to run to join my companions. After a short run I turned back to see if the bear were pursuing me. I saw the bear had disappeared in the dark wood. I arrived among my companions and told them that I had seen a bear. They were surprised at this news, and we decided to stay together. So we did. Our vessels were soon filled, and we started home.

206. [The tempest]

It was still about ten versts to the next village, but a big, dark lilac cloud turned quickly towards us. Far away, at a distance, it was lightening at intervals, and thundering in an undertone first, then increasingly louder, turning into ear-splitting thunder. The horses prick their ears, as if to breathe in fresh air coming from the approaching cloud. And the britzka rolls on more swiftly along the dusty road. I begin to be afraid and feel my blood run faster in my veins. And, see, the cloud begins to hide the sun. For the last time it casts a glance at the shining horizon's fearful, sad landscape, and then hides itself completely. Everything around us was suddenly changed and sorrowful. The aspen wood began to quiver. The crowns of the tall birch trees begin to bend and bow, and dry bunches of hay fly up along the dry road. Hardly had I made the horses move, when they were forced to stop by blinding lightning, and at the same time thundering was heard, and it seemed as if the vault of heaven was going to collapse above us.

207. The elk

The elk is a beast which is rarely found in our woods. It excels in strength, and sometimes in its fierceness. The elk can run fast and swim well. While running it breaks down bushes, boughs and dry trees that block its way. The swamp is nothing to it. Its broad hoofs hold it up in the swampy soil. When it sinks very deep, the elk rests on its belly, extends its fore legs and so pulls itself forward. Once upon a time there used to be many elks in our woods. Although it was dangerous to hunt them, the hunters often brought down an elk. The elks began to diminish in number. Vladimir Ilyich Lenin signed the decree on the protection of elk: it was forbidden to hunt for them. Our animal-breeders decided to accustom the elk to human beings and work as other domestic animals work. It was two years ago that the first elk farm in the world was established in the Moscow district. Today elk are used in transporting firewood, logs and everything needed on the farm.

208. *soboľ*

soboľ vetle̮·te̮ ke̮sti·śe̮me̮n. ke̮r polźas, sija lebźe̮, ki̮ǯ kaj ki̮k metr kuźa ćećća·le̮me̮n. a i̮ǯi̮t opa·snośť di̮rńi kaje̮ pu vi̮le̮ ki̮z ullez saje̮ ǯepśi·śe̮me̮n. opi·tne̮j soboľa·tńik soboľ vi̮le̮ kapkan sulte̮tike̮ objeza·ťeľno ti̮rte̮ aśśis śľedse̮. te̮wnas soboľ ńe e̮tik lun śe̮rna či̮gje̮n oli̮ke̮ pukale̮ li̮ma norai̮n. ke̮r aǯǯase̮ nora, ke̮dai̮n ole̮ źvero·kkez, ve̮rali·śśez ge̮ge̮rte̮ni̮ sije̮ śeťe̮n.

209. *iń-va ju*

pemi̮t ve̮rreze̮t, źeľo·ne̮j viǯǯez kuźa kote̮·rte̮ i ń - v a ju ńužale̮ma golube̮·j ćukľaśan ľentae̮n. ki̮nim i̮le̮·ži̮k, si̮nim loe̮ sija paśki̮tži̮k; kote̮·rte̮ i ń - v a, gaže̮·te̮ oťirse̮. ńokraśe̮ni̮ si̮ veśti̮n vi̮li̮n požummez da šuške̮ni̮ aśśini̮s peśńa-ni̮se̮. le̮ń si̮ vi̮li̮n ari̮n da te̮le̮n. moro·zzez paśte̮·te̮ni̮ sije̮ ki̮z ji̮e̮n, ńebi̮t li̮m veľťťe sije̮ ćoćkom šebrase̮n. šoni̮t si̮le̮ sečče̮m paś-ke̮m ultas.

210.

1. *tuli̮s. — šondia mića lunnez. i ń - v a ćapkas aśśis te̮lśa paś-ke̮mse̮, i̮žde̮m vanas veťas viǯǯese̮. ri̮te̮n loktan ju dore̮, di̮r viǯe̮·tan si̮ vi̮le̮, ńe-ki̮ǯ be̮r oz munśi̮.*

2. *gožumśa mića lune̮ mije̮ ińde̮·ććim i̮ǯi̮t ve̮re̮. jugde̮ gaža šondi. pe̮ľtis ńe-i̮ǯi̮t te̮lo·k. kolχozne̮j i̮bbez vi̮li̮n moreen juklaśis kuź da ček ruǯe̮·g. mi̮ććiślis le̮z vi̮ǯan id, gi̮riś rozja ze̮r. e̮tik-me̮di·klàn družne̮j koľľekťi·vvez ponde̮·ććise̮ vun-di̮ni̮. no vot i ve̮r. vozduχi̮s lois i̮rki̮·tži̮k da uľži̮k. ki̮nim i̮leži̮k pi̮ram ve̮ras, si̮nim pujes gi̮ri̮·śži̮keś, leśi̮·tži̮keś. uće̮·ťik kajo·kkez bi̮dlàn šurge̮me̮n lebale̮ni̮. ńe-di̮r mi̮jiś aǯǯim, gi̮riś bi̮tse̮n ńi voe̮m maľi·na. ćoža ti̮rtim i̮ǯi̮t tuji̮·ssezni̮me̮s i śi̮lte̮n munim gorte̮. — gožume̮n ćeľaď kote̮·rtise̮ va-de̮re̮. e̮teri̮s ve̮li šondia da žar. ečče̮m lune̮ bur ujalni̮ vai̮n. šoni̮t va seste̮mme̮, kokńite̮ vi̮l-tir. vot va-de̮r paśta pondis ki̮lni̮ gaža šum. e̮tikkez ćoža će̮lććise̮ da će̮lććise̮ và, me̮di·kkez ujalise̮ ńi da vuǯise̮ med beregas. kujme̮·ttez, ke̮dna eśśe̮· ez kuže̮ ujalni̮, pi̮rise̮ pole̮me̮n i tule̮ććise̮ bereg doras. ome̮n vase̮ veľťťise̮ pośńiťik oťir. pervo nija kupa·jććeni̮, ki̮ǯ biťťe̮ aśśini̮s kuže̮mse̮ toľko mi̮ććale̮me̮n, no ńe-di̮r mi̮jiś leptiśe̮ ni̮le̮n be̮bale̮m. reśśe̮ni̮ [ɔ: rezśe̮ni̮], šuńgi·śe̮ni̮ pi̮de̮·ži̮k, kośśe̮ni̮ ujale̮m ponda*

208. The sable

The sable arches its back when walking. When it gets frightened it flies away like a bird, with leaps two metres long. In times of great danger it will climb a tree and hide in the big branches. An experienced hunter will in any case hide his footmarks when setting a trap for sable. In winter the sable often sits for days starving in its snow-den. When hunters find the den in which the small beasts are living, they surround it with a net.

209. The River Ińva

The River Ińva flows through dark woods and green meadows, stretched out like a meandering blue ribbon. The further it flows, the wider it becomes. The Ińva flows and people take delight in it. Tall fir trees bow above it, humming their tunes. Calm spreads over it throughout the autumn and the winter. Ice sheets are thickly laid on it by frosts, and soft snow spreads a white cover on it. It feels warm in such a dress.

210. [About the seasons]

1. Spring. — Sunny days are coming. The Ińva doffs its winter clothes, inundating the fields with floods. In the evening you come to the river, looking at it for a long time; it has no intention whatever of retreating.

2. On a beautiful summer day we set off and went to the big wood. It is beautiful sunny weather. A little breeze was blowing. In the kolkhoz fields long-stalked, dense rye was waving like a sea. There were long stretches of bluish barley, and long-eared rye. At some places friendly collectives were starting harvesting. There you are now, there is the wood! The air becomes cooler and moister. The deeper we penetrate into the wood, the taller and more beautiful are the trees. Little birds fly in every direction, flashing to and fro. Soon we perceived that the raspberry was fully ripe. Quickly we filled our large vessels of birch-bark, and went home singing. — In summer the children ran to the river bank. It was sunny weather outdoors, and the air was hot. It is fine to swim on such a day. The warm water makes your body clean and light. Merry voices were heard along the bank. Some sprang into the water quickly, others had already been swimming, crossing the river to the other bank. Still others who could not yet swim were afraid to enter into the river, and stayed splashing by the bank. The water was full of small children everywhere. First they bathe, as if to display what they know, but soon they start to play pranks. They splash each other,

pe̯llez, poččez. bi̯di̯s stara·jćće̯ aǯǯi̯ni̯ kupa·jććemas mi̯j-ke̯ vi̯ľe̯s. vai̯n bur, no ti̯rmas, kole̯ petni̯ i ćeľad pervo žag-vi̯l, a si̯ be̯ri̯n kote̯re̯n e̯tik be̯rśań me̯di·k pete̯ni̯ vaśis.

3. *ar. — pujez vi̯li̯n ľisttez e̯ťi me̯di·lai̯n pondase̯ vežetni̯ e̯šše̯· avgust końe·ći̯n. śeńťabri̯n ki̯ǯ vi̯li̯n mi̯ćći·śase̯ sovśe·m vež, zoloťi·stej ullez. tuli̯se̯n med oǯ pučalis ki̯ǯ, a ari̯n sija med-e̯ǯ pondas vežetni̯. luniś-lune̯, śo una·ži̯k i una·ži̯k loase̯ vež ľisttez. e̯šše̯· ki̯k-kujim lun i pi-pu pondas sulalni̯ ge̯rd, bagro·ve̯j, zoloťi·stej. no vi̯na te̯l-ćik ľeťi̯·štas i ete̯ med-be̯rja me̯de̯ćća·nse̯ kokńiťik kośman ľisttese̯ vozduχi̯n berge̯tle̯me̯n sija veľťťas nije̯n uľ muse̯. i̯bbez žag-vi̯l kuša·mmase̯. ćvettez, e̯śase̯ i keľde̯te̯m turun ńoki̯rććas mu berde̯. toľke̯ e̯źim pondas leptiśni̯ rovne̯j, źeľo·ne̯j barχate̯n, no jona tomińik peta·ssezle̯ ćoža kolśas kulni̯. si̯ tuje̯ śu bi̯dmassezle̯n vuž-vežni̯s kujlase̯ li̯m ultas i tuli̯se̯n mi̯ćći·śase̯ źeľo·nej zao·kkeze̯n.*

211.

v o l o · ď a *kokńita i oχo·tne̯ja vele̯ććis. sposo·bnośťťez si̯le̯n ve̯lise̯ i̯ǯi̯te̯ś i ajni̯s vele̯·tis sije̯ uśi·ććivośť di̯ne̯, śete̯m zada·ńńoese̯ točne̯ja da vńima·ťeľne̯ja ti̯rte̯m di̯ne̯.* v o l o · ď a *vńima·ťeľne̯ja pi̯r ki̯lzis, ke̯r klassi̯n objaśńa·jtise̯ uro·k. aslas prekra·sne̯j sposo·bnośťťez di̯rji sija ez vune̯·tli̯ klassi̯n objaśńite̯m uro·kse̯ i gorti̯n si̯le̯ kolśis toľko sije povtori·tni̯. med-bi̯ gižni̯ sočińe·ńńo, sija li̯ďďe̯·tlis ńe-toľko uče·bńikkez da ki̯lzis uči·ťeľliś objaśńa·jte̯mse̯, a bośti̯vlis bibľioťe·kaiś kńigaez. i si̯le̯n sočińe·ńńoes ve̯lise̯ obstoja·ťeľne̯je̯ś da gižemaeś bur ľiťeratu·rnej ki̯le̯n. eďďe̯n matiś jorttez* v o l o · ď a *le̯n gimnaźi·ćeske̯j goddeze̯ ez ve̯le̯, no klassi̯n otnošeńńoez si̯le̯n ve̯lise̯ bure̯ś. sija objaśńa·jtlis ńe-veže̯rta·nase̯ peremenaez di̯rji, veśke̯·tlis perevoddez iľi sočińe·ńńoez, a muke̯dpi̯rśa otsavlis jorttesle̯ nije̯ gižni̯. sija voli̯vlis gimna·źijae̯ oǯǯi̯k, med-bi̯ vuǯe̯·tni̯ jorttesle̯ śe̯ki̯t mestaez grećeske̯j, ńe-to laťinske̯j ki̯l viliś, ńe-to objasńa·jtis śe̯ki̯t ťeore·ma. med-oǯi̯n munike̯ sija ki̯skis as śe̯ras i me̯di·kkeze̯s.*

212.

i̯rki̯t te̯lo·k kote̯·rtis menam ćuže̯m vi̯le̯. e̯šše̯ ńe-ki̯te̯·n ez ge̯rde̯t zaŕa, no asi̯llańi̯n ńeboi̯s ćoćkommis ńi, keť i umeľa e̯šše̯, no ge̯ge̯·r bide̯·s pondis ti̯dalni̯.

dive into the water, looking for planks or poles to swim with. Each one of them tries to find some new trick in bathing. It is fine to be in the water, but enough of it, it is time to get out, and one after the other, the children walk out, first with sluggish steps, then running, and leave the water.

3. Autumn. — The leaves of trees begin to grow yellow here and there as early as the end of August. In September there are completely yellow branches shining like gold on the birch-trees. In the spring the birch-trees are the first to burst into bud, in autumn they are again the first to turn yellow. Day by day the yellow leaves increase in number. In two or three days the aspen will stand there red and purple-coloured, shining like gold. But strong whirlwinds will strike at it, whirling the last remnants in the air, the leaves that are dry easily, strewing them over the damp earth. Slowly also the ploughed fields become bare. The flowers fall, and the yellow grass droops to the ground. Only the autumn crop begins to come up like smooth, green velvet, although the seeds that are too young are bound to perish at once. As against this, the young roots of the corn crop lie under the earth to sprout up with green stalks in spring.

211. [About the school-years of V. I. Lenin]

Volo·ďa learnt with ease and pleasure. His talents were great, and their father taught him perseverance and taught him to perform his school tasks with accuracy and care. *Volo·ďa* was always attentive when a lesson was explained in the form. Owing to his excellent gifts, he never forgot the lesson that had been explained in class, and at home he simply had to repeat it. When it came to a written test, he did not only read the text-books and listen to the teacher's explanations but he also borrowed books from the library. His exercises were well-founded and written in a good literary style. During his years in the secondary school, *Volo·ďa* did not have any close friends, although he maintained good relations with the rest of his class. In the breaks he clarified what was difficult for them to understand, corrected the translations or compositions, and even helped his companions in writing them occasionally. He went to the secondary school earlier than necessary so that he should be able to translate for his mates the difficult portions of Greek or Latin or to explain the theses. He went ahead and led other boys to follow him.

212. [At dawn]

The cold breeze struck at my face. Nowhere had the dawn sky yet turned red, but toward morning it began to turn white, although not yet distinctly,

me provorne̮ja ćećći da śibe̮·ćći zono·ćkaez di̮ne̮. bi̮de̮ ·nni̮s nija uźise̮ ńe-burika soććan kośťo·r ge̮ge̮·ri̮n. e̮tnas p a v e l lepti̮śi̮·štis da e̮ďďe̮n viǯe̮·tis me vi̮le̮. me kaći̮kńi·ti si̮le̮ jurnam i pondi munni̮ ju bereg dore̮t. me ge̮ge̮·r li̮s-vaa paśki̮t viǯ kuźa i oǯam i be̮ram pondise̮ kiśśi̮ni̮ šondi-juge̮·rrez. pervo nija ve̮lise ale̮je̮ś, si̮ be̮ri̮n loise̮ ge̮rde̮ś. bi̮dlai̮n almazzeze̮n jugjalise̮ li̮s-vale̮n gi̮riś voťťez. meni̮m pani̮t pondise̮ ki̮lni̮ kolokol-ši̮ez. drug me di̮ne̮t ge̮ńi·tis mi̮ććiśe̮m tabu·n, ke̮de̮ vaše̮·tise̮ menam te̮dsa zono·ćkaez.

213.

petna·ćate̮j veki̮n m o s k v ale̮n ćentra·ľne̮j ćaśť, ke̮da pondis šuśi̮ni̮ k r e mľ, ve̮li je̮rje̮ma vi̮li̮n da jon kirpi·ćne̮j śťena·e̮n. k r e m ľi̮n olise̮ car da bojara, a k r e m ľ saji̮n obslu·živajuššej oťir, ke̮dna śeľiććillise̮ aslani̮s spećia·ľnośťťez śe̮rti. m o s k v a ćentr di̮nśań šondi juge̮·rrez moz paśka·llise̮ e̮t-me̮dere̮ uľi·ćaez, ke̮dna nue̮·tlise̮ sośedne̮j goroddeze̮. sija mestai̮n, ki̮te̮·n ene̮ uľićaesse̮ poperegalise̮ śťenaes, ve̮lise̮ kere̮me̮ś voro·taez. e̮ni m o s k v a ju vi̮li̮n kere̮me̮ś paśki̮t possez, ke̮dna vi̮li̮na e̮šale̮ni̮ va veštas. torže·stvennej lunneze̮, para·ddez da ďemonstra·ćijaez di̮rńi k r a s n e̮ j p l o š š a ď vi̮le̮ lokte̮ni̮ m o s k v aiś uǯali·śśez, ke̮dna mi̮ćća·le̮ni̮ parťijake̮t da praviťe·ľstvoke̮t aśśi̮ni̮s jeďińe·ńńo.

214.

m i č u · r i n znameńi·te̮j sadovo·d. una·ži̮k petďeśa·ť godśa sija keris seče̮m uǯ, ke̮de̮ e̮ďďe̮n ľubi·tis. sija kerlis bi̮d-koď opi̮ttez, med-bi̮ bi̮tti̮ni̮ viľ sorta puez i ploddez. sija petke̮·tis seče̮m plodojage̮·dne̮j bi̮dmassez, ke̮dna oze̮ pole̮ ke̮ǯi̮tiś. gorodi̮s, ki̮te̮·n sija olis da uǯa·lis, šuśe̮ si̮ ńime̮n: m i č u · r i n s k. miču·rinske̮j sadi̮n eme̮ś seče̮m jablońaez, ke̮dna ulti̮n ńe̮ľki doźirajti·śśez pole̮ni̮ uźni̮. uśas-ke̮ ki̮me̮s vilad jablok, sek-že̮ kajas i̮ǯi̮t šval. med-bi̮ viǯni̮ seče̮m jablokse̮, kole̮ paśke̮·tni̮ ki̮knan kiiś ćuńńez. una ińťere·sne̮ji̮s miču·rinske̮j sadi̮n. taćće̮ volle̮ni̮ sadovo·ddez, med-bi̮ vele̮·ćći̮ni̮, kiǯ kole̮ bi̮tti̮ni̮ viľ sorta frukttez, karć da jage̮d. m i č u · r i nle̮n učeńi·kkez vele̮te̮ni̮ nije̮, kiǯ kole̮ viľ sorttese̮ bi̮tti̮ni̮. vele̮te̮ni̮ bi̮tti̮ni̮ sećći̮n, ki̮te̮·n ke̮ǯi̮t i gożumi̮s olle̮ ǯeńi̮t.

and things began to emerge all around. I jumped up briskly and joined the other little boys. None of them had slept well by the blazing camp-fire. Only *Pavel* rose, staring at me with a firm look. I nodded to him and started off along the bank. There was the dewy, wide meadow around me; before me and behind me the sun's rays began to pour down. First they were purple in colour, then red. Big drops of dew were glittering about like so many diamonds. In front of me the tinkle of bells could be heard. All of a sudden a herd of horses appeared and passed by at a swift gallop, the herd which my boy friends were chasing.

213. [Moscow]

In the fifteenth century the central part of Moscow, which began to be called the Kremlin, was surrounded by a high and strong brick wall. The Tsar and the boyars were living inside the Kremlin while the hosts of serfs settled according their trades behind the Kremlin. From the centre of Moscow, like the rays of the sun streets proceeded in every direction leading to neighbouring towns. At places where these streets were crossed by walls gates were made. Today there are broad bridges on the River Moscow, suspended high above the water. On festal occasions, when there are parades and processions, the workers of Moscow come to Red Square to express their unity with the Party and Government.

214. [About the Michurin garden]

Michurin was an important horticulturist. For more than fifty years he performed the work which he loved very much. He carried out all kinds of experiments to grow new kinds of trees and fruit. He produced fruit-bearing plants which can thrive in the cold. The city in which he lived and worked is called Michurinsk, after his name. In the Michurin garden there are apple-trees under which even the guards are afraid to fall asleep. If an apple falls on your forehead, a big swelling grows on it at once. If you want to hold such an apple in your hands, you must spread out the fingers of both your hands. There are many interesting things in the Michurin garden. Horticulturists come here to learn how to breed new kinds of fruit, vegetables and berries. The pupils of Michurin instruct them how to produce new stains. They are taught to apply production technique where the climate is cold and summer short.

215.

mijan žeńšinaez, kolχo·źńićaez akťivne̮ja peśśe̮ni̮ śeľske̮j χoźa·jstvo lepte̮m ponda. nija mune̮ni soćiaľiśťi·českej sorevnova·ńńo perve̮j ŕaddezi̮n, starajćće̮ni̮ bi̮tti̮ni̮ vi̮li̮n usto·jčive̮j uroža·jjez, razviva·jte̮ni̮ obše·stvenne̮j podali̮ś produkťi·vnośť. ti̮śećaez žeńšinaez uǯa·le̮ni̮ kolχo·zzezi̮n predśeda·ťeľľeze̮n. nija rukovoďi·te̮ni̮ poľevo·dčeske̮j da životnovo·dčeske̮j briga·daeze̮n, uǯa·le̮ni̮ traktori·stteze̮n, komba·jńorreze̮n, śeľske̮j χoźa·jstvoi̮n spećiaľi·stteze̮n. kolχo·zne̮j stroj leptis žeńšina kreśťa·nkaliś kuľtu·rne̮j uroveń. kolχo·źńićaez ovlaďeva·jte̮ni̮ peredove̮j agronomi·českej naukàn i kuže̮me̮n ispoľzu·jte̮ni̮ sije̮ aslas prakťi·-českej uǯi̮n. śeľske̮j χoźa·jstvoi̮n e̮ni ćentra·ľne̮j zada·čae̮n loe̮ razviva·jtni̮ obše·stvenne̮j životnovo·dstvo. ete̮ zada·čase̮ ti̮rte̮me̮n akťi·vne̮ja uča·stvujte̮ni̮ mijan žeńšinaez. godiś-gode̮ sode̮ni̮ životnovo·dstvoi̮n peredovi·kkez-žeńšinaez.

216.

1. *mijan śelo· e̮ďďen i̮ǯi̮·t i — ki̮ǯ meni̮m kažiććе̮ — base̮k. śelo· di̮ni̮n em k e̮ s - v a. krugo·m śelo· di̮ni̮n ve̮r. sećće̮ mije vetle̮tam jage̮·dla da čakla. ťer-ku mijan i̮ǯi̮·t. ťer-ku di̮ni̮n bi̮dme̮ni̮ base̮k ćveto·kkez. ťer-ku mijan sulale̮ samej base̮k uľića vi̮li̮n. ńe-i̮li̮n sulale̮ klub. sete̮n mi̮ććale̮ni̮ kino da konće·rttez. ri̮tteznas klubi̮s di̮ni̮n χe̮ť-kor una oťir, tom oťir. nija tonćujte̮ni̮, śile̮ni̮, orse̮ni maćen i je̮kte̮ni̮. pani̮t klubi̮sle̮ sulale̮ počta, a jeśśe̮· daľše̮ dvuχeta·žne̮j škola. sete̮n me veleććі. školai̮s meni̮m gľeńi·ććis, me ľubi·ti vele̮·ćći̮ni̮. meni̮m gľeńi·ććise̮ uči·ťeľľez.*

2. *oťir mijan śelo·iś uǯale̮ni̮ ve̮ri̮n. nija piľite̮ni̮ ve̮r, a poto·m splavľa·jte̮ni̮ sije̮s va vi̮lti. ve̮r mune̮ k e̮ s - v a vi̮lti i lokte̮ k a m a di̮ne̮ǯ. k a m ai̮s mijan di̮niś ńe-e̮ďďen i̮li̮n. śelo·i̮s di̮ni̮n em pośo·ľok k o r d o · n. śelo·i̮s i pośo·ľoki̮s počti̮ e̮tlaaśise̮. kor-ke̮ sete̮n ve̮li e̮ďďen śed ve̮r i sete̮n ńe-ťin ez ol. a e̮ni pośo·ľoki̮s lois e̮ďďen i̮ǯi̮t. sete̮n ole̮ni̮ rabo·čejjez, kodna uǯale̮ni̮ tože̮ ve̮ri̮n. no oťiri̮s uǯale̮ni̮ ńe-teľke̮ ve̮ri̮n, em kolχo·z. kolχozi̮s obje·ďińitis ńoľ ďere·vńa. tuli̮snas kolχo·źńikkezle̮n una rabo·ta. kole̮ ge̮rni̮ mu, saďitni̮, petke̮tle̮ni̮ naźom kartaes vi̮liś (kartaeziś). saďi·te̮ni̮ karto·ška, ke̮ǯe̮ni̮ ze̮r, šogdi ruǯe̮·g, ań-ki̮č. e̮ni saďi·-te̮ni̮ i kukuru·za.*

215. [Our peasant women]

Our women, the female workers of our kolkhoz, are actively working for the progress of agriculture. They are in the vanguard of socialist competition, endeavouring to raise the high-value of crop produce and to develop the profitability of the collective stock of animals. Thousands and thousands of women are working as presidents in the kolkhozes. They lead brigades engaged in tilling arable land and breading stock, and they also work as tractor-drivers, combine-mechanics, and agricultural specialists. The system of kolkhozes has done much to raise the cultural standards of the peasant women. The peasant women of the kolkhoz acquire the science of agriculture, which they apply with skill in their own practical work. In agriculture it is a central task today to develop the common stock of animals. In performing this task our women participate actively. The number of female ace-workers in the field of stock-breeding grows from year to year.

216. [Our village]

1. Our village is very large and — it seems to me — beautiful. Beside the village is the Kosa. The village is surrounded by woods. We go there to collect berries and pick mushrooms. Our house is large. Beautiful flowers grow by the house. Our house stands in the most beautiful street. The Club stands nearby. Cinema-shows and concerts are given there. Every evening many people, young people, gather together by the Club. They dance, sing, play football, and perform folk-dances. Opposite the Club stands the post office, and still further along is the two-storied school. I studied there. I liked the school and loved studying. I was pleased with my teachers.

2. People in our village work in the woods. They saw trees and float the timber down the river. The logs float down the Kosa and reach the Kama. The Kama is not far from us. There is a settlement by the village, called Kordon.

The village and the settlement are almost joined together. There used to be a dark wood there with no people living in it. Today, however, there is a settlement that has grown very large. Workers live there, who also work in the woods. But people do not only work in the woods, for there is a kolkhoz too. The kolkhoz unites four villages. In spring the kolkhoz peasants have much to do. They have to plough, plant and carry the manure out of the stables. They plant potatoes, oats, wheat, rye and peas. Today they also grow maize.

217. *menam babuška*

kor me veli uće·t, menam pondis šoga·lni mam i me bidmi babuška dinin. babuškais menes l'ubi·tis, no me sijes eg kilziś i si ponda sija menes vidlilis. me asja-ponśań pišjali gortiś i bidsa lun vetletli i teľke ritnas lokti gorte. sija eďďen polis, šte meket mij-ke lois. a kor me lokta, to ok [ɔ: og] sile viśtaś, kiten me veli i mij me ťeri. si ponda sija menes vidlis, no ńe-kor ez pes. sija viśtallis menim skazkaez.

(b) A Song

218.

me teda, lun-tir esten žeʒan,
panta·śam, kiʒ biťte en vel.
me polemen śinnezes leʒa
i ši śetteg sotta ośke·l.

proďitam, te bera·t viʒe·tan,
berge·ćća, miľa-ke i me.
kaźa·la i kila: gerde·ta
da naťte gerde·tan i te.

te menim bide·sen gľeńi·ććan:
i um i mige·r i ćužem;
no etiken me og miri·ćći:
te nilka-koď poliś-koď zon.

217. My grandmother

When I was little, my mother began to be ill, and I was raised by my grandmother. Grandmother loved me, but I did not obey her, and she often chid me. In the morning I ran off from home and came home late at night. She was very much afraid that something might happen to me. When I returned I did not tell her where I had been and what I had done. Therefore she chid me, but she never beat me. She told me tales.

218.

I know you are roaming there the whole day,
We meet as if you did not exist.
Timidly I cast down my eyes
And without saying a word I quicken my steps.

We pass by each other, you look back,
I turn back, why am I like this?
I perceive and feel that I am blushing,
And most likely you are blushing too.

You please me entirely —
Your brain, your figure, your face,
But there is one thing I am not reconciled to:
You are a lad as timid as a girl.

VIII. THE SOUTHERN PERMYAK DIALECT

I collected my Southern Permyak texts — like my Northern Permyak material — while staying in Syktyvkar, from college students in that city. One of the narratives, however, was noted down in Moscow, from the aspirant Rajsa Michajlovna B a t a l o v a (aged 32 in 1964). At present R. M. Batalova is working as a researcher at the Institute of Linguistics, Academy of Sciences of the USSR in Moscow. She was born in the village of Рудаково, situated on the left bank of Ińva, some 4—5 km SSE from the mouth of the River Juśva. As for the material collected in Syktyvkar, my informants were: Ilja Alekseevič J a r k o v (aged 18, Кудымкар), Galina Aleksandrovna K o ń š i n a (aged 18, Кудымкар), Galina Petrovna T a s k a e v a (aged 18, Веселый мыс, Kudymkar district). One narrative (No. 248) comes from Miss K o ľ č u r i n a, a student born in Kudymkar, another (No. 251) from undergraduate T a r a k a n o v, born in Verch-Ińva. I have no further particulars of these two informants.

All my informants spoke the so-called Kudymkar-Ińva dialect (see V. I. LYTKIN, ДиалХрест. 26). The major part of my texts represent the Kudymkar dialect, the smaller portion originates from other dialect areas (see above). Between the Kudymkar and the Rudakovo dialects, the most significant divergence is to be seen in Kudymkar *w* ~ Rudakovo *v*, both derived from **l*, and both showing peculiar features, depending on their phonetic position (see below). My informants have preserved a thorough command of their dialects, except for Tarakanov, whose speech is marked by a liberal use of Russian loanwords and Russian turns of speech. The influence of literary usage — except for Taskaeva and Tarakanov — is less conspicuous in their speech than in the case of my informants from the Northern Permyak area. This is understandable since Komi-Permyak literary usage is based essentially on the Kudymkar dialect.

The dialect has the following characteristic features:

1. The *w* phoneme deriving from old Permian *l* has the following allophones in the Kudymkar dialect: (a) *w* in the initial position in words or

syllables: *wokta* 'I come', *kinwe̮* 'to whom'; (b) *u̯* in the final position in words or syllables: *ve̮u̯* 'horse', *ou̯ni̮* 'to live'; (c) in the medial position Ø~*w*: *o*ˌ*a* ~ *owa* (in slow speech) 'I live', *su*ˌ*a·e̮* ~ *suwa·we̮* (in slow speech) 'he stands'. — Depending on the phonetic environment, the phoneme *v* (< *l*) has the following allophones in the Rudakovo dialect: (a) *v* in the initial position in words or syllables: *vun* 'day', *vokta* 'I come', *že̮ńi̮·ki̮sve̮* 'to the bridegroom'; (b) *u̯* in the final position in words and syllables: *ki̮u̯* 'tongue, word', *ni̮u̯ka* 'little girl'; (c) in the medial position Ø ~ *w*: *so*ˌ*a·e̮* ~ *sowa·we̮* (in slow speech) 'he salts (down)'. For reasons of simplicity I do not use the mark ˌ to denote syllabic limits. — For old Permian *l*, Southern Permyak *v*, or *w* (*u̯*, Ø,) see *П. С. Кузнецов*, Судьба твердого *л* в иньвенском диалекте коми-пермяцкого языка (Памяти академика Льва Владимировича Щербы (1880—1744). Сборник статей. Изд. ЛГУ им. А. А. Жданова. 1951. 188—90); *В. И. Лыткин*, ДиалХрест. 20, Совр. коми язык 48—9; Vászolyi: NyK 64:353—63; *А. С. Кривощекова-Гантман*: VFUJa. 1962: 212—28.

2. In Russian loanwords final *v* in words or syllables is realized as a *u̯* allophone in both the Kudymkar and the Rudakovo dialects, e.g. *goto·u̯* 'ready' < Russ. *готов*. In medial positions Ø or *w* is found: *goto·ite̮* ~ *goto·wite̮* 'he makes'. Thus the *v* phoneme of Russian loanwords is preserved as *v* in initial and post-consonantal positions (*vedra* 'bucket' < Russ. *ведро*, *kvaťi·t-* 'to seize' < Russ. *хватить*, *pritvoriććis* 'he pretended' < Russ. *притвориться*), while, in intervocalic, final, and preconsonantal positions it is replaced by the *w* in the Kudymkar dialect. Occasionally *v* is encountered in this last phonetic environment as well, or a vacillation may be observed: *iva·n* 'Ivan', *ńeve·sta* 'bride', *care·vić* 'tsarevich', *pervoj* 'first', *care·wna* ~ *care·vna* 'daughter of the tsar'. In the Rudakovo dialect the *v* phoneme of Russian loanwords naturally remains *v* in any phonetic environment.

3. Under the influence of more recent Russian loanwords the phonemes *(f)*, *(c)*, *(χ)* have also come into usage, for example, *funt* 'pound', *ofice·r* 'officer', *car* 'tsar', *dvore·c* 'manor-house', *χitrej* 'cunning', *oχotńi·k* 'hunter'. Sometimes variations can be observed: *staru·χa* ~ *staru·ka* 'old wife'.

4. Sporadically palatalized phonemes such as *ḿ*, *ṕ*, *b́*, *f'*, *ŕ*, *v́*, etc. occur in Russian loanwords, for example, *śḿeta·na* 'cream', *ṕatka* 'heel', *šof'o·r* 'driver', *oṕa·ť* 'again', *popeŕoga·is* 'it crossed', *kov́o·r* 'carpet'. If followed by a palatal vowel, palatalized *ṕ*, *b́*, *ḿ* occur also in original words, e.g. *ṕete̮ni̮* 'they go out', *b́eď* 'stick', *ḿe* 'I'.

5. In Russian loanwords the phonemes *ś* and *ź* are phonetically closer to the Russian *ś* and *ź* phonemes than to the *ś*, *ź* (= *ś̌*, *ź̌*) phonemes in original Zyrian words.

6. The phonemes *e̯* and *i̯* have the reduced allophones *ə̂* and *î* in absolute final positions: *munə̂* 'he goes', *ve̯rə̂* 'to the woods', *uje̯nî* 'they swim', *puka·-we̯nî* 'they sit'.

7. Substantives ending with a vowel drop the linking vowels of suffixes in rapid speech, which means that the sequence of vowels merges into a long or half-long phoneme. For example, *e̯škās* (< *e̯škae̯s*) 'the bull (acc.)', *e̯twàn* (< *e̯twai̯n*) 'together', *vojevo·dās* (< *vojevo·dai̯s*) 'voivod', *mùs* (< *mui̯s*) 'earth', *và* (< *vae̯*) 'into the water', *końušńà·* (< *końušńa·e̯*) 'into the stable', *si̯ pe̯rà* (< *si̯ pe̯rae̯*) 'at that time'. Sometimes a short vowel results: *pu kuźas* (< *pu kuźai̯s*) 'all along the tree'.

8. In the case of a consonant + *t*, the latter phoneme is often dropped in the absolute final position. For example, *bośǃ* 'take !', *eg wiś* 'I did not dare', *ćećće̯·wǃ* 'leap !' (~ *ćećće̯·wta* 'I leap'), *ez duma·jti̯š* 'he did not think' (~ *duma·jti̯šta* 'I think for a moment').

9. The sandhi-phenomenon occurs sporadically as in the following examples: *ki̯ď sija* (< *ki̯ǯ sija*) 'as he', *ki̯ć kote̯·rtis* (< *ki̯ǯ kote̯·rtis*) 'as he was running', *ok te̯d* (< *og te̯d*) 'I do not know', *sić-ke̯* (< *siǯ-ke̯*) 'for, since'.

10. The Northern Permyak group of *vi̯li̯n*, *vi̯liś*, *vi̯le̯* postpositions exists in Southern Permyak both as postpositions and transformed into suffixes, e.g. *spina vi̯was* 'on to his back', *be̯žis vi̯we̯* 'on to its tail', *tuj vi̯we̯t* 'on the road', *spina vi̯wśis* 'from his back' ~ *peľ-ponvas* 'on his shoulder', *be̯ži̯sve̯* 'on to its tail', *tujve̯t* 'on the road', *tropkavvas* 'on to the cork'.

11. The egressive suffix (*-śań*) has, rarely, a *-śiń* allomorph: *gortśiń* 'from home', *sekśiń* 'from that time onward', *pu vi̯wśiń* 'from the tree'.

12. The allative suffix sometimes assumes an accusative function, e.g. *i me̯dis se̯tni̯ kaji̯swe̯* 'and he started to beat the bird'; *ke̯ji·nwe̯ tože̯ oχo·ta veis viǯe̯·tni̯ gorša źverwe̯* 'the wolf also felt like taking a look at the hungry beast'.

13. Compared with the vacillations in the Northern Permyak, stress is more stable in the Southern Permyak, which means that certain morphemes are stressed, others unstressed. Stress is given for instance, to such morphemes as the deverbal noun formative suffixes *-a·n*, *-a·s*, *e̯·m*, *-e̯·t*, *-i·ś* and the verbal formative suffixes *-a·v-* (<*-a·l-*), *-a·ś-*, *-a·m-*, *-e̯·t-*, *-e̯·vt-*, etc. Such morphemes as: *-ka*, *-tor* (noun formatives), *-a*, *-sa*, *-śa*, *-e̯ś* (adjectival formatives) etc. remain unstressed. Case suffixes are always unstressed. I observed vacillation in several instances, e.g. *kore̯·m* ~ *kore̯m* 'request', *viśta·-we̯m* ~ *viśtave̯·m* 'he said, having said' *berge̯·ććis* ~ *berge̯ććis* 'transformed', *turu·n* ~ *turun* 'grass', *be̯ra·* ~ *be̯ra* 'again', *aǯǯi̯·wise̯* ~ *aǯǯi̯wise̯* 'they saw it'. Southern Permyak stress — since the place of it depends on the given morphemes (formative suffixes) — is termed "morphologized stress". For

Permyak accentuation, see Совр. коми язык 61—2; Коми-пермяцкий язык 90—5; *Р. М. Баталова:* SFU 1972:269—76.

Tales and narratives

219. *ruć da drozd*

1. *owis-ve̮wis kaj-drozd. si̮we̮n ve̮i poz. eta pozi̮n ve̮wise̮ si̮we̮n kaj-pijannez. e̮t-pi̮riś sećće̮ woktis ruć. rući̮s či̮g. sija pondis korni̮ kaji̮swiś pija·nnese̮, štobi̮ sije̮ śojni̮. no kaji̮s ez pondi̮ śetni̮ aśśis pija·nnese̮. sek rući̮s kajse̮ be̮be̮·tis. rući̮s viśta·wis, što sija be̮žnas pe̮re̮·tas puse̮. sek sija śojas kaj pija·nnese̮ i kajse̮ aśse̮. sek kaji̮s tože̮ be̮be̮·tas rućse̮. kaji̮s viśta·is rući̮swe̮, što sija verdas rućse̮. rući̮s sećće̮ jua·wis, ki̮ǯ sija verdas rućse̮. sećće̮ kajis viśta·is rući̮swe̮, štobi̮ sija ki̮wzis kajse̮. kaji̮s viśta·wis si̮we̮: i̮ǯi̮t tuj vi̮we̮t mune̮ni̮ ni̮woćka da babuška. babuškai̮swe̮n kias kuwši̮ni̮n ma, a ni̮woćkai̮s ne̮be̮tis uźelo·ki̮n pire̮žo·kkez. sete̮n kaj pritvori·ććis, što sija dojme̮m. sija pukśis niwkai̮s da babuškai̮s oǯe̮. ni̮woćkai̮s kaźa·is, što kaji̮s dojme̮m i koris babse̮, štobi̮ sija otsa·is kutni̮ kajse̮. nija puktise̮ pirožo·kkese̮ da mase̮ tuj bokas i ve̮ććise̮ kaji̮s śe̮re̮. kaji̮s ćećća·we̮me̮n pondis na di̮niś pi̮śśi̮ni̮. eta kade̮ rućis woktis koto·mkaes di̮ne̮, śojis pi̮rožo·kkese̮ da mase̮; eśśe̮ ǯebis. a kaji̮s si̮ be̮ri̮n ki̮ǯ biťte̮ ńem i ez ve̮w, webźis aswas poze̮. siǯ kajis verdis rućes.*

2. *ńe-di̮r mi̮jiś ruci̮s be̮r woktis pui̮s di̮ne̮ i koris kaji̮swiś pija·nnese̮. no sećće̮ kaji̮s viśta·is: "me tene̮ śas jukta·a. i̮ǯi̮t tujve̮t mune̮ ve̮e̮n mi̮ži̮·k. si̮e̮n ťeľe·gaas boćka sure̮n. sećće̮ webźi̮štis kaji̮s i pukśis boćka-tropkavvas (tuvvas). mi̮ži̮·ki̮s sije̮ vaše̮·tis boćkawiśis. sek kaji̮s pukśis ve̮w spina vi̮was. mi̮ži̮·ki̮s pľe̮ťe̮n vaše̮·tis spina vi̮wśis. kaji̮s be̮ra pukśis boćka-tropka vi̮was. sek mi̮ži̮·ki̮s we̮ga·śis. sija kvaťi·tis ćer i me̮dis se̮tni̮ kaji̮swe̮. no kaji̮s webźis, a mi̮ži̮·ki̮s inmis tropkaas. sija ćećće̮·wtis ťeľe·gaśis i ve̮ććis kaj śe̮ri̮n. a suri̮s eta kadi̮n boćkaśis pondis petni̮. sećće̮ wokti̮štis ruć i pe̮tte̮ǯ juis. si̮ be̮ri̮n ruci̮s be̮ra munis ve̮re̮. a kaji̮s webźis aswas poze̮.*

3. *ńe-di̮r mi̮jiś sećće̮ woktis kujme̮t-pi̮riś ruci̮s. pondis vartni̮ be̮žnas pu kuźas, a aći̮s eta pora·e̮ šuis: "me tenćit, kaj, puse̮ be̮žnam pe̮re̮·ta i śoja tenćit kaj-pija·nnese̮," kaj sećće̮ šuis, štobi̮ sija ez pe̮re̮·t puse̮ i ez śoj kaj-pija·nnese̮. ruci̮s pani̮t-šuis: "te mene̮ verdin?" a kaji̮s viśta·is: "verdi." a ruci̮s be̮ra juwa·wis: "te mene̮ jukta·in?" kaji̮s otve·ťitis: "jukta·wi." ruci̮s sećće̮ viśta·is kaji̮swe̮: "e̮ni mene̮ śere̮mte̮·t!" kaji̮s se̮gwaśi·ććis. sija nue̮·tis rućse̮ ďere·vńae̮ i*

219. The fox and the thrush

1. There once lived a thrush. She had a nest; her fledglings were in that nest. Once the fox came that way. The fox was hungry. It began to ask the bird for her young ones, which it wanted to eat. But the bird did not want to give it her young ones. Then the fox cheated the bird. The fox said it would overturn the tree with its tail. Then it would eat both the young ones and the bird, too. Then the bird cheated the fox in turn. The bird said to the fox that she would give it food to eat. Then the fox asked how she would feed it. Then the bird told the fox to obey her. The bird said to it: "A little girl and her grandmother are walking along the highway. The grandmother has a jar of honey in her hand, while the little girl is carrying pirogi in a small bag." There the bird pretended to be injured. She sat in front of the little girl and the grandmother. The little girl perceived that the bird was injured and asked her grandmother to help her catch the bird. They put down the honey and the pirogi by the road and set out to catch the bird. The bird began to run away, hopping along. Meanwhile the fox reached the shoulder-bags, ate the pirogi and the honey; and he also hid what remained. And after this the bird flew back to her nest as if nothing had happened. This is how the bird gave the fox food to eat.

2. In a short time the fox returned to the tree and asked the bird for her young ones. This time the bird said to it: "Now I will give you something to drink. A peasant is driving a horse along the road. There is a cask of beer on his cart." The bird flew and lighted on the plug of the cask. The peasant chased her away from the cask. Then the bird sat on the horse's back. The peasant chased her away from the back of the horse with his whip. The bird sat on the cask again. Then the peasant grew angry. He seized a hatchet and prepared to strike the bird. The bird flew away, and the peasant hit the plug. He jumped off the cart and made after the bird. Meanwhile the beer began to flow out of the cask. The fox came up and drank its fill. After this the fox returned to the woods again. And the bird flew back to her own nest.

3. After a while the fox came a third time. It began to strike at the tree with its tail, saying: "Bird, I will fell your tree with my tail and eat your young ones." The bird asked it not to fell the tree and not to eat the young ones. The fox answered: "Have you given me something to eat?" The bird said: "Yes, I have." The fox asked her once more: "Have you given me something to drink?" The bird answered: "Yes, I have." Then the fox said to the bird: "Now you must make me laugh!" The bird agreed. She took the fox into the village and hid it behind the fence. Grandfather,

ʒebis zabor saję. ogra·dain vęwisę ďed, bab da męs. ętwa-dęras ďed puka·wis da kįjis ńin-kęm, a babįs wįśtis męssę. kajįs pukśis babįswę peľ-ponvas. ďedįs sećće šuis: "te puka·w žagę·ńika, a me vija peľ-ponviśįt kajsę." starik węśę·ććis da sętis kajįs kuźa. no kajįs eta pora·ę webźis peľ-ponviśis i stari·kįs inmis staru·χaįswę peľ-ponas. uśis i kiśtis podo·ńćaśis jęwsę. sija ęďďęn węga·śis i pondis vidnį ďedsę, miľa sija sętis peľ-ponas. a eta pora·ę ruć viʒę·tis, śera·wis. a kajįs eta pora·ę bęra webźis aswas pozę.

4. *ńe-dįr mįjiś ruć bęra woktis kajįs poz dįnę i pondis vartnį bęžnas pu kuźa. a aćįs sećće šuę: "me tenćit pusę pęrę·ta, postę [ɔ: poztę] razęri·ta i pija·nnitę śoja." kaj sećće šuis: "en pęrę·t menćim pusę da en razęri·t menćim possę [ɔ: pozsę]!" ruć sećće jua·is: "te menę verdin?" kajįs otve·ťitis: "verdi." rućįs bęra jua·is: "te menę śeręmtę·tin?" kajįs viśta·is: "śeręmtę·ti" rućįs sećće šuis: "ęni te menę powźę·t!" kajįs sećće węga·śis i sįę viśta·is: "pędnaw śinnetę i kotę·rt me śerę!" kaj petkę·tis rućsę verśis veśkįta oχotńi·kkez dįnę ponnezęn. rućįs ęďďęn powźis i pondis pįššinį vęrę aswas nora· dįnę.no ponnes sįę kaźa·isę i pondisę vęććinį. rućįs ędva pįššis ponnes dįniś. kęr sija pįris aswas nora·ę, to sija pondis jua·śnį, kin sįę otsa·is pįššinį ponnes dįniś. sija pondis jua·śnį siʒ: "peľľez, peľľez, tiję mįj kerit?" peľľes viśta·isę: "miję kįwzimę, štobį otsa·wnį tenįt pįššinį ponnez dįniś." "śinnez, śinnez, tiję mįj kerit?" nija otve·ťitisę: "miję viʒę·timę, štobį otsa·wnį pįššinį tenįt ponnez dįniś." "kokkez, kokkez, tiję mįj kerit?" kokkez otve·ťitisę: "miję kotę·rtimę, štobį otsa·wnį pįššinį tenįt ponnez dįniś." "bęž, bęž, a te mįj kerin?" bęž otve·ťitis: "me kįša·świ kusttez da mįrrez berdę, štobį tenę kutisę ponnez." ruć węga·śis bęžįsvę (bęžįs vįwę) i kįskis nora·śis, štobį sįję śojisę ponnes. ponnes kvaťi·tisę bęžsę da ętwain bęžnas kįskisę nora·śis i rućsę.*

220. *ruć da rak*

ęt-pįriś kuććisę ruć da rak spori·tnį: kin nį koasiś ćožžįka kotra·śę. nija kaźa·isę turu·n zoro·d i kin nį koasiś ćožžįka kotę·rtas, to sija woas pobeďi·ťeľ. vot nija węśę·ććiśtisę i vot nija pondisę kotę·rtnį. ruć kotę·rtis, kotę·rtis i ʒar-ńitis bęras, štobį viʒę·tįštnį, kįććę. sija koľis raksę. rućįs raksę bęras ez kaźa·w. kęr rućįs woktis turu·n zoro·dis dįnę i suwtis, to jua·is raksę: "kįććę·ʒ te koľććin?" a rakįs sįwę otve·ťitis, što sija uže· važę·n ńi tatęn. rućis uďivi·ććis, što rakįs seććęm ćoźa kotę·rtis turu·n zoro·d dįnęʒ. a rakįs bębę·tis rućsę: kęd

grandmother and a cow were in the yard. The grandfather was sitting on one side weaving a shoe of bast, while the grandmother was milking the cow. The bird lighted on grandma's shoulder. Then grandfather said: "Sit quietly, and I will kill the bird on your shoulder." The old man got ready and struck the bird. Then the bird flew away from her shoulder, and the old man hit the old woman's shoulder. She fell and spilt the milk out of the pail. She was very angry and she began to scold the grandfather who had beaten her on the shoulder. Meanwhile the fox was looking and laughing at them. The bird returned once again to her nest.

4. After a while the fox came to the bird's nest once again and began to strike at the tree with its tail. He said: "I shall fell your tree, destroy your nest and eat your young ones." This time the bird begged it like this: "Do not fell my tree, do not destroy my nest!" Then the fox asked: "Have you given me food to eat?" The bird answered: "Yes, I have." Again the fox asked: "Have you made me laugh?" The bird answered: "Yes, I have." Then the fox said: "This time frighten me." The bird grew angry and said to it: "Close your eyes and run after me!" The bird led the fox out of the wood right to the hunters and their dogs. The fox was very frightened and began to run into the wood, back to its lair. But the dogs caught sight of it and started to chase it. The fox could hardly escape the dogs. As it entered its lair, it began to ask who had helped it escape from the dogs. It began to ask like this: "My ears, my ears, what were you doing?" Its ears answered: "We were listening so that we could help you escape the dogs." "My eyes, my eyes, what were you doing?" They answered: "We were looking, so that we could help you escape the dogs." "My feet, my feet, what were you doing?" The feet answered: "We were running so that we could help you escape the dogs." "My tail, my tail, what were you doing?" The tail answered: "I was caught in the bushes and stumps so that the dogs might catch you." The fox grew angry at its tail, thrust its tail out of the lair so that the dogs might eat it. The dogs seized its tail and pulled the fox as well as its tail out of the den.

220. The fox and the crab

Once the fox and the crab started a debate as to which of them could run faster. They caught sight of a haystack; whichever of the two could run to it first would win. They made preparations and began to run. The fox ran and ran, and looked back to see where it had left the crab. The fox did not see the crab behind it. When the fox arrived at the haystack, it stopped and asked the crab: "Where have you been?" The crab answered that it

pora· rući̯s węsę·ććis kotę·rtni̯, to raki̯s kuććiśis ruć bęž berdę. a kęr woktis turu·n zoro·d di̯nę, to bęra mezdi·śis ruć bęž berdiś. siǯ (sić) sija bębę·tis χitrej rućęs.

221. *koza· da ruć*

ęt-pi̯riś koza· woktis kowo·ďeć di̯nę i kaźa·wis, što kowo·ďećas uśęma ruć. a wuni̯s kak raz vęwi ęďďęn žar, a koza·wę vęwi oχo·ta ęďďęn juni̯. kęr sija jua·wis rućsę, mi̯j sija kerę seććin kowo·ďećas, to ruć si̯wę viśta·wis, što vi̯in ęďďen žar: "vot me i ćeććę·wti kowo·ďećas, sić-kę tatęn ęďďe·n i̯rki̯t. dava·j, ćeććę·w taććę koza·!" — šuis ruci̯s. estęn ęďďe·n ńi bur i i̯rki̯t. no koza· ez i duma·jti̯š, ki̯ć [ɔ: ki̯ǯ] śuris seććinę rući̯s da ćeććę·wtis rućis di̯nę kowo·ďećas. rućwę toľko etę i kowis. sija ćećće·wtis koza·wę śurrezvas, a ni̯śań ćeććę·wtis kooďećis i si̯ bęri̯n ćožži̯k pi̯ššis vęrę. a koza· di̯r puka·wis kowo·ďećas da gorę·twis, poka· siję ez ki̯skę seććiniś.

222. *kań da ruć*

1. *owis-vęwis mi̯ži̯·k. si̯węn vęi kań. eta kańi̯s vęi pęriś i ez pondi vermi̯ni̯ kuta·wni̯ śi̯rrezęs. sek χoźa·jini̯s pukśę·tis kańsę mešękę da nębętis vęrę, štobi̯ sija śojśę vęrśis źverrez. kań pondis owni̯ vęri̯n. sija pondis kuta·wni̯ kajjezęs da ućę·ťik źverrezęs.*

2. *ęt-pi̯riś kań panta·śis rućkęt. ruć powźi̯·štis kańi̯swiś i jua·wis: "kiśań te woktin?" kań si̯wę viśta·is, što siję pukśę·tisę eta vęrę vojevo·ďitni̯ bi̯dę·s źverrezęn. ruć sek koris kańsę aswas nora·ę. kań munis rućkęt i pondis si̯kęt owni̯. ruć vetwi̯·wwis oχo·ťiććini̯. sija vaja·wis una· śakej pętka. ęt-pi̯riś oχo·ta kostę ruć panta·śis kęjinkęt. i rući̯s viśta·wis kęjini̯swę, što ni̯ di̯nę vęras pukśę·-tisę viľ vojęvo·da. eta vojęvo·dai̯s ęďďen ńi węg. kejin pondis korni̯ rućsę, štobi̯ sija otsa·wis viǯę·tni̯ viľ vojęvo·dasę. ruć da kęjin setęn spori·ti̯štisę, no rući̯s śo-žę mędis otsa·wni̯ viǯę·tni̯ kęjini̯swę, štobi̯ kęjini̯s viǯę·tni woktis viľ vojęvo·-dasę ńe pustęj, a vajis baľaez. siǯ nija dogovori·ććisę i munisę aswani̯s tujęt. ńe-di̯r miji̯ś ruć panta·wis ošęs i ruć viśta·wis ošwę viľ vojęvo·da ji̯wiś. oš tožę mędis viǯę·tni̯ viľ vojęvo·dasę. sek ruć viśta·is, štobi̯ oš vajis ęškaęs (ęškās), a to vojęvo·dai̯s ęďďęn una· śoję. nija dogovori·ććisę, ki̯ććę nija woktasę kęjinkęt.*

3. *sek męd wunas oš vajis vęrę ęškaęs (ęškās), a kęjin baľās. ruć niję ǯebis siǯ, štobi̯ viľ vojęvo·dai̯s (vojęvo·dās) ośsę da kęjinsę ez kaźa·w. a nija štobi̯*

had been there for a long time. The fox was amazed to learn that the crab could run so quickly to the haystack. But the crab had cheated the fox. While the fox was preparing for the race, the crab clung to the fox's tail. And when it reached the haystack, the crab released itself from the fox's tail. This is how the crab cheated the sly fox.

221. The goat and the fox

Once the goat got to a well and perceived that the fox had fallen into the well. It was a very hot day, and the goat had a great desire to drink. When she asked the fox what it was doing down there in the well, the fox answered that it was very warm up above. "Well, I plunged into the well because it is very cold here. Come along, jump down here, goat!" — said the fox. The goat did not think about how the fox had got there but jumped right into the well to the fox. This was just the fox wanted. It leapt on the horns of the goat and then ran swiftly into the forest. But the goat sat for a long time in the well shouting until she was pulled out of it.

222. The cat and the fox

1. There once lived a peasant. He had a cat. This cat was already old, it could not catch mice. Then the master put the cat into a bag and took it to the forest so that the beasts of the forest might devour it. The cat began to live in the forest. It began to catch birds and small animals.

2. Once the cat met the fox. The fox was frightened of the cat and asked: "Where have you come from?" The cat answered that it had been made leader of all the beasts in the forest. Then the fox invited the cat to its own lair. The cat went with the fox and began to live with it. The fox went out hunting. It brought home all kinds of wild birds and a lot of them. Once while hunting the fox met the wolf. The fox told the wolf about the new voivode sent to them in the forest. This voivode was very angry now. The wolf asked the fox to help him in seeing the new voivode. The fox and the wolf debated there; the fox was willing to help the wolf only if he did not come empty-handed to see the new voivode but with a lamb. They agreed on this and started out, each on its own path. After a short time the fox met the bear and told him about the new voivode. The bear also wanted to see the new voivode. Then the fox told the bear to bring an ox because the voivode ate very much. They agreed where to meat the bear.

3. Next day the bear brought an ox and the wolf a lamb to the woods. The fox hid them so that the new voivode should not see the bear and the

aǯ́ǯ́ise̮, mi̮j vil' vojevo·dai̮s (vojevo·dās) kere̮, ke̮jinse̮ ruć ǯebis kustteze̮ i vewt'l'is sije̮ l'istteze̮n, a oš kajis pu vi̮we̮. ke̮r ruć nije̮ ǯebis, to ke̮će̮s ińde̮·tise̮, štobi woktis vil' voje̮vo·dās. kań woktis pol'a·navve̮ i każa·is bal'ās i e̮škās. sija uśke̮·ć-ćis ni̮ vi̮we̮ (ni̮vve̮) i pondis gorša mawzi̮me̮n śojni̮. eta kade̮ ke̮jin jua·wis oši̮swiś, mi̮j sija vi̮wśań aǯ́ǯ́e̮. oš otve·t'itis, što sija aǯ́ǯ́e uće̮·t'ik źvere̮s, ke̮da e̮d'd'e̮n żadne̮ja śoje̮. ke̮jinwe̮ tože̮ oχo·ta ve̮is viǯe̮·tni̮ gorša źverwe̮. sić-ke̮ [ɔ: siǯ-ke̮] sija vewt'l'e̮m l'isttezen ńem ez aǯ́ǯ́i̮, to sija żage̮·ńike̮n pondis kerni̮ ośta l'isttez koa·se̮t. eta bi̮de̮·s ki̮wis kań i sija duma·jtis, što kusttezas kotra·śe̮ ši̮r. sija uśke̮·ććis kusttezas da kuććis gi̮ǯǯeznas ke̮jinwe ni̮ras. ke̮jin e̮d'd'e̮n powźis. sija bi̮d vi̮niś uśke̮·ććis pišši̮ni̮. kańi̮s tože̮ powźis ke̮jini̮swiś i kajis pu vi̮we̮ (puvve̮) i inmis sija kak raz sija puvve̮, ki̮će̮· kajis oš. oš e̮d'd'e̮n ńi powźis. sija duma·jtis: 'vot kiče̮·m źveri̮s gorša! si̮we̮ daže̮ ječa bal'ās i e̮škās'. oš će̮će̮·wtis pu vi̮wśiń da pondis pišši̮ni̮. sekśiń bi̮de̮·s źverrez pondise̮ powni̮ vil' voje̮vo·daiś.

223. *kot, bara·n da koza·*

1. *owis-ve̮wis stari·k da staru·ka ni̮we̮n ve̮ise kań, bara·n da koza·. e̮t-pi̮riś stari·k da staru·ka viććise̮ ge̮śśeze̮s. nija we̮śe̮·ććise̮ nije̮ panta·wni̮ i e̮ktise̮ doze̮ śmeta·na. no kań kić-ke̮ [ɔ: kiǯ-ke̮] inmis eta doze̮ da śojis bi̮de̮·s śmeta·-nase̮. stari·k da staru·ka śmeta·nai̮s bol'še ez ve̮w i siǯ nija reši·tise̮ naćki̮wni̮ bal'ae̮s. kań ete̮ ki̮wis da petis e̮te̮re̮ ni̮we̮ viśta·wni̮. ke̮r ete̮ viśta·wis, to nija pondise̮ vidni̮ kańe̮s, mi̮l'a sija śojis śmeta·nase̮ dośśis [ɔ: dozśis].*

2. *štobi̮ bal'ase̮ ez naćki̮we̮, kań, bara·n da koza· pišśise̮ stari·k da staru·ka (staru·χa) di̮niś. nija kote̮·rtise̮, kote̮·rtise̮ i kańi̮s pondis kol'ćći̮ni̮, sić-ke̮ [ɔ: siǯ-ke̮] sija mi̮ǯis. sek sije̮ koza· pukśe̮·tis aswas spina· vi̮we. ke̮r ponde̮ććis ri̮t, to nija śo kote̮·rtise̮. ćoża nija suwtise̮ i reši·tise̮ kerni̮ bi (kośt'o·r). no ni̮we̮n ez ve̮we̮ spićkaez. to kań ni̮we̮ viśta·wis: "me we̮śe̮·ta sarta·s, a tije̮ l'uka·śe̮. ke̮r śinneśśiń [ɔ: śinnezśiń] pondase̮ će̮ćća·wni̮ bi-ćirrez, to me e̮zta sarta·sse̮ i siǯ mije̮ e̮ztame̮ kośt'o·r." nija aǯ́ǯ́e̮·tise̮ kośt'o·rse̮ i pukśise̮ šonti·śni̮. ńe-di̮r mijiś sećće̮ woktis oš. sija koris, štobi̮ sije̮ we̮ǯise̮ šonti·śni̮. siǯ nija ńol'e̮n šonti-śištise̮ i pondise̮ we̮śe̮·ćći̮ni̮ oj keže̮. kań kajis turu·n zoro·d vi̮we̮ (zoro·dve̮), a oš pi̮ris zoro·d uwte̮. bal'a i koza· kol'ććise̮ bi (kośt'o·r) di̮ne̮. sećće̮ woktise̮ ke̮jinnez. nija ve̮ise̮ čige̮ś. vot nija viśta·ise̮, što śojase̮ bal'ase̮ da koza·se̮. no nija viśta·ise̮,*

wolf. In order that they might see what the new voivode was going to do, the fox hid the wolf in the bushes and covered him with leaves of trees, while the bear climbed a tree. After the fox had hidden them, they sent the hare to tell the new voivode to come. The cat reached the clearing and perceived the lamb and the ox. It rushed at them and began to eat, mewing greedily. Meanwhile the wolf asked the bear what he could see from above. The bear answered that he saw a small animal eating very greedily. The wolf also wanted to look at the hungry animal. As he could not see anything because of the leaves he was covered with, he began silently to make a hole in the leaves. The cat heard the noise of this and thought there was a mouse running among the bushes. It dashed at the bushes and drove its claws into the wolf's nose. The wolf was very frightened. He wanted to flee with all his might. The cat was also frightened by the wolf and climbed the tree, that the bear had climbed. The bear was very frightened. He thought: "Look what a greedy animal he is! Even a lamb and an ox are not enough for him." The bear jumped down from the tree and took to its heels. From that time every animal began to fear the new voivode.

223. The tom-cat, the lamb and the goat

1. There once lived an old man and an old woman. They had a cat, a lamb and a goat. Once the old man and the old woman were waiting for guests to come. They prepared to receive them and collected sour cream in a vessel. But somehow the cat got to this vessel and ate up all the sour cream. The old man and the old woman had no more sour cream and therefore they decided to slaughter the lamb. The cat overheard them and went out to tell the animals about it. When he had finished, they began to scold the cat for having eaten the sour cream in the vessel.

2. In order to save the lamb from being slaughtered, the cat, the lamb and the goat fled from the old man and the old woman. They ran and ran, and the cat began to lag behind, since it was tired. Then the goat sat him on its back. At nightfall they were still running. Suddenly they stopped and made up their mind to make a fire. But they had no matches. Then the cat said to them: "I shall prepare chips of pine, and you will butt and butt. When sparks fly out of your eyes, I shall kindle the chips of pine, and we can light the fire in this way." They lit the fire and sat down to get warm. After a while the bear came to them. He asked their permission to warm himself. The four of them warmed themselves like this, and they prepared for the night. The cat climbed on top of a haystack, the bear crept under the stack. The lamb and the goat stayed by the fire. The wolves came that

štobi̮ ke̮jinnez ez we̮ge̮·te̮ pe̮riźži̮k [ɔ: pe̮riśži̮k] vonse̮ i korise̮ si̮wiś razreše·ńńe̮. oš eta pora·e̮ bura uźis i si̮wiś onse̮ ǯugise̮. sija we̮ga·śis da se̮tis ke̮jinwe̮. ke̮jinnes e̮ďďe̮n powźise̮ da pi̮ššise̮. asi̮wnas kań, bara·n da koza· pondise̮ kote̮·rtni̮ daľše̮ (be̮ra·).

3. *ke̮r nija kote̮·rtise̮ ve̮re̮t, to ni̮ śe̮re̮ ve̮ććise̮ be̮ra· ke̮jinnez. kań, bara·n da koza· kajise̮ puvve̮. kań veśki̮ta kajis same̮j ji̮wwas (ji̮wvas), a bara·n da koza· e̮še̮·ććise̮ uwiś uwwezve̮. koza· e̮ša·is, e̮ša·is da mi̮ǯis i potom uśis veśki̮ta ke̮jinnesve̮. kań sek vi̮wśań gore̮·tis: "viǯ ke̮jinnese̮, a me otsa·wa teni̮t vaše̮·tni̮." ke̮jinnes e̮ďďe̮n powźise̮ i nija pi̮ššise̮. sek kań, bara·n da koza· e̮kśise̮ uwi̮n i reši·tise̮ be̮ra· bertni̮ stari·k da staru·ka di̮ne̮. koza· pukśe̮·tis be̮ra· kańse̮ spina·vi̮we̮ da be̮r ińde̮·ććise̮ gortwańe̮.*

224. *ruć da turi*

1. *e̮t-pi̮riś ruć koris turie̮s ge̮śťi·tni̮. turi munis ruć di̮ne̮. ruć puis će̮ski̮t kaša. ete̮ kašase̮ sija tećis tare·ľkà (tare·ľkae̮) i pondis poću·jtni̮ turie̮s. turi pondis koka·wni̮ kašase̮, no mi̮mda sija ez koka·w kuź ni̮rnas, si̮we̮ e̮me̮ ńem ez šed. a ruć eta kade̮ žage̮·ńike̮n śojis bi̮de̮·s kašase̮. i si̮ be̮ri̮n šuis turii̮swe̮, štobi̮ sija rućse̮ ez osu·ďit.*

2. *me̮d wunas turi koris ge̮śťi·tni̮ ruće̮s. turi keris će̮ski̮t okro·ška (wuka-sow). wuka-sowse̮ turi keris gľińńane̮j goršo·ke̮ vekńi·ťik gorwi̮·škoe̮n. vot ruć woktis turi orde̮ i turi pondis sije̮ poću·jtni̮ okro·škae̮n eta goršo·kiś. ruć berga·is, berga·is goršo·k ge̮ge̮·ri̮n, no ez vermi̮ suǯe̮·tni̮ okro·škase̮. a turi suwa·wis bokas aswas kuź kokkezvi̮n da vi̮wśiń kuź e̮mnas suǯwa·is wuka-sowse̮. eta kadśań ruć da turi e̮štise̮ družbani̮se̮.*

225. *k u ź m a · skoroboga·te̮j*

1. *owis e̮tik i̮ǯi̮t ve̮ri̮n k u ź m a ·. sija ois e̮tnas i ve̮is si̮we̮n vit kure̮·g da petu·χ (petu·k) sija vetwi̮·wis ve̮re̮ bi̮d-koď pe̮tkavve̮. vot e̮t-pi̮riś sija munis ve̮re̮ ve̮ra·wni̮. ete̮ śľeďi·tis ruć, sija pi̮ris izbu·škà da śojis kure̮·ge̮s. ke̮r k u ź m a woktis gortas, to kaźa·wis, što e̮tik kure̮·g si̮we̮n oz ti̮rmi̮. me̮di·k wune̮ k u ź m a · munis tože̮ ve̮ra·wni̮. ruć siǯ-že̮ śojis me̮dik kure̮·ge̮s. ete̮ be̮ra· kaźa·wis k u ź m a · kujme̮t wune̮ k u ź m a · ośa·ť munis. no sija ez mun ve̮ra·wni̮, a pondis*

way. They were hungry. They said they would devour the lamb and the goat. They said that they must ask permission from their elder brother lest he should be angry. Meanwhile the bear was having a good sleep, but his dream was disturbed. He grew angry and struck one of the wolves. The wolves were very frightened and fled. In the morning the cat, the lamb and the goat continued their flight.

3. As they were running in the woods, the wolves again chased after them. The cat, the lamb and the goat climbed a tree. The cat climbed right up to the top of it, while the lamb and the goat clung to the lower branches. The goat hung and hung there, then he grew tired, and fell right into the midst of the wolves. Then the cat shouted down from above: "Look after the wolves, and I will help you chase them away!" The wolves were very frightened and fled. Then the cat, the lamb and the goat gathered together under the tree and decided to return to the old man and the old woman. Again the goat put the cat on its back, and they started for home.

224. The fox and the crane

1. Once the fox invited the crane to a feast. The crane went to see the fox. The fox cooked a dish of tasty mush. He put this mush on a plate and began to entertain the crane. The crane began to pick the mush, but he picked in vain with his long beak, for none of it got into his mouth. Meanwhile the fox slowly ate up all the mush. Then he asked the crane not to blame him.

2. Next day the crane invited the fox to feast. The crane prepared cold soup of salted onion. The crane put the salted onion into a pottery vessel that had long and narrow neck. The fox arrived at the crane's, the crane served cold sour soup in this jug to him. The fox turned round and round the jug but he was unable to reach the food. And the crane was standing by it on his long feet and was able to reach the salted onion from above with his long beak. From that time on, the fox and the crane were no longer friends.

225. Suddenly-enriched Kuzma

1. Kuzma lived in a large forest. He lived alone, he had five hens and a cock. He hunted all sorts of wild fowl in the forest. Once he went to hunt in the forest. A fox followed him, entered the hut and ate a hen. When Kuzma came home he noticed that one of his hens was missing. Next day Kuzma went hunting again. The fox ate the second hen as well. Again Kuzma noticed it. On the third day Kuzma went out again. But he did not go hunting,

śl'eďi·tni kerkuis śerin. vot k u ź m a · *kaźa·wis, kiď [ɔ: kiʒ] sija kerku dine kote·rtištis ruć i piris kerkuas.* k u ź m a · *kote·rtis gortas i kutis rućse. no ruć pondis korni* k u ź m a · *wiś, štobi sija weʒis sije. no* k u ź m a · *ez med weʒni. ruć viśta·wis, što sija keras* k u ź m à ·*s* (k u ź m a ·*es*) *skoroboga·tejen.* k u ź m a · *jua·wis sije, kiʒ keras sije skoroboga·tejen. ruć sek čektis žari·tni etik kure·ges i sije verdni. ruć śojis petteʒ kure·ges da si berin kote·rtis carskej pol'eezve (ibbezve). seććin ruć pondis tarowa·śni bokiś bokve. ete kaźa·wis keji·n i jua·wis rućiswiś, mij sija kere. ruć sek otveťitis kejiniswe: "me vei carskej pirvin. seććin jui, śoji petteʒ i vot tarowa·śa. eta pirvin ez vewe toľko keji·nnez." keji·nis pondis korśini, štobi ruć nebe·tis pirve. ruć sie viśta·wis, što sije etnase oz nebe·t i čektis ekśini keji·nnese sorok-soroko·w. ker keji·nnes ekśise, to nije ruć nebe·tis carskij pirve. ker nija woktise car orde, ruć viśta·wis cariswe, štobi sija primi·tis poda·rok* k u ź m a · s k o r o b o g a · t e *jśań, keji·nnezes sorok-soroko·w. car čektis pedna·wni keji·nnezes końu·śńà. ruć kote·rtis bera·* k u ź m a · *dine i čektis žari·tni eššе· etik kure·ges, ruć śojis ete kure·ges petteʒ da kote·rtis carskej ibbezve. seććin sija pondis tarowa·śni bokiś bokve. seti kak raz kote·rtis oš. i ośis jua·wis siwiś, mij rućis kere seten. ruć viśta·is, što sija vei carskej pirvin. seććin veise una· raznej źverrez, toľko ez vewe oššez. ruć čektis ekśini oššezes sorok-soroko·w. oš kote·rtis i ektis medi·k oššezes. sek ruć nije nebe·tis carskej pirve. ker nija woktise car orde, to ruć viśta·wis carwe, štobi sija primi·tis poda·rok* k u ź m a s k o r o b o g a ·-t e *jśań, oššezes sorok-soroko·w. car čektis pedna·wni oššezes końu·śńae. ruć bertis* k u ź m a · *dine i čektis žari·tni kure·ges da petu·kes. ete bide·s ruć śojis petteʒ da kote·rtis tupľa·śni carskej ibbezve. eta kade seććinet kote·rtis sobo·ľ. sobo·ľ jua·wis rućiswiś, mij sija kere seten. ruć siwe viśta·wis, što sija vei carskej pirvin, kiten veise una· raznej źverrez, toľko ez vewe sobo·ľľez da kuńi·caez. ruć nije čektis ekśini sorok-soroko·w. ker nija ekśise, to ruć nije nebe·tis carskej pirve. ker nija woktise car orde, to ruć viśta·wis carwe, štobi sija primi·tis poda·rok* k u ź m a s k o r o b o g a · t e *jśań, kuńi·caez da soboľľez sorok-soroko·w. car pondis daže ďivu·ććini sečem poda·rokkezve.*

2. *ruć ber bertis izbu·škàś i čektis ińdini* k u ź m a ·*we svattezes. poda·rok ińdis meše·k ďeńga. no* k u ź m a ·*wen simda ďeńga ez vew. sek nija rućket meše·k pide·sas tećise peso·k, a vewderas deńgaez. ruć nebe·tis ete poda·rokse carwe. car primi·tis poda·rokse i čektis woktini* k u ź m a ·*se si dine. ruć ber pondis kote·rtni* k u ź m a ·*dine. tujvas seććin vei pos. ruć piľi·tis pos uwtas*

rather he stood on guard behind the house. Kuzma noticed that a fox ran up to his house and entered the house. Kuzma ran home and caught the fox. But the fox began to beg Kuzma to let him go. But Kuzma refused to let him go. Then the fox said he would make Kuzma rich within a short time. Kuzma asked him how he would make him rich. The fox told him to roast a hen and give it to him. The fox had his fill of the hen, then hurried to the ploughed fields of the Tsar. There he began to roll from one side to the other. The wolf observed this and asked the fox what he was doing. Then the fox said to the wolf: "I have been feasting with the Tsar. I had my fill of food and drink there and now I am rolling. Only wolves were missing from this feast." The fox told him he would not take him there alone but ordered the wolves to gather together in groups of forty. When the wolves came together, the fox took them to the Tsar's feast. When they came to the Tsar, the fox told the Tsar to accept the gift from Suddenly-enriched Kuzma, the groups of forty wolves. The Tsar ordered the wolves to be locked in the stable. The fox again ran to Kuzma and had another hen roasted. The fox ate this hen as well and ran to the fields of the Tsar. He began to roll from one side to the other. Just then a bear came running by. And the bear asked him what the fox was doing there. The fox said that he had been at the Tsar's feast. There had been many beasts of all kinds there, only there had been no bears there. The fox commanded that the bears should gather together in groups of forty. The bear ran away and collected the other bears. Then the fox took them to the Tsar's feast. When they came to the Tsar, the fox told the Tsar to receive the gift of groups of forty bears from Suddenly-enriched Kuzma. The Tsar ordered the bears to be locked in the stable. The fox returned to Kuzma and had a hen and a cock roasted. The fox ate all this up and ran off to roll in the fields of the Tsar. In the meantime a sable came running by. The sable asked the fox what he was doing there. The fox said that he had been at the Tsar's feast where many beasts of all kind had been present, only sables and martens had been missing. The fox commanded them to gather together in groups of forty. When they had gathered together in groups of forty. When they had gathered together, the fox took them to the Tsar's feast. When they had come to the Tsar, the fox asked the Tsar to accept the gifts: the groups of forty martens and sables from Suddenly-enriched Kuzma. The Tsar was amazed at such gifts.

2. The fox returned to the hut and told Kuzma to send suitors to the Tsar. He sent a sack of money as a present. But Kuzma did not have so much money. Then he and the fox poured sand into the sack, and put coins on the top of it. The fox took this gift to the Tsar. The Tsar accepted this

stobbese̮ da woktis k u ź m a ·di̮ne̮. vot nija pondise̮ munni̮ k u ź m a ·ke̮t car di̮ne̮ i eta pose̮n nija uśise̮ vaas. ruć pondis gore̮·twi̮ni̮, što ve̮je̮ k u ź m a · s k o r o b o g a · t e̮ j. car ińde̮·tis morttezes, štobi̮ nija ki̮skise̮ k u ź m a ·e̮s. ke̮r nija ki̮skise̮ k u ź m a ·e̮s, to si̮we̮ śetise̮ bur paś-ke̮m (oďe·žda), štobi̮ sija vežis aśśis vame̮m paś-ke̮mse̮. eta be̮ri̮n k u ź m a · woktis car di̮ne̮. se̮te̮n nija pondise̮ pirujtni̮.

3. *ki̮ni̮·m-ke̮ wun be̮rti car koris, štobi̮ k u ź m a · mi̮ćća·wis aśśis vlaďe·ńńoese̮ (gosuda·rstvose̮). ruć pondis kote̮·rtni̮ carske̮j kare·ta oʒi̮n. sija kote̮·rtis, kote̮·rtis i kaźa·wis tabu·n baľaez. sija jua·wis pastu·kwiś, kinwe̮n eta tabu·ni̮s. pastu·k viśta·wis, što eta tabu·ni̮s ź m e j g o r n i̮ · ćwe̮n. ruć viśta·wis sek pastu·kwe̮, štobi̮ sija viśta·wis, što eta tabu·nis k u ź m a · s k o r o b o g a · t e̮ jwe̮n. jeśľi siʒ sija oz viśta·w, to sije̮ sotase̮ ćar-bi da ćar-moľńa (ćar-virda·wan). pastuk powźis etaiś i me̮dis siʒ viśta·wni̮, ki̮ʒ vewe̮·tis rući̮s. ruć kote̮·rtis daľše i kaźa·wis tabu·n porśśeze̮s. sija jua·wis pastukwiś, kinwe̮n eta tabu·ni̮s. pastuk viśta·wis, što eta tabu·ni̮s ź m e j g o r n i̮ ćwe̮n. ruć siʒ-že̮ pastu·kse̮ vewe̮·tis, štobi̮ sija viśta·wis, što tabu·ni̮s k u ź m a · s k o r o b o g a · t e̮ jwe̮n. ruć pondis kote·rtni̮ daľše i kaźa·wis tabu·n ve̮wweze̮s. se̮te̮n ve̮wi tože̮ pastuk. pastukse̮ ruć vewe̮·tis siʒ-že̮, štobi̮ sija viśta·wis, što ve̮w-tabu·ni̮s k u ź m a s k o r o b o g a · t e̮ jwe̮n. ruć pondis kote̮·rtni̮ daľše i panta·wis tabu·n verbľu·ddeze̮s. pastukse̮ sija vewe̮·tis siʒ-že̮, štobi̮ sija viśta·wis, što tabu·ni̮s s k o r o b o g a · t e̮ jwe̮n.*

4.. *eta be̮ri̮n ruć kote̮·rtis daľše i woktis dvore·ci̮s di̮ne̮. rući̮s pi̮ris seććine̮ i viśta·wis ź m e j g o r n i̮ · ć i̮ swe̮, što si̮ śe̮ri̮n wokte̮ni̮ ćar-bi da ćar-virda·wan. ź m e j g o r n i̮ · ć powźis i pondis korni̮ rućse̮, štobi̮ sija otsa·wis ʒebśi·śni̮ si̮we̮. ruć si̮we̮ viśta·wis, što sija e̮gra·dàń bi̮dme̮ gi̮rka dub. ź m e j g o r n i̮ · ć ʒebśi·śis eta dube̮. eta kade̮ k u ź m a · s k o r o b o g a · t e̮ j i cari̮s kare·tàn (kare·taen) woktise̮ baľa tabu·n di̮ne̮ i jua·wise̮, kinwe̮n eta tabu·ni̮s. pastuk viśta·wis, što k u ź m a s k o r o b o g a · t e̮ jwe̮n. nija munise̮ daľše i kaźa·wise̮ tabu·n ve̮wwezes. eta tabu·ni̮s tože̮ ve̮wi k u ź m a · s k o r o b o g a · t e̮ jwe̮n. car pondis ďivu·ćći̮ni̮, ki̮če̮·m boga·te̮j k u ź m à ·s (k u ź m a·i̮s). nija pondise̮ munni̮ daľše i kaźa·wise̮ tabu·n verbľu·ddeze̮s. eta tabu·ni̮s ve̮wi siʒ-že̮ k u ź m a·we̮n.*

5. *skoro nija woktise̮ dvore·c di̮ne̮ i pi̮rise̮ seććine̮. nije̮ panta·wis ruć. se̮te̮n nija pondise̮ pirujtni̮, weśe̮·tise̮ e̮twàn svaďba. eta svaďbai̮s da piri̮s kiśśis top ńeďe·ľa. no poto·m rući̮s viśta·wis k u ź m a ·we̮, što ź m e j g o r n i̮ ·ć ʒebśi·śis*

gift and invited Kuzma to see him. The fox started running back to Kuzma. There was a bridge on the way. The fox sawed through the piles under the bridge and returned to Kuzma. He and Kuzma started off to the Tsar's, and they fell into the water together with the bridge. The fox began to shout at once that Suddenly-enriched Kuzma was drowning. The Tsar sent men to pull Kuzma out. When they drew Kuzma out, they gave him fine clothes to exchange for his own clothes that had got wet. After this Kuzma came to the Tsar. There they began to feast.

3. A few days later the Tsar asked Kuzma to show him his own land. The fox began to run ahead of the Tsar's coach. He ran and ran, and caught sight of a flock of sheep. He asked the shepherd whom that flock belonged to. The shepherd said the flock belonged to the dragon *Gorni̯ć*. Then the fox told the shepherd to answer that the flock belonged to Suddenly-enriched Kuzma. Should he answer in a different way, he would be burnt up by lightning. The shepherd took fright at this, and answered as he had been instructed by the fox. The fox ran on and caught sight of a herd of pigs. He asked the swineherd whom the herd of pigs belonged to. The swineherd answered that the pigs belonged to the dragon *Gorni̯ć*. The fox instructed the swineherd in the same way to answer that the herd belonged to Suddenly-enriched Kuzma. The fox started running on again and caught sight of a herd of horses. There was also a horseherd there. The fox likewise instructed the horseherd to answer that the herd of horses belonged to Suddenly-enriched Kuzma. The fox started running on and met a herd of camels. Again he instructed the herdsman to answer that the herd belonged to Suddenly-enriched Kuzma.

4. After this the fox continued running and arrived at the palace. The fox entered it and said to the dragon *Gorni̯ć* that thunder and lightning were pursuing him. The dragon *Gorni̯ć* was frightened and asked the fox to help him hide. The fox said there was a hollow oak in his courtyard. The dragon *Gorni̯ć* hid in this oak-tree. Meanwhile Suddenly-enriched Kuzma and the Tsar arrived at the herd of sheep. The shepherd answered that it belonged to Suddenly-enriched Kuzma. They went on and caught sight of the herd of horses. That herd of horses also belonged to Suddenly-enriched Kuzma. The Tsar began to be astonished at the riches of Kuzma. They started to go on and caught sight of the herd of camels. As before, this herd also belonged to Kuzma.

5. Soon they arrived at the palace, and went in. The fox received them. There they began to feast, and together arranged a wedding. This wedding and feasting lasted for a week. After this the fox related to Kuzma that the dragon *Gorni̯ć* was hiding in the oak-tree. Kuzma and the Tsar took

gi̮rka dube̮. k u ź m a · da car bośtise̮ strela·ez da lukkez da viise̮ ź m e j g o r- n i̮ ·će̮s. eta kadśań k u ź m a s k o r o b o g a · t e̮ j i ińi̮s pondise̮ owni̮, a ruće̮s každe̮j wun verdise̮ kure̮·ge̮n.

226. *kroška χawro·ška*

1. *owis-ve̮wis staru·χa. si̮e̮n ve̮ise̮ kujim ni̮w. perve̮j ni̮wse̮ šuise̮ o d n o g l a · s- k a e̮n, me̮d ni̮wse̮ d v u g l a · s k a e̮n, a kujme̮·tse̮ t r e̮ g l a · s k a e̮n. si̮we̮n ve̮wi eše̮ primi·te̮m ni̮w, χ a w r o · š k a. eta primi·te̮m ni̮wi̮s ve̮i uće̮·ťik da e̮ďďe̮n base̮k. staru·ka pi̮r če̮ktis u̮ǯa·wni̮ χ a w r o · š k ae̮s. χ a w r o · š k a pi̮r keris med śe̮ki̮t rabo·ta(u̮ǯ). χ a w r o · š k a ńe-kin ez ľubi·te̮, bi̮de̮·nni̮s sije̮ ćuwjise̮ da vartise̮. a štobi̮ viśta·wni̮ bur ki̮w, sije̮ ńe-kin ez ker. χ a w r o · š- k a toľko ľubi·tis e̮tike̮: eta ve̮i staru·kai̮swe̮n me̮s, b u r j o · n u š k a.*

2. *e̮tik wune̮ staru·χa śetis χ a w r o · š k awe̮ vit pud ľon pećki̮ni̮ da ki̮jni̮ de̮ra. ete̮ sija śetis χ a w r o · š k awe̮ ki̮jni̮ e̮tik wune̮. χ a w r o · š k a munis b u r j o · n u š k a di̮ne̮ da si̮we̮ pondis žawu·ćći̮ni̮. drug b u r j o · n u š k a pondis baji·tni̮ χ a w r o · š k ake̮t mort-gowose̮n. b u r j o · n u š k a viśta·wis, štobi̮ χ a w r o · š k a pi̮ris si̮we̮ e̮t peľas da me̮das petis. χ a w r o · š k a siǯ i keris. si̮ be̮ri̮n sija toľko (toko) pondis e̮kti̮ni̮ de̮ra. siď ćoža keris χ a w r o · š- k ai̮s u̮ǯse̮. ke̮r sija vajis staru·χawe̮ goto·ve̮j de̮ra, to staru·χa uďiviććis, ki̮če̮·m sija ćoža keris śete̮m u̮ǯse̮. me̮d wunas staru·χa śetis eše̮· una·ži̮k ľonse̮, štobi̮ goto·vitni̮ de̮ra. χ a w r o · š k a munis be̮ra· b u r j o · n u š k a di̮ne̮ i si̮we̮ viśta·wis. b u r j o · n u š k a si̮we̮ be̮ra· siǯ-že̮ otsa·wis. kujme̮·t wunas staru·χa śetis eše̮ unaži̮k ľonse̮, štobi̮ ki̮jni̮ de̮ra. e̮twàn χ a w r o · š k ai̮ske̮t staru·χa ińde̮·tis o d n o g l a · s k ae̮s, štobi̮ sija śľeďi·tis, kin otsa·we̮ kerni̮ u̮ǯse̮ χ a w- r o · š k awe̮. ke̮r o d n o g l a · s k a woktis i̮bve̮, to sija pondis seććin kotra·śni̮ i be̮ba·wni̮. a ke̮r mi̮ǯis, to vodis. χ a w r o · š k a eše̮· viśta·wis: "kuńśi̮ śi- no·k!" eta be̮ri̮n b u r j o · n u š k a otsa·wis χ a w r o · š k awe̮ kerni̮ u̮ǯse̮. ke̮r ri̮tnas staru·χa jua·(w)is ni̮wi̮swiś, kin otsa·wis kerni̮ u̮ǯse̮, to o d n o g l a · s k a viśta·wis, što sija ńe-kine̮s ez a̮ǯǯiw. staru·χa we̮ga·śis i ašinas śetis rabo·tase̮ (u̮ǯse̮) eše̮· unaži̮k i ińde̮·tis śľeďitni̮ d v u g l a · s k a e̮ s. d v u g l a · s k a poľovi̮n (i̮bvi̮n) kotra·śi̮štis i poto·m (si̮ be̮ri̮n) vodis. χ a w r o · š k a sećće šuis: "uź, śino·k, uź me̮di·ki̮s!" ke̮d pora d v u g l a · s k a uźis, χ a w r o · š k a*

bows and arrows and killed the dragon *Gornič*. From that time forth Suddenly-enriched Kuzma and his wife lived there and each day gave the fox a hen to eat.

226. Kroška Xawroška

1. Once upon a time there lived an old woman. She had three daughters. The first was called *One-Eye,* the second *Two-Eyes,* and the third *Three-Eyes.* She had also an adopted daughter, *Xawroška.* This adopted daughter was small and very beautiful. The old woman had all the work done by *Xawroška. Xawroška* always did the most difficult jobs. *Xawroška* was loved by nobody, she was pushed and beaten by everybody. To say a kind word to her — well, there was no one to do so. There was only one thing *Xawroška* loved: the old woman's cow *Burjonuška.*

2. One day the old woman gave five puds of flax to *Xawroška,* telling her to spin it and weave linen with it. She gave it to her saying that it must be woven in a day. *Xawroška* went to *Burjonuška* and began to complain to her. All of a sudden, *Burjonuška* began to speak in a human voice to *Xawroška. Burjonuška* told *Xawroška* to walk into one of her ears and come out of the other. *Xawroška* did as was told. She began to weave the linen only after this. In this way *Xawroška* performed the work quickly. As she brought the linen complete to the old woman, the old woman was astonished how quickly she had performed the task she had set. Next day the old woman gave her even more flax, telling her to weave linen with it. *Xawroška* went again to *Burjonuška* and told her about it. *Burjonuška* helped her again. On the third day the old woman gave her still more flax telling her to weave linen. The old woman sent One-Eye with *Xawroška* to find out who was helping *Xawroška.* When One-Eye reached the meadow, she began to run about, playing mischievously. When she grew tired she lay down to rest. *Xawroška* said to her: "Close your pretty eye!" After this *Burjonuška* helped *Xawroška* to perform the task. When the old woman asked her daughter that evening who had helped to do the work, One-Eye said she had seen nobody. The old woman grew angry and gave out yet more work in the morning, and sent Two-Eyes to find out. Two-Eyes ran about a little in the field and then lay down. Then *Xawroška* said: "Sleep, pretty eye, sleep, the other one too!" While Two-Eyes was sleeping, *Xawroška* performed the work, helped by *Burjonuška.* In the evening the old woman began to enquire from her daughter whom she had seen; then Two-Eyes answered that she had seen nobody. The old woman grew still more angry and sent Three-Eyes to find out. Three-Eyes ran around a little,

b u r j o · n u š k aket kerisḙ śetḙm uǯsḙ. ri̮tnas staru·χa pondis jua·wni̮ ni̮wi̮s-wiś, kinḙs sija aǯǯiwis, to d v u g l a · s k a viśta·wis, što sija ńe-kinḙs ez aǯǯiw. staru·χa eśḙ· ḙdjḙnǯik wḙga·śis i ińdḙ·tis śl'eďi·tni̮ t ŕ o g l a · s k aḙs. t ŕ o g l a · - s k a kotraśi̮·štis i tožḙ vodis. χ a w r o · š k a seććḙ viśta·wis: "uź, śino·k, uź, mḙdik!" a kujmḙ·ti̮swḙ vunḙ·tis viśta·wni̮. sija duma·jtis, što t ŕ o g l a · s k aḙn uźḙni̮ kujimna·n (bi̮dḙs) śinnez. kḙr χ a w r o · š k a da b u r j o · n u š k a kerisḙ uǯsḙ, to t ŕ o g l a · s k aḙn ḙt śini̮s bi̮dḙ·s aǯǯi̮·wis. kḙr staru·χa pondis jua·wni̮, kin χ a w r o · š k awḙ otsa·wis, to t ŕ o g l a · s k a viśta·wis, što si̮wḙ otsa·wis b u r j o · n u š k a. sek staru·χa čḙktis stari·ksḙ naćki̮wni̮ mḙssḙ. stari·k pervo ez mḙd naćki̮wni̮, no staru·χa śo rowno· čḙktis (zastavi·tis).

3. *etḙ bi̮dḙs ki̮wis χ a w r o · š k a. sija munis b u r j o · n u š k a di̮nḙ da bi̮dḙ·s viśta·wis. sek b u r j o · n u š k a viśta·wis χ a w r o · š k awḙ, štobi̮ sija ez śoj si̮wiś jajsḙ, a koskasḙ ḙktis da ǯebis mu pi̮čkḙ sadi̮n. χ a w r o · š k a siǯ i keris. sija owis či̮gjḙn, no ez śoj jajsḙ.*

4. *skoro sija mestai̮n, ki̮tḙ·n kujwisḙ koskaez b u r j o · n u š k awḙn, bi̮dmis i̮ǯi̮t jablońńa. eta jablońńai̮n vḙisḙ rumja·nḙjḙś, i̮ǯi̮t jablokkez. vot ḙt-pi̮riś ni̮ sad di̮nḙt munis boga·tḙj barin i sija jua·wis, kinwḙn sečḙm jablońńai̮s bi̮dmḙ. sek ni̮wwes staru·χai̮swḙn viśta·wi̮sḙ, što jablońńai̮s ni̮wḙn. seććḙ barin viśta·wis, kin si̮wḙ śetas jablok eta jablońńa vi̮wśiń (vi̮wśań), to sijḙ bośtas ińḙn. staru·ka-wḙn ni̮wwes uśkḙ·ććisḙ jablońńa di̮nḙ, štobi̮ suǯḙ·tni̮ jablok. no drug jablońńai̮s wepti·śis vi̮wwańe. kiǯ nija ez stara·ććḙ suǯḙ·tni̮ jablok, no ni̮wwes staru·χaḙn suǯḙ·tni̮ ez vermḙ. sek seććḙ woktištis χ a w r o · š k a. jablońńa weǯis aśśis uwwesḙ top si̮ kijezeǯ. sija orḙ·tis jablok da śetis barinwḙ. barin viǯis aśśis ki̮wsḙ i boštis χawro·škasḙ as sajas.*

227. *jeme·l'a-dura·k*

1. *ḙtik stari·kwḙn vḙisḙ kujim zon. ki̮k zoni̮s vḙisḙ gḙti̮raḙś, a kujmḙ·ti̮s vḙi dura·k. vot kić-kḙ (kiǯ-kḙ) koris stari·k di̮nas zonnesḙ da viśta·wis, što sija ćoža kuwas i čḙktis ďel'i·tni̮ χoźa·jtvosḙ ḙta-mḙd koa·si̮n. skoro stari·k kuwis i sijḙ ǯebisḙ.*

2. *j e m e · l' a - d u r a k ńe-kḙr ez uǯa·w, a pi̮r puka·wis gorvi̮n. ḙt-pi̮riś tḙwḙn vonnes munnisḙ gorodḙ jarmarkavvḙ i nija zakaži·tisḙ j e m e · l' awḙ, štobi̮ sija otsa·wis ińńezni̮swe. pervo j e m e · l' a ńem ez kḙr, no aśi̮nas ińkaes ińdḙ·tisḙ j e m e · l' aḙs va-dḙrḙ kajḙ·tni̮ va. j e m e · l' a pervo ez mḙd munni. no ińńes vista·wisḙ, što nija viśta·wasḙ vonneswḙ, štobi̮ vonnes j e m e · l' awḙ ezḙ*

then lay down. *Xawroška* said: "Sleep, pretty eye, sleep, the other one, too!" She forgot to tell the third eye to sleep. She thought all three eyes of Three-Eyes were sleeping. When *Xawroška* and *Burjonuška* were working, Three-Eyes witnessed everything with one of her eyes. When the old woman asked her who had helped *Xawroška*, she replied that *Burjonuška* had been helping her. Then the old woman commanded the old man to slaughter the cow. First the old man did not want to slaughter her, but the old woman persuaded him in the end.

3. *Xawroška* overheard all this. She went to *Burjonuška* and told her everything. Then *Burjonuška* told *Xawroška* not to eat of her flesh, and to collect her bones and dig them into the ground in the garden. And *Xawroška* did so. She was starving, but she did not eat her flesh.

4. Soon a big apple-tree grew at the place where the bones of *Burjonuška* were lying. There were big red apples on that apple-tree. Once a rich landowner passed by their garden. He asked who had grown such a fine apple-tree. Then the old woman's daughters replied that the apple-tree belonged to them. Then the landowner said that he would marry whoever would give him an apple from that tree. The old woman's daughters ran to the apple-tree to reach and get an apple. But suddenly the apple-tree rose into the air. However much they tried to reach the apple, the old woman's daughters were unable to get one. Then *Xawroška* came up. The apple-tree lowered its branches close to her hand. She plucked the apple and handed it over to the landowner. The landowner was true to his word and married *Xawroška*.

227. Stupid Jemeľa

1. An old man had three sons. Two of his sons were married, the third was stupid. The old man called his sons somehow and said he was going to die in a short time, and ordered them to share his wealth among them. Soon the old man died, and he was buried.

2. Stupid Jemeľa never did any work but always sat on the top of the stove. Once in the winter they went to town to market, and told Jemeľa to help the wives. At first Jemeľa did not do anything, but in the morning the wives sent Jemeľa to the river bank to fetch water. At first Jemeľa did not want to go. However, the wives said to him they would tell his brothers not to buy him red boots and a good suit. Then Jemeľa got off the top of the stove, took the bucket and the water-carrying pole, and walked to the river bank. There he made an ice-hole and dipped the buckets in the water. He was just about to start home when he noticed a pike in the ice-hole.

boštę gęrd sapo·ggez da bur paś-kęm. sek j e m e · l'a weććis gorviś, boštis vedra·ęs da koro·mįswa da munis va-dęrę. seććin sija węśę·tis ośta da gumį·štis vedra·ezę và. toľko mędis kajnį gortas, kįž kaźais oštaas šukaęs. sija kutis šukasę da mędis kaję·tnį gortas. no drug šuka pondis baji·tnį sįkęt mort-gowosęn. sija pondis kornį j e m e · l'aęs, štobį sija weźis siję bęr vaas. no ez pondį weźnį. sek šukaįs vįšta·wis sįwę, što pondas kernį bįdę·s j e m e · l'a tuję. j e m e · l'a ez verit sįwę. sek šuka vįšta·wis, štobį sija ez vunę·t seččęm kįwwez: "šuka baji·tęm śęrti, menam koręm śęrti." j e m e · l'a sek vįšta·wis enę kįwwesę i čęktis vedra·esę aswįnįs kajnį gortas. i drug biľiś vedra·es aśnįs pondisę munnį gortanįs. sek j e m e · l'a šukaęs weźis bęr vaas.

3. *eta bęrśiń j e m e · l'a bęr woktis gortas i kajis gorvę. ińkaes pondisę čęktįnį j e m e · l'aęs kernį pes da pįrtwįnį kerkuę. j e m e · l'awę ńe oχo·ta vei weććįnį gor vįwśiń. sek sija seććin as śęrtas šuis: "šuka vįšta·węm śęrti i menam korę·m śęrti, noko ćer kera·w pes, a pesįs aś aśnįs ćeććawęnę kerkuę!" toľko ještis vįšta·wnį, kįď ćer ćeććę·wtis kerkuiś da pondis potkę·tnį pes. a pesses aśnįs pondisę ćećća·wnį kerkuę. męd wunas ińkaez pondisę ińdę·tnį j e m e ·-l'aęs peswę. j e m e · l'a paśta·śis, boštis ćer da puktis ćersę doďďę. a doďsę kįskis ogra·da šerę i pukśis doďďę. ińkaesę-že čęktis ośnį vorota: ińkaes sįvįn pondisę śera·wnį: "kįććę· te munan vęwtęg?" no oštisę vorota·sę. a j e m e · l'a eta kostaę žagę·ńikęn šuis: "šuka vįštawę·m śęrti, menam korę·m śęrti, noko doď, mun vęrę!" i doď ińdę·ććis vęrę. ińdę·ććis sija vęrę įźįt gorodęt. sić-kę j e m e · l'awę ńe oχo·ta vęi gorę·twįnį gorodas, to doďįs taľis una morttezęs. j e m e · l'a śerįn pondisę vęććįnį, no nija ćoža koľććisę, sić-kę doďįs ęďďęn ćoža. kęr j e m e · l'a woktis vęras, to sija šuis: "šuka vįštawę·m śęrti, menam korę·m śęrti, no ćer, kera·w pes, a pesįs aś vodęnį aśnįs doďďę da kęrta·śęnį!" ćer pondis kera·wnį puez, a pes aćįs vodis doďďę da kęrta·śis. eta bęrįn j e m e ·-l'a čęktis ćerįswę kera·wnį zor, krepįdźįkę. eta bęrin j e m e · l'a bęr ińdę·ććis gortwańę i eta-žę gorodęt. no siję eććin vićći·śisę užę·. j e m e · l'aęs kįskisę doďďiś da pondisę vartwįnį sį ponda, što sija taľis una morttezęs. sek j e m e ·l'a bęra· žagę·ńikęn šuis: "šuka vįštawę·m śęrti da menam kore·m śęrti, noko zoro·k, kresta·w nįwiś spinaesę!" zor ćeććę·wtis voz vįwśiń da pondis vartwįnį morttesę. j e m e · l'a bęr pukśis aswas doďďę da woktis gortas.*

4. *eta jįwiś kįwis car. sija ińdę·tis j e m e · l'a dįnę ofice·rę s da solda·ttezęs, štobį nija vaję·tisę j e m e · l'aęs car dįnę. ofice·r da solda·ttez pįrisę j e m e · l'a*

He caught the pike and wanted to take it home. But at once the pike began to speak in a human voice. It begged Jemeľa to let it back to the water. But he did not want to let it go. Then the pike said to him it would do everything instead of Jemeľa. Jemeľa did not believe it. Then the pike told him to remember the following words: "According to the pike's words, according to my own request." Jemeľa uttered these words and ordered the buckets to get home by themselves. And indeed the buckets did start for home at once. Then Jemeľa let the pike go back into the water.

3. After this Jemeľa came home and climbed up onto the stove. The wives commanded him to chop wood and fetch it into the house. Jemeľa did not feel like getting off the top of the stove. Then he said to himself: "According to the pike's words, according to my own request, go to it, hatchet and chop wood, and let the wood jump into the house by itself!" As soon as he uttered these words the hatchet jumped out of the house and began to chop firewood. The pieces of firewood began to leap into the house by themselves. Next day the wives sent Jemeľa to fetch firewood from the forest. Jemeľa put on his clothes, took the hatchet, and placed it in the sleigh. He pulled the sleigh to the middle of the courtyard and sat on it. He told the wives to open the gate. The wives started to laugh at him: "Where are you going without horses?" All the same, they opened the gate. Meanwhile Jemeľa said in a low voice: "According to the pike's words, according to my own request, go, sleigh, to the forest!" And the sleigh started for the forest. It went right through the large town, to the forest. As Jemeľa had no mind go through the town shouting, his sleigh ran over many people. People began to chase Jemeľa, but soon they were left behind as the sleigh rushed on swiftly. When Jemeľa arrived in the woods, he said: "According to the pike's words, according to my own request, hatchet, cut wood, and let the logs lie on the sleigh by themselves, and fasten themselves to it!" The hatchet began to cut wood, and the logs lay themselves on the sleigh and fastened themselves to it. Then Jemeľa ordered the hatchet to cut a club, a strong one. Then Jemeľa started for home through the same town. But people were waiting for Jemeľa to return: they pulled Jemeľa off the sleigh and started to thrash him because he had run over so many. Then Jemeľa again said in a low voice: "According to the pike's words, according to my own request, go to it, club, baptize their backs!" The club jumped off the sleigh and began to thrash the people. Jemeľa sat back on his sleigh and went home.

4. The Tsar heard of all this. He sent an officer and soldiers to Jemeľa to take him to the Tsar's. The officer and the soldiers went into the house to Jemeľa, and began to shout at him. Jemeľa grew angry and said in a low

di̮ne̮ kerkuas da pondise̮ gore̮twi̮ni̮ j e m e · l̕ a v i̮ n. j e m e · l̕ a we̮ga·śis da žage̮·ńike̮n šuis: "šuka viśtawe̮·m śe̮rti, menam kore·m śe̮rti, noko zoro·k, ćegwa·w ni̮wiś rebroese (ord-viese̮)!" zor pondis vartwi̮ni̮ nije̮ siʒ̆, što solda·ttez da ofiće̮·ri̮s jel̕e kokkezni̮se̮ ne̮be̮·tise̮. sek ćar ińde̮·tis me̮di·k morte̮s. eta morti̮s ve̮i χitre̮j. sija woktis d̕ere·wńaas da pervo ińkaeswiś jua·wis, mi̮j l̕ubi·te̮ j e m e · l̕ ai̮s. si̮ be̮ri̮n eta morti̮s bośtis ge̮śńe·ććez da woktis j e m e · l̕ a di̮ne̮. sija śetis j e m e · l̕ awe̮ ge̮śńe·ććez da viśta·wis, što sije̮ kore̮ car. pervo j e m e · l̕ a ez-že̮ me̮d munni̮, no poto·m viśta·wis eta mortwe̮, što woktas si̮ be̮ri̮n. tol̕ko morti̮s munis, j e m e · l̕ a žage̮·ńike̮n gorvas šuis: "noko gor, mun car di̮ne̮!" i gori̮s kerkuśis munis. munis tujve̮t car di̮ne̮. car sije̮ uže· vićći·śis. sija e̮d̕d̕e̮n ud̕ivi·ććis, ki̮ʒ̆ j e m e · l̕ a wokte̮ gorvas. car sek viśta·wis j e m e · l̕ awe̮, što si̮ve̮ em žawoba. ke̮r j e m e · l̕ a vetwis ve̮re̮, to sija dod̕nas tal̕is una mortteze̮s. eta kade̮ e̮śi̮·ni̮n mi̮ćći·śis cari̮swe̮n ni̮w. sija seče̮·m ve̮i base̮k, što j e m e · l̕ a srazu-že̮ pondis sije̮ l̕ubi·tni̮ i as śe̮rtis viśta·wis: "šuka viśtawe̮·m śe̮rti, menam kore̮·m śe̮rti, štobi̮ mene̮ l̕ubi·tis carske̮j ni̮wi̮s!" eta kadśiń carske̮j ni̮w e̮štis poko·jse̮. sija pondis korni̮ aji̮swiś, štobi̮ ge̮tra·śni̮ j e m e · l̕ ake̮t. car e̮d̕d̕e̮n we̮ga·śis etavve̮ i čektis vaje̮·tni̮ j e m e · l̕ ae̮s si̮ di̮ne̮. vaje̮·tni̮ be̮ra· munis j e m e · l̕ ae̮s pervoj ofice·ri̮s.

5. *ke̮r sija woktis d̕ere·wńaas, to sija bośtis bi̮d-kod̕ vina·ez da zaku·skaez. si̮ be̮ri̮n sija jukta·wis j e m e · l̕ ae̮s kode̮ʒ̆. puktis j e m e · l̕ ae̮s dod̕d̕e̮ da vaje̮·tis car di̮ne̮. seććin e̮twàn j e m e · l̕ ae̮s carske̮j ni̮wke̮t pukśe̮·tise̮ smol̕i·te̮m boćkae̮, pe̮dna·wise̮ da šukkise̮ okea·ne̮. di̮r miji̮ś j e m e · l̕ a sajmis i ez vermi̮ veže̮·rtni̮, ki̮te̮·n sija kujwe̮. sek carske̮j ni̮wi̮s si̮we̮ viśta·wis, što nija puka·we̮ni̮ e̮twai̮n smol̕i·te̮m boćkai̮n da uje̮ni̮ okea·ne̮t. sek carske̮j ni̮w pondis korni̮, štobi̮ kić-ke̮ petke̮·tis nije̮ muvve̮ da petke̮·tis boćkaiś. j e m e · l̕ a šuis as śe̮rtas: "šuka viśtawe̮·m śe̮rti, menam kore̮·m śe̮rti, noko petke̮·t boćkase̮ muvve̮ da ośti̮!" okea·n skoro nije̮ šukkis beregve̮ da ośtis boćkase̮. j e m e · l̕ a da carske̮j ni̮w petise̮ boćkaiś i pondise̮ vi̮ʒ̆e̮·tni̮ krugo·m: nija ve̮ise̮ ostrowi̮n. sek carske̮j ni̮w pondis korni̮ j e m e · l̕ ae̮s, štobi̮ sija keris kuče̮·m-ke̮ kerkuo·k. j e m e · l̕ a sek viśta·wis: "šuka viśtawe̮·m śe̮rti, menam kore̮·m śe̮rti eta mestai̮n aś wo dvore·c pose̮n carske̮j ni̮w gort di̮ne̮ʒ̆, a eta dvore·ci̮n aś owe̮ni̮ slugaez!" tol̕ko ještis viśta·wni̮ j e m e · l̕ a, kid̕ si̮ o̮ʒ̆i̮n bi̮dmis dvore·c i pos. j e m e · l̕ a da carske̮j ni̮w pi̮rise̮ eta dvore·ce̮ i pondise̮ sete̮n owni̮.*

voice: "According to the pike's words, according to my own request, go to it, club, break their ribs!" The club began to thrash them so thoroughly that the soldiers and the officer were hardly able to carry away their legs. Then the Tsar sent another man. This man was cunning. He arrived in the village and then asked the women what Jemeľa was fond of most. Then the man brought presents and came to Jemeľa. He gave the presents to Jemeľa and said that the Tsar summoned him. At first Jemeľa did not want to go but later he said to the man that he would follow him. No sooner had the man stepped outside than Jemeľa spoke up in a low voice on the top of the stove: "Stove, go to the Tsar!" And the stove went out of the house. It went along the road to the Tsar. The Tsar was waiting for him. He was astonished when he saw how Jemeľa was coming on top of the stove. Then the Tsar said to Jemeľa that people had complained about him. When Jemeľa had gone to the forest, he had run over many people with his sleigh. Then the Tsar's daughter appeared at the window. She was so very beautiful that Jemeľa at once fell in love with her. He said to himself: "According to the pike's words, according to my own request, let the Tsar's daughter fall in love with me!" From that time on the Tsar's daughter lost her peace of mind. She began to beg her father to let her marry Jemeľa. The Tsar grew very angry at this, and gave orders for Jemeľa to be brought to him. Again the former officer went to fetch Jemeľa.

5. When he arrived in the village, he bought wine and something to eat. Then he made Jemeľa drunk. He seated Jemeľa in the sleigh and took him to the Tsar. There they put Jemeľa and the daughter of the Tsar in a tarred barrel, shut them in and threw them into the ocean. It took a long time for Jemeľa to become sober again, and he could not find out where he was lying. Then the Tsar's daughter told him that they were sitting together in a barrel, floating in the ocean. The Tsar's daughter asked him to get her out of the water somehow or other onto land and free her from the barrel. Jemeľa said to himself: "According to the pike's words, according to my own request, take this barrel to dry land and open it!" The ocean soon cast them ashore and opened the barrel. Jemeľa and the Tsar's daughter stepped out of the barrel and looked round. They were standing on an island. The Tsar's daughter began to ask Jemeľa to build some kind of hut. Then Jemeľa said: "According to the pike's words, according to my own request, let there be a castle here and a bridge reaching to the home of the Tsar's daughter, and let there be servants in the castle!" No sooner had Jemeľa uttered these words than there appeared in front of them a castle and a bridge. Jemeľa and the Tsar's daughter entered the castle and began to live there.

6. *e̮t-pi̮riś carske̮j ni̮w pondis korni̮, štobi̮ j e m e · l'a owis base̮k. no j e m e ·- l'a višta·wis: "šuka vištawe̮·m śe̮rti, menam kore̮·m śe̮rti, štobi̮ me woi base̮k da umne̮j!" toľko višta·wis ene̮ (etne̮) ki̮wwese̮, ki̮ǯ wois base̮k da umne̮j. skoro nija korise̮ carske̮j ni̮wwiś ajse̮ geśťi·tni̮. e̮twàn nija sete̮n piru·jtise̮ da spravitise̮ svaďba. ke̮r aji̮s nije̮ pondis korni̮ gortani̮s owni̮, to nija eze̮ mune̮, a koľććise̮ ostrowas aswani̮s dvore·ci̮n.*

228. *ćorttez da solda·t*

1. *solda·t swuži·tis aśśis srokse̮ da ińde̮·ććis gortas. sija munis, munis i woktis i̮ǯi̮t gorod di̮ne̮. sija pi̮ris eta gorode̮ da suwtis oj keže̮ e̮tik staru·ka di̮ne̮. sija užna·jtis i pondis jua·śni̮ staru·kai̮swiś, mi̮j sete̮n gorodas bur em. staru·ka si̮we̮ višta·wis, što eta gorodi̮n bi̮de̮s bur em, toľko e̮tik ume̮ľ em. solda·t sek jua·wis: "mi̮j sečče̮m?" staru·ka višta·is, što carwe̮n šoga·we̮ ni̮w. každe̮j oj carske̮j ni̮w di̮ne̮ vowwe̮ni ćorttez. i vot sija solda·t munis car di̮ne̮. sija višta·wis si̮we̮, što sija vaše̮·tas ćorttese̮. a štobi̮ vaše̮·tni̮ nije̮, sija če̮ktis śetni̮ si̮we̮ funt greckej ore·kkez, funt ćugu·nne̮j puľaez, ki̮k kolo·da kartaez, kujim žeľe·zne̮j otre·zokkez i kľešši·ez i mort-koď meχańizm pruži̮naeze̮n.*

2. *vot ri̮tnas sija pi̮ris komnatà, pe̮dna·is bi̮de̮s e̮ši̮·nnez da i̮be̮·ssez i koľis ośte̮n e̮tik i̮be̮·s. vot ojnas woktis e̮tik ćort. sija me̮dis pi̮rni̮ e̮ši̮·ne̮t veśki̮ta, no nija bi̮de̮·s ve̮ise̮ pe̮da·nae̮ś. sija di̮r berga·is da koššis ośta. poto·m tožno di̮r mi̮jiś kaźa·wis ośta i̮be̮·s. toľko me̮dis pi̮rni̮, ki̮ď ćorte̮s kutis solda·t. ćort koris solda·tse̮, štobi̮ sija weǯis mući·tni̮ carske̮j ni̮wse̮. solda·t sek si̮we̮ višta·wis, što weǯas ćorte̮s mući·tni̮ sek, ke̮r sija vermas sije̮ ńe-e̮t-pi̮riś podŕad karta·eze̮n orsike̮. nija dogovori·ććise̮ siǯ, kin ćožži̮ka proigra·jtas das šowbane̮ǯ. vot nija pukśise̮ i pondise̮ orsni̮. ćort si̮wiś vi̮igrajtis kujim šowban i me̮dis śetni̮ srazu·-že̮. solda·t sek višta·wis, što nija eze̮ wokte eše̮· das šowbane̮ǯ. eta be̮ri̮n solda·t vi̮igrajtis ćorti̮swiś das šowban i pondis we̮śe̮·ćći̮ni̮ śetni̮ ćorti̮swe̮ šowba·nćikkez. solda·t pondis we̮śe̮·tni̮ kise̮, štobi̮ śeta·wni̮ šowba·nćikkez. sek ćort powźis, to solda·t višta·wis si̮we̮, što si̮we̮n em uće̮tǯi̮k von. i sija vaje̮·tis ćorte̮s maši·na di̮ne̮ pružinaeze̮n i zewe̮·tis e̮tik pružina. maši·nai̮s siď se̮tis ćorti̮swe̮, što sija webźis e̮ši̮n di̮ne̮ǯ i me̮dis pi̮šši̮ni̮. no solda·ti̮s i suwte̮·tis me̮d-pi̮riś. ke̮r se̮tis maši·nàs (mašina·i̮s), to ćort će̮će̮·wtis potowo·ke̮ǯ. soldat sije̮ suwte̮·tis kujme̮·t-pi̮rśa. i ki̮ď se̮tis maši·nàs, to ćort webźis komna·taiś e̮ši̮·ne̮t i pi̮ššis. me̮di·k oje̮ woktis me̮di·k ćort i si̮ke̮t sija-že̮ wois, ki̮ǯ i pervoji̮s-*

6. Once the Tsar's daughter began to ask Jemeľa to be handsome. Well, Jemeľa said: "According to the pike's words, according to my own request, let me be handsome and clever!" No sooner had he uttered these words than the grew handsome and clever. Shortly, they invited the father of the Tsar's daughter to a feast. They feasted and arranged a wedding together. When the father asked them to go and live at home, they did not go but stayed in their own palace on the island.

228. The devils and the soldier

1. The soldier had served his time and started for home. He went on and on, and arrived at a city. He went into the city and put up with an old woman for the night. He ate his supper and asked the old woman if there were any good news in the city. The old woman said to him that everything in that city was good; only one thing was bad. The soldier asked, "What is that?" The old woman related that the Tsar's daughter was ill. Every night the Tsar's daughter was visited by devils. This soldier went off to the Tsar. He said to the Tsar that he would chase away the devils. In order to be able to chase them away, he asked for a pound of nuts, a pound of cast iron bullets, two packs of cards, three pieces of iron, a pair of tongs, and also a machine with springs similar to a man.

2. At night he went into the room and locked all the windows and doors, leaving only one door open. At night one of the devils arrived. He wanted to get straight in through the window, but each of them was closed. He turned hither and thither for a long time, seeking the opening. It took him a long time to find the open door. Scarcely had he got in when the soldier seized the devil. The devil asked the soldier to allow him to torment the Tsar's daughter. The soldier said he would agree to his tormenting the girl if he succeeded in defeating him several times at cards. They decided that it would be the loser over ten tricks. They sat down to play. The devil won three tricks and wanted to be the dealer immediately. But the soldier said they had not yet got to the tenth trick. Then the soldier won ten tricks from the devil and prepared to strike the devil. The soldier raised his hand to strike him. The devil became frightened, then the soldier said he had a younger brother. He took the devil to the machine with springs and wound up one of the springs. The spring gave such a kick to the devil that he flew to the window and wanted to flee at once. But the soldier seized him and stood him there the second time. When the machine kicked, the devil jumped up to the ceiling. The soldier stood him there the third time as well. When the machine kicked him, he flew through the window out of

ke̮t. si̮ǯ vowwise̮ carske̮j ni̮w di̮ne̮ ćorttes trina·ce̮ťa. eta be̮ršiń woktis uže· aći̮s glavne̮j ćorti̮s. sija pukśis solda·tke̮t orsni̮ kartaeze̮n. solda·t orse̮ i śoje̮ greckej ore·kkez. ćorti̮swe̮ zavidno wois i sija koris solda·ti̮swiś ore·kkez. sek solda·t si̮we̮ śetis ńe greckej ore·kkez, a ćugu·nne̮j puľaez. ke̮d pora ćort kurćća·is ćugu·nne̮j puľa, to si̮ pora solda·ti̮s śojis ki̮k-das ore·k. eta kostae̮ ćorti̮s koľććis kartaeznas. drug ćorti̮s kaźa·wis bokśis kľešši·ese̮. sija jua·wis solda·ti̮swiś, mi̮jwe̮ ene̮ (etne̮) kľešši·ese̮. solda·t viśta·is, što ke̮dnija oze̮ kuže̮ orsni̮ balala·jkae̮n, to sija we̮śe̮·te̮ sije̮n ćuńńese̮. ćorti̮s kužis orsni̮ balala·jkàn, no ume̮ľa. sek sija če̮ktis solda·te̮s we̮śe̮·tni̮ si̮wiś ćuńńese̮. a solda·twe̮ toľko i kowis. sija zewe̮·tis kľešši·eznas ćorti̮swiś ćuńńese̮. si̮ be̮ri̮n bośtis žeľe·zne̮j šať (otre·zokse̮) da pondis vartwini̮ ćortse̮. sija vartis si̮je̮ di̮r, a si̮ be̮ri̮n we̮ǯis, i viśta·wis ćorti̮swe̮, štobi̮ sija boľše ńe-ke̮r ez mući·t carskej ni̮wse̮. a ćort pani̮t viśta·wis, štobi̮ solda·t ńe-ki̮će̮· ez vetwi̮ carskej dvore·c di̮nśań kujim-das versta i̮wi̮na.

3. *eta be̮ri̮n ćorttes dugdise̮ bespoko·jitni̮ carskej ni̮wse̮. car śetis ni̮wse̮ žeńik saje̮ eta solda·t saje̮. si̮ǯ nija di̮r owise̮ i ki̮ć-ke̮ carskej ni̮w koris solda·te̮s vetwini̮ prudve̮, ke̮da di̮ne̮ǯ ve̮i kujim-das versta. toľko solda·t ještis woktini̮ prud di̮ne̮ǯ, ki̮ď ćorttes ki̮skise̮ si̮je̮ và.*

229. *ćeriś kaša*

e̮tik staru·ka di̮ne̮ pi̮ris solda·t oj keže̮. staru·ka sek si̮we̮ viśta·wis: "mestase̮ oj kežas a̮ǯǯa, a vot užna·jtni̮ ńem abu. solda·t berga·i̮štis kerkui̮n, ćewććis da me̮dis pukśini̮ skamjavve̮. no drug sija kaźa·is, skamja uwti̮n kujwe̮ žeľe·zne̮j ćer, ćer pute̮g. sećće̮ solda·t rade̮n šuis: "nu raz em ćer, to uži̮n woas goto·w." staru·kawe̮ wois ďivo, ki̮ǯ sija me̮de̮ we̮śe̮·tni ćeriś uži̮n. solda·t koris goršo·k, sećće kištis va da puktis ćerse̮. si̮ be̮ri̮n eta bi̮de̮·s śuji̮štis gore̮. va pizis, pizis i solda·t bośtis proba. as śe̮rtas šuis: "bi̮de̮·s bur da toľko abu sow." staru·ka sećće̮ šuis: "sowi̮s em, jeśľi kowe̮ da boś!" i śetis si̮we̮ sowo·nkae̮n sow. solda·t sowa·wis vase̮ da be̮ra· śuji̮·štis gore̮. ńe-di̮r mi̮jiś solda·t be̮ra· ki̮skis gorśis goršo·kse̮, štobi̮ bośti̮ni̮ proba. pondi̮·wis vase̮ i šuis: "bur kašàs, toľko sećće̮ krupa· ńewno·ćka." staru·kawe̮ śo ďivo, ki̮ď solda·ti̮s kaša pue̮ i śetis si̮we̮ meše̮ćo·ke̮n krupa·. solda·t puktis krupa·se̮ goršo·ke̮ da me̮d-pi̮riś suji̮·štis gore̮. skoro kaša ve̮i gotow. pukśise̮ nija pi̮zan saje̮. solda·t koris e̮twàn si̮ke̮t śojni̮ i

the room and ran away. The second night the second devil appeared, and the same happened to him as to the first. So the devils came one after the other to the girl, thirteen in all. After them, the chief devil came himself. He sat down to play cards with the soldier. The soldier plays and nibbles at a nut. The devil was envious and asked the soldier for nuts. Then the soldier gave him cast iron bullets instead of nuts. While the devil was chewing the iron bullets, the soldier consumed twelve nuts. In the meantime the devil was lagging behind with the cards. Suddenly the devil caught a side glimpse of the tongs. He asked the soldier what those tongs were used for. The soldier said that he used them to mend the fingers of those who could not play the balalaika. The devil could play the balalaika a little, though badly. He asked the soldier to mend his fingers. This was all the soldier wanted. He squeezed the devil's fingers with the tongs. Then he took the iron stick and started to thrash the devil. He gave him a thorough thrashing, and then let him go, telling him not to torment the Tsar's daughter any longer. And the devil's reply was that the soldier should not go thirty versts in any direction from the Tsar's palace.

3. After this the devils stopped disturbing the Tsar's daughter. The Tsar gave his daughter in marriage to the soldier. They lived like this for a long time, but then the Tsar's daughter somehow got the soldier to walk to the lake which was at a distance of thirty versts from the palace. Hardly had the soldier arrived at the lake, when the devils pulled him into the water.

229. Mush from a hatchet

A soldier dropped in on an old woman for the night. The old woman said to him: "I can find a place for you for the night, but I have nothing to give you for supper." The soldier turned here and there in the house, undressed and sat down on the bench. Suddenly he caught sight of a hatchet lying under the bench. The hatchet had no handle. The soldier spoke up gladly: "If there is a hatchet here, then supper is all ready." The old woman wondered how he would make supper from the hatchet. The soldier asked for a pot; he poured water into it and put the hatchet in. Then he put all this into the oven. He said to himself: "Everything is all right, only we need some salt." Then the old woman said: "There is the salt, take some if you need it!" She passed him the salt-box containing salt. The soldier put salt into the water and pushed the pot into the oven. After a short time he drew the pot out of the oven to taste (the dish). He tasted the water and said: "It is a fine mush, only some groats are lacking." The old woman wondered more and more how the soldier was goint to cook mush and gave

staru·kae̯s. staru·ka pukśis, sećće̯ solda·ti̯s šuis: “eďďe̯n ńi će̯ski̯t kašàs, a eše̯ će̯ski̯tǯi̯k woas, jeśľi pukti̯ni̯ sećće vi.” staru·ka śetis si̯we̯ vi. e̯twàn nija śojise̯ kašase̯. a staru·ka śojis kašase̯ da oškis solda·te̯s si̯ ponda, mi̯ľa sija sečče̯m će̯ski̯ta puis kašase̯. siď solda·t skupo·j staru·ka ordi̯n puis ćeriś kaša.

230. *ki̯ǯ pome·śśik pe̯žis ve̯wweze̯s?*

1. *e̯tik mi̯ži̯·k tuwi̯se̯n saďi·tis ti̯kvaez. etna ti̯kvaez bi̯dmise̯ gožumnas i̯ǯi̯te̯ś. vot arnas ubira·jtis uroža·jse̯, tećis ťeľe·gae̯ ti̯kvaez da ne̯be̯·tis baza·re̯. tujvas mi̯ži̯·kwe̯ panta·śis pome·śśik, i vot pome·śśiki̯s jua·wis mi̯ži̯·ki̯swiś, mi̯j sija ne̯be̯·te̯ bazare̯. mi̯ži̯·k viśta·wis, što sija ne̯be̯·te̯ baza·re̯ uza·wni̯ koľťťez. pome·śśikwe̯ ďivo wois, mi̯ľa e̯ďďe̯n i̯ǯi̯te̯ś koľťťes. a mi̯ži̯·k sećće̯ viśta·wis, što etna koľťťeziś petase̯ ćańńez. pome·śśikwe̯ oχo·ta wois bośtni̯ (ńe̯bni̯) koľťťese̯. i pome·śśik če̯ktis vee̯·tni̯, ki̯ǯ kowe̯ koľťťese̯ pe̯žni̯. mi̯ži̯·k si̯we̯ viśta·wis, kowe̯ kerni̯ i̯ǯi̯t puvvi̯n poz i sete̯n puka·wni̯. pome·śśik sek jua·wis mi̯ži̯·ki̯swiś, oz-ja vermi̯ sija pe̯žni̯ koľťťese̯. mi̯ži̯·k sek si̯we̯ viśta·wis, što sija pondi̯·wis ńi pe̯žni̯, no si̯ koľťťeziś petise̯ śo boltunnez. vot pome·śśik sek če̯ktis mi̯ži̯·ki̯swe̯ kerni̯ poz i tećni̯ koľťťese̯. mi̯ži̯·k si̯ǯ i keris i če̯ktis pukśi̯ni̯ pome·śśikse̯ i ćećći̯wni̯ mestaiś sećće̯ǯ, kiće̯·ǯ koľťťeziś ńe-kin oz pete̯.*

2. *pome·śśik puka·wis wun, me̯dik, kujme̯·t, a ńoľe̯t wunas pondis berge̯·ćći̯ni̯ pozas i uśis e̯twai̯n poznas muvvas. eta pu uwti̯n kak raz kujwis keć. ke̯r pome·śśik poznas uśis, to kećis powźis da pondis korte̯·rtni̯ eta pu di̯nśań. pome·śśik ćećće̯·wtis mu vi̯wśań i kaźa·wis, što e̯tik koľťi̯s paza·we̯m. i sećće̯ šuis: “vi̯ǯe̯t-ko (∼ -ke̯), puka·wi toľko ńoľ wun i uže· pe̯ži e̯tik ćańe̯s. i ki̯čče̯m sija ćoža pi̯śśis me di̯niś, što toľko ṕatkaese̯ kaźa·wi a ki̯čče̯m-bi̯ ćoža kotra·śis jeśľi-bi̯ puka·wi di̯rži̯k.”*

231. *pop da solda·t*

solda·t pi̯ri̯s e̯t-pi̯riś e̯tik ďere·wńae̯ i vi̯ǯe̯·te̯, bi̯de̯·nni̯s mune̯ni̯ vićkue̯. no solda·t tože̯ pondis munni̯ ni̯ śe̯re̯, a ďeńga si̯we̯n ńe-mi̯nda ez ve̯w. woktis sija

him a small bag of groats. The soldier pured the groats into the pot and pushed it into the oven once more. Soon the mush was ready. They sat down to the table. The soldier invited the old woman to eat with him. The old woman sat down, and then the soldier said: "The mush is very fine now, but it will be still finer if we put some butter in it." The old woman gave him some butter. They consumed the mush together. The old woman ate the mush and praised the soldier for the fine mush he had cooked. This is how the soldier cooked a dish of mush from the hatchet at the miserly old woman's house.

230. How the landowner hatched horses

1. A peasant planted pumpkins in the spring. These pumpkins grew big in the summer. In the autumn he harvested the crop, loaded the pumpkins on a cart and took them to market. The peasant met the landowner on the way. The landowner asked the peasant what he was taking to market. The peasant said that he was taking eggs to sell at the market. The landowner was very surprised to see how big the eggs were. Then the peasant said that colts would be hatched from these eggs. The landowner felt like buying the eggs. The landowner ordered him to teach him how to hatch the eggs. The peasant told him to build a nest in a big tree and sit in it there. Then the landowner asked the peasant if he was not willing to hatch the eggs. The peasant answered that he had tired already, but his eggs proved to be sterile. Then the landowner ordered the peasant to build a nest and place the eggs in it. The peasant did as told and had the landowner sit on the eggs, and he told him not to move from the spot until the eggs were hatched.

2. The landowner sat there for one day, for two days, and he sat there for the third day already, and on the fourth day he began to toss and turn in the nest so that together with the nest he fell down on the ground. There was a hare lying just beneath that tree. When the landlord fell down together with the nest, the hare became frightened and ran away from the tree. The landowner sprang up from the ground and saw that one of the eggs was broken. He said: "Look, I have only been sitting for four days and I have already hatched a colt. But how quickly it ran away from me! I could hardly see its heels. And how much quicker the colt would have run if I had been sitting longer on the eggs."

231. The priest and the soldier

Once a soldier went into a village and saw that everybody was going to church. The soldier also set out after them, but he had no money whatever.

vićkuę greχχesę weʒni. a štobi weʒni greχχesę, kowis grive·ńńik ďeńga. solda·t pondis korni popęs, štobi sija siwę weʒis greχχesę ďeńgatęg. a pop sek siwę seććę višta·wis: "te — šuę — gušaw ďeńgasę, wok me dinę, me tenit weʒa bidęs greχχesę daj guša·śęm ponda." solda·t bergę·ććis da toľko mędis munni vićkuiś, kiď sija kaźa·wis, ńe-iwin, popis din ugewin kujweni siwęn beď da bur šapka. vot setęn solda·t i duma·jtištis: 'vaj-ko me guša·wa etę šapkasę da kaba·kin uza·wa. menam woas sek i grive·ńńik weʒni greχχesę daj pira·wni kaba·kę jui·śni vina·. solda·t sek guša·wis šapkasę da nebę·tis kaba·kę uza·wni. seććin sija uza·wis edďę·n donęn i śetisę solda·twę šapka ponda grive·ńńik weʒni greχχez da dvacať pať rubľe·j śuji·štisni karma·nas. vot solda·t bęr woktis vićkuę, śetis popwę grive·ńńik. i weʒis siwiś bidę·s greχχesę. solda·t bergę·ććis da munis kaba·kę. a ritnas pop kvaťi·ććis, a šapkais siwęn abu. sija kotę·rtis kaba·kę i pondis kęri·tni solda·tęs guśaśę·min. a solda·t siwę višta·wis: "te pę aćit weʒin meńćim wunnas greχχesę, a eni menam ńe-kičę·m greχ abu." siď solda·t veę·tis popęs.*

232. *boltľi·vej baba*

1. *owisę-vewisę miži·k da ińka. miži·kis mij-bi oz višta·w, kiʒ ińkais ďerę·wwńaas bidę·s vištaśas. eta miži·kis gęris mu, vetwis vęra·wni i kijis ćeri. vot ęt-piriś miži·k gęris aśśis poľosę i aʒʒis klad. i pondis duma·jtni, kiʒ-że-bi siję vajni gortas, štobi staru·χàs ńe-kinwę ez višta·ś. sija pondis dumajtni i munis prove·ritni kapka·n kęććezwę. kapka·nas siwęn śurema kęć. miži·k boštis kęćsę da śuji·štis aswas torbaę da munis rećka dinę prove·ritni śeť. siwę śeťas śuris šuka. starik kiskis šukasę da śeťas śuji·štis kęćęs, a šukasę nebę·tis da puktis kapka·nas.*

2. *eta bęrin woktis gortas da čęktis žari·tni bľinnez. a staru·χa višta·wis, mijwę śeća·s žari·tni blinnesę. no śo-żę žari·tis. miži·k ętik bľin śojas da kikę puktas torbaę. ińka daže pondis viććini: "mij tenit ta-wun seččęmis wois. te ta-wun una edďę·n ńi śojan bľinnesę." "ta-wun me — šuę — śoja krepidʒika, sić-kę muna me ojnas gortę vaja·wni klad." siʒ vot nija śojisę, a ritnas munisę vajni klad. stari·k munis oʒas i štobi ińis ez aʒʒi·w, žagę·ńikęn torbaśis ęświs bľinnesę puezvę. ińka munis, i šuę miži·kiswę: "mij eta seččęmis, edďę·n una bľinnez tujvanim". miži·k seććę višta·wis: "a etę mijan oʒin munis bľinowej kimę·r. vot sijęn i una bľinnes." eta kadę nija woktisę kapka·n dinęʒ. ińka viʒę·tę i ďivu·ććę: kapkanas śurema šuka. eta kapkan dinśiń nija munisę ju*

* A SR form.

He came to church to repent of his sins. Ten kopecks were necessary to obtain absolution. The soldier began to beg the priest to give him absolution without money. The priest said: "Go and steal money, come back to me, and I shall pardon all your crimes for the theft." The soldier turned round and was about to leave the church when he noticed the priest's stick and his fine cap lying in the corner near the priest. The soldier thought: "I will steal this cap and sell it at the inn. Then I shall have ten kopecks to obtain absolution with, and I can go into the inn to drink vodka." The soldier stole the cap and took it to the inn to sell it. There he sold it at a good price, for the cap he received the ten kopecks necessary for absolution, and a further twenty-five roubles were stuck into his pocket. The soldier returned to the church, and handed the ten kopecks over to the priest. And he pardoned all his sins. The soldier turned on his heels and went to the inn. In the evening the priest set out, but could not find his cap. He ran to the inn and began to scold the soldier for the theft. The soldier said: "This day you yourself pardoned my sins, so I have now no sin whatever." This is how the soldier taught the priest a lesson.

232. The wordy woman

1. There lived a peasant and his wife. Whatever the peasant said to her, she let it out in the village. The peasant ploughed his land, and he also went to hunt and fish. One day, as he was ploughing on his land, he found treasure. He began to ponder how he could bring it home without his wife telling anybody about it. He pondered and went to check the hare-trap. A hare was caught in the trap. He took the hare, put it in his knapsack and started for the little stream to check the net. A pike was caught in the net. The old man pulled the pike out of the net, pushed the hare into the net, and took the pike and put it into the trap.

2. After this he came home and had pancakes fried. The old woman asked why it was so urgent to fry pancakes. But she fried some. The peasant ate a pancake and put two into his knapsack. The old woman even began to scold him: "What happened to you today? You are eating a lot of pancakes today!" "Today I shall have something more solid to eat" — says he — "because tonight I am going out to fetch the treasure." They had their meal, and in the evening went out to fetch home the treasure. The old man took the lead so that his wife might not see him quietly hanging the pancakes he had in his bag on the trees. The wife walked on and on and said to her husband: "What is this? Why are so many pancakes along the way?" Then the peasant said: "A cloud of pancakes passed by in front

dine viže·tni šeťse. šeťe vei šurema keć. boštise nija keťse (kećse) šeranis i munise vajni kladse.

3. *vot nija woktise gortanis kladnas i ašinas ińka višta·šis ďere·wńaas, što siwen miži·kis aǯǯis klad. ete bides kiwis barin i sija koris miži·kes dinas i višta·wis siwe, štobi sija vajis kladse si dine. miži·k višta·wis, što sija ńe-kiče·m klad ez aǯǯi·w. sek barin koris ińse i siwiś pondis jua·šni. ińkàs i višta·wis, što nija kladse aǯǯise. a kiǯ nija vaja·wise kladse gortas? — juawis barin. ińka sek i višta·wis, što nija ritnas munise vere. sek, ker munisni*, ni vewderet bľinowej kime·r, potomu što una bľinnes eša·ise puezvin. ker nija woktise kapka·n dineǯ, to kapka·nas niwe vei šurema šuka, a šeťas šurema keć. barin pondis šera·wni ińkavvin da vaše·tis. a miži·kwe višta·wis: "kiǯ to toľko oan seččem ińkàtket?" a miži·k višta·wis sećće: "da vot siǯ i oam."*

233. *gľińńenej zonka*

1. *owise-vewise stari·k da staru·ka. owise nija kiken i ćeľaď ez vew. vot et-piriś stari·k puka·wis eši·n oǯin da viže·tis, kiǯ ćeľaďo·kkez eterin orseni. vot stari·k i šuis staru·kaiswe: "davaj kerame χoť aswinim gľińńenej zonkaes." kerise nija gľińńenej zonkaes kiken staru·kaket da puktise sije gorve, štobi sija košmis. ked pora zonkais košmis, starik pondis šekta·nen kijni ńin-kemmez, a staru·ka pukšis pećkini kuďeľ. vot seten nija puka·ištise siǯ i drug kiise, kiǯ gor viwšań kin-ke gore·tis: "me-bi šoja." stari·k ćećće·wtis da viže·tis, kin gore·tis gorvas. ete gore·tis gľińńenej zonka. stari·k da staru·ka šetise zonkawe šojni jew da ńań. šojis, šojis da eše· pondis korni. a sija uže· šojis šiži·m ćewpano·k ńań da krinka jew. stari·k da staru·kaen vei boľše ńemen verdni. sek zonka ćećće·wtis gor viwšań da šojis stari·kes šektannas da staru·kaes pećkannas.*

2. *si berin gľińńenej zonka petis etere da pondis munni, kiće· šinnez viže·teni. i siwe panta·šise miži·kkez kosa·ezen da ińkaez kura·nnezen. vot i nie šue: "ińkaez da miži·kkez, me tija·nes šoja." sivvin pondise šera·wni. sek gľińńenej zonka šojis ińkaezes kura·nnezen da mizikkezes kosa·ezen. eta berin sija pondis munni daľše. i siwe panta·šise ver-kerawi·ššez ćerrezen. i niwe pondis šiwni pešenka: "me owi bab ordin da ďed ordin. šoji šiži·m ćewpano·k ńań da krinka jew, stari·kes šekta·nnas da staru·kaes pećka·nnas, ińkaezes kura·nnezen da miži·kkezes kosa·ezen." ete toľko šiwis, kiď šrazu·-že šojis ver-kerawi·ššezes*

* A SR form.

of us. This is why there are so many pancakes." Meanwhile they got to the trap: the trap had caught a pike. From the trap they went to the river to take a look at the net. A hare had got into the net. Taking the hare with them, they went on to fetch the treasure.

3. They arrived home with the treasure, and next morning the wife told all the village that her husband had found treasure. The landlord also heard of this, and called the peasant to see him. He told him to fetch the treasure to his place. The peasant said he had not found any treasure. Then the landlord called for the woman and started to query her. The woman said they had found treasure. Well, how had they brought it home? the landlord asked. The woman replied that they had gone to the forest the night before. As they were going along, a cloud of pancakes must have been passing above them for many pancakes were hanging on the trees. When they arrived at the trap, a pike was caught in the trap, and a hare in the net. The landlord began to laugh at the woman and turned her out. At the same time he said to the peasant: "How can you live with such a woman?" The peasant replied: "Well, that is how we live!"

233. The son made of clay

1. There lived an old man and on old woman. They lived by themselves, they had no children. One day the old man was sitting by the window watching some children playing outdoors. The old man said to the old woman: "Let us make ourselves a son if only of clay." He and the old wife made a son of clay and put it on the stove to dry. While the son was drying, the old man was weaving shoes of bast with the big awl, and the old woman sat down to spin oakum. They were sitting like this for a while, until suddenly they heard somebody shout on the top of the stove: "I'm hungry!" The old man stood up to see who was shouting on the stove. It was the clay son who was shouting. The old man and the old woman gave the son milk to drink and bread to eat. He ate and ate and asked for more. He had eaten seven round loaves of bread and drunk seven jugs of milk. The old man and the old woman had nothing more to give him. Then the son jumped down from the stove and devoured the old man together with the awl, as well as the old woman together with the distaff.

2. Then the clay son went out into the street and started out wherever his eyes looked. He met peasants with scythes and women with rakes. He said to them: "Women and men, I shall devour you." They laughed at him. Then the clay son devoured the women with the rakes and the peasants with the scythes. Then he continued on his way. He met wood-

ćerrezen. si berin gľińńenej zonka munis daľše aswas tujen. i drug sija kaźa·wis koza·es i siwe śiwis peśenkase toľko: "me owi ďed da bab ordin, śoji śiźi·m ćewpano·k ńań da krinka jew, ďedes śekta·nnas da staru·kaes pećka·nnas, ińkaezes kura·nezen, miži·kkezes kosa·ezen da ver-kerawi·śśezes ćerrezen, me tene, koza·, tože śoja." toľko medis śojni koza·es, kiʒ koza· siwe śuis: "mijwe seten te pondan truďi·ććini? te wučše suwt kere·s uwte i emte oś, a me aćim ćećće·wta emat." gľińńenej zonka siʒ i keris. suwtis kere·s uwte, da ośtis emse. a koza· kere·s viwśań eʒʒe·ććis, si berin ćećće·wtis da inme· ććisńe emas, a veśkita kime·sas. siʒ torskis kime·sas gľińńenej zonkawe, što sija srazu· uśis da paza·wis. a kine·mśis petise stari·k śekta·nen, staru·ka pećka·nen, inkaes kura·nnezen, miži·kkez kosa·ezen da ver-kerawi·śśez ćerrezen.

234. *care·vna ľagu·śka*

1. *etik carwen veise kujim zon. ker woktis kadis carwe kuwni, to sija koris dinas zonnese i ćektis bośni niwe etik strela·en da luken. i ćektis nije petni ćistej poľovve i vijni ena strela·ese. kiće· uśas strela·is, seććiniś i bośni aswinis ińkaez. wijis pervoj zonis i siwen strela·is uśis boja·rskej ogra·dae i bośtis sek eta pervoj zonis boja·rskej niwes as sajas. wijis med zonis i uśis siwen strela·is kupe·ćeskej ogra·dae. bośtis sek med zonis as sajas kupe·ćeskej niwes. a kujme·t zonis — sije śuise i v a · n c a r e · v i ćen — wijis aśśis strela·se i munis kośśini sije, kiće· sija uśas. i aʒʒis strela·se bowo·to dorin. a strela·se emas viʒis ľagu·śka. i v a · n c a r e · v i ć pondis korni strewa·se ľagu·śkaiś. no sija viśta·is, śetas sek strela·se, ker i v a · n c a r e · v i ć bośtas sije as sajas. śekita vowźi·śiśtis i v a · n c a r e w i · ć i seglaśi· ććis.*

2. *i vot skoro car orsis srazu kuji·m svaďba. pervoj zonis getra·śis boja·rskej niwket, med zonis getra·śis kupe·ćeskej niwket, a i v a · n c a r e · v i ć getra·śis ľagu·śkaket. ńe-dir owise siʒ i vot et-piriś car koris zonnese dinas i*

cutters carrying axes. He began to sing a little song to them: "I was living with my grandmother and grandfather. I ate up seven round loaves of bread and drank up seven jugs of milk. I devoured the old man with his awl, the old woman with her distaff, I devoured the women with their rakes and the peasants with their scythes." No sooner had he ended his song than he devoured the woodcutters together with their axes. Then the clay son went on his way. Suddenly he caught sight of a goat and sang the song to it: "I was living with my grandfather and grandmother. I ate up seven round loaves of bread and drank up seven jugs of milk. I devoured grandfather with his awl and the old woman with her distaff, I ate up the women with their rakes and the peasants with their scythes, as well as the woodcutters with their axes. Goat, I shall eat you as well." He was just about to devour the goat when the goat said to him: "Why should you bother? It will be better if you stand at the foot of the hill and open your mouth, and I myself will jump into your mouth." The clay son did so. He stood at the foot of the hill and opened his mouth wide. And the goat started to run down the mound, then made a jump though not into his mouth but right at his forehead. He struck the forehead of the clay son so strongly that he fell and broke at once. Out of his belly there came the old man with his awl, the old woman with her distaff, the women with their rakes, the men with their scythes and the woodcutters with their axes.

234. The frog tsarevna

1. A Tsar had three sons. When the time came for the Tsar to die, he called his sons and ordered them to take an arrow and a bow each. He ordered them to go to a clearing and to shoot off their arrows. Where their arrows fall they must choose wives for themselves. The eldest son shot first, and his arrow fell into the courtyard of a nobleman. Then the eldest son married the nobleman's daughter. The next son shot, and his arrow fell into the courtyard of a merchant. The second son married the merchant's daughter. The third son — called Tsarevich Ivan — shot his arrow and started off to find out where it had fallen. He found his arrow beside a swamp. A frog was holding the arrow in its mouth. Tsarevich Ivan asked the frog to return his arrow, but the frog said it would not return it until Tsarevich Ivan had married it. Tsarevich Ivan breathed a heavy sigh and consented.

2. The Tsar soon arranged three weddings. The eldest son married the nobleman's daughter, the second son the merchant's daughter, and Tsarevich Ivan the frog. They had not been living long like this when the Tsar,

śetis ni̮we̮ zada·ńńo, štobi ni̮we̮n ińńes vurise̮ carwe̮ je̮rne̮·ssez. woktise̮ gortani̮s zonnes. i̮ǯi̮·tǯi̮k vonnes viśta·wise̮, mi̮j koris cari̮s, a uće̮·tǯi̮k, i v a · n c a r e v i · ć pukśis da pondis śe̮ki̮ta duma·jtni̮. vot si̮ di̮ne̮ ćećća·wis ľagu·ška ińi̮s i drug mort-gowose̮n jua·wis i v a · n c a r e · v i ćwiś, mi̮j sija siǯ duma·jte̮. i v a · n c a r e v i · ć si̮we viśta·wis, mi̮j če̮ktis kerni̮ aji̮s. ľagu·ška sek si̮we viśta·wis: “vod da uź, a aši̮n je̮rne̮·si̮s woas goto·w.” i v a · n c a r e v i ć ki̮wzis da vodis uźni̮. ľagu·ška ćećće̮·wtis pose̮·ǯe̮, šukkis aśśis ľagu·ša paśke̮m i wois v a ś i ľ i · s a p r e m u · d r e̮ je̮n. i sija gore̮·tis sek: “ńańkaez da služa·nkaez, ki̮je̮ je̮rne̮·s carwe̮, kiče̮·me̮ nowis menam aje̮!” je̮rne̮·s asi̮weǯ ve̮i goto·w. ke̮r i v a · n c a r e · v i ć ćeććis, to je̮rne̮·si̮s ve̮wi kaťťe̮m ći̮ške̮·te̮n. i v a · n c a r e · v i ć boštis je̮rne̮·sse̮ da munis aji̮s di̮ne. aji̮s kak raz prińima·jtis pe̮ri·źźi̮k vonnese̮. ke̮r pervoj voni̮s śetis je̮rne̮·sse̮ aji̮swe̮ i sija viǯe̮·tis, to viśta·wis, što eta je̮rne̮·se̮n toľko uǯa·wni̮ końu·šńàn. ke̮r śetis me̮d voni̮s je̮rne̮·sse̮ aji̮swe̮, to sija viśta·wis, što eta je̮rne̮·se̮n vetwi̮ni̮ toľko bańae̮. a ke̮r śetis i v a · n c a r e · v i ć, to eta je̮rne̮·si̮s ve̮wi vure̮ma zowotòn da śerebròn. sećće̮ car viśta·wis: “ete̮ je̮rne̮·sse̮ paśta·wwi̮ni toľko praźńikkeze̮n.” sećće̮ car śetis me̮di·k zada·ńńo zonnez ińńezwe̮. sija če̮ktis pe̮ža·wni̮ aši̮n kežas ńań. vot vonnes munise̮ si̮ di̮nśań, a i v a · n c a r e · v i ć wois ńeweśo·w. sek ľagu·ška be̮ra· si̮wiś jua·wis, mi̮j sija siǯ te̮ždi·śe̮. i v a · n c a r e · v i ć viśta·wis si̮we̮, što cari̮s če̮ktis pe̮ža·wni̮ ńań. ľagu·ška sek viśta·wis i v a · n c a r e · v i ćwe̮, štobi̮ sija vodis uźni̮. i v a · n c a r e v i · ć siǯ i keris, ľagu·ška toľko me̮dis šukki̮ni̮ aśśis ľagu·ša paśke̮mse̮, ki̮ď sija kaźa·wis, što si̮ śe̮riś śľeďite̮ služa·nka, ke̮dije̮ ińdise̮ ińkaes pe̮riźźi̮k vonneswe̮n, štobi̮ te̮dni̮, ki̮ǯ pondas pe̮ža·wni̮ ńańse̮ ľagu·ška. ľagu·ška veže̮·rtis bi̮de̮·s ete̮ i aśśis paśke̮mse̮ ez šukki. sija soro·wtis kvašńa·, a si̮ be̮ri̮n keris gor vi̮wśań ośta da sećće̮ kiśtis kvašńa·se̮. ete̮ bi̮de̮·s aǯǯi̮·wis služa·nkàs. žage̮·ńike̮n petis kerkuśis da kote̮·rtis pe̮ri·źźi̮k ińkaez di̮ne̮ i ni̮we̮ viśta·wis, ki̮ǯ pe̮ža·wis ńańse̮ care·vna ľagu·ška. nija siǯ-že̮ kerise̮. a care·vna ľagu·ška eta kade̮ šukkis aśśis ľagu·ša paśke̮mse̮ da be̮ra· wois v a ś i ľ i · s a p r e m u · d r e̮ je̮n. petis pose̮·ǯe̮ da gore̮·tis: “ńańkaez da služa·nkaez, pe̮ža·w meni̮m sečče̮m ńań, kiče̮·me̮ me śojwi̮wi̮ aj ordi̮n.” asi̮weǯ ńań ve̮i pe̮ža·we̮m, kaťťe̮m da pukte̮m pi̮za·nve̮, štobi̮ i v a · n c a r e v i ć ne̮be̮·tis ete̮ ńańse̮ carwe̮. cari̮s eta kade̮ prińima·jtis pe̮ri·źźi̮k zonnese̮. ke̮r sija viǯe̮·tis pe̮ža·we̮m ńańse̮ pervoj zoni̮swiś, to ińde̮·tis ete̮ ńańse̮ verdni̮ sluga·eze̮s. ke̮r viǯe̮·tis me̮d zoni̮swiś, to tože̮ ińde̮·tis verdni̮ sluga·eze̮s.

well, one day called his sons and set them a task: that their wives should sew shirts for him. The sons returned home. The older brothers recounted what the Tsar wanted. The youngest one, Tsarevich Ivan, sat down and began to rack his brains. His frog-wife jumped up to him and all of a sudden asked Tsarevich Ivan in a human voice what he was pondering about. Tsarevich Ivan told her what his father had commanded. Then the frog said to him: "Go to bed and sleep, the shirt will be ready in the morning." Tsarevich Ivan obeyed and went to bed. The frog jumped into the porch and casting off her frog's robe changed into Wise Vasilisa. Then she spoke in a loud voice: "Nurses and maidservants, weave such shirt for the Tsar as my father used to wear!" By next morning the shirt was ready. When Tsarevich Ivan got up, he found the shirt covered with a kerchief. Tsarevich Ivan took the shirt and went to his father. His father was just receiving the older brothers. When the eldest brother handed the shirt to his father, he looked at it and said: "This shirt is good enough only for working in the stable." When the second brother handed the shirt to his father, he said that one could only go to the bath-house in that shirt. And when Tsarevich Ivan handed over his shirt — and this shirt was embroidered with gold and silver — the Tsar said: "This shirt must only be worn on festive occasions." Then the Tsar gave a second task to the sons' wives. He ordered them to bake bread for the next morning. The brothers left, and Tsarevich Ivan was plunged into sorrow. Again the frog asked why he was so sad. Tsarevich Ivan told her about the Tsar commanding them to bake bread. The frog told Tsarevich Ivan to go to bed. Tsarevich Ivan did so. The frog was just about to doff her frog's clothes when she noticed that she was followed by a maidservant who had been sent by the elder brothers' wives to discover how she would bake bread. The frog understood all, and she did not doff her robe. She kneaded dough, then made a hole in the roof of the stove and poured in the dough. All this was seen by the maidservant. Slowly she walked out of the house and ran to the older wives, and told them how the Tsar's frog-daughter was baking bread. They did likewise. Meanwhile the Tsar's frog-daughter cast off her frog's robe and turned into Wise Vasilisa once more. She went to the porch and called out: "Nurses and maidservants, bake such bread for me as I used to eat in my father's court!" By next morning the bread was baked, and placed under a cover on the table so that Tsarevich Ivan might take it to the Tsar. Meanwhile the Tsar was receiving the older brothers. When he took a look at the bread of the first brother, he dismissed him saying that the bread should be given to the servants. When he took a look at the second brother's bread, he sent this too to the servants. When Tsarevich Ivan handed over his own bread,

a kẹr siwẹ śetis i v a · n c a r e · v i ćiś, to sija koľis sijẹ śojnị. eta bẹrịn car viśta·wis zonneswẹ, štobị nija woktisẹ ińkaeznanịs pirvẹ.

3. *pẹri·źźịk vonnes woktisẹ pirvẹ aswanịs ińkaeskẹt, a i v a · n c a r e · v i ć woktas ẹtnas. sịvvịn pondisẹ śera·wnị, mịľa sija ez vajẹ·t ińkasẹ. vot nija pondisẹ piru·jtnị i drug nija bịdẹ·nnịs powźisẹ, kịʒ pondis drẹži·tnị muịs (mùs) da šumi·tnị vozduχịs. etẹ woktis pirvẹ kare·taẹn i v a · n c a r e · v i ćwẹn ińịs: v a ś i ľ i · s a p r e m u · d r ẹ j. bịdẹ·nnịs pondisẹ ďivu·ććịnị, kịčẹ·m basẹk ińịs i v a · n c a r e · v i ćwẹn. kẹr nija pondisẹ piru·jtnị, to v a ś i ľ i · s a p r e m u · d r ẹ j vina·sẹ kiśtis ẹt sosas. a kẹr śojis ľebeďẹs, to koskaesẹ tećis mẹd sosas. etẹ kaźa·isẹ ińńes pẹri·źźịk vonneswẹn i kerisẹ siʒ-žẹ. ẹbẹ·d bẹrịn pondisẹ jẹktịnị. petis jẹktịnị ińịs pervoj voniswẹn. jẹktis, jẹktis sija da makńi·tis ẹt sosnas. kitẹ·n vẹi kiśtẹm jutẹm vina·ịs i vinanas rezis carsẹ. car wẹga·śis da vašẹ·tis ińsẹ pervoj zonịswiś. petis jẹktịnị ińịs mẹd zonịswẹn. sija jẹktis, jẹktis da makńi·tis sosnas siʒ, što koskaes webźisẹ sośśis da inmisẹ carịswẹ. car wẹga·śis ešẹ· ẹďďẹ·nžịk da vašẹ·tis ińsẹ mẹd zonịswiś. nị bẹrịn petis jẹktịnị ińịs i v a · n c a r e · v i ćwẹn. sija jẹktis, jẹktis da makńi·tis sosnas. kitẹ·n vẹwi kiśtem vina, to srazu-žẹ webźisẹ ńeboẹ zvezda·ez da tẹwiś (meśać). makńi·tis mẹd kinas, kitẹn vẹisẹ koskaez ľebeďwẹn, to sośśis webźisẹ ľebeďďez. a kịʒ pondis jẹktịnị, to bịdẹ·nnịs seččẹ·m ďivośań, to mestaiś dažẹ ez verźẹ·ććẹ.*

4. *eta kadẹ i v a · n c a r e · v i ć pukśis kare·taẹ da ćoźźịk gẹńi·tis gortas. aʒʒis ľagu·ša paśkẹmsẹ da sotis gorịn. skoro woktis v a ś i ľ i · s a p r e m u · d r ẹ j. sija jua·wis, kịćẹ voštis sịwiś paśkẹmsẹ. i v a · n c a r e · v i ć sek viśta·wis, što sija sotis paśkẹmsẹ gorịn. sek v a ś i ľ i · s a p r e m u · d r e j viśta·wis i v a · n c a r e · v i ćwẹ, što sịwẹ sowśe·m ńewno·ćka kowis vićći·śišnị, štobị sija aćịs šukkis ľagu·ša paśkẹmsẹ. v a ś i ľ i · s a p r e m u · d r ẹ jsẹ kowdujtis ajịs sị ponda, mịľa v a ś i ľ i · s ajs pondis bịdmịnị ajịsśa mudrẹjžịka. v a ś i ľ i · s a bergẹ·ććis kuku·škaẹn da webźis ośta ẹśi·nẹ.*

5. *i v a · n c a r e · v i ć gorzịštis da munis kośśịnị ińsẹ. sija munis dịr-ja iľi ńe-dịr, kịď sija panta·wis staricó·kes. staricó·k sịwiś jua·wis: "kịćẹ· te munan, bur moloďe·ć?" i v a · n c a r e · v i ć viśta·wis aśśis bedasẹ. sek stari·k śetis sịwẹ klubo·k i čẹktis munnị eta klubo·k śerịn. i viśta·wis, što eta klubo·kịs vajẹ·tas sijẹ seććinẹ, kitẹ·n sịwẹn ińịs. munis, munis i v a · n c a r e · v i ć i ćịstej poľovvịn kaźa·wis ośẹs. sija mẹdis sijẹ vijnị, a ośịs sịwẹ šuis mort-gowosẹn: "en vij menẹ, me tenịt prigoďi·ćća." i v a · n c a r e · v i ć źaľe·jtis sijẹ i ez vij, a munis aswas tujẹn. ćoźa mịjiś sija kaźa·wis, što webźẹ śeľeźeń. i v a · n c a r e · v i ć mẹdis vijnị sijẹ, no śeľeźeń mort-gowosẹn*

he kept it to eat it. Then the Tsar told the brothers to bring their wives to a feast in his home.

3. The older brothers arrived with their wives, but Tsarevich Ivan came alone. They began to mock him since he had not brought his wife. They began to feast, and all of a sudden they were frightened because the earth began to shake and the air to roar. Tsarevich Ivan's wife arrived in a coach for the supper: she was Wise Vasilisa. All were amazed at seeing how beautiful Tsarevich Ivan's wife was. When they began to feast, Wise Vasilisa poured the wine into the sleeve of her dress. When she was eating swan, she put the bones into the other sleeve of her dress. The older brothers' wives noticed this, and they did the same, too. After supper they began to dance. The eldest brother's wife went out to dance. She danced and danced, and waved the sleeve of her robe where she had poured the wine, and spattered the wine over the Tsar. The Tsar grew angry and expelled the eldest son's wife. The second son's wife went out do dance. She danced and danced and swung the sleeve of her dress so that the bones flew out it, hitting the Tsar. The Tsar grew still more angry and expelled the second son's wife. Following them, Tsarevich Ivan's wife went out to dance. She danced and danced and waved the sleeve of her dress. From the one the poured wine was in, stars and the moon shot up suddenly into the sky. She waved her other arm, and from where the swan's bones were hidden, swans flew out. When she started to dance, everybody was amazed; they could not even rise from their seats.

4. Meanwhile Tsarevich Ivan got into a coach and galloped home quickly. He found the frog's dress and burnt it in the stove. Soon Wise Vasilisa arrived. She asked where he had hidden her robe. Tsarevich Ivan related that he had burnt her clothes in the stove. Wise Vasilisa said to Tsarevich Ivan that he should have waited only for a short time then she herself would have thrown away her frog's robe. Wise Vasilisa had been bewitched by her own father because she was growing wiser than her father. Vasilisa turned into a cuckoo and flew out of the house through the window.

5. Tsarevich Ivan wept and started out to search for his wife. He went on a short time or a long time, when he met an old man. The old man asked: "Where are you going, my good young man?" Tsarevich Ivan told him about his sorrows. Then the old man gave him a reel of thread, telling him to follow that thread. He said the reel would lead him to the place where his wife was staying. Tsarevich Ivan went on and on, and caught a glimpse of a bear in a clearing. He wanted to kill it but the bear spoke in a human voice: "Do not kill me, I may be of some use to you!" Tsarevich Ivan took pity on it and did not kill it, but continued on his own way.

viśta·wis si̮we̮, štobi̮ sija ez vij sije̮. i v a · n c a r e · v i ć ki̮wzis i pondis munni̮ daľše. sija munis, munis i kaźa·wis ke̮će̮s. toľko me̮dis vijni̮ ke̮ći̮swe̮, ki̮ǯ ke̮ći̮s pondis mort-gowose̮n korni̮ štobi̮ sija ez vij ke̮ćse̮. sija eše· prigoďi·ććas si̮we̮. i v a · n c a r e · v i ć munis daľše. munis, munis i woktis śińej more di̮ne̮. i aǯǯe̮, bereg doras peso·kvi̮n kujwe̮ šuka. sija uže· jeľe wowa·we̮. sija pondis korni̮ i v a · n c a r e · v i će̮s, štobi sija šukkis sije̮ śińej moree̮. i v a · n c a r e · v i ć žaľe·jtis šukase̮ da šukkis moree̮. eta be̮ri̮n i v a · n c a r e · v i ć pondis munni̮ daľše.

6. *munis, munis i woktis śe̮d ve̮r di̮ne̮. poľanavvi̮n suwa·wis izbu·ška kure̮·g-kokkezvi̮n. i v a · n c a r e · v i ć sek šuis izbu·skai̮swe̮: "berge̮·ćći̮ be̮rnas ve̮rwańe̮, a oǯnas mewańe̮!" izbu·ška siǯ i keris. i v a · n c a r e · v i ć pi̮ris izbu·škaas i kaźa·wis baba-jaga·e̮s. si̮we̮n pińńes kujwise̮ powkavvi̮n, a ni̮ri̮s bi̮dme̮m potowo·ke̮ǯ. baba-jaga· juwawe̮ i v a · n c a r e · v i će̮s, ki̮će̮ sija mune̮. i v a · n c a r e · v i ć sek si̮we̮ otve·ťitis: "te pervo mene̮ verd, jukta·w, bańàn miśśe̮·t, a si̮ be̮ri̮n tožno i jua·ś!" baba-jaga· verdis, jukta·wis, miśśe̮·tis bańàn i votte̮·tis kojkavve̮. i pondis jua·śni i v a · n c a r e · v i ć-wiś. i v a · n c a r e · v i ć viśta·wis si̮we̮ bi̮de̮·s. baba-jaga· ńe-di̮r mi̮jiś viśta·wis, što v a ś i l' i · s a p r e m u · d r e̮ jwe̮n aji̮s k o š e · j b e ś m e · r t-n e̮ j i si̮we̮n śmerťi̮s jem-końe·ći̮n, a jemi̮s ǯebe̮m koľťi̮n, koľťi̮s utkai̮n, utkai̮s ke̮ći̮n, ke̮ći̮s kamenne̮j sundu·ki̮n, a eta sundu·ki̮s vi̮wi̮n (vi̮i̮n) dubvi̮n. ćue̮·tis ojse̮ i v a · n c a r e · v i ć baba-jaga· ordi̮n i aši̮nas munis kośši̮ni̮ ete̮ dubse̮. skoro sija aǯǯis ete̮ dubse̮, kite̮·n ve̮i kamenne̮j sundu·ki̮s. no kajni̮ eta sundu·k di̮ne̮ i v a · n c a r e · v i ć ez vermi̮. drug kiśa·ń-ke̮ petis oš. sija uśke̮·tis dubse̮ e̮twai̮n sundu·knas. sundu·ki̮s uśis da paza·wis. eta sundu·kiś ćećće̮·wtis ke̮ć i pondis pi̮šši̮ni̮. no si̮ śeri̮n ve̮ććis me̮di·k ke̮ć. ete̮ ke̮ćse̮ ve̮tis da orwawis torrezve̮. eta ke̮ćiś webźis utka. no drug ki̮me̮·rrezśań utkavve̮ uśke̮·ććis śe̮ľeźeń. utka uśke̮·tis koľťse̮ i koľťi̮s uśis moree̮. i v a · n c a r e · v i ć e̮ďďe̮n wois gažte̮m, što koľťi̮s uśis moree̮. no drug bereg doras mi̮ćći·śis šuka. sija e̮mas viǯis koľťse̮. i v a · n c a r e · v i ć radu·ććis i bośtis koľťse̮. žugdis sije̮, aǯǯis jem-końe·ćse̮ da pondis sije̮ ćegwa·wni̮. k o š e · j b e ś m e · r t n e̮ j eta kade̮ mući·ććis aswas śmerťke̮t da skoro sija kuwis, sić-ke̮ i v a · n ć a r e · v i ć ćege̮·tis jem-końe·ćse̮. eta be̮ri̮n i v a · n c a r e · v i ć munis ćoćkom dvore·će̮·. pani̮t si̮we̮ kote̮·rtis si̮we̮n ińi̮s, v a ś i l' i · s a p r e m u · d r e̮ j. i v a · n c a r e · v i ć oka·wis ińse̮ da nija be̮r munise̮ aswani̮s carstvoe̮. seććin nija di̮r owise̮.*

Soon he caught sight of a drake flying in the air. Tsarevich Ivan wanted to kill it, but the drake begged him in a human voice not to kill it. Tsarevich Ivan obeyed and started on. He went on and on, and caught sight of a hare. As he was about to kill the hare, it asked him in a human voice not to kill it. It would be of use to him later. Tsarevich Ivan continued on his way. He went on and on, and arrived at the blue sea. He saw a pike lying in the sand. It was hardly breathing. It asked Tsarevich Ivan to throw it back into the blue sea. Tsarevich Ivan took pity on the pike and threw it back into the sea. Then Tsarevich Ivan continued on his way.

6. He went on and on, and arrived at a dark forest. In a clearing there was a hut standing on hen's legs. Then Tsarevich Ivan said to the hut: "Turn your back part towards the wood, and your front part towards me!" The hut did as it was told. Tsarevich Ivan entered the hut and saw a witch in it. Her teeth were lying on a shelf while her nose reached up to the ceiling. The witch asked Tsarevich Ivan where he was going. Tsarevich Ivan answered: "First give me something to eat and drink, wash me in the bath-house, and only then ask me!" The witch gave him something to eat and drink, washed him in the bath-house, and put him to bed. And then she put many questions to Tsarevich Ivan. Tsarevich Ivan told her everything. After a short while the witch said to him: Wise Vasilisa's father was the Immortal Košej. His death is in the eye of a needle, the needle is hidden in an egg, the egg in a duck, the duck in a hare, the hare in a stone chest, and this stone chest is in the crown of a tall oak. Tsarevich Ivan spent the night with the witch and in the morning he set out to search for the oak. He soon found that oak with the chest of stone. But Tsarevich Ivan could not climb up to reach the chest. Suddenly a bear appeared from somewhere. It felled the oak together with the chest. The chest fell down and broke in pieces. The hare sprang out of the chest and ran away. Another hare set after it. The second hare caught the first one and tore it to pieces. The duck flew out of the hare. But suddenly from the clouds the drake attacked the duck. The duck dropped the egg and the egg fell into the sea. Tsarevich Ivan was very sorry to see the egg fall into the sea. The pike appeared on the shore. It was holding the egg in its mouth. Tsarevich Ivan was very glad at this, and he took hold of the egg. He broke it up and found the eye of the needle, and began to break it. Meanwhile Immortal Košej was struggling with his own death and soon he died, since Tsarevich Ivan broke the end of the needle. After this Tsarevich Ivan entered the white palace. His wife Wise Vasilisa ran to meet him. Tsarevich Ivan kissed his wife, and both of them returned to their own tsardom. They lived there a long time.

235. *śiwka-burka*

1. *e̮tik mi̮ži̮·k ke̮ǯis ńań. ńańi̮s bi̮dmis e̮ďďe̮n bur. no vot sija pondis peća·ľić-ći̮ni̮. každe̮j oj si̮ śu-polosavve̮ kin-ke̮ pondis vowwi̮ni̮. woktas ojnas i eča·ži̮k śojas śuse, a una·ži̮k taľas. vot sija e̮tik oje̮ ińde̮·tis karau·ľitni̮ śuse̮ i kutni̮ vore̮s med pe̮riś zonse̮. zon we̮śe̮·ććis oj keže. puka·is, puka·is, viǯe̮·te̮, ńe-kin oz wok i sije̮ pondis e̮deľe·jtni̮ on. sija munis sara·je̮, vodis da uźis osta·tki ojse̮. me̮d ojas ińde̮·tis karau·ľitni̮ śuse̮ śe̮re̮·t zonse̮. sija siǯ-že̮ puka·wis ńe-di̮rik, a si̮ be̮ri̮n sara·ji̮n uźis ojse̮. kujme̮·t ojas ińde̮·tis karau·ľitni̮ kujme̮·t zonse̮. sije̮ šuise̮ iva·n dura·ke̮n. bośtis gez da munis karau·ľitni̮ śu-polosa·se̮. sija pukśis i̮ǯi̮·t iz saje̮ i pondis vićći·śni̮ vorse̮. eta kade̮, štobi̮ ńe e̮nme̮·śśi̮ni̮, sija bośtis geziś kere̮m arka·n. no vori̮s śo eše· ez ve̮w. sije̮ pondis vermi̮ni̮ oni̮s sija pondis miśśi̮ni̮ rosa·e̮n. oj-bi̮te̮n sija ńe e̮t-pi̮riś miśśis rosa·e̮n, štobi̮ vaše̮·tni̮ onse̮. i vot uže· asja-ponas kaźa·wis, ki̮ć kote̮·rtis ni̮ śu polosa·vve̮ ve̮w da pondis śojni̮ śuse̮. eta ve̮wi̮s ńe prosto·j ve̮wi. si̮we̮n e̮tik ge̮ni̮s ve̮wi śere·bran-ne̮j, a me̮di̮s zowo·te̮j. vot iva·n dura·k we̮śe̮·ććištis da šukkis arka·nse̮ ve̮vve. ve̮w ďorńiććis da me̮dis pi̮śśi̮ni̮. no iva·n dura·k sije̮ viǯis aswas arka·ne̮n krepi̮ta. ve̮w pondis korni̮, štobi̮ sije̮ iva·n dura·ki̮s we̮ǯis. ve̮wi̮s sek si̮we̮ viśta·wis, što pondas kowni̮, jeśľi si̮we̮n koas otse̮t. a iva·n dura·k jua·śis, ki̮ď sije̮ a̮ǯǯi̮ni̮. ve̮w če̮ktis ńe vune̮·tni̮ sečče̮m ki̮wwez: "śiwka-burka, veśśe̮j kuaku·rka, suwt me o̮ǯi̮n, ki̮ď ľist turun o̮ǯi̮n!" ve̮w siǯ-že̮ soglaśi·ććis, što sija boľše oz pondi̮ śojni̮ ni̮wiś śuse̮. vot asi̮wnas woktis iva·n dura·k gortas i aji̮s si̮wiś jua·we: "kutin vorse̮?" iva·n dura·k viśta·wis, što sija vorse̮ kutis. vori̮s ve̮wi ve̮w. si̮we̮n e̮tik ge̮ni̮s ve̮wi śere·bran-ne̮j, a me̮di·ki̮s zowo·te̮j. aji̮s da vonnes śera·wištise̮ iva·n dura·kwi̮n, da ez verite̮. no eta be̮rśiń śuse̮ ńe-kin ez ve̮re̮·t.*

2. *eta kade̮ car objavi·tis, što si̮we̮n em ni̮w, ńeve·sta. sija puka·we̮ vi̮i̮n ťeremi̮n, e̮śi̮·n o̮ǯi̮n puka·we̮. kin seććine̮ǯ ćećće̮·wtas ve̮we̮n i suǯe̮·tas ćuń-ki̮·č, to si̮ saje̮ i śetas ińe̮n. vot iva·n dura·kwe̮n pondise̮ vonnes we̮śe̮·ćći̮ni̮ gorode̮, štobi̮ viǯe̮·tni̮, ki̮ǯ dobre̮j molode·ććez pondase̮ ćećća·wni̮ ve̮wweze̮n. iva·n dura·k tože̮ pondis korśi̮ni̮ ni̮ke̮t, no vonnes si̮vvi̮n śera·wise̮ da viśta·wise̮: "puka·w pe̮ iva·n dura·k gorti̮n aswat gorvi̮n da śi̮ en śet!" vot pe̮ri·žži̮k vonnes munise̮ gorode̮, a iva·n dura·k koris kor-*

235. Śiwka-burka

1. A peasant sowed corn. The corn grew very tall. He began to feel sorry. Every night somebody came to his rye-field. He arrives at night, eats a little and tramples down more. One night he sent his eldest son to guard the rye and catch the thief. The son prepared for the night. He sat and sat: he watches, but nobody comes, and he was overcome by sleep. He went into the barn, lay down and slept through the rest of the night. The next night he sent his middle son to watch the corn. He too sat for a short time, but then he spent the night sleeping in the barn. On the third night he sent out his third son on guard. He was called Stupid Ivan. He took a rope and went on watch in the rye-field. He sat behind a big stone and began to wait for the thief to come. Meanwhile, so that he should not fall asleep, he held the lasso he had made from the rope. But no thief appeared as yet. Sleep began to overcome him. He washed himself in dew. In the course of the night he washed several times in dew to drive away sleep. Towards dawn he noticed a horses running to their rye-field and feeding on the rye. This horse was by no means a common horse. One thread of its hair was silver, the other gold. Ivan gathered his strength and threw the lasso over the horse. The horse jerked and tried to escape. But Stupid Ivan held it tight with his lasso. The horse began to beg him to set it free. Then the horse said he would need him in case of necessity. Stupid Ivan asked how he would find it. The horse told him not to forget the following words: "*Śiwka-burka veššej kuaku·rka*, stop before me as a leaf stops before the grass!" At the same time the horse promised not to feed on their rye any longer. Stupid Ivan went home in the morning, and his father asked him: "Have you caught the thief?" Stupied Ivan said he had. The thief was a horse. One thread of its hair was silver, the other gold. Both the father and the brothers laughed at Stupid Ivan, and did not believe him. But from that time on nobody touched their rye.

2. It was about this time that the Tsar proclaimed that he had a daughter of marriageable age, who was sitting by the window in the uppermost tower room. Whoever could jump that high on his horse to reach the ring would be given her as his wife. Stupid Ivan's brothers got ready to go to town to see how the brave young men would jump on horseback. Stupid Ivan also asked for leave to go, but his brothers laughed at him, saying: "Stupid Ivan, stay at home sitting on the stove and do not say a word!" The older brothers went to town, while Stupid Ivan asked for a basket and started to pick mushrooms in the forest. When he reached the meadow, he suddenly threw his basket under a bush, whistled and shouted jauntily: "*Śiwka-burka,*

źi·nka da munis ve̮re̮ čakja·wni̮. toľko sija petis i̮bve̮, ki̮ǯ korźi·nkase̮ srazu·-že̮ šukkis kusttez uwte̮, a aći̮s šuťńe̮·wtis da gore̮·tis moloďe·ćkej gowose̮n: "śiwka-burka, veššej kuaku·rka, suwt me oǯi̮n, ki̮ǯ ľist turun oǯi̮n." toľko ještis viśta·wni̮, ki̮ǯ ve̮w suwa·wis si̮ oǯi̮n. i v a · n d u r a · k pi̮ris ve̮we̮ veśki̮t peľas da šuľgaas petis. i wois sečče̮m moloďeće̮n, ki̮če̮·m toľko owwe̮ skazkai̮n. sija pukśis ve̮vve̮ da ge̮ńi·tis gorode̮. tujvas sija ve̮tis aśśis vonnese̮. śetis pľeťe̮n ni̮ spina·ez kuźa da ge̮ńi·tis oǯwańe̮. woktis gorode̮, a sećći̮n naro·di̮s e̮kśe̮ma, ki̮ǯ śe̮d ki̮me̮·r. eta naro·di̮s woktis viǯe̮·tni̮ dobrej moloďe·ććeze̮s, ki̮ǯ nija pondase̮ suǯe̮·tni̮ cari̮s ni̮wwiś ćuń-ki̮·č. vot i v a · n duma·jti̮štis, śetis ve̮wi̮swe̮ bokkezas šolkovoj pľeťe̮n i ge̮ńi̮·tis, štobi̮ ćećće̮·wtni̮ vi̮wwańe̮, ki̮te̮n puka·is ńeve·stai̮s ćuń-ki̮·čke̮t. ćećće̮·wtis i v a · n d u r a · k ś i w k a - b u r k ake̮t da ez vermi̮ suǯni̮ toľko kuji·m vi̮i̮na. naro·d sećće̮ pondis gore̮·twi̮ni̮, kin sija sečče̮mi̮s, ki̮tiś. no nija aǯǯi̮·wise̮, ki̮ǯ i v a · n d u r a · k woktis, no ez aǯǯi̮·we̮, kiće̮· sija ge̮ńi·tis. i v a · n d u r a · k woktis i̮bvas, weǯis ve̮wse̮, aǯǯis aśśis korźi·nase̮, e̮ktis sećće̮ mu̮χomo·rrez da woktis gortas. si̮vvi̮n śera·wise̮, mi̮jwe̮ sija e̮ktis ete̮ čakse̮ da šukkise̮. eta kade̮ woktise̮ vonnes da pondise̮ viśta·śni̮, mi̮j nija aǯǯi̮·wise̮. vot nija viśta·wise̮, što tujvas nije̮ ve̮tis bur moloďe·ć. si̮ ve̮wwe̮n e̮tik ge̮ni̮s śere·brenne̮j, a me̮di̮s zowo·te̮j. sija se̮tis nije̮ pľeťe̮n da ge̮ńitis oǯwań gorodas. sija ćećće̮·wtis ńeve·sta di̮ne̮, no ez suǯe̮·t, toľko kuji·m ker vi̮i̮na. a i v a · n d u r a · k gor vi̮wśiń jua·wis: "a možet eta bur moloďe·ći̮s me." no vonnes si̮vvi̮n śera·wni̮ pondise̮. sek i v a · n d u r a · k boľše śi̮ ez śet.

3. *aśi̮nas vonnes be̮ra· we̮śe̮·ććise̮ gorode̮. pukśise̮ ve̮wwezve̮ da ge̮ńi·tise̮. i v a · n d u r a · k bośtis korźi·na da munis čakwe̮. petis i̮bbezve̮, šukkis korźi·nase̮ kusttez uwte̮ da be̮ra· šuťńe̮·wtis da gore̮·tis gora gowose̮n: "ś i w k a - b u r k a, veššej kuaku·rka, suwt me oǯi̮n, ki̮ǯ ľist turu·n oǯi̮n!" si̮ oǯe̮ be̮ra· woktis ś i w k a - b u r k a. i v a · n d u r a · k pi̮ris siwe̮ e̮t peľas da me̮das petis i be̮ra wois bur mowoďe·će̮n. sija pukśis ve̮vve̮ da ge̮ńi·tis gorode̮. tujvas sija ve̮tis vonnese̮. se̮tis šolkove̮j pľeťe̮n da koľis be̮ras. ke̮r gorode̮ bi̮de̮·nni̮s e̮kśise̮, i v a · n d u r a · k be̮ra· ćećće̮·wtis ťere̮m e̮śi̮n di̮ne̮, štobi̮ suǯe̮·tni̮ ćuń-ki̮·č, no ez vermi̮ ćećće̮·wtni̮ ćuń-ki̮·či̮s di̮neǯ toľko ki̮k ker vi̮i̮na. naro·d be̮ra pondis gore̮·twi̮ni̮, kin sija sečče̮mi̮s i ki̮tiś. no sije̮, aǯǯiwi̮se̮, ke̮r woktis, no ez aǯǯiwe̮, ki̮ǯ sija munis. i v a · n d u r a · k woktis i̮bve̮, weǯis ve̮wse̮, aǯǯis aśśis korźi·nase̮ da ti̮r sećće korźi-naas e̮ktis poga·nkaez. woktis gorte̮,*

veššej kuaku·rka, stop before me as a leaf stops before the grass!" No sooner had he uttered these words than the horse stood in front of him. Stupid Ivan entered the horse's right ear and came out through the left ear. He changed into a brave young man the like of whom can only be found in tales. He mounted the horse and rode to the town. He caught up with his brothers on the way. He gave them a cut with his whip and rode on. He arrived in the city where people were gathering together like a black cloud. These people had come along to see how the daring young men would reach the ring of the Tsar's daughter. Ivan stood thinking for a short time, then he struck the flank of his horse with his whip of silk, and galloped in order to jump where the bride was sitting with the ring. Stupid Ivan jumped up with Śiwka-burka, but he only reached the height of the third floor. Then people began to shout, eager to learn who he was and where he came from. They could see how Stupid Ivan had arrived but they could not see where he disappeared in a gallop. Stupid Ivan returned to the meadow, set free the horse, found his basket, picked fly-agaric and went home. They mocked at him because he had gathered these mushrooms, and threw them all out. In the meantime the brothers arrived and told what they had seen. They related that they had been overtaken on their way by a gallant young man. One thread of the hair of his horse was silver, the other gold. He had struck them with his whip and galloped to town before them. He made a jump up to the bride, though he could not reach her, jumping up to the height of the third floor. Stupid Ivan said to them from the stove: "That gallant young man may well be me!" But his brothers laughed at him. After this Stupid Ivan did not say a word.

3. Next morning the brothers prepared to go to town again. They mounted their horses and galloped away. Stupid Ivan took his basket and went to gather mushrooms. He walked out to the ploughed fields, threw his basket under a bush and whistled as before, then shouted in a loud voic: "*Śiwka-burka, veššej kuaku·rka*, stop before me as a leaf stops before the grass!" Stupid Ivan entered one of its ears and left through the other, and once more he changed into a gallant young man. He mounted the horse and galloped to town. On the way he overtook his brothers. He struck at them with his whip of silk and left them behind. When all the people were gathered together in the city, Stupid Ivan made a jump up to the window of the tower room to reach the ring, but he could not jump up to the ring, only to the height of two joists. Again the people shouted, eager to learn who he was and where he came from. They could see him when he arrived, but could not see how he left. Stupid Ivan came to the ploughed field, set free his horse, found his basket and filled it with toadstools. He came home,

no si̮vvi̮n e̮ṕať śera·wise̮ da šukkise̮ si̮wiś čakse̮. i v a · n d u r a · k kajis be̮ra· gorve̮ da pondis puka·wni̮. eta kade̮ woktise̮ si̮we̮n vonnes i pondise̮ viśta·śni̮, mi̮j nija aǯ́ǯ́i̮·wise̮. nija viśta·wise̮ siǯ́-že̮, što nije̮ tujvas ve̮tis sija bur mooďe·ći̮s, se̮tis nije̮ šolkovoj pľeťe̮n da nije̮ koľis. sija ćećće̮·wtis ńeve·sta di̮ne̮ i ez verme̮ suǯ́e̮·tn̮i̮ ćuń-ki̮·čse̮ ki̮k ker vi̮i̮na. i ńe-kin ez aǯ́ǯ́i̮·we̮, ki̮ď sija ge̮ńi·tis. "a možet ete̮ ve̮wi me." no vonnes si̮vvi̮n be̮ra śera·wise̮ i ez veri·te̮ si̮we̮.

4. kujme̮·t wunnas vonnez be̮ra· we̮śe̮·ććise̮ gorode̮. toľko nija munise̮, ki̮ǯ́ i v a · n d u r · a k boštis korźi·nka da munis ve̮re̮ čakjawni̮. toľko petis paśki̮t i̮bve̮, ki̮ď šukkis korźi·nase̮ kusttez uwte̮, šuťńe̮·wtis da gore̮·tis mooďe·ćke̮j gosse̮n: "ś i w k a - b u r k a, veššej kuaku·rka, suwt me oǯ́i̮n, ki̮ǯ́ ľist turun oǯ́i̮n!" toľko viśta·wis ene̮ ki̮wwese̮, a ś i w k a - b u r k a suwawis si̮ oǯ́i̮n ńi. i v a · n d u r a · k pi̮ris si̮we̮ e̮t peľas da me̮das petis i wois sija bur mooďe·-će̮n. pukśis ś i w k a - b u r k avve̮ da ge̮ńi·tis gorode̮. tujvas sija ve̮tis aśśis vonnese̮, se̮tis ni̮ spina·ez kuźa šolkove̮j pľeťe̮n da be̮ra· nije̮ koľis be̮ras. woktis gorodas, a naro·di̮s e̮kśe̮m, ki̮ď śed ki̮me̮·r, štobi̮ viǯ́e̮·tni̮, ki̮ǯ́ pondase̮ ćećća·wni̮. i v a · n d u r a · k se̮tis krute̮j bokkez ve̮w kuźa šolkove̮j pľeťe̮n da ćećće̮·wtis aswas ve̮wke̮t. suǯ́e̮·tis ćuń-ki̮·čse̮ i ještis oki̮·śni̮ ńeve·stase̮ rožo-banas. si̮ be̮ri̮n sija pondis ge̮ńitni̮. a naro·di̮s pondis gore̮·twi̮ni̮: "kute̮ sije̮, kute̮!" i si̮ śere̮ ve̮ććise̮ ve̮wweze̮n, štobi̮ kutni̮ i v a · n d u r a · ke̮s. no sije̮ kutni̮ ez verme̮. i v a · n d u r a · k woktis i̮bve̮, we̮ǯ́is ve̮wse̮, aǯ́ǯ́is aswas aśśis korźi·nkase̮ da woktis gortas. gortśis pondise̮ jua·wni̮, miľa si̮we̮n ćuńi̮s kaťťe̮m trepi·će̮n. sija viśta·wis, što čakse̮ e̮kti̮ke̮ ńećaja·nno dojdis uvve̮. eta kade̮ woktise̮ vonnes i pondise̮ viśta·śni̮: nije̮ be̮ra· tujvas ve̮tis bur mooďe·ći̮s, se̮tis nije̮ pľeťe̮n da koľis be̮ras. gorodas sija ćećće̮·wtis, suǯ́e̮·tis ćuń-ki̮čse̮, oki̮·štis ńeve·stase̮ da ki̮će̮·-ke̮ e̮śis. i v a · n d u r a · kwe̮ oχo·ta wois viǯ́e̮·tni̮ ćuń-ki̮čse̮. sija gorvas žage̮·ńike̮n perćća·wis ćuńse̮ i kerkui̮n srazu·-že̮ pondis jugja·wni̮. vonnes pondise̮ gore̮·twi̮ni̮ i v a · n d u r a · kwe̮: "te en be̮ba·w seććin binas, a sotan kerkuse̮." i v a · n d u r a · k ši̮ńńa·we̮me̮n be̮r ke̮rta·wis ćuńse̮.

5. ki̮ni̮·m-ke̮ wun be̮rti car če̮ktis wokti̮ni̮ bi̮de̮·nniswe̮ pirve̮. a ješľi kin oz wok, to si̮wiś jurse̮ kera·wase̮. vot vonnez we̮śe̮·ććise̮ munni̮ pirve̮ i boštise̮ śe̮rani̮s i v a · n d u r a · ke̮s. woktise̮ nija car orde̮ i vonnes pukśise pi̮za·nnez

again they laughed at him and threw out his toadstools. Stupid Ivan climbed up on the stove and sat there. In the meantime his brothers arrived and started to relate what they had seen. As before they told how the gallant young man had overtaken them on the way, and having struck them with his whip of silk, had left them behind. He made a jump to reach the bride; although could not get the ring, he could only reach the height of two joists. Nobody saw how he galloped away. "Maybe, it was me!" But again his brothers laughed at him and did not believe him.

4. On the third day the brothers prepared to go to town again. Hardly had they left when Ivan took his basket and went out to pick mushrooms in the forest. Hardly had he arrived in the broad meadow when he threw his basket under a bush, whistled once and shouted jauntily: "*Śiwka-burka, veššej kuaku·rka*, stop before me as a leaf stops before the grass!" No sooner had he uttered these words than Śiwka-burka stood in front of him. Stupid Ivan entered one of its ears and came out through the other, changing into a gallant young man. He mounted Śiwka-burka and galloped to town. On the way he caught up with his brothers, lashed their backs with the whip of silk and again left them behind. He arrived in the city; the people were gathered together like a black cloud to see how they would jump. Stupid Ivan struck at the horse with great flanks with his whip of silk and made his horse jump. He reached the ring, and he succeeded in kissing the bride's face. Then he began to gallop away. The people began to shout: "Catch him, catch him!" They set out after him on horseback, to catch Stupid Ivan. But they could not catch him. Stupid Ivan came to the meadow, set free the horse, found his own basket and came home. The folk at home asked him why his finger was wrapped in a rag. He said a branch had hurt it by chance while he was gathering mushrooms. Meanwhile the brothers arrived at home and started to tell their tale: again the gallant young man had overtaken them, lashed them with his whip of silk and left them behind. He had made a jump in the city, reached the ring and having kissed the bride had disappeared somewhere. Stupid Ivan felt like taking a look at the ring. On the stove he slowly unwrapped his finger, and the house was filled at once with a bright glow. The brothers shouted at Stupid Ivan: "Don't play around with the fire there, or you'll set the house on fire!" Smiling, Stupid Ivan wrapped his finger up again.

5. A few days later the Tsar invited everybody to a feast. Anyone who failed to come would be beheaded. Well, the brothers prepared for the feast and they took Stupid Ivan with them. They came to the Tsar, and the brothers sat down at the table while Stupid Ivan sat in the corner by the stove. The Tsar's daughter, the bride, offered wine and honey to everyone,

saje̮, a i v a · n d u r a · k pukśis gor koa·se̮. carske̮j ńeve·stàs aći̮s każde̮j mortwe̮ vajis vina· da ma i viǯe̮·tis, ke̮da si̮we̮n že̮ńi̮ki̮s. no ge̮śśes koa·si̮n pi̮za·n saji̮n že̮ńi̮·ki̮s ez ve̮w. no vot sija każa·wis gor koa·siś i v a · n d u r a · ke̮s i vajis si̮we̮ vina· da ma. ke̮r sija śetis vina·se̮ da mase̮ i v a · n d u r a · kwe̮, to jua·wis, mi̮ľa si̮we̮n ćuńi̮s ke̮rta·we̮m. i v a · n d u r a · k i viśta·wis, što sija vetwis ve̮re̮ čakja·wni̮ i dojdis ćuńse̮. sek ńeve·sta če̮ktis pe̮rćća·wni̮, štobi̮ viǯe̮·tni̮, ki̮ǯ dojdis. ke̮r sija pe̮rćća·wis ćuńse̮, to kerku srazu· pondis jugja·wni̮. sek neve·sta bośtis i v a · n d u r a · ke̮s kieťťas, vaje̮·tis aji̮s di̮ne̮ da viśta·wis: “vot menam že̮ńi̮ke̮!” i v a · n d u r a · ke̮s miśśe̮·tise̮, paśte̮·tise̮ i wois sečče̮m bur mooďe·će̮n, ki̮če̮·m toľko owwe̮ skazkai̮n. sete̮n car srazu·-že̮ orsis svaďba. a i v a · n d u r a · k aswas ińkake̮t di̮r owis pi̮di̮n goddeze̮ǯ.

236. mun seććine̮, og te̮d ki̮će̮·, vaj sije̮, og te̮d, mi̮j!

1. owis e̮tik strelo·k carwe̮n, šuise̮ sije̮ a n d r e · j e n. a n d r e · j bi̮d wun vetwi̮wis ve̮re̮, vijwis pe̮tka da vaja·wis carske̮j kuχńà. vot e̮tik wune̮ munis sija ve̮re̮. vetwe̮·tis, vetwe̮·tis i ńe-kine̮s ez aǯǯi̮. ke̮r sija pondis bertni̮ gortas, to każa·wis, što pu ji̮vvi̮n puka·we̮ kaj. a n d r e · j meťi·ććis da vijis. kajis uśis. sija voktis si̮ di̮ne̮, bośtis sije̮ kias i każa·wis, što sija rańi·te̮m. a n d r e · j me̮dis sije̮ vijni̮, no sećće̮ kaji̮s mort-gowose̮n viśta·wis, štobi̮ sija sije̮ ez vij, a ke̮r woktas gortas, aś pukśe̮·te̮ e̮ši·nve̮ i vićći·śe̮, ke̮r kaji̮s pondas suna·śni̮. a ke̮r kaji̮s pondas suna·śni̮, to sija bi̮d vi̮niś veśki̮t kinas se̮te̮ si̮we (kaji̮s kuźa). sek sija aǯǯas aśśis śťaśťe. a n d r e · jwe̮ ďiwo wois, što kaji̮s baji·te̮ mort-gowose̮n. sija siǯ i keris. woktis gortas, puktis e̮ši̮·nve̮, pondis vićći·śni̮, ke̮r sija pondas suna·śni̮. ńe-di̮r mi̮jiś kaji̮s pondis suna·śni̮. a n d r e · j bi̮d vi̮niś se̮tis kaji̮s kuźa. i kaji̮s uśis ǯoǯe̮ i srazu-že̮ berge̮·ććis m a r j a c a r e · w-n ae̮. m a r j a c a r e · w n a sek si̮we̮ šuis: “raz te mene̮ kutin da kuž i viǯni̮ ćožǯi̮k pirvi̮n!” a n d r e · j siǯ i keris. ćoża we̮śe̮·tis pir i nija orsise̮ svaďba. sija owis aswas ińke̮t da vetwi̮wwis ve̮re̮.

2. vot e̮t-pi̮riś ińis i šue̮: “mije̮ bedneja owame̮.” sija če̮ktis bośni̮ a n d r e ·-je̮s šolk sto rubľe·jwe̮. a n d r e · j munis aswas tova·riššez di̮ne̮, e̮ktis kinwiś rube̮n, kinwiś ki̮ke̮n, sto rubľe·j. bośtis raznej šolkkez da vajis m a r j awe̮. marja če̮ktis vodni̮ a n d r e · je̮s da uźni̮, a aći̮s eta kade̮ pukśis ki̮jni̮ kovo·r.

trying to find out which one of them her bridegroom might be. But her bridegroom was not sitting among the guests at table. She noticed Stupid Ivan sitting in the corner by the stove and brought him wine and honey. When she was handing over the wine and the honey to him, she asked why his finger was wrapped up. Stupid Ivan told her how he had hurt his finger while picking mushrooms in the forest. Then the bride told him to remove the bandage so that she might see how he had hurt his finger. When he unwrapped his finger, the house immediately began to glow. Then the bride took Stupid Ivan by the hand and leading him to her father, said: "Look, here is my bridegroom!" They washed Stupid Ivan, gave him new clothes, and he changed into a gallant young man the like of whom only exists in tales. The Tsar immediately arranged the wedding there. Stupid Ivan lived for a long time, for many years, together with his wife.

236. Go I-know-not-where, bring I-know-not-what!

1. Once upon a time the Tsar had a marksman called Andrej. Day by day Andrej went to the forest: he shot wild-fowl and brought them to the Tsar's kitchen. One day he walked into the forest. He walked and walked without finding anything. As he was about to return home, he noticed a bird sitting on the top of a tree. Andrej aimed at it and brought it down. The bird fell down. He walked over to it, took it in his hand and saw that it was hurt. Andrej was about to kill it, when it spoke up in a human voice, asking him not to kill it, but when he got home put it in the window and wait until it began to fall into slumber. When it began to fall into slumber, he must strike at the bird with all his might, with his right hand. Then he would find his own good fortune. Andrej marvelled at the bird speaking in a human voice. He did as was told. He came home and put the bird in the window and began to wait for it to fall asleep. In a short while the bird began to fall into slumber. With all his might Andrej struck at the bird. The bird fell down on the floor and changed immediately into the Tsar's daughter Marja. Then the Tsar's daughter Marja said to him: "Now that you have caught me, you must make a feast as soon as you can!" So Andrej did. He gave a feast and they arranged a wedding. He lived with his wife, and continued hunting in the forest.

2. Then one day his wife said: "We are living poorly." Andrej had a hundred roubles worth of silk bought. Andrej went around his friends and collected a hundred roubles: from this one, from that two. He bought various kinds of silk and took them to Marja. Marja told Andrej to go to

ętik ojęn sija kįjis kovo·rsę. ašįnas, kęr andre·j ćeććis, sija śetis sįwę kovo·rsę i čęktis uza·wnį. seććę marja viśta·wis andre·jwę, štobį sija uza·wis kovo·rsę sįwę, kin pervęj śetas ćena·sę. vot andre·j puktis kovo·rsę kivvas i munis torgo·węj wawkaez ożęt. sįwę panįt kotę·rtis kupe·ć i jua·wis andre·jwiś, uza·was-ľi sįwę kovo·rsę. andre·j viśta·wis, što uza·was. kupeć jua·wis: "mįmda koran kovo·rįs ponda?" andre·j ez pondį duma·jtnį i viśta·wis: "te mortįs torgo·węj, te i śet cena·sę!" eta kadę seććę ekśisę una· kupe·ććez i pondisę duma·jtnį, mįmda sįwę śetnį cena·sę. no ńe-kin ez vermį viśta·wnį ńem. seti kak raz kare·taęn munis carskęj sove·tńik. sija kaźa·wis, što kupe·ćces mįj-kę ekśęmaś i spori·tęnį. carskęj sove·tńik ćeććis da munis vįżę·tnį. sija jeľe pįris towpa· śęras andre·j dįnę. kęr sija kaźa·wis kovo·rsę, to sija dįr ńem ez vermį viśta·wnį. eta kovo·rvįn vęi bįdę·s carstvoįs goroddezęn, ďere·wńaezęn, įbbezęn, źverrezęn da kajjezęn. sija jua·wis andre·jwiś, mįmda sija korę cena·sę. andre·j viśta·wis, mįmda śetas, sįmda i wadnę woas. sek carskęj sove·tńik kįskis košeľo·k da śetis eta kovo·r ponda ďeśiť tįśić rubľe·j. boštis kovo·rsę da munis car ordę. woktis sija car dįnę i mįćća·wis sįwę kovo·rsę. car kįż vįżę·tis kovo·rvas, sįż viśta·wis: "mįj kowę, boś, a kovo·rsę og śet." car kįskis kęšeľo·kęn ďeńga da śetis sove·tńikiswę dvaćeť tįśić. a sove·tńik duma·jtįštis: 'no i wadnę, me eśę· buržįkę zakažįta.' sija pukśis kare·taę, woktis slobo·daę, kįtęn owis andre·j. ażźis kerkusę i pįris. sija ośtis įbę·ssę, ęt koknas pįris kerkuę, a mędnas ez ještį. sija kaźa·wis marja care·vnaęs i srazu· kįnmis mestaas, sečćęm sija vęi basęk. marja vićći·śis, vićći·śis, bergę·tis siję peľ-po·nnezęťťas da pędna·wis įbę·ssę.

3. *carskęj sove·tńik eta kadśiń śoję i oz śoj, juę i oz ju. etę kaźa·wis car i sija jua·wis, mįj sįkęt wois. carskęj sove·tńik viśta·is sįwę, miľa sija sečćęm wois. carwę oχo·ta wois vįżę·tnį strelo·kįs ińwę. sija paśtaśis prostę·j paśkęmę da munis andre·jis ordę. ośtis įbę·ssę, ęt koknas pįris, a mędnas ez ještį. sija srazu·-żę kįnmis mestaas. marja vićći·śis, vićći·śis, boštis caręs peľ-po·nnezęťťas, bergę·tis da pędna·wis įbę·ssę. car vęi gętįrtęm i sįwę uśis umeľ duma: miľa etę sį strelo·kwęn sečćęm basęk ińis, a sija gętįrtęm. marjawę ownį ńe streľči·χaęn, a ćare·vnaęn. woktis gortas car, koris carskęj sove·tńikes da viśta·wis, štobį sija duma·jtis, kićę· ińdę·tnį andre·jęs, štobį sija bęr ez bert.*

bed and sleep while she sat down to weave a carpet. She sat up the whole night and finished the carpet. When Andrej got up next morning, she handed him the carpet and ordered him to sell it. Marja told Andrej to sell the carpet to the first man that would pay its price. Taking the carpet on his arm, Andrej started out for the merchants' shops. A merchant has run up to him, and asked: "How much do you want for the carpet?" Not willing to give a thought to it, Andrej said: "You are a merchant, you fix its price." Meanwhile many merchants gathered together, and they tried to find it out how much they ought to pay. But nobody could say anything. The Tsar's counsellor happened to be passing by in his coach. He noticed that the merchants had come together and that they were having a debate. The Tsar's counsellor jumped down and went over to find out what the matter was. He had hardly reached Andrej in the middle of the crowd when he saw the carpet; for a long time he could not say a word. On that carpet there were to be seen all the towns, villages, fields, beasts and birds of the whole empire of the Tsar. He asked Andrej how much he wanted for it. Andrej replied that he would be contented with what the counsellor would give. Then the Tsar's counsellor produced his purse and handed him ten thousand roubles for the carpet. He took the carpet, and went to the Tsar. He came to the Tsar and showed him the carpet. As the Tsar caught a glimpse of the carpet, he said: "Take whatever you want, but I will not give you the carpet." The Tsar produced his purse and gave the counsellor twenty thousand. Then the counsellor thought to himself: "Very well, I shall order a still better one." He got in his coach and rode to the free village where Andrej was living. He found the house and entered it. He opened the door and put one leg inside, but was unable to move the other. He caught a glimpse of the Tsar's daughter Marja, and he froze to the spot, so beautiful was she. Marja waited and waited, then turned him round, seizing him by the shoulder, and closed the door.

3. From that time onwards the Tsar's counsellor was eating and was not eating, drinking and not drinking. The Tsar noticed this, and asked what had happened to him. The Tsar's counsellor told him all about it. The Tsar had a desire to see the marksman's wife. He dressed in simple clothes and went to Andrej's house. He opened the door, put one foot inside, but he was unable to move the other. At once he froze to the spot. Marja waited and waited, then she seized the Tsar by the shoulder, turned him round, and locked the door. The Tsar was unmarried, and a wicked thought occurred to him: why should the marksman have such a beautiful wife while he was unmarried? Marja ought to live not as a marksman's wife but as a Tsar's wife. The Tsar went home and called the Tsar's counsellor. He told

jeśľi sija oz duma·jt, to sija če̮ktas kera·wni̮ jurse̮ sove·tńikwe̮. sove·tńik te̮ž-di·śe̮me̮n munis gortas, no tujvas sija pi̮ris kaba·ke̮. koris vina· da pondis juni̮. si̮ di̮ne̮ kote̮·rti̮štis kaba·cke̮j ńišše̮j. sove·tńik si̮we̮ viśta·wis: "mun te tatiś, kabacke̮j ńišše̮j!" kaba·cke̮j ńišše̮j si̮we̮ višta·wis: "te meni̮m suwte̮·t lučše staka·n vina; a me teni̮t možet mi̮j-ńi-buď otsa·wa." carske̮j sove·tńik śetis ńiššejwe̮ staka·n vina· da bi̮de̮·s viśta·śis. kabacke̮j ńišše̮j viśta·wis, što a n d-r e · jse̮ možno ćoža ne̮be̮·tni̮, a vot ińi̮s si̮we̮n e̮ďďe̮·n ńi χitre̮j. i vot viśta·wis si̮we̮, štobi̮ a n d r e · j vetwis me̮d śvetas đa aʒ́ʒ́i̮wis poko·jne̮j car baťuskase̮. se̮ve·tńik siǯ i keris. munis car di̮ne̮ da viśta·wis, car koris di̮nas a n d r e · je̮s đa viśta·wis si̮we̮: "bura te meni̮m služi·tan. služi·t meni̮m e̮tik služba! vetwi̮ me̮d śvetas da aʒ́ʒ́i̮w menćim poko·jne̮j aje̮s!" a n d r e · j e̮še̮·tis jurse̮ đa woktis gortas. sija bi̮de̮·s viśta·wis ińi̮swe̮, mi̮j sije̮ če̮ktis kerni̮ cari̮s. m a r j a care·wna seće viśta·wis: "ete̮ toľko eše̮· službi·ška, a službai̮s voas oʒ́as." sija če̮ktis a n d r e · je̮s vodni̮. a m a r j ai̮s ośtis ńigaez da pondis wi̮ďďi̮ni̮, kiǯ munni̮ me̮d śvetas da aʒ́ʒ́i̮·wni̮ poko·jne̮j car baťuškase̮. aši̮nas, ke̮r a n d r e · j ćeććis, m a r j a śetis si̮we̮ koľe·ćko i če̮ktis munni̮ eta koľe·ćko śe̮ri̮n. a štobi̮ cari̮s veri·tis, to aś bośte̮ tova·rišše̮ carske̮j se̮ve·tńike̮s. a n d r e · j siǯ i keris. bośtis tova·rišše̮ carske̮j se̮ve·tńike̮s da munise̮ nija koľe·ćko śe̮ri̮n. di̮r nija munise̮ i vot woktise̮ nija pemi̮t ve̮re̮. koľe·ćko sek dugdis tare̮·wćći̮ni̮ daľše. sek a n d r e · j da se̮ve·tńik pukśise̮ da pondise̮ e̮be̮da·jtni̮ suχarreze̮n. eze̮ ješte̮ e̮be̮da·jtni̮, ki̮ǯ nija pervo ki̮wise̮, a si̮ be̮ri̮n kaźa·wise̮, ki̮ǯ ki̮k ćort dođďa·e̮-maś morte̮s ťeľe·gae̮, ki̮će̮· ve̮i teće̮ma una· pes. a n d r e · j kaźa·wis, što eta poko·jne̮j car baťuška. sija pondis korni̮ ćorttezwiś, štobi̮ nija weǯwise̮ ńe-di̮rik keže̮ poko·jne̮j carse̮ baji·ti̮šni̮. a ćorttes i šue̮ni̮: "a mije̮ aśni̮m ńi mi̮j-ľi ki̮skame̮ pesse̮?" a n d r e · j šuis: "me tijanwe̮ śeta poka· sveže̮j morte̮s." ćorttes weǯise̮ poko·jne̮j carse̮ da dođďa·wise̮ se̮ve·tńike̮s. a n d r e · j jua·wis cari̮swiś, ki̮ǯ owe̮mi̮s si̮we̮n. car i šuis, owe̮mi̮s si̮we̮n e̮ďďe̮·n ume̮ľ. i sija će̮ktis viśta·wni̮ a n d r e · jwe̮, štobi̮ zoni̮s ńem ume̮ľse̮ ez ker. eze̮ ješte̮ nija baji·tni̮, ki̮ď ćorttes proste̮·j ťeľe·gàn bertise̮ uže· be̮r. a n d r e · j boštis se̮ve·tńikse̮ da ińde̮·ććis gortwańe̮. ke̮r sija woktis i carwe̮ viśta·wis, što sija aʒ́ʒ́i̮wis poko·jne̮j car baťuškase̮ i poko·jne̮j car baťuška če̮ktis si̮we̮ ńem ume̮ľse̮ ńe kerni̮, car ez pondi̮ veri·tni̮. sek a n d r e · j viśta·wis, jeśľi sija oz veri·t, to aś jua·we̮ se̮ve·t-ńikse̮, ke̮dawe̮n emeś śińa·kkez polući·te̮me̮ś me̮d śvetas. car sek veri·tis i eše̮·

him to plan some journey on which Andrej might be sent never to return. If he failed to devise something, he would have the counsellor's head cut off. The counsellor returned home sadly, but on his way he entered the inn. He asked for wine and started to drink. The beggar at the inn ran up to him. The counsellor said to him: "Clear out, you beggar from the inn!" The beggar from the inn said to him: "Better set a glass of wine in front of me, for I might be of some use to you!" The Tsar's counsellor gave a glass of wine to the beggar and told him everything. The beggar said that Andrej could be removed quickly, but that his wife was very shrewd. He told him that Andrej should go to the nether world to find the deceased Father Tsar. The counsellor acted accordingly. He went to the Tsar and told him about the plan. The Tsar called Andrej and said to him: "You serve me well. Will you do a favour for me? Go to the nether world and find my deceased father!" Andrej lowered his head and walked home. He related to his wife all the Tsar had ordered him to do. The Tsar's daughter Marja said to him: "This is a minor duty to perform, the really difficult one is still in store for you." She told Andrej to go to bed. And Marja opened up the books and began to read how to go to the nether world to find the deceased Father Tsar. When Andrej got up in the morning, Marja gave him a ring, and ordered him to follow where the ring led. And in order to make the Tsar believe him, he should take the Tsar's counsellor as a companion on the way. Andrej acted accordingly. He took the Tsar's counsellor as his companion, and they started off after the ring. They followed the ring for a long time. They arrived in a dark forest. There Andrej and the Tsar's counsellor sat down and began to eat biscuits for lunch. They had not yet finished their lunch when first they heard, then they saw two devils harnessing a man to a cart loaded with a lot of wood. Andrej noticed that it was the deceased Father Tsar. He asked the devils to set the deceased Tsar free for a short while because he wanted to chat with him. But the devils said: "Are we to pull the load of wood ourselves?" Andrej replied: "I'll give you a fresh man instead." The devils set the deceased Tsar free and harnessed the counsellor to the cart. Andrej asked the Tsar how he was faring. The Tsar said he was leading a wretched life. He asked Andrej to tell his son not to do any evil deed. They had not yet finished their talk when the devils returned with the empty cart. Andrej took the counsellor and started for home. When he arrived home, and told the Tsar that he had found the deceased Father Tsar, who ordered his son not to do any evil deed, the Tsar refused to believe him. Then Andrej said to him that if he did not believe him he should consult the counsellor who had acquired blue bruises in the nether world. Then the Tsar believed him and grew

ed̕d̕ę·nžįk węga·śis. i čęktis duma·jtnį sęve·tńikwę, kįćę ińdę·tnį a n d r e · jęs, štobį sija bęr ez bert.

4. *sęve·tńik munis bęra· kaba-kę da vi̇śta·wis kabackęj ńiššęjwę. ńiššęj koris bęra· staka·n vina· da duma·jtįštis. sį bęrįn vi̇śta·wis, što seččęm gosuda·rstvòn em kot baju·n. sęve·tńik kotę·rtis car ordę da vi̇śta·wis, kįćę· ińdę·tnį a n d- r e · jęs. car, znaćit, srazu· koris a n d r e · jęs i čęktis vaję·tni k o t b a j u · nęs. a n d r e · j ešę ed̕d̕ę·nžįk ešę·tis jursę da woktis gortas i vi̇śta·śis bįdę·s ińįswę. ińįs čęktis vodnį a n d r e · jęs da uźnį. a m a r j às eta poraę čęktis kuźńeććez dornį kuji·m kęrtowęj kowpa·k, kl̕ešši·ez, kujim śat̕-kod̕ bed̕d̕ez: ętiksę kęrtowęję, mędsę mednęję, a kujmętsę olovja·nnęję. kęr ašįnas a n d r e · j ćeććis, to m a r j a śetis sįwę kuji·m kęrtowęj kowpa·k, kl̕ešši·ez i kuji·m śat̕-kod̕ bed̕ i vi̇śta·wis: te pę on wok k o t b a j u · nįs dįnęž kuji·m versta, kįž pondan suna·śnį, te en vod, a n d r e · j ! tol̕ko vodan, kįd̕ srazu·-že tenę k o t b a j u · nįs vijas.” a n d r e · j kįwzis etę i munis aswas tujęt. dįr sija munis i vot sija woktis k o t b a j u · n dįnęž. siję pondis vermįnį on, no a n d r e · j ez vod i woktis kotįs dįnęž. kotįs ćeććę·wtis a n d r e · jvę i žugdis kįk kowpa·ksę. tol̕ko mędis sija žugdįnį kujmę·tsę, no sija ez ještį. a n d r e · j kutis siję kl̕ešši·en i pondis vartwįnį kęrtowęj bedęn. vartwis dotovo· siję, što ćegwa·wis kęrto·węj bed̕sę. sija boštis mednęj bed̕sę i mednęj bed̕sė ćegwa·wis. sek a n d r e · j boštis olovja·nnęj bed̕sę i pondis sijęn vartwįnį. eta bed̕is vei ńebįt. sija oz ćeg, a kęsta·śę. sek k o t b a j u · n pondis kornį, štob a n d r e · j bol̕še ez vartwį siję. a n d r e · j sek sįwę vi̇śta·wis, štobį sija munis sį śerę. k o t b a j u · n munis a n d r e · jkęt. woktisę nija aššanįs carstvoę i munisę car ordę. i a n d r e · j mįćća·wis carwę k o t b a j u · nęs. car ešę ed̕d̕ę·nžįk węga·śis i čęktis sęve·tńikęs duma·jtnį ešę·, kįž a n d r e · jęs vijnį.*

5. *sęve·tńik munis bęra· kaba·kę i vi̇śta·wis etę kaba·ckęj ńiššęjwę. kaba·ckęj ńiššęj vi̇śta·wis sek, štob car ińdę·tis a n d r e · jęs seććinę, og tęd kįćę· i vajis siję, og tęd, mįj. car koris dįnas a n d r e · jęs i vi̇śta·wis, štob munis sija, og tęd, kįćę· i vajis siję, og tęd, mįj. a n d r e · j woktis m a r j a dįnę da vi̇śta·śis. m a r j a čęktis vodnį a n d r e · jęs. a aćįs koris bįd-kod̕ kajjezęs da źverrezęs i jua·wis nįwiś, kįćę· munnį, štob ažžįnį og-tęd-mįj. zverrez da kajjez ńem ez vi̇śta·w, sić-kę nija ez tędę. m a r j a sek koris kįk vel̕ika·nes i čęktis nębę·tnį okea·n šerę. vel̕ika·nnes nębę·tisę m a r j aęs okea·n šerę.*

still more angry, and ordered the counsellor to think where to send Andrej never to return.

4. The counsellor returned to the inn and told the beggar at the inn of his troubles. Again the beggar asked him for a glass of wine and began to ponder. Then he said that Tomcat Bajun was living in such and such a state. The counsellor hurried to the Tsar and told him where to send Andrej. The Tsar called Andrej and ordered him to go and fetch Tomcat Bajun. Andrej dropped his head still lower, went home and told the whole story to his wife. His wife told him to go to bed and sleep. Meanwhile Marja gave orders to the blacksmiths to forge three caps of iron, tongs and three sticks, one of iron, the second of copper and the third of tin. When Andrej got up next morning, Marja handed him the three iron caps, the tongs and the three sticks, saying: "When you get to within three miles of Tomcat Bajun, you will begin to feel sleepy, but do not lie down to sleep, Andrej! As soon as you lie down, Tomcat Bajun will kill you." Andrej listened to this and started on his way. He went on for a long time, and at last came to Tomcat Bajun. He was nearly overcome by sleep, but Andrej did not lie down, but went straight to the Tomcat. The Tomcat leapt at Andrej and broke two of the caps. He was just about to break the third, but he had not time to do so. Andrej seized him with the tongs and began to thresh him with the iron stick. He threshed him until the iron rod was broken. Then he took the copper rod, but the Tomcat broke the copper rod as well. Then Andrej took the tin rod and started to thresh with it. That rod was flexible, it did not break but bent. Then Tomcat Bajun asked Andrej not to beat him any longer. Andrej commanded him to follow him. Tomcat Bajun went along with Andrej. They arrived in their own tsardom, and went to the Tsar. And Andrej showed Tomcat Bajun to the Tsar. The Tsar grew still more angry and ordered the counsellor to think again and find out how to kill Andrej.

5. Again the counsellor went to the inn and told the story to the beggar at the inn. Then the beggar at the inn said that the Tsar should send Andrej to I-know-not-where and fetch I-know-not-what. The Tsar called Andrej and told him to go to I-know-not-where and fetch I-know-not-what. Andrej came to Marja and told her everything. Marja ordered him to go to bed. And she called all kinds of birds and beasts, asking them where to go to find I-know-not-what. The beasts and birds did not say anything, because they did not know. Then Marja called two giants, and commanded them to take her to the middle of the ocean. The giants carried Marja to the middle of the ocean. There Marja called the fish together and asked them where to find I-know-not-what. The fish did not know. When Andrej got up next morning, Marja gave him a ball of thread and a towel, telling him to dry

seććin m a r j a koris ćeriezes da pondis jua·wni̮, ki̮te̮·n em og-te̮d-mi̮j. ćeries tože ez te̮de̮. aši̮nas, ke̮r a n d r e · j ćeććis, m a r j a śetis siwe̮ kwubo·k suńi·se̮n da ćiške̮·t i če̮ktis ki̮te̮·n-bi̮ ez ve̮w ći̮ški·śni̮ toľko si̮ ćiške̮·te̮n. a n d r e · j munis i di̮r mi̮jiś woktis baba-jaga· orde̮. pi̮ris si̮ orde̮, a baba-jaga· puka·we̮ wabi·ć dori̮n da kuďe·ľ pećke̮. baba-jaga· i šuis seććе̮: "este̮n ńe ez ki̮w ruske̮j du̮χe̮n?" a e̮ni aći̮s sija woktis si̮ di̮ne̮. "vot me tene̮ žari·ta, śoja da koskaezvat tupľa·śa." a n d r e · j seććе̮ šuis: "me ve̮i di̮r tuji̮n, greźe̮·ś me, ume̮·ľći i woi ćori̮t. te mene̮ lučše mišše̮·t bańàn, verd da si̮ be̮ri̮n i śoj!" baba-jaga· wontis bańa, mišše̮·tis. ke̮r a n d r e · j pondis ći̮ški·śni̮ aswas ćiške̮·te̮n, to baba-jaga· jua·wis: "ki̮ti·ś tenat eta menam ni̮wwe̮n ći̮ške̮·ti̮s?" a n d r e · j viśta·wis, što sija si̮we̮n iń. baba-jaga· srazu·že̮ pukśe̮·tis pi̮za·n saje̮, pondis poću·jtni̮ bi̮d-koď vina·eze̮n da maeze̮n. eta kosta·e̮ a n d r e · j viśta·śis, kiće̮· sija mune̮. baba-jaga· duma·jti̮štis da viśta·wis, što sija oz te̮d, ki̮te̮·n sija em. no ete̮ dowže̮n te̮dni̮ si̮we̮n babi̮s ľagu·ška, ke̮da owe̮ bowo·tòn trista ľet. baba-jaga· votte̮·tis a n d r e · je̮s, a aći̮s ge̮ńi·tis rossezvi̮n bowo·to dore̮. sija koris ľagu·ška babe̮s da jua·wis, ki̮te̮·n em sija og-te̮d-mi̮j. ľagu·ška bab viśta·wis, što sija te̮de̮, ki̮te̮·n i sija otsa·was baba-jaga· źaťwe̮ sije̮ aǯǯi̮ni̮, toľko aś a n d r e · j krinkàn je̮we̮n ne̮be̮·te̮ ľagu·šase̮ bija ju di̮ne̮. a n d r e · j siǯ i keris. ne̮be̮·tis staru·kae̮s bija ju di̮ne̮ǯ i sije̮ seććin ki̮skis je̮wśis. ľagu·ša če̮ktis pukśi̮ni̮ a n d r e · je̮s si̮vve̮. a n d r e · j pukśis ľagu·škavve̮ i sija pondis pe̮ľći̮ni̮. pe̮ľććis, pe̮ľććis i wois wi̮i̮nži̮k śed ve̮rśa. ľagu·ška ćeććе̮·wtis bija juse̮ i če̮ktis munni̮ a n d r e · je̮s daľše. seććin sija kaźa·wis kerku ńe kerku, sara·j ńe sara·j. seććin sija dowže̮n pi̮rni̮ i ǯebśi·śni̮ gor saje̮. seććin sija aǯǯas og-te̮d-mi̮j. a n d r e · j munis, aǯǯis ete̮ kerkuse̮, pi̮ris seććine̮ da ǯebśi·śis gor saje̮. skoro sija ki̮wis, kiǯ bi̮de̮·s pondis gi̮ma·wni̮ da tre̮śi·ććini̮ kerku̮is. kerkuas pi̮ris miži̮ćo·k, ćuń i̮žda. sija pi̮ris i gore̮·tis: "svat n a u · m, vaj śojni̮!" i drug kiśa·ń-ke̮ kerku še̮re̮ kin-ke̮ suwte̮·tis pi̮za·n. pi̮za·nvas puktis puem me̮s-tuša· da boćo·nok sur. miži̮ćo·k ete̮ bi̮de̮·s śojis da munis. a n d r e · j powe̮me̮n petis gor sajiś da šuis: "svat n a u · m, dava·j śojni̮!" kerku še̮re̮ kin-ke̮ suwte̮·tis pi̮za·n razne̮j zaku·skaeze̮n da vina·eze̮n. a n d r e · j pukśis da śojis: "svat n a u · m, pukśi̮, śojame̮ e̮twai̮n!" i drug andre·j kaźa·wis, što pi̮za·nwiś śoja·nse̮ kin-ke̮ kiǯ rose̮n ćiške̮. vina·i̮s aći̮s kišše rumkaeze̮, a rumkaes skok da skok ćećća·e̮ni̮. a n d r e · j jua·wis: "svat n a u · m, munam meke̮t?" "muna, dobre̮j mort, me este̮n oa uže· ńe eča, a ńe-ke̮r eše̮ eg śoj." vot a n d r e · j woktis bija ju di̮ne̮, ćeććе̮·wtis ľagu·škake̮t bija ju vewde̮ret i

himself only with that towel wherever he might be. Andrej set out on the way, and after a long while he came to a witch. He entered her hut, and the witch was sitting on a bench, spinning oakum. Then the witch said: "Isn't that a Russian smell over there?" Well, he himself now came over to her. "I shall roast you and eat you, and I shall roll on your bones." Then Andrej answered: "I have come a long way, I am dirty, I have become lean and tough. Better give me a bath in the bath-house, then food, and then eat me!" The witch heated the bath-house and bathed him. When Andrej started to dry himself with his own towel, the witch asked him: "Where did you get my daughter's towel?" Andrej answered that she was his own wife. At once the witch seated him at the table and feasted him on all kinds of wine and honey. Meanwhile Andrej explained to her where he was going. The witch pondered for a little while and said that she did not know where the place was. But her frog-grandmother must know about it, having lived for three hundred years in the swamp. The witch put Andrej to bed, and she herself rode on her broomstick to the swamp. She asked her frog-grandmother where I-know-not-what was to be found. The frog-grandmother answered she knew where it was and she would help the witch's son-in-law to find it, only let Andrej take her (the frog) in a milk jug to the fiery river. Andrej acted accordingly. He took the old dame to the fiery river and there pulled her out of the milk. The frog ordered Andrej to sit on her. Andrej sat on the frog, and the frog began to puff herself up. She puffed and puffed until she had grown taller than the dark forest. The frog jumped over the fiery river and commanded Andrej to continue his way. There he would catch sight of something: a house, yet not a house, and a barn, yet not a barn. He must enter it and hide behind the stove. There he would find I-know-not-what. Andrej set out and found the house, entered it, and hid behind the stove. Soon he heard it beginning to thunder, and the house began to shake. A little man the size of a thumb entered. He entered and shouted: "My Spouse Naum, bring me something to eat!" All of a sudden a table was set by somebody in the middle of the house. A boiled cow's rump and a small barrel of beer were placed on the table. The small man ate and drank all this, and then went away. Andrej came fearfully out from behind the stove and said: "Spouse Naum, give me something to eat!" A table was laid by somebody in the middle of the house, with various bits of food and wine. Andrej sat down and began to eat: "Spouse Naum, sit down and let us eat together!" Andrej suddenly noticed that the food vanished from the table as if someone had swept it away with a broom. Wine was poured of its own accord into the glasses, and the glasses hopped around. Andrej asked: "Spouse Naum, will you come with me?"

weʒ́is sije̮. ńewwe̮ [ɔ: ńe-i̮we̮] munis a n d r e · j i jua·wis: "svat n a u · m, te tate̮n?" "me — šue̮ — muna te śe̮re̮." a n d r e · j munis, munis i mi̮ʒ́is i siʒ́ šuis: "vot-bi̮ gorte̮ wokni̮!" a svat n a u · m sećće̮ i ši̮a·śis: "važi̮·n ńi kowis viśta·wni̮. śića·s te woan gorti̮n." drug a n d r e · je̮s te̮w-ćik weptis ńeboas da pondis ne̮be̮·tni̮ gortwańe̮. ke̮r a n d r e · j webźis okea·n veśte̮·t, to si̮e̮n juri̮s pondis berga·wni̮. sija šuis: "šoćći·šni̮!" te̮w-ćik pondis weʒ́ni̮ a n d r e · je̮s okea·n še̮re̮ ostrovve̮. drug ostrowi̮n wois dvore·c. a n d r e · j pi̮ris eta dvore·ce̮. sete̮n nija svat n a · u mke̮t šoćći·śi̮štise̮ da e̮be̮da·jtise̮. svat n a u · m viśta·wis a n d r e · jwe̮, što skoro pondase̮ ujni̮ ostrowi̮s di̮ne̮t kuji·m kupe·ćeske̮j kora·beľ. ena kupe·ććezwe̮n eme̮ś kuji·m ďiko·wine̮j veššez. svat n a u · m če̮ktis vežni̮ a n d r e · je̮s sije̮ ena ďiko·wine̮j veššezve̮. skoro eta ostrovve̮ woktise̮ kuji·m kupe·ć. nija jua·wise̮ i pondise̮ korni̮ a n d r e · je̮s, štobi̮ sija vežis svat n a u · me̮s ďiko·wine̮j zorve̮, ćerve̮ da dudkave̮. a n d r e · j vežis svat n a u · me̮s etna veššezwe̮. a ge̮śśeze̮s a n d r e · j poću·jtis siʒ́, što nija ki̮te̮·n puka·wise̮, sete̮n i e̮nme̮·śśise̮.

6. a n d r e · j eta kade̮ svat n a u · nke̮t munise̮ aswani̮s carstvoe. woktis a n d r e · j gortas, a si̮we̮n kerku sote̮m, toľko e̮tik truba te̮rći·te̮. a ińi̮s abu. sek munis a n d r e · j more dore̮, pukśis i pondis te̮ždi·śni̮. eta kade̮ ki̮śa·ń-ke̮ webźi̮štis si̮ di̮ne̮ kaj, uśis muvve̮ i berge̮·ććis m a r j a care·wnae̮. svat n a u · m eta kade̮ bereg dore suwte̮·tis dvore·c. pondise̮ owni̮ eta dvore·ci̮n a n d r e · j aswas ińke̮t. e̮t-pi̮riś car munis oχoťićći̮ni̮ i kaźa·wis more dori̮n dvore·c. sija we̮ga·wis, kin ete̮ stroji·tis si̮ muvvi̮n ši̮ śetteg dvore·c. ke̮r si̮we̮ viśta·wise̮, što sete̮n owe̮ a n d r e · j m a r j a care·vnake̮t, eše̮· e̮dďe̮·nźik we̮ga·śis car. sija e̮ktis i̮ʒ́i̮t armija da ińde̮·ććis a n d r e · j dvore·cve̮. a n d-r e · j ki̮ʒ́ kaźa·wis, što si̮ dvore·c di̮ne̮ wokte̮ i̮ʒ́i̮t armija, to boštis ćer, berge̮·tis sije̮ ji̮wnas ue̮ i ćeri̮s aći̮s pondis maka·jtni̮. ki̮ʒ́ makńi·tas, siʒ́ i voe̮ kora·beľ matro·sseze̮n da puškaeze̮n. ćeri̮s makńi·tis stoiś voise̮ sto kora·beľ. eta be̮ri̮n a n d r e · j boštis dudka da pondis pe̮ľtni̮ e̮t końe·ćas i srazu·-že pondise̮ dud-kaiś ćećća·wni̮ solda·ttez. siʒ́ a n d r e · j e̮ktis i̮ʒ́i̮t armija i če̮ktis ponde̮·tni̮ sraže·ńńo. eta kade̮ a n d r e · j boštis zor da če̮ktis sije̮ vijni̮ ćarse̮. zor vijis carse̮, a armija pi̮ššis. naro·d sek koris owni̮ care̮n ni̮ gosuda·rstvòn a n d-r e · je̮s.

"I will, my friend. It is not a short time I have been living here yet I have never been offered anything to eat." Andrej and Spouse Naum started off. Andrej got to the fiery river; he jumped over the fiery river with the help of the frog, which he then dismissed. Andrej went a little farther on and asked: "Spouse Naum, are you there?" "I am following" — said he — "behind you." Andrej went on and on and grew tired. He said: "It is time we were at home!" Spouse Naum said: "You ought to have told me long before. You will be home immediately." Suddenly Andrej was lifted up in the air by a whirlwind, which began to take him home. When he flew over the ocean, Andrej began to feel giddy. He said: "Let us have a rest!" The whirlwind began to bring Andrej down to an island in the middle of the ocean. A palace suddenly appeared on the island. He entered the palace. Spouse Naum and he rested and lunched there. Spouse Naum said to Andrej that soon there would be three merchant ships sailing by the island. These merchants had three magic things. Spouse Naum told Andrej to exchange him for these magic things. Soon the three merchants arrived at the island. They questioned Andrej and begged him to exchange Spouse Naum for the magic stick, axe and bagpipes. Andrej exchanged Spouse Naum for these things. Andrej gave such a rich feast to the guests that they fell asleep where they were sitting.

6. In the meanwhile Andrej, together with Spouse Naum, arrived in their own tsardom. Andrej reached his house. His house was burnt down; only the chimmey remained standing. His wife was nowhere to be seen. Then Andrej went to the seashore and began to grieve. In the meanwhile a bird flew to him from somewhere, fell to the ground and changed into the Tsar's daughter Marja. Spouse Naum meanwhile erected a palace on the shore. Andrej began to live in this palace together with his wife. Once the Tsar went hunting and caught sight of the palace on the shore. He grew angry. Who had built a palace on his land without his permission? When he was told that Andrej and the Tsar's daughter Marja were living there, he was still more angry. He collected a powerful army and set out to attack the palace. When Andrej noticed the big army coming to the palace, he took the axe and turned it with its head down. The axe began to beat about by itself. As it swung to and fro, a ship arrived full of sailors and cannons. The axe made a hundred swings and a hundred ships arrived. Then Andrej took the bagpipes and began to blow them at one end, and soldiers sprang out of the bagpipe at once. In this way Andrej collected a large army and gave orders to start battle. Meanwhile Andrej took out the stick and commanded it to kill the Tsar. The Tsar was killed by the stick, and the army fled. Then the people asked Andrej to be the Tsar in their country.

237. *iva·n care·vić da ke̯ji·n*

1. *ois-ve̯is car b e r e · ń ď e j. si̯e̯n ve̯wise̯ kuji·m zon: i̯ǯi̯tǯi̯kse̯ šuise̯ ṕ o t r care·vić, še̯re̯·tse̯ šuise̯ f́ o d o r care·vić, a med tom zonse̯ šuise̯ i v a · n care·viće̯n. eta carwe̯n ve̯wi i̯ǯi̯t sad. i eta sadi̯n bi̯dmis si̯we̯n e̯tik jablońńa, ke̯da·we̯n jablokkez tomme̯·tise̯ bide̯·nni̯se̯. i vot sija kaźa·wis, što jablokkese̯ pondis kin-ke̯ guśa·wni̯. i vot sija ińde̯·tis e̯tik oje̯ karau·ľitni̯ med pe̯riś zonse̯. med pe̯riś zon ńe-di̯rik puka·i̯štis e̯te̯ras; pi̯ris sara·je̯ da ostatki ojse̯ uźis. ke̯r asi̯wnas woktis aji̯s di̯ne̯, to si̯we̯ viśta·wis, što sija ńe-kine̯·s ez aǯǯi̯·w. me̯d ojas munis karau·ľitni̯ jablokkez še̯re̯·t zoni̯s. no sija tože ńe-kine̯·s ez aǯǯi̯·w, sić-ke̯ ojse̯ sija uźis tože̯ sara·ji̯n. kujme̯t ojas munis karau·ľitni̯ i v a · n care·vić. sija puka·wis, puka·wis i drug kaźa·wis, što sadi̯n wois jugi̯tǯi̯k. sija woktis jablońńa di̯ne̯ i kaźa·wis, što jablokkese̯ śoje̯ žar-kaj. i v a · n care·vić žage̯·ńike̯n woktis da kutis be̯že̯ťťis kajse̯. no kaji̯s ďorńiććis i webźis. i v a · n kii̯n koľććis toľko e̯tik bord-ti̯(w)i̯p. asi̯wnas i v a · n care·vić woktis aji̯s di̯ne̯ da viśta· wis, što vorse̯ sija aǯǯi̯·wis, a kutni̯ ez vermi̯. i śetis aji̯swe̯ e̯tik bord-ti̯ipse̯ žar-kajwiś. eta kadśiń car wois veśo·le̯j. di̯r mi̯jiś sija viśta·wis pirvi̯n, kin si̯we̯ kutas da vajas žar-kaj, to si̯we̯ sija śetas ǯi̯n carstvose̯.*

2. *vot i tuje̯ ińde̯·ććis koššini̯ žar-kaje̯s ṕ o t r care·vići̯s. vot ṕ o t r care·-vići̯s pukśis ve̯vve̯ da ge̯ńi·tis tuje̯. woktis sija perekro·stokve̯ i aǯǯe̯, sete̯n pľita kujwe̯ i si̯vvi̯n ve̯i gižema: kin munas šuľga·vvas, to sija aśse̯ e̯štas, a ve̯wi̯s koľććas wowja; jeśľi sija munas veśki̯·tvas, to e̯štas ve̯wse̯ da aći̯s koľććas wowja; a jeśľi munas veśki̯ta, to sija aswi̯s aǯǯas ińes. i ṕ o t r care·vić munis veśki̯ta. woktis e̯tik dvore·c di̯ne̯, a pani̯t kote̯·rte̯ ni̯wka. ni̯wkai̯s otsa·wis care·vićwe̯ ćećći̯ni̯ ve̯w vi̯wśań da pi̯rtis dvore·cas. sećći̯n sije̯ pukśetis pi̯za·n saje̯, jukta·wis, verdis da votte̯·tis uźni̯. toľko ještis ṕ o t r care·vić uźni̯, kiǯ ni̯wka berge̯·tis kojkase̯ i ṕ o t r care·vić uśis jamà. skoro car e̯ktis me̯di·k pir. eta pirvi̯n viśta·wis, kin si̯we̯ vaje̯·tas žar-kaje̯s, to si̯we̯ śetas ǯi̯n carstvose̯. i tuje̯ ińde̯·ććis f́ o d o r care·vić. f́ o d o r care·vić tože̯ munis veśki̯ta. woktis eta ni̯wka di̯ne̯ i tože̯ ni̯wkàs f́ o d o r care·viće̯s uśke̯·tis jamà.*

3. *ńe-di̯r mi̯jiś i v a · n care·vić ińde̯·ććis tuje̯. ke̯r sija woktis perek-ro·stokwe̯, to sija munis šuľga·vvas, ki̯te̯·n e̯šti̯ni̯ ve̯wse̯, no aswi̯s koľćći̯ni̯ wowje̯n. i v a · n care·vić munis, munis da mi̯ǯis. ćeććis ve̯w vi̯wśań, ke̯rta·wis si̯wiś oǯi̯ś kokkese̯ da weǯis šoćći̯śni̯. a aći̯s vodis uźni̯. ke̯r i v a · n care·vić*

237. Tsarevich Ivan and the wolf

1. Once upon a time there lived a Tsar called Bereńďej. He had three sons. The eldest was called Tsarevich Ṕotr, the middle Tsarevich F́odor, the youngest Tsarevich Ivan. This Tsar had a large garden. In this garden grew an apple tree whose fruit rejuvenated everybody. He noticed that someone was beginning to steal the apples. One night he sent his eldest son to keep watch. The eldest son sat outside for a while, then went into the barn and slept the rest of the night. When he came to his father next morning, he told him that he had seen nobody. The following night the middle son went to guard the apples. Neither did he see anybody, since he too slept the night in the barn. On the third night Tsarevich Ivan went on guard. He sat and sat, and suddenly he perceived that it was growing lighter in the garden. He went up to the tree and saw that a fire-bird was eating the apples. Quietly Tsarevich Ivan drew near and caught the bird by the tail. But the bird freed itself with a jerk, only a feather from its tail was left behind. In the morning Tsarevich Ivan came to his father and told him that he had seen the thief but could not catch him. And he handed the tail-feather of the fire-bird to his father. From that time on, the Tsar was a happy man. After a time he announced at a feast that he would give half his realm to anyone who would catch and bring the fire-bird to him.

2. Well, Tsarevich Ṕotr set out to find the fire-brid. Tsarevich Ṕotr mounted his horse and galloped along the road. He arrived at a crossroad and saw a notice lying there, with the words: he who takes the left-hand road will lose himself but save his horse's life; he who takes the right-hand road will lose his horse but himself stay alive; and he who takes the road straight ahead will find himself a wife. Tsarevich Ṕotr went straight ahead. He arrived at a palace, a girl came running to meet him. The girl helped the Tsarevich to alight from his horse and showed him into the castle. She sat him at the table, gave him drink and food and put him to bed to sleep. Hardly had Tsarevich Ṕotr fallen asleep, when the girl turned the bed round, and Tsarevich Ṕotr fell into a pit. Soon the Tsar gave another feast. At that feast he announced that he would give half his realm to anyone who would bring the fire-bird to him. And Tsarevich F́odor set out. Tsarevich F́odor went straight ahead too. He came to that girl, and the girl made Tsarevich F́odor fall in the pit as well.

3. After a while Tsarevich Ivan set out. When he got to the crossroads, he turned to the left where one would lose one's horse but save one's own life. Tsarevich Ivan went on and on, and he grew tired. He dismounted from his horse, tethered its front feet and let it rest. He himself lay down

sajmis, to sija vewsę ez aǯǯi. sija pondis teždi·śni. sek si dinę woktis keji·n i viśta·wis, što vewsę siwiś śojis sija. "no·wadnę, me tenit otsa·wa sek aǯǯini žar-kajsę." i v a · n *care·vić pukśis keji·nvę. keji·n siję nebę·tis medi·k carstvoę, kitę·n owis žar-kajis. vot keji·nis i šuę: "miję woktim bur porà. bidę·s storožžes uźeni. te žagę·ńikęn pir, boś žagę·ńikęn žar-kajsę kleťkaiś, no aśsę kleťkasę en verę·t!"* i v a · n *care·vić siǯ i keris. piris dvore·cę, kiskis žar-kajsę i žaľko siwę wois koľni kleťkasę. sek sija medis bośni kleťkasę. no toľko ještis sija kuććiśni kleťkàs berdę, kiǯ bidę·s pondis šumi·tni. storožžes sajmisę i kvaťi·tisę* i v a · n *care·vićes. vaję·tisę caris dinę. i pondis caris siwiś jua·śni: kinwę·n sija, kiti·ś, kičę·m gosuda·rstvoiś.* i v a · n *care·vić sek viśta·wis, što sija zon car* b e r e · ń ď e *jwęn, što sija woktis guśa·wni žar-kajsę. sek sećće car viśta·wis: "jeśľi teit siǯ koę žar-kajis, to vetwi sečče·m-kę gosuda·rstvò i vaj menim si carwiś vewęs!" vot weǯisę* i v a · n *care·vićęs. i si dinę woktis keji·nis i šuis: "vot ed, en kiwzi menę i śurin bedaę."* i v a · n *care·vić viśta·śis keji·nwę, mij siwę čęktis kerni caris. keji·n sek viśta·wis, što sija otsa·was* i v a · n *care·vićwę guśa·wni vewsę. vot nija woktisę carstvoas. keji·n i šuę* i v a · n *care·vićwę: "pir pę końu·śńaas, kut vewsę da pet siket! a ewmę·ssę en verę·t!" vot* i v a · n *care·vić piris końu·śńà, kutis vewsę, a ewmę·ssę siwę žaľ wois koľni, sić-kę vei ećďę·n basęk. sija toľko kutis ewmę·ssę, kić kolokowwez pondisę zvońi·tni. storožžes sajmisę i kutisę* i v a · n *care·vićes i vaję·tisę car dinas. car jua·wis, kiti·ś sija, kinwę·n, kičę·m gosuda·rstvoiś i mijwę siwę kois vewis.* i v a · n *care·vić bidę·s viśta·śis. sek car šuis: "vewsę me tenit śeta, toľko te menim oǯǯik vaję·t* j e ľ e · n a p r e k r a · s n e *jęs med·ik gosuda·rstvoiś."* i v a · n *care·vićes weǯisę i si berin srazu·-žę woktis keji·n. i pondis sija vidni* i v a · n *care·vićes, miľa sija ez kiwzi.* i v a · n *care·vić bidę·s siwę viśta·śis. sek keji·n viśta·wis, što sija otsa·was siwę guśa·wni* j e ľ e · n a p r e k r a s n e *jęs. ker nija woktisę medi·k gosuda·rstvò, kitę·n owis* j e ľ e n a p r e k r a · s n e *j, to keji·n ińdę·tis* i v a · n*es gortwańę, a aćis munis guśa·wni* j e ľ e · n a p r e k r a · s n e *jęs. vot skoro* i v a · n *care·vićes vetis keji·n, a si spina·vvin puka·wę* j e ľ e · n a p r e k r a · s n e *j. woktisę nija med carstvoas, a* i v a · n *care·vićwę žaľ wois vežni* j e ľ e · n a p r e k r a · s n e *jęs vewwę. sek keji·n čęktis ǯebni* j e ľ e · n a*ęs verę. keji·n bergęććis setęn-žę* j e ľ e · n a p r e k r a · s n e *ję i* i v a · n *care·vić nebę·tis siję vežni vewwę. vežis vewwę, woktis verę. bośtis* j e ľ e · n a p r e k r a · s- n e *jęs da gęńi·tis gortas. tujvas niję bera· vetis keji·nis. woktisę nija pervoj carstvoę, kitę·n žar-kajis. keji·n siǯ-žę bergę·ććis vewę, vewsę da* j e ľ e · n a

to sleep. When Tsarevich Ivan woke up, he could not find his horse. He began to worry. The wolf came up to him and said that it was he who had eaten his horse. "All right then, I'll help you find the fire-bird." Tsarevich Ivan got on the wolf's back. The wolf took him to the next tsardom where the fire-bird was living. The wolf said: "We've arrived at the right time. All the guards are asleep. Go in quietly, take the fire-bird quietly out of the cage, but don't touch the cage itself!" Tsarevich Ivan did as he had been told. He entered the palace and took the fire-bird, but was sorry to leave the cage. He wanted to take away the cage. But hardly had he seized the cage when everything began to boom. The guards woke and seized Tsarevich Ivan. They took him to the Tsar. The Tsar asked him whom he belonged to, where and which state he had come from. Then Tsarevich Ivan said that he was Tsar Berenďej's son and that he had come to steal the fire-bird. Then the Tsar said: "If you want the fire-bird so much, go to such and such state and bring me the horse of that Tsar!" Tsarevich Ivan was set free. The wolf came up to him and said: "Well, you didn't listen to me, and you've got into a scrape." Tsarevich Ivan told the wolf what the Tsar had commanded him to do. Then the wolf said he would help Tsarevich Ivan to steal the horse. They arrived in the Tsar's realm. The wolf said to Tsarevich Ivan: "Go into the stable, take the horse and bring it out! But don't touch the bridle!" Tsarevich Ivan went into the stable and seized the horse, but was sorry to leave the bridle there since it was a very fine one. Hardly had he seized the bridle, when the bells began to ring. The guards woke up and caught Tsarevich Ivan, and took him to the Tsar. The Tsar asked where he came from, to whom he belonged, from which state, and what he wanted the horse for. Tsarevich Ivan told him everything. Then the Tsar said: "I'll give you the horse, only first bring me Fair Jelena of the next state." Tsarevich Ivan was set free, and the wolf appeared in no time. The wolf began to scold Tsarevich Ivan because of his disobedience. Tsarevich Ivan told him everything. Then the wolf said he would help him to kidnap Fair Jelena. When they arrived in the next state, where Fair Jelena was living, the wolf sent Ivan home and himself went to kidnap Fair Jelena. The wolf soon overtook Tsarevich Ivan; Fair Jelena was sitting on its back. They arrived in the second Tsar's realm, but Tsarevich Ivan was very sorry to exchange Fair Jelena for the horse. Then the wolf commanded him to hide Jelena in the forest. There the wolf changed into Fair Jelena, and Tsarevich Ivan took her off to exchange her for the horse. He exchanged her for the horse and returned to the forest. He seized Fair Jelena and galloped home. Again they were overtaken by the wolf on the way. They arrived in the first tsardom where the fire-bird was living. As before, the wolf changed

p r e k r a · s n e jse žebise vere. i v a · n care·vić bera· vežis berge·ććem keji·nse žar-kajwe.

4. *vot i v a · n care·vić, vew, j e ľ e · n a p r e k r a · s n e j da žar-kaj ińde·ććise gortwańe. tujvas i v a · n care·vić virućitis aśśis vonnese i munise nija etwàn. no vonnes duma·jtise umeľe tujvas. ker i v a · n care·vić vodis uźni, to vonnes šukkise sije propaśťe. dir kujwis i v a · n care·vić. eta jiliś tedis keji·n. sija kote·rtis i v a · n care·vić dine. viže·te, a sivvin puka·weni ńi raka da raka-pija·n. keji·n kvaťi·tis raka-pija·nse da viśta·wis rakawe, štobi sija vajis kuwšinin wowja va da kuwem va. raka vajis ete vase, a keji·n miśśe·tis i v a · n care·vićes. i i v a · n care·vić ćeććis i šuis, kiče·m sija dir uźis. sek keji·n viśta·wis, što sija uźis-bi pir, jeśľi-bi ńe keji·nis. i viśta·wis, mij siket kerise vonnes. sek keji·n pukśe·tis i v a · n care·vićes as viwas da vetis vonnese. keji·nis srazu·-že torrezve ľetis vonnese. a i v a · n care·vić woktis gortas, vajis ajiswe žar-kaj, a aswis bur vewes da ńewe·staes, sija bide·s viśta·śis: kite·n sija vewi, mij keris; viśta·wis kić kejinis ľetis vonnese. car teždi·śištis zonnes pondais, a si berin orsis veśo·lej pir da svaďba. a i v a · n care·vić aswas ńewe·staket dir owise da gosuda·rstvoen pravi·tise.*

238. *mijan kolχo·z*

1. *mijan kolχo·zin uža·eni kolχo·źńikkez. tewnas nija weśe·teni maši·naez. tewnas traktorrezen kiska·eni poľoezve udubre·ńiez. ker ponde·ćće tuwis, to nija weśe·ććeni gerni. ker gerase, to srazu·-že kuććeni kežni. a ker kežžase, to saďi·teni raznej owo·ššez. eta berin uže· ponde·ćće śenoko·s. maši·naezen ičkeni turu·n, kurteni i kiska·eni zoro·ddeze. seććin maši·naezen tećeni turu·nse zoro·de. si berin weśe·ććeni vundini oźimmez. oźimmez berin vundeni uže· ostaľne·j śu. poto·m-že arnas kereni owo·ššez. kiž eta bide·s kerase, pondeni gerni. a ker gerase, to bera· keženi oźimmez.*

2. *a tewnas mijan poľoezvin kereni śńegozaďerža·ńńoez. eta pondais poľoezveť vetweni traktoren, kereni borozdaez, štobi sećće ekśis wim iľi-že kereni wim-kućaez, iľi-že kereni vreme·nnej jer. a štobi pir seččem jer vei, to saďi·teni polosa·en ver.*

into a horse, and he hid the horse and Fair Jelena in the forest. Again Tsarevich Ivan exchanged the wolf turned into horse for the fire-bird.

4. Well, Tsarevich Ivan, the horse and Fair Jelena as well as the fire-bird started for home. On the way Tsarevich Ivan released his brothers, and they went on their way together. But the brothers thought evil on the way. When Tsarevich Ivan lay down to sleep, his brothers threw him into a ravine. Tsarevich Ivan lay there for a long time. The wolf got to hear of this. He ran to Tsarevich Ivan. He looks at him: crows and young crows are already perched on him. The wolf seized the young ones and told the old crow to fetch some water of life and death in a clay jar. The crow fetched the water, and the wolf washed Tsarevich Ivan. Tsarevich Ivan got up, saying: "I have been sleeping a long time." Then the wolf said he would have slept for ever had it not been for him. He told the story of what his brothers had done to him. The wolf put Tsarevich Ivan on his back, and overtook the brothers. At once the wolf tore the brothers to pieces. Tsarevich Ivan arrived home, he brought the fire-bird to his father and a good horse as well as a bride for himself. He told him everything: where he had been, what he had done; he told how the wolf had torn his brothers to pieces. The Tsar was sorry for his sons for a while, then he gave a lively feast and arranged a wedding. Tsarevich Ivan lived a long time, at the head of the state with his wife.

238. Our kolkhoz

1. Kolkhoz members work in our kolkhoz. During the winter they prepare the machines. During the winter they carry manure to the fields by tractor. When spring begins, they make preparations for ploughing. When they plough, they immediately begin to sow. When they sow, they also plant various vegetables. Then comes haymaking. They mow the grass with machines, rake the grass and stack it. They use machines for stacking the hay. After this they prepare to harvest the autumn crop. After the autumn crop they harvest the other kinds of corn. Then during autumn they gather in the vegetables. When all this is done, they begin to plough. After ploughing, they sow the autumn crop again.

2. During winter they raise snow-mounds on the ploughed fields. For this purpose they go out to the fields on tractors and make furrows to collect snow in them, or they make heaps of snow, or temporary fencing. For permanent windbreaks they plant forest belts.

239.

1. *ета ve̮wi ari̮n. sube̮·tae̮ škola be̮ri̮n mije̮ e̮kśime̮ ćel'ad'iske̮t i munime̮ ve̮re̮. śe̮rani̮m boštime̮ karto·ška, štobi̮ sije̮ seććin puni̮. mije̮ woktime̮ ve̮ras i pol'a·navi̮n kerime̮ kośt'o·r. karto·škase̮ puime̮ da śojime̮. si̮ be̮ri̮n mije̮ pondime̮ orsni̮ sete̮n. eta kade̮ mije̮ ki̮wime̮ pon-ši̮. eta poni̮s ve̮wi oχo·tńikwe̮n (ve̮raliśwe̮n)* [sić!]. *poni̮s vaše̮·tis ke̮ććeze̮s. sija vaše̮·tis ke̮ććese̮ mijan wade̮re̮. eta ke̮ći̮s pi̮ššis poni̮s di̮niś i ćećće̮wtis mijan di̮ne̮ǯ. ke̮ći̮s kote̮·rtis mijan boke̮t, metr kujim i̮wi̮na. sija kote̮·rtis veśki̮ta i̮b kuźa, pope̮ŕoga·jis tuj da pi̮ris me̮di·k ve̮re̮. a me̮d ke̮ći̮s ćećće̮·wtis i̮wi̮nžik i pondis pi̮šši̮ni poso·l'okwańas. sija tože̮ poto·m berge̮·ććis i pi̮ššis ve̮ras. a poni̮s ve̮rali·śi̮swe̮n* [sic!] *powźis i dal'še ez kote̮·rt.*

2. *e̮tik bur wune̮ me suwti li̮žiezve̮ da muni d'ere·wńa di̮ne̮ i̮swa·śni̮. ke̮r me wokti seććine̮ i i̮ske·wti gora uwtas, to me kaźa·i ke̮ć-śl'ed. ke̮r me viǯe̮·ti si̮wiś śl'edse̮, to me duma·jti̮šti, što ke̮ći̮s mati̮n kujwe̮. me reši·ti sije̮ wepti̮ni̮ mestaśis i pondi vetwe̮·tni̮ si̮ śl'ed kuźa. sete̮n me pondi wokni̮ śl'ed kuźas ke̮ći̮s di̮ne̮. ke̮ći̮s kaźa·is mene̮, ćećće̮·wtis da pi̮ššis ve̮re̮.*

240.

gožume̮n mije̮ e̮kśime̮ sośe·ddeske̮t da munime̮ ve̮re̮ čakja·wni̮. mije̮ maši·nae̮n munime̮ (woktime̮) ve̮re̮ǯ i ćeććime̮ seććin. si̮ be̮ri̮n pi̮rime̮ ve̮ras i pondime̮ e̮kti̮ni̮ čak. drug me ki̮wi, ki̮n-ke̮ jur vewde̮ram šumi·te̮. ke̮r me jure̮s wepti, to kaźa·wi ure̮s. uri̮s kajis puvve̮ i viǯe̮·tis mevve̮. si̮ be̮ri̮n sija pondis ćećća·wni̮ puviś puvve̮ i pi̮ris ve̮ras. sete̮n ešše̮· ńe-di̮r čakja·(w)ime̮ da munime̮ me̮d wade̮ras tuj di̮nśińi̮s. tol'ke̮ me ješti pi̮rni̮ ve̮ras, ki̮ǯ me oǯiś ćećće̮·wtis uće̮·t'ik ke̮ćo·k. me sije̮ di̮r viǯe̮·ti, ki̮ǯ sija kote̮·rtis. siǯ me čakja·(w)e̮m di̮ŕńi aǯǯi̮wi ure̮s i ke̮će̮s. a wun-še̮rnas mije̮ bertime̮ gorte̮.

241.

ki̮ć-ke̮ wune̮n mije̮ pondime̮ we̮śe̮·ćći̮ni̮ oj keže̮ ri̮ba·ćitni̮. ri̮ba·ćitni̮ mije̮ munime̮ kujime̮n. ri̮ba·ćitime̮ mije̮ ri̮tnas beregśań. oj keže̮ kerime̮ kośt'o·r. i sete̮n mije̮ ćuwe̮·tim ojse̮. no mije̮ sete̮n eg uźe̮, siǯ-ke̮ oji̮s ve̮i e̮d'd'e̮n gaža. a štobi̮ ńe uźni̮, mije̮ pondime̮ eta-medwe̮ viśta·śni̮ skazkaez. siǯ mijan ćuwa·(w)is oji̮s. oǯ asi̮wnas pukśime̮ pwotve̮ da ujime̮ ju še̮ras. seććin ke̮rta·ime̮ plotse̮ stowbik berde̮ i sete̮n pondime̮ ri̮ba·ćitni̮. asi̮wi̮s ve̮i e̮d'd'e̮n bur, to ćerii̮s

239. [Hare-hunting]

1. It was autumn. When school was over on Saturday, we children met together and walked to the forest. We took potatoes to cook there. We arrived in the forest and lit a fire in the clearing. We cooked the potatoes and ate them. Then we began to play there. While playing, we heard a dog bark. The dog belonged to the hunter. The dog was chasing hares. It chased the hares towards us. One hare escaped from the dogs and leapt towards us. The hare passed three metres away from us. It ran straight across the field, went over the road, and then entered the other forest. Another hare was leaping a little further away, and began to run towards the settlement. Then this one also turned and fled into the forest. And the hunter's dog became frightened and did not run any further.

2. One nice day I put on skis and started off to ski beside the village. When I arrived there and skied down to the foot of the hill, I detected a hare's tracks. When I noticed the tracks, I thought that the hare was near at hand. I made up my mind to catch it, and started following its tracks. Following the tracks, I began to approach the hare. The hare caught sight of me, sprang up and escaped into the forest.

240. [Gathering mushrooms]

In the summer we met together with our neighbours, and went to gather mushrooms in the forest. We went by car to the forest, and there we jumped down. Then we went into the forest and set to work picking mushrooms. Suddenly I was aware of something rustling above my head. When I raised my head, I saw a squirrel. The squirrel had climbed the tree and was looking at me. Then it began to leap from tree to tree and went into the forest. We went on picking mushrooms there for a while, then set out in a different direction from the road. Hardly had I entered the forest when a little hare jumped up in front of me. For a long time I watched how it ran. This is how I saw a squirrel and a hare while gathering mushrooms. At midday we went home.

241 [About fishing]

In the day-time we made preparations for fishing at night. Three of us went. In the evening we fished from the bank. We made a camp-fire for the night. We spent the night there. But we did not sleep as the night was very beautiful. We started to tell tales to each other, so as not to fall asleep. The night was spent like this. Early in the morning we got on a raft and floated to

pondis šedni̮ bura. mije̮ sete̮n ki̮jime̮ una ćeri, no i mezma·ise̮ una· ćeries krućo·kkez vi̮wśań. mezma·ise̮ ńe toľko uće̮·ťik ćeriez, no i i̮ǯi̮te̮ś. ke̮r dugdis koka·wni̮ ćerii̮s, mije̮ be̮r woktime̮ beregvas i munime̮ gorte̮.

242.

gožumnas, ke̮r me śeti ekza·mennez, ćeľaďi̮s si̮ pe̮rà kerise̮ pi̮ž. eta pi̮ži̮s ťerpitis toľko e̮tik morte̮s. sete̮n ve̮ise̮ siǯ-že̮ šeľľez, ki̮ti pi̮ris vàs (vai̮s). me e̮ďďe̮n ľubi·ti i̮swa·śni̮ pi̮žnas. e̮t-pi̮riś me pondi ujni̮ pi̮žnas bereg dore̮ťťis, a si̮ be̮ri̮n peti ju še̮ras. ju še̮ras menam pi̮že̮ pi̮ris una va. me pondi ujni̮ še̮rśis bereg ďoras, štobi̮ ńe ve̮jni̮ ju še̮ri̮n. toľko me ješti wokni̮ bereg doras, kiǯ e̮twai̮n pi̮žnas ve̮ji. no sete̮n uže· vei ńe pi̮di̮n. pi̮žse̮ me be̮r wepti, kiśti vase̮ setiś i be̮ra· pondi i̮swa·śni̮. no me ešše̮· ńe e̮t-pi̮riś eta pi̮že̮n ve̮jwi. no śo row- no· me sije̮n i̮swa·śi, χoťa· i ńe e̮t-pi̮riś kupa·ćći̮wi.

243.

eta ve̮i tuwi̮se̮n, maj meśaćći̮n. mene̮ ćeľaďi̮s korise̮ ju dore̮. mije̮ seććin obi·ćno be̮ba·wwim jabwońńez koa·si̮n. sete̮n mije̮ eg kaźa·we, ki̮ď ćua·wis kadi̮s. mije̮ pondime̮ munni̮ gorte̮. no sete̮n mijanwiś tujse̮ popeŕoga·jis va, ke̮da veśki̮ta kote̮·rtis i̮b kuźa. mijanwe̮ ńem ez koľćći̮ kerni̮, kiǯ veśki̮ta munni̮ vaeťťas. no vàs ve̮i uže· pi̮di̮n-koď i mije̮ e̮ktime̮ vase̮ sapo·g-goľeńi·ššeez vewde̮re̮t. no sić-ke̮ ve̮i mati̮n gorte̮, to me kote̮·rti i veži paś-ke̮me̮s i kok-ke̮m-ke̮t. siǯ mije̮ śurime̮ tuwi̮snas và (vae̮). eta be̮ri̮n mije̮ boľše siǯ ege̮ kere̮.

244.

ke̮r me ve̮i uće̮·ťik, to pape̮ke̮t korši rejse̮. sija uǯa·we̮ šof'o·re̮n, siǯ-ke̮ eta ve̮i te̮we̮n, to sija ez me̮d bośni̮ še̮ras. no me śo rowno· korši si̮ke̮t i sija mene̮ boštis. wuni̮s ve̮wi bur, mije̮ ve̮rźime̮ gortśiń (gortćiń) rejse̮. ke̮r mije̮ woktime̮ stancija di̮ne̮, kiće̮· kowis vajni̮ grusse̮ (gruzse̮), to pogo·ďďàs ume̮ľććis, weptiśis purga. ke̮r pape̮ śetis gruzse̮ i mije̮ be̮r ve̮rźime̮ gortwańe̮, to eta porà (porae̮) purgàs ti̮rtis tujse̮. mije̮ stancija di̮nśiń munime̮ ki̮ni̮m-ke̮ kilome·tr, daľše tuji̮s ve̮i ti̮rte̮m. mije̮ pondime̮ buksu·jtni̮, pape̮ be̮r pi̮ris ve̮re̮. seććin berge̮·ććis

the middle of the river. There we tied the raft to a stake, and began to fish. It was a very beautiful morning, and we caught a lot of fish. We caught a great many fish, although many fish also got free from the hook. Not only small fish but big ones also escaped. When the fish were no longer biting we went back to the bank and returned home.

242. [About boating]

After I had passed my examinations in the summer, the children made a boat. This boat could only take one person. There were also cracks in it that let in the water. I liked boating very much. Once I was rowing along the bank, then went to the middle of the river. A lot of water came into my boat in the middle of the river. I began to row to the bank, for fear of sinking in middle of the river. I had nearly reached the bank when I sank with my boat. But I did not sink very deep there. I lifted the boat out, poured the water out of it, and again began to row. But it was not the first time that I sank with that boat. Despite this, I continued boating with it, although I took a bath more than once.

243. [Playing on the river bank]

It was spring-time, in May. The children called me to go to the river bank. As a rule, we played about there among the apple-trees. We did not realize how time passed there. We started for home. Our way was blocked by water that was flowing right across the ploughed field. We had no other choice than to walk through the water. But the water was already deep, reaching above the legs of our boots. But as it was not a long way home, I ran home and changed my clothes and footwear. This is how we got into water in the spring. Afterwards we did not do this again.

244. [A ride in a snow-strom]

When I was a small child, I asked my dad to take me for a ride. He works as a driver. As it was wintertime, he did not want to take me with him. But I insisted, and he took me with him. It was a nice day, we started out from home along the road. When we arrived at the station where the load had to be taken, the weather grew worse, a snow-storm arose. After dad had delivered the load, we started for home, but in the meantime the snow-storm had blocked the way. We went a few kilometres away from the station; further on there was no way (because there was no snow there). We

i be̮r munime̮ stancijà. seććin si̮we̮n ve̮i e̮tik znakome̮j i mije̮ si̮ ordi̮n ćuwe̮·tim ojse̮. asi̮wnas mije̮ ve̮rźime̮ gorte̮. ojnas tujse̮ ćiśťi·tise̮ i mije̮ boľše eg buksu·jte̮. eta be̮rśiń pape̮ te̮wnas mene̮ boľše ńe-ki̮će̮· ez ne̮be̮·twi̮.

245.

me šogmi k u d i̮ m - k aras. mame̮ i pape̮ śića·s owe̮ni̮ k u d i̮ m - k aras. mian em aswani̮m kerku. sija suwa·we̮ centras. śića·s me końćiti ďeśiť klassow i pe̮stupi·ti ińśťitu·te̮. me ponda vewe̮·tni̮ ćeľaďe̮s, ke̮r końćita ińśťitu·tse̮. me vewe̮·ta inostra·nne̮j ki̮w. meni̮m gľeńi·ćće̮ angľijske̮j ki̮w. ke̮r końćita ińśťitu·tse̮, uǯa·wni̮ muna gorte̮, me ed seććin šogmi. — menam em aj i mam, ki̮k soj da ki̮k von. mame̮ uǯa·we̮, a pape̮ oz ńi uǯa·w. sija peńśijavi̮n. vonneze̮ i sojjeze̮ uǯa·we̮ni̮, nija tože̮ owe̮ni̮ gorodas.

246.

školaśiń woktim śore̮n. mamee̮ šua: "śoja-bi̮." mame̮ meni̮m šue̮: "me eg ješti̮ teni̮t weśe̮·tni̮, pu-ka aći̮t!" "mi̮j vaj pua?" "a mi̮j-bi̮ te śojan? ćiśťi·t karto·ška i pukti̮ puwni̮ poχľo·pka! en vune̮·ćći̮ soa·wni̮ vase̮!" "me važe̮n ńi pukti sowse̮." "śas, viǯe̮·t, štob ez pet. umeľa wonti·śe̮ gori̮s, sek kowe̮ pi̮rtni̮ pes." "me śas pi̮rta." pukti pesse̮ goras i pondis wonti·śni̮ gori̮s e̮ďďe̮n bura. i menam poχľo·pka pondis piźni̮ ćoža. "a ćajse̮ puktin piźe̮·tni̮? — juwa·wis mame̮. — nu vot i šuan: 'śoja-bi̮.' a e̮d poχľo·pkai̮t puśis ńi. boś pań i ćaška i pukti̮ poχľo·pkase̮! śoj skore·je!" "mame̮, te mi̮ľa on śoj?" "ńe-kor meni̮m. me peta e̮te̮re̮, kowe̮ ći̮škini̮ pos-e̮ǯ." "śoj meke̮t!" a poto·m me peta, ći̮ška pos-e̮ǯse̮." vot i užna·jtim mame̮ke̮t.

247.

e̮t-pi̮r gaža wuni̮n mije̮ mame̮ke̮t munim ve̮re̮. ve̮ras e̮ďďe̮·n gaža. di̮r mije̮ munim. tuji̮s e̮ďďe̮·n kuź. vot i woktim ve̮ras. ve̮ras suwa·we̮ ge̮ra: mije̮ pi̮rim ve̮ras. mame̮ e̮ďďe̮·n ćoža vetwe̮·te̮ i petis me di̮ne̮. si̮we̮n ti̮r ke̮rźi·nkàs jagedi̮s. a menam sowśe̮·m ječa. me pi̮ri ve̮ras. muni, muni i munśe̮m e̮ďďe̮·n i̮we̮. mame̮ ge̮re̮·twas, ge̮re̮·twas i oz ki̮w menśi̮m šise̮. me pondi gorzi̮ni̮. drug peti

began to slide; my dad drove into the forest. There he turned round and we went back to the station. An acquaintance of his was living nearby; we spent the night with him. Next morning we started for home. During the night the road was cleared and we did not slide any more. After this my dad would never take me anywhere with him in winter.

245. [My family]

I grew up in Kudymkar. My father and mother are still living in Kudymkar. We have a house of our own. It stands in the centre. I have just finished the tenth class, and have registered at the college. I shall teach children after finishing at college. I shall teach foreign languages. I like the English language. When I finish at college, I shall go home to work, after all. I grew up there. I have a father, mother, two sisters and two brothers. My mother still works, although my father does not. He has retired. My brothers and sisters are at work; they also live in the town.

246. [About cooking]

It was late when we arrived home from school. I say to mother: "I'd like something to eat." Mother says: "I had no time to get supper for you, cook it for yourself! Peel some potatoes and put the soup on to boil! Don't forget to put salt in the water!" "Oh, I put salt in it a long time ago!" "See that it doesn't boil over. If the stove doesn't burn well, put some more wood on the fire!" "I'll put some on immediately." I put wood into the stove, and the stove began to burn very well. My soup began to boil quickly. "And have you put on water for tea?" — asked my mother. — "Well, you see, you said: I'd like something to eat. Look, your soup is cooked already. Take a spoon and a bowl and have some soup. Eat it quickly! I myself have no time to eat. I'm going out, I must sweep the porch." "Eat with me! Then I'll go out and sweep the porch." So mother and I had supper together.

247. [Picking berries]

One fine day mother and I went into the forest. It is very beautiful in the forest. We walked for a long time. The path was very long. We arrived in the forest. There is a hill in the forest. We went into the wood. Mother walks very quickly, she came over to me. Her basket is full of berries. And I have very few in mine. I went on and on, and I got very far away. Mother calls and calls me, but cannot hear my voice. I began to shout. Suddenly I came

tujo·kve̮. muna, muna sija tujve̮t i panta·śe̮ starićo·k. “ki̮će̮· mune̮ ni̮woćka?” — šue̮ starićo·k. “e̮ši me, og aǯǯi̮ tujse̮ gorte̮.” “ki̮ti·ś te?” “b a r a · n e̮ v e̮ jiś.” višta·e̮ meni̮m ki̮ćće̮· munni̮: “veški̮ta eta tujve̮t mun! petan i̮bve̮ a seććin i mati̮n ďere·wńai̮s.” una me jage̮d e̮kti, a ćuť eg e̮š.

248.

1. *eta ve̮wi gožumi̮n, e̮tik bur wune̮. oǯ asi̮we̮n me bośti eťu·dńik i muni ve̮re̮ risu·jtni̮ eťu·ddes. asi̮w ve̮wi bur. ju-de̮ri̮n weptiśis tuma·n. ju-de̮ri̮n ńebo ve̮wi i̮ǯi̮·t da ćiste̮j. šondi toľke̮ ešše̮· weptiśis. vi̮i̮nas ńeboas weba·wis i̮b-šar. me muni tuj vi̮we̮t, ke̮da ne̮be̮·tis ve̮re̮. i̮b, bi̮de̮·s ve̮wi golube̮·j, sije̮n što śveťitis ľon. ve̮r poľa·na vi̮wi̮n ćveťitis žeľne̮g. eta ki̮ǯ-bi̮ višta·wis, što možno kupa·ćći̮ni̮. krugo·m ve̮wi seče̮m base̮k, što sije̮ ńeme̮n on giž. nastroje·ńie ve̮wi e̮ďďe̮n bur; ez ťerpi·ćći̮ bośni̮ kie̮ kiste̮ćka da kućći̮ni̮ risu·jtni̮. skore̮ me wokti ve̮r di̮ne̮. si̮ di̮ni̮n paχńite̮ śvežeśťe̮n. vetwe̮·ti ve̮r kuźa, me peti poľa·na vi̮we̮. poľa·na vi̮wi̮n kaźawi oz-je̮ge̮·d. sija ve̮wi sečče̮m una, što si̮ boke̮t ńe-ki̮ć oz tuj munni̮. me śoji je̮ge̮·dse̮ pette̮ǯ da muni daľše. vot kardon mi̮ććaśis. este̮n bi̮dme̮ni̮ ľistvińi·ćaez, ke̮dije̮ meni̮m oχo·ta i ve̮wi risu·jtni̮. keri ki̮k eťu·d. me muni daľše̮ ve̮re̮. vetwe̮·ti ve̮r kuźa, peti ju-de̮re̮. šondi ve̮wi uže̮ vi̮wi̮n i ńiša·dne̮ja sotis. ju koris di̮nas aswas i̮rki̮·te̮n. me i̮ǯi̮t oχo·tae̮n kupa·ćći, šoćći̮šti šondi vi̮wi̮n a si̮ be̮ri̮n pukśi risu·jtni̮ juse̮. kusttes e̮ďďe̮n wažme̮ta kusi̮·ńćise̮ ju vi̮wde̮t* [sic!]. *kajjez śi̮wise̮ seče̮m gore̮n, što gora·wise̮ peľľezi̮n. risu·jti juse̮ me, si̮ be̮ri̮n pi̮ri ve̮re̮. be̮ras me kaźa·i ure̮s, ke̮dija mene̮ e̮ďďe̮n ińťeresu·jtis. sić me muni uri̮s śere̮. me pi̮ri e̮ďďe̮n pi̮di̮na ve̮ras. ćoža me veže̮·rti, što sete̮n e̮ši.*

2. *vetwe̮·ti e̮ďďe̮n di̮r, no tujse̮ eg aǯ́ǯ́i̮. siǯ me vetwe̮·ti śor ri̮tte̮ǯ. peti ki̮če̮·m-ke̮ bolo·ta di̮ne̮. ve̮ri̮s wois pemi̮t. e̮ni me veže̮·rti, što vetwe̮·tni̮ bespoľe·zno. we̮śe̮·ti aswi̮m oj keže̮ mesta. toľko we̮śe̮·ćći oj keže̮, ki̮ć kin-ke̮ pondis śe̮ki̮ta wowa·wni̮. a si̮ be̮ri̮n pondis gore̮·twi̮ni̮. me kaźa·i as oǯam ke̮z vi̮wi̮n ki̮k i̮ǯi̮t vež śin. me siǯ powźi, što eg wiś ve̮rźe̮·ćći̮ni̮. si̮ be̮ri̮n tožno· te̮d vi̮wam uśis, što eta ve̮wi tupka. sija oj-bi̮t mene̮ powźe̮·tis. me siǯ ve̮wi powźe̮·te̮m, što eg kaźa·w, ki̮ć ćuwa·wis oji̮s. toľke̮ ponde̮·tis jugdi̮ni̮, me pondi be̮ra· košši̮ni̮ tujse̮. meni̮m ve̮wi ńe oχo·ta risu·jtni̮ da nastroje·ńńe ve̮wi ume̮ľ. me ve̮wi či̮k i me̮di uźni̮. mi̮ǯe̮mśań me uśi pu uwte̮ da e̮nme̮·śśi. me ek te̮d, mi̮j di̮ne̮ uźi. toľke̮ mene̮ sajme̮·tis pon vuwte̮m. pon ćećća·wis me ge̮ge̮re̮ (ge̮re̮) i rade̮ (rada) vuwtis.*

out on the road. I go on and on, and an old man is coming along the road from the opposite direction. "Where are you going, little girl?" – the old man asks. I've lost my way and can't find the way home." "Where do you live?" "At Baranẹvẹj." He explains where I have to go: "Go straight along this road. You will come out into the meadow, and the village is near to it." I picked a lot of berries but I almost lost my way.

248. [How I lost my way in the forest]

1. It was in summer, one beautiful day. Early in the morning I took my pad and went into the forest to sketch. It was a fine morning. Mist was rising from the river bank. Along the bank of the river the sky was high and clear. The sun had just risen. High in the sky a skylark was soaring. I followed the road leading into the forest. The meadow and everything were blue because the flax was in bloom. In the clearings in the forest wild roses were in bloom. All this seemed to say that it was time to bathe. All around was so very beautiful that I cannot find words to describe it. My spirits were excellent; I had no patience to take the brush in my hand and settle down to drawing. Soon I arrived in the forest. I walked in the forest and got to a clearing. I noticed strawberries there in the clearing. They grew in such abundance that it was impossible to pass them by. I ate my fill of strawberries and continued on my way. The foresters' hut appeared. Larch-trees grow there, which I desired to draw. I made two sketches. I continued my way into the forest. I walked in the forest and I went to the bank of the river. The sun was already high in the sky, and it shone down mercilessly. I was attracted by the river with its coldness. I bathed with much pleasure, had a rest in the sun, and then sat down to sketch the river. The bushes were leaning down very low above the river. The birds were singing so loudly that their songs echoed in one's ears. I sketched the river, then walked into the forest. I saw a squirrel next, which interested me very much. So I started off after the squirrel. I went very deep into the forest. Soon I realized that I had lost my way.

2. I walked for a very long time but I could not find the road. I walked around like this till late evening. I got to a sort of swamp. The forest grew dark. Now I understood that it was no use walking any more. I prepared a place for myself for the night. Hardly had I got ready for the night, when someone began to breathe heavily. Then it began to make a noise. I saw two big, green eyes in the spruce in front of me. Only later did it occur to me that it must have been a tawny owl. It kept frightening me throughout the night. I was so scared that I did not notice how the night passed by.

ńe-dir mijiś pues sajśań miććaśisę ńoľ mort. nija ketę·rtisę me dinę rad ćužę·m-mezen. si berin me tedi, što gortin edďen powźisę, miľa me dir og wokti gortę. papę koris aśśis tova·riššesę, štobi nija otsa·wise (atsa·wisę) koššini. nija koššisę menę bidę·s ojsę da eššę· wun ǯin. košši·śes wijwisę ružjo·eziś, gorę·twisę, no me ńem eg kiw, sić-kę edďen krepita uźi. no nilę atsa·wis koššini pon. ker me wokti gortę, to ńe-kin oz ted, mij kerni: vidni-ľi menę ľibę radu·jććini. no vśo-žę bidę·nnis edďen radu·jććisę. sekśiń me dugdi katra·śni urrez śerin. eni me teda, što pirteni pid verę.

249.

me ola permskej oblaśťin kudimkarskej rajonin; pośo·ľoksę šueni v e ś o · l ę j m i s. *mijan pośo·ľokis ńe-edďen iǯit. olę seććin una·žik rabo·čij jez. ńe-iwin pośo·ľok dinśis bidmę ver: una·žik kiǯǯez da kezzez. veras bidmeni čakkez da jaged. em seććin rika·* i ń - v a. *ńe-edďen pidin i paśkit. splavľajteni ver, paraχo·ddez ozę vetwę. no mijan pośo·ľokin ńoľ magaźi·n, iǯit klub, staďio·n. staďio·nvas emeś voľebo·ľnej plaša·dka, futplaša·dka i kotraśa·n tujo·kkez. ďetskej sad iǯit, jaśľi, no i škola. etikas velę·ććeni ńoľ klass, medi·kas velę·ććeni kekja·mis klass. mi olam šer pośo·ľokin, samej glavnej uľića vilin. kerku mijan ńe-edďen iǯit. kerkuis dinin saďik, seten bidmę kaľina, śed seter, ľem-puez. em maľi·na-kusťtez, ćveťiteni ćveto·kkez. em iššo· iǯit ogoro·ďeć; bidmę seten bidę·s ovošš.*

250. *svaďba jiliś*

1. *ker voktas getraśa·n kadis, sek pondeni košjini žeńi·kisvę ńeve·sta. nivkasę berjeni bid-ńož: kičę·m sija, bičę·m iľi ńoštem, jon-ľi, umeľ-ľi, kin sien aj-mamis, kičę·meś rodńa·is? bureś-ľi aj-mamis, em-ľi paś-kemnis da kem-ketis? kiǯ viǯę aśsę nivkais, kiǯ sija uǯa·e, kužę-ľi vęśę·ććini oťirket, mij kužę kerni? ker aǯǯasę ńeve·stasę, sek žeńi·kisven mamis da vež-a·ńis, iľi-že žeńi·kis-ven ajis da vež-a·jis, a mukę·d-pirśa aćis žeńi·kis asvas jortket iľi kinkę·t-kę išę muneni kora·śni ńeve·sta dinę. una·žiksę koraśeni tevnas, muneni veen. ker voktasę nivkais aj-mam dinę, pireni ker-kuas, zdorova·jććeni da pukśeni*

As soon as it began to grow light, I set out again to find a way. I did not feel like drawing, and I was in a bad mood. I felt hungry and wanted to sleep. I was so tired that I fell under a tree and went to sleep. It was only when a dog barked that I woke. The dog was jumping round me, barking joyfully. Soon four men appeared from behind the trees. They ran towards me with happy faces. Then I learned that folk at home had been very frightened that I had not come home for such a long time. My father called his companions out to help him find me. For a whole night and half a day they searched for me. The searchers had fired their guns and shouted, but I did not hear anything because I was fast asleep. But the dog also helped them to find me. When I arrived home, nobody knew what to do: should they scold me or be happy? Yet they were all very happy. From that time on I gave up running after squirrels. Now I know that they lead the way into deep forests.

249. [Our village]

I live in the Perm Region, in the district of Kudymkar; the settlement is called Veśo·lẹj Mi̮s. Our settlement is not very large. They are mostly workers who live there. Not far from the settlements there grows a wood consisting mainly of birch and spruce. Mushrooms and berries grow in the wood. The River Ińva is there. It is not very deep and wide. They float logs on it, but boats do not go along it. In our settlement there are four shops, a big club and a stadium. There is a volley-ball court, a football pitch and a race track in the stadium. The kindergarten is large, and there are a nursery and also schools. In one of them there are four classes, in the other eight classes. We are living in the central settlement, in the main street. Our house is not very large. There is a small garden beside the house, in which viburnum, black currant and wild-service grow. There are raspberry bushes, flowers blossoming. And there is a large vegetable garden, in which all kinds of vegetables are grown.

250. About weddings

1. When the time for marrying comes along, they begin to look for a bride for the bridegroom. The girl is examined in every way: what she is like, whether she is beautiful or ugly, strong or lean. Who are her parents, what are her relatives like? Are her parents good, has she clothes and shoes? How does the girl behave, how does she work, does she get on with people, what can she do? When a bride is found, the bridegroom's mother and godmother or the bridegroom's father and godfather, sometimes the bridegroom himself and his friends or other acquaintances go to the bride to make formal

oʒiś vabi·ćas i ponde̯·te̯ni̯ baśńi. viśta·e̯ni̯, mi̯jve̯ voktise̯: "voktim pe̯ kora·śni̯. tian pe̯ em toa·r, a mian pe̯ em kupe·ć. vot pe̯ i me̯dam bośni̯ tianviś toa·rni̯te̯." ni̯vkai̯sve̯n aji̯s da mami̯s śue̯ni̯: "mian pe̯ śetni̯te̯ ńe-kine̯s. ni̯vkai̯s pe̯ em da iše̯ tom. tije̯ pe̯ mune̯, kora·śe̯ me̯di·ke̯s!" a koraśi·śśes śue̯ni̯: "mi̯j pe̯ vek-ľi, mi̯j-ľi me̯dat viʒni̯ ni̯vkās? od-že̯ pe̯ ed soa·e̯? ni̯vka śogme̯ma, dak śo ńi śetśe̯. a mianve̯ tijan ni̯vkani̯t bura gľeńi·ćće̯. i mije̯ e̯ďďe̯n-bi̯ bośtame̯ sije̯ zonni̯m saje̯. mian zonni̯m oz ju, oz vetwe·t, e̯ďďe̯n uʒa·iś, bi̯de̯·s kuže̯ kerni̯, kiśis śake̯jis ṕete̯ da i tuša-rožavvas bi̯če̯m. oz vićći̯, ńe oz ti̯ška·ś, bi̯di̯ske̯t kuže̯ bai·tni̯, aj-mamse̯ uaža·jte̯. mi̯j-ne̯ iše̯ siśśa tia·nve̯ koe̯? ki̯če̯·m-ne̯ iše̯ burʒi̯k žeńi̯·ke̯s vićći·śat?" "da oge̯ ńe-kine̯s vićći·śe̯, toľko oʒ iše̯ śetni̯te̯. mi̯j i ker, ok [ɔ: og] te̯d ńem. vot bai·ććam śemja·i̯ske̯t da i viśta·am, mi̯j pondam kerni̯: śetam, iľi oge̯-ľi. vove̯ me̯di·-pi̯rśa!" koraśi·śśes sije̯n-sore̯n mune̯ni̯ gortani̯s da veśe̯·ćće̯ni̯ viľiś.

2. *vun me̯d be̯rti mune̯ni̯ upe·ť kora·śni̯. te̯dase̯, mi̯j viśta·ase̯ ni̯vkai̯sve̯n rodńa·i̯s, ki̯ʒ oz otkaži·te̯. možot ńeďe·ľa be̯rti ni̯vkase̯ jue̯ni̯. žeńi̯·ki̯s vaje̯ vina·, braga da sur, kore̯ni̯ rodńa·se̯ ńeve·stai̯svi̯ś. žeńi̯·ki̯s vina·se̯ da surse̯ da bragas, vaje̯ mami̯ske̯t da aji̯ske̯t e̯tvai̯n. vokte̯ni̯ žeńi̯·ki̯sve̯n vež-a·ji̯s da vež-a·ńi̯s. vaje̯ni̯ ni̯vkai̯sve̯ kożin pfaťťe̯vve̯, kovtavve̯, iľi jupkavve̯ da base̯k ćiśja·n kiče̯·me̯-ke̯. ni̯vkai̯s eta ri̯te̯ kożna·e̯ žeńi̯·ki̯sve̯ jerne̯·s da vešja·n, ke̯de̯ žeńi̯·ki̯s paśta·e̯ svaďba vunas. eta ri̯te̯ una· gaže̯·ćće̯eni̯, śie̯ni̯ da je̯kte̯ni̯. śore̯n ri̯tnas ge̯śśes mune̯ni̯ gortani̯s. ni̯vkai̯s orde̯ koľćće̯ni̯ sie̯n med-bur podru·škaes. a svaďbae̯ʒi̯s ena ni̯vkaez vurśe̯ni̯, ge̯rʒi̯·śe̯ni̯ da miśka·śe̯ni̯ da otsa·e̯ni̯ goto·ić-ći̯ni̯ svaďba kežas. kije̯ni̯ pokro·mmez, kuša·kkez, vońńez. vetve̯·te̯ni̯ ge̯śťi·tteń ni̯vkai̯s rodńa·e̯t.*

3. *vun ki̯k oʒti vokte̯ni̯ kutni̯ ki. ker kise̯ kutase̯, to ni̯vkai̯s oz ńi vermi̯ otkaži·ćći̯ni̯ žeńi̯·k sajas mune̯mi̯ś. svaďbase̯ kere̯ni̯ śereda·e̯, petńićae̯ da kreś-śe·ńńae̯. svaďbae̯ʒi̯s ńeve·stai̯s kere̯ una kożin. goto·ite̯ pi̯za·n-de̯raez, ńe ječaʒi̯k śeśśa, sur-tre̯pi·ć, una·ći̯ške̯·ttez, dvaćeť, trićeť iľi sorok štuk: e̯tikkese̯ pi̯r*

proposal of marriage. They usually go to ask for the girl's hand in marriage during the winter, and they go with horses. When they arrive at the girl's parents, they enter the house. They greet each other and conversation starts. They say why they have come. "We have come to ask for the girl's hand. You have goods to sell and we have a merchant. We want to buy your goods". The girl's father and mother say: "We have nobody to give to you. We have a daughter but she is too young as yet. Go and ask someone else!" The suitors say: "You are not going to leave her to be a maiden for good, are you? The girl has grown up, and that is the time a girl should be given away in marriage. Your daughter pleases us very much. We are anxious to take her to our son. Our son is not a drunkard, he is not a tramp, he is a good worker, he can do everything, he can turn his hand to anything, and his face and figure are handsome. He does not swear, does not quarrel, can talk to anybody, and honours his parents. What else do you want? Do you expect a better bridegroom?" "We do not expect anybody, only it is too early to give her away. We do not know what to do. We shall discuss the matter with the family and tell you what we are going to do. Whether we are going to give her away or not, come along again!" The suitors leave empty-handed, and prepare to try again.

2. Two days later the suitors are sent again. They know in advance what the girl's relatives are going to say: they are not going to refuse their request. Perhaps a week later they will drink the bride's health. The bridegroom brings vodka, home-brewed ale and beer, and invites the bride's relatives. The bridegroom brings the vodka, the beer and the home-brewed ale, together with his mother and father. The bridegroom's godfather and godmother also come. They bring presents for the bride, a nice kerchief to decorate her dress, jacket or skirt. On this evening the girl presents gifts of a shirt and under-pants to the bridegroom, and these he will put on on the day of the wedding. On this evening they entertain themselves with singing and dancing for a long time. Late at night the guests go home. Her best girl friends stay with the bride. Before the wedding, these girls sew, knot and wash, and help to make preparations for the wedding. They weave narrow as well as wide belts and braids for the sandals of bast. They go as guests to the girl's relatives.

3. Two days earlier the betrothal is held. After the betrothal the girl cannot withdraw from the marriage. The wedding is held on Wednesday, Friday or Sunday. Up to the wedding the bride prepares many presents. She makes tablecloths, never fewer than six, beer-napkins, towels, — twenty, thirty or forty of them, some of them for everyday use, others for special occasions. The bride makes all kinds of clothes for herself, all new from head

viǯnį, mędi·kkes praźńiśnęjjez. vurę asvįs ńeve·sta bįd-koď paś-kęm, jurśań kok utęǯ (~uvtęǯ) viľę. vurę paś-kęm žęńį·kįs aj-mamvę: mamįsvę vurę jernę·s da duba·s, ajįsve jernę·s, vešja·n da kįję jį. žęńį·kįs sojjezvę vurę jernęso·kkez. kįǯ emęś vonnez, to nię vurę jernęso·kkez da vešjano·kkez. mukę·d-kadę goto·itę nįvkao·kkesvę ľento·ćkiez. vurę jupka da kovta veža·ńńesvę, vešja·n iľi jernę·s veža·jjesvę. ćasto·žįksę ić-mo·ńįs koźna·ę bįdę·nnįsę, kin voktę svaďbavvas. mukę·dįsvę koźna·ę ćišjano·kkez da vońńez da mįj-kę śakęjsę, kįčę·m-kę ućę·ťik toro·kkez.

4. *svaďbanas voktęnį vun-šęrę·ǯįs. munęnį vęvvezęn. dođđa·ęnį košo(v)a·jez, vęvvesę męde·tęnį, baśi·tęnį kuša·kkezęn, ľento·ćkezęn, ęšę·tęnį duga· berdę kokoľe·ććez. dođđa·ęnį paťe, śemę, ďeviťę iľi oďi·nnaćeťę vęvvesę. dođđa·ęm vęvveznas voktęnį žęńį·kįs kerku dįnę. žęńį·kįs pukśę męde·k dođďę veža·jįskęt. oǯas puka·ę sięn von iľi oća-von. kujmę·t dođďas pukśęnį svakaez da žęńį·kįsvęn vež-a·ńįs. med-oǯa dođďas puka·ęnį zonkaez da nįvkaez žęńį·kįs rodńa·įś, kovdun, męd-ńož tįśećkęj. ajįs da mamįs koľva·ęnį zonnįsę dođďęǯįs, kresta·ęnį da višta·ęnį bur tuj. svaďbaįs ętdrug vęrźę·ććę žęńį·kįs ogra·da dįniś i gęńi·tęmęn munę ńeve·staįs ďere·vńaę. tujvas primeća·jtęnį, kįǯ munę svaďbaįs, bura-ľi, umęľa-ľi. ńeve·staįs ďere·vńaįn svaďbaįs suvtę ńeve·staįs kerku oǯę, a tįśećkęjįs ćeććę dođďiś da voktę vorota· dįnas i ćęktę ośnį. a vorota·įs nįvkaįsvęn pęda·na. stukę·ććęnį vokti·śśes vorota· panįt. pętę ńeve·staįsvęn ajįs i šuę: "śetat pę końin da vorota·se ośta." vokti·śśes šuęnį: "oś pę oś, śetam vina·". ajįs ośtę vorota·sę, juę vina·sę, korę svaďbasę pįrnį ogra·daas. pįrtęnį bįdę·s vęvvesę, svaďbovša·naįs ćeććęnį i vęśęććęnį pįrnį kerkuas. med-oǯas pįrę žęńį·kįs veža·jįskęt da tįśećkęjįskęt, a nį bęrįn pįręnį mukę·dįs. kęr pįrasę, zdorova·jććęnį i žęńį·kįs pukśę pįza·n saję da vićći·śę ńeve·stasę. a ńeve·staįs eta kadę puka·ę komas asvas jaššikvįn, sį gęgę·r sua·ęnį sięn jorttes, nįvkaes. nija sįję męde·tęnį, paśtę·tęnį, ić-mońkę·tęnį. žęńį·kįs termę·tę nįvkaesę, korę ńeve·stasę dįnas. a mamįs, vež-a·ńįs da męd·i·k ińkaes jukta·ęnį gęśśesę vina·ęn, suręn, bragaęn i įrę·šęn. vajęnį junį da śojnį, pįza·nvę puktęnį ńań i jajęn kapu·sta, ćeri-ńa·ń, vina·, braga, sur. ńeve·stasę petkę·tę veža·ńįs i gęgertę·tę pįza·n gęgę·reťis i pukśętę žęńį·kįskęt orććęn, bokas. gęgę·rtikas ńeve·staįs stara·jććę taľććinį žęńį·kįsvę kokvas, med-bį žęńį·kįs kįvzi·śis ińsę. a žęńį·kįs kokkesę ǯebę vabić uvtas, med-bį ić-mo·ńkaįs ez taľććį kokvas. kįǯi taľććas ńeve·staįs, to zonkaes da mįžį·kkes śera·ęnį žęńį·ksę. kęr juasę da śojasę, ćeććęnį pįza·n sajiś da ńebęnį pośťe·ľľase. pettęǯįs veža·jįs da tįśećkęjįs śetęnį ďeńga jaššikįs ponda, pas-kęmįs ponda. podu·škaesę (jurę·ǯsę) bośtęnį torjęn, siǯ-kįǯ nįvvįn puka·ęnį ćeľaď*

to foot. She makes clothes for the bridegroom's parents as well: a sarafan for his mother, a shirt, trousers and belt for his father. She makes little blouses for the bridegroom's sisters. If there are also brothers, she sews little shirts and trousers for them. Sometimes she makes ribbons for the little girls. She makes skirts and jackets for the godmothers and trousers or shirts for the godfathers. Often the new wife gives presents to all the guests at the wedding. Some of them receive from her gifts of kerchiefs, belts and the like, small objects.

4. People arrive before noon for the wedding. They come with horses. They harness them to festive sleighs which they decorate beautifully with belts and ribbons, while they hang bells from the yoke. They put five, seven, nine or eleven horses to the sleigh. They arrive at the bridegroom's house with their harnessed horses. The bridegroom and his godfather get on the second sleigh. In the front sits his brother or nephew. In the third sleigh sit the suitors and the bridegroom's godmother. In the first sleigh sit boys and girls related to the bridegroom, together with the master of ceremonies. The father and the mother see their son to the sleigh, make the sign of the cross over him and wish him a safe journey. The wedding procession starts at the same time from the bridegroom's courtyard and gallops off to the bride's village. People on the way watch how the wedding procession passes, whether it is going well or badly. In the bride's village the wedding procession stops in front of the bride's house, and the master of ceremonies leaps off the sleigh, hurries to the gate and tries to have it opened. But the girl's gate is closed. The newcomers rattle at the gate. The bride's father comes out and says: "I will give us presents." The newcomers answer: "Open it, open it, we will give you vodka." The father opens the gate, drinks up the vodka and invites the wedding party to enter the courtyard. All the horses are led in, the wedding party gets off the sleighs and goes into the house. The bridegroom, together with his godfather and the master of ceremonies, takes the lead, followed by the rest. When they are all inside, they greet each other, and the bridegroom sits at the table waiting for the bride to appear. Meanwhile the bride is sitting on her bridal chest in the kitchen, surrounded by her girl friends. They are busy adorning the bride, dressing her and tying a wife's kerchief on her head. The bridegroom urges on the girls, and calls the bride to come. The mother, the godmother and other women offer the guests vodka, beer, home-brewed ale and kvas. They bring in food and drink, and put bread and cabbage and meat, fish-pirogi, vodka, home-brewed ale and beer on the table. The bride is shown in by the godmother who leads her round the table and seats her by the bridegroom. While she is being led round it the bride tries hard to step on the feet of

iľi podru·škaez i nia kore̯ni̯ ďeńga. ki̯će̯ǯ oz vešte̯, sećeǯ oz i śete̯. ćeľaďo·kse̯ ćasto·ži̯k be̯be̯·te̯ni̯ kanpe·tkaeze̯n. eta be̯ri̯n paś-ke̯mse̯ ǯim-ǯurk kaťťase̯ da kurńi-verńi̯ petke̯·tase̯ e̯te̯re̯ da puktase̯ ńeve·stai̯s doďďe, ke̯dai̯n mune̯ni̯ aji̯s da mami̯s, sojjez da vonnez. petikas aji̯s da mami̯s bvagosvoi·te̯ni̯ ni̯vni̯se̯ bura ovni̯, ki̯vzi̯ni̯ žeńi̯·kse̯ da ńe śera·vni̯ ajse̯ da mamse̯. kresta·e̯ni̯ ni̯vni̯se̯ ńańćovpa·ne̯n da jene̯n. eta be̯ri̯n pete̯ni̯ kerkuśis da pukśe̯ni̯ doďďezas. med-pervo pukśe̯ni̯ že̯ńi̯·ki̯s da ńeve·stai̯s, a si̯ be̯ri̯n me̯di·kkez i pete̯ni̯ ogra·daśis. mune̯ni̯ ge̯ńa·jte̯me̯n. ni̯vkaes tujvas śi̯e̯ni̯ garmo·ńńa śerti. ke̯r voktase̯ že̯ńi̯·ki̯s kerku di̯ne̯, to suvte̯ni̯. med-oǯ ćećće̯ni̯ že̯ńi̯ki̯s da ić-mo·ńkai̯s i pi̯re̯ni̯ kerkuas. pose̯ǯas nie̯ panta·e̯ni̯ že̯ńi̯·ki̯sve̯n aji̯s da mami̯s. zdorova·jćće̯ni̯, će̯ktе̯ni̯ pi̯rni̯ kerkuas. ke̯r poro·gse̯ vožme̯vtase̯, jurbi̯·te̯ni̯ jenve̯ da pukśe̯ni̯ oži̯ś vabi·ćas. e̯kśase̯ bi̯de̯·s ge̯śśes, ponde̯ni̯ gaže̯·ćći̯ni̯. a že̯ńi̯·ki̯s da ńeve·stai̯s med-pe̯v paśta·śe̯ni̯ da pukśe̯ni̯ pi̯za·n saje̯ stou·jtni̯. eta kade̯ kožna·śe̯ni̯ že̯ńi̯·ki̯s rodńa·e̯, baśi·te̯ni̯ kerkuse̯. a kin bośte̯ poda·rokse̯, sie̯ paśta·e̯ i je̯kte̯. eta be̯ri̯n pukśe̯ni̯ śojni̯ da juni̯. jue̯ni̯ da śoje̯ni̯ śor oje̯ǯ. že̯ńi̯·kse̯ da ńeve·stase̯ verde̯ni̯ da jukta·e̯ni̯ e̯tik pańiś da e̯tik kruškaiś. una· oke̯·te̯ni̯ tommese̯. ke̯r pe̯tase̯, ponde̯ni̯ orsni̯, śi̯vni̯, je̯kti̯ni̯. śore̯n ri̯tnas iľi oj-śe̯rnas že̯ńi̯·kse̯ da ńeve·stase̯ votte̯·te̯ni̯ uźni̯ me̯di·k ži̯rje̯.

5. *ojnas ge̯śśes mune̯ni̯. asi̯vnas tommese̯ ki̯tsa·e veža·ji̯s. nia ćećće̯ni̯, miśśe̯ni̯. ić-mo·ńkai̯s ponde̯ otsa·vni̯ ańi̯sve̯ strepa·jtni̯, a že̯ńi̯·ki̯s panta·e̯ ge̯śśese̯. ke̯r śoja·ni̯s voas goto·v, to pukśe̯ni̯ piru·jtni̯. gaže̯·ćće̯ni̯ vun-ti̯r. ri̯tnas ge̯śśes mune̯ni̯ gortani̯s. mune̯ni̯ i aji̯s da mami̯s ńeve·stai̯sve̯n asvani̯s gorte̯, a ić-mo·ńkai̯s pondas ovni̯ že̯ńi̯·ki̯s ordi̯n.*

the bridegroom so that he may become obedient to his wife. But the bridegroom hides his feet under the bench to prevent the young wife from treading on his feet. If the bride succeeds in treading on them, the bridegroom will be laughed at by the lads and married men. When they have had their food and drink, they get up from the table and buy the bed. Before leaving the room, the godfather and the master of ceremonies give money for the chest and the clothes. The cushions are acquired separately since the children and girl friends, who are sitting on them, will ask ransom for them. Until they receive the ransom they will not hand them over. The small children are often tricked with sweets. Then the clothes are wrapped up swiftly and taken to the courtyard in a matter of minutes to be placed on the bride's sleigh in which the father, mother, the sisters and brothers are going to travel. While she leaves the house, the girl receives her father's and mother's blessing that she may have a good life and that she may not slight her father and mother. They make the sign of the cross over their daughter with a round loaf of bread and an icon. Then they go out of the house and get on the sleigh. First the bridegroom and the bride take their seats, then others follow them out of the courtyard. They go at a gallop. On the way the girls sing to an accordion. When they arrive at the bridegroom's house, they stop. First the bridegroom and the bride enter the house. They are received by the bridegroom's father and mother in the porch. They greet each other, and the guests are invited into the house. As they cross the threshold, they pray to God and sit on the first bench. The guests gather together and begin to enjoy themselves. The bridegroom and the bride change clothes for the second time, and sit at the table to eat. In the meanwhile presents are distributed among the relatives of the bridegroom and they decorate the house. Those given presents take the gifts and go to dance. Then they sit down to eat and drink. They drink and eat till late at night. The bridegroom and bride must eat with the same spoon and drink from the same jug. The young couple are made to kiss each other frequently. When they have their fill of food, they play, sing and dance. About midnight, or in any case late at night, they send the bridegroom and the bride to sleep in the next room.

5. The guests leave during the night. In the morning the godfather calls the young couple. They get up and wash. The young wife begins to help her mother-in-law to cook, while the bridegroom receives the guests. When the food is ready, they sit down to feast. They make merry the whole day long. In the evening the guests go home. The bride's father and mother also leave for their home, while the young wife begins her new life with the bridegroom.

1. *mijan dere·vńas suwa·we i ń v a di̯n. sija šuśe̯ v e r χ - i ń v a. ďere·wńa i̯ži̯·t, je̯zi̯s una owe̯ni̯. emeś i komiez i roććez. ďere·wńai̯n em kolχo·z. em ešo· dom kultu·ri, wawkaez, klub, biblioťe·ka, i̯ži̯·t boľńića, počta i me̯dikkez učrežďe·ńiez. škola mian viľ. pervo ve̯i puove̯j, e̯ni stroi·tise̯ viľ, kirpi·ćne̯je̯. škola i̯ži̯t dvuχetažne̯j. škola di̯n suwa·we̯ni̯ maśťerkaez, ki̯te̯n ćeľa·ďes u̯ža·e̯ni̯ (u̯ža·le̯ni̯) arnas. škoľńikkez u̯ža·(w)e̯ni̯ kolχo·zi̯n, priškoľne̯j učasto·kvi̯n, stroi·ťeľstvoi̯n. nija una stroi·tise̯: ińťernat, ťepľića, ťir-kerku. klubi̯s mijan bi̯vše̯j vićku. kwube̯ oťiri̯s wokte̯ šoćći·śni̯. vi̯že̯·tni̯ kino·, postano·wka, tanću·jtni̯, orsni̯ biľa·rde̯n. klub di̯n em i̯ži̯t sporťi·vne̯j plošša·dka, ki̯te̯n moloďo·ži̯s orse̯ voľebowe̯n, basket-bowe̯n, ťeńise̯n. klubi̯n pi̯r provo·ďićće̯ni̯ razne̯j meroprija·ťiez. este̯n i wi̯dďe̯ni̯ ľekćijaez, dokla·ddez, provoďi·te̯ni̯ beśe·ddez meždunaro·dne̯j ťemaezve̯. kuľtu·rno-prośveťi·ťeľne̯j rabo·ta klubi̯n mune̯ bura·. bibľioťe·ka mijan ńe-e̯dďe̯n i̯ži̯t, no kńigaez ti̯rme̯ni̯ naśeľeńńezve̯. ćita·ťeľľes una. este̯n i kolχo·źńikkez, i meχańiza·torrez ertèesśań, rabo·ćej-služa·ššejez, škoľńikkez, ćeľa·ďez. em ešo· mijan ki̯k ďetsa·d, jaśľi, kićće mammez kolve̯ni̯ aśśini̯s ćeľa·ďse̯, ke̯r mune̯ni̯ u̯ža·wni̯. jaśľeaz i ďetsa·ddezas u̯ža·e̯ kvalifići·rovanne̯j medpersona·l. boľńi·ća mijan i̯ži̯t-koď. meďi·kkez obslu·živajte̯ni̯ ďere·vńaese̯, ke̯dnija suwa·-we̯ni̯ v e r χ - i ń v a di̯n. medpersona·l boľńi·ćai̯n veďite̯ i̯ži̯t rabo·ta, med-bi̯ oťiri̯s ez šogaw. boľńi·ćai̯n emeś kvaľifići·rovanne̯j vraććez, feľšerrez akuše̯·rkaez (akše̯·rkaez).*

2. *kolχo·zi̯s mijan i̯ži̯·t. kolχo·źńikkez u̯ža·e̯ni̯ bura. kolχo·zi̯n emeś sečče̯m otraśľez, ki̯ž živo·tnovodstvo, źemľeďe·ľie, ogoro·dńićestvo, ovćevo·dstvo, śvinovo·dstvo, ľnovo·dstvo. kolχo·zi̯s mijan objeďińo·nne̯j. eće̯ fχoďat una briga·daez razne̯j ďere·vńaśiń. tuusnas kolχo·źńikkez pristupa·jte̯ni̯ śevve̯ źernove̯·j, ovo·šne̯j kuľtu·raeze̯, (kuľtu·rreze̯). ećće̯ wokte̯ i vŕema ubira·jtni̯ uroža·j. ďere·vńai̯n śelsove·ti̯s provo·ďite̯ blagoustro·jstvo: stroi·te̯ni̯ kolo·ďeććez, viľ kerkuez, u·ľićaez vewťťe̯ni̯ trotua·rreze̯n. ďere·wńai̯n emeś una śeľske̯j, gorodske̯·j i oblastne̯·j ďeputa·ttez. nija ispoľńa·jte̯ni̯ naka·z aśśini̯s naro·dśa (narodwe̯). tuisnas mijan owe̯ni̯ vi̯borrez, ki̯te̯n naro·di̯s vi̯dvigajte̯ med-bur zonnese̯ i nivvese̯ kańďida·ttezve̯ blo·ka kommuńi·stov i besparťi·jni̯χ (-k). ve̯ras mijan mune̯ ľesorazrabo·tka. emeś ľespromχo·zzes, ki̯te̯n maśťer ľesaez proizvo·ďite̯ni̯ ďelove̯j dreveśi·na. tui̯snas mijan owwe̯ každej god ľesosplaw. gosuda·rstvove̯ mijan ľesozagotovi·ťeľľez každej god śete̯ni̯ una kubometrrez ďelove̯j dreveśi·nase̯. ľespromχo·zzezas peredove̯j rabo·ćiezwe̯ prisvoi·tise̯ vi̯so·ke̯j zvańie: uda·rńik*

251. Our village

1. Our village is situated by theIńva. It is called Verch-Ińva. The village is large, many people live in it. There are Zyrians and Russians. There is a kolkhoz in the village. In addition there are a cultural centre, shops, a club, a library, a big hospital, a post-office and other institutions. Our school is a new one. First it was a wooden building, but recently a new one has been built of brick. The school is high, it has two stories. Beside the school stand the workshops in which the children work in the autumn. The schoolchildren work in the kolkhoz, on the plot next to the school; they work on a building-site. They have built many things: a hostel, a hothouse and a shooting gallery. Our club is the one-time church. People come to rest at the club, to see cinema and stage performances, to dance and play billiards. There is a large sports-ground by the club where the young folk play volley-ball, basket-ball and tennis. There are always various programmes arranged at the club. Papers and lectures are delivered and speeches given on international themes. The work of promoting culture and education goes on well at the club. Our library is not very large, although the books are sufficient for the inhabitants. There are many readers: kolkhoz members, mechanics from the technical repair station, workers, clerks, schoolboys and girls. There are in addition two kindergartens and a nursery where mothers take their children when they go to work. Qualified medical personnel work in the nurseries and kindergartens. Our hospital is a fairly large one. The medical staff serve the villages around Verch-Ińva. The medical personnel do great work in preventing people from falling sick. There are qualified physicians, medical staff and midwives in the hospital.

2. Our kolkhoz is large. The kolkhoz members work well. The kolkhoz has such departments as stock-breeding, agriculture, horticulture, sheep-breeding, pig-breeding and flax-growing. Our kolkhoz has been unified. Many brigades from various villages belong to it. In the spring, the kolkhoz members start to sow the grain crops and the vegetables. Then the time arrives for harvest. Community planning in our village is done by the village council: they build wells and new houses, and lay pavements along the streets. Many delegates representing their community, city and district live in our village. They implement the instructions they receive from their people. Elections here are held in the spring, when the people indicate in the list of communists and non-party members the sons and daughters who best represent them. In our woods there is a timber industry. There are forestries where the forestry experts produce finished hardwood. Every year in spring the logs are floated downstream. Our wood-workers supply

kommuńiśt́i·ćeskovo truda. krajḭs mijan boga·t. em estḛn i vḛr, i ćeri, i źvérrez, i muḭs bur. ḛni mijan gortḭn uǯa·ḛnḭ geo·logorazve·doćnḛj parťijaez, ućo·nḛjes predpologa·jtḛnḭ, što mijan rajonḭn em ńeft. a mijan okrugḭn voo·bše aǯǯisḛ ńeftsḛ m a j k o r dḭn.

3. *subo·taezḛn i kreśśe·ńńaezḛn oťirḭs šoććiśḛ, veśeľi·ććḛ. kin munḛ klubḛ, a kin vadḛ·rḛ iľi vḛrḛ. mukḛ·dḭs munḛ poχo·dḛ čakja·wnḭ, jagḛda·wnḭ (arnas). klubḭn subḛ·taezas i kreśśe·ńńaezas owwḛnḭ konćerttez, χudo·žestvennḛj samo-ďeje·ťeľnośťḭn tanćijez, kinoez, kḛr wḭďďḛnḭ i ľekćijaez raznḛj ťemaezvḛ. mukḛ·d-pḭrśa vośśḛ vḭjezdnej ťeatra·ľnḛj truppa k u d i m k arśań. arťisttes suwdḛtwḛnḭ raznḛj spekta·kľez, ṕessaez. naro·dḭs klubḭn pḭr poluća·jtḛ duχo·vnḛj piśśa. agita·torrez i ľektorrez pḭr prośvešša·jtḛnḭ kolχo·źńikkesḛ i rabo·ćejjesḛ. išo· owwḛnḭ arnas koma·ndnḛj strećaez voľebowḛn, ťeńisḛn, orsḛnḭ raznḛj briga·daez, raznḛj učrežďe·ńńez.*

many cubic metres of hardwood to the state. The ace-workers in the forestry have received high distinctions: that of ace-worker of communist work. Our region is rich. There are woods, fish and game, and it has good soil. Now groups of geological prospectors are working here; scholars believe that crude oil is to be found in our district. In general, crude oil has been found near Majkor in our district.

3. On Saturday and Sunday people rest and enjoy themselves. Some go to the club, others to the river bank or to the woods. Some join in collective excursions to pick mushrooms and berries. On Saturday and Sunday, as a rule, amateur concerts, dances and cinema-shows take place, or lectures are held on various topics. Occasionally theatrical groups travelling the country arrive here from Kudymkar. The actors put on various performances and plays. People visiting the club always receive some intellectual nourishment. The propagandists and speakers always supply information to the kolkhoz members and the workers. In autumn there are also volley-ball and tennis competitions. Various brigades and institutions come to play.

NOTES TO THE TEXTS

These notes contain linguistic observations on the individual texts. Explanations of certain ethnographical peculiarities are also added here and there in order to facilitate understanding, although it has not been my aim to enter into examinations of a folklore character.* Therefore I do not refer to variants of tales or songs. Nevertheless, certain features of the circumstances in which my notations were made are indicated. Further, the names of my informants, some topographical data, and references to Russian connections and literary or folklore affinities are given where necessary.

The tales and narratives published are divided into numbered paragraphs; the texts are thus easier to survey, and the relevant notes can be more readily found.

Irrelevant words and phrases repeatedly occurring in the performance of certain informants like *šue*, *šuas* 'he says', *šuis* 'he said', *mij-kẹ* '. . . er . . .', *znaćit* do., *sija*, *sijẹ* do., *mij-kẹ karẹ (kerẹ)* 'bother', *mij-kẹ karis (keris)* 'bothered' have been often omitted in the translation.

In songs — and especially in laments — for metrical and rhythmical reasons, line-filling words *(da, daj, i, kẹ, ke, taj, ved)*, i.e. inorganic sounds

* The following collections contain Zyrian texts of linguistic and folklore interest: Dávid Fokos, Zürjén népköltészeti mutatványok (Specimens of Zyrian Folk Poetry). Budapest, 1913; *Id* , Zürjén szövegek (Zyrian Texts). Budapest, 1916; *Id.*, Zürjén szövegek. I. Letka-vidéki szövegek (Zyrian Texts I. Letka-Region Texts). NyK 45 (1917—20): 401—68; *Id.*, Volksdichtung der Komi (Syrjänen). Budapest, 1951; В. В. Климов, Коми-пермяцкӧй народнӧй легендаэз, сказкаэз, песняэз, частуткаэз, пословицаэз, поговоркаэз. Кудымкар, 1961; А. К. Микушев—П. И. Чисталев, Коми народные песни 1. Сыктывкар, 1966; А. К. Микушев—П. И. Чисталев, Коми народные песни 11. Сыктывкар, 1968; А. К. Микушев, Коми эпические песни и баллады. Ленинград, 1969; А. К. Микушев, Шондiбанӧй олӧмӧй. Частушкаяс сборник. Сыктывкар, 1969; Ф. В. Плесовский, Ко ми мойдъяс, свыланкывъяс да пословицаяс. Сыктывкар, 1956; Ю. Г. Рочев, Челядь свыланкывъяс да мойдкывъяс. Сыктывкар, 1969; Y. Wichmann, Syrjänische Volksdichtung. MSFOu. XXXVIII. Helsinki, 1916; Т. И. Жилина—В. А. Сорвачева, Образцы коми-зырянской речи. Сыктывкар, 1971 etc.

or syllables in the final (or occasionally the medial) position *(i̯, i, e, j, ji, jej)* often appear. Hyphens are used to distinguish these sounds and syllables from the organic parts of the morpheme concerned. For example, *druž-i-ka* 'suitor', *me-jej* 'I', *nī̯-j ole̮me̮j* 'my maiden life'.

1.

Performed by Marija Semenovna Maľgina (Lug). — Semantic and rhythmical units and phrases pronounced with identical accentuation are separated by vertical lines.

1. *ne̮šol* 'load' (?).

2. *če̮lkat-* 'to clap' < R. *щёлкать* | *toče̮d-* 'to tap, to rap', *tuče̮d-* do. | *smotri·* 'look !' < R. *смотри* | *podveďit-* 'to bring into trouble' < R. *подвести* | *ńeńki-manki:* cf. (SrSlK) Vm. Skr. *ńeńki-mamki* 'мифитеские существа в сказках < R. *няньки-мамки* 'nurses'.

2.

Taken down from the same informant as the preceding tale.

1. *žemćugne̮j* 'pearly' < R. *жемчуг, жемчужный* | *aľeńkoj, aľeńke̮j* 'purple' < R. *алый* | *vopšem* 'in general' < R. *вообще* | *korošo* 'all right' < R. *хорошо.*

2. *toko* 'so it seems' < R. *токо* 'кажется, видится, думается' | *ńe̮žjammi̯-* 'to calm down'.

4. *ši̯ńal-* 'to stop speaking, to become silent'.

3.

Performed by Irina Semenovna Maľgina (Lug.).

1. *ić-iń-pom* 'надчерица; step-daughter'.

2. *sen same̮j i je̮kte̮ni̯, no tancujte̮ni̯* 'There they happen to be dancing'. Standing as the predicate, both verbs *(je̮kte̮ni̯, tancujte̮ni̯)* mean: 'they dance'. Although fairly rare in the Vm dialect, the informant — obviously accustomed to the use of the word — applies the Russian loanword *tancujt-* (< *танцевать, танцовать*) to the interpretation of the original verb *je̮kte̮ni̯* 'they dance' | *uďiraj* 'up and away' < R. *удирать.*

3. *tube·ń* 'directly' (?).

4. *zirajt-* 'to look around' < R. *зирать* | *svić* 'quickly' (?)

4.

Performed by Anastasija Petrovna Kozlova (Lug).

2. *jablońa e̮šale̮ seni veši̯s* 'nothing but apple-trees are there'; *vomnas kuććis sija jablońase̮ mi̯j-ke karni̯, šojni̯, kurććōni̯* 'he began to eat, biting the apple with his mouth'. Here the informant confused the word *jablońa* 'apple-tree' (< R. *яблоня*) with *jablok* 'apple (< R. *яблоко*). In the rest of her performance she uses the correct word | *reve·śńića* 'bride, spouse' R. *ровесница*, cf. (Fokos-Fuchs) Vm *reveśńića* 'Braut (eig. Altersgenossin)'.

5. *seśśa sija ʒ̑eľa kerkae̯ sle̯jmi, pete̯* 'then she got to the small house, goes out [ɔ: enters]'. Some confusion has occurred here: instead of *pete̯* 'goes out', the verb *pire̯* 'enters' would be correct in this sentence.

5.

Performed by Evgenija Grigorjevna Proševa (Šoški).

2. *te̯ke̯ńʒ̑i* 'чуть-чуть; 'hardly, a little'.

3. *tučke̯-točke̯* 'to hammer'.

6.

Performed by Anna Ivanovna Pudova (Šoški).

2. "*oj menam pi, menam si̯no·k, viďiś ti̯ kak, kuče̯m, no, viʒ̑e̯d te, kuče̯m*" "Oh, son, my little son, look, what it is like !" By mistake, he said the phrase *viďiś ti̯ kak* 'look, what it is like' first in Russian, then repeated it in Zyrian. Also the last sentence of this paragraph is in Russian: *no, no, no, no, korošo, korošo* 'Well, well, all right, all right'.

7.

Performed by Natalija Ivanovna Kučmeńëva (Turja).

1. *strośńića, trośńića* 'day-labouring woman' < R. *срочница* | *kazaćina* 'female farmhand' < R. *казачиха*, (Даль) *казачина* | *ki̯šuna vaľe̯k* 'boot consisting of felt upper and cloth leg reaching up to the thigh', cf. (SrSlK) Vm. *vaľe̯k* 'зимная обувь, состоящая из валеных головок и пришивных суконных или холщовых голениц'. *ki̯šuna* < **pi̯ši̯na* or *pi̯šna* (cf. Fokos-Fuchs: Ud *pi̯šna upaki* 'niedrige Filzschuhe mit Schaft', V Ud *pi̯ši̯n* 'Randsaum, Verbrämung an den Schuhen (V), Tuchschaft der Filzschuhe (Ud)'); the adjectival form may have been influenced by the verb *ki̯š-* 'anziehen'.

2. *ńe-stre̯je̯ve̯j* 'one performing auxiliary service' < R. *нестроевой*.

3. *vejjal-* 'to advance', cf. (Fokos-Fuchs) V. *voʒ̑avni̯*, Vm *vejjalni̯* 'überholen, zuvorkommen' | *(końi vomi̯ni̯n sija zej veśki̯d, vot vesľanaad kaige̯n aʒ̑ʒ̑ilin?)* 'at the *końi* stretch it is very straight (the river), after all, you realized it when you went to *vesľana*'. This remark was addressed by N. I.

Kučmeńёva to folklorist A. K. Mikušev, my fellow collector, who had visited the region at an earlier date.

5. *šeńel'* 'mantle' < R. *шинель*.

8.

Performed by Oľga Andreevna Nekrasova (Turja).

1. The first sentence reads on the tape-recorder as follows: *mijan zej bur olišjas veliṇ, glavnej olišjas* 'Very kind people lived with us, chief dwellers'. The phrase *glavnej olišjas* 'chief dwellers' is omitted as one not fitting in the context.

2. *ńe še jej, ńe še prestuž* 'not quite stupid, not quite sane', cf. (Fokos-Fuchs) V. *jej-ńi-še presuž* 'dumm, Maulaffe' | *me berdlam* 'we weep': *me* 'I' stands erroneously for *mi* 'we' as a slip of the tongue.

9.

Performed by Natalija Ivanovna Kučmeńёva (Turja).

ćerez demse 'one house farther on' < R. *через дом* | *vejp-in* 'that is the place where the engagement takes place' | *sešša bere-voẑe ńevesta pukšilan žeńik dore . . .* 'then the bride sits, back to back, beside the bridegroom . . .' The rest of the description is not quite clear. Unfortunately, I failed to note the situation presented by my informant.

10.

Dialogue between Natalija Ivanovna Kučmeńёva and Oľga Andreevna Nekrasova.

dvaceť pjatoje 'the twenty-fifth' < R. *двацать пятое, tricatoje* 'the thirtieth' < R. *тридцатое, ďešatoje* 'the tenth' < R. *десятое*. Calendar days in recent Zyrian are often referred to by Russian numerals. | Following the sentence *kik vežon mišťi karam svaďba* 'in two weeks we shall hold the wedding' there is a faulty section on the tape. | *leptiš-* 'boast of', cf. (KRSl.) *лэптысь-* 'кичиться, гордиться'.

11.

Performed by Natalija Ivanovna Kučmeńёva (Turja).

katert 'tablecloth' < R. *скатерть*, cf. (SrSlK) Vm *skaťert* do.

12.

The riddles originate from the villages of Šoški, Lug and Turja where I noted down them from the informants named in the introduction. Nearly all of them contributed to the material.

No. 1: *śor* 'cross-beam on which cooking vessels are hung' | No. 20: Chinks in the walls of log buildings are filled with moss. | No. 39: cf. No. 20 | No. 48: *ńemẹja voda* (literally 'mute water') folk etymology standing for *nemẹj vojevoda* 'dumb voivode' < R. *немой воевода*. Cf. VL *ńemẹj sar* 'dumb tsar'. | No. 64: *koloćka* 'crest' | No. 65: *jurblal-* 'to bow again and again'.

13.

I noted down the proverbs in Šoški.

Nos 14 and 15: These are used as a rule for unusual, chance occurrences.

14.

The idiomatic expression No. 23 was noted in Turja ,the others in Šoški.

No. 6: Usually said with reference to idle, useless things. | No. 21: *kernal-* 'выходить', cf. (Fokos-Fuchs) Vm *kernal-* 'hervorstarren': *vomśi̮s kẹrt kernalẹ̆* 'aus seinem Munde starrt Eisen hervor'.

15.

Sung by Natalija Ivanovna Kučmeńëva and Oľga Andreevna Nekrasova (Turja).

ešgẹdli̮- 'прицепить, навалить, развестить' | *vožgẹdli̮-* 'to separate', cf. (SrSlK) SR *vožgẹd-* ''широко расставить, раздвинуть (ноги)' | *juś ni̮r* (lit. 'swan's nose'): popular etymology for *jos̓ ni̮r* 'sharp-nosed' | *kẹnẹvatnẹj* < R. (Даль) *канаватый, канават* 'устарелая щелковая ткань, цветная и узорочная', linen' | *štopnẹj* 'made of patterned material' < R. *штофный* | *sborńik* 'головной убор замужной женщины' < R. сборник | *dokjan* 'jolting', cf. (SrSlK) Ud *dovjav-* 'качаться, шататься, раскачиваться', *dovkjav-* 'трясти, мотать (головой, о корове)'.

16.

Sung by Anastasija Petrovna Kozlova, Irina Semënovna Maľgina and Marija Semënovna Maľgina (Lug).

The song is Russian in origin, as indicated also by the Russian text portion (*t́elo druškaja* . . . lines 32—3).

17.

Sung by Evdokija Ivanovna Lapina, Lidija Parchačëva, Evgenija Grigorjevna Proševa, Aleksandra Semënovna Pudova and Anna Ivanovna Pudova (Šoški).

The personal name occurring in lines 4 and 8 may be optionally replaced by any other girl's or boy's name. Line 12: *palej roć ki vile* lit. 'on to the hand of a dead Russian', *palej* 'dead' < R. *палый* which well may be a corrupt form for: *paľ roẑ vile* 'into the pen on the clearing' | *ʒurkja-virkja* 'creaking; расшатанный, скрипучий' | *kalać-kē* '<cake-string<, on which cakes are stringed' | *katlan* 'jolting, cf. (Fokos-Fuchs) Pr *katlal-* 'sich nach rechts und links beugen, neigen'.

18.

This song was performed by the singers of the preceding one.

19.

Sung by Lidija Ivanovna Parchačëva (Šoški).

20.

Sung by Evdokija Ivanovna Lapina, Evgenija Grigorjevna Proševa and Anna Ivanovna Pudova (Šoški).

The song is Russian in origin.

21.

This song was performed by the singers of the preceding one.

The word *zon* 'Bursche' has a rhythm-filling function in the song, therefore I left it untranslated.

22.

Sung by Evdokija Ivanovna Lapina (Šoški). Fragment.

23.

Sung by Natalija Ivanovna Kučmeńëva and Oľga Andreevna Nekrasova (Turja).

verdan-verdiś 'sustainer, kind, dear', cf. (SrSlK) Vm *verdan-verdiś* 'кормилец' | *laća vile* 'hopefully', cf. (Fokos-Fuchs) V *laća vile*, *laćaen* 'с надеждой на кого-ниб.; auf jemand hoffend, sich auf jem. verlassend'.

24.

Sung by Natalija Ivanovna Kučmeńëva (Turja).

25.

Sung by Oľga Andreevna Nekrasova (Turja).

26.

Sung by Natalija Ivanovna Kučmeńëva (Turja).
krutnej̮ 'severe' < R. *крутой*, (Даль) *крутный* 'скорый, спешный, торопливый'.

27.

Sung by Irina Semënovna Maľgina (Lug). Fragment.
ľeń 'snake', cf. (SrSlK) Vm *ľeń* 'улитка, червяк, гусеница'.

28.

Sung by Evdokija Ivanovna Lapina (Šoški).

29.

Performed by Marija Dmitrievna Kokanina (Lug).
vika 'vetch' < R. *вика*.

30.

Performed by Irina Fëdorovna Bykova (Ibi̮). Phrases and rhythmic units accentuated identically are separated by perpendicular lines.
2. *vićko šer̮* 'in the middle of the church' (unaffixed adverb).

31.

Performed by the informant in the preceding text.

1. *śorkńi kez̮asni̮, una, repa* 'they sow beet, plenty of it'. After *śorkńi* 'beet' it seems redundant to mention *repa*, which is a Russian loanword for the same. | At the end of the first paragraph the same situation occurs as before, therefore the informant does not repeat it.

2. *ši̮rjovtni̮* 'затянуть веревкой; he makes a noose', cf. (Fokos-Fuchs) V *ši̮rkes̮* 'Schlinge zum Fangen von Tieren'.

3. *tark vart-* 'to knock', cf. (WUo.) *turk-tark ker-* 'klopfen, pochen', *tarked̮* -'klopfen (ans Fenster)' | *kes̮ti̮ga* 'crutch' < R. *костыль* | *kučem̮-ke̮ rańinejes* '(he spares the life of) a wounded man'. The accusative form — due perhaps to slip of the tongue — is connected with the predicate *(koľas)* of the previous sentence which has a double meaning: 'leave, stay'.

4. *pos-jịv* 'barn', cf. (Fokos-Fuchs) VL *tẹvar pukťis pos-jịlẹ* 'er lud die Ware in die Scheune (den Schuppen; на сарай)' | *buv-bov-bav ker-* 'to moo (the cow)', *ker-* 'machen, tun' is not a VL form.

5. *veďitẹ-babitẹ* 'she is nursing and petting' | *vẹrẹg* 'evil spirit' < R. *ворог* | *ďevka-ćerno·vka* 'black-haired girl' < R. *девка-чернявка..*

7. *lebalẹ* 'flies': slip of the tongue instead of *ujalẹ* 'swims' | *jataž* 'storey' < R. *этаж* | *kịšas* ('anziehen, überziehen'): possibly slip of the tongue for *nuas* 'takes it out'.

32.

Taken down from the informant of the previous two tales.

1. *pipiriśťi sokol* 'pipiriśťi falcon', cf. (WUo.) V *pipilịs, pipilịstị* 'Name eines Falken in einem Märchen', (Fokos-Fuchs) VL *pipiristi, pipiriski, pipilisti: p. sẹkẹl* '(in einem Märchen:) ein prächtiges Kleid od. ein Schmuck . . .; ein Falke . . .; Name eines Mannes, der sich zum zweitenmal verheiratet; dann kommt seine erste Frau hin und *p.s.* geht mit ihr weg. (Die Bedeutung soll?: 'Feuriger Falke, Feuerfalke' sein)' | *tịvk-tavk:* untranslatable word, yet cf. (WUo.) P *tịv* 'Schwung- od. Schwanzfeder', (SrSlK) SU Le *tịl* 'перо (птицы)' | *voć-* 'does sg.', cf. (SrSlK) *vẹć-* 'делать'.

4. *što da taja?* 'what is this?': *što* < R. *что* | *mịć* (sic!) 'what'.

6. *kurnan* 'rake' developed through contamination of the Vm *kurjan* and VL *narman* do. | *rịś-ńań* 'Passover cake; Easter meal made of curds', cf. (SrSlK) SU I *rịś-ńan* 'творожная пасха'.

33.

Performed by the informant of Nos 30, 31 and 32.

1. *ćetverik* 'measuring vessel' < R. *четверк* | *te ćevo, ńi-nẹm on tẹd* 'You know nothing': *ćevo* < R. *чего.*

2. *dve kopejki* 'two kopecks' < R. *две копейки.* Bilingual Zyrians often mingle Russian numerical attributive constructions with their Zyrian speech, like *kịk kẹpejka* for two kopecks etc. | *beda* 'very much' < R. *беда.*

3. *ka* 'ah!' | *smotri·* 'listen!' < R. *смотри.*

5. *tijanjasẹ* 'you (pl.)' rare vocative form: (Adess.-Gen.) *tijan* + (Plur.) *jas* + (PxlSg.) *ẹ* | At the end of her tale the informant, turning to her audience, added the following words: *pomaẹs mortẹ i karis. vot tenịd ruć, kučẹm śuś: važẹn taj: ruć kojd pẹ śuś. no, mića, abu?* 'It made a man of Poma. You see, how wise the fox is! Well, a long time ago (they said): He is clever as a fox. Well, is it nice or not?'

34.

Performed by Anna Petrovna Belova (Ibi̯).

1. *mes̯-ťuťiś ǯuǯidǯik* 'taller than the cock of a bull': possibly lapse of the tongue for *mes̯-ćupiś ǯuǯidǯik* 'taller than the udder of a cow' coming up below | *ďida kosa-mesań* 'scythed woman-cook from the stable', cf. (SrSlK) VL *mesań* 'хозяйка, стряпуха, повариха' | *e̯ksi̯ pili̯ jurbita . . .* 'Before the prince's son I bow . . .': probably a spell.

2. *zavedka* 'rope of withies for fastening the sleigh-shaft', cf. (Fokos-Fuchs) Ud *zavertka* 'Schlittenband (aus Ruten geflochten; mit diesem wird die Deichsel am Schlitten befestigt)', (SrSlK) Vm *zavetka*, VL *zavedki* 'завертка' | *ve̯vli̯ žvić vartas* 'he lashes at the horse'.

35.

Performed by Kristina Michajlovna Bykova (Ibi̯).

As K. M. Bykova is a teacher, it is only natural that turns of literary usage occur in her speech. For example, she uses the past-tense forms of the negative verb not as usual in the VL dialect but according to the literary norm: *eg*, *en*, *ez*, etc.

36.

Taken down from the informant of the previous tale.

ľok-gag 'lizard' literary form instead of VL *ćoǯiv*, *ćoǯuv* do.

37.

Performed by Klavdija Iljična Zinovjeva (Ibi̯).

dom 'house' < R. *дом* | *e̯ťi jure̯ keri̯štas* 'he cuts off one of its heads' (properly 'he strikes at one of its heads') | *slava bogu* 'thank God' < R. *слава богу*.

38.

Taken down from the informant of the previous tale.

39.

Performed by Elizaveta Michajlovna Kyzjurova (a, b, c) and Irina Fëdorovna Bykova (d, e, f, g) (Ibi̯).

(a) 2. *ić-mоń pire̯g-lun* 'the bride's pirogi-day': on this day the bridegroom has to carve pirogi at the bride's home. A piece of string is put in the pirogi to make the carving more difficult. If the bridegroom has no knife with him, this means that he is not a proper person, real man.

(b) *ćasa dvaeǯ* 'for two hours' < R. *часа два* 'two hours'. Zyr. *-ęǯ* terminative suffix. For numerical constructions of Russian origin, see No. 33 | *kęzla:* Kozlovka village soviet | *pol kilometra* 'half a kilometre distant' < R. *пол километра.*

(d) 1. *pęlęťentsi̯* 'towel' < R. *полотенце* | *ćugaręk* 'burnt chippings of fir' < R., cf. сгорать 'to burn, to be burnt' | *šmońaś-* 'to make a joke'.

(e) At the end of the narrative a woman present in the audience exclaimed: *ńe-kučem abu pravda, me og verit tajęli̯* 'Not a word of it is true, I do not believe this!'.

(f) *braććina* 'picnic party', cf. (Fokos-Fuchs) V *braččina*, Ud *braććina* 'Feiertag am 1. November; auf Grund einer Kollekte veranstaltetes gemeinsames Gastmahl (eig. Brüderschaft) (V), auf Grund einer Kollekte veranstaltetes gemeinsames Gastmahl in der Butterwoche (Ud)' < R. *братчина.*

(g) *vo gęgęrja bośtęm* 'the choosing of a mate for a year': Towards Christmas young people choose a mate to walk out with exclusively in the next year. | *pri̮ś*! 'boo!', cf. (SrSlK) *bri̮ś, pri̮ś* 'брысь' < R. | *muža svojevo* . . . 'Her own husband . . . (acc.)' Russian song | *χrusjedli̮-* 'quench'.

40.

The riddles were recorded at the village of Ibi̯, from nearly all of my informants.

No. 30: *bi̮ń*! 'splash!', cf. *zi̮ri̮mi̮d bi̮ń ki̮lę petis* 'your nose is running with snot, splash!' | *ľas* 'flattened', cf. (SrSlK) VL *ľas* 'приплюснутый, плоский' No. 32: *ǯęvjaś-* 'бегать только о глазах; to flatter', cf. (SrSlK) Ud *ǯęvkńit-* 'пронестись, быстро пробежать, проехать, проплыть' | No. 33: *kękjami̮s-pod* 'копыл на сани; runners of a sledge' No. 37: *ľus-ľas* 'slowly', cf. (WUo). V *ľus-ľas* 'langsam'.

41.

I also recorded the proverbs in Ibi̯.

No. 8: Said of a short person.

42.

The idiomatic expressions also come from the village of Ibi̯.

No. 2: said of a lazy person. | Nos 3 and 13: Addressed to the bride after the wedding is over as a warning to be careful and diligent. | No. 5: Useless futile work. | No. 6: It is a lie | No. 11: Said of children who are always ready to escape from home. | No. 12: Lamp with a dim light.

43.

Sung by Serafima Lukjanovna Popovceva (Ibi̯).

44.

Sung by Marfa Aleksandrovna Bykova (Ibi̯). Fragment.

The first word of line 5 sounds indistinct on the tape. | *dostojna:* that part of the mass where *достойно есть* . . . 'Worthy art thou' is sung.

45.

Sung by the informant of No. 43.

The portions of Zyrian in square brackets (recurrent stereotyped turns) are my complementary insertions. — Line 39 is missing; the informant had forgotten what the lover wanted to ransom the girl with. It can be heard from the tape that one of the audience whispers: *garmońńa vi̯le̯* 'with an accordion'.

46.

Sung by Elizaveta Michajlovna Kyzjurova (Ibi̯).

47.

Performed by several singers (Ibi̯).

48.

Variant (a) was sung by Marija Andreevna Kyzjurova and Anna Pavlovna Kyzjurova, and the fragmentary variant (b) by the choir of Ľaľi.

49.

Sung by two women of the village of Ibi̯.

kumać 'kumach cloth', cf. (Fokos-Fuchs) *kumać* 'rotes baumwollenes Zeug' < R. *кумач* | *kitajka* 'smooth cotton cloth; nankeen' < R. *китайка*.

50.

Sung by Elizaveta Iljinična Kyzjurova (Ibi̯).

51.

Performed by several singers (Ibi̯).

52.

Sung by the choir of Ľaľi (five women).

53.

Performed by the singers of No. 52.

54.

Performed, under the leadership of Nadežda Andreevna Igošina, by the choir of Ľaľi.

55.

Sung by Anna Pavlovna Kyzjurova (Ibi̯). Fragment.

56.

Sung by Anna Afanasevna Kyzjurova (Ibi̯). Fragment.
paľ: (SrSlK) Палевицы, Сыктывдинский район, or: 'паль, выжженное место в лесу'.

57.

Sung by Klavdija Iljična Zinovjeva (Ibi̯). Fragment.

58.

Performed by the choir of Ľaľi. Fragment.

59.

Sung by Oľga Pankratevna Popovceva (Ibi̯).

60.

Performed by the choir of Ľaľi. Fragment.

61.

Sung by Roza Pankratevna Popovceva (Ibi̯). Fragment.

62.

Sung by Marija Ignatevna Smirnova (Ibi̯). Fragment.

63.

Sung by Olga Pankratevna Popovceva (Ibi̯).

64.

This lament also was sung by Olga Pankratevna Popovceva (cf. No. 63).

65.

Sung by Anna Petrovna Kyzjurova, Marija Aleksandrovna Kyzjurova and Marija Vikentievna Popova (Ľaľi).

66.

Variant (a) sung by Marfa Aleksandrovna Bykova, and variant (b) by Irina Fedorovna Bykova (Ibi̯).

(a) *ši̯r-bľaď* 'мышка-пакостница; disgusting mouse' | *tūk-* 'to push', cf. (SrSlK) VL *tuvkńit-* 'толкнуть' | *jōk-* 'to displace', cf. (WUo). V *jovk-* 'verrücken' | *kojōt-* 'to overturn', cf. (WUo.) *koj-* 'gießen, ausgießen, ausschütten'. All three words *(tūk-, jōk-, kojōt-)* display Vm dialectal features *(ū, ō)* | *e̯ška-me̯ška* 'rainbow' | *ke̯ni pe̯če̯r-pe̯vsi̯s* 'Where is the nettle? (lit. 'where is the middle of the nettle?)': the word *pe̯vsi̯s* 'middle' occurs here most probably for reasons of rhythm. | *śivko da burko, meščanne̯j voronko* 'grey, blackish-brown magic steed', cf. Fokos-Fuchs (under *burko*).

(b) *sije vengrijae̯ nue̯dni̯* 'it will be taken to Hungary', *sije kare̯ nue̯dni̯* 'it will be taken to Syktyvkar': jocular improvization in honour of the guests.

67.

Performers: Variant (a): Serafima Lukjanovna Popovceva (Ibi̯); variant (b): Elizaveta Iljinična Kyzjurova (Ibi̯); variant (c): Klavdija Iljična Zinovjeva (Ibi̯); variant (d): Anna Stepanovna Kiselëva (Ľaľi); variant (e): Marija Vikentievna Popova (Ľaľi).

(a) *oš-mu*, correctly *mu-oš* 'mole': the parts of the compound are reversed in error.

(c) Line 7 is a distorted Russian text: *поиду в поляну, встречу Варвару* | Line 9: *kurka da re . . .*: Somebody dropped in during the recording, and the rest of the performance cannot be made out because of the loud conversation.

(d) *si̯ci̯* 'melted fat', cf. (SrSlK) I *ši̯ci̯ vi̯j* 'протопленное сало'.

(e) *końi-veńi:* incomprehensible combination of words | *pome̯s:* perhaps a place-name | *paľ:* place-name cf. SrSlK: Палевицы, Сыктывдинский район | *pi̯ž i potke̯dli̯śjas* 'the smashers of the boat': perhaps because they shatter the boat while playing and hopping about *gerd ku ektiśjas* 'collectors of red hides': possibly an allusion to their being thieves.

68.

Sung by an informant from Ibi̯.

69.

Sung by an informant from Ibi̯.

70.

Sung by Anna Aleksandrovna Kyzjurova (Ibi̯).

71.

Sung by Elizaveta Michajlovna Kyzjurova (Ibi̯).

72.

Sung by Klavdija Iljična Zinovjeva (Ibi̯).

73.

Sung by Kristina Michajlovna Bykova (Ibi̯).

74.

Sung by the six-year-old daughter of Kristina Michajlovna Bykova (Ibi̯). *kevdum* 'round loaf of bread': literary usage, in the VL dialect *keleb* do. is used. In all likelihood the little girl learnt the children's song from her mother who is a teacher.

75.

Sung by Nadežda Andreevna Igošina (Ľaľi).

From line 18 onwards the text contains untranslatable words, with the exception of *mij* 'what kind of'; these may be old Zyrian personal names. | *perenos* 'monstrance or amulet' < R. (Pawlwoski, Русско—немецкий словарь — Russisch-deutsches Wörterbuch) *перенос* 'die Übertragung der geweihten Gaben vom Opfertisch zum Altar; Talisman, Amulet'.

76.

Sung by Anna Ivanovna Karakčieva (Ľaľi).

77.

Sung by Nadežda Andreevna Igošina (Ľaľi).
From line 10 onwards there are no logical connections.

78.

Sung by Elizaveta Iljinična Kyzjurova (Ibi̯).

79.

Sung by Marfa Aleksandrovna Bykova (Ibi̯). Fragment.
bi̯ľkja ki̯mẹsa 'with a white forehead', cf. (WUo.) VL *bi̯ľkja-ki̯mẹsa* 'weißstirnig (Ochs; Mskr.: die ganze Stirn weiß)'.

80.

Performers: variant (a): Anna Aleksandrovna Kyzjurova (Ibi̯); variants (b), (c) and (d): Irina Fëdorovna Bykova (Ibi̯). The last three are fragments.

81.

The rhymes (chastushkas) were recorded at Ibi̯, with the exception of the last two chastushkas, which were collected at the village of Ľaľi.

Lines 6—12 of the twelfth chastushka were sung in Russian. | The word *śerbijanka* (< R. *сербиянка* 'Serbian woman') in the seventeenth chastushka means 'Gipsy girl'.

*

Here at the end of the notes to the VL texts I publish two counting songs which I recorded from Nadežda Andreevna Igošina in Ľaľi. It would be a difficult task to translate these logically incoherent rhythmic sequences. In the second verse the first words of the lines represent the Zyrian numerals from 1 to 10, while the second words of the lines are phonetic variants of the first ones generated by replacing the initial consonants, by bilabial consonants (except for two numbers). The change results in meaningful words in certain instances: *mi̯k, moľ, sit, šajt, pas*.

1.

eťile – mẹďile,
śẹd tar – pẹd tar,
pečẹr, poľe, bẹtala,
i̯b!

2.

ęt́ik – męt́ik,
ki̮k – mi̮k,
kujim – mujim,
ńoľ – moľ,
vit – sit,
kvajt – šajt,
siźim — biźim,
kękja·mi̮s – bękja·mi̮s,
ękmi̮s – bi̮kmi̮s,
das – pas.

82.

Performed by G. G. Baraksanov (Śośka).

2. *siʒ́-ke* (phonetically: *sić-kę*) 'значит; so, it means' | *i̮zbaz* 'шумом; noisily, clattering by' cf. (KRSl) *i̮z-baz: i̮. pi̮rni̮ vaę* 'с шумом войти в воду'.

83.

Taken down also from G. G. Baraksanov.

gorko 'bitter' < R. *горько* do. | *źveroboj* 'brandy matured on St. John's wort' < R. *зверобой* 'hollow-leaved St. John's wort; Hypericum perforatum' (Большая советская энциклопедия), *зверобойная* 'настойка, водка на зверобое настоенная' (Даль).

84.

Performed by Anna Nikolaevna Čalanova (Ust́-Kulom).

1. *pośked: pośkedis peľse* 'he pricked up his ears', cf. (SrSlK) VU *pośked-* 'насторожить, напрячь, навострить (уши)'.

3. *zaďeńejt-* 'to offend, to hurt' < R. *задеть* | *zaďevajt-* 'to insult' < R. *задевать* | *ćuń-kičte*, phonetically: *ćuń-kište* 'ring' (acc.).

4. *i sar objavitis stav narodes ćukarććini* 'the tsar proclaimed that all the people should be assembled': the verb *ćukarćći-* 'to come together' is due to a slip of the tongue, standing for *ćukart-* 'to call together' | *verćće* 'he takes nourishment': erroneously for *verde* 'he feeds' (trans.).

6. *ťikejaʒ́ik* 'in a calmer tone' < R. *тихий*! *pi̮ris* 'he went in', correctly 'he went out': erroneously for *petis* 'he went out'.

85.

Taken down from the informant of No. 84.

śpavgiś- 'to plop down somewhere' cf. KRSl. шпавгысь- 'падать' | *piśt* 'hole', cf. (Fokos-Fuchs) V *piś* (nicht in Syktyvkar) 'kleine Öffnung, Loch' | *ńikiľćišt-* 'to roll into a ball', cf. (SrSlK) Lu SC *ńigi̮ľtći-*, SU *ńiki̮ľtći-*, VU *ńugiľtći-* 'свернуться клубком'.

86.

Performed by Evgenij Semënovič Guljaev (1957, Derevjansk).
3. *mi̯j-śure̮* 'something; кое-что, что попало'.

87.

Taken down from the informant of No. 86.
2. *pe̮ś-vivśim*, *pe̮ś-vivśis* 'hot' (adv.); сгоряча'.

88.

Performed by the informant of the previous two narratives.
1. *goz-med* 'a few' | *pe̮d'd'azek* 'red-finned carp' < R. *подъязок*.
2. *d'erkjedli-* 'to jerk' < R. *дергать* | *žugil'-pi̯riś* 'listlessly'.

89.

Performed by Jurij Semënovič Guljaev (Derevjansk).
1. *li̯z-petl'a* 'winter snare', *te̮vśa petl'a* do.
2. *koj-bed'* 'shovel', cf. (Fokos-Fuchs) Pr *koj-bed* 'Schaufelstab'.
3. *ǯug* 'snare', cf. (Fokos-Fuchs) VU *ǯug* 'Schlinge, Falle für Vögel, Mäuse' | *sije unǯik li̯mse ve̮lem puktiśśe, ki̯zǯika da i ki̯vse, kapkan-ki̯vse abu sečem ćutkej* 'More snow was piled on it, more thickly, or the tongue of the trap would be less sensitive'. The use of *li̯mse* and *ki̯vse* in the acc. is incorrect. Obviously the informant wanted to use the transitive form yet he closed the sentence with a reflexive verb, or with a noun predicate. Hence the lapse.
5. *na* 'they' | *vot sija ve̮lem izjasse, na petaleni ve̮rśid i e̮kteni* 'They (the capercaillie) go out of the forest to collect stones'. — The capercaillie grinds the stones in its mouth but does not swallow them.
6. *bordjišt-* '(the bird) fights with its wings', cf. (SrSlK) VU *bordjiś-* 'драться крыльями (Напр., о петрухах)'.

90.

Performed by Boris Ivanovič Antonovskij (Derevjansk).
ot (phonetically: *o̮t)* 'look' < R. *вот*.

91.

The riddles were noted down in Ust́-Kulom.
No. 1: *va-gu* 'water cave', making no meaning here; parallelism with the word *mu-gu* 'cave (on land)' justifies its occurrence in the riddle. Cf. (WUo.)

V *vagu* 'unverständliches Wort in einem Rätsel' | No. 4: *iǯi-iǯi . . . aǯi-aǯi:* onomatopoeic words of unknown meaning. | No. 5: *ťūgun* 'nimble; шустрый' | No. 15: *śveńi-gered*, village name: *Źveńi-gorod;* Звенигородское', cf. (Fokos-Fuchs) S *źveńi-gorod:* Звенигородское (Dorf in der Визингск. вол. | No. 23: *śńari ji* 'thin ice', cf. (SrSlK) VU *ńar ji* 'шуга, тонкий, мелкий лёд на реке (перед ледоставом)'.

92.

This proverb was also noted down in Usť-Kulom.

93.

Charms and curses were taken down in Usť-Kulom. My informants: Anna Nikolaevna Čalanova: (b), (d); Irina Egorjevna Kipruševa: (e), (f), (g), (h); Lidija Dadovna Timuševa: (a), (c).

(c) *poma jokiš* 'Kama perch': *poma* de-etymologized word for *koma* 'of Kama', cf. (f) *koma jokiš* 'Kama perch' | (f) Said when the child loses its milk-teeth. | *kupaľńića:* name-day of St. John the Baptist (June 4) < R., cf. *Иван Купала*. The word *kupaľńića*, according to Fokos-Fuchs' vocabulary and the SrSlK means 'Ranunkel (Ranunculus acris); лютик'. Yet cf. R. (Даль) *купальница:* День 23 юня, св. Агрипины. Аграфены купальницы; начало купанья.

94.

Sung by: Agrafena Semënovna Zezegova, Elizaveta Semënovna Uľnyrova and Matrena Iljinična Uľnyrova (Ruć).

pľeť-i-śer nuvisni da kulak-śer nuvisni 'they took her away with the whip, they took her away with the fist', cf. (KRSl) *śer: ńajt śer mun-* обратиться в грязь', *vir śer mun-* 'истечь кровъю'.

95.

Performed by several singers led by Anna Nikolaevna Čalanova (Usť-Kulom).

In the first line the phrase *verdemej ďiťaj* 'my dear (prop. nourished) son' is illogical in the context. | *ľever* 'brother-in-law' < R. *деверь* | The phrase *ťom-i-nom ľesu* [< R. *в темном лесу*] — which came into the Zyrian text by mistake — well brings out the Russian origin of the song. | The expression *šondiej mamej* 'my pretty sun, dear mother' in line 19 is a stereotype turn, not appropriate in the context. | *ćuvki* 'stockings' < R. *чулки* | *ľutaja źmeja* 'bloodthirsty snake' < R. *лютая змея* do.

96.

Performed by several singers (Ruć).

97.

Performed by several singers (Ruć).

salatulati 'in Salatula': distorted form instead of *sarapula* 'Sarapul'. | *vi̯ľiś naževitteǯis* 'till her next marriage': (SrSlK) FV *naževit-* 'наживать, зарабатывать'.

98.

Performed by several singers led by Lidija Dadovna Timuševa (Usť-Kulom).

ťitsa 'bird' < R. *птица* | Numerals of Russian origin *(pervoja, toraja, treťťaja)* clearly indicate that the song's Russian variant is known at the place. As the song was finished A. N. Čalanova asked L. D. Timuševa: *mi̯jla te roćaśin* 'why were you talking Russian?'

99.

Sung by Anna Petrovna Kočanova (Nosim).

ďikej mu vilin 'in a wild land': *ďikej* (< R. *дикий*) may be an error, instead of the similarly Russian *ťikej* (<*тихий*).

100.

Performed by several singers (Ruć).

ńe-dekmi̯-šte 'not only' < R. (Даль) *не токмо*, *не токма-что* 'не только; мало того что' (see under токмо), cf. (WUo.) V *ńe-tẹkmi̯-štẹ* 'nicht nur (daß)' | In the last line (*arśa bi̯gen końerejes bi̯gedas* 'it dries the poor soul with the autumn wind [foam]') the word *bi̯gen* 'with foam' has replaced the logically expectable *tẹlen* 'with wind' under the influence of *bi̯gedas* (figura etymologica).

101.

Performed by several singers (Derevjansk).

102.

Sung by Lidija Dadovna Timuševa (Usť-Kulom).

103.

Performed by several singers (Ruć).

iń-pẹv 'kitchen part; кухонная часть; properly 'wives' side' | *berkńovt-* 'turn away (tr); повернуть' | *bekar* 'cup': this is not an VU word, but one widely known from the (SrSlK) SU Vm Lu Le VL SC dialects, yet cf. (WUo.) VU *bekar*. It follows, therefore, that we are dealing with a song of Russian origin — as indicated by the words *dunaj reka* 'Danube River' < *Дунай река* — which came from one of these dialects to Ruć. | *l'istevej* 'velvet' < R. *плистовый* | *rocnej:* de-etymologized form instead of *roć noj* 'Russian cloth' *aźam* 'kaftan' < R. (Даль) *азям* 'долгий и полный. . . кафтан'.

104.

Performed by several singers (Derevjansk).

vosadol'i 'accordion': the naming is based on the initial words of the Russian 'song' *(Во саду ли в огороде)* (cf. RÉDEI: NyK 76; 366). | The last two lines come from the Russian original.

105.

Sung by Anna Nikolaevna Čalanova and Lidija Timuševa.

106.

Performed by several singers (Derevjansk).

107.

Performed by several singers (Derevjansk). This song is literary in origin.

108.

Performed by several singers under Anastasija Ivanovna Kiprušëva's direction (Derevjansk).

This song is Russian in origin. *lutše* 'better < R. *лучше*.

109.

Performed by the singers of the previous song.

110.

Sung by Agrafena Michajlovna Rakina (Derevjansk).

111.

Sung by Marija Andrejevna Guljaeva (Derevjansk).

112.

Sung by Anna Nikolaevna Čalanova (Usť-Kulom).

113.

Performed by several singers led by Anna Nikolaevna Čalanova (Usť-Kulom).

114.

Performed by several singers led by Lidija Dadovna Timuševa (Usť-Kulom).

115.

Performed by several singers led by Anna Nikolaevna Čalanova (Usť-Kulom).

gęśťin 'present, gift'; in other dialects: SR. *gęśńeć*, SC *gęśńin* Ud (Vaš) *gęśťińća*, VU SU Vm I Lu Le Pec Ud (Gl) *gęśťińeć*, Vm VL *gęśťińʒi* do. < R. гостинэц | *pidaš/bidaš-gera:* 'P/B-hill' (geographical name) | *dorińō* 'slanting'.

116.

Performed by a group of singers directed by Anna Nikolaevna Čalanova (Usť-Kulom).

This song is of Russian origin.

117.

Sung by Anna Nikolaevna Čalanova (Usť-Kulom).

This song is of literary origin.

118.

Performed by a group of singers directed by Anna Nikolaevna Čalanova (Usť-Kulom).

119.

Sung by Anna Nikolaevna Čalanova and Lidija Dadovna Timuševa (Usť-Kulom).

This is a dance-song of Russian origin as indicated by the repetition of the incipit *ajgigla* (< R. Даль: *ой дид ладо*, cf. Fokos, ZürjNépkMut. 13, 15: *oj ďig lada*), further, by the second line which has been taken over — erroneously and in a corrupted form — from the Russian original: *źeľonej roščica alaja ćvetala ćvet*, meaning approximately: 'in the green grove there was a purple flower blooming'. Those engaged in dancing stand up in two rows at a certain distance from each other and sing the lines of the song alternately while approaching each other (cf. Fokos, op. cit. 15).

In lines 13—14 Čalanova replaced *kutan* 'you take me' by the plural *kutannid* 'you (pl.) take me'. Similarly in lines 23—24: *veštan* 'you redeem it' is replaced by *veštannid* 'you (pl.) redeem it'. | *mījen* 'with what': emphatic lengthening of *mijen* | Lines 27–28: Čalanova: *oz kov*, Timuševa: *oz kō* | *mijan polke sodi* 'our group has increased in number'; the form *polke* (PxlSg) is undoubtedly due to a slip of the tongue, the correct form being *mijan polknim* or *mijan polk*.

120.

Performed by the singers of No. 119.
korošoj 'good' < R. *хороший* (dialectal form *хорошой*).

121.

Performed by Anna Nikolaevna Čalanova and Lidija Dadovna Timuševa (Usť-Kulom).
kelaćse: phonetically *kelaťse* 'cake (acc.)'.

122.

Performed by Lidija Dadovna Timuševa (Usť-Kulom).
vićko-šor: geographical name, meaning 'church-brook'.

123.

Performed by the singers of No. 121.
In all likelihood this is a folksong originating from the Sysola region, as evidenced by the village name *viźin*, mentioned in the song (cf. SrSlK *viźin*: Визинга, Визингский с/с, Сысольский район), further, certain word-forms also referring to the Sysola region: *vorsan* 'accordion' (SrSlK: SU Lu SC VU *gudek*), line 54: *pul* 'cowberry' (in Usť-Kulom: *puv* or *pū*).

124.

Performed by Anna Nikolaevna Čalanova and Ekaterina Michajlovna Lipina (Usť-Kulom).
A song of literary origin.

125.

Performed by the singers of No. 124.
Zyrian popular version of a Russian song (Кирпичники) of urban origin in vogue in the twenties.

126.

Performed by the singers of the two preceding songs.

A popular version of a poem of Pavel Šebolkin (Vi̮l' Paš) 'Джуджыд керöсин (cf. P. Šebolkin, *Gi̮jasli̮ pani̮d.* Syktyvkar, 1964, p. 26.) Melody identical with that of No. 125.

Lines 28, 30: *bi̮rse ez lok?* (according to another informant: *bi̮rse̮-j ez lok?*) 'will he not return?' | Similarly, line 35: *aǯǯis* 'he caught sight of it' ∼ *aǯǯe* 'he catches sight of it, line 36: *lokte* 'he is coming' ∼ *loktis* 'he came'.

127.

Performed by Agrafena Semënovna Zezegova and Agrafena Andreevna Judina (Rué).

128.

Performed by Anna Nikolaevna Čalanova (Usť-Kulom).

129.

Performed by the singers of No. 127.

130.

Performed by Anastasija Ivanovna Kiprušëva (Derevjansk).

131.

Performed by Marija Dmitrievna Antonovskaja (Derevjansk).

l'el'-tor 'milk (dimin.)' (baby-talk), cf. (SrSlK) Lu SR SC *l'e̮l'*, SR SC Ud *l'e̮l'e̮*, VU *l'e̮l'e* (детск.) 'молочко'.

132.

Performed by the singer of No. 128.

mi̮l'kja pl'eša 'with a white forehead': the form *mi̮l'kja* is a de-etymologized word for (WUo.) *bi̮l'kja* 'weißstirnig'.

133.

Performed by Agrafena Semënovna Zezegova, Elizaveta Semënovna Ul'ni̮rova and Matrena Iljinična Ul'ni̮rova (Ruć).

krepki 'game of draughts (?)' < R. *крепки: играть в. к.* 'to play draughts'| The last line is a corrupted Russian text indicative, in all likelihood, of the Russian origin of the song.

134.

Performed by Anastasija Ivanovna Kiprušëva (Derevjansk).

sobanćik: probably a corrupted form of the Russian *собачник* 'dog-dealer' | *počitsa da ďevitsa:* Russian text; the meaning of the first word is unknown to me, the second is identical with *девица* 'young girl, maid, virgin' | *krebitki:* probably 'game of draughts' (cf. the word *krepki* in the preceding song) | Line 10: *za voroni koś iďot:* corrupted Russian text (cf. the last line of the preceding song).

135.

Performed by Anna Nikolaevna Čalanova (Usť-Kulom).

136.

Performed by the singer of No. 135.

137.

Performed by the singer of Nos 135 and 136.

138.

Performed by Lidija Dadovna Timuševa (Usť-Kulom).

139.

Performed by the singer of No. 138.

The melody agrees with that of No. 138. — *pulisoližanka* 'semi-maid servant; полуслужанка, полугорожанка' < R. *полуслужанка* | *vešeľanka* 'joker' < R. (Даль) *веселянка* 'веселый человек, забавник, потешник' | *ševkńit-* 'to slap gently'.

140

Performed by Marija Andreevna Guljaeva (Derevjansk).

parnij 'mate, bridegroom' < R. *парный* | *raźńićći-* 'differ, make a difference; особляться, отличаться' < R. *разниться.*

141.

Performed by the singer of No. 135.

142.

I notated the first three rhymes (chastushkas) in Ruć, the rest in Usť-Kulom.

*

Concluding the notes to the VU material, I publish four counting songs *(pudjaśem)*. The first three come from Anna Nikolaevna Čalanova, the fourth from Lidija Dadovna Timuševa. It would have been difficult — if not completely impossible — to translate these rhythmically connected, otherwise incoherent sequences of words, which practically make no sense. Nevertheless, the last ditty may provide valuable information for researchers into ancient Zyrian personal names.

1.

ęťik — šįťik,
kujim — ńujim,
ńoľ — moľ,
ćer — kok nasta,
šugu — rugu,
nare peďe,
dube — voje
krest!
te mįnin,

2.

ate — kate,
kįrme — ľoľe,
ćipan — ćoje,
rije — raje,
taľi — puťi,
kiki —vake,
šorom — bitom,
ľežneg — vežnev,
nęk — pęk — sęk.

3.

utjed — pered — goz,
utjed — pered — goz,
utjed — pered — goz,
utjed — pered — goz,
te mįnin.
utjed — pered — goz
me mįni.

4.

mędla-pęlin pon čįnale.
kod pon*? ľok pon.
kod ľok? rizi ľok.
kod rizi? tęle rizi.
kod tęle? moj tęle.
kod moj? šud-moj.
kod šud? ćaze šud.
kod ćaze? vęr ćaze.**
kod vęr? kįka vęr.

* also *pan*
** also *ćade*

kod ki̯ka? jen ki̯ka.
kod jen? baš jen.
kod baš? ẹgir baš.
kod ẹgir? ćuńa ẹgir.
kod ćuńa? mikit ćuńa.
kod mikit? makľa mikit.
kod makľa- ʒi makľa.
kod ʒi? kire ʒi.
kod kire? jodi̯ kire.
kod jodi̯? bur jodi̯.
kod bur? ńiken bur.
kod ńiken? soja ńiken.
kod soja? pedot ẹda.
kod pedot? sar pedot.
kod lar? viš lar.

143.

Performed by Evdokija Germogievna Michajlova (Nivšera).

A loose, somewhat anecdotal story. — *žarg-* 'to roast, to bake; жарить, шипиться (?) ɔ: шипеть'.

144.

Performed by Egor Archipovič Žižev (Nivšera).

1. *šud balakirov.* For the etymology of the name, cf. *šudbala kirov:* der berühmte Hofnarr Peters des Großen hieß: *шут* ('Narr, Spaßmacher') *Балакирёв* (Fokos-Fuchs, VdKomi 181). | *sija seśśa turin puktini munis ji vi̯le* 'Then he went to mow on the ice', (that is: went to mow the vegetation covering the frozen pond). | Since they are negligible features of my informant's style of performance, the vocatives *zonme* 'son' and *druge* 'friend' have been left untranslated in the majority of cases.

2. *voasni, ivanes kẹsjeni vini* 'They come, they want to kill Ivan'. My informant did not mention earlier that Balakirov's first name was Ivan. Most probably he called him Ivan — by a slip of the tongue — because the heroes of folk tales are frequently referred to by this name.

3. At this point the story becomes fragmentary and somewhat obscure. — *śem miľľion śemsot śemďeśat śem* 'seven million seven hundred and seventy-seven' < R. Russian numerals very often occurred in my informant's narrative.

145.

Performed by Kirill Vasiljevič Michajlov (Nivšera).

1. *dveśťi rubľej* 'two hundred roubles' < R. Larger numbers were often expressed by my informant — as well as by other people — in Russian (see below).

2. *munis kilometra dva iľi tri* 'he went for two or three kilometres': *dva iľi tri* 'two or three' < R. | *ľepjo·ški* 'pies' < R. *лепёшка* (pl. *лепёшки*) do. | *i pop tože nin metrov dvaceť munis* 'and the priest too has gone twenty metres already': *metrov dvaceť* 'twenty metres' < R. | *das-kękjamis aresa nin sija* 'he is already eighteen years old'. Slip of the tongue: earlier the son was said to have been lying ill for twenty-five years. | *dveśťi rubľej ne vaj:* 'Give me two hundred roubles!': *dveśťi rublej* 'two hundred roubles' < R.

3. *kamgini-zęreććini* 'to knock loudly, to bang on the door' | *šoj* ~ *šuj* 'corpse' | *sto rubľej pe tęľke bošta* 'I only ask you for a hundred roubles': *sto rubľej* 'a hundred roubles' < R. | Similarly: *trista rubľej* 'three hundred roubles', *šeśťsot rubľej* 'six hundred roubles' < R.

146.

This tale also was performed by K. V. Michajlov.

1. *žegdi-* 'to insult, to hurt'. SrSlK quotes this word only from the VL dialect; other dictionaries do not include it.

3. *kod* 'progress' < R. *ход* do. | *kilametrov ďešeť-ľi petnaceť* 'ten or fifteen kilometres (acc.)' < R. | *końuk* 'horseherd' < *конюх* do.

147.

Noted from the informant of the two preceding tales.

2. *buď spokojen:* 'keep quiet!' < R. *будь спокойным* do. Hybrid construction: the instructive suffix *-en* is Zyrian, while *buď spokoj-* is Russian. | *nęš-* 'to strike at' | *gęrǯǯilema* 'worn away' | *latka* 'patch' < R. (dial.) *платка* do. | *dvena·ceť ćaso·vin* 'at twelve o'clock' < R. (*-in* is the Zyrian inessive suffix).

3. *pańikaďile* 'chandelier' < R. *паникадило* 'church chandelier'.

4. *nadojeďit-* 'to get tired of sg.' < R. *надоесть, надоедать*' do. | *kir* 'snort; храп'.

148.

Performed by Ivan Kornilovič Michajlov (Nivšera).

(a) *šataj* 'stray animal (e.g. bear)' < R. cf. *шататься* 'roam', *шатун* 'roaming man, tramp' | *šorok-ši* 'swishing': *šorok* < R. *шорох* 'rattling, rustling, swishing'.

(b) *do smerťi* 'to death' < R. *до смерти* do. | *majdan* 'place', cf. (Wied.) *majdan* 'Lagersplatz', (SrSlK) FV Vm *majdan* ''утолока, утоптанное', вытоптанное место' | *kŕov* 'blood' < R. *кровь* do.

(c) *naśeľeńie* 'population' < R. *население* do. | *vel̮ďďal-* 'fresh snow is falling', cf. (SrSlK) VU Vm I Peč *vel̮ď*, Ud *vel̮ǵ* 'свежевыпавший снег, пороша'.

149.

Performed by Nina Andreevna Gabova (Bogorodsk).

My informant was an undergraduate in 1964. She could not speak the dialect of her village clearly, literary usage having strongly affected her style and pronunciation.

1. *tẹdćimenja* 'noticeably', a literary form; cf. (KRSl.) *тӧдчымӧн, тӧдчымӧнъя* 'заметно, значительно' | *gẹrbuš* 'sickle' < R. *горбуша* do. — Dialectal features retained in my informant's speech: *ńel̮ʼ* ~ (in other dialects) *ńolʼ* 'four', *og ńin ō* (~ V *og ńin ov*) 'I am not alive', *oz užō* (~ V *oz užav*) 'he does not work'.

150.

From the same informant as in the preceding narrative.

Dialectal features: *pū* (~ V *puv*) 'berry', *ū-tor* (~ V *uv-tor*) 'twig', *pōni* (~ V *povni* 'to be afraid'), *zē* (~ V *zev*) 'very much'; in non-initial syllables she pronounces *e*, *i* instead of *ẹ*, *ị* of the literary usage.

151.

Informant as before, N. A. Gabova.

ovošči 'kind of vegetable' < R. *овощи* do.

152.

Informant: N. A. Gabova.

153.

Performed by Dmitrij Vasiljevič Podorov (Bogorodsk).

vẹlem-ke 'obviously; оказалось'.

154.

Informant: D. V. Podorov.

155.

Performed by Evdokija Germogievna Michajlova (Nivšera).

ťikeja 'calm' < R. *тихий* do. The word *ťikeja* occurs most probably for *ďikeja* 'savage' < R. *дикий* which is found in the other variants. | *pervojja* 'first' < R. *первый*, *toraja* 'second' < *второй*, *treťťeja* 'third' < *третий* | The use of the adessive-genitive in lines 18, 20, 22: *per(i) vojja ćikišislen* 'for/of the first swallow' makes no sense, perhaps a slip of the tongue due to the influence of the adessive-genitive used correctly from the 24th line onwards.

156.

Performed by E. G. Michajlova.

A fragmentary song. The old man's replies contain the stereotyped phrase *ki̮ś nin eśke* . . . only in lines 28, 32 and 49.

157.

Performed by the singer of the two preceding songs.

158.

Performed by the singer of the three preceding songs.

159—171.

Performed by Nina Andreevna Gabova, Ija Michajlovna Ivaševa, Lija Vasiľjevna Ivaševa, Lija Aleksandrovna Mišarina (Bogorodsk). Song No. 160 was performed by E. G. Michajlova.

159: *ľas-* 'to shut with a bang', cf. (KRSl.) *ľas-* 'бросить. . .'

161: *pećenka* 'baked potato, turnip, gourd'.

165: line 27 was interpreted by my informant (N. A. Gabova) as *ki̮ǯi mijan e̮ľćizna* 'like our country': although *ki̮ǯi mijane̮ǯ ez na* 'as never before us' can be heard on the tape.

169: *roć akań* 'Russian doll, a beauty', cf. (SrSlK) *roć akań* 'куколка, красавица'.

172—179.

Performed by E. G. Michajlova.

172: line 6: *ti̮la* < *ti̮lae̮* (illative) | *ni̮r-pom* < **mi̮r-pom* 'bramble'; according to SrSlK, the Vm I Ud dialects have a *ni̮r-pom* form.

173: *ćerńeć* 'monk (here figuratively) bridegroom' < R. *чернец* 'monk' | *ćerńeć pe oz če̮kti* 'the bridegroom does not command' (that is, he does not command the bride to take leave of her relatives since she is going to a good place).

175: *i spas daj prićistaja* 'Saviour and the Holy Virgin': originating from Russian laments or church songs.

178: *ľubej* 'sweetheart': in place of *ľube* | *povod* 'bridle, leading rein (here figuratively) hair' < R. *повод* do.

179: *lučče* 'rather' < R. *лучше* do.

180.

Performed by Ju. G. Ročev (Mi̮ži).

1. *li̮kjedli̮-* 'to lie', cf. (SrSlK) I *li̮kjedli̮-* 'обманнывать, одурачивать' | *bi̮gjal-* 'to talk big', cf. (SrSlK) I *bi̮gjal-* ''болтать, молоть' | *ǯe̮m* 'just'.

2. *ośenćik* 'autumn ice (?)' | *protoha* 'tributary' < R. *протока* сиб. 'рукав реки, проран, побочное русло, связь озера с рекою' (Даль) | *vejśen* 'one on the other; один на другом' | *ńeodńik* 'fishing boat' < R. *неводник* do., cf. (SrSlK) I (Ob) *ńevodńik* 'неводник, рыбацкая лодка'.

181.

Performed by Ju. G. Ročev (Mi̮ži).

be̮ža-ku parka 'Ermine Coat' proper name, *jeǯi̮d ku parka* 'White Fur Coat' proper name.

182.

Performed by V. G. Ročev (Mi̮ži).

si̮rok 'kind of fish' < R. *сырок* 'морская рунная рыба; Salmo vimba' | *pi̮žjan* 'kind of fish ≶ ? Ostyak (KT 758) Ni Kaz *pĭšjan* 'ein Fisch' | *ńarhul* 'raw fish' < Ostyak *ńar χŭl* do. | *varka* 'dried fish'.

183.

Performed by V. G. Ročev (Mi̮ži).

pregit-, *pŕagit-* 'to harness a horse' < R. *прягать, прячь* do. (Даль).

* * *

In the following only those Northern Permyak texts will be referred to which require certain linguistic or ethnographical explanation to be understood. In the case of texts to which no explanatory notes have been given, the provenance can be adequately indicated by mentioning the informant's name and birthplace. Thus the relevant texts grouped by informants are the following: Ľubov Stepanovna Gribova (Petuchova): 184, 185, 186, 187, 191, 192, 193, 194, 195, 196, 198, 199, 200, 201, 202, 203, 204, 218; Anna Andreevna Minina (Boľšaja Koča): 197; Maria Makedonovna Pystogova (Kočevo): 188, 189, 190, 205, 206, 207, 208, 209, 210, 211, 212, 213, 214, 215; Larisa Nikolaevna Snigirova (Kosa): 216, 217. There are many more Russian loanwords in Permyak (Southern Zyrian) than in the Northern Zyrian dialect. Leaving out of consideration the readily identifiable loanwords, I mention in the notes only those, which deviate either phonetically or semantically from the literary or standard norms of Russian and which, therefore, are likely to raise difficulties of understanding even to Zyrian- or Russian-speaking readers.

185.

2. *pros* 'свободный; free' < R. прост 'simple' | *śvatkę·tni* 'стучать; to knock'.

3. *ńe śojnį, ńe junį abu, ńe paśtalnį ńem* 'We have nothing to eat and drink, nor clothes to put on': the particle *ńe* 'nor' (<R. 99) when in an unstressed position was pronounced *ńi* by my informant. | *voštįnį* 'to lose' is a literary form of Komi-Zyrian, corresponding to *ęštįnį* in the P dialect.

4. *mona·kkes va kaję·tnį* 'the friars are carrying water': the infinitive as a finite verb characteristically occurs also in the style of Russian performers of folk tales.

5. *ajka* 'муж; husband'.

186.

1. *šedtįnį* 'вытащить, нарубить дрова; to pull out, to cut wood' | *stram* 'nasty thing' < R. *срам* 'shame, ignominy, infamy' | *rušį·ťik* 'тепловатый; 'luke warm'.

2. *art* 'порядок, соображение; order, sense, consideration; *arta·lni* 'сообразить, привести в порядок; to consider, to put in order'; *arttęm* 'глупый, беспорядочный; stupid, untidy' | *įlęs* 'разум, ум, сообразительность, соображение; sense, brain, comprehension, consideration'; *įlęstęm* 'глупый, неразумный; stupid, insane'; *įlęsa* 'умный; clever' | *kuľnį* 'ударить, бить (ремнем, веником); снимать кожу; to beat, to strike (with lash or bundle of sticks); to flay' | *kińi·ććį-* 'кинуться; to dash at sy' < кинуться.

187.

1. *kęjića, kęji·ća* 'мешочек; small bag' | *gaľa* 'камень; stone' < R., cf. галька 'pebble' | *rozva·ľ* 'розвальни, сани; peasant sleigh' < R., cf. *розвальни* 'peasant sleigh (low, broadening towards the rear)' | *sua·lę* 'stands' (instead of *sula·lę*): the absence of *l* is conspicuous; omission of medial *l* (> *w*, Ø) being characteristic only of PS | *śiľka·n* 'bell' | *kaľa·n* 'черт; дьявол; devil, ghost' | *gor-vil-śord* 'место за печкой, середина печи; back of the oven, middle of the oven'.

3. *ńe-tę-lištę* 'не то лишто; let alone' | *ćula·lnį* 'проходить (о времени); to pass (time)', *lunnez ćula·lisę* 'the days passed away' | According to my informant, the verb *mędę·tnį* is exclusively used with the connotation 'to send' in the region. The word *ińdįnį* PS (Kudymkar) was unknown to her while she was living as a child at home; however, the form *ińdę·tnį* 'to send (with reference to a definite place)' is still extant among them.

188.

2. *vokta* 'I come': a PS (Kudymkar) form instead of *lokta* | *gi̮lja·ś-* 'полоскать; to rinse'.

189.

švi̮rkji̮- 'swim swiftly'.

190.

šuć 'always' | *śaďaś-* 'to come to one's senses' | *tuli̮-* 'притереть; to rub'.

191.

1. *jua·n* 'квас; kvas' | *ki̮j-* 'ловить; to grapple', here: 'выиграть; win'.

2. *sek pervo* 'раньше всего, прежде всего; first of all' | *śoronno* 'всё равно; all the same' < R.

3. *pe̮kre̮·m* 'пояс; narrow belt'.

4. *zapadńa* 'верхняя часть подполя около печи; upper part of the cellar by the oven' < R. *западня* 'западная дверь, подъемная крышка над лазом в подполье' (Даль) *prok* 'skilful', that is: 'умеет-ли что-нибудь делать? can she do anything?' < R. *прок* 'надежность, прочность, крепкое, стойкое, годное напредки; польза, толк, что обещает выгоду, добро' (Даль) | *re̮źńit-* 'разбрасывать; to scatter, to disperse' < R. *рознить*.

192.

ćiľke̮·t-, *ćiľke̮·tli̮-* 'доить; to milk'.

193.

1. *ľis* 'лист; foliage' < R. | *trepi·ć*, *trepi·ća* 'тряпки; rag' < R. тряпица | *ďerja·lni̮* 'рыдать, плакать навзрыд; to sob' | *koľinko·r* 'белый материал, коленкор; white material, calico'.

2. *streća* 'Троица; Holy Trinity, whitsun', cf. (Wied.) *streća-lun* 'Pfingsten' < R. *троица* do. | *voššini̮* 'кушать (в отношении мертвых); to eat (with reference to the dead)', *vošši̮ mijanke̮t* 'ешь с нами (только о мертвых); eat with us (with reference to the dead, to those alive only jokingly)', *vošše̮·tni̮* 'угощать умерших; to feast the dead one', cf. (WUo.) I *vošji̮ni̮*, Ud *vošji̮·ni̮s* 'anfangen, beginnen (I); (an etw.) anstoßen, streifen (Ud)', V *vošjej śibe̮dćej* 'nähert euch! (so sagt man zu den Geistern der Verstorbenen, der Eltern und der Vorfahren, wenn man ihrer in der Kirche auf russische Weise gedenkt)', P *aś vošje̮ni̮* 'mögen sie essen! (die Verstorbenen; so sagt man bei der Gedächtnisfeier)' | *gegere̮·n* 'кругом; round about', *gegere̮·ńńas* 'точно вокруг, определенно вокруг; exactly round, definitely round'.

194.

1. *ďiťťa·n* 'качели; swing', *ďiťťa·śni̮* 'качаться; 'to swing', *ďiťťe̮·t-* 'to swing, to rock' | *vež kaga* 'грудной ребенок; baby' | *ban-palak* 'большой кусок бересты; large piece of birch-bark' | *lɪťťan śor* 'гибкая палка, перекинут через забор или балку; flexible rod thrust through a partition wall (fence) or a support beam', cf. (Wied.) P *latjan śor* 'Brunnenschwengel'; *laťťit* 'качающийся; swinging, swaying' | *kom* 'kitchen' | *giće̮·tni̮* 'качать; to rock', cf. (Wied.) *gićedni̮* 'schaukeln, wiegen, hin und her bewegen'.

195.

1. *ćud* 'черт, нечистый дух; devil, unchaste spirit' < R. *чудо* 'marvel' | *bare̮·tni̮* 'расширить глаза и смотреть в упор; to stare, to make big eyes'.

2. *deźira·jtni̮* 'пасти лошадей, дозирать, дозёрить; to graze, to guard horses' < R. | *veršne̮j* 'mounted', *veršne̮je̮n* 'верхом, на лошади; on horseback' < R. *вершній* 'конный, сидящий верхом' (Даль) | *zēť-viʒni̮* 'блестеть, сверкать; to shine, to glow' | *poperega·lni̮* 'пересекать; to stand aside, to cross' < R., cf. *поперёк* 'across, crosswise' | *ńe-mij-ńe* 'nothing' | *kiwzini̮* 'кричать; to shout, to neigh'.

3. *naťte̮* 'наверно; probably' | *ńań-jaru·śńik* 'barley bread' | *peššo·rka* 'сумка из бересты; bag made from birch-bark' < R., cf. *пещер, пещор, пещур* 'большая, высокая корзина. . .' (Даль) | *toko* 'только; only' < R. | *baba* 'ящик, ларчик; mill-loading hopper' < R., cf. *бабка* 'брус с пазами, по которым (по двум бабкам) ходят мельничные вешняки, творила, и песты толчеи' (Даль) | *prostej* 'пустой; empty' < R. *простой* | *keke·rkai̮n, (-ān)* сидеть на корточках; to squat', *kekeri·ććini̮* присесть, нагнуться; to sit down, to bend down' | *riz-viʒni̮* 'расширяться, скалить зубы: to flash one's teeth' | *i̮ke̮·stni̮* 'крикнуть; to exclaim' | *te̮žne̮* 'тогда, только что; then, only then' < R. *тожно* 'тогда, в то время, в те поры' (Даль) | *kiše̮n sultni̮* 'дыбом подняться (о волосах); his hair stands on end' | *ʒuz-viʒni̮* '(чуть-чуть) светать (светить); it is dawning' | *ćiste̮* 'даже; moreover' < R. *чистый* | *torkśini̮* 'to perish', cf. (WUo.) V S Lu I *torkśini̮*, Ud *torkśi̮·ni̮s* 'sich irren, einen Irrtum begehen, sich verwirren (V S Lu Ud), sich verwirren (I)'.

196.

1. *komi-permak* 'Komi-Permyak': a term of literary usage, unknown in folk idiom; the Komi-Permyak, as well as the Northern Zyrians (Komi-Zyrians) call themselves *komi*. | *jaru·śńik* 'маленький каравай; small, round loaf' < R.

2. *seče·n* 'сочень (круглый как блин); pie (round in form like a pancake)', cf. (Wied.) *sečen* 'ein Fladen mit Fruchtmuß' < R. | *ńur-meľ* 'клюква; cranberry', cf. (WUo.) Lu Le *ńur-moľ* 'Moosbeere' | *śela-jaged* 'сжевика; bramble' | *bigre·t-* раскатывать тесто; knead, roll paste', cf. (Wied.) P *bigred-* 'zusammendrehen, zwirnen', *bigre·ććan* 'скалка; rolling-pin', cf. (Wied.) P *bygrödtšan* 'Rolle' | *uški* 'ушки; jam pockets' < R. | *ikra* 'грибная икра, разрубленные сушенные грибы; 'minced dried mushroom'.

3. *ťeri·tni* 'тереть, натирать, натереть; to rub, to grate' < R. | *kreši·tni* 'крошить; to crumble, to break in small pieces' < R.| *keča·n* 'кочан; cabbage', cf. (Wied.) *kečan* 'Kohl' < R. | *kaľe·g* 'брюква; Swedish turnip' | *luk-grez* 'гнездо лука; onion-bed'.

4. *direva·tka* 'глиняная посуда, корчага; pottery vessel' < R. *дыроватка* 'корчага с дырою повыше днаб для варки и спуска браги (Даль') | *ćes-vižan* 'слащавый; sweetish' | *ćuž-piź* 'солод; malt' | *ještem gor* 'истопившаяся печь; heated stove' | *suslo* 'сладкое, первое пиво, густое; wort, sweet beer, thick' < R. *сусло* | *vije·tni* 'выцеживать, пропускать через сито; to strain with a sieve, cf. (WUo.) P *vije·tni* 'gießen, ausgießen, tropfen'.

197.

1. *masľa·k* 'boletus', cf. (Wied.) *masľanka: kez-m.* 'ein Pilz', *masľeńik: jag-m.* 'ein Pilz' < R. масляк 'гриб козляк; Boletus granulatus' (Даль) | *śińa·wka* 'russula' < R. *синявка* 'гриб сыроежка' (Даль).

2. *ľaka·lni* 'мазать, to smear', cf. (Wied.) P *ľakal-*, *ľakav-* 'versiegeln; ankleben (intr.), anhaften'.

198.

1. *gegi·t, gogi·t* 'скребло, откуривают деревья, соскабливают кору деревьев; scraping, scratching tool, draw-knife, used to bark trees', cf. (Wied.) P *gogit*, (WUo.) P *gogin* 'Schabeisen, Schabmesser'.

2. *kapu·śńik* 'огород, огородец; kitchen-garden' < R. *капустник* 'cabbage-plot, cabbage-field' | *vire·ć* 'парник; hot-bed standing on poles', cf. (Wied.) *vireć, viric, viric* 'Baumschule, Pflanzschule' < R. *вырец* 'рассавник, срубец на столбах, для посева капусты' (Даль) | *esľa·ď* 'сваленные деревья; felled trees' < R. *оследь, ослядь* 'бревно, строевой лес' (Даль) | *ľito·vka* 'scythe' < R. *литовка* 'русская, большая коса' (Даль) | *ľož* 'ряд; swath, row', cf. (Wied.) *ľož* 'Schwaden'.

199.

2. *śed mu-śin* 'чернозем; chernozem' | *grad, gŕada* 'bed', cf. (Wied.) *gŕad, gŕada* 'Beet, Gartenbeet' < R. *гряда* | *ťape·tni* 'окучивать; to earth up', *ťapka* 'окучник; earthing hoe'.

200.

goľki 'круглые шарики, бомбошки из шерстяных ниток; rolls of wollen yarn' < R. cf. *голи* 'в игре зерни или кости. . .' (Даль).

202.

pi̭rke̮ćća·n 'трепалка; swingling machine', cf. (Wied.) *pyrködtšan* 'Schwinge, Flachsschwinge' | *preste̮·ď* 'пестредь; checked linen', cf. (SrSlK) VU Skr *pestreď* 'самотканый пестрый холст'.

203.

1. *ćuď* 'Chud', cf. (WUo.) V I *ćuď* ,S Lu Ud P *ćud* 'ein Volk (es war wild, dumm; es verschwand so, daß es sich lebendig in der Erde begrub) (V), id. (es begrub sich in seinen Städten — wovon es noch Spuren gibt —, damit die Feinde seine Reichtümer nicht bekommen sollten) (S), ein altes Volk der betr. Gegend (Lu P), ein Volk, das vormals auf dem Syrjänengebiete wohnte (es sprach syrjänisch, es war heidnisch) (I), ein unbekanntes Volk, das vormals auf dem Syrjänengebiete wohnte (die einen begruben sich in der Erde, die anderen flohen nach Norden; sie haben Grabhügel od. Kurgane mit Schätzen und Geld hinterlassen) (Ud)' | *kok-iž* 'чулок; stockings'.

204.

1. *e̮d* 'жар; heat of the bath-room'; men bathe first, women follow them; hence: "first heat", "second heat" | *baňa-pe̮l* 'предбанник; dressing-room (where people undress before bathing)' | *ve̮re̮ži·ćći̮ni̮* 'ворожить; to tell fortune, to spell' < R. | *gor-me̮ćća·n* 'кочерга; poker'.

205.

pu-jage̮d 'брусника; cowberry', cf. (WUo.) *pul*, *puv* 'Preiselbeere', *jage̮d* < R. *ягода* 'berry'.

206.

ćar-ńe̮l 'lightning', cf. (WUo.) S Lu *ćar: ćar-bi* 'Blitz', *ńe̮l* 'Pfeil' | *e̮zji̮vle̮* 'it catches fire': literary form | *saje̮wtni̮* 'to hide': literary form | *oklaśni̮* 'качаться; to bow, to sway', cf. (Wied.) P *oklaś-* 'schwanken, sich schaukeln', (SrSlK) SU *okleśni̮* 'качаться, шататься, пошатываться' | *ve̮rže̮·ćći̮ni̮* 'to stir': erroneously for *ve̮rže̮·dni̮* 'to move, to put in motion'.

207.

podpeši·t 'подписать; to sign' < R.

208.

ke̮sti̮ś- 'to bow', cf. (Wied.) P *ke̮sti̮ś-* 'sich biegen' | *te̮wnas* 'in winter'; literary form.

209.

šuški̮- 'to hum', cf. (WUo.) *šuški̮l'*: S Lu *s-ki̮lja* 'undeutlich sprechend', Lu *šuški̮·l'tni̮* 'lispeln, fehlerhaft sprechen (ohne alle Laute aussprechen zu können)'.

210.

2. *ińde̮ćći̮-* 'to start, to set out' | *juklaś-* 'to undulate' | *se̮ste̮mmi̮-* 'to become clean': erroneously for *se̮ste̮mti̮-* 'to clean' | *tule̮ćći̮-* 'барахтаться; to roll about, to kick about' | *šuńgi·ś-* 'to dive'.

3. *me̮de̮ćća·n* 'остатки; remainder, what is left' | *kušammi̮-* 'to become bare'.

211.

uśi·ććivośt' 'perseverance' < R. *усидчивость* | *bośti̮vli̮-* 'to take out, to borrow': literary form | *otsavli̮-* 'to help': literary form | *voli̮vli̮-* 'to come': literary form.

214.

ńel'ki 'даже; moreover, even . . . though', cf. (Wied.) *ńel'ki* 'wirklich (Frage)' < R., cf. *нель* 'не только, не то-что, не токмо' (Даль) | *šval* 'tumour, swelling' < ? R. | *karć* 'овощи; kind of vegetable', cf. (SrSlK) under волога (Lu Le Ud *karć*, Ud *karć-marć* 'харчи, пища (кроме хлеба, воды, напитков)'.

* * *

The Southern Permyak texts are grouped by informants as follows: Rajsa Michajlovna Batalova (Rudakovo): 250; Ilja Aleksejevič Jarkov (Kudymkar): 219—44; Kol'čurina (Kudymkar): 248; Galina Aleksandrovna Końšina (Kudymkar): 245—47; Tarakanov (Verch-Ińva): 251; Galina Petrovna Taskajeva (Vesëlyj Mys): 249. Only those Southern Permyak texts are referred to in the following notes which require some linguistic or ethnographical explanation to be understood.

219.

1. *sećće̮* 'thither', here and below often: 'then'. This latter meaning has developed, obviously, under the influence of the Russian *тут* 'here, then'.

2. *boćka-tropka* 'bung': *tropka* < R. *пробка* 'bung' (*p-* > *t-* by way of dissimilation).

3. *ogra·da* 'courtyard' < R. *ограда* 'fence, wall, hedge; (Даль) in Siberia: двор' | *podo·ńća* 'milking yard' < R. *подойница* do.

220.

bẹr ǯarńit- 'to glance back, to look back', cf. (Wied.) P *ǯarjav-* 'schauen, gaffen, besehen', (WUo.) P *ǯarjav-* 'sich nach allen Seiten umschauen'.

225.

1. *tarowa·ś-* переворочиться; to roll about', cf. (WUo.) P *tarva·ś-* 'sich wälzen, rollen (intr.)'.

226.

krośka χawro·śka: a name of Russian origin, the first constituent being identical with the Russian word *крошка* '(a small piece) crumble; little one, tiny tot, pretty child'.

228.

2. *śowban* 'шёлбанчик; flip (at card-playing, the loser will receive from the winner as many smacks on the forehead as the number of cards he has lost)'.

231.

śujị·śtisnị 'they hid': my informant picked up this form in Syktyvkar, and uses it instead of P *śujị·śtisẹ.*

232.

3. *munisnị* 'they proceeded': an SR form replacing P *munisẹ.*

234.

2. *car orsis . . . kujim svaďba* 'The tsar . . . arranged three weddings', cf. < R. *играть свадьбу* 'celebrate a wedding'.

4. *vośtis* 'he juggled it away': my informant acquired this form in Syktyvkar and uses it instead of P *ẹśtis.*

235.

4. *śịńńa·w-* to 'smile', cf. (WUo.) S *śịńjal-*, V *śịńjav-* 'die Ohren hängen lassen (Pferd) (S); lächeln (V)'.

236.

2. *uza·w-* 'to sell': *vu-* > *u-*, cf. (WUo.) P *vuza·v-* 'verkaufen'.

5. *skok da skok* 'hey presto!' < R. *скок-поскок* do.

237.

1. *bord-ti̯(w)i̯p* 'tail-feather', cf. (WUo.) P *ti̯v-bord* 'Schwung- od. Schwanzfeder', (Wied.) P *ti̯lep* 'Faser', *jur-śi-t* 'Haar'.

3. *ęwmęs* 'уздечка; bridle, leading-rein', cf. (Fokos-Fuchs) V *ovmęs* 'Habe, Vermögen'.

238.

1. *udubre·ńie* 'dung' < R. *удобрение* do.

239.

1. *vęraliś, vęrali·s* 'hunter': literary form (the Kudymkar dialect has the form *vęrawi·ś)* | *poperoga·jis tuj* 'crossed the road': *popeŕoga·w-* 'to cross' < R., cf. *поперек* 'across, crosswise'.

240.

1. *oz-jęgę·d* 'strawberry': *oz* 'Erdbeere' + *jęgę·d* (< *jagę·d*) 'Beere'.

2. *mi̯j di̯nę uźi* 'how long have I been sleeping?' | *me gęrę* (< *gęgęrę*) 'around me': the form *gęrę* is due to haplology | *atsa·wisę* < *otsa·wisę* 'they helped': the vowel *a* in the first syllable can be explained by the analogical influence of the Russian *akańje*.

250.

1. *śo ńi* 'обычно, всегда; in general, as a rule, always' | *sijęn-soręn* 'ни с чем; with nothing, with empty hands'.

3. *sur-trępić* 'особым образом вытканное полотно, применяемое для приготовления пива; linen woven with a special technique and used for brewing beer'.

4. *košo(v)a* 'прездничные сани, похожие на кибитку; festive sleigh similar to the kibitka' | *kokole·ć* 'колоколец, звонок; bell' < R. *колоколец* do. | *ti̯śećkej* 'тот человек, который знает все правила свадьбы, является организатором, обычно приглашают в свадьбы; master of ceremonies' < R. (Даль) *тысяцкий* 'старший свадебный чин; обычно это крестный, он же и посаженный отец жениха: он распорядитель поезда и обрядов, благословляет и увозит жениха, меняет кольца четы, платит за свадьбу и привозит домой молодых' | *e̜t-drug* 'одновременно; simultaneously' | *ić-mońke̜·t-* 'надевать женский головной убор; the bride's kerchief is tied at the nape as is usual with wives' | *pośt'e·ľľa* 'bed' < R. *постеля* do. | *bośt-* 'nehmen, bekommen', here: 'выкупать; to redeem' | *siʒ-kiʒ* 'since, as': calque of Russian *так как* | *ʒim-ʒurk* 'очень быстро; very quickly, in a hurry' | *kurńi-verńi* 'мигом, очень быстро; in the matter of a moment, very quickly'.

251.

In order to demonstrate the intensity of Russian linguistic influence, I list here the Russian turns of speech and phrases (disregarding, of course, the Russian loanwords which, though profuse, can be readily discerned).

1. *dom kultu·ri̯* 'house of culture' < R. *дом культуры* 'do' | *ertèes* = R. ремонтно-техническая станция 'mechanical repair station' | *medpersona·l* 'health personnel' < R. *мед(ицинский) персонал* do.

2. *eće̜ fχoďat una briga·daez* 'this comprises many brigades': *fχoďat* < R. *входят* 'join in, belong to' | *kańďida·ttezve̜ blo·ka kommuńi·stov i bespart'i·jni̯χ* (~ -*k*) 'as representatives of the communist block, as well as of the non-party block < R. *блок коммуничтов и беспартийных* 'the block of communists and non-party members' | *ľespromχo·z* 'forestry' < R. *леспромхоз* (лесопромышленное хозяйство) do. | *maśt'er ľesaez* 'forestry inspectors' < R. *мастер леса* 'forestry inspector'.

3. *suwde̜·t-* 'to set up, to introduce', cf. P *suvte̜·t-* 'aufstehen machen, zum Aufstehen bringen; stellen, hinstellen, aufstellen, aufrichten'.

APPENDICES

Type-Numbers of Tales according to the Aarne-Thompson System*

1. A married couple and a son. AaTh 465 *The Man Persecuted Because of his Beautiful Wife.*
2. The merchant who was a widower. AaTh 425C *Beauty and the Beast.*
3. The little peasant. AaTh 510A *Cinderella.*
4. [The Tsarevich and the girl who was driven out.] AaTh 706 *The Maiden Withouth Hands.*
5. The rich brother and the poor brother. AaTh 875 III. *The Clever Peasant Girl* (J1191.1. Reductio ad absurdum: The decision about the colt. AaTh 735A *Bad Luck Imprisoned.*
6. [The soldier and the priest.] AaTh 1424 *Friar Adds Missing Nose (fingers) to Unborn Child.* AaTh 1563 "*Both*".

27. Cf. AaTh 2034A *The Wormwood does not Rock the Sparrow.*
28. Cf. AaTh 2015 *The Goat, who Would not go Home.*
28. Cf. AaTh 2015 *The Goat, who Would not go Home.*
30. [The priest's cows.] AaTh 1737 "*Who Gives his Own Goods, Receives it Back Tenfold.*"
31. Tsarevich Ivan. AaTh 530;I. *The Princess on the Glass Mountain.* Reward for the Vigil.* + AaTh 1130 *Counting out Pay* + AaTh 532* *Son of the Cow* + AaTh 1045 *Pulling the Lake Together* + AaTh 1152 *The Ogre Overawed by Displaying Objects* + AaTh 590A *The Treacherous Wife.*
32. Pipiristťi falcon. AaTh 432 *The Prince as Bird* + AaTh 425A *The Monster (Animal) as Bridegroom.*

* For those interested in Zyrian tales and their international variants the following two works are recommended: 1. István Kecskeméti and Heikki Paunonen, Die Märchentypen in den Publikationen der Finnisch-Ugrischen Gesellschaft. JSFOu. 73:205—265; 2. Antti Aarne and Stith Thompson: *The Types of the Folktale.* Second Revision. Helsinki 1961. FFC 184.

33. About Poma. AaTh 545B *Puss in Boots.*

34. Uncle Noriṃe̥. AaTh 1655 *The Profitable Exchange* + AaTh 158 *The Wild Animals in the Sleigh.*

35. Father Re̥man. AaTh ?

36. [The mother curses her daughter.] AaTh ?

37. About the three dragons. AaTh ?

38. [The three sisters.] AaTh 780 *The Singing Bone.*

65.a. AaTh 2018 "*Where is the Warehouse?*"

66.b. AaTh 2018 "*Where is the Warehouse?*"

71. Verse insert, cf. No. 85. AaTh ?

73. Cumulative tale. AaTh ?

74. Formula tale. AaTh ?

75. Formula tale. AaTh ?

76. Cf. AaTh 2034A *The Wormwood Does not Want to Rock the Sparrow.*

84. [Lazy Ivan.] AaTh 530 *The Princess on the Glass Mountain* + AaTh 532 *Son of the Cow.*

85. The mouse travels down and up the river. Animal tale with song inserts. Cf. AaTh 158. *The Wild Animals on the Sleigh.*

127. AaTh 2018 "*Where is the Warehouse?*"

128. AaTh 2018 "*Where is the Warehouse?*"

129. AaTh 2018 *From Iron a Hatchet.*

130. Formula tale AaTh ?

131. AaTh 2018 *From Iron a Hatchet.*

132. Formula tale AaTh ?

137. AaTh 1415 *Lucky Hans.*

139. AaTh 2022B *The Hen Lays an Egg. The Mouse Breaks it.*

143. [Petruš and the fugitives.] Aath 1653 *The Robbers under the Tree.*

144. [Stupid Balakirov.] AaTh 1539 *Cleverness and Guillibility* (AaTh 1538 *The Jester-bride*)

145. About the priest. AaTh 1829A *Saint's Image Smeared with Milk* + AaTh 785 *Who Ate the Lamb's Heart* (AaTh 753A *Unsuccessful Resuscitation*).

146. [Ivan and Tsar Gr im.] AaTh 545B *Puss in Boots.*

147. [The miraculous lamp.] AaTh 561 *Aladdin.*

180. About a lying old man. AaTh 1960J *The Great Bird.* AaTh 1960B *The Great Fish.*

184. About Al'onuška. AaTh 780 *The Singing Bone.*

185. About rich Marko. AaTh 930 *The Prophecy.*

186. [The witch and the two girls.] AaTh 480 *The Kind and Unkind Girls.*

187. [The ghost and the two girls.] AaTh 431 *The House in the Wood.*

188. [How Ivan rescued the Tsar's daughters from the dragons.] AaTh 301A *Quest for a Vanished Princess.*
203. About the Chuds. AaTh 1202 *The Grain Harvesting*, AaTh 1260A* *Flour in River.*
219. The fox and the thrush. AaTh 56C *The Fox Sits in a Pit and Threatens to Eat the Bird's Young.*
220. The fox and the crab. AaTh 275 *The Race of the Fox and the Crayfish.*
222. The cat and the fox. AaTh 103A* *Cat Claims to be King.*
223. The tom-cat, the lamb and the goat. AaTh 126A* *The Frightened Wolves.*
224. The fox and the crane. AaTh 60 *Fox and Crane Invite Each Other.*
225. Suddenly-enriched Kuzma. AaTh 545B *Puss in Boots.*
226. Kroška Xawroška AaTh 511 *One-Eye, Two-Eyes, Three Eyes.*
227. Stupid Jemeľa. AaTh 675 *The Lazy Boy.*
228. The devils and the soldier. AaTh 330 *The Smith Outwits the Devil.* (AaTh 1159 *The Ogre Wants to Learn to Play*).
229. Mush from a hatchet. AaTh 1548 *The Soup-stone.*
230. How the landowner hatched horses? AaTh 1319 *Pumpkin Sold as an Ass's Egg.*
231. The priest and the soldier. AaTh 1842A* *The Avaricious Priest.*
232. The wordy woman. AaTh 1381 *The Talkative Wife and the Discovered Treasure* (AaTh 1381B *The Sausage Rain*).
233. The son made of clay. Cf. AaTh 2028 *The Troll who was Cut Open* (AaTh 122M* *The Ram Runs Straight into the Wolf's Stomach*).
234. The frog tsarevna. AaTh 402 *The Mouse (Cat, Frog, etc.) Bride* + AaTh 302 *The Ogre's (Devil's) Heart in the Egg.*
235. Śiwka-burka. AaTh 530 *The Princess on the Glass Mountain.*
236. Go I-know-not-where, bring I-know-not-what! AaTh 465A *The Quest for the Unknown.*
237. Tsarevich Ivan and the wolf. AaTh 550 *Search for the Golden Bird.*

MUSICAL EXAMPLES

Introduction

As an appendix to the volume, we publish here twenty-nine tunes — a small selection from the rich material of this collection. In compiling it, we had to choose between two alternatives: either to represent each dialect area by a characteristic example of the genres typical of the area, or renouncing any claim for a comprehensive survey, to introduce only a few genres of Zyrian folk music, and these with several examples. We decided on the second of these. Thus our selection includes thirteen children's songs, ten laments and six ballads or songs not linked with any particular event. About one-third of these tunes originate from one region along the Višera. The bulk of this material is unison in nature, since this style of performance has been better preserved by the archaic children's songs and laments than by certain other genres in which polyphony has come to prevail increasingly under the influence of Russian music.

During the past twenty years four works have appeared in the Soviet Union which present a comprehensive view — both adequate in size and well supplied with analytical studies and explanatory notes — of every genre and each area of Zyrian folk music. First of all, the three-volume series by Mikušev and Čistalëv must be mentioned in this connection.*

The rich material in these volumes offers possibilities of a general survey of the melodic stock. Since, however, only the first few lines of each melody are given, no analysis in depth of the individual melodies is feasible. But from the first melodic lines one may see that while the songs appear to be simple in construction and melodic patterns, their external simplicity is amply compensated for by their rich internal "microvariation" technique.

* М. И.—С. А. Кондратевы, Коми народная песня (= Kondr) (Москва 1959); А. К. Микушев—П. И. Чисталев, Коми народные песни I. Сыктывкар, 1966 (= Komi n. p. I.); А. К. Микушев—П. И. Чисталев, Коми народные песни II. Сыктывкар, 1968; А. К. Микушев—П. И. Чисталев—Ю. Г. Рочев, Коми народные песни III. Сыктывкар, 1971 (= Komi n.p. III.).

A closer examination shows that the recurrent lines that seem to be identical at first hearing are never completely identical: within the narrow confines of the basic construction and melodic pattern there are practically endless possibilities of variation. This is why we chose to publish the melodies here in their full forms, either as they were recorded and notated or by reference to their variants (with the sole exception of No. 29 in which instance this is not necessary). This method is all the more justified since in certain regions it is a characteristic feature of the style of performance that almost every syllable of the text is augmented by filling notes. If the texts alone are published, such filling notes need not be specially marked, but in the case of singing performance the filling notes answer to full-value musical notes, in other words, they belong unconditionally to the music.

General Comments on the Melodies

The first number at the head of the melody is the number of the melody (1—29) while the second shows the place the song occupies in the texts.

The melodies have been transposed uniformly to end on g^1. The metronome tempi and those of the original closing note *(T.f.)* are given in brackets, because standard *a* is missing from the tape-recording and consequently neither the tempo nor the original pitch could be determined exactly.

In cases where the song ends in an ordinary speaking voice, the initial note *(T.i.)* is given instead of the closing note.

Time signatures are not given: in general, the unit of the melodies published is the 2/4 bar which, however, extends occasionally to 3/4 or even longer bars (owing to augmentations in the words, intervening pauses, lengthened cadences, etc.).

The filling notes are not differentiated from the basic ones; but by collation with the text they can be clearly discerned.

Such sounds which are not audible on the tape-recording but logically belong to the song are put in brackets.

The cadence signatures given in the notes to the tunes of strophic construction indicate on what note of the scale (reduced to g^1) the final notes of the individual lines fall.

Explanation of Symbols

T.f. = *tonus finalis*, the original closing note of the melody

T.i. = *tonus initialis*, the original starting note

↑● = intoned a little higher

↓● = intoned a little lower

∩ = slightly lengthened note or group of notes

∪ = slightly shortened note or group of notes

ϡ = pitch uncertain, roughly at the given pitch

⤥ = slide, touching the intermediate notes

╲ = slide, the tone falls as if with moaning

× = stop, mistake

∨ = strongly audible breath (only in No. 14)

ɔ = short stop

Notes to the Tunes

1. Children's song. Basic unit consisting of two bars in 2/4 time. Note set: trichord with a minor third, the nucleus of the melody being a step of a minor third. On the tape-recording, the pitch gradually slides downwards from the sixth bar onwards.

2. Children's song. Two-bar construction, the melody being developed from a single two-bar phrase by repetitive variation. Note set: tetrachord with a major third. Congruent articulation in words and melody: the first half of the two bars including the question, the second the answer.

The singer performs the first four bars in a somewhat quicker tempo; from the fifth bar the tempo becomes fixed.

Var. Komi n.p. I. 86, 89, 91, 94, 95.
Komi n.p. III. 35, 44, 63.

3. Children's song. Two-bar construction, the melody being developed from one single two-bar phrase by repetitive variation. Note set: tetrachord with a major third. Congruent articulation in melody and words: the first two-bar phrase including the question, the second the answer.

The singer also separates the two-bar phrases by shortening the last note of every second bar and stressing the first note of the next bar.

The performer finds the proper tonality at about the ninth bar.

Var. Komi n.p. I. 86, 98.
Komi n.p. III. 35, 44, 63.

4. Children's song. Two-bar construction. Note set: trichord with a minor third. The singer does not articulate the two-bars, performing six, eight and even ten bars with one breath.

Stops and mistakes occur fairly often in the performance.

Towards the end of the song, a gradual change occurs from the singing to the speaking manner of performance.

The symbol [ˇ] indicates that the ligature refers to only one of the repeated melodic forms.

5. Song inserted into the tale, occurring four times during the performance of the narrative. The two-bar construction shows a certain degree of similarity to that of the children's songs. Note set: tetrachord with a minor third.

6. Children's songs. The two-bar basic unit is sometimes enlarged to a unit of three bars. Note set: tetrachord with a minor third and lower changing note.

7. Children's song. Two-bar construction, although a tendency to construct in larger units can be observed in the combination of four and even as many as eight bars. Two two-bar phrases constitute a melodic line of eight bars, and in general two lines, one with a descending, the other with an ascending trend complement each other, forming a period. The articulation of the text is congruent with that of the melody. Each melodic line corresponds to a "question-reply" pair. Note set: pentachord with minor third.

8. Mocking song. Two-bar construction, variegated with three-bar units. There is a certain regularity in the sequence of the two-bar phrases: two main types alternate, responding to each other: with g^1 taken as the mean, the one ranges within the ambit of an ascending minor third, the other of a descending fourth.

Var. Komi n.p. III. 34.

9. Children's song. Two-bar construction. A certain regularity can be observed in the sequence of the two-bar phrases: two main types alternate responding to each other: with g^1 taken as the mean, the one ranges above it within the ambit of a fourth, the other to a third below it. The note set is basically pentatonic, with frequent pien notes. The articulation of text and melody agrees: the first half of the two-bar phrase represents the question, the second gives the answer.

Var. Komi n.p. I. 63, 72.

10. Children's song. Two-bar construction, a close variant of the preceding song.

Var. Komi n.p. III. 41.

11. Children's song. Transition between the two-bar and the strophic construction patterns. Note set: pentachord with minor third.

12. Children's song. Strophic construction. The informant often commits errors, therefore we chose to publish the second strophe as the main form, this being the completest of all; the melodic divergences in the other stanzas are added as variants.

13. Children's song. Two-bar construction. Performed by two voices, the lower representing the melody proper, the upper being a kind of accompaniment which the singer hums softly.

14. Lament. Half-way towards the strophic form, it consists of musical sections with fixed motifs continuously varied in the course of repetition. The first two musical sections are composed of twelve bars, the rest of nine. The main caesura always falls in the middle of the sixth bar. The motifs vary in length from one and a half to four bars. A markedly melismatic style of performance. The signature of slow tempo seems to contradict the method of notation in semi-quavers, yet the performance audible from the tape suggests this kind of metric pulse. Note set: plagal, major.

Exceptionally in this song, each single moment of respiration has been marked; unnatural as they may seem, the audible breaths follow in a regular sequence; this suggests that they should be considered a characteristic feature of the performance. Accordingly, the singer often performs an incredibly long passage in one breath, almost never stopping at the ends of the passages but slurring the long cadences to the first note of the next passage.

Var. Komi n.p. III. 53.

15. Lament. A sequence of musical passages of varying length (from five to ten bars) constructed on a common motif. Note set: tetrachord with major third.

Only the first part of the text has been recorded. The recording was broken where indicated in the notation.

16. Lament. Two-line construction. Repetition of varied periods of nine bars which are asymmetrically divided (5 . 4). The cadence in the first line falls on the second note of the scale. Note set: hexachord with minor third and minor sixth.

Var. Komi n.p. III. 49.

17. Lament. Two-line construction. Repetition of varied periods of eight bars which are symmetrically divided (4 + 4). The cadence in the first line falls on the second note of the scale. Note set: pentachord with minor third. Incomplete recording, with a portion missing from the beginning.

Var. Komi n.p. III. 51.

18. Lament. Two-line construction. Repetition of varied periods of eight bars which are symmetrically divided (4 + 4). The cadence in the first line falls on the second note of the scale. Note set: pentachord with major third. The informant finds the proper tonality at about the third line. Where indicated by the symbol + the informant stops, others are heard whispering the text, then another woman joins in the singing: thus a bar including two voices develops.

Nos 19—26 are performed by the same female informant. Characteristic features of her archaic manner of performance are the following: a strained, hoarse voice, brisk, rhythmic singing, frequency of filling notes: the pitch of her tones cannot be adequately rendered by the traditional method of musical notation: the tonic and the fourth are usually lower while the third higher than required by tempered scales which, however, does not mean that her singing is false. (The phenomenon is well known in the music of other peoples, especially in territories where the archaic style of performance still prevails.) She extends the cadences of the two-lined periods considerably, singing them with a characteristic, hoarse tone. She produces these tones by a different position of the larynx (guttural tones), and occasionally even the "shifts" can be heard.

19. Lament. Two-line construction. Repetition of varied periods consisting of eight bars and a half (4 1/2 + 4). The cadence of the first line falls on the tonic. Note set: pentachord with major third.

20. Lament. Two-line construction. Varied repetitions of periods consisting of seven bars which are asymmetrically divided (4 + 3). The cadence in the first line falls on the tonic. The informant sings the last note of the first line somewhat short and staccato. Note set: tetrachord with major third. (She performs the first line in brackets even faster and also somewhat out of tune.)

21. Lament. Two-line construction. Repetitions of varied periods of nine bars which are asymmetrically divided (5 + 4). The cadence in the first line falls either on the tonic or on the second note of the scale. Note set: pentachord with major third and lower note changing.

22. Lament. A continuation of the preceding song. See note above.

23. Lament song. A continuation of the preceding song. See note above. From the words "*ćećći že mįššį*" a three-bar motif enters as a new element.

24. Ballad. Two-line construction. Consisting of eight-bar periods symmetrically divided (4 + 4). In the last three sections this division is replaced by a nine-bar period (3 + 3 + 3). Note set: pentachord with major third.

25. Ballad. A close variant of the preceding ballad.

26. Ballad. Two-line construction. Varied repetition of periods of eight bars which are symmetrically divided (4 + 4). The cadence of the first line falls on the tonic. Note set: tetrachord with major third.

27. Mocking song. Two-line construction. Slightly varied repetition of periods of six bars which are symmetrically divided (3 + 3). Apart from the cadences, there are no differences between the two parts of the periods. Regular changes in the bars occur with the intervention of 2/4 and 3/4 times. Note set: hexachord with major third, major sixth. Syllabic manner of performance.

28. Lyrical song. Slightly varied repetition of four-bar lines. Note set: pentachord with major third. Syllabic manner of performance. One of the most popular Zyrian songs, mostly performed polyphonically (see the next melody).

Var. Kondr. 9.

Komi n.p. I. 32, 34, 36, 37, 41, 42, 49, 124, 126, 127.

Komi n.p. III. 20, 24.

29. Lyrical song. Melody as preceding, in a performance by two voices. The melody proper is represented by the lower voice. Exceptionally, only the first part is published, since the performance extends to many stanzas without any considerable differences in the melodic pattern.

Var. see the notes to the preceding song.

1/71

2/71

** See: Notes to the Texts, p. 582

3/66 b

T.i.
(♩= 96 → 118)
du - dẹ, bo - bẹ, kịć - će vet - lin?
ćo - žẹ gu - ẹ.
mịj - nẹ va - jin?
vị-ja ńań va - ji. kịć - će puk - tin?
šeg-jes po - mẹ puk-ti. a - bu taj da vẹv-lẹ - ma.
śẹd pon pịš - je-dẹ-ma, śe-ra pon vẹ - tẹ - dẹ - ma,
po-čịs ko-la-sẹ i śib - dẹ - ma. kẹn i - nẹ po-čị - sịs?
bi so - tẹ - ma. kẹn i - nẹ bi - ịs?
va ku-sẹ - dẹ - ma. kẹn i - nẹ va - ịs?
ẹš-ka-mẹška ju - ẹ - ma. kẹn i - nẹ da ẹš-ka - mẹš-ka - ịs?
ị - bẹ ćeć-će-ma. kẹn i - nẹ ị - bịs?
ćer ke-ra - lẹ - ma. kẹn ị - nẹ će - rịs?
zud ľa - mẹ - ma. ken i - nẹ zud - jis?
pe-čẹr pẹvstẹ u - še - ma. kẹn i - nẹ pe - čẹ - rịs?
śo vẹ-la-ća-ńa ǯu-gẹ-ma-ẹś da ľa-kẹ-ma-ẹś bị - dẹn da
ľok kar-ta-ẹ pị-rẹ-ma - ẹś
continues in speech

3/66 b

T.i.
(♩= 96 → 118)
du - dẹ, bo - bẹ, ki̯ć - će vet - lin?
ćo - žẹ gu - ẹ.
mij - nẹ va - jin?
vi̯ - ja ńań va - ji. ki̯ć - će puk - tin?
šẹg-jes po - mẹ puk-ti. a - bu taj da vẹv - lẹ - ma.
śẹd pon pi̯š - je - dẹ - ma, śe - ra pon vẹ - lẹ - dẹ - ma,
po-či̯s ko - la - sẹ i śib - dẹ - ma. kẹn i - nẹ po-či̯ - si̯s?
bi so - tẹ - ma. kẹn i - nẹ bi - i̯s?
va ku-sẹ - dẹ - ma. kẹn i - nẹ va - i̯s?
ẹš-ka-mẹška ju - ẹ - ma. kẹn i - nẹ da ẹš-ka - mẹš-ka - i̯s?
i̯ - bẹ ćeć-će-ma. kẹn i - nẹ i̯ - bi̯s?
ćer ke-ra - lẹ - ma. kẹn i̯ - nẹ će - ri̯s?
zud ľa - mẹ - ma. ken i - nẹ zud - jis?
pe-čẹr pẹvstẹ u - śe - ma. kẹn i - nẹ pe - čẹ - ri̯s?
śo vẹ - la - ća - ńa źu - gẹ - ma - ẹś da ľa - kẹ - ma-ẹś bi̯ - dẹn da
ľok kar - ta - ẹ pi̯ - rẹ - ma - ẹś
continues in speech

(♩ = 120—138)
T.i.
ľe - ńe, ľe - ńe, pi̮š - ji! śe̮d ši - ke̮ - ǯi̮d śi̮ - jad,
pa - la - u - zi̮di ju - rad.
ľeń si - ja oz piš - ji. gez - je, gez - je, ľeń - li̮ ǯa - ge̮d!
gez si - ja oz ǯa - ge̮d. ši̮ - re̮, ši̮ - re̮, ľeń - li̮ ke - rav!
ši̮r si - ja oz ke - rav. ka - ńe, ka - ńe, ši̮r - li̮ ki̮j!
či̮n si - ja oz pe̮d - ti̮. bi - je, bi - je, či̮n - li̮ sot!
kań si - ja oz ki̮j. či̮ - ne̮, či̮ - ne̮, kań - li̮ pe̮d - ti̮!
bi si - ja oz sot. va - e̮, va - e̮, bi - li̮ ku - se̮d!
va si - ja oz ku - se̮d. e̮š si - ja oz ju.
e̮š - ke̮, e̮š - ke̮, va - li̮ ju!
će - re̮, će - re̮, e̮š - li̮ nać - ki̮! ćer si - ja oz nać - ki.
zud - je, zud - je, ćer - li̮ ľam!
zud si - ja oz lam. zud zi̮ - re̮ - das ćer vi̮ - le̮,
ćer zi̮ - re̮ - das e̮š vi̮ - le̮,
e̮š zi̮ - re̮ - das va vi̮ - le̮,
va zi̮ - re̮ - das bi vi̮ - le̮,
bi zi̮ - re̮ - das či̮n vi̮ - le̮,
či̮n zi̮ - re̮ - das kań vi̮ - le̮,
kań zi̮ - re̮ - das ši̮r vi̮ - le̮,
ši̮r zi̮ - re̮ - das gez vi̮ - le̮,
gez zi̮ - re̮ - das ľeń vi̮ - le̮,
ľeń zi̮ - re̮ - das... continues in gabbling speech

5/85

(♩=76)
1. šir kī - te, ka - te ka-ča - kẹ - ja pị - ža,
moj - lop-ta pe - li - sa vurd - bẹž zib - ja.
(♩=72→76)
1) 3. 4.
2-4. šir kī - te, ka - te, ka-ča - kẹ - ja pị - ža,
2) 3. 4.
moj - lop - ta pe - li - sa, vurd - bẹž zib - ja,
3) 4.
kị-rə-kečə dori-se sị - niš - tam lị - va - dorise zib-jiš - tam.

6/141

T. i.
(♩=92)
kị - su - ľej, ka - ńu-ľej, śẹd śor kuźad en vet-ted-li!
kok-pị - de - sid śẹ - da - śas, śẹ - da-śas. po-paď-ďadliś
vij - te, nẹkte en kurt, en kurt! paććer - se-re-gad ka, da brịz - ńit! (sa)

7/128

T. i.
(𝅗𝅥=100 → 126)
bo-be, bo-be kiḉ- ći vet-lin? ćo-že gu- e vet - li.
mịj ne va - jin? vị - ja ńań va - ji.
kiḉ - ći ne puk - tin? pos-voʒ́ ʒaʒje puk - ti.
a - bu taj ne! śẹd pon nu - ve - ma.
kẹn - že śẹd ponjis? počis kos- te śil-de- ma.
kẹn - že po-či - sis? bi taj ku - se - de - ma.
kẹn - že bi - is? va ku - se - de - ma.
kẹn - že va - is? ẹš-ka-mẹška ju - ve - ma.
kẹn - že ẹš - ka-mẹš-kas? ị - be ka-je- ma.
kẹn - ne šị - ris? naľk- je še - de- ma.
kẹn - že ị - bis? šir taj kị - red-le - ma.
kẹn - ne naľk - jis? čer taj ke - ra - le - ma.
kẹn - že će - ris? zud taj na-ľe - ma.
kẹn ne zud - jis? ʒuʒid pe-čer pi-je šị - bi- ti da
continues in speech
daskịk ća-ńa - vẹ - la piź - pẹ - jim(e) pe - tis - ni:

8/75

(♩=116→140)
mur-ja-mar-ja, ććć - ći-žẹ ććć - ći!
as-ja-ko-ra - śid vo-is, rit-ja nu-i̭ - śid vo-is. mar-ja ććć - ćis.
ẹ - tẹ -rẹ-kẹ gur - gar, mẹ-dẹ-rẹ-kẹ ǵir-gar, ved-ra-sẹ-kẹ kva-ťi-tis,
ved-ra - i̭s pi̭- dẹs-tẹm, kẹš - sẹ - kẹ kva-ťi - tis,
kẹ - ši̭s nud - tẹm, kar-nan-sẹ-kẹ kva-ťi-tis,
kar-na-ni̭s ču-pẹd-tẹm. va-la mẹ-dẹććis, pop voć - ća lo-i,
tu-run vevt ćuž-jiš-tis, jur śi - i̭s ľoź - mis.
ni̭-lẹ, ni̭-lẹ, mij či̭n či̭-na-lẹ? mij či̭n? ki̭-rẹd či̭n.
mij-ki̭-rẹd? ća - dẹ ki̭-rẹd. mij ća-dẹ. bur ća-dẹ. mij bur? ńi-ki̭ľ-bur.
mij ńi-ki̭ľ? i̭b ńi-ki̭ľ! i̭b šẹ-ri̭n pẹ pe-re-no-sẹn pi̭-rẹ-ni̭ i pe-tẹ-ni̭.
T. f.

(♩=108)
ťęs ku-źa ko-ter-tis. ko - đis-že ko-ter-tis?
ka - ťa-že ko-ter-tis. kįć - će-že sū - tis?
šťe-pan ę - ńe pos-po-me. ko - dis-že pe - tis?
jo - gor-že pe - tis. kį - ti-že kva-ťi-tis?
kos-šę - re-dis kva-ťi-tis. kįć - će-že pįr - tis?
kre - va-ťas pir - tis.
T. f.

10/139

(♩=92)
važen o - lis iń - ka, va-žen o - lis aj - ka
strej ka-ga - bab - ka, pu-li̯ so-li žan - ka,
veś ve-še - lan - ka. ku - reg-tor vẹ - li,
koľk - tor va-jiš - tis, iz- ki po-me puk-te-ma.
šir loktis, tuv - kis, šir lok-tis, tav - kis,
bẹž - nas ševkńi - tis. u - ši, žu-ga-li,
u - ši da pa-za-li. iń - ka-is bẹr - de,
aj - ka-is tẹž - de. ẹ-šin ẹ - že-si klupka - klopka ki̯- le,
ẹ-žes žir-ki da vir-ki ki̯ - le.
T.f.

11/135

(♩=152)
kuč - kuč ko- ča - nẹj muč-ki-rə - mač-ki-rə ma-ka - rej,
jẹ - la - vị - ja to - ta - ra jen- li kẹs-jis kvajt-šo ur
kvajtšo ur-li lo - pi - ćań lo-pi - ćań-li ẹs - tap
ẹs - tap-li pẹs - tap vịj - ću - ńa - liś ẹ - ďạ.
vịj-ću- ńa-liś ẹ - ďa rị-nịš-tup-jed ma - lań
sa-peg-ko-ka pe - deś śi - zim u - ra jo - gor.
T.f.

12/132

(♩=138 → 158)
2. ruj, ruj, kịć-ći vet-lin?
1)
mẹs-kes korśni vet - li.
2) 3)
kuš-čem te-nad mẹs - kid?
miľk - ja pľe - ša.
T.f.
1) 6.7. 3
3) 1.
2) 6.7.

13/140

(♩=118)
tu-ru-ru-ru - ru-ru-ru, ke̯-bi-la-li vi̯l' me-gir
as - lim vi̯l' ćer-pu, ba - ba-li vi̯l' ža-ket,
nas-ta-li par - nij, i-zo-śim-li ge̯rd paś,
sa-me-var, sa-me-var, kiǯ ku-žan da raz-ńić-ći!
Tf.

14/60

(♩=54)
i šo - ni - di̯ - e̯ - ba - ne̯-ji - ke̯ me -
na - mi taj ni̯ - vi da ke̯ - sa -
e̯j đe-vi-jej da kra - sa - e̯j,
ko - ľi - ni̯ taj me - nam ko - ńer-le̯-ni daj pon-
dis daji ni̯vi ke̯ - sa -
e̯j, đe-vijej da kra - sa - e̯j,
i vo - ši taj me - nam ko - ńe-re̯ - ji-le̯n daj
ni̯v daj ni̯vi ke̯ - sa - e̯j,
ko - riš - ni̯ e̯d si - je ko - le̯ menši-mi ko-
ńe - re̯j - len daj ni̯vi ke̯ - sa - e̯j.
ko- ri̯ - še̯ že̯ mu - sa vok - ja - se̯-ji menšimi
zar - ńi ni̯v daj ni̯vi ke̯ - sa - e̯s,

14/60 *(continue)*

5/61

(♩=108 – 126)
šon - di̯-ba-neį pe̜ me-na-mi daj ba-ťu-ši-ko-e̜j,
mu-nin že̜ te me di-niś da końe-re̜-ji di-niś.
ki̯ ki̯ćće-će ne̜ mene̜ te me̜-di-ni da to-jiš-ti-ni̯-se̜?
ku-ži-ni taj ne̜š-na bit-ti-ni̯-se̜
da-ji, ku-žin taj me-ne̜ daj śe-ti-ni̯-se̜.
ńe pa-śi-be̜ že̜ tenid, ba-ťu-ši-ko-e̜j,
le-ćidi ko-sa-nad te-ni̯d daj i̯čke̜-te̜-mi̯di vi̯-le̜,
pa-śi-be̜ že̜ te-nid, ba-ťu-ši-ko e̜j,
ko-ki-ńi narə-man-nad me-ńe̜ kuri-te̜-de̜ mi̯di vi̯-le̜.
i-ni taj me-ne̜ u-be̜-li-ti-li̯ ke̜-gi-di vi̯-las pe-ti-ni̯-se̜.
e̜ ni vedi me seć-će-mu-na da og kuž vi-gedi-li̯-nis

15/61 b *(continue)*

15/61 c *(continue)*

* takes a breath

(♩ = 69 → 76)
… i šęd pę ved da-ji kį - mę - ri kojd.
dru-ži - ka taj kį - lę, lo - ki - tę
į - ǯį - di pę ved daj tu - ća kojd.
dru-ži - ka taj kį - lę, lo - ki - tę
daj šę-di pe - mį-di vę - rį kojd.
ə dru-ži - ka ved kį - lę, lo-ki - tę
ǯu - og i - ǯa-si kojd
da-je l'o-ki mį - gę - ri - nas.
dru - ži - ka taj kį - lę, lok - tę
rį - nį - ši tup - l'ęd kojd ju-ri - nas.
dru-ži-ka taj kį - lę, lo - ki - tę
ko - sa da nud kojd da soj - jas - nas.

17/24 *(continue)*

18/25

(♩=82 → 88)
a - ji ve - ri - da-ni ve - ri - di̯ - śe̯j,
dru-ži - ka taj ki̯ - le̯ daj vo - e̯ - ma
ro - ći - ba ja - ri kojd da mi̯ - ge̯ - ri - nas,
ver - da-ni ve - ri - di̯ - śe̯j,
roć pre - ńik kojd da ću - že̯ - mi - nas,
druž - ka taj ki̯ - le̯ daj vo - e̯ - e̯ ma
roć a - ka - ńi kojd da mi̯ - ge̯ - ri - nas.
druž - ka taj ki̯ - le̯ daj vo - e̯ - e̯ - ma
i̯ - žid ge̯ś - nas da - ji ge̯ś - ťa - nas,
druž - ka taj ki̯ - le̯ daj vo - e̯ - ma
i̯ - ži̯-di - ge̯ś - nas daj ge̯ś - ťa - nas.
T. f.

19/172

(♩=98→108)
menam vȩ - li śȩ-di šȩ - ki l'entoć-ka, vo - ši si - ja
śȩ-di vȩr šȩ - re.
menam vȩ - li lȩ-zi šȩ-ki l'e-ni-toć - ka, vo - ši si - ja
menam vȩ - li gȩr-di šȩ-ki l'e-ni-toć - ka, vo - ši si - ja
ćȩ-di-ja ja - ge.
o-zi-ja tį - la.
menam vȩ - li je-ǯid šȩ-ki l'e-ni-toć - ka, vo - ši si - ja
ja - a ja - ge.
(speaks)
me-nam vȩ - li ja-lej šȩ-ki l'e-ni-toć - ka, vo - ši si - jaj
ȩ-mį-ǯa kus - te.
menam vȩ - li vi-ži šȩ-ki le-ni-toć - ka, vo - ši si - ja
nir-po-ma nu - rȩ.
menam vȩ - li gȩ-lu-be-ji šȩ-ki l'e-ni-toć - ka, vo - ši si - ja
ćȩd la-ća kus - te.

19/172 *(continue)*

(♩=76→98)
i ri-ti-ja pe vo - je ma - tuš-ka, me-ne da rẹ - ďi-tin.
da vo-ji-šẹ-ri ka - de, ma - tuš-ka, ka-rab ij
eš - te - din.
(speaks)
da ju-gi-da-ni do - re, ma - tuš-ka, me-ne da
mẹ - de - din.
i prẹši-šaji pe prẹš - šaj, ďi - ťot-ka, ra-di pe me
prẹ - šajć - ća.
će - ri - ńe-ći pe-ji jo-zi čẹ-ki - ti da ka - ra - abij
o-zi sū-ti - li.
da kin - ta pe kị-ni-ta da, ma - tuš-ka, vo-ji šẹ-ri
mo - χo-ro - zen,
i sī - da pe sī - da, ma - tuš-ka, ạ-si-ja da
šo - χondi - en,

20/173 *(continue)*

21/175

(♩ = 104 — 120)
i spasi daji pri - ći-si-ta - ja
(speaks)
i jeni-śa-ńi pe ve-di me - ni-mi bu-ri - śi - in.
je-ni-ta lu-ni-ja da lu - u - ni-si ku - źa,
(speaks, coughs)
i buri - śi že da-ji bla - go-si-le - vit e - ta lu-ni-
ja lu - nis ku- źa.
i je-ni-śa-ńi pe ve-di me - ni-mi bu-ri - śi i
jeni ko - ǯu - li-si mi̯ - daj,
i va-śań pe vedi me - ni-mi bu-ri - śi va - će -
ri - ji-si mi̯ - daj.
i mu-śań pe vedi me - ni-mi bu-ri - śi i ve-ži tu -
ri - ni - si mi̯ - daj.
i bu-ri-śi že da-ji me-χe ni-mi ko-ńe-rej-li i
bla - go - si - le - vit!

21/175 *(continue)*

(♩=122)
i ju - gid šo-ni-di - je - χe-ji da me-nam i nī
vẹ - ľa ji da
(speaks)
i nī vẹ - ľa-ji pe da me - nam i į
žį - di vẹ - ľaj
i ko-ľi ve-di ko - ľi me - nam i ko -
ńe - re - ji - len.
i ju - gid šo-ni-di - je - χe-ji da me-nam i ve-ti-le-mi-
mu - ne - mej.
i tuj ku - źa vedi me-χe - je-ji vet - li i tu-ji-se da
še - red - lig tir - ja,
i tuj ku - źa vedi me vet - li i tuji-sẹ da
mo - ľe - dig-tir - ja.
i ćuńi-pomi pe vedi me - je-ji vet-li i ču-li-ki
da - ji čo - li - ki,

22/176 *(continue)*

23/177

(♩ = 120—136)
i veti - la me že ve - χe-ti - la me i ze̯-le - ta-ja -
se-ji da-ji pe̯ - di ru - ga-ja - sej.
i nu - le že, nu - le me - ne i me̯ - di -
be̯ - ri - ja - šis!
i ze̯ - le - ta - ja se - χe-ji da me-nam i bu - ri
zo - ni - ja - sej,
nu - le že me-ne go - ra da-ji gu - u - de-kə-na - nid!
i vet - la - me že ve - ti - la - me i mi - ća daj
a - ri - t́e-lə - na - nim,
tu-ji-se mo - l'e-di - li - gi ti̯ - ri-ja da i še - re-di-
li - gi - ti̯ - ri - ja.
(speaks)
i ćeć - ći že pe mi̯ - ši - ši!
(speaks)
ćeć - ći že miš - ši!
ne - pe̯ - ra uz - ni, pe̯ - ra će-ći-ći - ni. o-nə - ke
ve̯-di ćeć - ći,

23/177 I *(continue)*

25/156

(♩=112—118)
da i̯ - lin, i̯ - lin va sa - jin vil̓ sle̯ - be - da
ti̯ - da - le,
vil̓ sle̯ - be - das tom de̯- vaj o - le̯, tom de̯ - vas - len
tom že ni̯ vi̯ - jim.
i - će - t́ik› da ʒ́e̯ - t́a - ńik, ge̯g - res ću - že-ma,
še̯d šin-tas-ja - sa,
(coughs)
ge̯g - res ću - že-ma, še̯d šin-tasja - sa, ro - ža vi̯-[las]
a - lej vir vor - se,
(coughs)
da ši - ni-ja - si-nas pe da vo-mi-ja-si - nas da čeč že
si - ja vo-ri-seć - ćej.
da e - ti-ja sla - va ku - ʒ́a sta - rik sa - je
lo - ve mu - ni.
kiǯ pe ved taj ul̓ pu ńukl̓a - še, siǯ - že me - nim
sla-va lok - te.

25/156 b *(continue)*

25/156 c *(continue)*

25/156 d *(continue)*

(♩ = 118 → 134)
nḙ va-la leć - će da čaj va-la leć - će. zon voj jukta - le da
mi-ća pu-ka - le,
zē ved si - ja i la - si - kov, zē ved si - ja da
pri- me - t́it.
ḙ - le da ka- a - re mḙ - de da joz ḙ - le
ka - re mḙd,
ka - za - ńi ka - re da ka - zań - ju pe
vi - zī - tej.
oz ka - za - ńi - ju vi - zīt. ḙ - le ka -
re mḙ - de.
(speaks)
ka - zań ju pe vi - zī - te daj oz ka - za - ńi -
ju vi - zīt.
gḙ - ra jḙ - las-ke vi - ǯed - lam da stá - vis sḙ - ni

26/157 b *(continue)*

27/50

(♩=76→90)
gę - tị - rej me - nę oz ľu - bit, krę - vať vị - liś me - nę jęt - kis,
krę - vať vị - liś me - nę jęt - kis da ki - je - ko - kę menam vẹr - źis,
ki - je ko - kę me-nam vẹr - źis da vet - la žę me vol-ga vị - lę,
vet - la žę me vol-ga vị - lę da boś - ta žę me le - ćid brit - va,
boś - ta že me le - ćid brit - va da bri - ta žę me vež kud...kudri - jas,
bri - ta žę me vež kud - ri - jas da šon - di - ba - nej vež kud - ri - jej!
T. f.

28/160

(𝅗𝅥=98→110)
ći - ki - šes ko - le kij - ni da sa - de - ge ko - le jęrt - ni.
sa - de - ge ko - le - jęrt - ni da kęj - di - śis na ve - sō - tem.
kęj - di - sis na ve - sō - tem da ver - di - śis na bịt - ti - tem.
ver - di - śis na bịt - ti - tem da kęž pos ku - źa lok - te - ma.
kęž pos ku - źa lok - te - ma da kęrt - ke - re - si - ni bịd - me - ma.
T. f.

29/95

(♩=60)
T. i.
3
šon-di - ej ma - mej daj ve-ri- ďi-ni - mej ďi - ťaj,
di̯-ri vedi nōled - lin daj ćas ve-ďi re̥- ďi - tin.
re̥ - ďi - ti - ni, ma - tuška, mi - ća - ja, bu - ra,
bi̯t - tin, ma - tuš - ka, be - ri - ba- iś ǯu - ǯid,
ve - le - di - ni, ma - tuš - ka, ško-li - ne-ji mańe - re,
e - ni ke̥s-ji-li, ma - tuš - ka, i̯ - le - je śet - ni.
śe - ti - ni, ma - tuš - ka, i̯ - le że-mi-ľa - je,
i̯ - le że-mi-ľa - e daj u - na śe-mi-ja - e,...

PHOTOGRAPHS

1. Zyrian women of the village of Šoška

2. Informant E. I. Lapina, Šoška

3. River Vym

4. Zyrian women of the village of Ľaľi

5. Zyrian village scene